EU BANKING UNION AND THE SINGLE SUPERVISORY MECHANISM

ELGAR FINANCIAL LAW AND PRACTICE

Series editor: Jeffrey Golden KC (Hon), *Arbitrator and Mediator, Joint Head of Chambers, 3 Hare Court; Founder and Chair Emeritus of the P.R.I.M.E. Finance Foundation*

The Elgar Financial Law and Practice series is a library of works by leading practitioners and scholars covering discrete areas of law in the field of banking and finance. Each title will be both analytical and descriptive in approach, highlighting and unpicking the legal issues that are most critical and relevant to practice. Designed to be detailed, focused reference works, the books in this series should aim to offer an authoritative statement on the law and practice in key topics within the field, from Financial Collateral to Private Equity, from Secured Transactions to Financial Crime, and from Financial Derivatives and Hedge Funds to Bank Resolution and Bank Capital.

For a full list of Edward Elgar published titles, including the titles in this series, visit our website at www.e-elgar.com.

EU BANKING UNION AND THE SINGLE SUPERVISORY MECHANISM

CARLOS BOSQUE ARGACHAL

Legal Counsel, European Investment Bank, Luxembourg, Adjunct Professor of Law, University Carlos III, Spain and European Banking Institute Fellow

ELGAR FINANCIAL LAW AND PRACTICE

Edward Elgar PUBLISHING

Cheltenham, UK · Northampton, MA, USA

Published by

Edward Elgar Publishing Limited
The Lypiatts
15 Lansdown Road
Cheltenham
Glos GL50 2JA
UK

Edward Elgar Publishing, Inc.
William Pratt House
9 Dewey Court
Northampton
Massachusetts 01060
USA

Authorised representative in the EU for GPSR queries only: Easy Access System Europe – Mustamäe tee 50, 10621 Tallinn, Estonia, gpsr.requests@easproject.com

A catalogue record for this book is available from the British Library

Library of Congress Control Number: 2025947073

This book is available electronically in the Elgaronline Law subject collection
https://doi.org/10.4337/9781035355280

MIX
Paper | Supporting responsible forestry
FSC® C013604

ISBN 978 1 0353 5527 3 (cased)
ISBN 978 1 0353 5528 0 (eBook)
ISBN 978 1 0353 8496 9 (ePub)

Printed and bound by CPI Group (UK) Ltd, Croydon, CR0 4YY

To Anne-Céline; without you, this work (and many other things) would have not been possible.

CONTENTS

EXTENDED CONTENTS

PREFACE

There are cases where a Preface gives its writer the opportunity to honour a colleague. In this case, the honour is only mine and a testimony of the author's generosity.

This book is written by an outstanding scholar. Carlos Bosque Argachal has been a practicing lawyer, who has worked in a large private firm, a legal counsel at a national supervisor (Bank of Spain), a lawyer at a European institution and also an academic, with rich experience in teaching and research.

This helps explain why this book is unique. There are great academic works on the Banking Union, covering its political and policy drivers, issues of Treaty mandates or constitutional implications. There are also excellent works dealing with the specific allocation of powers and tasks within the system, based on the SSM and SSM Framework Regulations. There are also great works that cover the role of the courts in construing and interpreting the SSM and ensuring its judicial accountability. And, finally, there are great analyses of some applicative aspects of the SSM and their practical implications.

What is harder to find, and what this book provides, is a comprehensive account where the reader can understand the intricacies of the actual functioning of the SSM and, at the same time, trace these practical details back to their origins in the specific design choices in the system, its constitutional determinants and/or their construction by the courts.

The work developed by the author here has been the product of a deep and thorough analysis of the existing literature, case law and practice manuals but, also and distinctly, his own reflection. I can attest to that, having spent many fruitful hours sharing impressions and insights as well as doubts. The SSM architecture is a work in progress. This work, like the best works do, acknowledges the certainties and the open questions.

The book begins with a deep analysis of the Banking Union as a further step in the EU's construction of the monetary union. Financial markets were the linchpin of institutional ingenuity in the post-Financial Crisis, and the discussion explains the conditions under which the ECB was vested with supervisory powers, which, however, did not entail full trust by the Member States, and why this results in limitations in design and constitutional tensions. His reflection on the meaning of "specific tasks", on the ECB's "regulatory" role and on the tensions between the supervisory tasks and the monetary "mandate" invite academic reflection and pave the way for the practical challenges.

In subsequent chapters, the author continues the discussion of "competences", "tasks" and "powers". Far from a question of semantics, these are the basic concepts used to allocate functions within the system. This acts as an anchor to ensure that the proposal to construe the system by appealing to its finality and rationale is, nonetheless, solidly tied to the letter of the law. After explaining the "tasks", the subsequent discussion of "procedures" is the natural next step. Here, the author combines a critical analysis of the European system and, e.g., the problems of gold-plating with a more classic view of procedural administrative law and the need to accommodate regular procedures and sanctioning procedures. The reader, however, will be well-advised to keep in mind this part. The topic may be classic, but the angle taken is anything but. The discussion of the comparison between regular administrative procedures and sanctioning procedures is as insightful as it is provocative. This is because, in the end, distinguishing between one and another is easier said than done. And yet, drawing on the case law of the Court of Justice and the European Court of Human Rights (ECtHR), the author manages to offer answers that are both clear and constitutionally sound.

One could read only this previous part and think that this is a very good monograph. What makes this work special is the fact that right after comes what could well be another great monograph, this one analysing the SSM's practical implications and its composite nature. And yet, this is done maintaining full cohesion. Each detail is traced back to its origins, helping the reader find practical answers as easily as their conceptual underpinnings.

The characterisation of "composite procedures" is extremely useful to differentiate them from other forms of cooperation between authorities and to assess their implications for purposes of judicial review and the application of procedural safeguards.

Then, all this basis helps the author offer a minute analysis of different procedures, including the granting and withdrawal of banking licenses and authorisations or the assessment of acquisition of qualifying holdings. What is impressive is not the attention to detail in each step but the ability of the author to ensure that this is not a discussion of detail for detail's sake. Diagrams and lists of criteria (essential if one wishes to keep the account close to reality) are combined with an analysis of the safeguards, legal challenges and remedies.

The practitioner working for a law firm or public institution will find this as useful as the academic looking for examples where constitutional tensions come to a head.

The author reserves the crown jewel for the end. Very often, sanctions and sanctioning procedures are seen as their own universe, disconnected from other considerations. Here, I believe, they are put in their proper place – both as a continuation that follows other administrative procedures, as a piece that has to fit within a complex system, which has its own finality and internal coherence, and a piece that is distinct, that acts as both a linchpin and test bed of the effectiveness of the system and its constitutional soundness.

The author shows this not by engaging in abstractions. One can find all that in previous chapters. Instead, he presents sanctioning procedures in all their complexity and all their steps. Questions about safeguards and remedies are then addressed thoroughly and precisely, with concrete answers and solutions, which link together procedural rules, supervisory practice and case law, and using a sequence that is as informative and predictable as it is intellectually stimulating.

To sum up, the author grants me a great honour in allowing me to write these lines. I can only hope to not that repay this honour by writing a Preface that meanders around or sidetracks a reader kind enough to read a Preface. If I did, it would be a disservice to this truly excellent work. I enjoyed reading it as much as exchanging ideas with its author. This work is unique and has much to offer to academics, policymakers and practitioners. I can only thank the reader for being so patient, and invite you to proceed to the real work in the next pages.

LIST OF ABBREVIATIONS

AboR	Administrative Board of Review.
AG	Advocate General.
AML	anti-money laundering.
BRRD	Bank Recovery and Resolution Directive.
BU	Banking Union.
BverfG	*Bundesverfassungsgericht.* German Constitutional Court.
CCPs	Central clearing counterparties.
CEBS	Committee of European Banking Supervisors.
CEIOPS	Committee of European Insurance and Occupational Pensions Supervisors.
CESR	Committee of European Securities Regulators.
Charter	European Charter of Fundamental Rights.
Commission or **EC**	European Commission.
CPR	Common Provisions Regulation.
CRD IV	Capital Requirements Directive.
CRR	Capital Requirements Regulation.
DGS	Directive on deposit guarantee schemes.
EBA Regulation	Regulation establishing the EBA.
EBA	European Banking Authority.
ECA	European Court of Auditors.
ECB	European Central Bank.
ECHR	European Convention on Human Rights.
ECtHR	European Court of Human Rights.
EDIS	European Deposit Insurance Scheme.
EFSF	European Financial Stability Facility.
EFSM	European Financial Stabilisation Mechanism.
EMU	Economic and Monetary Union.
EP or **Parliament**	European Parliament.
ESCB	European System of Central Banks.
ESFS	European System of Financial Supervisors.
ESM	European Stability Mechanism.

ESMA	European Securities and Markets Authority.
ESRB	European Systemic Risk Board.
FED	Federal Reserve System.
FSA	Financial Services Authority.
GO&Ds	ECB Guideline (EU) 2017/697 of 4 April 2017 on the exercise of options and discretions available in Union law by national competent authorities in relation to less significant institutions (ECB/2017/9).
IFR	Investment Firms Regulation.
IMF	International Monetary Fund.
ITS	Implementing Technical standards.
JSTs	Joint Supervisory Teams.
LSIs	Less Significant Institutions.
MIFID	Markets in financial instruments Directive.
MS(s)	Member State(s). The term will be used to refer interchangeably, and as the context may require, to (i) participating member states as defined in art. 2(1) SSM R or (ii) to EU member states.
NCAs	National Competent Authorities.
NCB	National Central Banks.
NPLs	Non-performing loans.
NRA	National Resolutions Authorities.
O&Ds	Options and discretions.
P2G	Pillar 2 Guidance.
P2R	Pillar 2 Requirements.
PSD2	Payment services Directive 2.
RTS	Regulatory Technical Standards.
SESCB	Protocol no 4 – to the TFEU– on the Statute of the European System of Central Banks and of the European Central Bank.
SIs	Significant Institutions.
SO	Statement of Objections.
SRB	Single Resolution Board.
SREP	Supervisory Review and Evaluation Process.
SRM R	Single Resolution Mechanism Regulation.
SRM	Single Resolution Mechanism.
SSM Fr	Single Supervisory Mechanism Framework Regulation.
SSM R	Single Supervisory Mechanism Regulation.

SSM	Single Supervisory Mechanism.
Supervisory Board	Supervisory Board of the SSM.
TAT	Total Annual Turnover.
TFEU	Treaty on the Functioning of the European Union.

TABLE OF CASES

European Court of Human Rights

European Union

Germany

Spain

TABLE OF LEGISLATION

EUROPEAN UNION

Treaties

Regulations

Directives

Decisions

INTERNATIONAL

NATIONAL

Austria

France

Ireland

Italy

Spain

INTRODUCTORY REMARKS ON THE SINGLE SUPERVISORY MECHANISM (SSM)[1]

I.001 Before even introducing the objectives of this work, and with a view to understand its objectives and challenges, it is necessary to offer a quick overview on its main object of study: the SSM.

I.002 This introduction does not seek to exhaustively describe each and every aspect of the functioning of the SSM (or the Banking Union (BU)). It merely seeks to sketch the basic features of the SSM in order to provide an adequate basis for addressing, later, the main topics covered in this book.

I.003 The SSM was introduced by Council Regulation (EU) No 1024/2013 of 15 October 2013 conferring specific tasks on the European Central Bank concerning policies relating to the prudential supervision of credit institutions (SSM R), which came into force on 3 November 2013.[2] After a transitory period of one year,[3] on 4 November 2014, the SSM became operational.

I.004 Broadly speaking, the implementation of the SSM was motivated by the financial crisis that globally started in 2007–2008 and that, by 2010, mutated in the European Union (EU) into a sovereign debt crisis, affecting the real economy, the financial sector and Member States' (MSs) public debt.[4] The EU perceived, then, the need for a comprehensive and consolidated approach and proposed advancing towards "*a Genuine Economic and Monetary Union*"[5]

---

1 NB: The cut-off date of this work is 1 January 2025. Any publications and judicial developments occurring after that date are not considered. Additionally, all internet links shared herein are working and functional as of this cut-off date.

2 For a comprehensive SSM timeline, see Milestones (europa.eu).

3 See art. 33(2) SSM R.

4 Particularly, creating a vicious circle between those latter ones.

5 So-called *Four Presidents Report*. See European Council Report: TOWARDS A GENUINE ECONOMIC AND MONETARY UNION. Report by President of the European Council Herman Van Rompuy. Brussels, 26 June 2012 (EUCO 120/12): 2012-06-26_towards_genuine_economic_and_monetary_union.pl.pdf (europa.eu). The Report was elaborated in close cooperation with the presidents

(EMU). Within that EMU, it was presented the idea of a BU, composed of the SSM, a Single Resolution Mechanism (SRM) and a European Deposit Insurance Scheme (EDIS).

The SSM constitutes, indeed, the first leg of the BU and, as it will be discussed below, was set up upon a barely used treaty basis: art. 127(6) of the Treaty of the Functioning of the European Union (TFEU).[6] Under such Treaty foundations, the ECB could be conferred "*specific tasks* (…) *concerning policies relating to the prudential supervision of credit institutions and other financial institutions*". **I.005**

The SSM is a *mechanism* (not vested with legal personality), composed by the European Central Bank (ECB) and the National Competent Authorities (NCAs) of the participating MSs.[7] The term *participating MSs*[8] encompasses both (i) Eurocurrency MSs and (ii) MSs which have entered into a close cooperation agreement to join the SSM, pursuant to art. 7 SSM R. **I.006**

The main objective of the SSM is that of "*contributing to the safety and soundness of credit institutions and the stability of the financial system within the Union and each Member State*".[9] In other words, the SSM aims at ensuring a sound prudential supervision in the area falling under its remit. **I.007**

Pursuant to art. 6(1) SSM R, the ECB is solely responsible for the (smooth) functioning of the *mechanism*. In this vein, the ECB is made exclusively competent to carry out the micro-prudential tasks foreseen in arts. 4(1) and 4(2) SSM R. In addition, the ECB is also vested with some (limited) macro-prudential tasks under article 5 SSM R. **I.008**

Concerning those micro-prudential tasks, they encompass a broad number of activities, ranging from granting (and withdrawing) banking licenses and **I.009**

---

of (i) the EC (José Manuel Barroso), (ii) The Eurogroup (Jean-Claude Juncker) and (iii) the ECB (Mario Draghi).

6 This foundational basis was already used for the first time in 2010 to assign certain specific tasks to the ECB concerning the European Systemic Risk Board (ESRB) by means of Council Regulation 1096/2010 of 17 November 2010 conferring specific tasks upon the European Central Bank concerning the functioning of the European Systemic Risk Board.

7 Cf art. 6(1) SSM R. The terms MSs or participating MSs may be used interchangably across this work, as the context may require.

8 Art. 2(1) SSM R.

9 Art. 1.I SSM R.

authorising the acquisition of qualifying holdings[10] on credit institutions to performing diary supervision tasks[11] and early intervention duties.[12]

I.010 Such tasks are only directly exercised by the ECB as regards the entities that are considered more relevant for the financial system on the basis of several criteria.[13] Those entities are named *Significant Institutions* (SIs). On the other side, those entities not considered *significant* (i.e., *Less Significant Institutions* (LSIs)) are directly supervised by the relevant NCAs.[14] Cooperation between the ECB and NCAs is pivotal in the SSM R.[15] In this regard, the ECB relies completely on them as regards the supervision of LSIs (exercising an *indirect* supervisory role). Further, the ECB is also heavily reliant on the NCAs' expertise (and personnel[16]) to carry out the supervision of SIs.

I.011 Within the SSM, art. 4(3) SSM R contemplates the application of a wide panoply of different rules. Those include, of course, EU Regulations but also national rules transposing relevant prudential Directives. Such an application of national rules by the ECB (an EU institution) constitutes an absolute novelty within EU law.

I.012 The SSM R further vests the ECB with supervisory and investigatory powers[17] to carry out the tasks indicated right above. Such powers include the usual powers vested on prudential supervisors, such as the power to request information[18] and perform on-site inspections,[19] imposing additional stringent obligations to prevent or contain any actual or potential prudential issues,[20] and certain sanctioning powers to punish entities[21] which have incurred a breach of their prudential obligations.

---

10 Indents (a) and (c) of art. 4(1) SSM R. Those tasks are exclusively exercised directly by the ECB over any supervised entity.

11 Cf art. 4(1)(d)–(e) SSM R.

12 Art. 4(1)(i) SSM R.

13 Cf art. 6(4) SSM R.

14 Art. 2(2) SSM R.

15 Cf art. 6(2) SSM R.

16 As the supervision of those SIs is carried out by Joint Supervisory Teams (JSTs), composed of NCAs and ECB staff, headed by an ECB manager.

17 Art. 9 SSM R.

18 Arts. 10–11 SSM R.

19 Art. 12 SSM R.

20 Cf art. 16 SSM R.

21 Art. 18 SSM R. Due to constitutional limitations, the ECB is only entitled to impose pecuniary penalties over supervised entities (legal persons). It cannot impose non-pecuniary penalties, nor directly sanction natural persons.

As regards the decision-making process concerning the adoption of supervisory decisions and regulations, the SSM has sketched a two-step procedure with a view to ensure the separation of the prudential supervisory tasks allocated to the ECB from its statutory and treaty-founded monetary policy functions.[22] **I.013**

To this end, the SSM has established a *Supervisory Board* formed by a Chair, a Vice-Chair,[23] four representatives of the ECB[24] and one representative from the relevant NCA of each participating MS. Further, the SSM R contemplates a *Steering Board*, composed by the Chair, the Vice-Chair of the Supervisory Board, one additional member from the ECB and several members of the NCAs of the participating MSs.[25] This Steering Committee has the main objective of preparing the Supervisory Board meetings and helping it to fulfil its tasks. **I.014**

As a general rule, the Supervisory Board adopts its decisions by simple majority of its members. Hence, with a view to preserve the statutory structure of the ECB,[26] draft decisions approved by the Supervisory Board need to be approved by the Governing Council through a non-objection procedure. Hence, the Governing Council is given up to ten working days to object to the draft supervisory decisions submitted.[27] In the case that it objects, it must provide the reason leading to such objection, in particular, highlighting any *monetary policy concerns* it may have.[28] **I.015**

The SSM R also implements an internal body tasked with the purpose of carrying out "*an internal administrative review of the decisions taken by the ECB in the exercise of the powers conferred on it*".[29] Such a body, named the Administrative Board of Review (ABoR), is composed of five independent individuals (and five alternates) of high repute and expertise in the financial field who are not ECB nor NCAs staff. The ABoR will issue, upon request of the supervisees, non-binding opinions addressed to the Supervisory Board on the compliance **I.016**

22 Cf art. 25 SSM R.

23 Appointed by the council, upon proposal from the Parliament. Candidates proposed by the Parliament to the Council are proposed by the ECB. Cf art. 26(3) SSM R.

24 Art. 26(5) SSM R.

25 Art. 26(10) SSM R.

26 Where the Governing Council is the ultimate decision-making body of the ECB. Cf arts. 129(1) TFEU and 9(3) and 10 Protocol on the Statute of the European System of Central Banks and of the European Central Bank (SESCB).

27 Art. 26(8) SSM R.

28 Ibidem.

29 Art. 24(1) SSM R.

of supervisory decisions with procedural safeguards and substantive rules foreseen in the SSM R.

I.017 Concerning the mentioned procedural safeguards, art. 22 SSM R expressly contemplates the minimum due process rights and binds the ECB to observe them, regarding the adoption of supervisory decisions.

I.018 On the independence dimension, art. 19 SSM R reinforces ECB independence when carrying out the tasks attributed to it under the SSM R. To this end, the ECB, and also the NCAs, must act independently. Further, art. 19(2) SSM R calls other EU bodies and institutions and "*the governments of the Member States*" to respect such independence.

I.019 The SSM foresees, also, measures to ensure the democratic accountability of the ECB in the exercise of its new supervisory tasks. To this end, it is expressly indicated that the ECB shall be accountable to the European Parliament (EP or European Parliament, indistinctively) and to the Council as regards the implementation of the SSM R, in the terms contemplated therein.[30]

I.020 Those terms foresee the issuance of a yearly report to the Parliament, to be presented by the Chair of the Supervisory Board. Also, the Regulation contemplates that further exchanges with the Chair of the Supervisory Board may take place on request of the Parliament (including *ad hoc* requests formulated both orally or in writing) and, eventually, confidential sessions with the Chair and Vice-Chairs of competent parliamentary committees.[31]

I.021 Additionally, the ECB will be subject to the operational scrutiny of the Court of Auditors[32] as regards the exercise of the supervisory task allocated under the SSM R.

I.022 To conclude, the SSM R simply enunciates the basic rule that those affected (negatively in principle) by a decision adopted by the ECB may bring an action before the Court of Justice of the EU (CJEU). The vague reference enunciated in art. 24(11) SSM R must be read in conjunction with its Recital (60), which expressly indicates that: "*Pursuant to Article 263 TFEU, the CJEU is to review*

30 Art. 20(1) SSM R.
31 Cf art. 20(2)–(6) and (8) SSM R.
32 Art. 20(7) SSM R.

the legality of acts of, inter alia, the ECB, other than recommendations and opinions, intended to produce legal effects vis-à-vis third parties".

This schematic picture, though, does not do justice to the nuances and mismatches linked to the SSM and the SSM R, which are multiple and legally complex. These constitute this book's main focus. **I.023**

PART I

SSM ORIGINS AND TREATY FOUNDATIONS: SOLID AS A ROCK OR CAPABLE OF BEING CHALLENGED?

1

FROM EUROPEAN AND MONETARY UNION (EMU) TO BU, ARCHITECTURE OF THE BU

A. THE EVOLUTION OF THE ECB

1. From the European Monetary Institute to the ECB as a supervisor

1.001 To an outside perspective, it may seem natural that central banks (or *ad hoc* agencies, functionally similar in nature) carry out micro– and macro-prudential supervision tasks. Economic, governmental and legal operators have intuitively incorporated this approach into their mindset. However, it is not.

1.002 Central banks' duties have come a long way from their initial purposes, mainly providing finance to the Crown or the government facing the costs of expensive wars.[1] In addition, tracking the origins of Central Banks sometimes reveals their private or public-private origins, focused on providing finance to a vigorous merchant class – or to the general public.[2] These early war-financing

1 See Goodhart, C. A. E. (2010). The changing role of central banks. *BIS Working Papers* No 326. At p. 1. The author refers to the central banks of England and France which are, indeed, two of the first central banks ever established.

Looking back at the history of central banks, mention must be made to the Bank of the Estates of the Realm of Sweden (nowadays, the *Sveriges Riksbank*) (see Lastra, R. M. (2011). The Evolution of the European Central Bank. *Queen Mary University of London, School of Law Legal Studies Research* Paper No. 99/2012. At p. 3). The Sveriges Riksbank was founded in 1668, becoming the world's first central bank. The primarily objective allocated on this central bank was not specially related with providing war finance, but with procuring price stability. See: History | Sveriges Riksbank.

2 The Bank of England, which was set up as a private entity, intended precisely to provide finance to the public and to the merchant class. See Bagehot, W. (1873). Lombard Street: a Description of the Money Market. *Henry S. King & Co.*, London. This was also the case of the Banco de España (the Central Bank

and private-financing tasks were combined (later on) with a more well-known duty: providing price stability in the national territory.

In this regard, the ECB is not an exception. As a starting point, it must be noted that the Treaty of Rome[3] did not contemplate a monetary Union (not even dare to dream it). It was not until 1988 when talks on the need to enhance economic union and set out – to the extent possible – monetary union led to the establishment of the Delors Committee.[4] The report issued by such committee (the Delors Report[5]) proposed a new hybrid EU Institution, the very first experiment of this kind, formed by a central institution[6] and the National Central Banks (NCB) (together the *European System of Central Banks* (ESCB)). Within this architecture, the Delors report aimed at entrusting the coordination not only of monetary policies – which was, and still is, the principal function of the ESCB[7] – but, in the long run, the system should also play a role in banking supervision.[8] **1.003**

The Maastricht Treaty[9] grandfathered, later on, such an approach and introduced two sets of provisions relevant to understand the set of powers allocated to the ECB under the SSM: *first*, the Protocol on the Statute of the European **1.004**

---

of Spain), originally funded by means of royal decree on 2 June 1782 and named as *Banco Nacional de San Carlos*. Although it was promoted by the crown, its capital was fully private and divided into shares.

3 Treaty establishing the European Economic Community made in Rome on 25 March 1957 (TEC or Treaty of Rome).

4 This committee was chaired by himself and composed by the governors of the MSs' central banks and three additional members: Alexandre Lamfalussy, Miguel Boyer and Niels Thygesen.

5 Report on economic and monetary union in the European Community Presented on 17 April 1989 (hereafter the Delors report): http://aei.pitt.edu/1007/1/monetary_delors.pdf).

6 This was later called the European Monetary Institute (cf art. 109f of the Maastricht Treaty). This *ephemeral* body – which constituted the prelude to the ECB – played a brief but rather decisive role laying the foundations of the ESCB as we know it nowadays.

Having initiated its activities in 1994 – as foreseen in the Maastricht Treaty – its existence ceased on 1 June 1998, once the ECB was established. See Lastra, R. M. & Louis, J. V. (2013). European Economic and Monetary Union: history, trends, and prospects. *Queen Mary University of London, School of Law. Legal Studies Research Paper* No. 136/2013, at pp. 12–13; and the ECB webpage on the Stage 2 of the EMU: https://www.ecb.europa.eu/ecb/history/emu/html/index.en.html.

7 On the predominance of the ECB monetary policy mandate, see Lamandini, M., Ramos Muñoz, D. & Solana, J. (2015). Depicting the Limits to the SSM's Supervisory Powers: The Role of Constitutional Mandates and of Fundamental Rights' Protection. *Quaderni di Ricerca Giuridica*, (79), at pp. 40–43; and Lamandini, M., Ramos, D. & Solana, J. (2016). The European Central Bank (ECB) as a Catalyst for Change in EU Law, Part 1: The ECB's Mandates. *Colum. J. Eur. L.*, *23*, 1, at pp. 46–48.

8 "*the System would participate in the coordination of banking supervision policies of the supervisory authorities*" (see the Delors Report at Para. 32, p. 22). In addition, the advising/coordinating function on banking supervision attributed to the ESCB was not *brand new* at all. It was already foreseen in the *first* step drawn in the Delors Report. However, it must be conceded that the report attributed these tasks to an *advisory committee*.

A deeper analysis may suggest that the Delors report aimed at allocating to the ESCB a greater role on this matter, enabling it to carry out not only regular *consultations* but also the *coordination* of banking supervision policies.

9 Treaty on European Union (Maastricht Treaty) signed on 7 February 1992 (in force on 1 November 1993).

System of Central Banks and of the European Central Bank (SESCB) and, *second*, art. 105(6) to the TEC.

1.005 Arts. 25(2) SESCB and 105(6) TEC (as amended by the Maastricht Treaty), provided for an enabling clause to allocate upon the ECB *specific* tasks concerning prudential supervision of credit institutions.[10]

1.006 The institutional architecture designed by the Maastricht Treaty remained unchanged after the Treaty of Amsterdam. Successively, the Treaty of Nice[11] did not impact this matter; the wording of art. 105(6) TEC remained untouched.[12] Fifteen years later after the Maastricht Treaty, a modification of the *enabling clause* was performed by the Lisbon Treaty.[13] Such modification constitutes, in the view of the author, a mere clerical amendment. In this regard, the two modifications performed consist of: (i) suppressing the EC's initiative to submit to the Council a draft Regulation proposing the allocation of supervisory competences to the ECB, and (ii) the explicit reference to the kind of legal instrument – *Regulations* – to be used for these purposes.[14]

---

10 By means of this provision is instituted the so-called *enabling* clause, whose literal wording is as follows: "*6. The Council may, acting unanimously on a proposal from the Commission and after consulting the ECB and after receiving the assent of the European Parliament, confer upon the ECB specific tasks concerning policies relating to the prudential supervision of credit institutions and other financial institutions with the exception of insurance undertakings*".

The necessity for such clause was early foreseen by the *Committee of Governors of the Central Banks of the Member States of the European Economic Community* in its *Commentary to draft statute of the European System of Central Banks and of the European Central Bank, issued on 27 November 1990* (https://www.ecb.europa.eu/ecb/access_to_documents/document/cog_pubaccess/shared/data/ecb.dr.parcg2007_0001annex1.en.pdf?2ff91099977119d7bb19fff1465b3128). Said commentary referred that: "*Any future transferral of competence to the ECB should be specified by Community legislation for which the Treaty would have to provide an enabling clause*".

It must be noted that the Committee did not make reference to a precise legal act but simply to *legislation*. Therefore, it is implied that in its mind, the Committee may have understood that the transferral of supervisory competences could take place, potentially, through other legal means than through a *Regulation.*

11 Treaty of Nice amending the Treaty on European Union, the Treaties establishing the European Communities and certain related acts. This Treaty was signed on 26 February 2001 and entered into force on 1 April 2003 (however, the applicability of some of its provision was postponed).

12 The impact of the Draft Treaty establishing a Constitution for Europe is not analysed here because it was not finally enacted. However, it seems that it did not materially impact on the enabling clause. See Smits, R. (2005). The role of the ESCB. In *Banking supervision. Legal Aspects of the European System of Central Banks*. In *Liber amicorum Paolo Zamboni Garavelli* (pp. 199–212). Frankfurt am Main: European Central Bank. At p. 204.

13 Treaty of Lisbon amending the Treaty on European Union and the Treaty establishing the European Community. This Treaty was signed on 13 December 2007 and entered into force on 1 December 2009.

The Treaty of Lisbon amended the TEC and renamed it as the Treaty on the Functioning of the European Union (TFEU). In addition, the mentioned Treaty of Lisbon renumbered the TEC and its protocols, and therefore, art. 105 TEC passed to be current art. 127 TFEU. Furthermore, the *Protocol on the Statute of the European System of Central Banks and of the ECB* is now listed as protocol nº 14 of TFEU.

14 An additional minor modification would be the qualification of the legislative procedure to be followed as *special.*

Such enabling clause (art. 127(6) TFEU), introduced in the Treaties already in 1992, was only activated for the first time 2010.[15] More than 21 years later (in 2013), the financial and economic crisis prompted the activation of the enabling clause with a view to implement the SSM (which became operative one year later in November 2014). Accordingly, the ECB, who was born as a monetary policy authority, was finally dressed in supervisory clothes. **1.007**

2. The (in)complete architecture of the BU, a temple without its final pillar

Building upon the evocative image of a Greek temple façade, the BU is, at the time these lines are being written, a work in progress. Its well-founded basement, the Single Rulebook,[16] has been operating – almost in its entirety – since the beginning of 2014 and refined under the aegis of the EBA, fostering its horizontal character.[17] **1.008**

In this façade, the BU's *first pillar*, the SSM, became reality already in October 2013. The *second pillar*, the SRM was established the next year, merging seamlessly its geographical remit (the Eurozone and the participating MSs) with that of the SSM. At the same time, BRRD catered for the adequate material basis for the SRM to carry out its resolution tasks. **1.009**

Finally, the *third pillar*, the EDIS, seems still utopic nowadays. Whereas the Five Presidents Report situated the time horizon for the political agreement by 2015–2017, the impasse of the negotiations is today more patent than ever before.[18] In October 2017, the EC again urged the EP, the Council, the ECB, the Economic and Social Committee and the Committee of Regions to *complete the Banking Union*.[19] **1.010**

---

15 To assign certain specific tasks to the ECB concerning the European Systemic Risk Board (ESRB) by means of Council Regulation 1096/2010 of 17 November 2010 conferring specific tasks upon the European Central Bank concerning the functioning of the European Systemic Risk Board.

16 The set of material rules that operates within the BU, basically, CRR, CRDIV, DGS and BRRD; those rules are sometimes referred as Level 1 texts.

17 At this point, it is worth mentioning that the CRR has been amended 17 seventeen times by during its relatively short life. A consolidated version of this Regulation, indicating in chronological order all its amendments, can be found here: EUR-Lex – 02013R0575-20240709 – EN – EUR-Lex (europa.eu).

On its side, CRD IV was amended nine times. A consolidated version of this Regulation, indicating in chronological order all its amendments, can be found here: EUR-Lex – 02013L0036-20240729 – EN – EUR-Lex (europa.eu).

18 At a political level, Germany appears to be the only country opposing the deployment of such a necessary Pillar. Domestic preferences and competitive advantages enjoyed by the German banking sector under their current regulatory environment motivate this fierce opposition. (See the analyses carried out by Isabel Schnabel (member of the German Council of Economic Experts) in the Financial Times on 29 August 2018 (https://www.ft.com/content/4a3d048a-a9fb-11e8-8253-48106866cd8a).

19 Communication to the European parliament, the Council, the European Central Bank, the European Economic and Social Committee and the Committee of the Regions on completing the Banking Union. COM(2017) 592 final.

1.011 As the EC's proposal on the establishment of a European Deposit Insurance Scheme clearly summarises:[20] "*EDIS addresses the misalignment between the Union supervision and resolution of banks in the participating Member States, on the one hand, and the effectiveness and credibility of national DGSs in case of failure of those same banks pursuant to the Directive 2014/59/EU on Deposit Guarantee Schemes (DGS Directive), on the other*". Therefore, the instrument is not only the final step of a fully-fledged BU but also an essential requisite to maintain financial stability, provide equal protection to depositors and definitively tackle domestic discretions affecting banking services competition.

1.012 At the present time, negotiations between the EP and the Council are stuck. The MSs' preferences show different sensibilities concerning the design of the EDIS when fully phased-in and its willingness towards more (or not) fiscal unions and how to properly handle the issue of non-performing loans (NPLs). The EC has acknowledged the progress made in reducing non-performing loans and its material decrease so far. For the ECB, the impact of NPLs on credit institutions' profitability has become a major concern for the ECB as its chair, Andrea Enria, soon spotted.[21]

1.013 In early December 2018, the Economic and Financial Affairs Council discussed thoroughly a technical report on the progress of the negotiations concerning the EDIS.[22] The conclusions of the following Euro Summit, held on 14 December, reflected the lack of consensus about the path to be followed; the statement that followed this Euro Summit does not make any reference to the EDIs.[23]

1.014 Only the Economic and Financial Affairs Council's press release made a brief reference to the ongoing negotiations,[24] postponing further decision for June

---

20 Proposal for a Regulation of the European Parliament and of the Council amending Regulation (EU) 806/2014 in order to establish a European Deposit Insurance Scheme. COM(2015) 586 final: http://www.europarl.europa.eu/RegData/docs_autres_institutions/commission_europeenne/com/2015/0586/COM_COM(2015)0586_EN.pdf.

21 During its first interview in the media, stating: "*We still have the legacy issue of non-performing loans. And the macroeconomic outlook seems to be deteriorating. You need to complete this process of cleaning the bank's balance sheets before you enter the next recession*". (See Interview with Andrea Enria, Chair of the Supervisory Board of the ECB, conducted by Claire Jones on 13 March 2019 and published on 19 March 2019: https://www.bankingsupervision.europa.eu/press/interviews/date/2019/html/ssm.in190319~3a9b32fbbc.en.html?utm_source=ecb_linkedin&utm_medium=social&utm_campaign=190319_interview_enria).

22 See the conclusions of the Economic and Financial Affairs Council of 4 December 2018: https://www.consilium.europa.eu/media/37280/st15085-en18.pdf.

23 Euro Summit statement EURO 503/18: https://www.consilium.europa.eu/media/37563/20181214-euro-summit-statement.pdf.

24 See: https://www.consilium.europa.eu/en/press/press-releases/2018/12/04/eurogroup-report-to-leaders-on-emu-deepening/.

2019. The last development on this matter took place in March 2024, when the Committee on Economic and Monetary Affairs of the EP issued a report proposing the adoption of the EDIS regulation[25] in a phased manner (i.e., funded progressively over the coming years and steered at an EU level). After the issuance of such report, the ball sits on EC's and MSs' court. The former should refer to the EP in case it intends to substantially amend such a proposal, and the latter should push forwards the adoption of such a proposal.

Despite this latest development, the author notes that nothing augurs that in the short nor middle term; the BU's third pillar will be set out. **1.015**

B. SSM BASIC PRINCIPLES: LEVEL PLAYING FIELD & PROPORTIONALITY

It is time now to explore the pure will of the *legislators*[26] (and of the agents involved in the drafting process of the SSM R). **1.016**

The purpose is twofold: *(a)* firstly, to (try to) find a principle or set of principles guiding the general interpretation of the SSM R and its rationale; and *(b)* secondly, to attribute a determined *weighting* to the key principles of the SSM R, capable of helping prioritise or postpone feasible legal solutions when the particular acts of application of the SSM R generate frictions. **1.017**

In the pursuit of the principle or principles that should guide the interpretation of the SSM R, indefectible attention must be paid to the will of Parliament, as it was a major player that, indeed, refined and amended severely the EC draft proposal. Accordingly, the structure of the parliamentary debates favours this principle-based analysis. **1.018**

From the outset, following the draft SSM R presented by the EC,[27] concerns of the SSM R being an instrument tailor-made to deal with systemic institutions,[28] and designed somehow to reinforce their credibility before the **1.019**

---

25 Actually, a regulation that amends the SRM R.

26 The term *legislators* is used on purpose here. Art. 127(6) TFEU attributes to the Council the possibility of "*confer*[ring] *specific tasks upon the European Central Bank concerning policies relating to the prudential supervision*". That is, without seeking the Parliament's formal approval, although its involvement must be sought through consultation. Yet, the EP involvement was so decisive and thorough that the SSM R overcomes a substantive co-decision procedure.

27 Proposal for a Council regulation conferring specific tasks on the European Central Bank concerning policies relating to the prudential supervision of credit institutions (COM(2012) 511 final.

28 See, on the topic of the SSM being designed in the form of *one size fits all*, the interesting contribution of Joosen, B., Lamandini, M., Lehmann, M., Lieverse, K. & Tirado, I. (2018). Stability, Flexibility and Proportionality: Towards a Two-Tiered European Banking Law? *European Banking Institute Working Paper Series* 2018 no. 29.

markets, spread. Middle-size and local entities would take part in a model too complex, too burdensome to deal and capture their specificities.

1.020 The words deployed in the draft texts point towards absolute harmonisation, that is, level playing field. The first and intermediate version of the draft report issued by the Committee on Constitutional Affairs of the Parliament[29] (depicting the legislative measure) contained clearer and a greater number of explicit references to the concept of *level playing field*, which were suppressed in the approved SSM R. However, we can still find an explicit reference to this principle in Recital 41 SSM R. Yet, unlike in the previous versions, the SSM R does not include an explicit reference to this principle in its normative part.

1.021 Does the envisaged level playing field mean that "one size fit all"? One may argue not, and I argue that this is what, precisely, the legislators' will. The SSM R articulates mechanisms capable of dealing with (if properly managed) the variety of business models, sizes and banking traditions.

1.022 Accusations against the mechanism for being insensitive to the wide variety of entities subject to supervision (directly or indirectly) were expressly made during the debate.[30] Some of the opinions submitted by national Parliaments show certain concerns on the capability of the SSM of copying with national features and specialities. In early November 2012, the Swedish Parliament issued fierce critics on the draft report presented by the Committee on Constitutional Affairs of the Parliament. It openly considered that the proposed Regulation conflicted with the principles of proportionality and subsidiarity. The Swedish Parliament argued that it was against the principle of subsidiarity that the MSs would not be capable of rising autonomously the capital requirements of its national credit institutions.[31]

29 The several versions of the draft SSM R issued during the parliamentary discussion can be consulted here: Verbatim report of proceedings – Specific tasks for the European Central Bank concerning policies relating to the prudential supervision of credit institutions (A7-0392/2012 – Marianne Thyssen) (vote) – Wednesday, 22 May 2013 (europa.eu).

30 In this token, the member of Parliament John Bufton (EFD) stated: "*This proposed banking union represents a single one-size-fits-all approach that does not show the slightest regard for the hugely complex nature of the financial crisis we currently find ourselves in*". See also Joosen, B., Lamandini, M., Lehmann, M., Lieverse, K. & Tirado, I. (2018). Stability, Flexibility and Proportionality: Towards a Two-Tiered European Banking Law? *European Banking Institute Working Paper Series* 2018 no. 29.

31 Opinion accessible here: http://www.ipex.eu/IPEXL-WEB/dossier/files/download/082dbcc539edbbe6013ae51481b2079a.do).

This observation was taken on board and, in the draft proposal, presented in the Parliament on 14 May 2013, and a new art. 4a (*macroprudential tools*) was included (actually art. 5 SSMR).

Although those concerns were legitimate, the SSM R is vested with a panoply of instruments to ensure homogeneity and a level playing field while treating differently those situations which deserve being treated differently. Consequently, the system would respect the principle of proportionality in the abstract: **1.023**

First, when carrying out its supervisory tasks, the ECB is bound by the principle of proportionality. That means treating different what is different. In this regard, art. 1(III) of the SSM R stresses this policy mandate by establishing that "*the ECB shall have full regard to the different types, business models and sizes of credit institutions.*"[32] What makes this general policy mandate particularly strong is that it is triggered whenever the ECB carries out the tasks entrusted under the SSM R. **1.024**

Second, the provisions defining the mechanism to set out the perimeter of entities subject to ECB direct supervision provide the substantial materialisation of this principle.[33] Subjecting the most relevant credit institutions and financial groups to the same consolidated supranational supervisor allows the consolidated supervisor to harmonise its prudential approach while, at the same time, it enriches its own experience, comparing and contrasting the different business models of the entities under its remit. But what is most important is that the system provides for two different approaches based on the importance and level of complexity of the credit institutions/financial groups; those thought to be most relevant are subject to the direct supervision of the ECB whereas those not considered significant remain under NCAs direct supervision. **1.025**

Finally, the basic *bricks* upon which the mechanism bases its day-to-day supervisory activity, that is, the JSTs provide for elements to take on board national supervisory practices and approaches. It also allows the ECB to benefit from national expertise built up by years of supervisory practice. Being JSTs composed by NCAs members, acting under the aegis of ECB coordinators,[34] can ensure an adequate representation of the domestic supervisory traditions. **1.026**

All in all, even if the objective of the SSM is achieving supranational harmonised supervision (level playing field) delinked from any national pressure, it does not disregard the wide variety of models and previous supervisory traditions. In fact, it establishes a policy-guiding principle that should bound the **1.027**

32 Cf Recital 17.

33 See art. 6(4) SSM R and Part IV of the SSM Fr (arts. 39–72). See further in *Chapter 6. Allocation of tasks within the SSM.*

34 Arts. 3–6 SSM Fr.

ECB action (having *full regard to the different types, business models and sizes of credit institutions*) and a wide range of concrete mechanisms that materialise that principle and fully put it into practice.

1.028 Hereby, I submit that when interpreting the provisions of the SSM, we have to find an adequate balance between two forces, two principles of equal force and opposed direction: level playing field within a proportionality approach.

1.029 Further, when interpreting SSM provisions one needs to bear in mind also the principle of "equivalence and effectiveness" foreseen in art. 19(1) TEU.[35] Pursuant to this principle of long standing tradition,[36] MS are required to establish a system of legal remedies and procedures capable of protecting the rights conferred on individuals by EU law.[37]

1.030 Although pursuant to the principle of *procedural autonomy*,[38] it is for the MSs to freely establish the remedies and procedures they may deem appropriate; they must ensure that those ensure effective judicial protection of concerned individuals.[39]

1.031 The principles of equivalence and effectiveness act, then, as a limit to the procedural autonomy of MSs, which must ensure that the substantive rules provided under EU law are capable of being enforced with enough guarantees.[40] Accordingly, when construing the provisions enshrined in the SSM R (and national substantive provisions allowing its implementation), this must be done in full compliance with the principle of equivalence and effectiveness, with a view to ensure that the *mechanism* remains effective in such a fractious legislative setting.[41]

---

35 Extensively on this matter, see Lenaerts, K. (2011). National remedies for private parties in the light of the EU law principles of equivalence and effectiveness. *Irish Jurist (1966–)*, Vol. 46, pp. 13–37, and Lenaerts, K., Maselis, I. and Gutman, K. (2015). *EU procedural law*. OUP Oxford.

36 See Court of Justice judgment in case 45–76 (*Comet BV v Produktschap voor Siergewassen*) of 16 December 1976 (ECLI:EU:C:1976:191). At Para. 13.

37 See Lenaerts 2011 at p. 13–14. See also Court of Justice Judgement in case C-93/12 (*ET Agrokonsulting-04-Velko Stoyanov*) of 27 June 2013 (ECLI:EU:C:2013:432), at Paras. 35–36.

38 See Court of Justice judgment in case C-224/01 (*Gerhard Köbler v Republik Österreich*) of 30 September 2003 (ECLI:EU:C:2003:513). At Para. 47.

39 See Court of Justice judgment in case C-12/08 (*Mono Car Styling SA*) of 16 July 2009 (ECLI:EU:C:2009:466).

40 Lenaerts 2011 at p. 15.

41 See Section A.2. (*The (problematic) application by the ECB of national law: some considerations*) in Chapter 7.

2

CONSTITUTIONAL FOUNDATIONS OF THE SSM

The so-called enabling clause (art. 127(6) TFEU) is the keystone upon which the SSM is built. The use of this constitutional basis was already contemplated in the Four Presidents Report and in the EC's draft legislative proposal.[1] The Parliament fully embraced the proposed constitutional basis. Neither the report issued by the competent parliamentary committee nor the three committees which submitted their opinions in writing raised any concern on the foundational basis chosen.[2] However, the Parliamentary debate cast serious **2.001**

1 See Section B. (*SSM basic principles: level playing field & proportionality*) in Chapter 1. In addition, the EC, in its communication COM(2012) 777 final (*A blueprint for a deep and genuine economic and monetary union Launching a European Debate*), insisted on recurring to art. 127(6) TFEU for settling the SSM (at p. 39).

2 Ibidem.

doubts on the validity of the Treaty basis used for setting out the SSM or, better said, for establishing it in the manner that it was.[3]

2.002 The EC itself conceded the necessity of reviewing the basis to settle the SSM by expressing that:

> *Article 127 paragraph 6 TFEU could be amended to make the ordinary legislative procedure applicable and to eliminate some of the legal constraints it currently places on the design of the SSM (e.g., enshrine a direct and irrevocable opt-in by non-euro area Member States to the SSM, beyond the model of 'close cooperation', grant non-euro area Member States participating in the SSM fully equal rights in the ECB's decision-making, and go even further in the internal separation of decision-making on monetary policy and on supervision).*

2.003 Does art. 127(6) constitute a sound legal basis for establishing the SSM as depicted by the SSM R? The question is multifaceted and cannot be reduced to whether the system is valid or has gone far beyond the remit of its constitutional foundations (however, I believe that its foundations are solid enough). The previous query puts on the table at least three additional questions that show the *open texture* of this main question. One: at the time it was drafted, was art. 127(6) TFEU designed to cope with a fully-fledged supranational supervisory system? I argue that it was not. Two: if so, can constitutional evolution explain and protect the SSM as conceived by the SSM R? And, focusing on the standard of judicial review developed by the CJEU, is there any chance that the System may be overturned? I strongly believe that there is not. Three: is the SSM effective from a legal perspective or, in other words, given its original constitutional shortcomings, can we make it work? I strongly believe that this is possible, and the objective of this research is to detect those shortcomings related to sanctioning (and supervisory) proceedings and overcome them.

A. CONSTITUTIONAL CONSTRAINS OF THE ENABLING CLAUSE

2.004 Examining the enabling clause requires analysing two separated features: *(a)* the material (objective) scope of the clause (the matters that can be entrusted to the ECB) and *(b)* the subjective scope of the supervisory powers that may be attributed to the ECB.

2.005 This analysis cannot be understood without recourse to the original will of the agents that modelled the wording of the enabling clause, but also taking into

3 See Section B. (*SSM basic principles: level playing field & proportionality*) in Chapter 1.

account the evolution and maturation experienced by the EU in general and the EMU in particular.[4]

When tracing back the origins of and discussion on the enabling clause, it is easy to realise that the involvement of the ECB in supervisory matters was much less ambitious than it is in the SSM. This can be explained by the polarised debate that lead to the adoption of the final wording of this clause. The compromise reached modelled the clause in two ways. *Firstly*, it restricted its activation by establishing that the allocation of *tasks* regarding supervisory *policies* to the ECB would require the Council's unanimity. *Secondly*, the enabling clause also imposed objective limitations, concerning the scope of the tasks that could be allocated to the ECB, and subjective limitations as well, excluding *insurance companies* from its remit. **2.006**

1. Material limitations of the basis chosen: depicting the concepts of "specific" and "tasks"

(a) Material limitations I: the concept of "specific tasks" and the tasks actually transferred to the ECB

The adjective *specific*,[5] as opposed to *general*, implies that only certain selected tasks can be transferred to the ECB. **2.007**

This limitation creates some frictions with the SSM R constitutional foundations. It is arguable whether the huge armoury of tasks attributed to the ECB under the SSM R may allow to qualify them as *specific*.[6] Just to recall, art. 4 SSM R transfers to the ECB not only the core supervisory tasks – such as the authorisation and withdrawal of banking licenses, the assessment of the acquisition and disposal of qualifying holdings and the establishment of regulatory capital above the minimum regulatory levels[7] – but also other more subtle or less evident prudential tasks, such as relevant role attributed in relation to recovery plans and early intervention.[8] In addition, the ECB has also been **2.008**

4 See in Section A.1 (*From the European Monetary Institute to the ECB as a supervisor*) in Chapter 1 above.

5 *Spécifiques*, in French; *específicas*, in Spanish; *specifici*, in Italian.

6 Capolino, O. (2013). Il Testo unico bancario e il diritto dell'Unione Europea. In *Dal Testo unico bancario all'Unione bancaria: tecniche normative e allocazione di poteri* (pp. 51–73). Quaderni di Ricerca Giuridica della Consulenza Legale (Banca D'italia), n.75. At pp. 68 and ss. See, also, Gortsos, C. V. (2019). European Banking Union Within the System of European Banking and Monetary Law. In *The Palgrave Handbook of European Banking Union Law* (pp. 19–40). Palgrave Macmillan, Cham.

7 Indents a), c) and d) of art. 4(1) SSM R.

8 Indent i) of art. 4(1) SSM R.

equipped with a greater involvement concerning macro-prudential supervisory tasks.[9]

2.009 Additionally, the ECB has developed a teleological reading on the functions and powers attributed to it. This approach is prone to facilitating the expansion of involvement in supervisory matters, to the point that all the relevant supervisory powers concerning SIs are captured and therefore exercised by the ECB (even for powers stated by national statutes not aiming at transposing CRD IV). This expansive potential is rooted in the letters addressed to the ECB in 2016 and 2017 to all SIs.[10] As detailed in those letters and following art. 9(1) SSM R,[11] the ECB is given the power to decide, for example, on the amendments of institutions' bylaws, the approval of their external auditors or the appointment of *key function holders*.

2.010 Consequently, in practice and concerning SIs, only tasks and functions pertaining to consumer protection,[12] anti-money laundering,[13] purely competition matters,[14] supervision of the external auditors and similar matters[15] remain outside the ECB's remit.

(b) Material limitations II: the territorial scope of the SSM and the decentralised exercise of competences

2.011 As per the foregoing, it is hard thinking of supervisory tasks that are not allocated to the ECB, as regards SIs at least. Hence, the majority of the *core* micro-prudential tasks have been allocated to the ECB. This *massive* transferal of supervisory tasks – is it at odds with art. 127(6) TFEU, overstretching its limits (*specific tasks*) or not?

2.012 One may argue that the material transfer of a vast list of supervisory tasks can be compliant with the limits imposed by the enabling clause should we

---

9 Art. 5 SSM R.

10 See "Additional clarification regarding the ECB's competence to exercise supervisory powers granted under national law": https://www.bankingsupervision.europa.eu/press/letterstobanks/shared/pdf/2017/Letter_to_SI_Entry_point_information_letter.pdf?cb0801df81ba2db9d450ce4fb53065c8. See further in Section B.1. (*Tasks included vs. tasks excluded*) in Chapter 6.

11 The ECB is vested with the national powers foreseen in national law, provided that those powers strictly relate to any of the supervisory tasks listed on arts. 4 and 5 SSM R and as regards SIs.

12 The conditions attached to the commercialisation of banking products (*product rules*). See the letter cited in previous footnote 10 at p. 2.

13 Court of Justice judgment in case C-803/21 P (*Versobank AS v ECB*) of 7 September 2023 (ECLI:EU:C:2023:630) at Para. 97.

14 Ibidem at p. 2.

15 Recital 25 SSM R.

be capable of looking at the broader picture, that is, (*a*) considering the geographical scope of the SSM and (*b*) the decentralised exercise of the supervisory tasks envisaged by the SSM R.

As per the territorial argument, it must be emphasised that although the regulations approved on the basis of the enabling clause are applicable to all EU MSs,[16] the SSM R applies only to participating member states (art 2(1) SSM R), that is, euro currency MS and non euro-currency MS, which have established a close cooperation.[17] The tension generated between the *ins* and the *outs* paradoxically has contributed to reinforce the compatibility of the SSM with its treaty basis. By construing the term *specific* in a comprehensive way, it becomes reasonable to state that the tasks attributed to the ECB are *specific* insofar as they are deployed only within the monetary union and the territory of the participating MSs. **2.013**

Attention must be also paid in the *decentralised way those tasks are executed.* Whereas the EC's initial proposal[18] envisaged attributing (directly) to the ECB the abovementioned supervisory tasks concerning *all* credit institutions, the final text of the SSM R tempered this ambitious proposal. The CJEU has further confirmed that the ECB is exclusively competent to supervise all credit institutions included within the scope of the SSM.[19] However, the Court has also ruled that the prudential tasks referred to in art. 4(1) SSM R are implemented within a decentralised framework and, in this regard, the intensity of ECB's oversight when carrying them out is directly correlated with the type of institution: SIs or LSIs. Therefore, it can be concluded that the tasks attributed to the ECB under the SSM R are *specific*, as they are performed with a different degree of intensity depending on the relevance of the institution supervised.[20] **2.014**

To conclude, given that (a) the mechanism results are applicable only to the *ins* participating MS (and not to the whole of the EU MSs), plus (b) only **2.015**

16 See Smits, R. (1997). *The European Central Bank: Institutional Aspects*. The Hague: Kluwer Law International. At pp. 359–360. Accordingly, Regulation 1096/2010, based on art. 127(6) TFEU, applies to all EU MSs as well.

17 See, on this matter, also, Teixeira, P. G. (2017). The legal history of the Banking Union. *European Business Organization Law Review*, *18*, pp. 535–565.

18 See COM(2012) 511 final: http://www.europarl.europa.eu/registre/docs_autres_institutions/commission_europeenne/com/2012/0511/COM_COM(2012)0511_EN.pdf.

19 See *L-bank case* at Paras. 54–58, as confirmed by the *L-Bank appeal*, at Paras. 37–38. See also, more recently, General Court judgment in joined cases T-351/18 and T-584/18 (*Ukrselhosprom PCF LLC v ECB* and *Versobank AS v ECB*, respectively) of 6 October 2021 (ECLI:EU:T:2021:669), at Para. 133.

20 However, authorisation (and withdrawal) of credit institutions and the assessment of acquisition and disposal of qualifying holdings remain entirely on the hands of the ECB as regards both SIs and LSIs (cf arts. 4(1)(a) and (c) and 6 (4) SSM R).

a number of tasks are directly implemented by the ECB (mainly as regards SIs), it can be considered that, indeed, the tasks allocated to the consolidated supervisor are *specific* and that the wording of the enabling clause is respected.

(c) Material limitations III: allocation of tasks but not of powers

2.016 The strict reading of the enabling clause provides the possibility of allocating, exclusively, *tasks* but not the *powers* necessary to carry those out.[21]

2.017 The controversy, though, is more apparent than real. *Firstly*, because from a hermeneutical perspective, the discussion is pointless. Allocating tasks to an EU body or institution without equipping it with the necessary implied powers to carry them out would result in the absurdity of rendering the transfer ineffective.[22] The apagogic argument obliges to admit that the enabling clause allows allocating the tasks *and* (necessary) powers to the ECB to implement them (i.e., without needing to issue a separate regulation subject eventually to a different treaty basis[23]). *Secondly*, the SSM R furnishes the ECB with an adequate set of powers, including "*the powers conferred on competent authorities by Union law*".[24] Those powers are sometimes expressly mentioned in the SSM R (e.g., investigatory powers[25]) and other times are implied and must be construed in light of art. 9 SSM R. *Thirdly*, because of the Parliament involvement in the legislative procedure,[26] there was no need to run a parallel legislative procedure, funded upon a complementary treaty basis to vest the ECB with the powers required to perform its functions under the SSM. This involvement of the Parliament, precisely, ensures compliance with the relevant CJEU case law addressed to ensure that the involvement of the Parliament is not

21 See Lackhoff, K. (2017). *Single supervisory mechanism: European banking supervision by the SSM: a practitioner's guide*. CH Beck [Lackhoff, K. (2017)(i)], at p. 16.

22 D'Ambrosio, R. The ECB and NCA liability within the single supervisory mechanism. *Quaderni di Ricerca giuridica della Consulenza Legale* (Banca d'Italia), nº 78, at p. 72.

23 It is worth recalling that the CJEU has ruled that, when necessary, the functioning of decision-making bodies needs to be ensured by allowing them to delegate some of their decision-making powers. This was the understanding of the Court in, among others, judgments C-5/85 (*AKZO Chemie v Commission*) of 23 September 1986 (ECLI:EU:C:1986:328), at Para. 37; and C-301/02 P (*Carmine Salvatore Tralli v ECB*), of 26 May 2005 (ECLI:EU:C:2005:306), at Para. 59.

Implicitly, the Court recognises that, to implement the tasks allocated on the decision-making bodies of an EU body, it should be vested with the necessary powers to do so, including the possibility of issuing a certain set of rules impacting its hierarchical units. Applying the same logic, it must be conceded that, to perform its tasks, the ECB must be vested with the necessary powers to do so.

24 Cf Recitals 45 and 55 SSM R.

25 See arts. 10–13 SSM R.

26 Which turned the legislative procedure into a truly co-decision one despite the strict wording of the enabling clause. See footnote 26 in Chapter 1 above.

circumvented by the Council by making use of a Treaty basis that artificially would exclude its full participation from the legislative procedure.[27]

Yet, even when it is clear that the political aim of the enabling clause, at the time it was drafted, did not envisage such a wide transferral of tasks to the ECB, it would not be reasonable to analyse this provision with the perspective of almost 30 years ago. The Treaties evolve and adapt to the reality, and therefore, they must be construed in accordance with the time they must be applied to. Similarly, at the time the Treaty of Rome was ratified, who would ever imagine that more than 40 years later, the *Community* would be regulating the use of Genetically Modified Organisms (GMOs)?[28] Nobody, and basically, because the matter to regulate was not existent at the time that Treaty was drafted. **2.018**

2. Subjective limitations: the enabling clause and insurance undertakings

The enabling clause excludes from its scope the transferral of tasks related to insurance undertakings. This natural limitation puts the SSM under additional pressure since the evolution of financial holdings in modern times has determined that they encompass not only the investment and banking business but also insurance undertakings under the same corporate umbrella. **2.019**

The intertwine between the financial and the insurance sector has turned this reference outdated,[29] adding burdens to the practical implementation of the SSM. To overcome this intrinsic limit, the SSM R rather contemplates that the ECB exercises its powers in connection with the tasks listed in arts. 4(1) and 5 SSM R over financial holdings and credit institutions. However, is this mechanism effective enough to prevent the violation of the limits of the enabling clause? I am afraid it is not, but the explanation is certainly more interesting than the bold answer itself. **2.020**

Some practical examples of frictions, between this limit imposed by the enabling clause and the functions allocated to the ECB, can be spotted in the **2.021**

27 In its judgment C-490/10 (*European Parliament v Council of the European Union*) of 6 September 2012 (ECLI:EU:C:2012:525), the Court of Justice annulled Regulation 617/2010 insofar that the chosen Treaty bases were incorrect and prevented the Parliament to fully participate in the ordinary legislative procedure. The Court held the same interpretation in its judgments in cases C-166/07 (*European Parliament v Council of the European Union*) of 3 September 2009 (ECLI:EU:C:2009:499) and C-414/04 (*European Parliament v Council of the European Union*) of 28 November 2006 (ECLI:EU:C:2006:742).

28 See Council Directive 90/220/EEC of 23 April 1990 on the deliberate release into the environment of genetically modified organisms: https://eur-lex.europa.eu/legal-content/EN/TXT/?uri=celex:31990L0220.

29 Lastra, R. M. (2011), at p. 12.

SSM R. *Firstly*, it must be highlighted that art. 4(1)(h) SSM R sets forth the possibility of the ECB being appointed as a coordinator as regards the supplementary supervision of a financial conglomerate.[30] In such quality, the ECB would be vested with limited competences concerning insurance undertakings.[31] Aligning those limited competences with the limits arising from the enabling clause can be complex under the best of circumstances when not almost impossible. To ensure compliance with the Treaty basis, the ECB should self-restrain from participating, advising or deciding any issue directly and materially impacting the insurance undertakings that form part of the conglomerate. Even with that caution, it is arguable whether the mere participation in the supplementary supervision of the financial conglomerate does not violate the limits of the enabling clause. Furthermore, one could argue that any decision affecting directly the conglomerate may impact indirectly the insurance undertaking. Therefore, even if this argumentation is conservative, the risks persist.

2.022 *Secondly*, the same issue can arise when dealing with the investigatory powers attributed to the ECB.[32] Bearing in mind that the investigatory powers attributed to the ECB may be exercised towards financial and mixed financial holding companies, and the personnel belonging to them,[33] it is not impossible that those powers may be exercised somehow over insurance undertakings as well. For example, if the relevant JST or investigating unit[34] decides to examine or request intragroups contracts, being one of the signatories of the insurance branch of the conglomerate, or to interview a representative of a parent holding financial company regarding a large exposures breach, the latter also having a seat within the supervisory board of an insurance undertaking pertaining to the group (and that can be potentially linked to the breach investigated). In addition, and given the fact that art. 10(1)(f) SSM R allows exercising those investigatory powers towards third companies outsourced with functions by financial entities, could the ECB exercise those powers if the outsourcing entity is an insurance undertaking? The variety of the situations exposes the lack of sense of the limitation included in the enabling clause. A strict reading

30 Cf Directive 2002/87/EC of the European Parliament and of the Council of 16 December 2002 on the supplementary supervision of credit institutions, insurance undertakings and investment firms in a financial conglomerate and amending Council Directives 73/239/EEC, 79/267/EEC, 92/49/EEC, 92/96/EEC, 93/6/EEC and 93/22/EEC; and Directives 98/78/EC and 2000/12/EC of the European Parliament and of the Council.

31 See Lackhoff, K. (2017) at p. 17.

32 See arts. 10–13 SSM R.

33 Cf art. 10(1)(b) to (f) SSM R.

34 Art. 125 SSM Fr.

of the enabling clause should prevent the ECB from exercising those powers whenever it entails a material and direct interaction with insurance undertakings. At the same time, this shortcoming could jeopardise the ability of the ECB to perform its tasks under the SSM R (and to exercise a complete and not fragmented supervision).

Finally, additional frictions can be detected as regards of the amounts of the administrative penalties that can be imposed by the ECB.[35] Whereas the fines that the ECB may impose in the cases falling within its remit can amount up to 10% of the total annual turnover, art. 18(2) SSM R determines that, where the sanctioned entity is a subsidiary of a parent undertaking, the total annual turnover shall be calculated from the "*consolidated account of the ultimate parent undertaking*". Since this consolidated account could potentially include the revenue from insurance undertakings belonging to the same holding, the issue is problematic.[36] To address this mismatch, one potential alternative would entail reading the said provision in conjunction with art. 127(6) TFEU and excluding from the consolidated account the contributions coming from any insurance undertaking when imposing fines. Nevertheless, one may object that this could be contrary to the aim of the legislators of considering the *whole* consolidated account of the financial holding at stake. **2.023**

In this regard, some scholars have claimed a Treaty amendment to deal with the shortcomings resulting from the limits imposed by the enabling clause concerning the exercise of supervisory tasks by the ECB over insurance undertakings[37] providing compliance with the principle of conferral, as depicted by the CJEU.[38] The author agrees that this would be the swiftest and most preferable solution. However, realistically, it is difficult to think that a Treaty amendment will occur in the short and midterm, as not even the financial crisis was capable of prompting it. An alternative to the proposed Treaty amendment entails using a finalistic approach linked to the main objective of the SSM: ensuring financial stability.[39] With a view to preserve financial stability, it may be construed that what is forbidden by the Treaty is to directly entrust the ECB with direct supervision over insurance undertakings but not **2.024**

35 Art. 18(1) SSM R.

36 See, on this point, Lamandini, M., Ramos, D. & Solana, J. (2016), at p. 242.

37 Ibidem; and Lackhoff, K. (2017), at p. 17.

38 Cf art. 13(2) TFEU. See, among many others, Court of Justice judgment in case C-133/06 (*Safe Countries of Origin*) of 6 May 2008 (ECLI:EU:C:2008:257) at Para. 44.

39 Cf art. 1(I) SSM R: "(…) *with a view to contributing to the safety and soundness of credit institutions and the stability of the financial system within the Union and each Member State*".

indirect supervision via financial or mixed financial holdings (matrix companies). Three arguments back this proposal:

2.025 *First*, the literal wording of the enabling clause only prevents the ECB from directly supervising insurance companies.

2.026 *Second*, this approach would be, indeed, required in order to ensure that the ECB conducts a sound prudential supervision, ensuring that financial stability is so maintained.[40] This would be, broadly speaking, compatible with the latest judicial developments that advocate to ascertain whether the act is appropriate to attaining the objectives pursued by the legislation without going beyond what is necessary to achieve it.[41] This approach demands weighing the specific act performed by the ECB to ensure prudential supervision (relating to the indirect oversight over insurance undertakings) against the need to ensure sound prudential supervision and financial stability and performing a subsidiarity test to ascertain whether the ECB did not go beyond what was strictly necessary to attain those objectives.

2.027 *Thirdly*, the evolutionary nature of the banking industry also demands an evolutionary interpretation of the enabling clause wording, suitable to present times and needs. The complexity of financial holdings and their expansion towards any financial market, including the insurance business, impedes simply tearing apart insurance undertakings from the consolidated supervision. Limiting ECB indirect supervision over those holdings may undermine the effectiveness of the SSM and compromise the possibility of attaining a sound prudential supervision.

2.028 Nevertheless, it may be still argued that a violation of the Treaty basis exists and that the above-mentioned arguments overstretch the treaty basis upon which the SSM is founded, violating the principle of conferral. Then it is worth asking whether the CJEU would be prone to review the current structure of the SSM R and should this be likely to happen given the restrictive standing rights to seek that judicial review.

---

40 Cf Recital 55 SSM R and *L-Bank appeal* at Para. 86.

41 Cf case *Gauweiler* at Para 67 and *L-Bank* at Para. 45.

B. THE ECB AS A "REGULATOR"

This Section aims at assessing whether the legal basis of the SSM would allow the ECB to exercise regulatory powers as regards the options and discretions (O&Ds) or, broadly, *ad extra* regulatory powers. **2.029**

1. Introduction: allocation of regulatory competences and the range of regulatory competences allocated to the ECB under the SSM

(a) Depicting the distribution of regulatory tasks between the ECB and the EBA

The ESFS model entrusted the ESAS, in general, and the EBA, in particular, with the tasks of developing the secondary level of legislation (RTS and ITS) to be formally approved by the Commission.[42] In this vein, the EBA is vested with *quasi-regulatory* powers to enact technical standards completing Level 1 legislation. **2.030**

This model interplays with the non-euro currency countries supervisory models and, of course, with the SSM. The broad picture situates the ECB, at the level of *enforcement* (Level 4) as supervisor, bound to apply the Level 2 legislation drafted by the EBA (and also Level 1 legislation). Accordingly, the financial architecture presents the dichotomy of separating *regulatory tasks*,[43] attributed to the EBA, from *enforcement-supervisory* tasks, entrusted to the ECB.[44] **2.031**

Still, the boundaries between regulatory/enforcing-supervising tasks are blurry. This is because *(i)* in accordance with art. 4(3)II SSM R, the ECB *is bound to* apply the ITS and IRS and, what is most relevant, even the EBA's soft-law instruments, such as the *guidelines* and *recommendations*.[45] By acting through these guidelines and recommendations (by definition, even more detailed than the rules included in the Single Rulebook), it may be argued that the EBA can limit the supervisory judgment of the ECB, restricting its discretion. *(ii)* The ECB is capable of exercising indirect influence on the EBA since, via art. 4(3) **2.032**

---

42 Ibidem. Cf also arts. 10(1)(v) and 15(1)(iv) EBA Regulation.

43 Not completely separated, considering the fact that at least the ESMA is vested with some *enforcing competences*, as the adoption of executive measures in accordance with art. 28 of Regulation No. 236/2012 on short selling and certain aspects of credit default swaps (cf *ESMA short selling* case at Paras. 63–64).

44 Grundmann, S. (2019). European Banking Union and Integration. In *European Banking Union and Constitution* (pp. 85–120). Oxford: Bloomsbury Publishing, at pp. 98, 112–115 and 119–120.

45 Cf, also, Recital 32 SSM R. Art. 4(3)II SSM R makes a cross-reference to art. 16 of the EBA Regulation, which allows the EBA to issue, subject to certain conditions, recommendations and guidelines.

Given the extensive wording of this article, one may argue that the ECB would be subject to the Q&A tool developed by the EBA on the basis of art. 29(2) of the EBA Regulation and now expressely covered in its art. 16b. And this, even if in compliance with this regulatory tool, is not subject to the *comply or explain* mechanism that the guidelines and recommendations enjoy (cf art. 16(2) of the EBA Regulation).

V SSM R, the ECB is entitled to draw the attention of the EBA to the need of issuing new or amending existing RTS or ITS. *(iii)* Finally, the non-voting member of the EBA Board of Supervisors nominated by the ECB[46] enjoys a pre-eminent position as the representative of the competent authority[47] supervising the greatest number of systemic credit institutions.[48] And its proposals and impulse are duly considered.

2.033 In short, the post financial crisis model contemplates (a) the EBA, entrusted with the regulatory task of developing the Single Rulebook, and (b), for the Eurosystem (and potentially beyond[49]), a consolidated supranational supervisor (the ECB) in charge of enforcing the Single Rulebook but not provided with regulatory powers to develop the Single Rulebook. This view was shared by ECB senior managers who acknowledged that "*[b]eyond our primary mandate for price stability, it is worth remembering that we are not regulators, neither for financial markets nor for banks*".[50]

(b) CRR and CRD IV: options and discretions

2.034 CRR and CRD IV contain several O&Ds. For the sake of clarity, a distinction must be drawn here on the concept of O&Ds. An *Option* refers to the case where "*competent authorities or Member States are given the choice on how to comply with a given provision, selecting from a range of alternatives set forth in Community legislation*".[51] A *Discretion* means "*a situation in which "competent authorities or Member States are given a choice as to whether to implement, or not implement, a given provision*".[52]

2.035 *Options* are numerous. Just citing some examples: (i) the possibility of waiving the application of prudential requirements on an individual basis (art. 7(1) CRR); (ii) the possibility of waiving the application of liquidity requirements on an individual basis (art. 8(1) CRR); and (iii) the possibility of waiving

46 Cf art. 40(1)(d) EBA Regulation.

47 EBA regulation classifies the ECB as another "competent authority" (cf art. 14 EBA Regulation).

48 See Grundmann, S. (2019). European Banking Union and Integration. In *European Banking Union and Constitution* (pp. 85–120). Oxford: Bloomsbury Publishing, at p. 120.

49 See immediately above concerning participating Member States (Cf arts. 2(1) and 7 SSM R).

50 Speech passed by Yves Mersch Member of the Executive Board of the ECB titled *Climate change and central banking* on 27 November 2018 in Frankfurt: https://www.ecb.europa.eu/press/key/date/2018/html/ecb.sp181127.en.html.

51 See Brescia Morra, C. (2014). From the Single Supervisory Mechanism to the Banking Union: The Role of the ECB and the EBA. *Luiss Guido Carli Working Paper 2/2014*, at pp. 12–13. See, also, on the scope and application of the GO&D, Witte, A. (2021). The application of national law by the ECB, including options and discretions, and its impact on the judicial review. In *Judicial Review in the European Banking Union* (pp. 236–250). Edward Elgar Publishing.

52 Ibidem.

certain requirements relating to securitisation[53] for entities situated in the same MS and which are permanently affiliated to a central body which supervises them (art. 10 CRR).[54]

Concerning *Discretions*, some examples can be also easily found in CRD IV, for example: (i) the possibility of exempting particular categories of credit institutions from the minimum initial capital requirements (art. 12(4) CRDIV); (ii) defining the causes of withdrawal of the banking license (art. 18 CRD IV); and (iii) the possibility of host MSs requiring all credit institutions that have branches within its territory to report periodically on their activities in that MS – only for information or statistical purposes (art. 40 CRD IV).[55] **2.036**

Those *alternatives* were vested on both MSs and Competent Authorities as the mechanism to provide a certain degree of flexibility when addressing supervisory issues.[56] Precisely, those O&Ds put additional tensions on the level playing field envisaged by the Single Rulebook, of which CRR and CRD IV represent its cornerstone.[57] **2.037**

(c) Range of "regulatory" competences allocated to the ECB: *ad intra* regulatory competences

When drafting the SSM R, the legislators vested the ECB with more or less identifiable *ad intra* powers to organise the modalities of cooperation between the NCAs and the ECB.[58] This expressly authorised regulatory powers crystallised in the SSM Fr. **2.038**

Digging in the SSM R, it is possible to find another example of expressly authorised *ad intra* regulatory powers: the ECB Decision on the methodology and procedures for the determination and collection of data regarding **2.039**

53 Under Regulation (EU) 2017/2402 of the European Parliament and of the Council of 12 December 2017 laying down a general framework for securitisation and creating a specific framework for simple, transparent and standardised securitisation and amending Directives 2009/65/EC, 2009/138/EC and 2011/61/EU and Regulations (EC) No. 1060/2009 and (EU) No. 648/2012.

54 Further examples would include (i) the prohibition of qualifying holdings outside the financial sector (art. 89(3) CRR); (ii) the definition of the default of an obligor (art. 178(1)(b) CRR); (iii) netting of own funds for position risks (art. 327(2) CRR); and (iv) waiver of determined own funds requirements calculations in case of major failures of the settlement or clearing systems (art. 380 CRR).

55 For a detailed assessment of O&Ds and its implications in the context of the SSM, see Bassani, G. (2019). *The Legal Framework Applicable to the Single Supervisory Mechanism: Tapestry Or Patchwork?* Kluwer Law International BV.

56 The *options* and *discretions* were, in fact, a sort of compromise reached in the *trialogues* between the EC, the Parliament and the Council, as regards the cases where finding a common understanding was not possible.

57 See Arranz Alonso, L. (2017). Level playing field: towards a more uniform application of banking legislation. In *ESCB Legal Conference 2016* (pp. 260–270). Frankfurt am Main, ECB. At p. 261.

58 Art. 6(7) SSM R and Recital 7 SSM Fr.

the fee factors used to calculate annual supervisory fees (art. 30(2) SSM Fr).[59] Accordingly, it can be concluded that the issuance of the aforementioned general Decision would be also covered by the general authorisation contemplated in art. 6(7) SSM R.[60] Therefore, the allocation of regulatory powers concerning *ad intra* matters does not stir up controversy, since those *ad intra* regulatory powers are specifically contemplated and delineated in the SSM R and aligned with its Treaty legal basis.

(d) Codification of O&Ds by the ECB and the basis provided in the SSM

2.040 Art. 4(3) of the SSM R provides for the possibility of the ECB adopting regulations "*to organise or specify the arrangements for the carrying out of the tasks conferred*" by the SSM R (and only to the extent this becomes necessary).

2.041 Building upon arts. 132 TFEU and 34 SESCB,[61] and in the cited art. 4(3) SSM R, the ECB has already issued several regulatory legal acts anchored in the SSM R.[62] Most notably, the RO&Ds[63] can be regarded as the expression of the ECB's will to become a prudential *legislator*. By means of this legal instrument, the ECB seized the opportunity to exercise regulatory powers concerning the options granted by CRR/CRD IV to NCAs (not having been gold-plated by means of national statutes).

2.042 Those regulatory powers have been exercised in two ways: (i) *first*, in a strong way, by means of a legally binding act,[64] as it is the case of RO&Ds and (ii) *second*, in a more *subtle* but equally regulatory way, by means of general

59 Decision (EU) 2019/2158 of the European Central Bank of 5 December 2019 on the methodology and procedures for the determination and collection of data regarding fee factors used to calculate annual supervisory fees (ECB/2019/38). Cf D'Ambrosio, R. (2015), at p. 101.

60 In the author's view, such Decision stirs also *ad extra* effects (*vis-à-vis* the supervisees obliged to pay the annual supervisory fees, in accordance with the methods set out in that Decision).

61 Cf art. 25(2) SESCB.

62 For example, the RO&Ds; the Regulation 2015/534 of the European Central Bank of 17 March 2015 on reporting supervisory financial information (ECB/2015/13); and the Regulation 2018/1845 of the European Central Bank of 21 November 2018 on the exercise of the discretion under art. 178(2)(d) of Regulation (EU) No. 575/2013 in relation to the threshold for assessing the materiality of credit obligations past due (ECB/2018/26).

63 Regulation ECB 2016/445 of 14 March 2016 on the exercise of options and discretions available in Union law (ECB/2016/4) (RO&Ds).

64 Cf arts. 288 and 297 TFEU on the classification of EU legal acts of the Union and, between the legally binding ones, the distinction drawn between *legislative* and *non-legislative* acts depending on the procedure that led to their approval.

recommendations, guides and similar instruments, as it has been the case of the ECB Guide on Options and Discretions.[65][66]

The RO&Ds and GO&Ds materialise this debated competence. The debate on the suitability of the legal basis provided for in the TFEU[67] and SESCB,[68] 2.043

65 Of March 2022. Available at: https://www.bankingsupervision.europa.eu/ecb/pub/pdf/ssm.supervisory_guides2022_ond.en.pdf.

This Guide, applicable to SIs, should be clearly differentiated from the GO&Ds (and not only because the latter indirectly applies to LSIs). This GO&Ds constitutes, indeed, a truly legally binding instrument addressed to NCAs by means of which the ECB actually has indirectly exercised some CRR options as regards LSIs for the purposes of ensuring consistent (uniform) application of supervisory standards (i.e., level playing field). On the legally binding nature of the ECB Guidelines, see Bax, R. and Witte, A. (2019). The taxonomy of ECB instruments available for banking supervision. *Economic Bulletin Articles, 6.* See also Witte, A. (2021).

Further to the GO&Ds, the ECB also issued the Recommendation of the European Central Bank of 4 April 2017 on common specifications for the exercise of some options and discretions available in Union law by national competent authorities in relation to less significant institutions (ECB/2017/10). As the GO&Ds, this Recommendation is addressed to NCAs (and indirectly to the LSIs they supervise). However, it has a non-binding character and expresses the ECB's expectations as regards the use of options and discretions *vis-à-vis* LSIs.

66 Whereas the Guide on Options and Discretions states that it "*does not establish new regulatory requirements and the specifications and principles included herein should not be construed as being legally binding rules*" (Para. 9), I am persuaded that the Guide itself must be regarded as the product of the exercise of regulatory powers. It is more than debatable that the Guide itself, despite its *denomination* (a guide, a soft law instrument), may not constitute a plain *soft law* instrument. A number of arguments support this view. *First,* the CJEU has constantly held that those rules are somehow binding for the issuing administration (see the Court of Justice judgments in the joined cases C-189/02 P, C-202/02 P, C-205/02 P to C-208/02 P and C-213/02 (*Dansk Rørindustri A/S and others v Commission*) of 28 June 2005 (ECLI:EU:C:2005:408) at Paras. 209). Following this case law, the referred administration must justify the reasons supporting any deviation from the application of its general *guidance* concerning a particular individual.

Second, the intrinsic appearance of the Guide, that is, an articled text composed of chapters, sections and commentaries on articles, does create the appearance of a legislative text (cf Conseil d'Etat. (2013). *Etude annuelle 2013 – Le droit souple.* La Documentation française. At pp. 61–63). *Third,* the actual menace for the supervisees of being subject to enforcement or sanctioning procedures in the case they do not observe the Guide on Options and Discretions. *Fourth,* linked to the previous *first point,* it may produce *certain legal* effects and, in this regard, indirectly, could be subject to judicial review (see cases C-16/16 P (*Kingdom of Belgium v European Commission*), delivered on 20 February 2018 (ECLI:EU:C:2018:79) at Paras. 29; and C-399/12 (*Germany v the Council*) of 7 October 2014 (ECLI:EU:C:2014:2258), at Paras. 64 and ss.). In the same vein, they may be used as a yardstick by Courts to gauge the conformity of ECB behaviour, and in the same vein, indirectly, it may contribute to set out a standard of review as per ECB supervisory decisions.

For a comprehensive approach on the topic of EU soft law, the opinions of AGs Cruz Villalón and Bobek must be highly praised. See, respectively, (i) Opinion of AG Cruz Villalón in case C-399/12 (*Germany v Council*). Delivered on 9 April 2014 (EU:C:2014:289), at Paras. 97 and ss. and (ii) Opinions of AG Bobek in case C-16/16 P (*Kingdom of Belgium v European Commission*), delivered on 12 December 2017 (ECLI:EU:C:2017:959) at Paras. 80 and ss., and in case C-911/19 (*Fédération bancaire française (FBF) v Autorité de contrôle prudentiel et de résolution (ACPR)*) delivered on 15 April 2021 (ECLI:EU:C:2021:294) at Paras. 56, 85 and 132. In the same topic, see Kovacs, A., Toth, T. & Forgacs, A. (2016). The Legal Effects of European Soft Law and Their Recognition at National Administrative Courts. *ELTE LJ*, 53, pp. 53–70.

67 Art. 132 TFEU.

68 Art. 34 SESCB.

allowing the ECB to exercise the referred O&Ds, is not settled. The positions are polarised between those who advocate construing the SSM R in a finalistic way and, therefore, supporting the possibility of ECB exercising supervisory powers[69] and those who opt to adopt a rather strict reading of the legal text.[70] In the absence of case law, we must be cautious when expressing preference towards any of the (apparently) two available options.

2.044 Yet, even if in the view of the author, the former option may be preferred; the controversy must be split into two parts: the exercise of O&Ds as regards SIs and as regards LSIs. *In the first place* and as per the exercise of O&Ds impacting SIs, the direct involvement granted to the ECB and its characterisation as *competent* supervisory authority allows to construe its entitlement to issue a regulatory act codifying its supervisory preferences.

2.045 *In the second place* and as per LSIs, the abovementioned reasoning sits badly when extrapolated to them. Even if the ECB is the *only* competent authority as regards the tasks listed in the SSM R,[71] the decentralised way in which these tasks are performed, relying upon the NCAs, seems to militate against the ECB exercising O&Ds pertaining those authorities. The wording under art. 6(5)(a) of the SSM R, when contrasted to art. 4(3), puts in doubt the possibility of the ECB exercising O&Ds as regards LSIs.[72] This is because *(i)* art. 6(5)(a) refers to the possibility of issuing guidelines or instructions addressed to NCAs concerning how to exercise the tasks listed in art. 4(1) (except for points (a) and (c), which belong exclusively to ECB). Delimiting the O&Ds to be exercised is a policy exercise preceding LSIs oversight and, consequently, would not be clearly covered by the SSM R.[73]

2.046 *(ii)* NCAs are called to exercise direct oversight on LSIs (except for the tasks indicated in indents (a) and (c) of art. 4 SSM R) and, hence, overcoming such limitation seems challenging.

---

69 See. Lamandini, M., Ramos, D. & Solana, J. (2016), at pp. 32–36; Lamandini, M., Ramos Muñoz, D. & Solana, J. (2015), at pp. 28–36; and D'Ambrosio, R. (2015), at pp. 101–107.

70 Lackhoff, K. (2017), at pp. 32–33, hypothesising about the solidness of the legal basis vested on the ECB to exercise regulatory powers.

71 Cf art. 4(1) SSM R and *L-Bank Appeal* at Paras. 36–38.

72 Nevertheless, these were precisely the legal bases utilised by the ECB to issue the GO&Ds.

73 This argument seamlessly links the principle of conferral (art. 13(2) TFEU), upon which EU bodies and Institutions must exercise their powers, within the scope they were granted. Cf Alexander, K. (2018). The European Central Bank's supervisory powers: the need for enhanced macro-prudential supervision. In *ECB Legal Conference 2017, Shaping a new legal order for Europe: a tale of crises and opportunities* (pp. 349–369). Frankfurt am Main, ECB. At pp. 359–360.

2.047 Finally, (*iii*) even if the ECB is considered the competent authority as regards the tasks listed in art. 4(1) SSM R,[74] it is only directly vested with the powers listed in that Regulation.[75] When no direct power is expressively attributed to the ECB under the SSM R, it may require NCAs to use the powers granted by national statutes on its behalf. Given the fact that no direct *regulatory* power is granted to the ECB to exercise O&Ds as regards LSIs, the decision-making powers may remain at a national level.[76]

2.048 However, as the ECB is directly responsible for issuing (or withdrawing) banking licenses and assessing the acquisition (or disposal) of qualifying holdings as regards both SIs and LSIs, it might be acceptable and even desirable that the ECB exercises O&Ds only as regards those tasks, listed in points (a) and (c) of art. 4(1) SSM R. More precisely, when the relevant O&Ds to be applied as regards LSIs directly impact the previously referred tasks.[77] The wording of art. 6(5)(a) SSM R, further proportionality reasons and the need to ensure that the *entry* to the banking market and the trading of shares of credit institutions are subject to the same regulatory discretion (level playing field) favour this approach.

C. JUDICIAL REVIEW OF THE LEGAL FOUNDATIONS OF THE SSM R

2.049 It has been concluded above that the legal foundations upon which the SSM was built may not be solid enough to support the structure as it was designed[78] or, at least, to raise grounded questions on the suitability of the basis.

2.050 The questions that arise, then, are whether the weakness of such a legal basis is amenable to judicial review and, if in the affirmative case, who may be entitled to initiate such procedure.

---

74 Cf art. 9(1) SSM R.

75 Art. 9(1)II SSM R.

76 And this seems to be also compliant with the principle of proportionality as balanced by the pursuit of *level playing field* (cf art. 1.IV SSM R).

77 Cf, as a mere sample, art. 21(1) CRD IV, that allows NCAs to exempt credit institutions permanently affiliated to a central body from the requirements set out in arts. 10, 12 and 13(1) of CRD IV (which relate to the taking up of business of credit institutions).

78 This is particularly true as per the exercise of supervisory tasks indirectly impacting insurance activities; see right below.

1. Who may challenge the SSM R?

2.051 It seems rather obvious that neither the Commission nor the Parliament, MSs or the ECB are likely to question the nature and constitutional foundations of the SSM.

2.052 It is also doubtful whether, under certain circumstances and for strategic purposes, any credit institution[79] would dare challenge the institutional structure that supports the supervision of its business and furnish it with credibility. The situation appears merely hypothetical today, but maybe it will not in the future.[80]

2.053 In the affirmative case, the restrictive doctrine set out by the Court of Justice in *Plaumann*[81] imposes severe obstacles to the possibility of directly challenging the SSM R as such.[82] Under *Plaumann*, the Court requires[83] that (i) "*the measure affects them by reason of certain attributes which are peculiar to them or by reason of circumstances in which they are differentiated from all other persons and by virtue of these factors distinguishes them individually just as in the case of the person addressed*" (*individual concern*); and (ii) there must be *a direct concern* for the applicant.[84] As stated by the Court, this latter requisite demands the existence

79 And the persons closely related to them (e.g., their shareholders). However, the doctrine set out by the Court of Justice in its judgment of joined cases C-663/17 P, C-665/17 P and C-669/17 P (*Trasta Komercbanka appeal*) of 5 November 2019 (ECLI:EU:C:2019:923) has prevented direct and indirect shareholders of a credit institution from challenging an ECB supervisory decision as they were not "*directly concerned by the decision at issue for the purposes of the fourth paragraph of Article 263 TFEU*" (cf Para. 115).

80 E.g., an ECB decision that places the credit institution at stake in a fatal situation that most likely leads to the withdrawal of its banking license and/or resolution. Under this pushy scenario, an individual may be more prone to make the whole system *fall*, in order to survive, without balancing the consequences that the action may entail for the entirety of the banking business.

81 Court of Justice judgment in case C-25/62 (*Plaumann & Co. v Commission*) of 15 July 1963 (ECLI:EU:C:1963:17).

82 I will focus here on the *material* constraints concerning the *locus standi*, whereas below I will examine the associated *time* constrains. On these matters, see Lehmann, M. (2021). Jurisdiction, *locus standi* and the circulation of judgments in the Banking Union. In *Judicial Review in the European Banking Union* (pp. 77–96). Edward Elgar Publishing.

83 Although heavily criticised by scholars, this doctrine has been applied constantly until the present moment. In this sense, see Court of Justice judgments in cases C-263/02 P (*Commission v Jégo-Quéré & Cie SA*) of 1 April 2004 (ECLI:EU:C:2004:210); and C-583/11 (*Inuit Tapiriit Kanatami v European Parliament and Council*) of 3 October 2013 (ECLI:EU:C:2013:625).

For an analytical and comprehensive explanation of the *Plaumman* doctrine and its recent developments, see also Eliantonio, M. & Stratieva, N. (2010). From Plaumann, through UPA and Jégo-Quéré, to the Lisbon Treaty: The locus standi of private applicants under art. 230 (4) EC through a political lens. *RRDE*, 43.

84 Direct concern has two dimensions. Firstly, a direct, causal link between the act that is being challenged and the damage the applicant has suffered is needed. The second dimension requires that the challenged measure imposes on the addressee(s) the obligation to act in a certain predefined way, leaving no discretion to them on how to behave. See Kucko, M. (2017). The Status of Natural or Legal Persons According

of a direct link between the challenged act and the damage allegedly suffered. The challenged act must "*leave no discretion to the addressees of the measure, who are entrusted with the task of implementing it*".[85] In addition, the interest disturbed by the legal act must be of legal nature, i.e., legally protected.[86]

2.054 The rigidity of the *Plaumann* doctrine[87] may be tempered through the practices developed by the Commission and the General Court. That was the case in recent case *Dyson*[88] or in other cases dated many years before, such as one like *Toyo Bearing*[89] or *Sony v Commission.*[90] In the former case, the applicant challenged the Delegated Regulation implementing act related to energy labelling of vacuum cleaners, without its *locus standi* being challenged or questioned by the defendant or by the Court.

2.055 Building upon the *Plaumann doctrine* and their further developments,[91] it seems hard to justify the *individual* and *direct concern* elements required for granting standing to challenge a regulation of general scope, and this way of action must be disregarded. The applicants' *individual concern* would be missing since the SSM R is addressed to a plurality of private individuals (credit institutions). Since the requisites for granting standing are cumulative,[92] the lack of individual concern directly determines that standing may not be granted for the foregoing purpose. *Additionally,* it seems difficult to argue that the SSM R is of *direct concern* for the applicant, given that, indeed, its organising character (addressed mainly to the ECB and NCAs) requires *implementing* decisions and, indirectly, leaves a margin of discretion on how to apply it.

---

to the Annulment Procedure Post-Lisbon. *LSE Law Review, 2*, pp. 101–119, at p. 106; and Lenaerts, K., Maselis, I. and Gutman, K. (2015) at pp. 315 and ss.

85 Court of Justice judgment in case C-386/96 P (*Dreyfus v Commission*) of 5 May 1998 (ECLI:EU:C:1998:193) at Paras. 43 and 44.

86 See Kucko, M. (2017) at. p. 106.

87 Here, it must be noted that the *Plaumann* test has to be overcome, even in the case of formal Regulations. In Court of Justice judgment in case C-309/89 (*Codorniu v Council*) of 18 May 1994 (ECLI:EU:C:1994:197), the Court opened the door to consider Regulations being of *individual concern* for the applicants at stake. This encouraging approach was later on watered in the said judgment by subjecting the assessment of the *individual concern* to the same orthodox rules depicted in *Plaumann.*

88 See General Court judgment in case T-544/13 (*Dyson Ltd. v. Commission*) 8 November 2018, (ECLI:EU:T:2018:761). See Lamandini, M., Ramos, D. & Solana, J. (2016), at p. 251.

89 Court judgment in case 113/77 (*Toyo Bearing Company Ltd and others v Council*) of 29 March 1979 (ECLI:EU:C:1979:91), at Para. 11.

90 Court of First Instance in case T-243/01 DEP (*Sony Computer Entertainment Europe Ltd v Commission*) of 18 March 2005 (ECLI:EU:T:2005:113), at Paras. 63–78.

91 See footnote 83 above.

92 See Order of the General Court in case T-507/13 (*Solar World AG & Others v Commission*) of 14 June 2015 (ECLI:EU:T:2015:23) at Paras. 40.

2.056 Alternatively, the clear way (I submit) to put the abovementioned weakness of the legal foundations of the SSM on the CJEU's table would be bringing them as a preliminary (or first) plea on an action for annulment. Challenging the foundations of the SSM R upon which a supervisory or sanctioning decision is issued allows overcoming the rigidity of the *Plaumann* test[93] to a certain extent. However, it cannot be discarded that the Court may understand that the argument is inadmissible, since it can be regarded as an artificial way of gaining standing that otherwise would have been denied. Furthermore, closely linked to this fact, it is debatable whether this indirect way of challenging the Treaty basis must be subject to the same short deadline of the *direct* action addressed against the legal act.[94] In addition, strategically, questioning the validity of the legal basis of the SSM R may undermine the strength of the action brought and raise some issues related to the internal coherence of the action. For instance, if the applicant seeks to not annul entirely the supervisory decision but modify some of its grounds, why then challenge the validity of the system as a whole? The acceptance of the mentioned preliminary argument concerning the SSM R legal basis should be translated into a carefully drafted *request,* contemplating subsidiary petitions.

2.057 Another potential indirect path that could be followed would be based on a preliminary reference (cf art. 267 TFEU). The involvement of national courts[95] raises additional questions and adds extra complexity stemming from the composite nature of the SSM.

2.058 For the avoidance of doubt, the possibility of challenging the legal basis of the SSM is explored here as per the cases where NCAs dictate acts following ECB instructions which do not entail margin of discretion.[96]

93 Cf Art. 263. IV TFEU.

94 See Section C.2. (*Time constrains for challenging the SSM R: can they be overcome?*) right below in this chapter.

95 For instance, national courts (in the sense predicated by the CJEU) are the only entities capable of bringing a preliminary ruling before the CJEU. Even if under art. 267 TFEU, the national court should file the preliminary ruling when against its ruling "*there is no judicial remedy under national law*", it remains under its discretion whether to file that preliminary request or not.

96 See Lamandini, M., Ramos, D. & Solana, J. (2016), at p. 249. Given the issues and limitations as regards (i) its reviewability, (ii) the *locus standi* to be granted to the applicants and (iii) the standard of review to be deployed by the Court, (a) decisions of the NCAs issued upon a delegation regarding less significant institutions, but executing tasks attributed to the ECB, and (b) decisions of the ECB in application of EU soft law and national legislation are disregarded in this analysis. Ibidem at p. 249. See also, on this matter, for a dedicated analysis on the possibility of challenging ECB instructions addressed to NCAs under art. 9(1)III SSM R, Hernández Saseta, C. (2021). The legal review of ECB instructions under article 9 SSM regulation. In *Judicial Review in the European Banking Union* (pp. 304–315). Edward Elgar Publishing.

Finally, another possible way to eventually challenge the SSM set-up would entail questioning incidentally its conformity with its Treaty basis and, in general, with the Treaties and principles of EU law by resorting to art. 277 TFEU. Such possibility would be subject to the filing of an action for annulment by a private actor against an ECB supervisory decision affecting it (or a similar act of direct concern). This will be addressed below. **2.059**

2. Time constrains for challenging the SSM R: can they be overcome?

Actions for annulment are subject to a very short exercising period of only two months.[97] Therefore, even if applicants could potentially overcome the *Plaumann* test (which is unlikely, as stated above), the time lapse for filing action for annulment would have elapsed already. **2.060**

As per the possibility of requesting a preliminary ruling indirectly calling into question the legality of the SSM R, it must be highlighted that the Court has constantly held that this remedy is not available when the applicant could have potentially challenged the direct measure or legal act under art. 263. IV TFEU.[98] Reasons of legal certainty are adduced by the Court to support this approach.[99] **2.061**

The question that arises is whether the Court may accede to review the validity of a regulation, when the applicant has no *locus standi* to file an action for annulment against the original decision and once the time limit to directly challenge the said legal act has elapsed. **2.062**

The judgment of the Court in case *Canadian Solar v Council* looks encouraging in this regard.[100] Even if the Court dismissed the arguments brought by the appellants, it hypothesised about the possibility of challenging indirectly the lawfulness of a regulation by means of a preliminary ruling. The Court stated that the case law established in *TWD Textilwerke Deggendorf*[101] would not constitute an obstacle to proceed this way, provided that the interest in **2.063**

97 Cf art. 263(5) TFEU. However, the Court has also held that if the legislative act is amended, the two-month period to challenge the general act is restarted. This, not only as regards the new provisions or the provisions amended, but as regards the entire legislative act. See Court of Justice judgment in case C-299/05 (*Commission v Parliament and Council*) of 18 October 2007 (ECLI:EU:C:2007:608) at Para. 30.

98 Court of Justice judgments in cases C-188/92 (*TWD Textilwerke Deggendorf GmbH v Bundesrepublik Deutschland*) of 9 March 1994 (ECLI:EU:C:1994:90) at Paras. 24–26; and C-442/04 (*Spain v Council*) of 15 May 2008 (ECLI:EU:C:2008:276) at Para. 22.

99 See Court of Justice judgment in case C-667/13 (*Estado português v Banco Privado Português SA*) of 5 March 2015 (ECLI:EU:C:2015:151), at Para. 28.

100 Judgment in case C-237/17 P (*Canadian Solar v Council*) of 27 March 2019 (ECLI:EU:C:2019:259).

101 See footnote 97 above.

bringing such action "*arose after the expiry of the two-month period referred to in the sixth paragraph of Article 263 TFEU*".[102] Similarly, the Court held this view also in cases (i) *European Union Copper Task Force v Commission* and (ii) *T & L Sugars Ltd and Sidul Açúcares v Commission*,[103] although it was not so detailed about *when* the interest in bringing the action should have arisen.

2.064 As per the possibility of questioning the lawfulness of the SSM R incidentally within an action for annulment, the viability of the action, in terms of legal standing, seems easier. Building upon art. 277 TFEU,[104] the Court and the General Court have stated that: "(…) *it should be borne in mind that the possibility afforded by Article 277 TFEU of pleading the inapplicability of a measure of general application does not constitute an independent right of action and recourse may be had to it only as an incidental plea*".[105] Hence, the Court has made clear that the remedy contemplated in art. 277 TFEU may not be used for the only purpose of circumventing the standing rights granted upon art. 263 TFEU.

2.065 As per the requisites for making use of the incidental mechanism foreseen in art. 277 TFEU, the General Court in case T-787/14 P[106] provided a helpful systematic approach. In accordance with this judgment, the viability of this kind of pleas requires the concurrence of the following requisites:

> *(i) a plea of illegality can be relied on only incidentally, in the course of an independent action brought before the Courts of the European Union and against an individual decision adversely affecting the applicant, (ii) the independent action must itself be admissible, (iii) the plea is admissible only in so far as the applicant is not entitled to bring a direct action against the act of general application that is connected to the individual decision adversely affecting him, (iv) it is for the Courts of the European Union to declare inapplicable the act of general application which it finds to be unlawful and to draw the consequences of that inapplicability on the individual act adversely affecting the applicant and (iv)* [(v) sic] *that declaration of inapplicability has the*

102 *Canadian Solar v Council* at Para. 87.

103 See, respectively, Court of Justice judgment in cases C-384/16 P (*European Union Copper Task Force v Commission*) of 13 March 2018 (ECLI:EU:C:2018:176) at Paras. 116–120, and C-456/13 P (*T & L Sugars Ltd and Sidul Açúcares v Commission*) of 28 April 2015 (ECLI:EU:C:2015:284) at Paras. 45–49.

104 "*Notwithstanding the expiry of the period laid down in Article 263, sixth paragraph, any party may, in proceedings in which an act of general application adopted by an institution, body, office or agency of the Union is at issue, plead the grounds specified in Article 263, second paragraph, in order to invoke before the Court of Justice of the European Union the inapplicability of that act*".

105 See, among others, the General Court orders in cases T-392/13 DEP (*Leone La Ferla v Commission and European Chemicals Agency*) of 14 December 2017 (ECLI:EU:T:2017:929), at Para. 40; T-194/95 (*Area Cova SA and Others v Council*) of 8 July 1999 (ECLI:EU:T:1999:141) at Para. 78; and Court of Justice judgment in joined cases 87, 130/77, 22/83, 9 and 10/84 (*Salerno and Others v Commission and Council*) of 11 July 1985 (ECLI:EU:C:1985:318) at Para. 36.

106 General Court judgment in case T-787/14 P (*European Central Bank v Maria Concetta Cerafogli*) of 27 October 2016 (ECLI:EU:T:2016:633).

force of res judicata only with regard to the parties to the dispute and does not have erga omnes effect".[107]

Looking into these requisites, those listed in numerals (i) to (iv) do not seem to entail much of a problem. Provided that the ECB decision entails adversary effect to the applicant, it would be able to bring the plea of illegality under art. 277 TFEU, challenging the suitability of the SSM R legal basis. However, point (v) raises some issues on the nature of the effects derived from a potential judgment rendering *inapplicable* the SSM R. Those effects will be appropriately explored in the following Section C.3. right below. **2.066**

As per art 277 TFEU,[108] the lapse of the two-month period provided for in art. 263.VI TFEU would not preclude the possibility of indirectly challenging the Treaty basis of the SSM R.[109] **2.067**

3. Under which circumstances would the CJEU review the SSM R and to which extent? Legal consequences

When the Court has been given the chance to examine the validity of the legal basis of an act of general application[110] following an action for annulment, it has been systematically inclined to maintain the effects of the challenged general act until the entry into force of the new act or provisions, adopted upon the correct legal basis.[111] Reasons of legal certainty and the need to avoid any legal uncertainty for the economic operators[112] have made the Court prone to make use of the second paragraph of art. 264 TFEU.[113] **2.068**

---

107 Ibidem at Para. 46.

108 See General Court judgment in case T-168/12 (*Aguy Clement Georgias and Others v Council of the European Union and European Commission*) of 18 September 2014 (ECLI:EU:T:2014:781), at Para. 34; Ibidem case T-787/14 P (*European Central Bank v Maria Concetta Cerafogli*) at Paras. 41 and 45.

109 In this regard, see Horspool, M. & Humphreys, M. (2012). *European Union Law*. Oxford University Press, at P. 260.

110 In this chapter, the suitability of the legal basis chosen to build up the SSM (i.e., art. 127(6) TFEU) is solely examined.

In Chapter 3 *(Potential) Conflicts between ECB competences and Treaty basis*, the possibility of challenging the SSM R on the grounds of eventually contradicting EU primary law because of the conflict of the price stability mandate with the supervisory mandate allocated to the ECB under the SSM R will be explored.

111 See Court of Justice judgments in cases C-113/14 (*Germany v Parliament and Council*) of 7 September 2016 (ECLI:EU:C:2016:635) at Paras. 79–85; and C-299/05 (*Commission v Parliament and Council*) of 18 October 2007 (ECLI:EU:C:2007:608) at Paras. 74–75.

112 See Court of Justice judgment in case C-414/04 (*Parliament v Council*) of 28 November 2006 (ECLI:EU:C:2006:742) at Para. 56.

113 "*However, the Court shall, if it considers this necessary, state which of the effects of the act which it has declared void shall be considered as definitive*".

2.069 As stated above in Section C.1. (*Who may challenge the SSM R?*), the possibility of the SSM R being directly challenged does not seem possible or viable. However, the approach followed by the Court in those circumstances must be used as a yardstick to guide the consequences of a court judgment adjudicating in favour of credit institutions in actions rather brought indirectly. As it will be examined below, the particularity of the case makes necessary to explore *unchartered waters* to determine the most suitable remedy.

2.070 When the Court has adjudicated on the validity of an EU legislative act under a preliminary ruling, it has held that such a decision has *erga omnes* effects, even if the reference was made by a particular national court.[114] In this regard, the Court has applied, by analogy, arts. 264 and 266 TFEU to proceedings related to preliminary rulings.[115] By doing so, the Court has sometimes determined that the invalidity of certain provisions set forth in a legislative act (basically, a Regulation) would have *ex nunc* effects, i.e., from the moment that the legislative act was determined onwards.

2.071 The question that subsequently arises is whether the approach held by the Court in action for annulment in cases where the application is granted can be followed also in cases concerning preliminary rulings. I am inclined to concede that the answer to that question is "yes", but given the scarcity of judicial precedent, this approach may be taken cautiously.

2.072 Yet, in the well-known *Kadi* case,[116] even if the Court decided to annul Council Regulation No. 881/2002, it maintained the effects of the challenged Regulation in respect of the applicants "*for a brief period to be fixed in such a way as to allow the Council to remedy the infringements found, but which also takes due account of the considerable impact of the restrictive measures concerned on the appellants' rights and freedoms*". Given the particularities surroundings this case, its outcome may be taken with the outmost precaution. Nevertheless, the author is of the opinion that the matters debated in the *Kadi* proceeding[117] and its outcome provide a valuable guidance.

---

114 See Court of Justice judgments in case 66 at Paras. 13–14. See Craig, P. (2018). *EU administrative law*. Oxford. University Press, at pp. 679 and ss.

115 See Court of Justice judgment in joined cases C-92/09 and C-93/09 (*Volker und Markus Schecke GbR (C-92/09) and Hartmut Eifert (C-93/09) v Land Hessen*) of 9 November 2010 (ECLI:EU:C:2010:662) at Paras. 93–94.

116 Court of Justice judgment in joined cases C-402/05 P and C-415/05 P (*Kadi and Al Barakaat International Foundation v Council and Commission*) of 3 September 2009 (ECLI:EU:C:2008:461).

117 For an insightful resume and analysis of the *Kadi* case, see Kokott, J. & Sobotta, C. (2012). The Kadi case – constitutional core values and international law – finding the balance? *European Journal of International Law, 23(4)*, pp. 1015–1024.

Consequently, it can be argued that in cases founded upon art. 267 TFEU, the CJEU would feel inclined to grant a grace period to adapt the former regulation or to issue a new one of similar content as the case may be. The duration of that potential *standby* period raises additional questions due to the lack of consistency concerning the duration of that period and its application to the present case. In some cases, the Court has used a rather generic formula, stating that: *"the effects of the contested decision should be maintained until the entry into force, within a reasonable period from the date of delivery of the present judgment, of a new decision"*.[118] Whereas in other cases it has set a maximum deadline to issue the new legislations.[119] **2.073**

As per the indirect challenge of the Treaty basis of the SSM R through a plea of illegality, the issue becomes thornier. In this regard, the Court has held that a judgment declaring incidentally the invalidity of an act of general application does not have *erga omnes* effects;[120] it only renders *inapplicable* such an act as regards the applicants.[121] The rationale behind this construction seems to be twofold: (i) on the one hand, based on the language used in art. 277 TFEU, which uses the word "*inapplicability*" when referring to the effects of granting the application (and not the words *invalid* or *illegal*), and (ii) on the other hand, founded upon reasons of legal certainty, since the act of general application under judicial scrutiny would have become *unchallengeable* after the expiry of the two-month period foreseen in art. 263.VI TFEU.[122] **2.074**

Thus, the different extent of the effects attributed to this remedy, when compared to arts. 263 and 277 TFEU, adds extra complexity to the case at stake. If the Court grants the application in this case and understands that the SSM R is founded in **2.075**

---

118 See Court of Justice judgment in cases C-28/12 (*Commission v Parliament and Council*) of 28 April 2015 (ECLI:EU:C:2015:282) at Para. 63; and joined cases C-103/12 and C-165/12 (*Parliament and Commission v Council*) of 26 November 2014 (ECLI:EU:C:2014:2400) at Para. 93.

119 See Court of Justice judgment in cases C-389/15 (*Commission and Parliament v Council*) of 25 October 2017 (ECLI:EU:C:2017:798) at Para. 84 (six months from the date of delivery of the judgment); joined cases C-124/13 and C-125/13 (*Parliament and Commission v Council*) of 1 December 2015 (ECLI:EU:C:2015:790) at Para. 90 (12 months starting from 1 January of the year following the date of delivery of the judgment); and *Kadi* at Para. 376 (three months running from the date of delivery of the judgment).

120 See General Court judgment in case T-787/14 P (*European Central Bank v Maria Concetta Cerafogli*) of 27 October 2016 (ECLI:EU:T:2016:633) at Para. 53:

> *"(…), while the finding of illegality made by the court, as it does not have erga omnes effect, entails the illegality of the individual contested decision, but leaves the act of general application in the legal order without affecting the legality of other acts which have been adopted pursuant thereto and which were not challenged within the period for appeal* (…)".

121 See General Court judgment in case T-286/15 (*KF v European Union Satellite Centre (SatCen)*) of 25 October 2018 (ECLI:EU:T:2018:718) at Para. 157.

122 Ibidem in case T-787/14 P at Para. 45.

incorrect or insufficient Treaty basis, (i) would it directly annul the decision challenged by the applicant since the Regulation providing for the possibility of issuing that decision is ill-founded?; (ii) otherwise, would the Court decide to keep the SSM R in *standby* because of the serious disturbances that would generate for the applicant?; (iii) considering art. 266 TFEU, may the Court invite the Council (and the Parliament) to rethink the legal basis of the SSM R?[123]

2.076 Regrettably, the jurisprudence is not capable of providing answers for such specific questions. As per the two first questions ((i) and (ii) right above), a proportional interpretation, aligned with the case law settled by the CJEU in cases involving actions for annulment, would demand a case-by-case analysis.[124] In this vein, if the challenged ECB decision refers to a financial holding composed by several insurance undertakings, the said decision has an impact on the insurance business of that financial conglomerate, and the suitability of the Treaty basis to allocate indirectly to the ECB competences affecting insurance undertakings is questioned; the Court may be prone to render the SSM R inapplicable, so far as it concerns insurance undertakings. Should a more general approach be taken by the applicant, challenging the lawfulness of the SSM R as a whole, the outcome is more uncertain and the CJEU may be ready to decline the plea of illegality arguing lack of legal concern as per the dispute at stake.

2.077 Answering the third question demands considering the institutional balance existing between the Council, the Commission and the Court; and the limits to the functions of the latter imposed precisely by art. 277 TFEU. In this regard, it results that the Court could not require the Council (and the Parliament) reviewing the legal basis of the SSM R. Nevertheless, should a judgment of this kind be made in favour of an applicant, it would encourage more entities to file similar claims before the CJEU.[125] In such a case, the Commission, the Council and the Parliament may decide to promptly review the legal basis of the SSM R on their own initiative, exploring the possibility of setting out the mechanism under other or an additional Treaty basis. Those alternatives will be explored soon below.

---

123 It is here assumed that the Council and the Parliament, as *legislators* (see footnote 26 in Chapter 1), should be called to the trial in case a plea of illegality questioning the legal basis of the SSM R is brought (cf art. 266 TFEU).

124 See General Court judgment in case T-155/13 (*Zanjani v Council*) of 3 July 2014 (ECLI:EU:T:2014:605) at Paras. 80–86.

125 Since a declaration of inapplicability under art. 277 TFEU may be also invoked as regards any subsequent unfavourable decision by the same applicant (and potentially by other applicants in the same situation), this would prevent the systematical application of the SSM R. See, in this regard, Steiner, J., Woods, L. & Watson, P. (2012). *Steiner & Woods EU Law*. Oxford University Press, at p. 290.

3

(POTENTIAL) CONFLICTS BETWEEN ECB COMPETENCES AND TREATY BASIS

Whether interferences from supervisory tasks[1] (potentially undermining ECB's monetary policy) could lead to the annulment of the SSM R is a relevant legal and practical question. **3.001**

Maintaining price stability is depicted as the primary objective or competence of the ESCB/ECB.[2] Defining and implementing the monetary policy is ranked as the top task entrusted to the ECB,[3] whereas conducting prudential supervision is depicted as a *secondary* task ranking under the latter one (Section A below). **3.002**

1 References made here to *tasks* and *competences* are used in an interchangeable way as meaning the concrete duties or functions allocated to the ECB.

2 Arts. 127(1) and 282(1) TFEU. See Gortsos, C. V. (2018). Legal Aspects of the European Central Bank (ECB) – The ECB within the European System of Central Banks (ESCB) and the European System of Financial Supervision (ESFS) – Second (Extended and Updated) Edition. *SSRN 3162024*. At pp. 35–36; and Ioannidis, M., Murphy, S. J. H. & Zilioli, C. (2021). The mandate of the ECB: Legal considerations in the ECB's monetary policy strategy review. *ECB Occasional papers* No. 276. European Central Bank. At pp. 7–11.

3 Art. 127(2) TFEU.

3.003 In this chapter, it will be analysed whether the SSM R, in the way it was set out, may lead to a conflict with the primary objective and core tasks entrusted to the ECB (price stability and monetary policy, respectively (Section B below)). In addition, assuming that, indeed, prudential supervisory tasks may conflict with monetary ones, it will be assessed whether it is possible to argue that SSM R, as a secondary legislation, does not conform with a superior provision established in the Treaty and, consequently, should be removed from the legal framework (Section C below).

A. ECB CONSTITUTIONAL MANDATE AND MAIN TASKS: FRICTION WITH THE SUPERVISORY TASKS ENTRUSTED UNDER THE SSM R

3.004 Whereas in the post-financial crisis world, the idea of attributing the exercise of monetary policy and prudential supervisory tasks to the same entity (naturally, a Central Bank or comparable authority) seems to gain momentum,[4] the debate is far away from being completely settled.[5]

3.005 Against this generally accepted view, Principle 2 of the Basel Core Principles for Effective Banking Supervision[6] would demand prudential supervision to be conducted independently from other monetary policymaking tasks.[7]

3.006 Being the model embraced by the EU, an integrative one, mandating the ECB with both monetary and prudential supervision tasks, it is necessary to examine (a) how these competences interact between them and (b) whether interferences between the two functions may occur. The answer must be anticipated; interferences are unlikely to happen, but they can happen.[8]

---

4 See Policy Department A: Economic and Scientific Policy (European Parliament). (2015). Interaction Between Monetary Policy And Bank Regulation, European Parliament Doc. IPOL_IDA(2015)563458. For a comprehensive analysis run in the pre-crisis era, see Goodhart, C. & Schoenmaker, D. (1995). Should the functions of monetary policy and banking supervision be separated? *Oxford Economic Papers*, pp. 539–560.

5 On the academic voices that claim for the two functions to be separated to avoid potential conflicts of interests, see Eijffinger, S. & Nijskens, R. (2012). Monetary policy and banking supervision. *VoxEU*, 19 December: https://voxeu.org/article/monetary-policy-and-banking-supervision.

6 See Basel Committee on Banking Supervision. Core Principles for Effective Banking Supervision, September 2012.

7 Supporting this view, see Alexander, K. (2018). At p. 364.

8 See Lamandini, M., Ramos, D. & Solana, J. (2016), at pp. 48 and ss.

1. Hierarchy between the tasks entrusted to the ECB: are the mechanisms foreseen to avoid the conflicts of interests ultimately effective?

Despite statements produced by senior ECB officials,[9] the author submits that there is a hierarchical dependence between the objectives relating to price stability and prudential supervision. **3.007**

Price stability does constitute the ECB's primary goal.[10] Conducting the monetary policy of the Union is the first one of the ECB's basic tasks,[11] whereas prudential supervision is somehow a task added to the backlog of the ECB, entrusted also by means of Secondary legislation.[12] **3.008**

Price stability mandate and monetary policy tasks are entrusted to the ECB through Primary legislation. On the contrary, the allocation of prudential supervisory tasks required a piece of secondary legislation to be enacted (cf art. 127(6) TFEU). The differentiated way of attribution of tasks, and the *derivative* nature of the prudential or financial stability competence, indicates that the latter should rank below the price stability one (and so the tasks associated to it).[13] **3.009**

The mechanisms established in the SSM R,[14] and the arrangements placed outside it[15] to ensure the separation between the monetary and prudential supervisory tasks, are not totally capable of isolating the exercise of those competences. This concern can be found in Recital 85 SSM R, which suggests the possibility of implementing further arrangements leading to greater separation between the two functions, leaving even the door open to a Treaty amendment **3.010**

---

9 Based on art. 25 SSM R, Ignazio Angeloni seems to build a principle of separation between prudential supervisory tasks attributed to the ECB as regards the SSM and monetary tasks, which ultimately would amount as equaling both sets of tasks. See speech passed by Ignazio Angeloni (Member of the Supervisory Board of the ECB) at Halle on 2 February 2017: https://www.bankingsupervision.europa.eu/press/speeches/date/2017/html/se170202_1.en.html.

10 Cf art. 127(1) TFEU. Such primary objective would be followed by a secondary one (ranked lower), that is "(...) *support the general economic policies in the Union with a view to contributing to the achievement of the objectives of the Union as laid down in Article 3 of the Treaty on European Union*".

See, in this regard, Ioannidis, M., Murphy, S. J. H. & Zilioli, C. (2021) and Gortsos, C. V. (2020) European Central Banking Law: The Role of the European Central Bank and National Central Banks under European Law. Cham: Palgrave Macmillan. At p. 186.

11 Art. 127(2) TFEU.

12 Thus, objectives related to financial stability are set out in the SSM R, not in the Treaties. Art. 1(1) SSM R implies that "*contributing to the safety and soundness of credit institutions and the stability of the financial system within the Union states*" constitutes SSM main purpose.

13 Cf Ioannidis, M., Murphy, S. J. H. & Zilioli, C. (2021). See Gortsos, C. V. (2018) at pp. 35–36.

14 Cf Arts. 25 and 29(1) SSM R.

15 See ECB Decision of 17 September 2014 on the implementation of separation between the monetary policy and supervision functions of the European Central Bank (ECB/2014/39).

entrusting the decisions related to monetary policy and the ones linked to financial stability to two different decision-making bodies.[16]

3.011 But even if these conflicts happen, they should be solved by means of principle-weighting and self-restraint (i.e., the ECB itself refraining from taking any supervisory action compromising its monetary function). Since the objective of maintaining price stability ranks higher than the financial stability one, priority should be given, ultimately, by the Governing Council to the former in case a potential of real conflict is spotted.

3.012 Furthermore, given that prudential supervision tasks are granularly implemented through continuous operational acts, not forming part of the formal decision-making process,[17] ECB – and particularly staff conduct day-to-day supervision – should apply self-restraint when those acts may impair the transmission of the monetary policy.

B. MONETARY POLICY MEASURES UNDERMINING PRUDENTIAL SUPERVISION APPROACHES (AND VICE VERSA)

3.013 Even if the SSM R foresees diverse mechanisms to keep prudential supervisory tasks' exercise separated from monetary policy tasks,[18] it is agreed that the mechanisms foreseen do not make absolutely impossible[19] the appearance of a *friction* or a *conflict* between them. It is agreed and observed that mutual influence may happen.[20]

3.014 Not pretending to enumerate (nor even acknowledge) whether this task is feasible, I will depict two samples of these interferences:[21]

---

16 Actually, the Governing Council constitutes the ultimate decision-making body for both monetary policy and (micro- and macro-) prudential measures.

17 See ECB SSM Supervisory Manual: European Banking Supervision: Functioning of the SSM and supervisory approach (March 2018) (SSM Supervisory Manual) at p. 21 (https://www.bankingsupervision.europa.eu/ecb/pub/pdf/ssm.supervisorymanual201803.en.pdf).

18 Cf Decision of the European Central Bank of 17 September 2014 on the implementation of separation between the monetary policy and supervision functions of the European Central Bank (ECB/2014/39), art. 25 SSM R, art. 26(5) and (8) SSM R.

19 Even considering the *independence* or "*chacun pour soi*" principle as regards the performance of the prudential supervisory tasks enshrined in art. 25 SSM R.

20 See Lamandini, M., Ramos Muñoz, D. & Solana, J. (2016), at pp. 48 and ss.

21 See the speech referred to in footnote 9.

1. Monetary policy measures jeopardising financial stability policies

In a context of crisis, one of the first measures that central banks are eased to arrange is lowering interest rates under its remit[22] to stimulate credit flowing through the monetary policy transmission channels. **3.015**

In a context of low interest-linked profitability, maintained during a long period (e.g., the pre-COVID outbreak situation), credit institutions would be prone to increase its risk appetite, engaging into riskier business to compensate and/or obtain the profit that they cannot obtain as a result of a prolonged seasons of low interests. Economic studies corroborate this.[23] **3.016**

This increased appetite for risk rows exactly in the opposite direction that supervisors would try to guarantee, as it is in their interests that supervisees conduct their business in a safe and sound way, not posing too excessive risk on the individual entities themselves nor in the whole financial system, creating a macro-prudential risk. As a result, one may observe that, indeed, monetary policy conducted at times of recession may impair supervisory policies conducted by bank supervisors, watering down its efforts to support and promote a *sound* management of the credit business, avoiding taking up excessive risks. **3.017**

In the opposite side, when the ECB pursues a tight monetary policy (e.g., by increasing or maintaining a high deposit facility rate), this may affect the survival or the soundness of institutions, particularly of those which may find difficulties in transitioning or adapting to high rates or which have businesses heavily reliant on low interest monetary policies (e.g., credit institutions, which focused on the commercial and housing mortgage market).[24] **3.018**

2. Prudential supervisory measures undermining monetary policy

If considered appropriate, the ECB may use some of the supervisory powers granted under art. 16(2) SSM R, such as requiring the use of net profits to strengthen its own funds,[25] increasing the level of its own funds as regards risks **3.019**

---

22 Basically, (i) the interest rate on the main refinancing operations (MRO), (ii) the rate on the deposit facility and (iii) the rate on the marginal lending facility.

23 Altunbas, Y., Gambacorta, L. & Marques-Ibanez, D. (2010). Does monetary policy affect banks' risk-taking. *BIS working paper* 298.

24 Heller, H. R. (1991). 5 Prudential Supervision and Monetary Policy. In *The Evolving Role of Central Banks.* International Monetary Fund, and Gortsos, C. (2022). Evolving key risks in the banking sector, and related priorities for the SRB: the impact of the current "inflation crisis". *Economic Governance Support Unit (EGOV).*

25 Art. 16(2)(h) SSM R.

not covered by relevant union acts,[26] or applying specific provisioning requirements and the treatment of assets in terms of its own funds requirements.[27]

3.020 All these measures, impacting the level of its own funds held by financial institutions and potentially playing with the risk weight attributed to different risk factors, are capable of watering down monetary measures related to interest rate adjustments.[28] More precisely, interests rate increases may be counterbalanced (or the impact of such measures lingered) through a benevolent treatment of the risk-weighted assets (RWAs) used to calculate its own funds (to soften them).

3.021 Conversely, in a high interest scenario linked to a tight monetary policy, the ECB may feel keen to eventually delay or set up more generous deadlines to comply with supervisory requests issued in use of its supervisory powers (cf art. 16(2) SSM R). For example, setting lower Pillar 2 Regulatory (P2R) requirements or Pillar 2 Guidance (P2G) requirements or providing more time to meet those as regards specific supervisory decisions.[29]

C. IS THERE ANY REAL CONFLICT BETWEEN THE SSM R AND SUPERIOR TREATY PROVISIONS? ASSESSING HOW TO CLASSIFY POTENTIAL FLAWS AS REGARDS THE ECB DUAL MANDATE

3.022 If the regulatory *brakes* contemplated in the SSM R (and outside its remit) and its associated *principle weighting* fail, then the prudential supervisory competence may be prioritised over the principal financial stability objective and the price stability tasks. This, not as a general rule but as per the samples drawn previously, in some particular cases.

3.023 Then, one may submit that the fact that art. 127(6) TFEU contemplates the possibility of entrusting the ECB with *specific* supervisory tasks does not mitigate the fact that the SSM R itself should have been built up in such a way that does not conflict, at any time, with the core objective of the ECB referred to in art. 127(1) TFEU (i.e., maintaining price stability).

3.024 Also, one may argue that, in a specific case, if a prudential measure, decision or operational act has undermined or has been prioritised over price stability,

26 Art. 16(2)(a) SSM R.

27 Art. 16(2)(d) SSM R.

28 The same seems to happen with prudential measures impacting liquidity ratios. See Lamandini, M., Ramos, D. & Solana, J. (2016), at pp. 50–51.

29 See footnote 24.

this would amount to having issued an act in contravention of the Treaties or against a regulatory provision ranking higher.

Academic literature, in line with CJEU jurisprudence, unanimously agrees that secondary legislation must be annulled, purged and extricated from the EU legal framework should it conflict with a provision or principle enshrined in the Treaties.[30] **3.025**

The fact that some supervisory *acts of application* of the SSM R may potentially clash with the monetary tasks entrusted to the ECB, undermining them, would not equate to a real constitutional conflict between Treaty provisions (art. 127 TFEU) and secondary legislation (SSM R), nor even to a conflict between competences (that should be always resolved, after weighting the interests at stake, in favour of the price stability one). **3.026**

The TFEU has designed a hierarchy among objectives entrusted to the ECB (affirming price stability as the ECB's primary goal) and tasks (*core tasks* related to, among others, monetary policy[31] and prudential supervisory tasks). Furthermore, the SSM has placed a mechanism to try to insulate supervisory decisions from monetary ones.[32] Even if the mechanism is imperfect, because the final decision-making body, the Governing Council, is at the end the ultimate decision-making body for both mandates, it should safeguard the appropriate weight and priority attributed to each mandate. Consequently, it should be discarded that the SSM R conflicts with superior Treaty provisions. **3.027**

Additionally, the author considers that flaws, if potentially occurring, are expected to be circumscribed to crisis times and limited to certain specific cases within a general policy action. If that is the case and the ECB prioritises its supervisory objective over the price stability, this may amount to a misuse of powers (*détournement de pouvoir*).[33] As the Court of Justice has stated, misuse of powers amounts to adopting an act by an EU body or institution "*with the exclusive purpose, any rate the main purpose, of achieving an end other than that stated or evading a procedure specifically prescribed by the Treaty for dealing with the circumstances of the case*".[34] **3.028**

---

30 See Klamert, M. (2014). *The principle of loyalty in EU law*. OUP Oxford, at p. 222; and Blanke, H. J., Villalón, P. C., Klein, T. & Ziller, J. (2015). *Common European Legal Thinking*. Springer, at p. 226.

31 Art. 127(2)(I) TFEU.

32 Cf art. 25 SSM R and ECB Decision of 17 September 2014 on the implementation of separation between the monetary policy and supervision functions of the European Central Bank (ECB/2014/39).

33 Cf art. 263. II TFEU.

34 See, among many others, Court of Justice judgment in case C-331/88 (*Fédesa and Others*) of 13 November 1990 (ECLI:EU:C:1990:391) at Para. 58. More specifically, in an SSM context see also General Court

3.029 The Court considers an act to be vitiated by misuse of powers if it appears, "*on the basis of objective, relevant and consistent evidence, to have been taken with the exclusive or main purpose of achieving an end other than that stated*".[35] Should the ECB adopt a supervisory act, as regards one single supervisee or a group of them, for the purpose[36] of diminishing or eroding a monetary measure adopted, to facilitate its prudential mandate, the act at stake may be challengeable before the CJEU.

3.030 As misuse of powers constitutes a rather casuistic matter, it is not possible to elaborate further whether an action of such kind may succeed. Difficulties linked to the necessity to objectively demonstrate such *detournement* jeopardise the feasibility of the action. Yet, one may question whether the supervisees would be up to seeking the annulment of such acts, especially if they produce some indirect benefits, such as loosening the effects of a strict monetary policy, adopted during an expansive cycle.

judgement in cases T-323/22 (*Socrates Capital Ltd and others v ECB*) of 10 July 2024 (ECLI:EU:T:2024:460) at Paras. 471–472.

35 See Court of Justice judgment in joined cases C-186/02 P and C-188/02 P (*Ramondín and Others v Commission* and *Territorio Histórico de Álava v Commission*) of 11 November 2004 (ECLI:EU:C:2004:702) at Para. 44.

36 According to the abovementioned case law, it does not have to be the exclusive purpose but at least the *main* or principal one. In accordance with this, other valid and well-grounded supervisory purposes may also be found.

4

CONCLUSIONS OF PART I

Building upon the analysis carried out in Chapter 1 (*From European and Monetary Union (EMU) to BU, architecture of the BU*), the following conclusions can be distilled: **4.001**

First, the idea of allocating prudential supervision coordinating powers as a basic task on the ESCB/ECB was disregarded in the Maastricht Treaty. Yet, that Treaty introduced the possibility of allocating on the ECB *specific* tasks concerning prudential supervision of credit institutions (cf arts. 25(2) SESCB and 105(6) TEC). **4.002**

Second, prudential supervision remained being exercised at a national level until the advent of the SSM, which took place amid (and was propelled by) the financial crisis. The previous national-based model remained unchallenged until the outbreak of the financial crisis. **4.003**

Third, as per the institutional architecture of the BU, whereas the BU's first two pillars (the SSM and the SRM) are completed and functioning, its third pillar (the EDIS) is still missing with nothing indicating that it will be set up in the short– or mid-term. **4.004**

The issue of legacy NPLs seems to be one of the major elements dragging the adoption of the EDIS. In this token, nothing augurs that, in the short nor in the middle term, the BU's third pillar will be set out. The foregoing undermines the capacity of the system to provide a complete and coherent approach, as deposits protection remains at national level whereas banking supervision and resolution is exercised at supranational level within the Eurozone and as regards those MSs who entered into close-cooperation arrangements (cf art. 7 SSM R). **4.005**

Fourth, the examination of the draft SSM R proposal, together with the thorough legislative debate, occurred in the Parliament; and the final text of the SSM R itself allows one to identify that there are two principles of equal force **4.006** and opposed direction beating deeply in the mentioned Regulation: level playing field within a proportionality approach.

4.007 These two basic principles should be regarded as the guiding principles which together provide the bedrock of the SSM. Those should be able to provide certain guidance when in doubt as regards how to conjugate different interests at stake and shed light on how to construe ambiguous or contradictory SSM R provisions.

4.008 Accordingly, when construing the provisions enshrined in the SSM R (and national substantive provisions allowing its implementation), this must be done in full compliance with the principle of equivalence and effectiveness with a view to ensure that the *mechanism* remains effective in such a fractious legislative setting.

4.009 Considering the analysis carried out in Chapter 2 (*Constitutional foundations of the SSM*), it can be concluded that:

4.010 *First*, the legal basis of the SSM Regulation (while at times pushed to its limits) was sufficient to establish the mechanism as designed. By contrast, the validity of the foundations of certain ECB decisions remains debatable (for example, those touching on the indirect or direct supervision of insurance undertakings) and would call either for supervisory self-restraint to avoid insurmountable legal issues or for a far-reaching purposive/teleological interpretation. In any event, the limited judicial mechanisms catering for the review of the legal basis of the SSM R shield it (almost perfectly) from the attack of private entities.

4.011 *Second*, the resource to the preliminary ruling and the plea of illegality (both indirect remedies to challenge the lawfulness of EU legislative acts) is most likely to lead, to a judgment granting a *grace period* to adapt the SSM R or to issue a new Regulation to similar content. Consequently, it can be argued that the general effects attached of these potential applications would be negligible. However, in certain cases (and following a case-by-case analysis), these applications can be beneficial for the applicant entities, allowing them to be granted the application sought (i.e., the annulment of an unfavourable ECB decision).

4.012 Finally, in Chapter 3 (*(Potential) Conflicts between ECB competences and Treaty basis*), it was assessed whether the exercise of the supervisory tasks allocated to the ECB could undermine its basic task relating to the implementation of the monetary policy and, ultimately, its primary objective of maintaining price stability. There, it was concluded as follows:

First, that even if the SSM R contemplates diverse mechanisms to keep prudential supervisory tasks' exercise separated from monetary policy tasks, the mechanisms foreseen do not make absolutely impossible the materialisation of a *friction* or a *conflict* between them. **4.013**

The fact that some supervisory *acts of application* of the SSM R may potentially clash with the monetary tasks entrusted to the ECB, undermining them, would not equate to a real constitutional conflict between Treaty provisions (art. 127 TFEU) and secondary legislation (SSM R) nor even to a conflict between competences (that should be always resolved, after weighting the interests at stake, in favour of the price stability one). **4.014**

However, in a specific case, if a prudential measure, decision or operational act has undermined or has been prioritised over price stability, this would amount to having issued an act in contravention of the Treaties or against a regulatory provision ranking higher. Should this be the case, such measure or act should (and could, by bringing an appropriate action before the CJEU) be purged and extricated from the EU legal framework. **4.015**

PART II

COMPETENCES, TASKS AND PROCEDURES UNDER THE SSM: TACKLING COMPLEXITY IN A COMPOSITE FRAMEWORK

5

TASKS, POWERS AND COMPETENCES: BUILDING DISTINCTIONS

This whole Part II aims at providing the technical basis to analyse (and eventually to overcome) the practical frictions embedded in the system itself. The legal angle of those tensions will be analysed below and include, among others: the application of national rules vs. the application of EU law by the ECB; frictions between level playing field and proportionate approaches; and national vs. EU judicial systems, established under different rules aiming at protecting fundamental rights.[1] **5.001**

The objective broadly depicted above cannot be achieved without appropriate tools, that is, precise and unequivocal concepts capable of capturing the legal categories and notions they may encompass. Concept imprecisions must be especially avoided when assessing SSM-related legal issues.[2] The difficulty of delimiting the meaning of broadly used legal terms has been well noted and addressed in the classic law-philosophy debate,[3] and here, acknowledging such a difficulty, the definition of some basic legal notions relevant for the SSM will be addressed herein. **5.002**

1 See further in Chapter 13 (*Procedural and substantive safeguards in composite procedures*).

2 Poetically noted by Luis Rosales, "*imprecision is the hell we know*" (free translation from Spanish). See Rosales, L. (2005). *Antología poética*. Rialp, Madrid.

3 Dworkin, R. (2013). *Taking rights seriously*. Bloomsbury.

A. THE SSM CONCEPTS: COMPETENCES, TASKS AND POWERS

1. The "competence" concept in legal philosophy and legal reasoning

5.003 At the beginning of the 20th century, Hohfeld identified in a classical doctrinal paper[4] that the tendency to mingle legal and non-legal concepts led to the ambiguity of legal conceptions, which resulted in misconceptions.[5] Such ambiguity and undesired obscurity can appear (and in fact happens) when core legal terms bearing several meanings are used and the sense in which they are intended to be used is not made clear by the writer to the readers.[6] Such core legal terms in the legal reasoning include concepts such as *power*, *competence*, *task*; all of them present in the laws regulating or interacting with the SSM.

5.004 The reasons behind the ambiguity of those *core* legal concepts are, indeed, connected with its polysemy. Additionally, its abstract character makes difficult its definition. The foregoing technical difficulties lead to the conclusion that such concepts are "*not secured by any technique independent of the use of other words*".[7] Put differently, the jurist must provide a definition of those concepts to specify their content in a given context or discussion. Building upon these notions, the concept of *competence*, *task* and *power* in connection with the SSM R will be examined.

2. The "competence" concept in the Treaties

5.005 The term *competence* is deeply embedded in the Treaties yet not defined. Post-Lisbon Treaty, the concept of *competence* seems to be linked to the distribution of general areas of action between MSs and the EU.[8] Building upon article 5(1) TEU, competence evokes rather wide areas on which the EU would have the exclusive (or shared) exercise of policy actions. At the same time, the concept would act as a limit (*conferral*), applicable on the EU globally considered

4 Hohfeld, W. N. (1917). Fundamental legal conceptions as applied in judicial reasoning. *The Yale Law Journal, 13*(1), pp. 16–59.

5 Ibidem at p. 21.

6 Cf Ibidem at pp. 28–29. The need to procure terminological precision has also been noted as regards the implementation of SSM. See Brito Bastos, F. (2021). Composite procedures in the SSM and SRM – an analytical overview. In *Judicial Review in the European Banking Union* (pp. 97–113). Edward Elgar Publishing. At p. 99.

7 Shuman, S. I. (1955). Jurisprudence and the analysis of fundamental legal terms. *Journal of Legal Education, 8(4)*, pp. 437–468. At p. 439.

8 Cf arts. 2 to 4 TFEU. Here, it must be noted that the EU is identified as a single actor, in line with its international legal personality.

(and on each and every Institution, body or emanation of it,[9] preventing them from acting beyond the areas conferred.

It is not possible to find a legal definition of *competence* within the Treaties.[10] In addition, the term seems to have an interchangeable character with the equivalent concept of *power*. This can be illustrated simply by looking at art. 7 TFEU, where it is referred that "*[t]he Union shall ensure consistency between its policies and activities, (...) in accordance with the* ***principle of conferral of powers***" (emphasis added). **5.006**

Indeed, when referring to the principle of conferral enshrined in art. 5(1) TEU, it is equivalent to speaking about conferral of *powers* and conferral of *competences*.[11] Reasons of that equivalence may be found in the previous wording of art. 5 TEC, which referred to *powers* when phrasing the principle of conferral.[12] In general, some authors point out that, in the field of EU constitutional law, *competences* and *powers* are interchangeable terms.[13] **5.007**

This view is indeed supported by the case law systemically produced by the CJEU, in particular, in cases regarding the disentanglement of competences between the Union and its MSs. For instance, in its recent case C-157/21 (*Republic of Poland and Hungary v. the European Parliament and the Council*),[14] examining the validity of the controversial Rule of Law Regulation,[15] the **5.008**

9 On the principle of conferral, see Schütze, R. & Tridimas, T. (Eds.). (2017). *Oxford principles of European Union law* (Vol. 1). Oxford: Oxford University Press. At pp. 1113 and ss. and Craig, P. & de Búrca, G. (2020). *EU Law-Text, Cases, and Material.* Oxford: Oxford University Press. For an analysis article-by-article of the TFEU, see Blanke, H. J. & Mangiameli, S. (Eds.). (2020). *Treaty on the Functioning of the European Union: A Commentary*. Springer.

10 See Schütze, R. (2015). Union Competences. In *An Introduction to European Law* (pp. 65–89). Cambridge: Cambridge University Press.

11 See the opinion of AG Mengozzi in case C-589/15 P (*Alexios Anagnostakis v Commission*), delivered on 7 March 2017 (ECLI:EU:C:2017:175) at Para. 61 (and case law cited in footnote 71 of this Opinion).

12 Craig, P. & de Búrca, G. (2020). at p. 74.

13 See Mayer, F. C. (2003). The debate on European powers and competencies. Seeing the trees but not the forest. *Walter Hallstein Institut-Working Paper* 18/03. The author suggests that the broad utilisation of the term *competence* in EU constitutional law vocabulary would be the result of a hasty translation from German *Kompetenz* and also considers that drawing a clear distinction between *competence* and *power* would be advisable.

14 Court of Justice judgment in case C-157/21 (*Republic of Poland and Hungary v the European Parliament and the Council*) of 16 February 2021 (ECLI:EU:C:2022:98).

15 Regulation 2020/2092 of the European Parliament and of the Council of 16 December 2020 on a general regime of conditionality for the protection of the Union budget.

CJEU seems to assimilate the concept of *competence* to the ability of the EU to act[16] within the legal framework.[17]

5.009 Focusing on the ECB, it is worth analysing the TFEU provisions relating to it.[18] In this vein, only arts. 127(4) TFEU and 4 SESCB refer to *competence*,[19] in the sense that the ECB shall be consulted concerning Union or national draft *legislative* proposals relating to its *fields of competence*. Considering that Para. 2 of the same article lists the tasks entrusted to the ECB, it can be construed that *competence* means the *tasks* entrusted to the ESCB as a whole under that paragraph.[20]

5.010 The so-called *OLAF* case,[21] which assessed the scope of the consultation powers attributed to the ECB concerning its *fields of competence*, identifies these fields of competence with the basic tasks listed under article 127(2) TFEU, as referred to above.[22] Yet the Court, on purpose or not, uses the terms *tasks* and responsibilities interchangeably.[23] In light of the above, there seems to be a certain confusion in the terms used in the TFEU as regards the definition of *competences* attributed to the ECB and the ESCB.

3. The "competence" concept under the SSM R and ECB decisions under it

5.011 The term *competence* is scarcely used in the SSM R and in the SSM Fr when compared to the term *tasks*.[24] In the SSM R, the term competence is not used to refer to the set of specific tasks and powers conferred on the ECB under this regulation but to name the scope of action attributed to MSs and EU

16 It is worth also mentioning here the opinion of AG Campos Sánchez-Bordona in case C-724/19 (*Spetsializirana prokuratura v HP*), delivered on 20 May 2021 (ECLI:EU:C:2021:974) and its attempt to define competence in a unitary manner in Para. 49 (possibly the clearer attempt to define *competence* within the CJEU related procedures).

17 Cf Paras. 237–242.

18 Basically, arts. 127 to 133, 282 to 284 and 219 TFEU. The ECB is also mentioned in articles referring to transparency (art. 15 TFEU), EMU (art. 66 TFEU), privileged legal standing (art. 263.III TFEU), annulment of decisions (art. 265 TFEU), etc.

19 See, also, art. 282(5) TFEU, which refers to the areas "*falling within the responsibility*" of the ECB.

20 Following art. 127(6) TFEU, the specific supervisory tasks conferred to the ECB by the SSM R now will be added to the Treaty-conferred ones. Supporting this view, see Section 3.3. (*fields of competence*) of the ECB *Guide to consultation of the European Central Bank by national authorities regarding draft legislative provisions* (October 2015): https://www.ecb.europa.eu/pub/pdf/other/consultationguide201510.en.pdf.

21 Court of Justice judgment in case C-11/00 (*Commission v ECB*) of 10 July 2003 (ECLI:EU:C:2003:395).

22 *OLAF* case at Para. 109. See, also, the opinion of AG Jacobs delivered on 3 October 2003 in this the *OLAF* case at Para. 140 (ECLI:EU:C:2002:556).

23 Ibidem at Paras. 109, 111 and 114.

24 Seven mentions against 149 ones, in the case of the SSM R, and 20 mentions against 68 as per the SSM Fr respectively.

Institutions, in accordance with the principle of conferral.[25] This is particularly clear in arts. 3(3)[26] and 8[27] SSM R, where reference is made to the *tasks* conferred to the ECB under this Regulation and the *competences* attributed to MSs and EU Institutions (in particular, to the ESFS).

Furthermore, art. 48 SSM Fr, which deals with the change of competent supervisory authority, constantly refers to *change in competence*. This implies a broader use of the concept of competence grouping all the supervisory tasks conferred to the ECB under the SSM R. Consequently, the concept of *competence* would group the specific micro– and macro-prudential tasks vested on the ECB under the SSM R.[28] The SSM Supervisory Manual and some ECB decisions developing the SSM legal framework[29] seem to use an even wider concept of the term *competence*, which would include not only the specific supervisory tasks entrusted under the SSM R but also the explicit and implicit powers conferred on the ECB.[30] **5.012**

The CJEU has not contributed to create a clear concept of *competence* in the context of the SSM, even if it has already had several opportunities to draw the contours of the term. In the *L-Bank* case, the term usually encompasses the micro-prudential tasks attributed to the ECB under article 4(1) SSMR.[31] Yet, the General Court in that judgment sometimes refers to these specific tasks as *competences*, creating some interferences. Additionally, in the *L-Bank Appeal* the Court of Justice upholds the criterion proposed by the General Court and utilises the term *competence* as inclusive of all the specific tasks conferred on the ECB.[32] **5.013**

25 See above. Cf arts. 7 TFEU and 5(1) TEU.

26 Cf Recital 31 SSM R.

27 Cf Recital 51 SSM R.

28 Cf arts. 4(1) and (2), and 5 SSM R. Those tasks correspond to the *specific tasks* referred to in article 127(6) TFEU. Cf Section A.1.(a). (*material limitations I: the concept of "specific tasks" and the tasks actually transferred to the ECB*) in Chapter 2. See, also, Lastra, R. M. & Psaroudakis, G. (2020). Prudential supervisory tasks (Article 127 (6) TFEU, monetary policy vs. prudential supervision): "Kissing awake the Sleeping Beauty provision". In *The EU Law of Economic and Monetary Union* (pp. 751–787). OUP.

29 Cf Recital 3 of ECB Decision of 31 January 2019 on delegation of the power to adopt decisions regarding supervisory powers granted under national law (ECB/2019/4).

30 See arts. 9 to 18 SSM R. See Section A.1.(a). (*material limitations I: the concept of "specific tasks" and the tasks actually transferred to the ECB*) in Chapter 2, where it is reasoned that the ECB has developed a teleological reading of the powers attributed to it under the SSM R, leading to an increase of the *implicit* powers that it actually exercises.

31 Cf Para. 63 of the *L-Bank case*. Similar consequences can be drawn from General Court judgment in joined cases T-351/18 and T-584/18 (*Ukrselhosprom PCF LLC v ECB* and *Versobank AS v ECB*, respectively) of 6 October 2021 (ECLI:EU:T:2021:669), at Paras. 133, 144, 156 and 187.

32 Cf Paras. 37–38 and 49 of the *L-Bank Appeal*.

4. The "competence" concept: conclusion

5.014 The SSM R and the SSM Fr referred to ECB (and NCAs) *competences* without defining such a term. Also, legal literature refers to the *competences* attributed to the ECB without precising too much the meaning given to that term. Furthermore, the Treaties and the CJEU seem to refer to *competence* in a loose way, sometimes as a term which is synonymous to *power* and some other times as an attribution to an act that needs to be carried out by means of powers.

5.015 Against this approach, one may object that art. 127(6) TFEU actually refers to the conferral of *tasks* upon the ECB (rather than to competences). Even if it is a valid objection, it must be disregarded as it based on one single isolated element and not on a systematic analysis of the Treaty and Regulation provisions impacting this matter. Additionally, being the *enabling* clause, the result of intense negotiations and the outcome of common understanding reached between antagonistic positions,[33] the precision of the language was sacrificed to find a solution agreeable by the parties.

5.016 However, considering the literal wording of art. 6(1) SSM R, the following two-fold distinction should be maintained when referring to ECB competence(s):

(a) *Competence* should encompass all the micro– and macro-prudential tasks conferred on the ECB, as a whole. Within this concept, it is possible to distinguish between (specific) micro– and macro-prudential tasks, as a kind of subdivision.
(b) *Competence* in this context would also mean the ECB overall liability for the effective and efficient functioning of the SSM.[34]

5.017 The context would allow to distinguish one meaning from the other. For the sake of accuracy, the author would endeavour to utilise the term in the sense depicted above unless otherwise expressly indicated.

B. FROM ECB "COMPETENCE" TO ITS "TASKS" UNDER THE SSM

5.018 It is quite relevant to define the scope of *task*, as references across the SSM R and the SSM Fr are multiple but are also in the judicial interpretations provided by the Court of Justice (and the General Court) and academic ones. Such references do not always encompass the same notion.

33 See Smits, R. (1997), at pp. 336–337.

34 Cf arts. 6(1) and (5)(c) SSM R.

Building upon art. 127(6) TFEU, the specific tasks allocated to the ECB under the SSM R can include both micro– and macro-prudential supervision. Consequently, when referring generally to tasks, the term must be construed as comprising the whole spectrum of supervisory policies. 5.019

Terminologically speaking, it seems more precise to reserve the term micro-prudential tasks to the tasks listed and expressly conferred upon the ECB in arts. 4(1) and (2) SSM R, including those other tasks that, by means of a teleological interpretation, should fall under the ECB's remit to ensure a consistent supervision. 5.020

Yet, it is not the intention of the author to generate the impression that the ECB is entrusted with a kind of fragmented supervision, built upon compartmented blocks of tasks. This seems to be against the principal objective of the SSM R that, as established in art. 1(I) SSM R, would be to ensure the safety and soundness of credit institutions and to secure the stability of the financial system as whole. The CJEU seems to have construed the specific tasks allocated to the ECB in this finalistic way.[35] 5.021

The precision depicted above must be understood in a context of dogmatic precision, to avoid, whenever possible, any mismatch or explanatory flaws. Accordingly, when referring to *tasks* in the context of the SSM R this term will encompass the specific tasks listed in art. 4(1) and (2) and 5 SSM R.[36] These *specific* tasks, as indicated, can be split into micro– and macro-prudential tasks. 5.022

C. FROM "TASKS" TO "POWERS"

Chapter III of SSM R is titled *Powers of the ECB*, yet no express definition of the term is provided in article 2 (nor in its Recitals). 5.023

The concept of legal power is one those *unclear* concepts through which jurists try to describe the law.[37] In abstract terms, we can think about the *separation of powers*.[38] We can also recall the doctrine of the conferral of *powers* as referred above in this chapter. We can even discuss *decision-making powers*, powers executive or not in nature and so on. 5.024

---

35 Cf *L-Bank Appeal* at Para. 86.

36 Yet, the term *tasks* may be utilised in another more common sense. The context should be enough to distinguish one sense from another. Whenever deemed necessary, additional clarifications will be provided.

37 Cf Dworkin, R. (2013).

38 Identifying a legislative, an executive and a jurisdictional power. For a classical reference, see Montesquieu (de Secondat, C.-L.). (2012). *De l'esprit de lois.* Norph Nop.

5.025 EU Law authors have assimilated sometimes the concept of powers to the one of *competence*, at least from a semantic perspective.[39] Intuitively, specialised scholars use the term *function* as a synonym to *powers*,[40] potentially building upon the literal wording of the Treaties.[41] This latter constitutes an accurate starting point; the term power would encompass the exercise of precise functions in a field or policy area in which the EU bodies or Institutions have been attributed *competence*.

5.026 When looking into the SSM R in detail, confusion between the terms *task* and *power* can be spotted. In Recital 28 SSMR, it is referred that: "Supervisory tasks not conferred on the ECB should remain with the national authorities. *Those tasks* should include *the power to receive notifications* from credit institutions in relation to the right of establishment and the free provision of services" (emphasis added). This first confusion seems to be more a drafting flaw than a result sought on purpose by the *legislators*.[42] That conclusion is reached after looking at Recital 34 SSM R, that sets forth that: "*For the carrying out of its tasks and the exercise of its supervisory powers,* (...)". This latter approach is confirmed by Recital 35 SSM R, which deepens the distinction between *tasks* and the *powers* required to successfully develop the tasks allocated to the ECB under the SSM.[43]

5.027 The nature of the powers attributed to the ECB in the context of the SSM R can be understood by carefully looking into art. 9 SSM R.[44] The first paragraph of this provision determines the functional nature of the powers: the powers conferred on the ECB under the SSM R and/or under any other relevant Union law (in its capacity of *competent authority*[45]) are granted for the exclusive purpose of carrying out the tasks entrusted to it in arts. 4(1), 4(2) and

39 See Konstadinides, T. (2009). *Division of powers in European Union law: the delimitation of internal competence between the EU and the member states.* Kluwer Law International BV. See, also, Lenaerts, K. & Gutiérrez-Fons, J. A. (2010). The constitutional allocation of powers and general principles of EU law. *Common Market Law Review, 47*(6), pp. 1629–1669.

40 See Craig, P. & de Búrca, G. (2020).

41 Cf for instance, art. 16(1) TEU which speaks about the budgetary and legislative functions attributed to the Council, jointly with the European Parliament.

42 Cf footnote 26 in Chapter 1.

43 The Recital refers to the particular tasks concerning *early intervention* matters (cf art. 4(1)(i) SSM R) where the ECB is not equipped with the powers to carry out directly these tasks. Following art. 9(1)III SSM R, the ECB may require in this regard national authorities to make use of their powers, in accordance with the conditions set out in their respective national law.

44 See further in Chapter 7 below.

45 Cf art. 9(1)I SSM R. As a *competent* authority, the ECB is vested with the powers attributed by Union law concerning *competent authorities* and, in this vein, is capable of exercising *options* and discretions regarding SIs (and also of codifying these options and discretions in legally binding instruments). See Section B.1.(d). (*codification of O&Ds by the ECB and the basis provided in the SSM*) in Chapter 2.

5(2) SSM R.[46] Therefore, *powers* are accessory, a tool to perform effectively the SSM specific supervisory tasks.

As art. 9(1)III SSM R preludes, it may happen that the ECB is entrusted with the performance of a task but is not equipped with the relevant powers to that end. Following that provision, the ECB can request *national authorities* to make use of its powers conferred under pure national law in accordance with national procedures. **5.028**

In accordance with the foregoing, it results that powers have an instrumental character. Whereas a specific task (under the SSM R) may exist without the ECB being granted an explicit power to fulfil it, the equation does not work the other way around. It cannot be a power without an associated task to which it serves. **5.029**

Hence, in the view of the author, powers may be defined as the precise set of administrative functions granted directly (or indirectly[47]) to the ECB for the purposes of fulfilling the specific supervisory tasks contemplated in arts. 4(1)–(2) and 5(2) SSM R. **5.030**

Within the general category of *powers* (Chapter III of the SSM R), a threefold category of them can be depicted: (i) investigatory, (ii) supervisory and (iii) sanctioning powers. Basically, (i) we can distinguish investigatory or *monitoring* powers[48] under arts. 10 to 13 SSM R. (ii) Supervisory powers would come later on. Within those supervisory powers, the author distinguishes *specific* supervisory powers, which would encompass the so-called common procedures: (a) granting and withdrawing the authorisation to take up the business of credit institutions[49] and (b) carrying out the assessment of acquisitions (and disposals) of qualifying holdings in credit institutions.[50] A set of *broad* supervisory powers can be also found in art. 16 SSM R, which list a vast panoply of supervisory powers, mirroring almost literally art. 104 CRD IV. (iii) Finally, art. 18 SSM R confers to the ECB the sanctioning powers enabling it to exercise all the enforcement stages, i.e., monitoring, investigating and sanctioning powers.[51] **5.031**

46 See Lackhoff, K. (2017)(i) at pp. 25 and 37.
47 See art. 9(1)III SSM R and immediately above.
48 Using the classification provided Scholten, M. (2017). Mind the trend! Enforcement of EU law has been moving to "Brussels". *Journal of European Public Policy, 24*(9), pp. 1.348–1.366.
49 Art. 14 SSM R and arts. 70–84 SSM Fr. See, also, section 3.1.1 of the SSM Supervisory Manual.
50 Art. 15 SSM R and arts. 85–87 SSM Fr. See, also, section 3.1.2 of the SSM Supervisory Manual.
51 See Scholten, M. (2017).

5.032 In light of the above, for reasons of precision, it is advisable to use the term *powers,* in the context of the SSM R, as comprising functions granted explicitly to the ECB to perform a task included in the SSM R itself or in Union law. Powers are accessory to the tasks allocated to the ECB and must serve to its fulfilment; hence, they are ancillary to purpose and cannot constitute an end themselves.

6

ALLOCATION OF TASKS WITHIN THE SSM

In this chapter, attention will be paid to the manner in which the specific micro-prudential supervisory tasks (and sanctioning powers) allocated to the ECB are exercised in a *decentralised manner*.[1] **6.001**

Accordingly, in Section A, the perimeter of entities subject to the supervision exercised by the ECB will be analysed. A twofold approach will be followed, depicting first the subjective nature of the entities subject to the SSM R. Subsequently, looking in detail into the allocation of micro-prudential supervisory tasks, examining the rationale in which the model is embedded (Section B). Finally, the distribution of sanctioning powers will be subject to separate scrutiny given its particular nature and the competence limitations that obliged to formulate it in a manner that does not actually follow the micro-prudential tasks allocation model (Section C). **6.002**

1 Cf *L-Bank case* at Paras. 54, 63 and 72, and *L-Bank Appeal* at Paras. 41 and 49.

A. DEFINING THE SUBJECTIVE AND OBJECTIVE PERIMETER

1. Subjects of the SSM supervision

6.003 Micro-prudential supervisory tasks are exercised in relation to *supervised entities*.[2] This term encompasses a fourfold classification of entities over which the ECB exercised its powers.[3] The types of tasks and powers that the ECB carries out varies[4] depending on the types of institutions.

6.004 The rationale guiding the perimeter of subjects comprised the SSM R is that stability risks impacting a credit institution, may arise at an individual level or at a consolidated level.[5]

(a) The entities originally subject to ECB supervision under the SSM

6.005 With a view to ensure a complete response to ensure the safety and soundness of credit institutions and the financial system as a whole, it is necessary to act at the highest level of consolidation within a financial group. Supervisory response would be inefficient if it is only capable of overviewing the activity of credit institutions, usually included within a bigger financial group (and of which is not necessarily the holding or *head* company). Within the *supervised entities*, it is possible to distinguishing the following institutions:

(i) *Credit institutions*, defined as undertakings authorised "*to take deposits or other repayable funds from the public and to grant credits for its own account*".[6] Over these institutions, the competences, powers and tasks attributed to the ECB are more intense. The policy reasons justifying this more intensive approach may be found in the *enabling clause*[7] serving as the basis of the SSM R, which expressly refers to credit institutions.

Concerning credit institutions, (a) the ECB is entitled to carry out the supervisory tasks listed in art. 4(1) SSM R, (b) may exercise its supervisory powers in connection with these tasks, including (c) the sanctioning powers generally depicted in art. 18.

2 Cf art. 2(20) SSM Fr.
3 See Gortsos, C. V. (2019) at p. 187.
4 In the case of powers, in intensity.
5 Cf Recital 26 SSM R.
6 Cf arts. 2(3) SSMR and 4(1)(1) CRR. See, on this topic, particularly as regards the definition of credit institution, financial holding company and mixed financial holding company, Binder, J., Gortsos, C. V., Lackhoff, K. & Ohler, C. (Ed.). (2022). *European banking union: Brussels commentary*. Baden-Baden: Nomos. At pp. 13–23.
7 Art. 127(6) TFEU.

(ii) *Financial holding companies*,[8] meaning financial institutions[9] that do not fall under the concept of mixed financial holding companies, which have a least one subsidiary constituting an *institution*[10] and which also meet certain indicators on a steady basis concerning the institutions, and financial institutions that are their subsidiaries.[11]

(iii) *Mixed financial holding companies*,[12] meaning parent undertakings[13] which form a financial conglomerate. This would mean that at least one of the entities forming the financial conglomerate dominated by the parent undertaking would be a credit institution, an insurance undertaking, a reinsurance undertaking, an investment firm, an asset management company or an alternative investment fund manager having its registered office within the EU.

Concerning the two preceding types of entities, pursuant to art. 4(1)(g) SSM R, the ECB may (a) carry out supervision on a consolidated level,[14] (b) participate, as the case may be, in the relevant college of supervisors[15] and (c) participate in supplementary supervision of financial conglomerates[16] (including assuming the tasks of a coordinator for the conglomerate[17]).

(iv) Finally, *branches established in a participating MS by a credit institution which is established in a non-participating MS* are the last type of entities subject to the supervisory perimeter of the SMM R.

In accordance with art. 4(2) SSM R,[18] the ECB is entrusted to carry out the tasks listed in art. 4(1) SSM R, which are actually allocated to the NCAs (*host competences*). Overall, this may be understood as allocating all the relevant supervisory tasks, referred to above, over these branches. **6.006**

8 Cf art. 2(4) SSMR and 4(1)(20) CRR.

9 That is, undertakings whose main activity is to acquire holdings in credit institutions or investment firms and/or to pursue certain financial activities included within CRD IV, which are not a credit institution or an investment firm. Cf art. 4(1)(3) and (26) CRR.

10 Which comprises not only the entities that fall within the traditional concept of credit institutions as indicated above (arts. 4(1)(1)(a) CRR and 8 CRD IV), but also big investment firms which fall under arts. 4(1)(1)(b) CRR and 8a(3) CRD IV. See also immediately below in the following Section.

11 These indicators refer to equity, assets, revenues and personnel (and eventually others, as may deemed appropriate by the relevant NCA or the ECB). Art. 4(1)(20) CRR.

12 Art. 4(1)(21) CRR. See also art. 2(15) of Directive 2002/87/EC of the European Parliament and of the Council of 16 December 2002 on the supplementary supervision of credit institutions, insurance undertakings and investment firms in a financial conglomerate (Directive 2002/87/EC).

13 See art. 2(9) of Directive 2002/87/EC. Basically, a controlling entity which would not be a credit institution, an insurance undertaking, a reinsurance undertaking, an investment firm, an asset management company or an alternative investment fund manager (cf art. 2(4) Directive 2002/87/EC).

14 Provided that they are parent undertakings of credit institutions established in one participating MS.

15 Participating thus in the consolidated supervision (together with NCAs, if applicable) when the parent company of the credit institution at stake is not established in a participating MS.

16 See art. 2(14) Directive 2002/87/EC.

17 Cf art. 10 of Directive 2002/87/EC.

18 See also art. 14 SSM Fr.

6.007 Concerning the range of subjects included within the SSM subjective perimeter, there is an issue relating to scope of the specific supervisory powers comprised in art. 16 SSM R (which can be overcome using some interpretation). The issue arises when the first paragraph of this art. 16 refers to the possibility of the ECB exercising these broad supervisory powers in connection with credit institutions, financial holdings and mixed financial holdings (naming them expressly), whereas the second paragraph only refers to *institutions*.

6.008 One potential (rather strict) approach would entail considering the reference to institutions as exclusively made to *credit institutions*.[19] This option leveraged on the literal meaning of the provision must be discarded as undermining the effectiveness of the range of powers conferred on the ECB. Such approach is also inconsistent with the first sub-paragraph of art. 16, which expressly contemplated the possibility of the ECB making use of these powers as regards credit institutions, financial holdings and mixed financial holdings.

6.009 One legally sound approach (also one ensuring the full effectivity of the powers granted to the ECB over the referred entities) entails considering the term *institution* in art. 16(2) SSM R as encompassing the threefold type of institutions. This reasoning presupposes, somehow, a clerical flaw by the *legislators*, which is saved recurring to a systematic interpretation and also to a teleological one. In addition, given that the term *institution(s)* is not defined in the SSM R,[20] the interpreter should not be bound to recur to a term defined in EU banking law.[21] All in all, considering that the reference made to *institutions* in art. 16(2) SSM R includes all the institutions referred to above (including, also, branches of credit institutions established in a non-participating MS) ensures full consistency with the far-reaching powers of the ECB.

(b) Expansion of the SSM subjective perimeter

6.010 The structure and risks borne by large investment firms look like those of credit institutions. Additionally, some of those large risks, by performing activities

19 D'Ambrosio also explores (and later seems to discard) the possibility of considering the reference made to *institutions* as made to credit institutions and investment firms, in line with art. 4(1)(3) CRR. See D'Ambrosio, R. (2013). Due process and safeguards of the persons subject to SSM supervisory and sanctioning proceedings. *Quaderni di Ricerca giuridica della Consulenza Legale* (Banca d'Italia), nº 74. At pp. 23–24.

20 Nor in the SSM Fr.

21 See D'Ambrosio, R. (2013) at p. 23.

very close to taking repayable deposits from the public,[22] are capable of posing a similar risk for the financial stability of the whole system.[23]

In December 2017, the Commission started proposing a review of the prudential rules applicable to investment firms and a revision of the MIFID.[24] The purpose of this revision was to devise and update the prudential rules applicable to investment firms. The foregoing was done with the aim of subjecting them to different levels of prudential supervision depending precisely on their size and on the potential risk that they may entail for the system. Secondarily, the proposal aimed at tackling the potential regulatory arbitrage that may occur between credit institutions and the largest investment firms, if less stringent prudential requirements could apply to the latter ones.[25] **6.011**

On 5 December 2019, the IFR and the Directive 2019/2034 on the prudential supervision of investment firms were simultaneously published in the Official Journal. **6.012**

Art. 62(3) IFR modified art. 4(1) CRR and enlarged the definition of credit institution (expanding consequently the perimeter of entities subject to the prudential supervision within the SSM[26]). The said art. 62 IFR[27] devises the definition of credit institution around two basic types of entities: on the one hand, institutions taking repayable funds from the public and granting credits for its own account (indent (a) of article 4(1) CRR); on the other, (b) large investment firms (indent (b) of art. 4(1) CRR). **6.013**

Those large investment firms, in order to fall under the scope of CRR and being subject to the supervision of the NCAs/ECB, need to fulfil, cumulatively, the following requisites: **6.014**

---

22 For instance, cf points (1) to (6) of Appendix A of Directive 2014/65/EU of the European Parliament and of the Council of 15 May 2014 on markets in financial instruments and amending Directive 2002/92/EC and Directive 2011/61/EU ("MIFID").

23 Cf Recital 37 of Regulation 2019/2033 of the European Parliament and of the Council of 27 November 2019 on the prudential requirements of investment firms and amending Regulations (EU) No 1093/2010, (EU) No 575/2013, (EU) No 600/2014 and (EU) No 806/2014 ("IFR").

24 See (i) Proposal for a Directive on the prudential supervision of investment firms and amending Directives 2013/36/EU and 2014/65/EU (COM/2017/0791 final); and (ii) Proposal for a Regulation on the prudential requirements of investment firms and amending Regulations (EU) No 575/2013, (EU) No 600/2014 and (EU) No 1093/201 (COM/2017/0790 final).

25 Cf the *Opinion of the European Central Bank of 22 August 2018 on the review of prudential treatment of investment firms* (CON/2018/36).

26 Anticipating the change, see Busch, D. and van Rijn, M. (2018). Regulating systemic risk: A cross sectoral approach. In *European Financial Regulation: Levelling the Cross-Sectoral Playing Field. A Research Agenda* (pp. 107–129). Oxford: Hart Publishing. At p. 113.

27 Applicable as from 26 June 2021 pursuant to art. 66(2) IFR.

(i) Their business includes dealing on own their account and/or underwriting or placing financial instruments on a firm commitment basis.[28]

(ii) It is not a commodity and emission allowance dealer, a collective investment undertaking, an insurance undertaking or an investment firm for which the authorisation as a credit institution is waived in accordance with art. 8a of CRD IV.[29]

(iii) The total value of their consolidated assets of the undertaking individually consolidated is equal to or exceeds 30 billion euros.

In addition, this requisite may be also fulfilled if the total value of the assets of the undertaking is less than 30 billion euros and is part of a group in which the total value of the consolidated assets of all undertakings in that group, that individually have total assets of less than 30 billion euros and that carry out any of the activities referred to above, is equal to or exceeds 30 billion euros.

Finally, this requisite may be deemed fulfilled if the consolidated supervisor so decides (upon consultation with the supervisory college), when the total value of the assets of the undertaking is less than 30 billion euros and the undertaking is part of a group in which the total value of the consolidated assets of all undertakings in the group that carry out any of the activities referred to in indent (i) above is equal to or exceeds 30 billion euros.

6.015 Furthermore, investment firms already forming part of a consolidated group may continue to be subject to prudential supervision of the competent authorities, if competent authorities so decide.[30]

2. Perimeter of entities included within the ECB direct supervision

6.016 A close look at art. 4(1) SSM R evidences that the ECB is exclusively competent[31] to carry out the specific micro-prudential supervisory tasks listed in that article.[32] This exclusive ownership founds its intrinsic limit in the same article, according to which this exclusive competence can be only exercised for *prudential supervisory purposes*.[33] The foregoing mandates the ECB to use the competence and powers granted under this regulation for prudential purposes

---

28 Cf Points (3) and (6) of Annex I MIFID.

29 This precision was included by Regulation 2024/1623 (CRR III).

30 Cf art. 1(5) IFR.

31 *L-Bank* Appeal at Paras. 37–38 and Recital 2 SSM Fr. Art. 6(5) SSM R makes additional reference to the exclusivity of the competence of the ECB over *all* credit institutions.

32 In its Paras. (1) and (2).

33 Art. 4(1) SSM R. Such term not defined and then susceptible of being shaped by the ECB itself, building upon the EU banking law *corpus* and different national legal traditions. Ultimately, however, the delimitation of such open-texture concept belongs to the CJEU.

A parallelism may be draw here with the delimitation of economic vs. monetary activities, as in the *Gauweiler* and *Weiss* cases. Cf Court of Justice judgments in cases C-62/14 (*Gauweiler and Others v Deutscher Bundestag*) of 16 June 2015 (ECLI:EU:C:2015:400) and C-493/17 (*Heinrich Weiss and Others*) of 11 December 2018 (ECLI:EU:C:2018:1000).

only, separating them from the performance of its constitutional price stability mandate.[34] Several provisions of the SSM R actually highlight this duty, whose breach may lead to a situation potentially constituting *détournement de pouvoir*.[35]

6.017 Additionally, even if the ECB enjoys exclusivity, the exercise of these tasks is allocated between the ECB and the NCAs. This will be specifically addressed in Section B. (*Allocation of micro-prudential tasks*) below. As provided by the not-so-evident interplay of arts. 4(1) and 6(4) SSM R, the specific tasks are allocated between the NCAs and the ECB following a twofold classification between entities: SIs and LSIs.

6.018 Except for the tasks listed under indents (a) (authorisation and withdrawal of the authorisation to pursuit the business of credit institutions) and (c) (the assessment of acquisitions and disposals of qualifying holdings) of art. 4 SSM R, the ECB exercises direct oversight on SIs. NCAs, on their side, directly supervise LSIs. Art. 6(4) SSM R sets forth a (basic) triple benchmark to assess the significance of credit institutions – and supervised groups: (a) size; (b) relative size for the economy of the EU or the MS at stake; and (c) the significance of cross-border activities.[36]

6.019 Even if these three features do constitute the basic yardstick to measure significance, the SSM R and the SSM Fr build up on six criteria that actually determine when an entity must be subject to the direct supervision of the ECB.[37] These criteria can be summarised as follows:

---

34 Cf art. 127(1) TFEU.

35 See supra Section C (*Is there any real conflict between the SSM R and superior Treaty provisions? Assessing how to classify potential flaws as regards the ECB dual mandate*) in Chapter 3.

36 Significance shall be assessed at the highest level of consolidation, applying, in general, a parent-undertaking approach (as opposed to a horizontal approach). See arts. 6(4) SSM R and 40 SSM Fr and, more specifically, arts. 70 to 72 SSM Fr. On this topic, see Ugena Torrejón, R. (2014). El Mecanismo Único de Supervisión Europeo. *Actualidad Jurídica Uría Menéndez*, no. 36-2014, pp. 7–18.

37 Cf Section 3.2 of the SSM Supervisory Manual (pp. 57–61). On this matter, see, among others: (i) Wymeersch, E. (2014). The Single Supervisory Mechanism or "SSM", Part One of the Banking Union. *National Bank of Belgium Working Paper*, (255); (ii) Torrejón Ugena, R. (2014); (iii) D'Ambrosio, R. (ed.). (2020). Law and Practice of the Banking Union and of its governing Institutions (Cases and Materials). *Quaderni di Ricerca Giuridica*, (88). At pp. 41–42; (iv) D'Ambrosio, R. (2015) at pp. 82–83 [D'Ambrosio, R. (ed.). (2020)(i)]; (v) Lamandini, M., Ramos Muñoz, D. & Solana, J. (2015) at p. 24; (vi) Lamandini, M., Ramos Muñoz, D. & Solana, J. (2016) at p. 25; (vii) Gortsos, C. V. (2019) at p. 188; and (viii) Parchimowicz, K. M. (2019). Missed targets and misplaced incentives? The case of parent undertaking requirement in the USA and in the EU. *Journal of Banking Regulation*, pp. 1–12. (as regards the mismatch on the Intermediate EU parent undertaking).

(i) In accordance with the *size criterion*, entities whose assets' total value is above 30 billion euros will be subject to the ECB direct supervision.[38]

(ii) Pursuant to the *economic importance criterion*,[39] entities will be subject to the ECB when the ratio of its total assets over the GDP of the relevant participating MS of establishment exceeds 20%, (provided that the total value of their assets is greater than 5 bn euros).

(iii) Following the *cross-border activities criterion*,[40] the entity at stake is considered to be of significant relevance where it has established banking subsidiaries in more than one participating MS and its cross-border assets or liabilities represent a significant part of its total assets or liabilities.

In particular, pursuant to the SSM Fr, the entity at stake is expected to meet these requirements when (a) the total value of its assets exceeds 5 bn euros and (b) (*1*) the ratio of its cross-border assets to its total assets is above 20%; or (*2*) the ratio of its cross-border liabilities to its total liabilities is above 20%.

(iv) In accordance with the *assistance criterion*,[41] an entity which has requested or received directly aid from the EFSF or the ESM will be considered as *significant*.

(v) The *national champions criterion*[42] determines that the three most relevant credit institutions in each participating MS are considered significant.

Here, it is worth nothing that, unlike the other criteria, the SSM R refers explicitly to *credit institutions* (and not to *institutions*). Prudence demands construing the reference restrictively as referred only to credit institutions (excluding the other entities falling within the scope of the SSM supervision).

Additionally, a specific waiver from this criterion is expressly granted; if particular circumstances so demand, the most significant credit institutions in the participating member state may nevertheless remain subject to the supervision of the NCAs.

The circumstances on which the ECB may decide not to subject any of the three most significant credit institutions in a given participating MS are not entirely clear. One may argue that these reasons should be aligned with the scarce CJEU jurisprudence and relate to the equivalence between the supervision that may be exercised by the ECB and by the relevant NCA.[43] Conversely, the author is of the view that this objection is more linked to the lack of relevance

38 Cf arts. 6(4) SSM R and 50 to 55 SSM Fr. According to Wymeersch, this would be the most relevant criterion. See Wymeersch, E. (2014) at p. 29. The same threshold (30 billion euros) is used to determine (together with other requirements) that an investment firm may qualify as a *credit institution* under CRR (cf art. 4(1)(b)(i) CRR).

39 Cf arts. 6(4) SSM R and 56 to 58 SSM Fr.

40 Cf arts. 6(4) SSM R and 59 and 60 SSM Fr.

41 Cf arts. 6(4) SSM R and 61 to 64 SSM Fr.

42 Cf arts. 6(4) SSM R and 65 to 66 SSM Fr.

43 Cf *L-Bank Appeal* at Paras. 60–65. See also the *L-Bank case* at Para. 80 and Opinion of AG Hogan in the former case at Para. 74. Basically, the Court stated that (a) it was for the ECB making use of its discretion to define the extent of the concept of *specific circumstances* foreseen in art. 6(4) SSM R (which, actually, it did when it drafted arts. 70 to 72 SSM Fr); (b) additionally, the Court understands that it is implied that these specific circumstances may occur when "*direct prudential supervision by the national authorities is better able to attain those objectives and those principles, in particular, the need to ensure the consistent application of high supervisory standards, than by direct prudential supervision by the ECB*".

and *significance per se* that the three most significant credit institutions of a given country may have (and the risk they actually represent for the Union financial system).

(vi) Finally, less significant institutions may be classified as significant when "*necessary to ensure consistent application of high supervisory standards*" or when the relevant NCAs so request to the ECB and it may deem it appropriate.[44]

Some examples of the criteria that may justify the reclassification of an entity as significant are preluded in art. 6(5)(b) SSM R and further devised in art. 67(2) SSM Fr.[45]

Regarding this latter criterion, its flip side can be found in art. 6(4) SSM R itself, as it establishes that, in "*particular circumstances*", entities classified as significant may be *declassified* as less significant. Making use of its regulatory discretion, the ECB should indicate when these *particular circumstances* may concur.[46] The open texture of the concepts *specific and factual circumstances*[47] demands a purposive lecture. Also, further judicial guidance will be more than welcome (as it was the case in the *L-Bank* saga). Pursuant to the *L-Bank Appeal*, these particular circumstances may be identified with the possibility of NCAs being in a better position than the ECB to exercise their direct prudential supervision.[48] **6.020**

B. ALLOCATION OF MICRO-PRUDENTIAL TASKS

Dealing with the allocation of micro-prudential tasks within the SSM requires, first of all, delimiting what tasks are actually allocated to the ECB and comprised within the SSM, distinguishing them from those that remain under the remit of the NCAs. Drawing this distinction is not straightforward. The foregoing is due to the tension that sometimes arises between the strict and plain wording of the SSM R (Section B.1 below), and the principal objective **6.021**

44 Cf arts. 6(5)(b) SSM R and 67 to 69 SSM Fr. The author is of the view that this exception well deserves to constitute a separated criterion, taking into account that the SSM Fr devotes a separate Title (Title 8 within Part IV) and that six credit institutions were subject to the ECB direct supervision based on these criteria in 2019. Other authors seem to follow a different approach, treating this *criterion* as a sort of exception to the general rule. Cf Wymeersch, E. (2014) at p. 30 and Gortsos, C. V. (2019) at p. 188.

45 Including, among others: the fact that ECB instructions have not been followed by the relevant NCA, the fact that the entity at stake has received or requested indirect financial support from the EFSF or ESM and the interconnectedness of the given LSI (or group) with other credit institutions.

46 See arts. 70 to 72 SSM Fr (reference to them is also made in art. 39(4) SSM Fr). See footnote 43.

47 Cf art. 70(1) SSM Fr. These circumstances relate to the objectives and principles of the SSM R and the necessity to ensure the consistent application of high supervisory standards (cf art. 1(1) SSM R). In addition, art. 71(1) sets forth that the mentioned analysis must be done on a case-by-case basis, excluding the possibility of being carried out per categories of entities.

48 See footnote 43.

pursued by the *mechanism*, which is to protect "*the safety and soundness of credit institutions and the stability of the financial system*".[49]

6.022 Once determined what tasks are actually allocated upon the SSM (ECB), it is worth devising a twofold distribution approach. First, a *vertical* distribution of tasks between the ECB and the NCAs following the decentralised model[50] (Section B.2 below).

6.023 Second, a *horizontal* distribution scheme can be also depicted, building upon the SSM R and outside that legal text[51] (Section B.3 below). This horizontal distribution of task comprises the distribution of tasks (and powers) between the SSM (ECB/NCAs), the ESAS (specially the EBA), the SRM (SRB) and other EU Institutions (mainly the Commission). The term horizontal denotes that the distribution of those tasks is not funded in a principal-agent or hierarchical structure but on the principle of conferral, to which any EU body must comply with.

6.024 The general framework regulating the allocation of micro-prudential supervisory tasks leads to certain conclusions on the rationale and logic of the model that are driven ultimately (in the view of the author) by the guiding principle of level playing field as balanced by the equally ranked principle of proportionality.

1. Tasks included vs. tasks excluded

6.025 Para. 6 of art. 1 SSM R reserves to the NCAs the supervisory tasks not conferred to the ECB under such Regulation. This means that the NCAs would retain the exclusive competence of those tasks not allocated to the ECB.[52] Additionally, the SSM R reinforces the idea that the NCAs may be vested with macro-prudential powers not grounded in EU Law.[53] The exercise of

---

49 Cf art. 1(1) and Recitals 17 and 65 SSM R.

50 See footnote 43 and also Montemaggi, S. Case-study: Judgments of the General Court and of the ECJ on the Landeskreditbank (General Court, T-122/15 and ECJ, C-450/17 P). In D'Ambrosio, R. (ed.). (2020) (i). In *Law and Practice of the Banking Union and of its governing Institutions (Cases and Materials)* (pp. 217–231). Quaderni di Ricerca Giuridica, (88).

51 Cf SRM, EBA Regulation and Regulations 1094/2010 and 1095/2010.

52 As stated in the *L-Bank case* and in the *L-Bank Appeal*, the ECB would retain the exclusive competence over the tasks listed in article 4(1) SSM R.

53 Cf arts. 1(VII) and 5 SSM R. See also arts. 130 and 134 and ss. CRD IV relating to the requirements and setting out of the countercyclical capital buffer.

As an example of the national macro-prudential measures that could be adopted without grounds in EU law, one may imagine specific sectorial buffers. For instance, buffers linked to sectors that may constate the main sources of economic wealth for the country at stake (e.g., tourism-linked buffers, energy-dependent buffers, etc.).

these powers falls outside the remit of the competence entrusted to the ECB and should be exercised by the NCAs in accordance with their national rules.

The specific micro-prudential tasks conferred on the SSM are listed in arts. 4(1) and (2) SSM R. These tasks cover, in abstract, the main aspects of daily supervision over credit institutions and beyond.[54] These tasks are susceptible of being classified pursuant to the following scheme: **6.026**

(i) Authorising tasks, which includes authorising credit institutions (and withdrawing such authorisations), as well as branches, and assessing (authorising) the acquisition of qualifying holdings.[55]

(ii) Daily supervisory tasks:[56] these envisage to ensure compliance with capital requirements, securitisations, large exposure limits, leverage and disclosure of information concerning these and other matters. These tasks also comprise functions relating to governance and internal control functions[57] (i.e., ensuring that robust governance arrangements are put in place).

Functions relating to supervisory reviews (SREP)[58] can be included within this category of tasks (developed in collaboration with the EBA). Moreover, these tasks encompass the performance of consolidated supervision over credit institution's parent undertakings. Finally, within this set of tasks, the participation of the ECB in supplementary supervision of financial conglomerates can be included.[59]

(iii) Home-host competences:[60] within the general framework distributing the ECB and NCAs' involvement as regards the tasks listed in art. 4(1) SSM R (cf art. 6(4) SSM R), it falls within the SSM's remit exercising supervisory competences as regards branches of credit institutions established in a non-participating MS, willing to establish a branch or provide cross-border services within the SSM geographical area.[61]

Additionally, it cannot be discarded that in order to cope with the *transition risks* relating to a sustainable economy, macro-prudential measures may be put in place adopting a variable geometry – for example, by imposing levies to finance a national *transition fund* to finance those sectors of strategic interest for the state that need extra resources to complete its transition to sustainable finance.

54 Wymeersch, E. (2014) at. p. 37.

55 Cf art. 4(1)(a)–(c) and arts. 14 and 15 SSM R; arts. 11, 17 and 73–87 SSM Fr.

56 As per this block of tasks, see arts. 4(1)(d), (e), (f), (g) and (h); 16 SSM R; and 89–95 SSM Fr.

57 Cf arts. 93 and 94 SSM Fr, as regards fit and proper assessments of the persons responsible for managing credit institutions. See also the ECB Guide to fit and proper assessments (December 2021): https://www.bankingsupervision.europa.eu/ecb/pub/pdf/ssm.fit_and_proper_guide_update202112~d66f230eca.en.pdf.

58 Broadly on the SREP topic, see the comprehensive analysis undertaken in Lamandini, M., Ramos Muñoz, D. and D'Ambrosio, R. (2022). 18 Supervisory Review and Evaluation Process (SREP) in the Context of the Exercise of Supervisory Powers and Extraordinary Measures. In *Capital and Liquidity Requirements for European Banks* (pp. 526–547). OUP.

59 See Section A.1. (*Subjects of the SSM supervision*) above.

60 Cf arts. 4(2) SSM R and 13 and 14 SSM Fr.

61 Which would include the Eurosystem and, potentially, the territories of those participating MSs whose currency is not the Euro but which have entered into close cooperation agreements (cf art. 7 SSM R and 106–119 SSM Fr).

(iv) Early intervention: finally, tasks concerning the assessment and approval of recovery plans fall within SSM scope.[62]

6.027 As one may intuitively guess, those specific tasks not expressly conferred on the SSM will remain under MSs' (and national authorities') remit. In this regard, Recital 28 SSM R clarifies that: "*Supervisory tasks not conferred on the ECB should remain with the national authorities*".[63] Following these Recitals, the following tasks would remain with the NCAs (and outside the scope of the SSM):[64]

(i) Tasks relating to consumer protection,[65] anti-money laundering[66] and terrorism financing.
(ii) Matters relating purely or predominantly to competition law (within the remit of the competences vested on MSs). This would include the approval of mergers from a competition side, and the imposition of penalties to offset the profits generated from a breach of prudential requirements serving primarily to competition purposes.[67]

---

62 Cf Recital 27, arts. 4(1)(i) SSM R; Supervisory Manual (section 4.10); arts. 5–9, 20–28, 27–30 and 32 BRRD and the ECB *Report on recovery plans* (July 2018): https://www.bankingsupervision.europa.eu/ecb/pub/pdf/ssm.reportrecoveryplans201807.en.pdf.

63 See art. 1(II) and (V) SSM R. Pursuant to D'Ambrosio, these tasks are *non-supervisory tasks*. In the view of the author, this exclusion proves to be problematic due to the interplay that some of these tasks may have as regards the prudential supervision (within the SSM remit) of the credit institutions and supervised groups. D'Ambrosio, R. (ed.). (2020)(i) at p. 44. See also D'Ambrosio, R. (2019). Single Supervisory Mechanism: Organ and Procedures. In *The Palgrave Handbook of European Banking Union Law* (pp. 157–183). Palgrave Macmillan.

64 See Lackhoff, K. (2017)(i) at pp. 195–211.

65 See as regards the exclusion of consumer-related matters Wymeersch, E. (2019) at p. 48.
Actually, the EBA has been vested with the task (and powers) of promoting *consumer protection*. Cf arts. 1(5)(f), 8(1) and 9 of the EBA Regulation. See also Gortsos, C. V. (2016). The role of the European Banking Authority (EBA) after the establishment of the Single Supervisory Mechanism (SSM). In *Regulating and Supervising European Financial Markets* (pp. 277–297). Springer, Cham.

66 See, in this regard, General Court judgment in joined cases T-351/18 and T-584/18 (*Ukrselhosprom PCF LLC v ECB* and *Versobank AS v ECB*, respectively) of 6 October 2021 (ECLI:EU:T:2021:669) and Court of Justice judgment in case C-803/21 P (*Versobank AS v ECB*) of 7 September 2023 (ECLI:EU:C:2023:630) at Para. 97. There, the Court clarified in Para. 142 that: "(…) *it is apparent from recitals 28 and 29 of the Basic SSM Regulation that the task of preventing the use of the financial system for the purposes of money laundering and terrorist financing remains a national competence and that the ECB has, in that regard, a duty of cooperation vis-à-vis the national authorities*". See, in the same vein CJEU judgement in case C-579/22 P (*Anglo Austrian AAB AG and others v ECB*) of 12 September 2024 (ECLI:EU:C:2024:731) at Para. 137.

67 See, also, footnote 4 in the letter issued by the ECB dated on 31 March 2017: "Additional clarification regarding the ECB's competence to exercise supervisory powers granted under national law":
https://www.bankingsupervision.europa.eu/press/letterstobanks/shared/pdf/2017/Letter_to_SI_Entry_point_information_letter.pdf?cb0801df81ba2db9d450ce4fb53065c8.
This footnote also refers that the "supervision" will remain within the scope of the NCAs. This competence does not fit easily within any other category of competences depicted here and would serve, more broadly, to corporate law purposes.

(iii) Exclusions from the scope of the SSM based on subjective or objective requirements:

A third group of tasks falling outside the scope of the SSM can be identified. Those tasks are heterogenous, and the reasons motivating their exclusion from SSM R relate, mainly, to the constitutional limitations of the mechanism itself. Furthermore, such exclusions can be of an objective nature or of a subjective character. The former ones relate to matters that could not be attributed to the ECB as they fall outside the remit of the enabling clause (art. 127(6) TFEU). The latter ones refer to the types of entities that the ECB can, in principle, supervise (and are authorised by the SSM R). Those include the following tasks:

1. Supervision of financial intermediaries and other entities excluded from the scope of the SSM R[68] (for instance, central clearing counterparties (CCPs)).
2. Supervisory tasks concerning credit institutions from third countries establishing a branch or providing cross-border services in the EU.
3. The supervision of payment services.
4. Supervisory functions relating to day-to-day verifications of credit institutions (which would be, in principle, included within the remit of SSM R[69]).
5. Functions pertaining to competent authorities over credit institutions in relation to markets in financial instruments (MIFID).[70]
6. Supervisory tasks regarding bodies which are not covered by the definition of credit institutions under Union law but which are supervised as credit institutions under national law.[71] It must be recalled that, in some participating MSs, some financial intermediaries' central securities/stock depositories and CCPs are required to hold a banking license based on purely national requirements. These entities must be excluded as such from the SSM scope. However, they may ultimately remain subject to the ECB supervision as being part of a consolidated group.
7. Finally, following the said Recital 27 SSM R, the reception of notifications from credit institutions in relation to the right of establishment and the free provision of services would remain within the scope of national authorities.[72]

The delimitation of these tasks is contemplated in the SSM Fr[73] and relates (a) to the freedom of establishment *within* the geographical area of the SSM and **6.028**

---

68 Arts. 1(I) SSM R and 2(5) CRD IV.

69 Cf Recital 37 SSM R and also art. 3 SSM Fr. D'Ambrosio, R. (2020). The involvement of the NCAs in the ECB's supervisory proceedings. In *Law and Practice of the Banking Union and of its governing Institutions (Cases and Materials)* (pp. 163–181). Quaderni di Ricerca Giuridica, (88) [D'Ambrosio, R. (2020)(ii)].

70 See below in Section B.2. (*Vertical allocation? Examining the decentralised mode of implementing the specific supervisory tasks*).

71 For a detailed analysis of this question see. Wymeersch, E. (2014) at pp. 31–32. See also Gurlit, E. (2022). Art. 14 Authorisation. In *European banking union: Brussels commentary* (pp. 189–215). Baden-Baden: Nomos [Gurlit, E. (2022)(i)]. At Para. 10.

72 See Gortsos, C. V. (2019) at p. 191.

73 See above and in arts. 4(1)(b) and 4(2) SSM R; and 11–12, 13–16 and 17 SSM Fr.

(b) to the establishment and freedom of credit institutions established in non-participating MSs to provide services within the SSM.[74]

2. Vertical allocation? Examining the decentralised mode of implementing the specific supervisory tasks

> *[T]he Council has delegated to the ECB exclusive competence in respect of the tasks laid down in Article 4(1) of the Basic Regulation (…) the sole purpose of Article 6 of that same regulation is to enable decentralised implementation under the SSM of that competence by the national authorities, under the control of the ECB, in respect of the less significant entities and in respect of the tasks listed in Article 4(1)(b) and (d) to (i).*[75]

6.029 As stated in the *L-Bank case*,[76] and further confirmed in the *L-Bank Appeal*,[77] the SSM R vests the ECB with the exclusive competence regarding the specific micro-prudential tasks listed in arts. 4(1)–(2).[78] The conclusion is supported by three interlinked arguments:[79]

6.030 The *first* one is based on Recitals 15 and 28 SSM R and their interplay with art. 4(1) SSM R. Pursuant to this reasoning, tasks remaining within the remit of national authorities are listed (not exhaustively) in the mentioned Recital 28 and consequently not mentioned in art. 4(1).

6.031 The *second* argument explores the subordinate nature of the NCAs intervention. It is noted here that the ECB is capable of directing NCAs activities concerning LSIs via general instructions.[80] Furthermore, despite the ECB not being capable of issuing individual binding instructions to NCAs concerning

---

74 As indicated somewhere above, supervisory tasks concerning credit institutions from third countries establishing a branch or providing cross-border services in the EU remain within the remit of national authorities.

75 See *L-Bank case* at Para. 63. In this regard, see also, among others: Annunziata, F. (2020). European Banking Supervision in the Age of the ECB: Landeskreditbank Baden-Württemberg – Förderbank v. ECB. *Bocconi Legal Studies Research Paper No. 0*, pp. 1–39; D'Ambrosio, R. (2015) at pp. 71–90; and D'Ambrosio, R. (ed.). (2020)(i) at pp. 39–53, 173–181 and 203–217.

76 Not without some contestation from some members of the Academia; see Tröger, T. (2017). How not to do banking law in the 21st century. *SAFE Policy Letter*, no. 56.

77 See footnote 32 in Chapter 5.

78 Same reasoning would apply, in the view of the author, as regards the tasks comprised in the second paragraph of this art. 4(1) – which are not mentioned in Recitals 28 and 29 as remaining within the NCAs' remit.

79 Cf *L-Bank case* at Paras. 56–62. Cf Lamandini, M. & Ramos Muñoz, D. (2017) at pp. 194–195.

80 Cf art. 6(5)(a) SSM R. On the subordinated nature of the NCAs see Gortsos, C. V. (2015). Competence sharing between the ECB and the national competent supervisory authorities within the Single Supervisory Mechanism (SSM). *European Business Organization Law Review, 16*, pp. 401–420 [Gortsos, C. V. (2015)(i)]. At pp. 410–11.

such LSIs,[81] it may claim the exercise of direct supervision over a determined (or several) LSI(s). NCAs are therefore placed on a subordinated place *vis-à-vis* the ECB, which ultimately remains responsible for the effective and consistent functioning of the *mechanism*.[82]

In *third* place, it is highlighted that SIs may only be *declassified* (turned into LSIs) and subject to the direct supervision of NCAs only when justified "*particular circumstances*" so determine.[83] This would constitute the flip of the coin of the previous argument. 6.032

Later on, it will be discussed what are the implications of the *nonstandard* mechanism used by the legislators to distribute not the competences concerning specific micro-prudential tasks, but the *responsibilities* regarding the performance of those tasks. First it will be briefly analysed how, actually, those responsibilities are distributed, except as regards the exercise of sanctioning powers, which would be addressed in Section C. (*Allocation of sanctioning competences: a specialty over the general rule?*) below in this chapter. 6.033

Pursuant to the foregoing scheme, discussing the vertical allocation of responsibilities[84] requires focusing on the meaning of Para. 4 of art. 6 SSM R.[85] 6.034

An intuitive and basic approach on the distribution of responsibilities leads to understanding that the ECB carries out directly the supervision over SIs, whereas NCAs assume an equivalent intervention concerning LSIs (under the ECB aegis). 6.035

81 Which does not discard the issuance of informal indications and/or even the exercise of naming and shaming in the course of discussions within the Supervisory Board.

82 Cf art. 6(1) SSM R.

83 Cf arts. 6(4) SSM R and 39(4) and 70 to 72 SSM Fr.

84 To be noted, the difference between competences under the SSM R (as referred in Chapter 5 above) and *responsibilities*. The later determines who effectively carries out the material functions as regards LSIs (NCAs) or SIs (ECB). This is aligned with CJEU views on the exercise of functions pertaining to SSM-related competences. See *L-Bank case* at Para. 54.

85 The provision is not easy to read, and its structure sometimes does not follow a clear logic; first, it is established that, for the tasks listed in art. 4(1) (except for points (a) and (c)), the ECB will have the competences established in Para. 4 of this provision and, as regards NCAs, will have the responsibilities established in paragraph 6. These latter responsibilities will be exercised within the framework set out in Para. 7 (by the ECB, i.e., the SSM Fr).

The paragraph continues stating the basic criteria used to determine the significance of supervised entities. However, despite focusing on the determination of the significative character of supervised entities, this paragraph refers to competences that the ECB shall have as regards *less significant* entities.

6.036 This basic reasoning acquires further complexity as regards the tasks contemplated in letters (a) and (c) of art. 4 SSMR, i.e., authorisation and withdrawal of *banking* licenses and the assessment of acquisition and disposals of qualifying holdings in credit institutions. These tasks are entrusted exclusively to the ECB regarding any types of entities and/or supervised groups, irrespectively of their status (i.e., SIs or LSIs).

6.037 The expansive reading of the tasks entrusted to the ECB[86] is susceptible of further enlarging the remit of these *super-exclusive* tasks. And in this sense, the ECB would be competent to approve changes in any institution's bylaw, as these tasks would be "*instrumental for ensuring compliance with the authorisation to take up the business of a credit institution's requirements, which is an exclusive task of the ECB under Article 4(1)(a) of the SSM Regulation*".[87] The same would apply as regards the authorisation to carry out any additional activity to the ones contemplated in a banking license[88] (or to the removal of any of those additional activities from the banking license).

6.038 At this point, it is worth splitting the analysis of the allocation of vertical prudential competences into two: (i) focusing first on the distribution of tasks regarding SIs and (ii) differentiating later the intervention of the ECB and NCAs concerning LSIs.

(a) Vertical distribution of micro-prudential tasks concerning SIs

6.039 SIs are directly subject to the ECB purview. NCAs on their side are subject to a specific sincere cooperation obligation,[89] rooted in art. 6(1) and (2) SSM R. Pursuant to art. 6(7) SSM R, this cooperation is further devised in the SSM Fr, establishing the practical arrangements required for this purpose.

6.040 Within the scope and in accordance with the specific procedures set out in the SSM Fr,[90] NCAs serve the ECB to fulfil its responsibilities.[91] Under this setup, and following a *principal-agent* model, NCAs cooperate with the ECB in two differentiated ways:

---

86 See above and also in footnote 67 above.

87 Ibidem previous footnote 67 at p. 10. See also, on the expansive scope of the tasks exercised directly by the ECB as regards SIs pursuant to art. 9(1)II SSM R, Hernández Saseta, C. (2021) at pp. 306–307 and Bassani, G. (2019).

88 Ibidem footnote 67 at p. 13. See, also, art. 78(5) SSM Fr.

89 Which, as regards supervisory and investigatory powers, are extended to national designated authorities (cf art. 9(2) SSM R).

90 Cf art. 6(2)II and (7) SSM R

91 Cf art. 6(1) SSM R.

The *first one* is within the JSTs established to monitor each and every one of the SIs. Under the coordination and direction of the JSTs,[92] NCAs compulsorily allocate staff to serve in the supervision of SIs, which, before the SSM came into force, was carried out by NCAs themselves. **6.041**

Even if mandated and subject to JSTs, the NCAs' staff serving in JSTs are still *national* staff and not subject to EU staff regulation.[93] Accordingly, and even if they perform functionally equal tasks to ECB colleagues, the NCAs' personnel would not be covered by the EU privileges and immunities. Art. 22 of the Protocol no. 7 to the TFEU on the *privileges and immunities of the European Union* only attributes these privileges and immunities to ECB staff and the members of its organs.[94] This fact situates NCAs' staff in a comparably worse situation regarding its coverage by the EU legal framework (considering that they are carrying out functions for an EU Institution, under and in compliance to an EU Regulation).[95] **6.042**

This undesirable mismatch could be swiftly corrected through a simple amendment in the ECB's Conditions of Employment for Staff. Part 1(1) of those conditions could be easily modified by the General Council[96] to include the NCAs' staff only to extend to them the privileges and immunities of Protocol no. 7 during the performance of their tasks within the established JSTs. Another possibility would entail subscribing short-term secondment contracts with NCAs' staff involved in the JSTs. ESCB/IO types of contracts[97] could be easily adapted to this end. However, for the time being at least, it seems to be resistance from NCAs (as accepted by the ECB) that make broad use of these kinds of contracts. The use of these contracts seems to have been restricted to staff (inspectors) from a non-home/host NCA who go on a cross-border mission or a mixed team mission.[98] Consequently, these contracts are not used, **6.043**

92 See art. 6(1) SSM Fr. See, also, arts. 3 to 6 SSM Fr.

93 Neither to the ECB staff regulations.

94 Cf art. 40 SESCB. Pursuant to Part 1(1) of the *Conditions of Employment for Staff of the European Central Bank* determines that *staff* means any person employed by the ECB by means of an employment contract for an indefinite or defined period: https://www.ecb.europa.eu/careers/pdf/conditions_of_employment.pdf.

95 D'Ambrosio concisely also expresses some doubts regarding the applicability of the privileges and immunities of Protocol no. 7 to the NCAs' staff working within a JST. See D'Ambrosio, R. (2015) at p. 123.

96 Pursuant to arts. 21 and 12(1) of the Rules of Procedure.

97 Cf ECB Annex IIb of the *Conditions of Employment for Staff of the European Central Bank* (Annex IIb Conditions of Short-Term Employment).

98 Cf ECB explanatory note on the Application of the existing ECB Framework regarding ESCB/IO contracts to NCA on-site inspectors dated on 24 April 2019: https://www.ecb.europa.eu/ecb/access_to_documents/document/pa_document/shared/data/ecb.dr.par2019_0107_ExplanatoryNoteOnESCB_IOContractsForNCAInspectors.en.pdf?ddb4b2dcefb7e85055902a675719d7b1.

in principle, as regards staff carrying out tasks in their respective MS within a JSTs.

6.044 The *second one*, implies the collaboration and assistance of NCAs in the course of the so-called common procedures.[99] Within the course of these procedures, NCAs act as a focal point where supervisees must address their request.[100] They prepare draft decisions addressed to the ECB and prescreen the request to check whether it complies with relevant national law conditions.[101]

(b) Vertical distribution of micro-prudential tasks concerning LSIs

6.045 As regards LSIs, the NCAs' intervention increases its intensity, but always respecting its subordinating nature *vis-à-vis* the ECB. Whereas NCAs directly supervise LSIs, they must carry out these tasks not only in compliance with general acts (EU regulations, EBA standards and guidelines, and national law transposing EU law) but also abiding to ECB general instructions (and recommendations).[102]

6.046 The SSM Fr devotes Part VII (*Procedures for the supervision of less significant entities*)[103] to arrange the supervision of LSIs and regulate information flows to be provided by NCAs concerning those entities. Section 5 of the SSM Supervisory Manual complements the SSM Fr regarding this matter.[104] The intensity of ECB implication depends on the priority rank attributed to each LSI.[105] LSIs' rank depends on its "*riskiness and systemic impact*".[106] Accordingly, the degree of ex ante, ongoing and ex post reporting depends on the risk classification of the respective LSI. It follows from arts. 99 and 100 SSM Fr that the ECB can classify those LSIs according to their risk profile. The criteria that trigger the classification of a given LSI as a *High Priority* LSI were only made available to the general public in 2022 in the *ECB LSI Supervisory report.*[107]

---

99 See Section C. (*From "tasks" to "powers"*) in Chapter 5 above.

100 Which would be in line with the tasks remaining within the remit of the NCAs. See above in Section B.1. (*Tasks included vs. tasks excluded*).

101 See, for example, art. 14(2) SSM R and 15(2) SSM R.

102 Cf art. 6(6) SSM R.

103 Arts. 96 and ss.

104 Within the ECB, Directorate Specialised Institutions & LSIs deals with the supervision of LSIs and the relationship with NCAs concerning this type of entity.

105 Cf arts. 6(5)(a)II SSM R and 99, 100 and 117(2) SSM Fr.

106 Cf Section 5.4 (*Oversight of LSIs and LSI sectors*) of the SSM supervisory manual. The assessment of the importance of the LSI depends, among other factors, on (i) its potential impact for financial stability, (ii) the proximity to meet any of the threshold that would lead to its classification as SIs and (iii) whether the relevant LSI is in a crisis situation (cf SSM Supervisory Manual at p. 106).

107 Which can be consulted here, together with other practical information on the oversight exercised by the ECB over LSIs (including a list of *High Priority* LSIs): Supervisory approach and methodologies (europa.eu).

Those criteria include (i) the size (> €15 billion); (ii) the importance for the economy of the relevant participating MS; (iii) the degree of cross-border activities; and (iv) the type of business model.

ECB orders may adopt the form of general regulations,[108] legally binding, or more subtle recommendations[109] and/or policy stances. The SSM R sets out a double limitation as regards the type of instructions that the ECB may issue; it cannot directly address orders or supervisory acts directly to LSIs[110] nor to the NCAs individually.[111] Hence, the ECB may only issue general instructions to manage and coordinate LSIs' oversight. **6.047**

These limitations may be counterbalanced by means of symmetric prerogatives vested on the ECB. On the one hand, following art. 6(5)(e) SSM R, the ECB can request NCAs to submit, on *ad hoc* basis, information regarding supervision conducted on LSIs. In this regard, the ECB may request specific information regarding individual LSIs and, by means of its scrutiny and critic, this can (and thus may be) used as manner to directly instruct NCAs. The foregoing is capable of rightly showing to NCAs what the standards the ECB expects from them to achieve are, which methodologies to follow, and what deviations are not going to be tolerated. **6.048**

On the other hand, the ECB may claim the direct supervision over certain LSIs if it suspects that NCAs are not carrying out a coherent supervision capable of ensuring the application of high supervisory standards.[112] This power shows the subordinate character of the NCAs intervention, even as regards LSIs. **6.049**

Concerning both SIs and LSIs, NCAs intervention must be read in key of subordination, where the NCAs assume the role of satellites or subsidiaries (agents) of the ECB.[113] However, the author cannot avoid noting the lack of a truly *ad hoc* corrective mechanism. This punitive mechanism would be **6.050**

108 As it would be the case of the GO&Ds.

109 This would be the case of the Recommendation on common specifications for the exercise of some options and discretions available in Union law by national competent authorities in relation to less significant institutions (ECB/2017/10).

110 With the exceptions relating to the tasks listed on letters (a) and (c) of art. 4(1) SSM R.

111 However, see footnote 80 above.

112 Cf art. 6(5)(b) SSM R. See also Section A.2. (*Perimeter of entities included within the ECB direct supervision)* above.

113 Bosque Argachal, C. (2019). Sanctioning powers of the Banco de España within the SSM. General overview and challenges faced. In *Aspecte cheie in activitatea financiar-bancara. Conferinta internationala* (pp. 26–40). C. H. Beck.

activated in case any NCA objects to or resists implementing and/or following ECB general instructions (or make difficult the implementation of ECB tasks and mission under the SSM).[114]

6.051 A basic corrective tool in the form of *naming* can be found, as regards close cooperation, in art. 7(5) SSM R. Following this provision, the ECB may issue a warning addressed to the MS concerned that the close cooperation may be suspended or terminated unless *decisive* corrective action is taken.[115] The matter may heat and escalate, leading to the suspension or the termination of the close cooperation on ECB's initiative.[116]

6.052 Not being expressly contemplated is the possibility to *punish* undisciplined NCAs of participating MSs whose currency is the euro; the ECB can only

---

114 The foregoing disregarding the resource to an infringement procedure pursuant to art. 258 TFEU. The exercise of such a mechanism corresponds to the Commission and not to the ECB (who could always report a violation of EU law committed by a MSs). Also, such a mechanism does not seem ideal as it is usually quite lengthy and incapable of providing a swift response. The only indirect way to make diverging NCAs return to the path of compliance seems to be provided in art. 258 TFEU.

Notwithstanding the foregoing, acting on the basis of art. 271(d) TFEU is debatable. This provision contemplates that the ECB, upon the decision of the Governing Council, can bring an infringement procedure against an NCB in the case of breach of *an obligation under the Treaties* (including the SESCB, which forms part of them). It does not seem feasible to activate this clause in the case of MSs not complying with ECB guidance and instructions under the SSM: *first*, because this provision strictly refers to NCBs, which would not cover NCAs who are not NCBs; *second*, because it is unclear whether the infringement derives directly from the Treaties and the SESCB (cf art. 127(6) TFEU and art. 25(2) SESCB) or from secondary regulation. The EBA Regulation provides some arguments to consider the latter, relegating the former to clear duties established under the Treaties and the SESCB. In this regard, arts. 17(6), 18(4) and 19(6) of the EBA Regulation state that in the case of non-observance of an EBA binding formal opinion, resource to art. 258 TFEU infringement proceeding is expedited. Consequently, the infringement related to the deviation or incorrect application of supervisory ECB supervisory instructions by NCAs falls within the remit of art. 258 TFEU. Although construing these provisions the other way around is also possible, resource to the infringement procedure is not broadly referred to the infringement of EU Law but to the inobservance of an EU agency individual decision addressed to the NCA at stake. Being aware of these confronted interpretations, and taking a restrictive interpretation, as infringement rules so demand, art. 271(d) TFEU should be applied to situations that clearly fall within the remit of the Treaties and the SESCB. This approach also ensures that the same procedure applies to all the NCAs within the SSM, preserving this way the principles of proportionality and equal treatment. This strict approach seems to be followed in AG Kokott in its opinions in cases C-202/18 (*Ilmārs Rimšēvičs v Republic of Latvia*) and C-238/18 (*European Central Bank v Republic of Latvia*), delivered on 19 December 2018 (ECLI:EU:C:2018:1030), at footnote 25.

115 It must be noted that art. 7 SSM R constantly refers to *Member State* whereas, in the SSM Fr (arts. 106 and ss.), reference is made to *NCA in close cooperation*. In the view of the author, the references made in the SSM R must be construed as made to NCAs in close cooperation – e.g., as regards disagreement with an SB's draft decision or an objection of the Governing Council. However, in some cases, it seems appropriate to construe or maintain the reference made to MS in close cooperation. This would be the case in indents (a) and (c) of art. 7. The previous example relates to obligations that can be complied solely by the relevant MS, as they are enacting national laws and notifying to the ECB, EBA and other MSs its intention to enter into a close cooperation under art. 7 SSM R.

116 Cf arts. 7(5)(7) and 119(4) SSM Fr.

react through an infringement procedure.[117] This ensures that all NCAs are subject to the same level of correction or punishment.[118]

Nevertheless, this appears to be a residual and not a very practical way to dissuade NCAs, which disregarded the ECB's instructions and guidance given that: (i) NCAs are not the ultimate subjects to the infringement procedure (as those are MSs), which contributes to blur its deterrent effect. (ii) Pursuant to art. 258 TFEU, the Commission (and not the ECB) would decide whether to initiate such proceeding and how to steer it. Future reviews of the SSM R may decide to include mechanisms to deter NCAs from not observing ECB guidance, in order to overcome the issue generated.[119] **6.053**

(c) Rationale of the system

In the light of the foregoing, we can draw conclusions about (i) the specific micro-prudential tasks allocated to the ECB under the SSM and (ii) how those tasks must be exercised. **6.054**

(a) On the one hand, the *L-Bank Appeal* has clarified the exclusivity of the specific micro-prudential tasks allocated to the ECB under the SSM (those contemplated in art. 4(1)–(2) SSM R) as regards all credit institutions established in the participating MSs. By doing so, the Court has also emphasised that those tasks not comprised within the four corners of the mentioned provision continue to be exercised by NCAs.[120]
(b) On the other hand, and as per the way those specific micro-prudential tasks must be exercised, the General Court first and the Court of Justice later have confirmed that these tasks are carried out via a *decentralised implementation*[121] model.

The paucity of the reference made by the Court does not provide enough clarity of what such a decentralised way of implementation actually means. The issue is not simply theoretical or hypothetical, as the definition of *decentralised implementation* does affect the attributability of supervisory decisions and, **6.055**

---

117 Cf arts. 258 and 260 TFEU.

118 Ibidem footnote 114 above. On the lack of proper coercive tools, see Karagianni, A. & Scholten, M. (2018). Accountability Gaps in the Single Supervisory Mechanism SSM Framework. *Utrecht J. Int'l & Eur. L.*, *34*, pp. 185–194.

119 As the proposed mechanism does not have a clear basis on the SSM R, any attempt to devise it directly in the SSM Fr, without amending SSM R, may be considered unfunded and, consequently, *ultra vires.*

120 Cf Recital 28 SSM R. See Section B.1. (*Tasks included vs. tasks excluded*) above.
Similar conclusion has been recently drawn by the General Court in its judgment in joined cases T-351/18 and T-584/18 (*Ukrselhosprom PCF LLC v ECB* and *Versobank AS v ECB*, respectively) of 6 October 2021 (ECLI:EU:T:2021:669) at Para. 114.

121 Cf *L-Bank Appeal* at Para. 41, *L-Bank case* at Paras. 63, 65 and 72 and the Opinion of AG Hogan at Paras. 49 and ss.

in general, of supervisory acts, the jurisdiction competent to determine the potential liability of the ECB and/or NCAs (national vs. EU) and, consequently, the standard of review to be applied.

6.056 In the view of the author, only subsequent rulings may be able to elucidate and precise such key reference. Lacking such judicial precision, the interaction and distribution of tasks within the SSM and the scope of the *cooperation* duties[122] has raised a persistent, ongoing and unsolved debate in the academia.[123]

6.057 A cautious reading of the SSM R, together with the relevant rulings affecting this topic, would lead, in the view of the author, to the following conclusions:[124]

6.058 As regards the mechanism of distribution of tasks within the SSM, the SSM R implies that the *legislators* have distributed by ministry of the law the *functions* relating to the different tasks allocated to the ECB. This reading can be also inferred from the *L-Bank* saga.

6.059 One cannot deny that the delegation mechanism deployed in the SSM R does not fit within the classical *principal-agent* canon, preferentially used in the EU architecture to allocate missions and corresponding powers to agencies. This would be the case, for instance, of the ESMA or the EBA.[125].

6.060 Nevertheless, and as noted by the Court of Justice in the *ESMA short selling* case, the mechanisms expressly contemplated in the TFEU[126] do not preclude the existence of other forms of delegation.[127] This may be one of them: an anomalous mechanism of distribution of the functions pertaining to the tasks

---

122 Which, in the view of the author, may refer to multiple realities (e.g., cooperation in its functional meaning, cooperation outside the scope of the SSM as regards the mechanism to get an authorisation from a judicial to enter into premises, a general sincere cooperation duty, etc.).

123 For a complete summary of the positions held in the academia, see Annunziata, F. (2020) at pp. 15–17.

124 And ultimately, CJEU jurisprudence may advance in the direction presented immediately below.

125 See *landmark* cases Meroni and Romano: Court of Justice judgments in cases (i) C-9/56 (*Meroni & Co., Industrie Metallurgiche, SpA v High Authority of the European Coal and Steel Community*) of 13 June 1958 (ECLI:EU:C:1958:7); and (ii) C-10/56 (*Meroni & Co., Industrie Metallurgiche, società in accomandita semplice v High Authority of the European Coal and Steel Community*) of 13 June 1958 (ECLI:EU:C:1958:8) and (iii) 98/80 (*Giuseppe Romano v Institut national d'assurance maladie-invalidité*) of 14 May 1981 (ECLI:EU:C:1981:104).

126 Court of Justice in its judgment in case C-270/12 (*United Kingdom v Parliament and Council*) of 22 January 2014 (ECLI:EU:C:2014:18) at Paras. 106–108 (hereafter, the *ESMA short selling case*). See references contained to, in particular, with reference to arts. 290 and 291 TFEU.

127 See Gortsos, C. V. & Lagaria, K. (2020). The European Supervisory Authorities (ESAs) As "Direct" Supervisors in the EU Financial System. *European Banking Institute Working Paper Series* No. 57. The authors note that: "*The CJEU also considered that 'specific professional and technical expertise' can provide grounds for delegations of powers that can be exercised in special circumstances, in which cases there is no question of administrative discretion*" (at. p. 12).

conferred exclusively on the ECB.[128] In this case, the legislators would have conferred on the ECB the exclusive competence to carry out specific micro-prudential tasks. But instead of leaving up to it the decision of how to set up the distribution of functions pertaining to the SSM, they went a step forward and directly devised the perimeter, tools and forms of the cooperation.

Under this scenario, the intervention of NCAs must be read in terms of subordination, as satellites or subsidiaries of the ECB, only to the extent that they are rendered accountable for their performance of the functions entrusted. This subordination can be sustained without too much effort,[129] as fuelled by the *L-Bank* saga. However, the lack of a specific mechanism capable of correcting and deterring those NCAs that deliberately decide not to observe the ECB's instructions or indications casts some doubts on the effectiveness of the *mechanism*[130] regarding the ability of the ECB to retain full oversight over the *mechanism*. **6.061**

Leaving aside these shortcomings, several reasons justify or explain this atypical distribution of functions between the NCAs and the ECB. The main one may be an attempt not to overstretch the principle of proportionality. This is even more understandable if one recalls the pressure that the *mechanism* itself supposes for its legal basis and the progressive expansion of the tasks vested to the ECB via specification, including as regards regulatory competences. An excessive stress regarding the principle of proportionality, cumulated to the debated legal basis upon which the SSM was erected, may have resulted (or invited at least) in questioning, by some MSs or even by members of the EP and/or stakeholders, the constitutionality of the mechanism more deeply. **6.062**

Other reasons that justify the decentralised implementation of the functions relate to the necessity of leveraging on the NCAs' expertise and staff to fulfil its duties.[131] Since the ECB is expected to apply national law transposing EU directives and to request NCAs to use the powers vested under pure national law, it is logical that the *legislators* cautiously attributed a relevant role to **6.063**

128 Cf Lamandini, M. & Ramos Muñoz, D. (2017) at p. 194.

129 See Smits, R. (2018). Interplay of administrative review and judicial protection in European prudential supervision. Some issues and concerns. In *Judicial review in the Banking Union and in the EU financial architecture*. Quaderni di Ricerca Giuridica della Consulenza Legale, Banca d'Italia. At p. 42.

130 Except for, and in a tempered way, concerning NCAs of participating MSs subject to close cooperation agreement. See above in this Section.

131 See in this regard Wissink, L. (2017). Challenges to an Efficient European Centralised Banking Supervision (SSM): Single Rulebook, Joint Supervisory Teams and Split Supervisory Tasks. *European Business Organization Law Review*, *18*(3), pp 431–456.

NCAs. They are naturally better placed to serve the ECB to fulfil its principal objective under the SSM R.

(d) On the scope of the micro-prudential supervisory task contemplated in arts. 4(1) and 4(2) SSM R: teleological interpretation

6.064 The (on purpose[132]) exhaustive list of specific supervisory tasks depicted in art. 4(1) SSM R[133] may generate the misleading idea that such a list is exhaustive and not merely exemplary.[134] In this regard, a source of tension can be easily spotted:[135] the constitutional basis encompassing a number of *specific* or limited tasks capable of being allocated on the ECB vs. the need to provide a comprehensive reading avoiding any loophole that may undermine the *safety and soundness* of credit institutions and of the EU financial system as a whole. This tension will be summarised below.

6.065 Art. 127(6) TFEU foresees that *specific tasks,* pertaining to prudential supervision, may be conferred on the ECB. As addressed in Part I before, the specificity of the tasks conferred on the SSM must be assessed against (i) the degree of intensity upon which the ECB exercises those competences. Hence, even if the ECB is conferred upon all the micro-prudential tasks foreseen in art. 4(1)–(2) SSM R, it only *directly* carries out them concerning SIs.[136]

6.066 Additionally, (ii) the geographical area within which these competences are exercised (the territory of the participating MSs) contributes defining these tasks as specific.

6.067 Finally, (iii) the number of excluded tasks acts as a third constraining factor. Cumulatively, these three factors constitute a sound basis to consider these as specific supervisory tasks, there also including the ones that intuitively may be comprised within but that have not been expressly listed.

6.068 A narrow reading of the tasks actually allocated to the ECB under such TFEU provision and also under the SSM R itself may render the *mechanism* toothless and their main objectives simply unreachable. The foregoing is due to the fact

132 In order to justify that the tasks conferred upon the ECB/SSM are *so that* and, consequently, meeting the limits imposed by the enabling clause (see Chapter 2).

133 To which paragraph 2 of the same article must be added.

134 See, in this regard, Annunziata, F. (2020) at p. 21.

135 Cf Section A.1.(a). (*Material limitations I: the concept of "specific tasks" and the tasks actually transferred to the ECB*) in Chapter 2.

136 With the exceptions of the granting and withdrawing authorisations and the assessment of acquisition and disposal of qualifying holdings on credit institutions that are performed by the ECB as regards all credit institutions established in the participating MSs (arts. 4(1)(a) and (c) SSM R).

that such an approach would imply that the ECB would have a compartmentalised role in the supervision of entities.

The alternative, that is, squaring the tasks allocated to the ECB within the four corners of arts. 4(1) and 4(2) SSM R, amounts to deprive the *mechanism* from the possibility of attaining its first and main objective: ensuring financial stability.[137] **6.069**

If the prudential supervision was expected to be solely exercised as regards the tasks listed in arts. 4(1) and 4(2), following a modular or segmented approach, it would be impossible to ensure a comprehensive supervision capable of ensuring a level playing field within the territories of the participating MSs. A limited reading of this provision would generate a multiplicity of loopholes from which effective supervision could be dragged. **6.070**

BOX 6.1 EXAMPLE

Following the abovementioned approach, if the ECB was supposed to only take care of granting banking authorisations, in a strict sense, the system would present multiple gaps. There are multiple *authorisations* that credit institutions may seek during their existence, and those may need to be amended (to expand its remit or to limit it) over time. That would be the case, for instance, when given credit institutions statutes are amended to cater for a capital increase or a capital decrease. Certain MSs adopted legislations providing that such statutes amendments should be approved by the relevant NCA.

Exercising such competence is ancillary or instrumental to keeping control over granting banking licenses; plus, it also related to ensuring that entities have in place strong governance requirements.[138]

If the ECB would be able to exercise only a *general* competence to authorise credit institutions and not to grant other (instrumentally) related authorisations, ECB *control-of-entry* competence would be seriously diminished.

The foregoing concerns are shared by the Commission, which expressed some fears about the "*remaining competences of NCAs, and the way they may be used for circumventing the distribution of responsibilities within the SSM*".[139] **6.071**

Favouring a strict reading goes also against the logic and will of the *legislators*. It is rather obvious that it would go against any rationale, creating a mechanism addressed to care of the safety and soundness of the financial market for **6.072**

137 Art. 1(1) SSM R.

138 Cf arts. 4(1)(e) SSM R and 8(2), 10 and 19 CRD IV.

139 *Report from the Commission to the European Parliament and the Council on the Single Supervisory Mechanism established pursuant to Regulation (EU) No 1024/2013* (COM(2017) 591 final): https://eur-lex.europa.eu/legal-content/EN/TXT/PDF/?uri=CELEX:52017DC0591&from=en. At p. 8.

depriving it from all effectiveness. If this was the purpose, the objective of the SSM R would have needed to be drafted in a less ambitious way – and the rhetoric used in its preamble tempered. Art. 9(1)II SSM R, attributing to the ECB the powers that "*competent and designated authorities shall have under the relevant Union law*" for the purposes of carrying out the tasks contemplated in art. 4(1)–(2) SSM R, militates in favour of this approach.[140]

6.073 This view is favoured, for the time being at least; the Court of Justice, which in the *Crédit Mutuel* cases joined cases C-152/18 and 153/18 P, declared that:[141] "*the exercise of the prudential banking supervision functions referred to in Article 127(6) TFEU is aimed at protecting the safety and soundness of credit institutions*".[142] This understanding is subtly enshrined also in the *L-Bank case.*[143] However, if the *development* or specification of the tasks contemplated in arts. 4(1) and (2) SSM R start interfering with other tasks expressly excluded from the ECB's remit, and/or if even that expansion is perceived as going beyond what is necessary to attain SSM objectives (in breach of the principle of proportionality), it cannot be discarded that (i) the industry and/or NCAs and other national authorities (acting together with the relevant organs of the MSs at stake) challenge that expansive approach; and (ii) in that case, the Court may be tempted to reconsider its current approach based on a teleological and effective argumentation, using the principle of proportionality as the decisive standard of review.

6.074 The ECB has followed this well-tested path, evidencing such a position in two successive letters issued in summer 2016 and on 31 March 2017.[144] In the two annexes of the letter issued on 31 March 2017,[145] the ECB specifies in detail a number of tasks that will be directly exercised by itself (in accordance with the terms established by national law). The reason to exercise those tasks

140 See Hernández Saseta, C. (2021) at p. 307 and more generally on the interpretation of art. 9 SSM R Gruber, G. (2022). Art. 9 SSMR Supervisory and investigatory powers. In *European banking union: Brussels commentary* (pp. 146–158). Baden-Baden: Nomos. On the examination of this provision see further in Section B.4. (*Supervisory and investigatory powers to exercise those tasks below*) below.

141 See Court of Justice judgment in joined cases C-152/18 P and C-153/18 P (*Crédit Mutuel Arkéa v ECB*) of 2 October 2019 (ECLI:EU:C:2019:810) at Paras. 52 and ss. The conclusions drafted by AG Pitruzzella earlier on 18 June 2019 seem to be assumed by the Court. See conclusions of AG Pitruzzella in this latter case at Paras. 51–62.

142 Ibidem at Para. 55.

143 Cf Para. 56.

144 See ECB letter to banks, "Additional clarification regarding the ECB's competence to exercise supervisory powers granted under national law": https://www.bankingsupervision.europa.eu/press/letterstobanks/shared/pdf/2017/Letter_to_SI_Entry_point_information_letter.en.pdf?d01637f249f9109f54a70a6803078b66.

145 Being Annex I, the template of the letter already sent to all SIs in summer 2016.

is grounded in art. 9(1) SSM R, pursuant to which, "*for the exclusive purpose of carrying out the tasks conferred on it by Article 4(1) of the same Regulation, the ECB is considered the competent authority in the participating Member States as established by the relevant Union law*".[146] Although ultimately anchored on the specific tasks listed in arts. 4(1) and 4(2) SSM R, they were not expressly provided herein and until that moment, exercised by or in close cooperation with the NCAs.[147] As regards some of them, the ECB deploys the utmost care in referencing the specific tasks contemplated in art. 4(1), used as a basis to expand its scope towards further tasks, that would be implicitly comprised within its remit.[148]

By way of conclusion, it must be noted that, at least for the time being, the views of the Commission, the ECB and, most important, the CJEU are aligned so as to understand the tasks listed in art. 4(1)–(2) SSM R in a finalistic manner. That means that (i) the tasks listed in those provisions are exemplary. (ii) With a view to attaining the objective of ensuring financial stability, the ECB should also exercise those tasks which are instrumental to the tasks depicted therein. The foregoing to allow the SSM attaining its objective of protecting the stability of the financial system within the EU. **6.075**

A narrow reading of the specific micro-prudential tasks conferred on the ECB may impinge SSM implementation, rendering its ultimate objective unattainable. However, this finalistic interpretation needs to strike a balance with the literal wording of art. 4(1) and (2) SSM R and with the tasks that remain within the remit of NCAs and/or national authorities. **6.076**

Ensuring that the mentioned balance is respected demands, in the view of the author, a two-step approach. First, a trustful and sincere cooperation between **6.077**

146 ECB model letter, dated 31 March 2017 at p. 2. Vid footnote 144 above.

147 These tasks include: (1) approval of acquisitions by SIs of holdings in a non-credit institution or a credit institution outside the EU; (2) approval of mergers/demergers involving SIs; (3) approval of asset transfers/divestments involving SIs; (4) approval of SIs' statutes; (5) approval of the appointment of key function holders in SIs; (6) approval/objection to the appointment of external auditors (to the extent that such powers are linked to ensuring compliance with prudential requirements) of SIs; (7) approval of specific banking activities relating to licensing; (8) approval of strategic decisions of SIs; (9) operations of SSM credit institutions in third countries; (10) outsourcing of activities; (11) supervisory powers *vis-à-vis* a credit institution's shareholders; (12) provisions imposing the compliance with specific requirements as an ancillary condition to the authorisation as a credit institution; and (13) limitations of credits to related parties.

148 Further reference to these letters may be checked in Smits, R. (2017). After L-Bank: how the Eurosystem and the Single Supervisory Mechanism may develop. *ADEMU Working Papers* (WP 2017/077). At p. 18; and Grundmann, S. and Micklitz, H.-W. (ed). (2019). In *The European Banking Union and Constitution: Beacon for Advanced Integration or Death-knell for Democracy?* (pp. 85–120). Oxford. Hart Publishing, at p. 120. See also Hernández Saseta, C. (2021).

the ECB and the NCAs[149] and national authorities in charge of performing the tasks excluded expressly from the SSM R remit (e.g., money laundering and consumer protection) should be in place. The avenues are multiple, for instance, extending formally or informally the cooperation with NCAs (already participating within the SSM), or eventually the ECB could enter into Memorandums of Understanding with those national authorities which are not NCAs.[150] Second, the ECB should be ready to assess the risks that any potential expansion of the tasks may entail and, consequently, self-restrain from any attempt to go beyond the SSM legal framework.

6.078 If the abovementioned mechanisms fall short, or are examined in landmark cases,[151] the CJEU would need to set clear limits in general and on a case-by-case basis. CJEU's future reaction cannot be anticipated. However, it may not be as favourable to this *expansive* interpretation as it has been until today.

6.079 In particular, the CJEU would need to adjudicate and assess whether the ECB has expanded its tasks beyond what is required to attain the SSM purposes – in other words, whether the ECB has respected the proportionality principle embedded in the *mechanism*. Such tensions and consequential litigious cases are susceptible of appearing regarding front line *competences*, that is, those tasks expressly (or subtly) excluded from the scope of the SSM but capable of directly affecting financial stability (for example, AML and terrorism financing matters).

3. Horizontal allocation: relationship with the EBA (and within the ESFS)

6.080 Concerning the tasks allocated to the ECB, there exists a number of relationships with other *supervisory* authorities in the broad sense that are to be understood in a *horizontal* manner. These follow a compartmental approach, where each authority or body exercise its competences within the limits established by the law and cooperates with other bodies entrusted with bordering tasks.

6.081 The SSM R does not alter the allocation of tasks and powers made under EU law to other EU bodies and Institutions, in particular, the EBA.[152] Thus, this horizontal allocation may be found in the following fields:

149 See art. 6 SSM R.

150 And which may exercise micro-prudential tasks not falling within the remit of arts. 4(1) and 4(2) SSM R but which eventually could impact the risk profile of supervised entities: e.g., as AML control.

151 Which may be brought by the supervisees or even by MSs, spoiled by national authorities and/or NCAs.

152 Cf Recital 31 SSM R. See also Council conclusions of 18 October 2012, at p. 8: https://www.consilium.europa.eu/uedocs/cms_Data/docs/pressdata/en/ec/133004.pdf.

(i) Within the general scope of cooperation, art. 3(1) SSM R insists on the fact that the ECB *shall* cooperate closely with the ESMA, EIOPA, EBA and the ESRB (i.e., with the ESFS). These relationships would be governed and guided by the principle of sincere and loyal cooperation between EU bodies.[153]

Further, the SSM R declares in art. 3(3) that, as an emanation from the principle of conferral, the mentioned authorities will perform their tasks in accordance with that Regulation and with the EU framework in general.

(ii) As regards the specific micro-prudential tasks conferred to the ECB in art. 4(1) SSM R, we can identify some bordering tasks that do constitute an expression of this horizontal allocation of tasks.

Early intervention[154] and subsequent resolution of credit institution would be one of those, being the ECB called to assess the resolvability of the entity at stake.[155]

Performance of stress tests would be the most evident of these bordering tasks, as art. 4(1)(f) SSM R directly calls for collaboration between the EBA and the ECB. The EBA is the competent authority for coordinating the stress test exercise and determining the relevant methodology[156] (in cooperation with the ESRB). In this scenario, and pursuant to the SSM R, the ECB assumes an *executive* role, equal to the one attributed to other supervisors of non-participating MSs, and abides to the methodology and guidelines issued by the EBA.[157]

(iii) It is also possibly referring to pure horizontal distribution as regards the development of the Single Rulebook.[158] These tasks remain within the EBA and are carried out through ITS, RTS (eventually approved by the EC), non-legally binding guidelines and recommendations and the Q&A tool.[159]

The SSM formally does not alter the mission, purpose and powers attributed to the EBA.[160] Thus, the ECB is expressly bound by the regulatory instruments promoted by the EBA and also by its guidelines and recommendations,[161] as any other *national* competent authority.[162]

---

153 See Weismann, P. (2018). The European Central Bank under the Single Supervisory Mechanism. Cooperation, Delegation, and Reverse Majority Voting. *European Journal of Current Legal Issues*, *24*(1). For an analysis of art. 3 SSM R, see Kaufhold, A.-K. (2022). Art. 3 SSM R Cooperation. In *European banking union: Brussels commentary* (pp. 23–37). Baden-Baden: Nomos.

154 Art. 4(1)(i) SSM R.

155 Cf art. 18(1) SRM Fr.

156 Cf arts. 21(2), 23(1) and 32 of the EBA Regulation.

157 Cf art. 4(3)(II) SSM R. In this regard, following art. 16 SSM R, the ECB would be subject to the *comply or explain* rule. Cf *EBA Guidelines on institutions' stress testing* (EBA/GL/2018/04) of 19 July 2018, at p. 5.

158 On this matter, see Wymeersch, E. (2014) at pp. 66 and ss.

159 See Section B.1.(a). (*Depicting the distribution of regulatory tasks between the ECB and the EBA*) in Chapter 2. Cf art. 16a EBA Regulation, as amended by Regulation (EU) 2019/2175.

160 Report from the Commission to the European Parliament and the Council on the Single Supervisory Mechanism established pursuant to Regulation (EU) No. 1024/2013 (COM(2017) 591 final), issued on 11 October 2017 at p. 15–16: https://ec.europa.eu/info/sites/info/files/171011-ssm-review-report_en.pdf.

161 Art. 3(3) and 4(3) SSM R.

162 As defined in art. 4(2) of the EBA Regulation. It is worth emphasising the distinctive perimeter of action of the EBA versus the SSM. Whereas the former extends over the 27 (after Brexit) MSs, the latter one

To maintain existing checks and balances between the ECB and the EBA, concerning their respective areas of action and objectives, the EBA Regulation was amended (simultaneously to the issuance of the SSM R).[163] The mentioned amendment sought to strike a balance between participating and non-participating MSs, the former being subject to the ECB aegis.[164] Thus, the reform tried to avoid that the ECB captured, somehow, the EBA governing bodies.[165]

The role and responsibilities of the EBA and the ECB are close but, in the view of the author, do not necessarily overlap (provided that each authority exercises its powers in full compliance with the principle of conferral). Nevertheless, it is impossible not to appreciate the bizarre institutional equilibrium operating in this field. The ECB, an EU Institution, is subject and must comply with the regulatory interpretations and rules proposed by an EU agency.[166] The arrangement gets even more odd when one recalls that the ECB, by means of the Treaties, is granted a reinforced independent status.[167]

Another point of friction relates to the regulatory powers granted to both entities. The borders between the EBA regulatory powers and the limited regulatory powers granted to the ECB[168] can be reconciled considering the scope of the latter ones. ECB regulatory powers should be understood always *ad intra* and circumscribed to the purpose of performing the tasks conferred by means of the SSM R.

This power is distinct from the power to make use of options and discretions. However, it is closely linked to it. The foregoing because these options and discretions, concerning both LSIs and SIs, need to be systematised and expressed by means of a legally binding instrument to which NCAs, in the former case, and entities, in the latter case, must abide.[169] The ECB must exercise those reg-

---

relates only to the Eurocurrency MS and those MSs who decide to participate freely, subscribing an agreement with the ECB to this end.

163 See arts. 44(1) and 81a of the SSM R.

164 But, eventually, also non-euro Eurocurrency MSs which entered into close cooperation, as it has been the case of Bulgaria.

165 Further provisions were included, depriving the ECB from voting capacity. Cf arts. 40(1)(d) and 44(4)II of the EBA Regulation.

166 See footnote 161.

167 Cf arts. 130 TFEU and 7 SESCB. One may argue that this broad independence should only cover monetary policy-related tasks conferred directly by the Treaties. This interpretation is founded in the literal wording of the provisions, which refers to "*tasks and duties conferred upon them by this Treaty and this Statute*". Since the specific prudential supervisory tasks that can be conferred on the ECB under the enabling clause are not directly contemplated in such clause, but require to be determined by a special regulation, one soundly may argue that statutory independence should not cover ECB activity as a prudential supervisor (at least not less than any other national supervisor). Against this opinion, see Zilioli, C. (2016). The independence of the European Central Bank and its new banking supervisory competences. In *Independence and Legitimacy in the Institutional System of the European Union* (pp. 125–179). OUP; and ANGELONI. Speech by Ignazio Angeloni (Member of the Supervisory Board of the ECB) on 22 March 2019 at the ECB colloquium "Challenges for Supervisors and Central Bankers". Frankfurt am Main: https://www.bankingsupervision.europa.eu/press/speeches/date/2019/html/ssm.sp190322~c231d57793.en.html.

168 See Section B. (*The ECB as a "regulator"*) in Chapter 2.

169 Cf the G&ODs and the RO&Ds; and also, the ECB Guide on options and discretions available in Union law. March 2022: https://www.bankingsupervision.europa.eu/ecb/pub/pdf/ssm.supervisory_guides2022_ond.en.pdf.

ulatory powers in full compliance with the EBA general guidance, including EBA soft-law instruments, i.e., guidelines and recommendations, opinions and questions and answers.[170]

On its side, EBA regulatory powers are expressly provided by CRR/CRD IV. Consequently, those powers are provided with a view to further precise (innovating somehow) the existing legal framework applicable to the 27 MSs. They enjoy a *vis atractiva* that, as mentioned before, oblige national supervisors to comply with (or potentially explain as regards recommendations), including *vis-à-vis*, the ECB.

4. Supervisory and investigatory powers to exercise those tasks

Art. 9 of the SSM R sets out (or tries to set out, at least) a broad picture of the different powers actually conferred on the ECB as a supranational supervisor. The wording of this article indeed reminds or seems to be inspired by the wording of another well-known provision within the SSM R: art. 4(3).[171] **6.082**

Considering more specifically Para. 1 of this article,[172] a threefold classification of these powers can be established.[173] (1) First, the most basic approach is that the ECB is vested with the powers (and obligations) established in the SSM R.[174] (2) Second, it will have, also, the powers attributed to competent and designated authorities under the Union law, unless provided in the SSM R otherwise. (3) Third, the ECB can require (by means of instructions) national authorities to make use of their national powers when it has not been vested with the powers but has been conferred the task pursuant to art. 4(1)–(2) SSM R. **6.083**

The second and third sentences of the second sub-paragraph of art. 9(1) SSM R deserve some consideration.[175] From a legislative technique perspective, one cannot avoid noting that the mentioned second sentence reiterates the content **6.084**

170 Cf arts. 4(3)II SSMR and 16, 16a and 16b of the EBA Regulation (the latter two provisions being introduced by Regulation (EU) 2019/2175). The foregoing SSM R provision could refer to art. 16 of the EBA Regulation, since, at the time it was drafted, arts. 16a and 16b were not in force.

171 Interaction between the two articles has created not a few controversies on the conferral of real regulatory powers on the ECB (which, to some extent, are still ongoing). See, in this regard, Lamandini, M., Ramos Muñoz, D. & Solana, J. (2016) at pp. 33 y ss.

172 In the same vein, see Recitals 34, 35 and 45 SSM R.

173 See also section 4.11.1 (Supervisory powers) of the SSM supervisory Manual at pp. 98–99.

174 Art. 9(1)II SSM R.

175 These sentences from the second sub-paragraph of art. 9(1) SSM R read as follows: "(...). *It shall also have all the powers and obligations, which competent and designated authorities shall have under the relevant Union law, unless otherwise provided for by this Regulation. In particular, the ECB shall have the powers listed in Sections 1 and 2 of this Chapter*".

of the first sub-paragraph of art. 9 SSM (which, at the same time, builds upon the wording of art. 4(3)I SSM R). Additionally, one could ask what the limitations (within the SSM R) to the exercise of those powers are. A careful look at the Regulation shows that there is no express, nor obvious, indication of what these limits may be.

6.085 Furthermore, the spirit of this second sentence stirs some controversy.[176] From a general perspective, art. 9(1) starts framing the powers granted to the ECB. These are provided "*[f]or the exclusive purpose of carrying out the tasks conferred on it by Articles 4(1), 4(2) and 5(2)*". Under this prism, whatever powers that fall beyond or are unrelated or delinked from the specific micro-prudential tasks (and macro-prudential tasks contemplated in art. 5 SSM R) would not be covered by the allocation of powers provided for in the second sentence of the second sub-paragraph of art. 9(1) SSM R.

6.086 Yet, the referred sentence states that the powers conferred to the ECB will be those of competent (and designated) authorities under "relevant Union law". The term is broad and can be read in at least two different ways. The first one would encompass relevant Union law as *directly* applicable Union law (i.e., CRR).

6.087 This narrow reading seems less adequate than a broader interpretation. Pursuant to this interpretation, Union law must be interpreted as encompassing directly applicable Union rules and also national law transposing such Union rules (e.g., national rules transposing CRD IV). This reading seems to be more aligned with art. 4(3) SSM R,[177] which, as a master guideline, provides that the ECB should apply all the relevant substantive rules pertaining to prudential supervision (required to fulfil the tasks conferred under arts. 4(1), (2) and 5 SSM R).[178] This reading contributes to preserve the level playing field and to ensure a uniform supervisory approach and, thus, must be preferred.[179]

---

176 See D'Ambrosio, R. (ed.). (2020) at pp. 171–172.

177 And with Recital 34 SSM R as well.

178 By means of this provision (art. 9(1)II SSM R), the ECB has factored in a wide variety of tasks relating to the approval of modifications to credit institution' statutes, the appointment of external auditors, authorisation relating to mergers (from a prudential perspective), etc. See immediately above in this Chapter and also Hernández Saseta, C. (2021).

179 This seems to be the perception of the Commission. Cf Report from the Commission to the European Parliament and the Council on the Supervisory Mechanism established pursuant to Regulation (EU) No. 1024/2013 (COM(2017) 591 final): https://ec.europa.eu/info/sites/info/files/171011-ssm-review-report_en.pdf.

Nevertheless, such an approach may not be maintained in cases where national law has either not transposed or defectively transposed relevant Union law. Issues relating to this matter and the remedies that can be applied to mitigate them will be explored in Chapter 7 below. **6.088**

Finally, as indicated above, the third sub-paragraph of art. 9(1) SSM R introduces the possibility for the ECB to request national authorities to use the powers conferred under *pure* national law. Using this rather indirect mechanism entails a situation where the ECB is entrusted with the tasks under the SSM R but is not equipped with the powers (i.e., the ECB cannot exercise the supervisory powers conferred under the SSM R).[180] Consequently, and as noted by some scholars, "*the scope for powers exercise through instructions under Article 91(1) third sub-paragraph is narrow*".[181] **6.089**

This implies that the national legislation conferring the powers to the national authorities constitutes pure national regulation, which goes beyond what is strictly required by Union rules (mainly the transposition of the minimum requirements set out in the relevant prudential Directives).[182] Operationally-wise, the ECB may issue more or less detailed instructions addressed to NCAs (and national designated authorities) concerning specific SIs,[183] and they should make use of their national powers accordingly (and reporting after to the ECB). **6.090**

Considering the wording of art. 9(1)III SSM R, one may question whether those instructions are binding to NCAs or not. **6.091**

180 Cf art. 22 SSM Fr, which reads in a very similar manner (including not only NCAs but also national designated authorities within the scope of the potential ECB requests). See Hernández Saseta, C. (2021) at p. 307.

181 Ibidem.

182 This would be the case, for instance, of additional powers allocated to national authorities not stemming from arts. 64(1), 102 and 104 CRD IV. Examples of this would include additional investigatory powers to request information from clients of counterparts of the entities at stake that would not fall within a list of relevant subjects of art. 10(1) SSM R.

When reference is made to *prudential Directives* in this work, such a term is covering directives affecting the prudential supervision of the entities falling under the scope of the SSM and whose content would be comprised within the specific prudential supervisory tasks allocated to the ECB under arts. 4.1, 4.2 and 5 SSM R.

183 Even if this is not expressly indicated in art. 9(1)III SSM R nor in art. 22 SSM Fr, these instructions must be understood as referred to specific entities falling under the direct supervision of the ECB, i.e., SIs and LSI as regards the task contemplated in art. 4(1)(a) and (c) SSM R. See Hernández Saseta, C. (2021) at p. 307.

6.092 Some authors have reached the conclusion that, indeed, they are.[184] The reasons put forward by those authors relate to (i) the fact that the word *require* used in this provision (and correlated in Recital 35 SSM R) indicates that ECB requests are binding to the NCAs/national designated authorities. (ii) Further, art. 6(3) SSM R, concerning the general instructions provided by the ECB to NCAs, sets forth that they must abide to ECB instructions. Finally (iii), it is also construed that these instructions have an analogous value to those foreseen in art. 14(3) SESCB, which are actually binding to NCBs.[185] Yet, this interpretation also acknowledges that these instructions can be very detailed or broader, leaving considerable leeway to the NCAs/national designated authorities to implement them. In the latter case, the authors seem to accept that these could not bind national authorities.[186]

6.093 On the contrary, other authors argue that instructions issued by the ECB under art. 9(1)III SSM R would not be binding to NCAs/national designated authorities.[187] They derive this conclusion from the fact that the ECB has no (sanctioning or enforcement) powers to compel the relevant authorities to comply with these requests.[188] It has been also pointed out that these instructions only encompass a duty of *information* from the NCAs on the use of their national powers (and presumably also of the *way* they have been used).[189]

6.094 Procedurally, such powers must be exercised by the relevant NCA (or designated authority) pursuant to its national law. This means that the national authority must determine whether or not the conditions, established under which such powers can be exercised, are met and, accordingly, may refuse to use these powers in the way prescribed by the ECB (or indicate any impossibility to use those[190]). This circumstance seems to be foreseen in the third sub-paragraph of art. 9(1) SSM R, as it contemplates an obligation for the

184 See Hernández Saseta, C. (2021) at p. 307. Although in a more implicit manner, see also D'Ambrosio, R. (2021). The legal review of SSM administrative sanctions. In *Judicial Review in the European Banking Union* (pp. 316–332). Edward Elgar Publishing. At p. 324.

185 Ibidem at pp. 307–308.

186 Ibidem at p. 308; and D'Ambrosio, R. (2021) at p. 324.

As indicated by Saseta, the discretion granted on NCAs to comply with these requests also affects their reviewability dimension. If no discretion is allocated to them, according to this author, the CJEU would be exclusively competent to adjudicate on any direct action brought by the SI affected by those. Conversely, if the instruction is broad and much discretion is placed on the NCAs to comply with it, national courts would be competent to adjudicate (requesting the CJEU to issue a preliminary ruling, eventually, to ensure a consistent approach among national jurisdictions).

187 Bassani, G. (2019).

188 Cf footnote 114.

189 Bassani, G. (2019).

190 Ibidem.

competent authority to report on the "*exercise of such powers*" but not to compulsorily exercise them. Consequently, the author is of the view that ECB instructions addressed to NCAs/national designated authorities under art. 9(1)III SSM R always entail a margin of discretion for the NCAs to enforce them, based on their procedural and material national law. Consequently, it is submitted that these instructions should not be binding on the NCAs, on account that they ultimately need to weight how (and *if)* national rules allow following those in the manner requested by the ECB.[191]

At this point, it is worth recalling the difficulties that this indirect exercise of **6.095** powers by the ECB entails. The use of supervisory powers requires balancing, sometimes, a set of facts and weighting the interests at stake – pursuant to a yardstick that is rarely determined by the law itself but, rather, by the case law applying statutory or constitutional law. Additionally, this assessment involves sometimes considering other rules that fall outside the standard supervisory legal environment (e.g., competence rules and procedural rules dictating the elapsing time to exercise such powers). It results from this third sub-paragraph that this weighing of factors must be done pursuant to national law, which implies that, evidently, the ultimate interpretation shall be made by the relevant competent authority pursuant to its national law and its own judgement. Thus, even if not shared, the ECB would need to follow national authorities' interpretation, as, in this case, it is not vested with the possibility of applying such national powers directly.

C. ALLOCATION OF SANCTIONING COMPETENCES: A SPECIALTY OVER THE GENERAL RULE?

Whereas the distribution of the specific supervisory tasks between NCAs and **6.096** the ECB follows, in general terms, a subjective approach (i.e., SIs supervision vs. LSIs supervision), this intuitive scheme no longer applies as regards sanctioning competences.

Despite ECB sanctioning competences being framed under section 2 (*Specific* **6.097** *supervisory powers*) of Chapter III (*Powers of the ECB*) SSM R, and hence eventually being subject to the allocation rules contemplated in art. 6(4) SSM R, they do not follow this logic. ECB sanctioning competences under the SSM are allocated pursuant to three criteria: (i) a subjective criterion, depending

191 However, it remains to be seen what the position of the CJEU would be. For the time being, the CJEU has not dealt with this specific case.

on the nature of the infringing entity/individual;[192] (ii) an objective criterion which depends on the nature of the legal act or regulation supposedly breached; and (iii) the type of sanction to be imposed (pecuniary or non-pecuniary sanctions).

6.098 In order to frame the issue, it must be recalled that setting out a credible and deterrent system of corrective actions is enshrined within the Basel III core principles.[193] Furthermore, art. 34(3) SESCB contemplates that the ECB may impose, on undertakings, fines or periodic penalty payments as regards failures to comply with ECB decisions and regulations.[194] This constitutes a statutory limitation to the ECB's sanctioning powers, preventing it from sanctioning natural persons. Potential future reforms of the SSM R leading to the allocation of additional competences to the ECB may not be able to alter this statutory limitation, and as regards natural persons, competences and investigatory powers may remain within the remit of NCAs.[195]

6.099 Particularly, the SESCB contemplates two categories of *sanctions* – in a broad sense. The first category (including *fines* and *periodic penalty payments*) has been referred to above, and it is contemplated in art. 34(3) SESCB.[196] ECB sanctioning powers, in this regard, are further regulated by Regulation 2532/98 of 23 November 1998 concerning the powers of the European Central Bank to impose sanctions ("Regulation 2532/98").[197] When the ECB imposes fines

---

192 Riso refers to size criterion, but in the view of the author, it is more accurately speaking about a general *subjective criterion*. As exposed before, the size criterion may constitute one of the criteria used to classify an entity as significant. However, other criteria not linked to the actual size of the relevant entity may lead to the classification of the relevant entity as such (e.g., relative importance of the entity for the economy participating MS or being one of the three major entities of such MS). See Riso, A. L. (2014). The power of the ECB to impose sanctions in the context of the SSM. *Bančni vestnik, Letnik, 63*, pp. 32–35. See also Schneider, Sven H. (2014). Sanctioning by the ECB and National Authorities Within the Single Supervisory Mechanism. *European Journal of Business Law*. EuZW-Beilage 18; Loosveld, S. (2013). The ECB's investigatory and sanctioning powers under the future single supervisory mechanism. *Journal of International Banking Law and Regulation, 28*(10), pp. 422–425; and Gortsos, C. V. (2015). The Power of the ECB to Impose Administrative Penalties as a Supervisory Authority: An Analysis of Article 18 of the SSM Regulation. *ECEFIL Working Paper Series No 2015/11* [Gortsos, C. V. (2015)(ii)].

193 In particular, see core Principles 1 and 11: https://www.bis.org/basel_framework/chapter/BCP/01.htm?inforce=20191215. Additional references may be found under Principle 1 (Para. 01.67(6)), Principle 2 (Para. 01.67(5)) and Principle 10 (Para. 01.85(8)).

194 Cf art. 132 TFEU and 34(1) SESCB on the power of the ECB to issue general regulations.

195 Cf art. 67(2)(f) CRD IV, which contemplates the possibility of imposing pecuniary penalties of up to EUR 5 million (or equivalent value, if the currency is not the euro) to natural persons for the commission of the breaches listed in the previous Para. 1 of the same provision.

196 And further referred to in arts. 18(7) SSM R and 121 SSM Fr.

197 Amended after the entrance into force of the SSM R by means of Council Regulation (EU) 2015/159 amending Regulation (EC) No. 2532/98 concerning the powers of the European Central Bank to impose sanctions ("Regulation 2015/159").

and periodic penalty payments for breaches of ECB decisions and Regulations concerning the specific supervisory tasks under its remit (art. 18(7) SSM R), it must do so in accordance with the procedural guarantees and rules contemplated in Regulation 2532/98 (which may be complemented accordingly with those foreseen in the SSM R and SSM Fr[198]).

Secondly, and probably more unknown, are the statutory sanctioning powers conferred on the ECB as regards minimum reserves (art. 19(1) and (2) SESCB). Technically these sanctioning powers are a mere specification of the general category established under 34(3) SESCB and subject to the limits and guarantees established therein.[199] Yet one should not forget (a) that they are established in a different provision, (b) that provision is enshrined within the general Chapter IV of the SESCB dealing with ECB/ESCB monetary policy operations, which constitute indeed a basic task of the ESCB,[200] and (c) finally, that the imposition of these specific sanctions is subject to a special procedure, established in ECB Regulation 2157/1999. **6.100**

Given that there are different typologies of *sanctions* that the ECB can impose based on the SESCB (and Regulation 2532/98) and on SSM R, it is important to distinguish between them. Using the terminology proposed in art. 120 SSM Fr, the term *fines and periodic penalty payments* will be used as regards sanctions provided in art. 2 of Regulation 2532/1998 "*and imposed under art. 18(7) SSM R*".[201] The term *Administrative pecuniary penalties* will be used to define the sanctions contemplated in art. 18(1) SSM R. As per the initial sentence of that provision, all sanctions referred to above will be generically referred to as *administrative penalties*. **6.101**

Looking at the sanctioning powers vested on the ECB under art. 18 SSM R,[202] the following principles for the allocation of sanctioning competences can be distinguished:[203] **6.102**

198 Cf art. 121. SSM Fr. See Section B. (*ECB direct sanctioning powers: Procedure for the imposition of administrative pecuniary penalties and fines*) in Chapter 15 for a comparison between the safeguards foreseen in the SSM Fr and those contemplated in the Regulation 2532/1998.
See, also, D'Ambrosio, R. (2021) at p. 321 and Riso, A. L. (2014). at pp. 32–35.

199 Recitals 1 and 2 of the ECB Regulation 2157/1999 of 23 September 1999 on the powers of the European Central Bank to impose sanctions ("ECB Regulation 2157/1999") clearly support this approach.

200 In particular, the application of minimum reserves pursuant to Council Regulation (EC) No. 2531/98 of 23 November 1998 concerning the application of minimum reserves by the European Central Bank.

201 Cf art. 18(7) SM R. Also referred jointly as *sanctions* by art. 1(7) of Regulation 2532/1998.

202 See also arts. 120 to 137 SSM Fr.

203 See in this regard: (i) Mancini, M. (2013). Dalla vigilanza nazionale armonizzata alla Banking Union. *Quaderni di Ricerca Giuridica della Consulenza Legale Banca d'Italia, No 73.* At pp. 27 and ss.; (ii) D'Ambrosio, R. (2013) at pp. 38–49; (iii) D'Ambrosio, R. (2015) at pp. 89 and ss.; (iv) Allegrezza, S.

(i) Pursuant to arts. 18(1) SSM R and 124(a) SSM Fr, the ECB is exclusively competent to impose administrative pecuniary penalties on SIs in case of breaches of directly applicable Union Law.

Although art. 18(1) SSM R does not make any distinction as regards SIs and LSIs, and thus it could be concluded that the ECB may be competent to sanction any breach of directly applicable Union law,[204] art. 124(a) SSM Fr has specified that this competence may be exercised only as regards SIs.[205] The rationale for this is the need to facilitate ECB sanctioning action. In this vein, the ECB is in charge of sanctioning breaches committed by entities which are directly supervised by it (i.e., by the relevant JSTs) and, consequently, from which it receives a direct flow of information and where the supervisory dialogue is led by itself. The academic debate seems to be, after the SSM Fr came into force, settled.[206]

Nevertheless, it is not entirely clear how the abovementioned scheme should stand as regards the specific supervisory competences on which the ECB is exclusively competent as regards both LSIs and SIs,[207] that is, the authorisation and withdrawal of banking licenses and the assessment of acquisition and disposal of qualifying holdings (art. 4(1)(a) and (c) SSM R). Accordingly, as the ECB retains the exclusive competence on those tasks, it should be entrusted to sanction breaches related to common procedures, even as regards LSIs.

In the view of the author, a functional criterion may be followed in this regard, particularly as regards LSIs, mirroring the approach defined in art. 120(a) SSM Fr. However, it must be noted that for breaches concerning the scope and limits of banking licences, the NCAs may be in a better position to determine the eventual commission of breaches (in particular of the requisites pertaining purely to national law[208]). This would not be the case concerning the assessment of qualifying holdings. Given the ECB general involvement in the relevant common procedure,[209] in certain cases, the ECB may become aware of breaches of directly applicable Union rules committed by LSIs.

& Voordeckers, O. (2015). Investigative and sanctioning powers of the ECB in the framework of the Single Supervisory Mechanism: mapping the complexity of a new enforcement model. *EUCRIM*, *4*, pp. 151–160; (v) Lamandini, M., Ramos Muñoz, D. & Solana, J. (2015) at p. 91; and (vi) Allegrezza, S. (ed.). (2020). *The enforcement dimension of the single supervisory mechanism*. Wolters Kluwer.

204 "(...) *to which administrative pecuniary penalties shall be made available to competent authorities under the relevant Union law*". This requisite will be further analysed in Section C. (*Substantive law & sanctioning proceedings: issues and proposals to overcome them*) in Chapter 7.

205 Art. 124(a) refers to breaches "*committed by a significant supervised entity having its head office in a euro area Member State*" and detected by the ECB during the performance of the specific supervisory tasks allocated to it under the SSM R. See. Allegrezza, S. & Voordeckers, O. (2015). at p. 156. See also Felisatti, V. (2018). Sanctioning Powers of the European Central Bank and the Ne Bis In Idem Principle within the Single Supervisory Mechanism. *EuCLR European Criminal Law Review*, *8*(3), pp. 378–403. At pp. 383–388.

206 See Recital 36 SSM R and D'Ambrosio, R. (2015) at pp. 38–39.

207 See D'Ambrosio, R. (2021) at p. 322.

208 See, for in more detail, Section B.1. (*Authorisation/licensing of credit institutions*) in Chapter 14.

209 See above Section B.2. (*Vertical allocation? Examining the decentralised mode of implementing the specific supervisory tasks*) and further in Section C. (*Assessment of the acquisition of qualifying holdings*) in Chapter 14.

In order to maintain a uniform supervisory approach and level playing field, in these cases, the ECB should control at least the initiation of sanctioning procedures. In this regard, the ECB should be entitled to request NCAs to open sanctioning procedures against LSIs for breaches relating to common procedures pursuant to art. 18(5).[210]

It must be noted that the subjective scope of this art. 18(1) SSM R refers only to *credit institutions, financial holding companies and mixed financial holding companies*. Consequently, the ECB will not be able to sanction central entities, with which credit institutions are affiliated and which do not fall within the previous categories.[211] This should not affect the quality and completeness of the supervision conducted by the ECB, as the Court of Justice has recently clarified.[212]

(ii) Pursuant to arts. 18(7) SSM R and 124(b) SSM Fr, the ECB is also competent to impose (pecuniary) *fines* on SIs and LSIs for breaches of ECB decisions or regulations affecting them (that is, imposing obligations *vis-à-vis* the ECB).

In order to accommodate the interplay of Regulation 2532/98, with the general procedural guarantees contemplated in the SSM R[213] and with the general objectives that the imposition of fines should pursue:[214] (a) the SSM Fr further clarifies the relationship between the SSM R/SSM Fr and Regulation 2532/98, stating that "(…) *the procedural rules contained in this Regulation shall complement those laid down in Regulation (EC) No 2532/98 and shall be applied in accordance with Articles 25 and 26 of the SSM Regulation*".[215] (b) Additionally, Regulation 2015/159 amended Regulation 2532/1998 so as to align the procedural regime (including the procedural guarantees) to the one depicted in the SSM R – and further developed in the SSM Fr.[216]

210 On the scope of the application of art. 18(5) SSM R, which regulates ECB *indirect* sanction powers, see immediately below.

It must be noted that this approach seems to be in line with the sanctioning practice followed by the ECB. See the ECB Annual Report on Sanctioning Activities in the SSM in 2021: Annual Report on Sanctioning Activities in the SSM in 2021 (europa.eu). At footnote 2. See also Fernandez-Bollo, E. & Teixeira, P. G. (2021). Fostering a compliance culture in the European banking system. ECB. The supervision blog: Fostering a compliance culture in the European banking system (europa.eu).

In favour of this interpretation is also D'Ambrosio, who understands that, as regards both granting and withdrawing banking licenses to LSIs and the assessment of acquisition and disposal of qualifying holdings on LSIs, the ECB would always have the power to request the NCAs to open the relevant sanctioning procedure pursuant to art. 18(5) SSM R. See D'Ambrosio, R (ed.). (2020) at p. 55 and D'Ambrosio, R. (2021) at p. 322.

211 See General Court judgment in case T-712/15 (*Crédit Mutuel Arkéa v ECB*) of 13 December 2017 (ECLI:EU:T:2017:900) at Para. 93 and Court of Justice judgment in joined cases C-152/18 P and 153/18 P (*Crédit Mutuel Arkéa v ECB*) of 2 October 2019 (ECLI:EU:C:2019:810) at Paras. 74–77.

212 See Court of Justice judgment in case C-152/18 P (*Crédit Mutuel Arkéa v ECB*) of 2 October 2019 (ECLI:EU:C:2019:810) at Para. 75.

213 Cf art. 22 SSM R which expressly contemplates due process guarantees (e.g., right to be heard, access to documents, right to be informed of the infringement one may be accused of, etc.). See, also, arts. 25–35 SSM Fr, which further develop the foregoing provision.

214 That is, being *effective, proportionate and dissuasive* (art. 18(3) SSM R).

215 See in this regard Allegrezza, S. & Voordeckers, O. (2015) at p. 156. The flaws pointed out by Riso were spotted before both the SSM Fr and Regulation 2015/159 came into force. See Riso, A. L. (2014) at p. 34.

216 See at the beginning of this Section.

(iii) Art. 18(5) SSM R regulates, in an open-ended manner, the cases in which the ECB may request NCAs to open sanctioning procedures when it cannot directly sanction a given entity or natural person. Accordingly, NCAs are only capable of opening the relevant procedure upon a request received from the ECB.[217]

Following arts. 18(5) SSM R and 134 and 135 SSM Fr,[218] the ECB is neither empowered to impose directly non-pecuniary penalties nor to sanction natural persons (e.g., managers or members of the board of a credit institution[219]).

Additionally, the ECB lacks direct powers to impose non-pecuniary sanctions to SIs for breaches of directly applicable Union law and also cannot impose pecuniary and non-pecuniary sanctions on these entities as regards national law transposing EU law.[220]

Instead, for that purpose, the ECB has the exclusive competence to require the NCAs to open proceedings to ensure that appropriate penalties are imposed (according to their national law).[221] In summary, the following cases fall under the remit of the ECB indirect sanctioning competences pursuant to art. 18(5) SSM R:

1. Imposition of pecuniary and non-pecuniary penalties on natural persons belonging to SIs (e.g., managers or members of the board of a credit institution) for breaches of directly applicable Union rules.
2. Imposition of pecuniary and non-pecuniary penalties on natural persons belonging to SIs for breaches of national laws transposing prudential Directives or of national rules that attribute the relevant NCA specific powers not required by EU law but closely connected with prudential rules.[222]
3. Imposition of non-pecuniary penalties to SIs for breaches of directly applicable EU law.
4. Imposition of pecuniary and non-pecuniary penalties to SIs as regards breaches of national law transposing EU law or of national rules that attribute the relevant NCA specific powers not required by EU law but closely connected with prudential rules.[223]
5. Regarding LSIs, imposition of penalties concerning "breaches of "common procedures", for which the ECB remains exclusively competent.

(iv) NCAs, for their part, are exclusively competent to impose administrative penalties (both pecuniary and non-pecuniary) on LSIs and on the natural persons

217 See D'Ambrosio, R. (2021).

218 Cf Recital 53 SSM R.

219 In general, the individuals "*who under national law are responsible for a breach by a credit institution, financial holding company or mixed financial holding company*" (art. 18(5)II SSM R). See above as regards the statutory limitation discussed (art. 34(3) SESCB).

220 See in this regard, Lackhoff, K. (2017)(i) at pp. 211–217. See, also, SSM Supervisory Manual at p. 102.

221 See D'Ambrosio, R. (2015) at p. 89.

222 I.e., (i) they fall under the scope of the specific micro-prudential tasks allocated to the ECB under the SSM R and (ii) underpin a supervisory function foreseen under EU law. See Section A.2.(b).(2). (*What happens when the national statute allocates powers in excess to the ones foreseen in a prudential Directive?*) in Chapter 7.

223 Ibidem.

who are responsible for them.[224] Furthermore, they are competent for imposing any kind of sanction to SIs and LSIs (and the natural persons responsible for them) according to their national law – on matters excluded from the scope of the SSM Regulation

For the sake of clarity, the complex distribution of sanctioning tasks depicted above is summarised in Figure 6.1. **6.103**

As regards the use by the ECB of the direct sanctioning competences under Paras. 1 and 7 of art. 18 SSM R, and also concerning the indirect powers foreseen in Para. 5 of the same provision, one should recall that the consolidated supervisor is not obliged to initiate a sanctioning procedure (or request its initiation) regarding each and every potential breach of which it may become aware.[225] **6.104**

This can be inferred from the use of the verb *may* in the relevant provision, as opposed to the compulsory form *shall*. The same approach is followed in arts. 66(2) and 67(2) CRD IV, which depict sanctioning powers as a mechanism to which competent authorities should have access (but not compulsorily use it every time a potential infringement is detected). However, art. 122 SSM Fr expressly states that "*[t]he ECB shall impose administrative penalties* (...) *if there is a failure to comply with obligations under ECB regulations or decisions*". This would imply an automatic punitive reaction each and every time the ECB became aware of an infringement. This wording needs to be encompassed with the SSM R, to which it develops, and be understood as merely enunciating the possibility of initiating sanctioning procedures if infringements falling within the remit of the ECB direct sanctioning powers are detected. This is also the understanding that stems from the SSM Supervisory Manual[226] and that would be applied by the relevant JST and the Enforcement and Sanctions Division (under the Directorate General SSM Governance & Operations). **6.105**

In addition to the above, art. 18(3) SSM R leaves some leeway to the ECB as to whether or not to impose a penalty. To that end, ECB shall apply the legal acts referred to in art. 4(3) SSM R, which would include the possibility of the adopting guidelines, decision (of general scope) and regulations determining when or which conducts would be (preferably) pursued by the ECB and how **6.106**

224 Members of the board and individuals responsible for the breach under national law. See footnote 219 above.

225 For a dedicated analysis on this topic, see Section B.1.(b).(2) (*Legal challenges (and potential remedies)*) in Chapter 15.

226 Cf SSM Supervisory manual at p. 102.

their severity would be assessed (e.g., taking into account the intentionality in the commission of the potential breach, its duration, if the offender took any (effective) remedial measures before the sanctioning procedure was initiated, etc.).

6.107 In any event, the possibility of sanctioning is built upon the subjective element of intent or negligence (at least),[227] and the ECB (and NCAs, as the case may be) would need to prove so during the sanctioning procedure. This topic will be analysed further in Section B.3.(b).(i). (*Procedural safeguards: the subjective element of the infringement (intention and negligence)*) in Chapter 15.

6.108 Furthermore, administrative pecuniary penalties provided for in art. 18(1) SSM R are further subject to an *availability* requirement.[228] In this vein, the foregoing provision demands that such penalties must be *made* available to competent authorities. Otherwise, the ECB will not be able to impose such pecuniary penalties. This matter will be analysed in Chapter 7 below.

6.109 The amount of penalties that can be imposed[229] pursuant to this provision and paragraph 7 of the same article, its calculation,[230] and the determination (and eventual publication) of the penalty[231] (including the factors used to calculate its amount[232]) will be addressed in Part III when specifically referring to the sanctioning proceeding. And finally, the not-so-easy relationship between administrative measures (referred to expressly in art. 18(5) SSM R) and the factors used to draw a distinction between them will be explored in Chapter 8.

---

227 Cf arts. 18(1) SSM R. However, art. 1a(1) Regulation 2532/98 seems to require only *failure to comply with obligations arising from ECB decision or regulations*, hence obviating the subjective element of liability. SSM Fr rules may complement Regulation 2532/98 in this regard as requiring this subjective element (which should be also present as regards sanctions imposed by NCAs upon request of the ECB, in accordance with national law).

228 "(…) *in relation to which administrative pecuniary penalties shall be made available to competent authorities under the relevant Union law* (…)".

229 Cf arts. 18(1) SSM and 4a(1) Regulation 2532/98.

230 Cf art. 128 SSM Fr.

231 Which, in the view of the Court, eventually, should be published. See recent General Court judgments in cases T-576/18 (*Crédit agricole v ECB*), T-577/18 (*Crédit agricole Corporate and Investment Bank v ECB*) and T-578/18 (*CA Consumer Finance v ECB*) of 8 July 2020 (ECLI:EU:T:2020:304, ECLI:EU:T:2020:305 and ECLI:EU:T:2020:306, respectively) at Paras. 138 and 139; 121 and 122; and 124 and 125, respectively. Following those judgments, the ECB issued the *Guide to the method of setting administrative pecuniary penalties pursuant to Article 18(1) and (7) of Council Regulation (EU) No 1024/2013. March 2021:* https://www.bankingsupervision.europa.eu/ecb/pub/pdf/ssm.guidetothemethodofsettingadministrativepecuniarypenalties_202103~400cbafa55.en.pdf (Guide for the calculation of administrative pecuniary penalties).

232 Which should mirror the ones contemplated in art. 70(1) CRD IV.

<table>
<tr><th colspan="2" rowspan="2">Breaches/penalties</th><th colspan="2">SIs</th><th colspan="2">LSIs</th></tr>
<tr><th>Entities</th><th>Natural persons</th><th>Entities</th><th>Natural persons</th></tr>
<tr><td rowspan="2">Directly applicable Union Law</td><td>Pecuniary penalties</td><td>ECB (art. 18(1) SSM Regulation)</td><td></td><td colspan="2" rowspan="4">NCAs*</td></tr>
<tr><td>Non-pecuniary penalties</td><td colspan="2" rowspan="3">NCAs at the request of the ECB (art. 18.5 SSM R)</td></tr>
<tr><td rowspan="2">National Law implementing Union Law</td><td>Pecuniary penalties</td></tr>
<tr><td>Non-pecuniary penalties</td></tr>
<tr><td rowspan="3">ECB Decisions and regulations</td><td rowspan="2">Pecuniary penalties</td><td rowspan="2">ECB (art. 18(7) SSM Regulation)</td><td rowspan="2">NCAs at the request of the ECB (art. 18.5 SSM R)</td><td>ECB (art. 18(7) SSM Regulation)</td><td>NCAs (at the request of the ECB. Art. 18(5) and (7) of the SSM R)</td></tr>
<tr><td colspan="2">NCAs (if obligation vis-à-vis the NCAs)</td></tr>
<tr><td>Non-pecuniary penalties</td><td colspan="2">NCAs at the request of the ECB (art. 18(5) and (7) of the SSM R)</td><td colspan="2">NCAs at the request of the ECB</td></tr>
<tr><td>National Law (matters outside the scope of the SSM)</td><td colspan="5">NCAs</td></tr>
</table>

Note: * Except as regards the specific supervisory task contemplated in arts. 4(1)(a) and 4(1)(c) (the granting of banking licenses and assessment of qualifying holdings), concerning which the NCAs may initiate the relevant sanctioning procedure only upon request from the ECB.

Figure 6.1 Allocation of sanctioning powers within the SSM

7

THE SUBSTANTIVE AND PROCEDURAL LAW APPLIED BY THE ECB UNDER THE SSM (WITH PARTICULAR REFERENCE TO THE USE OF NATIONAL LAW BY THE ECB: FILLING GAPS)

7.001 The powers granted to the ECB to exercise the specific supervisory tasks are grounded in two different legal frameworks: EU law and also national law. This chapter aims at presenting briefly the substantive and procedural rules applied by the ECB under the SSM and highlighting some of the issues that the application of national law may entail. This chapter also seeks to summarise (and develop) the state of the question as it is today, therefore contributing to increasing the legal *corpus* that continues generating debate (and on which the CJEU will have a major role to play in the coming years)[1].

In this chapter, a general overview on the several substantive sets of rules applied by the ECB will be given first (Section A). This Section provides a classification of the legal instruments to be applied by the ECB, highlighting some of the issues related to the application of national law by the ECB (and some potential remedies as well). In Section B, the procedural law applied by the ECB under the SSM will be analysed. Finally, in Section C, the analysis will focus on the troubled relationship between national substantive law and ECB sanctioning powers. **7.002**

1 Without being exhaustive, some of the articles that have contributed to the development of this matter are: (i) D'Ambrosio, R. (2020). The application of national law by the ECB. In *Law and Practice of the Banking Union and of its Governing Institutions (Cases and Materials)* (pp. 129–147). *Quaderni di Ricerca Giuridica*, (88) [D'Ambrosio, R. (2020)(iii)]; (ii) Gagliardi, E. & Wissink, L. (2020). Ensuring effective judicial protection in case of ECB decisions based on national law. *Review of European Administrative Law, 13*(1), pp. 41–71; (iii) Witte, A. (2014). The Application of National Banking Supervision Law by the ECB: three Parallel modes of executing EU law? *Maastricht journal of European and comparative law, 21*(1), pp. 89–109; (iv) Coman-Kund, F. & Amtenbrink. F. (2018). On the Scope and Limits of the Application of National Law by the European Central Bank within the Single Supervisory Mechanism. *Banking & Finance Law Review*, Vol. 33, Iss. 2, pp. 133–172; (v) Amtenbrink, F. (2019). The application of national law by the European Central Bank: challenging European legal doctrine? In *Building bridges: central banking law in an interconnected world. ECB Legal Conference 2019* (pp. 136–151). Frankfurt am Main, ECB; (vi) Lo Schiavo, G. (2019). The ECB and its application of national law in the SSM. In *The European Banking Union and the Role of Law* (pp. 177–196). Edward Elgar Publishing; (vii) Boucon, L. & Jaros, D. (2017). The Application of National Law by the European Central Bank within the EU Banking Union's Single Supervisory Mechanism: A New Mode of European Integration. *Eur. J. Legal Stud., 10*, pp. 155–187; (viii) Di Bucci, V. (2018). Quelques questions concernant le contrôle jurisdictionnel sur le mécanisme de surveillance unique. In *Liber Amicorum Antonio Tizzano. De la Cour CECA à la Cour de l'Union: le long parcours de la justice européenne* (pp. 317–331). Torino; (ix) Witte, A. (2017). When does a national law transpose a directive? In *ESCB Legal Conference 2016* (pp. 247–260). Frankfurt am Main, ECB. (x) Arranz, L. (2017); (xi) Kornezov, A. (2017). The application of national law by the ECB – a maze of (un) answered questions. In *ESCB Legal Conference 2016* (pp. 260–270). Frankfurt am Main, ECB; and (xii) Banks, K. (2019). Incorrect implementation of EU directives: what effects for the ECB and the CJEU, and what mechanisms for rectification? In *ECB Legal Conference 2019. Building bridges: central banking law in an interconnected world* (pp. 121–129). Frankfurt am Main, ECB.

A. THE SUBSTANTIVE RULES APPLIED BY THE ECB UNDER THE SSM

1. Classification of the material rules to be applied by the ECB

7.003 Art. 4(3) SSM R[2] determines the *material*[3] rules to be applied by the ECB to carry out the tasks entrusted by the SSM R, and exercises the supervisory powers conferred by that regulation.[4] Following the literal wording of this provision, the ECB is bound to apply EU Regulation in the field of supervision (including the SSM R itself) and other pieces of directly applicable Union law, such as CRR.

7.004 Following this framework, the ECB is bound to apply national law transposing such Union Law, as clarified by Recital 34 SSM R. The author is of the view that the reading of art. 4(3) SSM R must be encompassed with the lecture of art. 9(1) SSM R.[5] The reference made in the first sentence of Recital 34 SSM R to "*supervisory powers*", which constitutes part of the title of art. 9 SSM R, points also towards this direction.

7.005 Additionally, in the specific case of prudential Regulations (in particular CRR), where such Regulations grant options and discretions for MSs, the ECB must apply such options and discretions as determined by the national legislation.[6]

7.006 At this point, it must be noted that art. 4(3) SSM R refers exclusively to the options and discretions conferred upon MSs. Those are meant to be exercised

---

2 As constant reference to the first sub-paragraph of this article is going to be made, it is reproduced herein: "*3. For the purpose of carrying out the tasks conferred on it by this Regulation, and with the objective of ensuring high standards of supervision, the ECB shall apply all relevant Union law, and where this Union law is composed of Directives, the national legislation transposing those Directives. Where the relevant Union law is composed of Regulations and where currently those Regulations explicitly grant options for Member States, the ECB shall apply also the national legislation exercising those options*".

3 Cf Recital 34 SSM R. See. D'Ambrosio, R. (2020)(iii) at p. 131.

4 Cf art. 9(1) SSM R.

5 See the analysis of that provision in Section B.4. (*Supervisory and investigatory powers to exercise those tasks*) in Chapter 6.

6 It must be noted that SSM R, in general, and art. 4(3) SSM R, in particular, only refer to options and not to discretions. Yet, following systematic and comprehensive interpretations, discretions should be also included therein. See Gortsos, C. V. (2023). Options and Discretions under the Capital Requirements Directive IV. *EBI working* no. 155.

For a short yet comprehensive analysis on options and discretion, see Directorate-General for internal policies. (2017). National options and discretions (NODs) in EU banking regulation: European Parliament: https://www.europarl.europa.eu/RegData/etudes/BRIE/2016/574403/IPOL_BRI(2016)574403_EN.pdf. In particular, the categorisation of options and discretions pursuant to a quintuple scheme depending on (i) their legal basis (CRR/CRD IV)), (ii) level of decision (MS vs. NCA), (iii) time horizon (permanent vs. temporary), (iv) perspective (micro– or macro-prudential) and (v) scope (horizontal vs. case-by-case) results very practical.

through proper legislative acts. Thus, the options and discretions referred in the said art. 4(3) SSM R would not be those allocated to NCAs or designated authorities,[7] for which the ECB will be considered as the competent (or designated) authority in the participating MSs pursuant to the first sub-paragraph of art. 9(1) SSM R. Consequently, the ECB itself may exercise those latter options and discretions.

There would be a debatable exception to the foregoing: MSs may gold-plate the options and discretions allocated to NCAs or designated authorities by enacting statutes materialising the relevant option or discretion. In those cases, it is debatable whether the ECB would be bound to apply the national statute exercising an option or discretion that the EU legislators wanted to allocate to the relevant NCAs or designated authorities. This problem will be explored in Section A.2.(a). (*Gold-plating national options and discretions*) below. **7.007**

Furthermore, under art. 9(1) SSM R,[8] as regards SIs (and LSIs as per licensing and acquisition of qualifying holdings), the ECB would be entitled to exercise powers granted under national law not expressly referred to under Union Law.[9] The ECB is entitled to directly exercise those powers[10] in accordance with the conditions set forth in the relevant national law.[11] **7.008**

Finally, the second sub-paragraph of art. 4(3) SSM R emphasises the principle of legislative hierarchy. In this vein, both ECB *regulatory*[12] and super- **7.009**

---

7 As Recital 8 RO&Ds indicates: "*Such options and discretions do not include those available only to competent authorities, which the ECB is solely competent to exercise and should exercise as appropriate*".

8 Cf Lackhoff, K. (2017)(i) at pp. 26–27 for a succinct discussion on the *national powers* issue.

9 Provided that "*they (i) fall within the scope of the ECB's tasks under Articles 4 and 5 of the 4 SSM Regulation and (ii) underpin a supervisory function under Union law*". Cf the model letter issued by the ECB on 31 March 2017 titled "Additional clarification regarding the ECB's competence to exercise supervisory powers granted under national law":
https://www.bankingsupervision.europa.eu/press/letterstobanks/shared/pdf/2017/Letter_to_SI_Entry_point_information_letter.pdf?cb0801df81ba2db9d450ce4fb53065c8.

10 Which means that, ultimately, it would not need to request the assistance from the relevant NCAs pursuant to the third sub-paragraph of art. 9(1) SSM R.

11 Against this interpretation, one may argue that the plain strict reading of the reference made to *Union law* (made in both sub-paragraphs (1) and (2) of art. 9(1) SSM R) would limit, in fact, the powers of the ECB solely to those expressly based on such Union law. This would imply that the ECB could not make use of powers granted to NCAs *in addition* to the ones foreseen in EU law and, hence, could not apply national law as regards such powers.
This argument falls short of considering the broader picture, which is to ensure a coherent and comprehensive supervision, building teleologically upon the notion of tasks and powers. See further: Section B.2.(d). (*On the scope of the micro-prudential supervisory task contemplated in arts. 4(1) and 4(2) SSM R: Teleological interpretation*) in Chapter 6.

12 The adoption of guidelines (legally binding to the addresses (NCAs)) and recommendations (non-legally binding).

visory activities are subject to delegated or implemented regulations (issued by the Commission) and by national rules easing the implementation of such delegated or implemented acts. The ECB is also bound by the EBA's RTS and ITS (as approved by the Commission).[13] The ECB must also abide by the *soft law* issued by the EBA.[14] The foregoing generates a particular and unprecedented phenomenon: that an EU Institution (although dressed in agency clothes) follows the guidance issued by an EU agency. The direct reference to art. 16 of the EBA Regulation should be construed as allowing the ECB to make use of the *comply or explain* mechanism foreseen in such provision. The opposite interpretation, i.e., arguing that the ECB would be always obliged to follow EBA guidelines, would be inconsistent with the plain wording of the article. In addition, this approach would place the ECB in a worse position than that of a national authority (which are granted some leeway to decide whether they plan to comply with such EBA guidelines and recommendations or not).

7.010 The end of the antepenultimate sentence of the second sub-paragraph of art. 4(3) SSM R stipulates that the ECB will be also subject "*to the provisions of that Regulation on the European supervisory handbook developed by EBA in accordance with that Regulation*". Pursuant to art. 29 of the EBA Regulation, the EBA is responsible for developing and maintaining updated the supervisory handbook in order to foster best supervisory practices across the EU.

7.011 One thing to consider is whether the ECB must take into account the Q&A published in the EBA website. This modern and dynamic supervisory tool was formally included within the EBA Regulation (as new art. 16b), applying as from 1 January 2020. The mechanism provides for the possibility of competent authorities, as well as natural and legal persons, to submit to the EBA questions on the practical application and implementation of the single rulebook. Pursuant to art. 16b(2) of the EBA Regulation, answers provided by the EBA are non-binding.

7.012 The SSM R could not refer to such a new provision of the EBA Regulation, as this was devised more than six years after the approval of such Regulation. Nevertheless, the principle of normative hierarchy and the principle of primacy of EU law favours that the ECB considers the EBA's Q&A. A systematic

---

13 Cf arts. 10 to 15 of the EBA Regulation.

14 Cf art. 4(3)II SSM R. Art. 16 of the EBA Regulation referred to in this provision regulates the issuance by the EBA of *soft law* instruments, specifically, guidelines and recommendations. The former would have a general scope, being addressed to all competent authorities, whereas the latter would contain individual recommendations targeting certain competent authorities. See also Recital 32 of the SSM R.

interpretation of art. 4(3) seems also to suggest so, building upon the reference made to art. 16 of the EBA. Given the similarity between the Q&A tool made available to the EBA and its guidelines and recommendations (being both soft law instruments), they should be given a similar treatment and apply to the ECB as the EBA Regulation so foresees: as a non-binding instrument.

2. The (problematic) application by the ECB of national law: some considerations

The application of national law by an EU institution is a total novelty in EU law[15] and, as any novelty in the legal realm, is not absent of controversy. This phenomenon is not limited purely to material law but also to the procedural safeguards required to apply such national law and the scope (and procedures) ensuring the review of ECB decisions taken on the basis of such national law. **7.013**

The purpose of this Section is not to exhaustively analyse this phenomenon, not even evidence all the issues pertaining to this field. The purpose of this segment is way more modest and aims at identifying some of the key flaws of this singularity in order to provide a smoother analysis of the challenges that sanctioning and supervisory procedures handled by ECB may pose.[16] **7.014**

For these purposes, (i) the issues relating to the gold-plating of certain options and discretions will be analysed first. Second, (ii) it will be assessed when it can be considered that a national law actually transposes a Directive. In connection with this matter, it will be assessed whether some remedies can be devised in the case of deficient or (directly) no transposition of prudential Directives allocating powers to NCAs (to be exercised by the ECB under national law). And finally, (iii) on the basis of this analysis, some policy considerations and potential initiatives that would allow to overcome these issues will be put forward.[17] **7.015**

---

15 This novelty has been replicated only recently in art. 5(6) of the Regulation (EU) 2024/1620 establishing the Authority for Anti-Money Laundering and Countering the Financing of Terrorism and amending Regulations (EU) No. 1093/2010, (EU) No 1094/2010 and (EU) No 1095/2010. Such provision reproduces (almost exactly) art. 4(3)I SSM R.

16 In addition, a separate Section will be devoted on the topic of substantive law transposition and ECB direct sanctioning powers. See Section C. (*Substantive law & sanctioning proceedings: issues and proposals to overcome them*) below in this chapter.

17 Some of the specific *judicial* issues linked to the application of national law by the ECB will be referred to later in Part III when dealing with the specific problematics linked to supervisory and sanctioning proceedings.

(a) Gold-plating national options and discretions

7.016 Participating MSs have crystalised, by means of national statutes, some particular options and discretions allocated to NCAs or designated authorities. The practice can be even more complex and subtle, as some national acts may not fully eliminate the margin of discretion allocated to such national authorities but may subject it to certain parameters.[18] The more precise those parameters are, the less discretion is left to NCAs.

(i) Issues relating to the gold-plating of options and discretions allocated to NCAs and designated authorities in prudential Directives

7.017 As foreseen in art. 162 CRD IV, MSs were obliged to transpose this Directive in their national legal system by 31 December 2013. This means that before the deadline to transpose CRD IV had expired, the SSM R was in force (although the SSM as such was not operative until 4 November 2014).

7.018 Pursuant to the information available,[19] a few MSs partially transposed CRD IV before 31 December 2013 (as established in that Directive), and the majority of them took, on average, almost one additional year. This is meant to emphasise the awareness and purposive approach of MSs as regards gold-plating certain provisions enshrined in CRD IV. I will not explore the reasons behind such technique. They may be, indeed, multiple and obeying several circumstances, ranging from preferences towards already-known legislative approaches, to ease the banking business and also to purposively limit ECB discretion.

7.019 As indicated previously, pursuant to article 4(3) SSM R, the ECB must apply national law *transposing* prudential Directives. The issue that arises here is what happens in cases where MSs have legislatively gold-plated certain rules, exercising options and discretions that, in principle and based on CRD IV, should be exercised by NCAs (limiting thus the NCAs' discretion). Is the ECB obliged to apply them, or may it escape from such gold-plated rules?

7.020 The debate needs to be framed, *first* considering the externalities that this gold-plating practice may generate. Gold-plated provisions may limit the supervisory discretion that EU legislators allocated to NCAs. Consequently, this may impinge the possibility of exercising a coherent supranational supervision by

18 See, for example, art. 30a of the Austrian Banking Act (*Bankwesengesetz*), which precises the criteria to exempt credit institutions affiliated permanently to a central body from complying with certain regulatory requirements (cf art. 10, 12 and 13(1) of CRD IV).

19 See the general description of the national transposition measures provided by EUR-Lex: https://eur-lex.europa.eu/legal-content/EN/NIM/?uri=CELEX:32013L0036.

the ECB, as it would be bound to apply a discretion (or option) over which it should, in principle, be free to decide how to apply (and in which way). The SSM key principle of level playing field and the equally relevant one of proportionality are then endangered.[20]

It must be noted that the issue here is different from the one on *national powers*[21] and of a different type. Concluding that limiting ECB discretion impacts its ability to exercise a consistent supervision over the entities it has been allocated with direct supervisory powers, the question that follows is whether the ECB is bound to apply national legislations gold-plating options of discretions allocated to NCAs. **7.021**

In the view of the author, the answer is "no". The foregoing because of the principles of primacy of Union law and equivalence and effectiveness and the plain wording of art. 9(1) SSM R. Three arguments support this conclusion and are presented below. **7.022**

Firstly, from a pure textual perspective, one needs to acknowledge that art. 4(3)I SSM R binds the ECB to apply only national legislation exercising options and discretions allocated to MSs (not to NCAs).[22] Art. 9(1)II SSM R also emphasises that the ECB shall have (as being considered as the *competent authority*[23]) all the powers of obligations established under Union Law. In the light of the foregoing, it can be concluded that (i) the ECB is meant to apply national legislation exercising options and discretions only when they are granted to MSs (and not other type of legislative exercise of such options). And (ii) the ECB as a competent authority may rightfully exercise options and discretions granted to NCAs without considering any national law gold-plating them (at least for SIs).[24] **7.023**

20 See Section B. (*SSM basic principles: level playing field & proportionality*) in Chapter 1. Following the illustrative sample provided Sabine Lautenschläger (Member of the Executive Board of the ECB and Vice-Chair of the Supervisory Board of the ECB), the consequence of this fragmented regulatory landscape collocates the ECB in the position of a referee in a football match bound to apply different rules depending on the football player. See keynote speech by Sabine Lautenschläger, at the Workshop of the European Banking Institute (EBI) hosted by the ECB, Frankfurt, 27 January 2016: https://www.bankingsupervision.europa.eu/press/speeches/date/2016/html/se160127.en.html.

21 See Section A.1. (*Classification of the material rules to be applied by the ECB*) above. See also, extensively on this topic, Bassani, G. (2019). Additionally, see Lackhoff, K. (2017)(i) at pp. 24–27.

22 Recital 34 SSM R is even clearer when it states that: "*Such options should be construed as excluding options available only to competent or designated authorities*".

23 Including both NCAs and national designated authorities, as applicable. To be noted that designated authorities would encompass those authorities designated pursuant to art. 136 CRD IV.

24 See Witte, A. (2021).

7.024 National legislation seizing options and discretions granted to NCAs would operate at a purely national level, hence being applicable only as regards LSIs, which remain subject to the direct supervision of NCAs (and under the overall oversight of the ECB). In short, art. 9(1)II SSM R supports that national statutes gold-plating options and discretions available to NCAs would not be able to limit the ECB discretion as regards SIs.

7.025 *Secondly*, and linked to the previous argument, it is worth noting that by virtue of the primacy of EU law, such pieces of legislation are rendered inapplicable to the ECB. Recital 34 SSM R precisely refers to this long-standing cornerstone principle[25] as a manner of warning or reminder presumably for these cases.

7.026 *Thirdly*, it is worth noting that building upon the principle of level playing field, interpretations fostering an integrated uniform banking market should be preferred. In this vein, subjecting, eventually, the ECB to such divergent national regulations would jeopardise equal treatment of credit institution, generating, in fact, regulatory arbitrage.[26]

7.027 The foregoing interpretation would be also respectful with the democratic rationale of the SSM. This has stirred some controversy that has reached some MSs constitutional courts, most notably the Federal German Constitutional Court (BverfG).[27] In its judgment, dated 30 July 2019,[28] the BverfG acknowledged that the SSM would comply with accountability standards as the ECB would be bound by primary law and secondary regulation (mainly the SSM R).[29]

7.028 In *conclusion*, the ECB should apply (as *competent authority* by ministry of EU law[30]) the options granted to the NCAs in prudential Directives. In doing so, the ECB acts validly, disregarding national legislation gold-plating options

---

25 Devised at the very beginning of the initiation of the Communities back in 1964 in the landmark case *Costa v. Enel.* See Court of Justice judgment in case 6/64 (*Flaminio Costa v E.N.E.L.*) of 15 July 1994 (ECLI:EU:C:1964:66).

26 Running then contrarily to art. 1(1) SSM R. See, in this regard, the ECB Opinion of 2 September 2015 on bank resolution (CON/2015/31) (as regards a German federal law adapting internal legal framework to the SRM). At. Para. 3.1.4.

27 See in this regard D'Ambrosio, R. (2020)(iii) at p. 136.

28 Judgment 2 BvR 1685/14, 2 BvR 2631/14. An English version of the judgment can be consulted here: https://www.bundesverfassungsgericht.de/SharedDocs/Downloads/EN/2019/07/rs20190730_2bvr168514en.pdf?__blob=publicationFile&v=1.

29 Ibidem at Para. 212.

30 Art. 9(1) SSM R.

and discretions which were entrusted to NCAs (and designated authorities) under such Directives.

This approach seems to be followed by the ECB, perhaps without evidencing the reasoning in such a bold way as done above. This is clearly evidenced in the RO&Ds, which establishes in its Recital 8 that "*Such options and discretions do not include those available only to competent authorities, which the ECB is solely competent to exercise and should exercise as appropriate*". This Recital works as an accurate closing to the reasoning devised above. **7.029**

(ii) Issues relating to the gold-plating of options and discretions allocated to NCAs and designated authorities in CRR

CRD IV grants options and discretions to both MSs[31] and NCAS,[32][33] also CRR does. When MSs exercise the options and discretions allocated to those NCAs, the same question that was answered above arises: is the ECB bound to apply national statutes that have gold-plated options and discretions allocated to NCAs under CRR? **7.030**

Again, the answer must be no. The reasons motivating such an answer are grounded in the very wording of the SSM R and also, on the primacy of EU law that manifests here, perhaps, in a stronger manner than in the case presented before.[34] **7.031**

First, it must be recalled that pursuant to art. 4(3)I SSM R, "*Where the relevant Union law is composed of Regulations and where currently those Regulations explicitly grant options for Member States, the ECB shall apply also the national legislation exercising those options*". **7.032**

Consequently, the ECB is bound to apply the national law exercising options and discretions granted by Regulations to MSs. However, this provision also **7.033**

31 For example, in art. 412(5) CRR as regards the introduction of provisions in the area of liquidity requirements before minimum standards for liquidity coverage requirements are made available and applicable in the EU pursuant to art. 460 CRR.

32 For example, in art. 284(9) CRR as regards the possibility of permitting entities to use their own estimates of alpha for the calculation of the Effective EPE (cf art. 284(4) CRR).

33 Sometimes CRR allocates such competence to both: MSs or NCAs. In those cases, and to the extent that MSs have the competence to exercise the relevant option or discretion, the ECB must apply the national statute exercising such option or discretion.

A good example of the foregoing can be found in art. 412(5) CRR, pursuant to which: "*Member States or competent authorities may require domestically authorised institutions* (...)". (Emphasis added).

34 Regarding the gold-plating of options and discretions foreseen in prudential Directives allocated to NCAs.

acts as a limit and, hence, prevents the ECB from applying national provisions exercising options and discretions allocated to NCAs.

7.034 Recital 34 SSM R is even clearer when it states that: "(…) *Such options should be construed as excluding options available only to competent or designated authorities. This is without prejudice to the principle of the primacy of Union law*". (Emphasis added).

7.035 The foregoing outlines the fact that the ECB is solely competent to exercise the options and discretions allocated to NCAs (or designated authorities) under relevant Regulations. Such approach is consistent with art. 9(1)I SSM R, which turns the ECB into the *competent* (or designated) *authority* in the MSs and allocates to it all the powers vested under relevant Union Law.

7.036 *Second*, the primacy of Union renders the national statutes gold-plating the options and discretions allocated to NCAs under CRR inapplicable to the ECB.[35]

7.037 In *conclusion*, the ECB is not bound by national law exercising options and discretions granted by EU Regulations (mainly CRR) to NCAs and designated authorities.

(b) When does national law transpose a Directive?

7.038 The following Section devotes to summarising the issues relating to national law transposing prudential Directives, mainly CRD IV. Such transposing national law, by means of art. 4(3) SSM R, is also part of the legal instruments that the ECB must apply.

7.039 The reference to issues, in plural, made in the previous paragraphs was done on purpose; the problematic linked to this innovative application of national law entails several issues (of a multifaceted nature). Below, the following interlinked topics will be analysed: *first*, it seems appropriate to start from the simplest matter, that is, how to identify national laws transposing prudential Directives. *Second*, continuing this path from simpler to more complicated issues, it is appropriate to explore what happens when a MS has indeed transposed a prudential Directive but allocated powers to the respective NCA in excess of the minimum content foreseen in the directive. Plus, it is necessary to determine what happens if such a national statute imposes additional requisites to exercise Directive-related faculties, tasks and powers. *Third*, it

35 See immediately above.

will be assessed what the consequences of a national statute not transposing a prudential Directive (or when that national act has transposed it wrongly) are. *To conclude*, and building on the foregoing analysis, some general policy and action proposals will be proposed to ensure that a coherent, consistent and comprehensive set of rules is applied on entities subject to SSM supervision.

(i) Assessing when national law transposes a Directive

Ascertaining when a national statute actually transposes a prudential Directive (mainly CRDIV) is the first step for the ECB to apply national law under arts. 4(3) and 9(1) SSM R, and sometimes not an easy one. **7.040**

The very first step entails identifying what national statute transposes the directive at stake. From a practical perspective, national statutes provide, sometimes, clear hints that, at the minimum, national law is related with the Directive, which is envisaged to be transposed. Such hints may be included in the title itself of the national statute, by referencing the directive to be transposed.[36] Other national statutes contain more subtle references to prudential requirements[37] that may be helpful to identify the prudential Directive transposed. **7.041**

EU law has not imposed a specific requirement to MSs to include a clear cross-reference between the directive transposed and the national statute.[38] Yet, MSs do have a duty to notify to the Commission – and eventually to other involved EU bodies or agencies – the transposition of such a measure.[39] EUR-lex, the official website of EU law and the public documents of the EU, **7.042**

36 This would be the case of the Legislative Decree of the Italian Republic of 12 May 2015 titled as follows: Attuazione della direttiva 2013/36/UE, che modifica la direttiva 2002/87/CE e abroga le direttive 2006/48/CE e 2006/49/CE, per quanto concerne l'accesso all'attivita' degli enti creditizi e la vigilanza prudenziale sugli enti creditizi e sulle imprese di investimento. Modifiche al decreto legislativo 1° settembre 1993, n. 385 e al decreto legislativo 24 febbraio 1998, n. 58. (15G00087) (GU Serie Generale n.134 del 12-06-2015).

A similar example, regarding this time the exercise of options and discretions of CRR, would be the Luxembourgish regulation, titled: Règlement CSSF N° 14-01 sur l'implémentation de certaines discrétions contenues dans le règlement (UE) n° 575/2013.

37 See, for instance, the Irish S. I. No. 158/2014 – European Union (Capital Requirements) Regulations 2014.

38 Concerning failures to transpose a Directive see Lenaerts, K., Maselis, I. and Gutman, K. (2015) at pp. 169–170.

39 See for instance art. 162(1)III CRD IV, which obliges MSs to communicate to the Commission and the EBA their national measures transposing such Directive. On the latest jurisdictional developments concerning communication of national measures transposing a given directive, see Court of Justice judgment C-543/17 (*Commission v Belgium*) of 8 July 2019 (ECLI:EU:C:2019:573). On this topic, see also Finke, D. & Dannwolf, T. (2015). Who let the dogs out? The effect of parliamentary scrutiny on compliance with EU law, *Journal of European Public Policy*, 22:8, pp. 1127–1147.

provides a tool to search the measures of national transposition communicated by MSs,[40] including sometimes links to the official publication of such national legislative measures in their respective official journal. This tool proves to be quite effective, at least to preliminarily identifying whether or not an MS has transposed a given statute – acknowledging that such publication has a merely informative (not official) character.

7.043 In the course of notifying such measures of national transposition, some MSs have completed such required notification with explanatory memos and/or correlation tables.[41] These explanatory memos and/or correlation charts, when publicly available, can ease the process of determining which national statute transposes what directive (or which part of it). Special mention must be made here to the charts published by the EBA, in accordance with art. 162(1) CRD IV.[42] These charts display "*the text of the main provisions of national law which they adopt in the field covered by this Directive*". Like as occurred with the explanatory memos and correlation tables indicated above, these prove to be a very useful tool to identify, at least, the text of the national rules implementing CRD IV.

7.044 Notwithstanding the foregoing, preambles of national statutes (when not directly the legal text of such statutes) contain reference to the fact that the respective statute aims at transposing such a Directive.[43]

7.045 All in all, monitoring and tracking the processes of national transposition of prudential Directives and detecting national law resulting from those processes appear to be for the ECB. Hence, on top of the practices and proceedings depicted above to identify such national statutes, the ECB could organise a permanent network or working group aimed at identifying and/or providing updated information on the national measures transposing prudential Directives. Such a net would rely on the legal departments of the NCAs, which would increase the synergies derived from its periodical analysis or intervention in the public consultations of national bills transposing prudential Directive. The final goal of such a structure would be to produce an updated and easily readable rulebook of national measures transposing CRD

40 https://eur-lex.europa.eu/collection/n-law/mne.html.

41 Of very different quality level, as acknowledged by the EP. See Smith, M. (2018). Challenges in the implementation of EU Law at national level. *European Parliament Briefing*.

42 Accessible here: Rules and guidance | European Banking Authority (europa.eu).

43 This would be the case of Spanish Law 10/2014 on Solvency, Supervision and Ordination of Credit Institutions (*Ley 10/2014, de 26 de junio, de ordenación, supervisión y solvencia de entidades de crédito*) whose Preamble indicates, in Section II, that this law aims indeed at transposing CRD IV.

IV, facilitating ECB tasks of identifying the national law that, in principle, would be subject to apply (or to require to apply pursuant to art. 9(1)III SSM R).

The second step of this process would involve understanding whether the national statutes transpose the minimum requirements foreseen in the directive at stake.[44] This assessment may be as easy as localising the relevant provisions copy-pasting the text of the directive, without performing much more adaptations. In other cases, it may imply diving into the existing national legal compilation.[45] **7.046**

The key point to be checked as regards this step is that, at the minimum, the basic elements foreseen in the CRD IV can be found and make the provision *recognisable*. The latter entails a subjective-driven exercise that should be presided by a teleological approach. The foregoing cannot (and does not) entail a purely mechanical exercise, and insofar qualitative considerations come into play, this analysis cannot provide a "*comply-or-not*" clear answer.[46] **7.047**

In substance, within this step, at a minimum, the following two operations are meant to occur: (i) firstly, identifying the core content of the provision of the directive to be transposed. Such minimum content must be, at the minimum, related to three elements which are: (*a*) the field in which a given provision is deemed to be applied. This may cover financial services in general or only banking services. What is relevant to understand is whether the national provision transposing the relevant prudential Directive captures, in its remit, banking services or credit institution's activities. (*b*) Secondly, one needs to ascertain the key powers or functions to be performed by the NCA. This allows to distinguish between the minimum set of powers to be allocated from whatever other additional powers may be allocated to the NCA (and eventually to the ECB). (*c*) Finally, one needs to identify whether, as regards the minimum powers foreseen in the prudential Directive, the national transposing legislation imposes additional elements to be considered by the NCA, restricting in **7.048**

44 One may note that, as per CRD IV, it is indeed a Directive providing minimum harmonisation. See Arranz, L. (2017) at p. 264. The foregoing, except for the provisions regulating the acquisition of qualifying holdings in credit institutions, which provide for maximum harmonisation as Bassaninotes. See Bassani, G. (2019).

45 For instance, this would be the case of the Italian Unique Banking Text (Testo Unico Bancario), which aims at compiling and structuring Italian supervisory banking law. See Porzio, M. (2010). *Testo unico bancario: commentario.* Giuffrè Editor and Banca D'Italia, R. (2012). Legislazione bancaria, finanziaria e assicurativa: la storia, il presente, il futuro. *Quaderni di Ricerca Giuridica della Consulenza Legale Banca d'Italia No 72.*

46 See, in this vein, Witte, A. (2017).

any manner its discretion. This would have an impact not in the transposition *per se* but on whether the transposition performed makes the power recognisable (which could be regarded as a wrongful transposition).

7.049 (ii) The second phase would aim at determining (on the basis of the previous one) if the national legislation has or has not transposed a given directive (or, better said, a certain provision of a prudential Directive). The latter case would collocate the MSs in a default position, similar to the case of a wrongful transposition.[47]

7.050 In the case that the core elements of the directive's provision are respected, one would still need to assess whether the national statutes add on to the content of the directive. As the case may be, the analysis should be focused on whether the respective provision (a) actually gold-plates the requirements steaming from EU law or (b) adds on the powers made available to the NCA. Yet, provided that the provision allocates additional powers, it needs to be determined if those powers are (i) clearly disconnected from the ones foreseen in the directive (*autonomous supervisory powers*) and (ii) clearly linked to the tasks foreseen in the directive and falling within the specific micro-prudential tasks allocated to the ECB under arts. 4(1) and 4(2) SSM R.

(ii) What happens when the national statute allocates powers in excess to the ones foreseen in a prudential Directive?

7.051 This Section continues with the two steps of analysis regarding the transposition of prudential Directives by MSs provided immediately above it; aims at depicting a third step of analysis regarding those cases the respective MSs have *added* on the minimum content established by the prudential Directive.

7.052 The main aim is to ascertain when the ECB may exercise powers vested under national statute directly (under arts. 9(1)II and 4(3) SSM R) or indirectly (under art. 9(1)III SSMR). The route would be as follows.[48] First, it needs to be determined whether the tasks regulated by the national act fall under any of the specific micro-prudential supervisory tasks depicted in arts. 4(1) and 4(2) SSM R,[49] broadly construed. The result of such assessment needs to be positive so that the ECB can be allowed to exercise the powers contemplated in the national statute.

47 Which would be referred later on below.

48 See also on the national powers issue Section B.4. (*Supervisory and investigatory powers to exercise those tasks*) in Chapter 6.

49 In principle, the same would apply to macro-prudential tasks described in art. 5 SSM R, but these do not form part of the following analysis.

Second, one needs to check whether the national statute actually implements, in a broad sense, the content of EU Law. And here comes the dividing line; if such correlation between the national act and the EU rule can be inferred, the ECB may exercise directly the powers granted under the national statute.[50] Otherwise, provided that the exercise of the powers granted to the relevant NCA is necessary to fulfil any of the specific prudential tasks conferred on the ECB, it may request the relevant NCA to exercise such powers on its behalf. **7.053**

The NCA must exercise such powers, then, in accordance with and subject to the national framework, which includes national procedural rules and jurisprudential interpretations.[51] This means that, in principle, it does not matter how direct or clear the ECB instructions may be; the NCA is ultimately better placed to construe the national law to be applied. Such law must be construed as a whole complete system and not as an isolated provision (the one, eventually, the ECB may request the NCA to apply). The result of these considerations may lead the NCA to, despite attending the ECB request, after judging the applicable framework, discard it (or attend it in a different matter). **7.054**

Determining when, actually, a national statute grants a supervisory power (additional or not to the ones foreseen under Union Law) that falls within the specific supervisory tasks allocated to the ECB[52] implies an exercise of calibration which must be undertaken on a case-by-case basis.[53] However, the following criteria may be considered when performing such analysis: **7.055**

(i) Examining the overall scope of the prudential Directive in order to determine what the core powers are which needed to be transposed into the national law (and to which specific supervisory task contemplated in the SSM R they may relate).
(ii) To ascertain the core powers which need to be transposed intonational law, it is necessary to examine whether those additional (not foreseen) powers are connected with the core powers to be transposed. To do so, the following yardsticks may be used:
    a. Analysing the subsidiarity and/or autonomy of the powers granted. If the power granted cannot be exercised (or can be exercised in a deficit manner) without resource to the core power foreseen in the prudential Directive, it may be considered as a form of implementation of Union law.

50 Witte, A. (2017) at pp. 251–252.

51 Which may substantiate on concepts having a long-standing national jurisdictional tradition, such as, *good faith*, *control*, *liability*, etc.

52 Cf Recital 3 of ECB Decision 2019/322 on delegation of the power to adopt decisions regarding supervisory powers granted under national law (ECB/2019/4).

53 The same conclusion is shared by BASSANI, after a deep examination of CJEU case law regarding the transposition of Directives. See Bassani, G. (2019).

b. Attending to the complementarity of the additional powers introduced by means of national law. If they enhance or contribute to complying the tasks allocated to the ECB, it is a strong sign of being considered as a *transposition* of the prudential Directive.

BOX 7.1 EXAMPLE: APPROVAL OF MODIFICATIONS OF THE BY-LAWS OF A SI

This chart aims at testing how the above criteria would work in practice when confronted to a real case, for instance, the approval of modifications of by-laws of SIs.[54] Such a tool is foreseen in the legal acquis of some MSs.[55]

As a starting point, one may consider that CRD IV requests credit institution to be duly authorised to pursue the business of credit institutions (art. 8(1)) in connection with the activities listed in Annex I[56]). Also, CRD IV contains multiples references so as to ensure that robust governance arrangements are set up[57] and that internal control mechanism are capable of detecting and preventing business risks.[58] These tasks are specifically transferred to the ECB pursuant to letters (a), I and (f) of art. 4(1) SSM R.

It is possible to see a clear connection between the basic powers pertaining to authorising credit institutions and supervising their corporate governance arrangements. One can easily perceive that this power presents a subsidiarity character from the main supervisory powers (*subsidiarity test*[59]) and at the same time enhances the supervisory options available to the relevant supervisor, easing the fulfilment of its tasks (*complementarity test*). Based on the foregoing, these types of powers can be regarded as supervisory powers not expressly foreseen in a prudential Directive but nevertheless falling under the tasks allocated to the ECB by the SSM R and, hence, pursuant to arts. 4(3) and 9(1)II SSM R, exercisable directly by the ECB.

---

54 To clarify, these amendments do not refer to changes in the subscribed capital of the entity at stake as these tasks would be clearly comprised within art. 4(1)(a) SSM R.

55 For instance, in France (art. L.511-58, L.511-12-1 II, L.532-3-1, L.511-13-1 and L.511-3-2 of the *Code monétaire et financier* and ACPR Position 2014-P-04 – *relative à l'utilisation de la forme juridique de société par actions simplifiée par des établissements de crédit ou des entreprises d'investissement dans le contexte de la directive CRD 4*) and Spain art. 4.2(c) of Law 10/2014 on Ordination, Supervision and Solvency of credit institutions, art. 10 Royal Decree 84/2015 developing the previous Law and art. 1.4 of Royal Decree 84/1993 on credit cooperatives.

56 Cf also art. 10 and 33.

57 Cf art. 74(1) and arts. 88 and ss. CRD IV. The General Court has already examined some governance requirement arising from CRD IV, in particular, regarding the combination of the roles of Chairman of the Board of Directors and CEO within the same institution. Joined cases T-133/16 to T-136/16 (*Caisse régionale de crédit agricole mutuel Alpes Provence and Others v European Central Bank*) of 24 April 2018 (ECLI:EU:T:2018:219). For a dedicated commentary on this judgment, see Gortsos, C. V. (2021). The Crédit Agricole cases: banking corporate governance and application of national law by the ECB. In *Judicial Review in the European Banking Union* (pp. 510–520). Edward Elgar Publishing.

58 Cf arts. 74 to 87 CRD IV.

59 The exercise of such by-laws' approval powers would not appear as the main supervisory function and cannot be understood as an autonomous power. Its exercise only makes sense when connected with/within broader supervisory powers.

(iii) What happens when a MS has not transposed (or has deficiently transposed) a Directive. Are there any remedies?

It rests to be assessed what happens when a given MS has not transposed or has transposed wrongly a given prudential Directive. The analysis below adds to the general (and pretty creative) debate on the remedies available to the ECB in cases where a MSs has not transposed (or has deficiently transposed) a prudential Directive. The consequence of such defective transposition entails depriving the ECB, eventually, from the possibility to exercise certain powers that should have been captured in the relevant national law transposing the prudential Directive.[60] **7.056**

The reaction to such a potential issue can be twofold: (i) enforcement, by resorting to the mechanisms foreseen in the Treaties to compel a given MS to transpose a relevant prudential Directive (or to do so in a proper way), or (ii) interpretative, trying to overcome the potential *lacunae* (or wrongful transposition) by means of legal interpretation. Reference will be made first to the former approach and, subsequently, the second reaction will be developed. **7.057**

The *first reaction* to the lack of transposition or incorrect transposition of prudential Directives is to make use of the mechanisms of enforcement for violation of EU law, that is, the infringement procedure.[61] However, the average duration of such procedures prevents them from being the swift tool that a prudential supervisor needs.[62] Some authors have also suggested the possibility to make use of art. 271(d) TFEU, which allows the ECB to start infringement proceedings on their own account against NCBs failing to fulfil their **7.058**

---

60 See Lo Schiavo, G. L. (2019); Coman-Kund, F. & Amtenbrink, F. (2018), pp. 133–172; Kornezov, A. (2017); Banks, K. (2019); Di Bucci, V. (2018); and Annunziata, F. and D'Ambrosio, R. (2019). L'applicazione del diritto degli Stati membri da parte della Banca Centrale Europea. *Giur. Comm.*, Vol. 46. Fas. 4.

61 Cf art. 258 TFEU.

62 On average, infringements procedures last 34.8 months according to the data provided by the Commission. See *Single Market Scoreboard* (2018–2019): The Single Market Scoreboard | Single Market Scoreboard (europa.eu).

As a matter of example, concerning CRD IV, which was supposed to be fully transposed by MSs by 31 December 2013 (not considering any amendments occurring thereafter), the Commission issued on 16 October 2014 (almost one year later) a reasoned opinion requesting Cyprus, Italy, Lithuania, Poland, Portugal and Slovenia to transpose such a directive. In such opinion, the Commission gave those countries two months to communicate and undergo the necessary transposing measures before instituting an infringements procedure before the CJEU. Despite such a deadline, the effective transposition of CRD IV provision took place, in some cases, almost one year and a half later. That was the case of Italy, which transposed the sanctioning provisions on 12 May 2015 via the Legislative Decree of 12 May 2015, n. 72 (GU n.134 of 12 of June 2015) and on 17 May 2016 by means of the *Provvedimento Banca d'Italia 3 maggio 2016* (GU n. 114 of 17 May 2016).

obligations under the Treaties and SESCB.[63] As indicated above,[64] resource to such provision seems doubtful in the context of the SSM and also as regards the possibility of making use of it *vis-à-vis* NCAs, which are not NCBs. It is worth noting also that MSs seem to have fully transposed CRD IV. However, looking forward and, in particular, as regards the transposition of CRD V (established by 28 December 2020) or any further prudential Directive, it cannot be discarded that MSs continue not to transpose such text into national framework on time. In fact, one may expect such a situation to constitute the *usual* rule, not the exception.

7.059 The second approach would entail finding interpretative avenues to overcome the defective transposition of prudential Directives. The interpretative available techniques are analysed below.

7.060 First of all, when assessing the potential remedies available to cope with such delayed or wrongly transposed [prudential] Directives, there seems to be at least two extrinsic limiting factors (to be added on top of the constitutional and regulatory conditionalities of the SSM itself, which will be referred to also below). Those are, *firstly*, the fact that Directives in general are addressed to MSs, not to EU bodies or institutions. From this perspective, one may argue that the legitimacy of the ECB to somehow re-construe a text that is meant to be implemented (most likely) by the legislative chambers of MSs is rather limited. In addition, such an interaction casts some doubts regarding the principle of subsidiarity, as if the ECB could freely decide how to directly apply certain provisions of the CRD IV;[65] this would amount to circumvent the main aim of directives.[66]

7.061 *Secondly*, there seems to be an insurmountable limitation on the legal interpretation; directives cannot produce a *reverse* direct effect on individuals (i.e., they cannot be applied directly against individuals by the MSs that failed to transpose them). Early examples of this can be found in the *Kolpinghuis* case.[67] The

63 See Kornezov, A. (2017) at p. 271.

64 See footnote 114 in Chapter 6.

65 In cases of defective or no transposition of CRD IV.

66 See, in this very sense, the General Court judgment in case T-502/19 (*Francesca Corneli v the ECB*) of 12 October 2022 (ECLI:EU:T:2022:627), hereafter **Corneli case**. At Para. 112.

As the subsidiarity assessment would have revealed that there is no need for a completely uniform approach which could be achieved only by means of Regulations. On the interplay of the principles of conferral and subsidiarity (and also proportionality), see Lenaerts, K. (2022). Proportionality as a matrix principle promoting the effectiveness of EU law and the legitimacy of EU action – Keynote speech. In *ECB Legal Conference 2021. Continuity and change – how the challenges of today prepare the ground for tomorrow* (pp. 27–45). Frankfurt am Main, ECB.

67 Ibidem. See also Court of Justice judgment in case C-80/86 (*Kolpinghuis Nijmegen*) of 8 October 1987 (ECLI:EU:C:1987:431). Paras. 8–10.

same doctrine has been maintained invariably by the CJEU. We can track this unchanged line of reasoning, among many other samples, in the *Kofoed* case.[68] Qualified authors have indicated that such doctrine does not seem likely to be modified any time soon;'[69] hence, the ECB may not be able to rely on a lingered version of such doctrine.

The assessment of the available remedies needs to differentiate the two basic types of breaches concerning prudential Directives' transposition. Those are (a) the complete lack of transposition of the Directive[70] and (b) the wrong transposition of the given Directive.[71] **7.062**

Concerning *(a)* (*lack of transposition of prudential Directives*), the structural limitation imposed by art. 4(3) SSM R leaves very little leeway to explore the possibility of reverse direct application. Pursuant to such provision, the ECB is bound to apply national law transposing prudential Directives.[72] **7.063**

Such set-up is inextricably linked to the constitutional foundations of the SSM[73] and is an element that vests it with a degree of democratic legitimacy by ensuring the enforcement and application of rules approved by national legislators regarding areas in which the Union cannot act via directly applicable Regulations. Such approach is shared by the BverfG, which, in its judgment on the Banking Union,[74] indicated that the application of national legislation by the ECB (contributed) to achieve democratic accountability and legitimacy. **7.064**

Additionally, it is worth assessing whether the ECB could rely on the *Mangold* doctrine[75] to apply directly a given prudential Directive. In *Mangold* (and some later judgments), the Court held that MSs' courts must set aside national provisions conflicting with general Union law principles enshrined **7.065**

68 Court of Justice judgment in case C-321/05 (*Hans Markus Kofoed v Skatteministeriet*) of 5 July 2007 (ECLI:EU:C:2007:408), Para. 42. See also Court of Justice judgment in case C-573/17 (*Popławski*) of 24 June 2019 (ECLI:EU:C:2019:530).

69 Banks, K. (2019) at p. 122.

70 Which entails a failure to transpose into the national legal framework the relevant directive before the deadline foreseen in such directive expires.

71 Partial or incomplete transposition by MSs can be assimilated to any of the two previous situations.

72 See Section A.1. (*Classification of the material rules to be applied by the ECB*) above. In this regard, see Amtenbrink, F. (2019).

73 See Section A. (*Constitutional constrains of the enabling clause*) in Chapter 2.

74 BVerfG's judgment of 30 July 2019 (2 BvR 1685/14, 2 BvR 2631/14). A partial version translated into English can be accessed here: https://www.bundesverfassungsgericht.de/SharedDocs/Entscheidungen/EN/2019/07/rs20190730_2bvr168514en.html;jsessionid=2A05FF166B43919DB70531AE5216416B.2_cid386.

75 Court of Justice judgment in case C-144/04 (*Werner Mangold v Rüdiger Helm*) of 22 November 2005 (ECLI:EU:C:2005:709).

in directives (even when the deadlines for their transposition have not expired yet).[76] The *Mangold* doctrine has been developed further but not uniformly applied, which leads to the conclusion that such doctrine demands a careful case-by-case assessment[77] in a twofold manner, as regards the examination of an undisputed, well-established Union principle and regarding the precise rule (or set of national rules) to be disapplied.

7.066 It proves to be complicated (at its best) understanding that prudential Directives may give expression to a general principle of Union Law,[78] leading to its direct application. In *Mangold,* for instance, the principle at stake was non-discrimination (on grounds of age), which was easily recognisable and is nowadays contemplated in art. 21 of the Charter. It seems indeed difficult to identify such a type of general Union law principles enshrined in prudential Directives.

7.067 Also, in *Mangold,*[79] the case at stake related to a horizontal relationship, where an individual (an employee) actioned against another private party (his employer, a sole practitioner) seeking to apply a general EU principle materialised in a given directive.[80] Under the SSM, there is not such a *horizontal* relationship but one of a more vertical nature; within the SSM, the ECB acts a prudential authority, and the entities it supervises are bound to observe its decisions.

7.068 Hence, the author is of the view that such an interpretative avenue may not be pursued by the ECB, unless the CJEU creates a tailor-made approach for it.

7.069 With this picture in mind, the only possibility that would allow the ECB to make use of a sort of reverse direct effect *vis-à-vis* supervised entities seems to depend on whether they may be considered as an *emanation of the state.*[81] In cases were a MS has failed to transpose a Directive, an entity which is to be considered an emanation of the state cannot take advantage of the MS's failure to transpose such directive.[82] In the case of the ECB, the application of

---

76 Ibidem at Para. 78.

77 Kornezov, A. (2017) at pp. 276–277.

78 Ibidem, in favour of such approach but expressing some concerns.

79 As well, in case *Kücükdeveci:* Court of Justice judgment in case C-555/07 (*Seda Kücükdeveci v Swedex GmbH & Co. KG*) of 9 January 2010 (ECLI:EU:C:2010:21).

80 And most importantly: "(...) *even where the period prescribed for transposition of that directive has not yet expired*". See *Mangold* at Para. 78.

81 On the criteria that allows to identify when an entity may be considered an emanation of the state, see Opinion of AG Sharpston in case C-413/15 (*Elaine Farrell v Alan Whitty*), delivered on 22 June 2017 (ECLI:EU:C:2017:492).

82 In this regard, see Court of Justice judgment in case C-6/05 (*Medipac-Kazantzidis AE V Venizelio-Pananio (PE.S.Y. KRITIS)*) of 14 June 2007 (ECLI:EU:C:2007:337). In Para. 43 (and cited case law), the Court

such doctrine requires an additional twist (which seems legally feasible tough). Evidently, the ECB is not a *MS*; however, it acts as a NCA per substitution,[83] and hence, it exercises the powers generally allocated to MSs. Consequently, the ECB may directly apply directives[84] *vis-à-vis* entities which may constitute an emanation of the respective MSs.

In the aftermath of the crisis, a number of institutions were nationalised or somehow received state aid support, which led to the MSs to exercise a degree of control which would make them qualify as *state entities*.[85] Such kind of reverse application of directives still would require that the provisions of such directives are clear and unconditional. In the light of the foregoing, even such reverse application of directives seems to be materially limited, given that prudential Directives' provisions are sometimes far from being specific and unconditional but rather contain a multiplicity of elements to be calibrated, open-texture concepts and indeterminate notions required to be specified. Hence, even the innovative avenue depicted above, applicable only to a reduced number of supervisees, falls sort of ensuring a seamless and consistent application of the regulatory framework. **7.070**

As regards *(b)* the *wrongful transposition of the given prudential Directive*, the tools to ensure compliance with Union law must be realistically curtailed.[86] The main reason advising contention when proposing any alternative addressed to substitute a wrong or inaccurate transposition of prudential Directives is the mandate enshrined in art. 4(3) SSM R. Pursuant to such provision, the ECB is bound to apply national rules transposing Union law. This is actually the approach held for the time being by the General Court. In the recent *Corneli case*, the General Court using a rather formalistic approach implied **7.071**

held that: "*It follows from the Court's settled case-law that the obligations arising from Community directives are binding, inter alia, on bodies or entities which are subject to the authority or control of a public authority or the State*". More recently, see Court of Justice judgment case C-425/12 (*Portgás*) of 12 December 2013 (ECLI:EU:C:2013:829) at Paras. 35–36.

83 See art. 9(1) SSM R.

84 In principle, when the provisions of such a directive are clear and unconditional enough, which may be also problematic. See Banks, K. (2019).

85 For an updated overview on the current level of nationalisation of credit institutions within the Eurozone, see Véron, N. (2017). *The governance and ownership of significant euro-area banks* (No. 2017/15). Bruegel Policy Contribution, Issue no. 14, May 2017.

86 On the alternatives proposed by some relevant authors, see: Di Bucci (2018). Quelques questions concernant le contrôle juridictionnel sur le mécanisme de surveillance unique. In *Liber Amicorum Antonio Tizzano* (pp. 316–331). Torino, G. Giappichelli Editore; and Kornezov, A. (2017). The application of national law by the ECB – a maze of (un) answered questions. In *ESCB Legal Conference 2016* (pp. 260–270). Frankfurt am Main, ECB.

that, following the principle of legality, the ECB should apply national rules transposing CRD IV, even if such transposition could be held defective.[87]

7.072 The second capital reason resides in the primacy of EU Law[88] and the principle of conferral,[89] pursuant to which the action of the ECB under the SSM must not deviate from the powers conferred on it, and the check and balances of the mechanism may not be altered.[90]

7.073 The institutional set-up of the mechanism in this regard favours exploring the application of interpretative solutions aiming at ensuring compliance of national rules with the directives they should have transposed into the national legal framework.

7.074 Therefore, the main alternative seems to be making use (to the very limit) of the consistent interpretation technique or "*interprétation conforme*". Pursuant to this interpretative mechanism, when national authorities apply national rules, they must "*interpret it, so far as possible, in the light of the wording and the purpose of the directive concerned in order to achieve the result sought by the directive and consequently comply with the third paragraph of Article 288 TFEU*".[91] In a number of cases, such interpretative resource should suffice to cure ambivalent provisions or semantic ambiguities. The foregoing requires, to some extent, that the ECB makes an autonomous interpretation which, in some cases, may lead to disregarding the systematic approach of the whole national act and/or the judicial interpretation of some terms by national courts (in case they may exist[92]).

---

87 Paras. 111–112. It must be noted that this judgement is under appeal, and so it may be reverted. In any event, even if confirmed by the CJEU, it constitutes an isolated case for the moment. See Petit, C. A. and Beck, T. (2024). 10 years of Banking Union case law – how did CJEU judgments shape supervision and resolution practice in the Banking Union? Economic Governance Support Unit (EGOV). At pp. 20–21.

For an analysis of the *Corneli case,* see also: (i) Lamandini, M. & Ramos Muñoz, D. (2024). 10 years of Banking Union's case-law: How did European courts shape supervision and resolution practice in the Banking Union? Economic Governance Support Unit (EGOV); (ii) Joosen, B., Pulgar Ezquerra, J., Tröger, T. (2024). 10 years of Banking Union case law How did CJEU – judgments shape supervision and resolution practice in the Banking Union? Economic Governance Support Unit (EGOV); (iii) Gortsos, C.V. (2024). 10 years of Banking Union case-law: How did CJEU judgments shape supervision and resolution practice in the Banking Union? Economic Governance Support Unit (EGOV); (v) Lamandini, M. & Muñoz, D. R. (2024). *Finance, Law, and the Courts.* Oxford University Press; and (vi) Annunziata, F. & Braga de Arruda, T. (2023). The Corneli Case and the Application of National Law by the European Central Bank. *Bocconi Legal Studies Research Paper,* (4477503).

88 Cf Recital 34 SSM R.

89 Art. 5(1) TEU.

90 See immediately above.

91 See Court of Justice judgment in case C-282/10 (*Maribel Dominguez v Centre informatique du Centre Ouest Atlantique and Préfet de la région Centre*) of 24 January 2012 (ECLI:EU:C:2012:33), at Para. 24. See also *Corneli case* at Para. 105 and Court of Justice judgment in case C-555/07 (*Seda Kücükdeveci v Swedex GmbH & Co. KG*) of 19 January 2010 (ECLI:EU:C:2010:21), at Para. 48.

92 In General Court judgement, in case T 667/21 (*BAWAG PSK Bank v ECB*) of 28 February 2024 (ECLI:EU:T:2024:131), the court concluded that "*the interpretation of national courts is sufficient to establish*

Yet, such interpretative resource has its limits. The *first one* entails that such consistent interpretation cannot go against the written national law (*contra legem*).[93] Such interpretation must not amount to rewrite the relevant national act as it "*would undermine the national legislative process*".[94] The foregoing seems to be a hard limit, which must be respected at all costs, not to alter the *mechanism* checks and balances (in particular, its democratic legitimacy) referred above in this Section. In the *Corneli case*, the General Court clarified that any interpretation should consider the legal transposition of prudential directives (i.e., national rules to be applied). Accordingly, it is not possible to construe art. 4(3) SSM R in a way in which both directives and national rules are binding to the ECB.[95] **7.075**

The *second limit* is constituted by a minimum degree of legal certainty so as to ensure that such interpretation, conforming with the directive at stake, was foreseeable beforehand and not unexpected.[96] **7.076**

Finally, the *third limit* refers to the principle of non-retroactivity of criminal law, meaning that such consistent interpretation cannot result in aggravating (or imposing) a criminal penalty.[97] In principle, concerning administrative penalties, the powers conferred to the ECB are more restrictive than as regards *general* supervisory powers.[98] Building upon art. 18 SSM R, the only **7.077**

---

the scope of that national law where it results in a finding that it is compatible with the directive which it transposes" (Para. 58). However, when the interpretation of such national courts does not render national rules compatible with a prudential directive, the General Court is called to act like it is a national court and apply tested interpretative remedies to try to achieve the objectives pursued in that directive (at Paras. 59–62).

In the absence of such judicial interpretation, it does not seem to be an obstacle to cater for such autonomous ECB interpretations. See General Court judgment in T-712/15 (*Crédit Mutuel Arkéa v ECB*) of 13 December 2017 (ECLI:EU:T:2017:900) at Para. 132.

See also Sarmiento, D. (2019). National Law as a Point of Law in Appeals at the Court of Justice. The case of Crédit Mutuel Arkéa/ECB. *EU law live*: https://eulawlive.com/blog/2019/10/08/national-law-as-a-point-of-law-in-appeals-at-the-court-of-justice-the-case-of-credit-mutuel-arkea-ecb/.

93 See Court of Justice judgment in case C-495/19 (*Kancelaria Medius SA*) of 4 June 2020 (ECLI:EU:C:2020:431) at Paras. 49–52.

94 See opinion of AG Hogan in case C-427/19 (*Bulstrad Vienna Insurance Group AD*), delivered on 16 July 2020 (ECLI:EU:C:2020:589), at Para. 75 and cited case law in footnote 32 therein.

95 *Corneli case* at Para. 112.

96 See Court of Justice judgments in case C-526/19 (*Entoma SAS*) of 1 October 2020 (ECLI:EU:C:2020:769), at Para. 43, and in case C-268/06 (*Impact v Minister for Agriculture and Food and Others*) of 15 April 2008 (ECLI:EU:C:2008:223) at Para. 100. Similarly, see *Corneli case* at para. 112. On this topic, see Raitio, J. (2003). *The principle of legal certainty in EC law*. Kluwer Academic Publishers. See, also, Whelan, P. (2012).

97 See Court of Justice judgment in joined cases C-387/02, C-391/02 and C-403/02 (*Silvio Berlusconi and others*) of 3 May 2005 (EU:C:2005:270), Paras. 70–77. See in this regard Amtenbrink, F. (2019) at pp. 140–141.

98 See further Section C. (*Substantive law & sanctioning proceedings: issues and proposals to overcome them*) below.

situation on which the SSM may come across this limit concerns art. 18(5) SSM R. Pursuant to such provision, the ECB may request NCAs to open sanctioning proceedings to SIs (and relevant natural persons linked to them).

7.078 It is evident that consistent interpretation has its limits and may not be able to deal with manifestly wrongful transpositions. Thus, should the ECB apply national rules in breach of EU law? Art. 4(3) SSM R implies that MSs have transposed correctly the relevant prudential Directives. Consequently, and under this prism, the ECB would be only obliged to apply national law transposing correctly prudential Directives. Otherwise, it would be unconceivable that an EU institution is compelled to apply national acts in breach of Union law (even in the form of a directive). However, in the (under appeal) *Corneli case*, the General Court implied that the ECB should still apply national rules that transpose, wrongfully or incompletely, prudential directives.[99]

7.079 In these cases and notwithstanding the previous *Corneli case*, the author submits that, following the previous reasoning and CJEU doctrine, relevant national provisions must be disapplied by the ECB on its own motion.[100] This may, however, not cure the issue, particularly when the sole basis for the action of the ECB is based on a provision or set of provisions that, if disapplied, can leave the ECB action without legal basis. In such cases, one potential approach would reside in exploring the interchangeability of supervisory tools.

BOX 7.2 EXAMPLE: ADDRESSING DIVERGENCES VIA PILLAR 2

Just hypothesising: the absence of an ex ante authorisation mechanism[101] may be compensated via Pillar 2, demanding the supervisee to hold their own funds in excess to mitigate potential risks (broadly read as an activity or action of any kind) which were not subject to such *ex ante* authorisation (after assessing the given risks in the SREP). The foregoing is but a mere example, and a case-by-case approach must be necessarily followed in such cases.

7.080 As a conclusion, it can be noted that gaps and open points due to the lack or incorrect transposition of prudential Directives into the domestic framework are – and continue being in the near future – inherent to the SSM. Pursuing

99 *Corneli case* at Para. 112 and Petit, C. A. and Beck, T. (2024) at p. 20.

100 See Court of Justice judgment in joined cases C-419/18 and C-483/18 (*Profi Credit Polska S.A.*) of 7 November 2019 (ECLI:EU:C:2019:930) at Para. 76.

101 Which would be foreseen in the prudential Directive but not transposed into the domestic legislation.

the level playing field envisaged as an objective by the SSM R requires minimising such externalities. To do so, legal interpreters and mostly the ECB need to rely on existing and well-established solutions tested and approved by the CJEU (such as consistent interpretation).

Accommodating such solutions may require some ingenuity, always within the four corners of the written text of the SSM R and CJEU jurisprudence. Advocating in favour of the CJEU developing and applying a sort of exceptional jurisprudence for SSM-related matters can be appealing. Nevertheless, a cautious approach requires considering that the CJEU would be more prone to stick to its guns rather than devising a single-case exceptional doctrine. **7.081**

Additionally, promoting any remedy based on a direct application of prudential Directives to supervisees – when those cannot be considered an emanation of the state – needs to be balanced against two limits: *first*, the literal wording of art. 4(3) SSM R. Such provision demands that the ECB applies national laws (correctly) implementing Union law. **7.082**

The *second* limit relates to the constitutional set-up of the *mechanism*. The democratic legitimacy of the system would suffer if the ECB could directly apply prudential Directives. The foregoing could create an imbalance within the constitutional checks and balances of the *mechanism*, whose restrictive legal foundations were already stretchered to the maximum. And not only that but also a potential flaw in EU law may also happen, as allowing the ECB to rely on the reverse direct effect of prudential Directive would amount to allowing the Union to act via directly implementable instruments in areas where (a) it may lack exclusive competences or (b) it was judged not necessary acting via Regulations following the subsidiarity principle. **7.083**

The limited panoply of remedies available in case of non-transposition or deviant transposition may generate another undesired and Treaty-barred effect; such externality could be eventually exploited by MSs to shield certain interests. The foregoing would entail that MSs deliberately do not transpose (or deliberately delay the transposition) or wrongly transpose prudential Directive with the aim of benefiting national champions by preventing the ECB from applying certain regulatory provisions restricting their business or generating additional operational or structural costs. Such practice is susceptible of producing competitive advantages as, eventually, some supervisees would not be required to meet (nor even be compelled to comply with) those stricter prudential requirements. **7.084**

7.085 All in all, beside the *reactive remedies* depicted in this Section, there may be other *preventive* remedies aiming at ensuring greater consistency that are worth exploring. They will be referred to immediately below.

(c) Some proposals to cater for further harmonisation

7.086 In the previous Sections, it has been analysed what (some of) the issues relating to the application of national law by the ECB pursuant to the mandate enshrined in art. 4(3) SSM R are. Furthermore, some avenues to overcome the challenges in the application of national law have been also depicted. Finally, it has been argued how such avenues must find their limits in the abovementioned mandate, which, in fact, does constitute an expression of the constitutional and democratic balance upon which the SSM is erected.

7.087 Having gained awareness of the issues that the lack of harmonisation and the *chacun pour soi* approach in the transposition of prudential Directives[102] creates, this Section is aimed at depicting implementable solutions catering for further harmonisation and levelling the playing field.[103]

7.088 The obvious starting point would be joining those who demand more directly applicable Union rules (*aka* Regulations) instead of directives. This constitutes more a *desideratum* than an achievable reality. Juggling the political preferences of MSs with those of the Commission and of the members of the Parliament is always difficult. Shifting towards Regulations *solely*, when it comes to regulating the financial sector, does not seem to happen any time in the near future. Not to mention that the foregoing would need to comply with the principle of subsidiarity,[104] and hence, there should be enough justifications that the objectives of the EU action cannot be sufficiently achieved at a national level.

7.089 Linked to the above, limiting the number of options and discretions in future pieces of legislation (both directives and regulations) does not seem to be an implementable option. As indicated somewhere in Part I,[105] they were the result of high-level political compromise, and one may argue that it would be rather difficult to sketch a compromise in this regard. Beside such political constrains, there may be other constrains of constitutional nature. In this

102 Or going way beyond what the *minimum harmonisation* directive prescribed. See Section A.2.(b). (*When does national law transpose a Directive?*) above.

103 See, in this regard, Arranz, L. (2017) and Banks, K. (2019).

104 Art. 5 TEU and Protocol 2 to the TFEU.

105 See Section B.1.(b). (*CRR and CRD IV: Options and discretions*) in Chapter 2.

regard, the BverfG's judgment on the Banking Union[106] in its Para. 212 insists on the fact that the application of the options exercised by national parliaments by the ECB acts as a counterweight to the discretion granted to the ECB when adopting supervisory decisions. This (together with other factors[107]) ensures sufficient democratic accountability and legitimacy. The lack of one of such levers may be compensated by the others, but the overall equilibrium may be affected. In that case, one would need to reassess the checks and balances granted to the ECB as regards its legitimacy and democratic accountability. Such reassessment should be done to determine if a minimum equilibrium is still maintained, or other levers would need to be added to compensate (e.g., attributing a greater role to the ABoR[108]).

More realistically, what could be done is exploring the possibility of enhancing maximum harmonisation concerning prudential Directives. Subject to the conduct of a subsidiarity and proportionality test, ensuring level playing field within the SSM seems to demand a more uniform approach, at least regarding SIs, which group the majority of assets and liabilities within the mechanism.[109] **7.090**

Additionally, advancing towards further harmonisation is possible by using binding and non-binding instruments addressed to NCAs. As regards the first group, pursuant to arts. 6(5)(a) and 6(5)(c) SSM R, the ECB can use the possibility of issuing binding guidelines guiding the action of NCAs (as regards the supervision of LSIs). This option has already been exercised, for instance, as regards the use of options and discretions, ensuring a minimum harmonisation **7.091**

106 BVerfG's judgment of 30 July 2019 (2 BvR 1685/14, 2 BvR 2631/14). A partial version translated into English can be accessed here: https://www.bundesverfassungsgericht.de/SharedDocs/Entscheidungen/EN/2019/07/rs20190730_2bvr168514en.html;jsessionid=2A05FF166B43919DB70531AE5216416B.2_cid386. See also, in this regard, Annunziata, F., Lamandini, M. & Ramos Muñoz, D. (2020). Weiss and EU Union Banking Law. A Test for the Fundamental Principles of the Treaty. *EBI Working Paper Series* 2020 – no. 67.

107 Such is the appointment of the members of the ECB decision-making bodies [sic] and the fact that the ECB is bound by primary Union law when implementing the SSM (e.g., the principles of conferral and proportionality).

108 Lamandini, M. & Ramos Muñoz, D. (2019). Appeal bodies of EU financial regulatory agencies: are we where we should be? In *ECB Legal Conference 2019. Building bridges: central banking law in an interconnected world* (pp. 384–399). Frankfurt am Main, ECB; and Morra, C. B., Smits, R. & Magliari, A. (2017). The administrative board of review of the European Central Bank: experience after 2 years. *European Business Organization Law Review, 18*(3), pp. 567–589.

109 The foregoing without disregarding the interplay with the principle of proportionality and the respect to the different business models of capital importance concerning LSIs (art. 1 SSM R). In this regard, ensuring that such a proportionality principle is observed at a regulatory and enforcement level may demand the creation of a tailor-made regime for LSIs. See Joosen, B., Lamandini, M., Lehmann, M., Lieverse, K. & Tirado, I. (2018). See also Section B. (*SSM basic principles: level playing field & proportionality*) in Chapter 1.

in the use of options and discretions concerning LSIs and SIs. The second option entails making use of a wide variety of internal[110] and external non-binding instruments, which include guides, policy stances, supervisory expectations and even public consultations as regards certain topics. Resource to both sets of instruments should be exercised to ensure wider consistency on the methodological and on the supervisory outcome all across the SSM but also between LSIs and SIs.[111] Considering the impact on the supervisees of any of the two types of measures (mostly indirectly), its publication (if so applicable) and implementation should be subject to broader *vacatio legis* terms. The foregoing, in order not to frustrate or affect the principle of legitimate expectations and leave enough time to the supervisees to consider the strategies and resources to deal with them.

7.092 Building upon the constitutional basis of art. 114 TFEU, some authors have proposed exploring the possibility of replicating the SRM Regulation approach and endorsing a sort of *SSM substantive set of rules*.[112] Although appealing, the proposal does not seem to fully align with the SSM constitutional basis, the SSM R mandate to apply national rules and the rationale of the mechanism (including the conception of *single market*).

7.093 First, bearing in mind that the SSM is built upon the *enabling* clause,[113] it seems difficult to combine such basis with an *ad hoc* regulation to be applied by the ECB under the SSM. The situation is far from being equivalent to transform the ECB into a *NCA* by substitution (as regards the specific supervisory powers which are vested under SSM R[114]). From the perspective of the checks and balances of the SSM, it seems indeed difficult to elude the mandate contained in art. 4(3) SSM R, which commands the ECB to apply national law. As indicated somehow above,[115] it is debatable whether (a) this could actually be done and (b) if so, what the implications on the whole SSM architecture would be, as this would create an imbalance in the democratic legitimacy equilibrium.

---

110 Internal-working documents drafted commonly (or at least in cooperation) between the ECB and the NCAs with the aim of determining common working approaches. In principle, those documents are not published or made available to the public, even if in certain cases it is not totally clear whether they may produce legal effects (even indirectly) on the supervisees, which would make their publication desirable in the light of the principle of transparency (and eventually due process rights).

111 To the extent that this is compliant with the principle of proportionality and respectful with the different business models existing across participating MSs.

112 See, basically, Arranz, L. (2017).

113 Art. 127(6) TFEU. See Section A. (*Constitutional constrains of the enabling clause*) in Chapter 2.

114 See Amtenbrink, F. (2019) at. p. 141.

115 In this Section but also in the previous one.

Finally, from the perspective of the mechanism, it must be recalled that what it could make sense under the SRM R, in the light of the absence of directly applicable union rules,[116] does not seem to follow the rationale of the SSM. Whereas the SRM lacked such directly applicable Union rules, the existence of CRR ensures a *corpus* of directly applicable rules. There was already a detailed set of directly applicable union rules regarding banking supervision (CRR) that the ECB could apply. The application of national rules transposing prudential Directives would help, then, to complement the democratic and legitimacy foundations on which the SSM was erected. **7.094**

B. THE ADMINISTRATIVE PROCEDURAL LAW APPLIED BY ECB

Applying the material rules the ECB is bound to apply pursuant to art. 4(3) SSM R requires appropriate procedures[117] and a *critical mass* of procedural rules. For the moment, there is not a single Regulation or equivalent legal text crystallising the administrative procedural *acquis* to be applied uniformly by all EU Institutions and bodies in direct administration.[118] Despite the EP having called towards this direction,[119] very little progress has been made. **7.095**

EU administrative procedural law is a patchwork formed from elements coming from multiple sources.[120] Quoting the EP's words: "*existing rules and principles on good administration are scattered across a wide variety of sources: primary law, case-law of the Court of Justice of the European Union, secondary legislation, soft law and unilateral commitments by the Union's institutions*".[121] **7.096**

---

116 Being the BRRD, the main instrument guiding the resolution of credit institutions within the Union, the SRB would lack the rules to be directly applicable by itself. Such circumstance would indeed hamper the application of a uniform resolution framework (not to mention that it would be rather paradoxical). To remedy this circumstance, the SRM R contains a set of rules to be applicable directly by the SRM as regards the participating member states. Such rules, as one can imagine, do constitute a kind of transposition of a Union level of some of the rules established in the BRRD.

117 See Chapter 8 (*Distinguishing between supervisory and sanctioning procedures. Is it possible?*) below and Chapter 14 (*Supervisory procedures: common procedures*) and Chapter 15 (*Sanctioning procedures*).

118 I.e., in procedures directly managed by the respective EU body or Institution.

119 Cf EP resolution of 15 January 2013 with recommendations to the Commission on a Law of Administrative Procedure of the European Union ((2012/2024(INL)). See also, Galetta, D-U, Hofmann, H. C., Mir Puigpelat, O. & Ziller, J. (2015). The General Principles of EU Administrative Procedural Law In-depth Analysis. European Parliament, Brussels.

120 See Craig, P. (2018) at p. 246.

121 See footnote 119.

7.097 Depicting, then, the rules to be applied by the ECB when dealing with SSM procedures (under direct administration[122]) requires looking at the different sources available and, in particular, to the secondary law which allocates the specific supervisory competences on the ECB.[123] This is precisely the aim of this Section. First, (a) it will be examined what the sources that nourish EU administrative procedural law are. Second, (b) it will be assessed what rules and principles must, indeed, the ECB apply. In particular, it will be examined whether national procedural rules must be applied and, if so, to what extent.

1. The sources of administrative procedural law for the ECB under the SSM

7.098 Principles (and rules)[124] of EU administrative law can be traced from a wide variety of EU law sources, including, for the purpose of this analysis, SSM secondary legislation. Following a top-down sequence, it seems appropriate starting from primary law sources, ending with those having the lesser binding character (self-regulation or soft law instruments).

7.099 As regards *primary law*, we can find some principles of administrative procedural law distributed within the Treaties. Among them, those having, in the view of the author, interest for the supervisory and sanctioning proceedings handled by the ECB are: the principle of transparency,[125] the principle of openness[126] (as regards the SSM administrative structure), the due process principle,[127] the principle of proportionality[128] and the duty to state reasons.[129]

7.100 The Charter, which has the same value as the Treaties,[130] also contemplates some relevant administrative procedural principles to which the ECB

---

122 Which would exclude those supervisory procedures – or part of them – which fall under the entire remit of NCAs (e.g., direct supervision of LSIs).

123 On this matter see Wojcik, K-P (2017). Primary law requirements for administrative procedures in the case-law of the court of justice. In *ESCB Legal Conference 2016* (pp. 211–220). Frankfurt am Main, ECB. See also Lackhoff, K. (2017)(i) at pp. 107 and ss.

124 The *Dworkinian* distinction here does not matter: See Dworkin, R. (2013); and Galetta, D-U., Hofmann, H. C., Mir Puigpelat, O. & Ziller, J. (2015).

125 Arts. 11 and 15 TFEU.

126 Art. 1 and 10 TEU.

127 Or *rule of law* principle, contemplated in art. 2 TEU.

128 Art. 5 TEU, in connection with the principle of conferral art. 5 TFEU.

129 Art. 296 TFEU.

130 Pursuant to article 6 TEU.

must abide.[131] These include right to good administration,[132] right of access to documents,[133] the right to an effective remedy and to a fair trial,[134] the presumption of innocence,[135] the legality principle[136] and the *ne bis in idem* principle.[137]

The CJEU has also derived many administrative principles, from constitutional traditions common to MSs.[138] These principles (and, in general, principles of EU law) must be applied even in the absence of rules as pure principles guiding the judicial and administrative action of EU bodies and institutions.[139] **7.101**

Secondary legislation may contain detailed or general principles and administrative procedural rules to be applied by EU bodies and Institutions.[140] In particular, as regards the SSM, the SSM R and the SSM Fr contain multiple procedural administrative rules and principles.[141] The basic anchor for these procedural rules is contained in article 22 SSM R, which frames the basic principle of *due process*, which includes, based on this provision, the right to be heard, the right to access files and the duty to state reasons (motivation). **7.102**

131 See Hofmann, H. C. & Mihaescu, C. (2013). The relation between the charter's fundamental rights and the unwritten general principles of EU law: good administration as the test case. *European Constitutional Law Review*, *9*(1), pp. 73–101, and Hofmann, H. C. (2014). General Principles of EU law and EU administrative law. *European Union Law*, pp. 196–225.

132 Art. 41 of the Charter.

133 Art. 42 Charter. Understood in a broad way as the right to access documents produced by EU bodies and institutions and not only to those pertaining to a file in which the requester may have a direct interest. See, in this regard, the Regulation 1049/2001 regarding public access to the European Parliament, Council and Commission documents and, specifically regarding the ECB, the Decision of the European Central Bank of 4 March 2004 on public access to European Central Bank documents (ECB/2004/3) (applicable also to NCBs and NCAs).

134 Art. 47 of the Charter.

135 Art. 48 of the Charter. This principle would also include the right not to incriminate oneself. Cf Recital 25 of Directive 2016/343 on the strengthening of certain aspects of the presumption of innocence and of the right to be present at the trial in criminal proceedings.

136 Art. 49 of the Charter.

137 Art. 50 of the Charter.

138 Cf art. 6(3) TEU and 52(3) of the Charter. See Court of Justice judgment in cases C-663/17 P, C-665/17 P and C-669/17 P (*Trasta Komercbanka AS*) of 5 November 2019 (ECLI:EU:C:2019:923), at Para. 55.

139 See Court of Justice judgment joined cases C-48/90 and C-66/90 (*the Netherlands, and others v Commission*) of 12 February 1992 (ECLI:EU:C:1992:63), Paras. 37 and 44. See Wojcik, K-P. (2017).

140 One may note that there is no closed list of those principles and there is, in principle, no hierarchy between them because of their source of origin (e.g., Primary law based, enshrined in the Charter, derived by the CJEU from the constitutional traditions of MSs, etc.). Cf Galetta, D-U., Hofmann, H. C., Mir Puigpelat, O. & Ziller, J. (2015).

141 See Lackhoff, K. (2017)(i) and Lackhoff, K. (2017). The SSM Framework regulation as a source of ECB administrative procedural Law. In *ESCB Legal Conference 2016* (pp. 202–211). Frankfurt am Main, ECB [Lackhoff, K. (2017)(ii)].

7.103 One thing to be observed is that the first paragraph of this provision extends these procedural rules to supervisory decisions, as comprised in art. 4 and Section 2 of Chapter III of the SSM R, which would expressly cover the administrative penalties contemplated in art. 18 SSM R.[142] One thing to note is that the second sub-paragraph of art. 22(1) SSM R seems to imply that, in case of urgency, the persons (entities) concerned may be deprived from the right to be heard. This exception, as clarified later on in the SSM Fr,[143] does not apply to sanctioning proceedings as (i) by definition, there is no such urgency (as damage to the financial system may not be directly corrected by means of the imposition of an administrative penalty to an entity) and (ii) this would be contrary to the rights of defence of the persons concerned, which are specially reinforced in sanctioning procedures, in particular those having a criminal nature.[144]

BOX 7.3 ADMINISTRATIVE PROCEDURAL RULES AND THE SSM: DEPICTING SOME SOURCES

Beside this provision, other procedural administrative rules are scattered around the SSM R. For instance, rules on cooperation and exchange of information,[145] rules on (non-binding) administrative review[146] and detailed rules on how to conduct the so-called common procedures.[147]

These rules are expanded, completed and detailed in the SSM Fr.[148] Arts. 25 to 38 comprise a broad set of administrative procedural rules and principles (procedural guarantees if one may prefer to name it in such way).[149] On top of these basic common rules, additional detailed administrative procedural rules may be found enshrined in the common procedures,[150] in close cooperation procedures[151] and in sanctioning procedures[152] (and even beyond).

142 Understood as such administrative penalties that the ECB is directly entitled to impose itself. See Section C. (*Allocation of sanctioning competences: a specialty over the general rule?*) in Chapter 6.

143 See art. 31(6) SSM Fr.

144 See Chapter 8. (*Distinguishing between supervisory and sanctioning procedures. Is it possible?*) below.

145 Arts. 3, 17 and 27 SSM R.

146 Art. 24 SSM R.

147 Art. 14, 15 and 17 SSM R.

148 See, for an almost article by article analysis, Lackhoff, K. (2017)(i). Particularly as regards the right to be heard see Kaufhold, A-K. (2022). Art. 22 SSMR Due process for adopting supervisory decisions. In *European banking union: Brussels commentary* (pp. 307–318). Baden-Baden: Nomos.

149 These are integrated in Titles 2 (*General provisions relating to due process for adopting ECB supervisory decisions*) and 3 (*Reporting of breaches*) of Part III (*General provisions applying to the operation of the SSM*) of the SSM Fr.

150 Arts. 73 and ss. SSM Fr.

151 Arts. 109 and ss. SSM Fr.

152 Arts. 120 and ss. SSM Fr.

Additionally, it is fair to say that the ECB is bound by the EU administrative procedural principles mentioned herein and, consequently, not by national administrative rules and principles. However, considering that the ECB must apply, pursuant to art. 4(3) SSM R, national rules transposing directives and/or exercising options and discretions allocated to MSs,[153] it is arguable if (and to which extent) it may apply national prudential administrative rules that, for this purpose, can be identified with substantive rules.

Also, additional secondary legislation rules, to be applied by the ECB in the context of the SSM, may be found outside the SSM/SSM FR binomial. For instance, the rules of procedure relating to the administrative review performed by the ABoR.[154]

Private or agreed arrangements may be also a source of administrative procedural rules. For instance, as regards the SSM, art. 24(2) SSM Fr[155] provides for the possibility for the supervisees to agree on the use of an official language regarding supervisory communications. This agreement, making use of the possibility foreseen in this provision, constitutes the actual source of procedural rules. Such arrangements may be as simple or as refined as the parties may agree.[156]

For example, fit-and-proper proceedings may be agreed to be held in the language of the place of incorporation of the supervised entity whereas SREP review and/or authorisation-related communications may be held in English (to facilitate communication to shareholders and/or to address publication obligations under capital markets regulations).

Finally, soft law[157] (in whatever form) may also create procedural administrative rules for EU bodies and institutions. This would especially be the case when an EU body has decided to commit itself to respect or abide by a certain piece of soft law.[158] We can find several examples of administrative procedural principles in the non-binding instruments issued by the ECB. 7.104

For example, in the ECB supervisory, expectations periodically disclosed[159] and applied individually to each supervised entity. Also, relevant guides may 7.105

153 See Section A. (*The substantive rules applied by the ECB under the* SSM) above.

154 Decision (EU) 2019/1378 of the European Central Bank of 9 August 2019, amending Decision ECB/2014/16 concerning the establishment of an Administrative Board of Review and its Operating Rules (ECB/2019/27) and also the Methodology for the apportionment of the costs of the review incurred by the applicant and by the European Central Bank in the context of a review by the Administrative Board (OJ 28.8.2019; L 224/11).

155 Lackhoff also extends this possibility to communicate with the persons referred to in art. 10(2) SSM R regarding investigatory proceedings. This conclusion is reached because of the lack of rules in this regard and, furthermost, because the legal principle which establishes that upon agreement cannot exist under any violation (*volenti non fit inuiria*). See. Lackhoff, K. (2017)(i) at p. 244.

156 In principle, the initiative and settling power is given to the supervisee (and/or the natural person subject to ECB supervisory proceedings). However, final acknowledgement is required from the ECB side, so it is fair to say that these arrangements are bilateral. Also, ECB must still control that the limits established by art. 24(1) SSM Fr are respected (e.g., communications taking place in one of the official languages of the EU and no other languages).

157 See, on this matter, Sarmiento, D. (2008). *El "soft law" administrativo: un estudio de los efectos jurídicos de las normas no vinculantes de la Administración*. Thomson Civitas.

158 This proves to be especially true when the EU body has generated a legitimate expectation for the administrative subjects, who reasonable expect the respective body to behave in such a given manner.

159 For example, ECB *Communication on supervisory coverage expectations for NPEs*: https://www.bankingsupervision.europa.eu/press/letterstobanks/shared/pdf/2019/ssm.supervisory_coverage_expectations_for_NPEs_201908.en.pdf.

define further, in broad, administrative procedural rules. A clear example would be the *Guide to fit and proper assessments*,[160] which defines and emphasises the principle of due process and fairness in Chapter 3 (Principle 4).

7.106 Or even ECB recommendations may contain procedural administrative rules to be taken into due consideration.

BOX 7.4 EXAMPLE: ECB RECOMENDATIONS AND PROCEDURAL ADMINISTRATIVE RULES

Just citing an example, it is worth mentioning the ECB recommendation on dividend distributions during the COVID-19 pandemic and repealing Recommendation ECB/2020/19, which are embedded in the principle of *complain or explain* with regulatory guidance, enshrined in the EBA Regulation.[161]

2. Administrative procedural rules (and principles) to be applied by the ECB: a general overview and particular analysis of procedural rules contained in national law transposing prudential Directives

7.107 When the ECB deals with supervisory and sanctioning proceedings under direct administration, it must be subject to the EU legal framework. This preliminary *intuition* stands to be true even when the ECB may apply *national* administrative procedural law enshrined in the O&Ds legislatively exercised by MSs or national rules transposing prudential Directives (as it does in a derivative way, obeying an EU law mandate).

7.108 A more detailed assessment of the SSM R definitely points towards this direction. First, art. 4(3) SSM R (and also art. 9(1)) refers to *Union law* as the basic framework to be applied by the ECB. Second, one may also recall that Recital 34 SSM R emphasises the primacy of Union, outlining that the ECB must base its decisions on and act in accordance with "*the relevant Union Law*". Third, the specific provision relating to the due process included in the SSM R (art. 22) aims at constituting a standard itself; hence, one may argue that, when construed, this must be done in accordance with EU law. Also, and more importantly, it must be noted, when enunciating the due process principles applicable to supervisory decisions, that there is no express mandate

160 See *Guide to fit and proper assessments (December 2021)*: https://www.bankingsupervision.europa.eu/ecb/pub/pdf/ssm.fit_and_proper_guide_update202112~d66f230eca.en.pdf.

161 Typically applicable to NCAs. Cf art. 16(3) EBA Regulation.

to consider national procedural rules. The application of national rules seems therefore to be confined to those presenting a substantive or material nature.

Having said that, the question is whether there is any case in which the ECB must apply national administrative procedural rules and, in the affirmative, to what extent. **7.109**

In the view of the author, this would be the case at least when the ECB is obliged to apply national law pursuant to art. 4(3) SSM R; that is, national rules transposing EU law[162] and national law exercising options and discretions allocated to MSs.[163] This would include the specific procedural rules contained in those pieces of national legislation and/or the relevant time lapses but not the principles of procedural national rules. In addition, it would be arguable that the ECB would have to apply national case law construing certain procedural provisions.[164] Compliance with the principle of level playing field and the need to ensure a coherent supervision seems to favour that the ECB must not be bound by national case law.[165] In addition, it is relevant to emphasise that such national law is applied by ministry of an EU law mandate and, consequently, in a derivative manner. **7.110**

The most relevant cases of such application relate to (a) notifications and (b) time lapses to exercise a given power (generally of approval). **7.111**

(a) As regards the former, one may note that national administrative provisions transposing CRD IV, when defining the need to notify a given supervisory decision, may enunciate such obligation – or construe such administrative duty – in the light of national law. Arts. 93(1) SSM Fr supports this approach by implying that decisions, regarding fit and proper need to be notified in accordance with national law[166] (and within the period established in such an act[167]).
(b) Regarding the deadlines to take relevant decisions, one may challenge its procedural nature as the lapse of the relevant deadline would deprive the prudential supervisor[168] from the opportunity to exercise its powers. Hence, they would present a material nature and would need to be considered as substantive rules and applied as such.

---

162 Including those national rules that allocated powers in addition to the minimum required by prudential Directives but that can be considered as a transposition of EU rules. See Section A.2.(b). (*When does national law transpose a Directive?*) above.

163 Which, as indicated above, would exclude national legislation gold-plating options granted to NCAs. See Section A.2.(a). (*Gold-plating national options and discretions*) above.

164 Arranz, L. (2017).

165 See, further, Section B. (*Judicial review in composite procedures: the CJEU's Berlusconi-Fininvest case law in perspective*) in Chapter 12.

166 See Lackhoff, K. (2017)(i) at p. 244.

167 In the same vein and regarding the acquisition of qualifying holdings, see art. 85(3) SSM Fr.

168 The ECB as regards SIs or the NCAs as regards LSIs.

7.112 The SSM Fr has showed a particular sensitivity towards this feature, depicting these types of rules as truly material rules to be applied by the ECB.[169] This is particularly clear as regards the deadline to notify the approval (or rejection) of applications to take up the business of credit institutions. Here, art. 73(2) SSM Fr imposes on the relevant NCA the duty to notify the time limit within which the decision on the application has to be taken "in accordance with the relevant national law".

C. SUBSTANTIVE LAW & SANCTIONING PROCEEDINGS: ISSUES AND PROPOSALS TO OVERCOME THEM

7.113 Besides the application of national law by the ECB when conducting specific supervisory tasks, there is also a close interconnection between the sanctioning powers attributed to the ECB and the national statutes transposing the prudential supervision directives.

7.114 This phenomenon also constitutes a novelty,[170] making ECB sanctioning powers eventually dependent on the availability of sanctioning tools under relevant national law. This arrangement stands far away from the classical administrative punitive law schemes, where a *sole* authority was empowered to sanction breaches under the sole basis of *its* (European or national) law. The legal framework set forth in the SSM R is singular and sometimes falls outside the classical dogmatic categories provided by the European and/or administrative law. Consequently, new approaches and new categories should be defined to properly address the particularities of this new scheme.[171]

7.115 Along this Section, (i) the interplay between national rules and ECB sanctioning powers to impose administrative pecuniary penalties pursuant to art.

169 See arts. 73(2), 85(3), 93(1) and 94 SSM Fr.

170 It is, in fact, a novelty introduced by the SSM. Direct reliance of the powers of the ECB on national law of member states and, in some cases, application of the choices introduced by national law constitute an absolute novelty. However, interaction between EU Agencies and member states, based on national law, was not absolutely unknown in the Union. In this regard, WITTE points that the execution of EU law was not unknown for the ESAs. For example, the EBA could give instructions addressed to MSs in case an emergency situation arose (art. 18 EBA Regulation) or to settle a dispute between national authorities in a binding manner (art. 19 EBA Regulation). See Witte, A. (2014) at pp. 89–109.

171 Some scholars have called to explore new approaches to further develop the implementation of the SSM legal environment, especially in connection with the reliance of the action of the ECB on domestic law.
In this vein see Smits, R. (2017). Competences and alignment in an emerging future after L-Bank: how the Eurosystem and the Single Supervisory Mechanism may develop. *Ademu Working Paper Series*, WP 2017/077. The author emphasises in this paper the necessity of developing new tools to foster the applicability of the regime established in the SSM and enhance its capacity.

18(1) SSM R will be examined. As it will be assessed, national rules transposing prudential Directives (*a*) constitute an element that enables the ECB to make use of foregoing powers and (*b*) may condition the way such penalties are imposed (narrowing or enlarging ECB sanctioning powers in this regard). In addition, (ii) some additional references will be made to the extent of the instructions that the ECB may address to the NCA in order to open sanctioning proceedings under art. 18(5) SSM R.

1. National laws and administrative pecuniary penalties I: to which extent national legislation may limit ECB direct sanctioning powers under art. 18(1) SSM R

(a) Introduction

National law transposing prudential Directives raises some issues concerning ECB sanctioning powers. For example, some transitional issues may arise, regarding the possibility to impose penalties on SIs pursuant to art. 18(1) SSM R or to initiate a sanctioning proceeding by a NCA, at the request of the ECB (art. 18(5) SSM R), in cases where prudential Directives were not transposed in due time, wrongly transposed or transposed with variations. **7.116**

Also, it is worth considering whether the SSM structure aims at establishing a system where credit institutions are subject to different levels of punitive measures, based on its "*nationality*". The answer seems negative.[172] These issues are not purely theoretical but, rather, practical, since they may affect the procedural safeguards of the persons involved in sanctioning proceedings arising from the SSM framework, and they may even impact the competition between SIs.[173] **7.117**

These concerns lead to important questions, such as: can art. 18(1) SSM R be interpreted in a manner that ensures its compatibility with basic procedural safeguards of sanctioning proceedings and with the level playing field (equivalence) principle? And also, can the national transposition[174] of the sanctioning provisions set forth in CRD IV modulate the punitive pressure that may be **7.118**

172 See, further, the analysis in Section B. (*SSM basic principles: level playing field & proportionality*) in Chapter 1. As indicated, the answer must be negative, as level playing field (equivalence) has been identified as one of the top principles guiding the application of the SSM R.

173 SIs subject, eventually, to a lesser sanctioning pressure may enjoy a distinctive advantage. They would have, in principle, an incentive to perform riskier conducts, eventually resulting in breach of directly applicable EU rules as the consequences of a breach would be economically (not reputationally) less severe. This creates, indirectly, a dangerous regulatory arbitrage that the SSM R aims to prevent (cf art. 1.I SSM R).

174 Or by delaying the transposition in breach of the obligation imposed under EU law.

exercised by ECB on SIs pursuant to art. 18(1) SSM R? What are the limits of that potential modulation?

7.119 Using these questions as a starting point, it is possible to construe a coherent approach from a twofold perspective: (i) first, according to the systematic purposes of the SSM R and (ii) secondly, attending to the general principles embedded in the Union Law.

7.120 Pursuant to this approach, the right place to start is the text of the provisions themselves – in particular, art. 18(1) of SSM R.[175] This paragraph allocates to the ECB the direct powers to sanction SIs for breaches of directly applicable EU law.[176] This paragraph delimits the kind of breaches that fall within the remit of the ECB sanctioning powers: breaches of directly applicable Union Law "*in relation to which administrative pecuniary penalties shall be made available to competent authorities under the relevant Union law*" (and committed by SIs – emphasis added).

7.121 Further, and as a necessary complement to ensure an adequate level playing field, Para. 5 of this art. 18 provides that the ECB (acting under its sole and exclusive competency) may require NCAs to initiate sanctioning proceedings (governed by the national law of the required NCA).[177] Having resource to art. 18(5) SSM R allows to somehow overcome ECB statutory limitations relating to the impossibility of imposing non-pecuniary penalties and not being able to punish natural persons.[178]

175 Which reads as follows: "*1. For the purpose of carrying out the tasks conferred on it by this Regulation, where credit institutions, financial holding companies, or mixed financial holding companies, intentionally or negligently, breach a requirement under relevant directly applicable acts of Union law in relation to which administrative pecuniary penalties shall be made available to competent authorities under the relevant Union law, the ECB may impose administrative pecuniary penalties of up to twice the amount of the profits gained or losses avoided because of the breach where those can be determined, or up to 10 % of the total annual turnover, as defined in relevant Union law, of a legal person in the preceding business year or such other pecuniary penalties as may be provided for in relevant Union law*".

176 See Section C. (*Allocation of sanctioning competences: a specialty over the general rule?*) in Chapter 6.

177 This provision reads as follows: "*5. In the cases not covered by paragraph 1 of this Article, where necessary for the purpose of carrying out the tasks conferred on it by this Regulation, the ECB may require national competent authorities to open proceedings with a view to taking action in order to ensure that appropriate penalties are imposed in accordance with the acts referred to in the first subparagraph of Article 4(3) and any relevant national legislation which confers specific powers which are currently not required by Union law. The penalties applied by national competent authorities shall be effective, proportionate and dissuasive*".

178 See Section C. (*Allocation of sanctioning competences: a specialty over the general rule?*) in Chapter 6.

(b) Exploring the limits of article 18(1) SSM R: is there any interpretation that can ensure a minimum level playing field? Possible interpretations of article 18(1) SSM R

Art. 18(1) SSM R confers on the ECB the possibility of imposing administrative pecuniary penalties for breaches of directly applicable EU acts "*in relation to which administrative pecuniary penalties shall be made available to competent authorities under the relevant Union law*". 7.122

This wording implies a sort of acquiescence for the ECB, allowing it to act when pecuniary penalties have been made available to competent authorities under Union Law. The issue strives in how to construe the term "made available". Two interpretations are possible: 7.123

The first one would follow the literal wording of this provision. According to such literal interpretation, the ECB could impose administrative pecuniary penalties on SIs only if the national law has provided for the possibility of sanctioning the breaches allegedly committed. *Made available* would then mean that penalties have to be contemplated under national law.[179] 7.124

Under this understanding, ensuring that the ECB can use the sanctioning powers provided for in art. 18(1) SSM R would require that MSs have transposed the provisions settled in CRD IV (specially in its arts. 66 and 67 CRD IV[180]), which refer to material breaches of requirements foreseen in CRR. These provisions include a minimum set of punishable infringements, which can be found in the first paragraphs of articles 66[181] and 67.[182] These infringements relate mainly to (i) severe infringements regarding the authorisation regime to take up the business of credit institutions (e.g., initiating the activity of credit institutions without being duly authorised),[183] (ii) the assessment 7.125

179 It is worth noting that those *administrative pecuniary penalties* are the ones that need to be made available. This is because the referred provision only speaks about them and not about *penalties* in general. Hence, if only non-pecuniary penalties are foreseen in the relevant national law, the ECB could not sanction the alleged breach of directly applicable Union rules.

180 References to art. 66 and 67 CRD IV are made to the latest wording given by Directive 2024/1619 (CRD VI), in force from 9 July 2024 (for the majority of its provisions) and due to be transposed by 10 January 2026, with some exceptions (i.e., some provisions are expected to be transposed by July 2026 or even January 2027).

See, also, art. 65 CRD IV which contemplates (i) the interplay between administrative penalties and criminal offences of banking regulation provisions, (ii) the subjects that can be sanctioned (Paras. (2) and (4)) and (iii) the scope of the investigatory powers necessary to exercise such sanctioning powers (Para. 4, cf arts. 10–13 SSM R).

181 Concerning the acquisition and disposal of qualifying holdings and the requirements for acquisitions or divestiture of material holdings, material transfers of assets and liabilities, mergers, or divisions.

182 Which relates to the most basic infringements of CRD IV and CRR.

183 Art. 66(1)(a) CRD IV.

of the acquisition (and disposal) of qualifying holdings[184] and (iii) a wide set of breaches related to the prudential basic requirements stated in CRR (e.g., exceeding the thresholds for large exposures foreseen in art. 395 of CRR[185]).

7.126 For the foregoing breaches (when committed by legal persons), CRD IV requires MSs to contemplate minimum penalties of up to 10% of the offender's annual turnover[186] or twice of the amount of the profits gained or losses avoided.[187]

7.127 However, MSs can define other infringements different from those contemplated in the mentioned arts. 66(1) and 67(1) CRD IV.[188] For those infringements, not subject to the minimum harmonisation rules established in CRD IV, MSs could contemplate different caps (in principle, lower than those referred to in the preceding paragraph). It follows from the foregoing that the possibility for the ECB to impose administrative pecuniary penalties would depend on whether the respective MSs would have foreseen such breaches (and the caps for such penalties would be those foreseen under national law, which would make them *available*[189]).

7.128 The previous interpretation, in some way, makes the ECB's direct sanctioning powers dependent on the national laws. These national laws can expand or constrain the scope of the ECB sanctioning powers.

7.129 The second interpretation of Para. 1 of art. 18 SSM R entails an autonomous understanding of the availability of such penalties under Union law, delinking them from national transposition or implementation.

7.130 Hence, it is possible to argue that, since art. 67(2)(a) CRD IV envisages that certain administrative pecuniary penalties[190] are applied for, at least, certain

---

184 Art. 66(1)(d) CRD IV.

185 Art. 67(1)(g) CRD IV.

186 Arts. 66(2)(a)(i) and 67(2)(a)(i) CRD IV.

187 Arts. 66(2)(a)(iii) and 67(2)(a)(iii) CRD IV.

188 In fact the first Para. of arts. 66 and 67 would enunciate the material breaches for which administrative penalties, periodic penalty payments and other administrative measures should apply.

189 As indicated above, a minimum set of infringements are foreseen in arts. 66(1) and 67(1) of CRD IV, for which administrative pecuniary penalties would be capped pursuant to arts. 66(2)(a)(i) and (ii) and 67(a)(i) and (iii) CRD IV.

190 Those pecuniary penalties are mirrored in art. 18(1) SSM R. Sub-Paras. (i) and (iii) of art. 67(2)(a) read as follows:

> *"(a) administrative penalties:*
>
> *(i) in the case of a legal person, administrative pecuniary penalties of up to 10 % of the total annual net turnover of the undertaking;*
>
> (...)

infringements established in art. 67(1) would have been made available under Union law to the ECB, and it could sanction those infringements of directly applicable EU rules (i.e., CRR provisions[191]). The same reasoning would apply as regards the infringement included in art. 66(1)(b) CRD IV,[192] for which the administrative pecuniary penalties set forth in art. 66(2)(a)[193] are foreseen.

This second interpretation makes the ECB direct sanctioning powers under art. 18(1) SSM R less dependent upon national rules, rendering the exercise of the specific supervisory tasks conferred on the ECB more autonomous, enhancing the achievement of the level playing field.[194] However, this construction is subject to a number of arguments in favour and against, which are systematised below. **7.131**

Additionally, one may note that, for those infringements of CRR not listed in arts. 67(1)[195] and 66(1)(b) CRR, the possibility for the ECB to apply administrative pecuniary penalties is subject to the availability of penalties[196] under national law (and the first interpretation depicted at the beginning of this Section would apply).[197] **7.132**

(iii) administrative pecuniary penalties of up to twice the amount of the profits gained or losses avoided because of the breach, where those profits gained or losses avoided can be determined".

191 It must be noted that art. 67(1) CRD IV also contemplates infringements of CRD IV (e.g., indents (b), (c), (d) and (t)) which, in principle, would not constitute directly applicable Union law as national transposition would be required.

192 "*(b) at least one of the activities referred to in Article 4(1), point (1)(b), of Regulation (EU) No 575/2013 is carried out by an entity that meets the threshold indicated in that point and that is not authorised as a credit institution, except for entities requesting the waiver under Article 8a of this Directive*".

193 Identical to those foreseen in art. 18(1) SSM R and art. 67(2)(a)(i) and (iii) CRD IV. See footnote 190 above.

194 FELISATTI is also of this view. This author states that the material scope of art. 18(1) SSM R would be defined by art. 67(2) CRD IV. See Felisatti, V. (2018) at pp. 390 and 402. Similarly, and as cited by FELISATTI, see Allegrezza, S. & Voordeckers, O. (2015) at p. 159.

195 Relating exclusively to CRR and other Regulations infringements.

196 Subject to the definition and penalties' thresholds foreseen in national rules. See, immediately above, the reference to the possibility of MSs regulating other infringements different from those contemplated in the mentioned arts. 66(1) and 67(1) CRD IV.

197 Going way beyond, one could argue that since art. 67(1) CRD IV contemplates a minimum set of breaches of CRD IV and CRR provisions (*at least*), NCAs would be, in general, entitled to sanction any infringement of CRR/CRD IV. Hence, the ECB would be entitled to sanction any CRR breach, and penalties would have been made available. This interpretation seems to be, *a priori*, too broad, and the pure literal analysis of art. 67(1) CRD IV does not seems to resist such expansive reading.

(i) Arguments favouring an interpretation of art. 18(1) SSM R in which the possibility for the ECB of imposing administrative pecuniary penalties is non-dependent on the availability of such penalties under national law

7.133 *First*, the main element that appears to favour the interpretation described immediately above is closely linked to the principle of equivalence (level playing field). More precisely, it is the aim of the European legislators to ensure a level playing field and a common supervisory framework for all SIs. As indicated in Part I, the author is of the view that this would be one of the top principles to be followed when construing unclear SSM R provisions.[198] In this regard, it is clear that when interpreting the provisions of the SSM R, one must always keep an eye on the Regulation's main goal: to provide a uniform supervisory framework that ensures a level playing field and prevents regulatory arbitrage.[199] Additionally, it results from a constant case law that, when interpreting an isolated provision, attention must be paid to the aim and objectives sought by the legislator when approving the piece of legislation at stake.[200]

7.134 *Second*, the proposed interpretation fosters supervisory convergence, leading to a minimum set of infringements that can be sanctioned by the ECB in all the member states in an equal way, since the level of the pecuniary penalties is the same for all MSs. The practical implications of this interpretation have received some favourable attention by the academia.[201]

7.135 In this sense, SMITS postulates that in cases of no implementation, in order to ensure supervision of the highest quality, action could be taken on the basis of the combined grounds of the SSM R plus the relevant provisions of CRD IV that are intended to be applied. The author considers that this entails a kind of circumvention of the well-developed case law principle, entailing that directives cannot be invoked against individuals; that is, no direct effect can be derived from directives imposing obligations on their addressees.[202] From

---

198 See Section B. (*SSM basic principles: level playing field & proportionality*) in Chapter 1.

199 See art. 1.I SSM R.

200 See *L-Bank* case at Para. 39: "*In order to respond to the questions of interpretation thus raised and determine the exact scope of Article 70(1) of the SSM Framework Regulation, account must be taken not only of its wording but also of its context and of the objectives pursued by the set of rules of which it forms a part (see, to that effect, judgment of 7 June 2005, VEMW and Others, C-17/03, EU:C:2005:362, paragraph 41 and the case-law cited)*".

201 See Smits, R. (2017) at pp. 16–19.

202 Provided that the directive at stake has not been transposed. See opinion of AG Whal in case C-425/12 (*Portgás – Sociedade de Produção e Distribuição de Gás*), delivered on 18 September 2013 (ECLI:EU:C:2013:623), at Para. 31. There, the corner-stone case law surrounding this question is perfectly synthesised. See also Court of Justice judgments in cases C-152/84 (*Marshall*) of 26 February 1986 (ECLI:EU:C:1986:84) – Para. 47, C-80/86 (*Kolpinghuis Nijmegen*) of 8 October 1987

a practical perspective, this author outlines the strategic opportunity for the ECB acting under this legal ground of "*gaining*" some time before the supervisory decision is challenged and, if any annulled, giving some time to correct an extremely urgent situation in which the ECB would lack powers due to the defective transposition of CRD IV.

The point made here is slightly different from the one discussed by SMITS, **7.136** as the interpretation suggested above does not entail a kind of reverse direct application of CRD IV but rather an authentic interpretation of the first paragraph of art. 18 SSM R; the ECB would be empowered to impose administrative pecuniary penalties as regards infringements contemplated in art. 67(1) relating to CRR provisions and art. 66(1)(b) CRD IV, since penalties for such breaches are made available to national competent authorities by Union law. A different separate matter is whether and how MSs have materialised such a minimum set of sanctioning powers over those specific infringements.

Third, digging into the precedents of the SSM R is capable of shedding **7.137** some light on the origin and actual meaning of the discussed provision. The Commission draft SSM R proposal contemplated the clearer expression: "*in relation to which administrative pecuniary sanctions shall be available to competent authorities under Union law*".[203] Based on the precedent drafts, one may argue that the *legislators* aimed at empowering the ECB with, at least, the same minimum sanctioning powers for breaches of directly applicable EU law to which NCAs are entitled under CRD IV.

Finally, such interpretation would be consistent with the plain reading of art. **7.138** 18(1) SSM R, which would not need to be stretched as administrative penalties have been made available to NCAs under art. 67(1) and art. 66(1)(b) CRD IV; the ECB would be entitled to sanction, at least, the infringements foreseen therein relating to CRR provisions.

(ECLI:EU:C:1987:431) (Para. 9) and C-168/95 (*Arcaro)* of 26 September 1996 (ECLI:EU:C:1996:363) (Para. 36).

203 Proposal for a Council Regulation conferring specific tasks on the European Central Bank concerning policies relating to the prudential supervision of credit institutions COM(2012) 511 final: https://www.europarl.europa.eu/registre/docs_autres_institutions/commission_europeenne/com/2012/0511/COM_COM(2012)0511_EN.pdf.

(ii) Arguments against an interpretation of art. 18(1) SSM R in which the possibility for the ECB of imposing administrative pecuniary penalties is non-dependent on the availability of such penalties under national law

7.139 A number of legal arguments can be brought against the interpretation proposed at the end of this Section, and it is fair to examine its validity and the possibility to quash it.

7.140 *In the first place*, and regarding the nature of the legal act that would enable the ECB to act, attention must be paid to the fact that CRD IV is a directive and, so, a legal instrument addressed to member states that requires them to implement it.[204] The use by the ECB of CRD IV as a *basic* legal instrument to deploy its sanctioning powers can be objected to as lacking competence.

7.141 The *counter-argument* to this objection is rooted in the SSM framework. Since the ECB is considered under the SSM R the competent authority to supervise SIs,[205] it is reasonable to assume that the ECB should also be vested with the powers and material rules provided to under CRD IV.[206] Otherwise, there would be competence without deterrence.

7.142 *Secondly*, in the field of sanctioning (and criminal) measures, we should be reluctant to accept any extensive interpretation that may entail unfavourable effects for the persons concerned. This has been the constant position held by the ECtHR.[207] From this consistent case law,[208] it can be inferred that

204 As stated in art. 288 TFEU: "(...) *A directive shall be binding, as to the result to be achieved, upon each Member State to which it is addressed, but shall leave to the national authorities the choice of form and methods.* (...)".

In this vein, see the opinion of AG Sharpston in the case C-413/15 (*Elaine Farrell*), delivered on 22 June 2017 (ECLI:EU:C:2017:492). In Para. 28 AG Sharpston outlines the idea that directives are addressed solely to MSs, imposing on them the burden to transpose directives by means of the legal instrument that they may consider appropriate.

At the same time, there is other kind of legal instruments that grant powers or impose obligations directly on EU institutions (or its staff), such as the Protocols attached to the TFEU (e.g., Protocol No. 7 of the TFEU on the privileges and immunities of the European Union) or Regulations (e.g., the Regulation 2018/1725 on the protection of natural persons with regard to the processing of personal data by the Union institutions, bodies, offices and agencies and on the free movement of such data).

205 Cf Chapter 6. (*Allocation of tasks within the SSM*).

206 Cf Recital 5 of the RO&Ds, which expressly states that "*The ECB is the competent authority in the participating Member States as established by relevant Union law*". See also Lamandini, M., Ramos Muñoz, D. & Solana, J. (2016).

207 See ECtHR Judgment in *S.W. v. the United Kingdom* (Application no. 20166/92). Despite being referred this case law to *criminal law*, it is perfectly applicable to the sanctioning procedures instructed by the ECB. The foregoing results from the criminal nature of the administrative pecuniary penalties foreseen in art. 18(1) SSM R (see Section C. (*Are the supervisory and sanctioning procedures foreseen in the SSM criminal "in nature"?*) in Chapter 8 below).

208 Which, in principle, based on art. 52(3) of the Charter, the CJEU should consider. See, in this regard, CJEU judgment in case C-617-10 (*Åklagaren v Hans Åkerberg Fransson*) of 26 September 2013 (ECLI:EU:C:2013:105). At Paras. 19 and 44.

sanctioning provisions must be construed in a restrictive and literal way, avoiding going any far beyond from its literal wording. However, the ECtHR has also accepted that sanctioning provisions can use some abstract notions to capture cases that cannot be exactly defined beforehand. Such abstract notions must be consistent with the essence of the offense.[209]

In relation to this, under a well-established case law, one may note that directives cannot impose obligations on the individuals, unless they are (correctly) transposed.[210] **7.143**

The *counter-argument* to these arguments would be based on the literal wording of the provision. A textual, plain reading of art. 18(1) SSM R cannot entail an "extensive" interpretation of art. 18.1 SSMR but a literal one. The ECB would be using their direct sanctioning powers only with regard to the sanctions made available to MSs. Also, the ECB would not be directly applying a directive (CRD IV) in a disadvantageous way to the persons concerned but would be directly applying art. 18(1) SSM R, which is a rule that was meant to be directly applicable. In this regard, the legitimacy of the ECB to use its direct sanctioning powers would arise from a clearly defined and foreseeable directly applicable provision, whose conditions for application rely on clear Union provisions – art. 67(1) CRD IV. **7.144**

Thirdly, an additional objection relates to the principle of legal certainty, which is a core principle of sanctioning proceedings. The principle of legal certainty requires legal sanctioning consequences to be foreseeable in advance in a clear and unambiguous way.[211] Taking into consideration article 7 ECHR and the well-established case law of the ECtHR, the CJEU has constantly determined that the principle of legality requires that any infringement must be "*clearly* **7.145**

---

209 See footnote 207. Despite this constituting well-settled ECtHR case law, the CJEU has not used it in its judgments. Only a few samples can be found in the opinions of AGs, who also uses direct reference to the ECtHR judgments. See, for example, opinion of AG Ruíz-Jarabo Colomer in the case C-303/05 (*Advocaten voor de Wereld VZW v Leden van de Ministerraad*) delivered on 12 September.

210 Focusing on the case law related to delayed implementation of Directives that may produce unfavourable effects on individuals, it seems clear that the CJEU has declared that the direct effect cannot take place (see Witte, A. (2014) at p. 106. In this regard, see Court of Justice judgments in cases C-80/86 (*Kolpinghuis Nijmegen*) of 8 October 1987 (ECLI:EU:C:1987:431), Para. 8; and C-457/02 (*Antonio Niselli*) of 11 November 2004 (ECLI:EU:C:2004:707), Para. 29.

In addition, some other authors have gone even further proposing granting direct effects under the SSM to non-transposed or incorrectly transposed directives. See Kornezov, A. (2017).

211 See Whelan, P. (2012). Legal certainty and cartel criminalisation within the EU member states. *The Cambridge Law Journal*, *71*(3), pp. 677–702.

defined by the law".[212] In this sense, the aforementioned interpretation can be found as somehow "artificial" and insufficiently predetermined, jeopardising its legal standing in case of a legal appeal before the CJEU.

7.146 However, that line of case law is not absolute, and the *counter-argument* to this reasoning can be found in itself. The ECtHR has recalled that, in determining the extent and scope of the infringements and penalties, the concerned parties may rely on (i) the court's interpretation and (ii) "*after taking appropriate legal advice*"[213] (i.e., emphasising the importance of the legal advice received). Consequently, considering (i) the high degree of professionalisation and specialisation that credit institutions are presumed to have, operating in a highly qualified and regulated market, and (ii) its access to high-level legal assessment and the possibility to directly ask the consolidated Supervisor, there would be some grounds to lawfully hold that the proposed interpretation was foreseeable and clear enough for the mentioned subjects in this highly specialised context.

7.147 Furthermore, one may argue that, indeed, art. 18(1) SSM R offers no doubt about the limited set of infringements that the ECB can actually punish without relying on national transposition, as these would be listed in arts. 67(1) and 66(1)(b) CRD IV in connection with CRR provisions as directly applicable Union law. The limited number of conducts that, in the view of the European legislator, contributes to reinforcing the predictability of the consequences, leads to a more than acceptable certainty of the sanctioning consequences attached to those infringements.

7.148 *Finally,* and from a practical point of view, the main objection that can be held against this interpretation relates to its naturally limited scope. It would only cover a limited set of infringements (not, in principle, the totality of infringements relating to CRR[214]). This brings us back, partially at least, to the corrosive *regulatory arbitrage.*

7.149 After having analysed the arguments in favour and against the second *(ii)* interpretation of art. 18(1) proposed at the beginning of this, it results that the

---

212 General Court judgment in case T-99/04 (*AC-Treuhand AG v Commission of the European Communities*) of 8 July 2008 (ECLI:EU:T:2008:256) at Para. 83. Influence of the ECtHR in the reasoning held in this regard by the CJEU seems decisive. Reference to the requisite of infringements of being *clearly defined by the law* can be tracked back to the cornerstone case of the ECtHR *Cantoni v. France* (Application no. 17862/91) – in the same vein, see, also, case *Del Río Prada v. Spain* (Application no. 42750/09).

213 Ibidem *Del Río Prada* at Para. 79.

214 For which ECB should rely on the national *availability* under national law.

arguments for outweigh the arguments against and, consequently, it must be followed.

(iii) Conclusion

Concluding this part requires rethinking not only the feasibility of construing article 18(1) SSM R (and so, the direct sanctioning powers attributed to the ECB) but also the interpretative techniques that should be used to deal with the ambiguous regime depicted by the SSM; in particular, regarding the interaction between national law and EU Law, and the blurry boundaries that are formed when the ECB (a European Institution trapped in an EU agency body) must apply or is constricted by national law.[215] **7.150**

The interdependence and the links between national law and the powers attributed to the ECB is a constant in the framework traced by the SSM R.[216] However, it is in the definition of the sanctioning powers of the ECB (the ultimate expression *imperium* that can be attributed to an Institution) where the national law perhaps most strongly modulates the extension and intensity of the punitive capacities of the ECB. Is this justifiable? From a political perspective, probably it is, since MSs may have interest in modulating the intensity of the punitive powers that can be exercised on supervised entities established in their country and that, in the end, generate their revenues in this territory. From the perspective of the aims and objectives pursued by the SSM, and the broader interest pursued by the establishment of the under-construction BU, it is not justifiable; it may affect directly the level playing field in an area that constitutes the very last resort to make supervised entities to comply with the material rules of the Single Rulebook.[217] **7.151**

In this scenario, the traditional ways of interpreting and implementing European and national law might need to be revisited for this particular system. New times require new solutions to ensure efficiently the level playing aimed by the SSM R. In this regard, actual dogmatic approaches, based on the area of the law concerned (i.e., administrative law, competition law, European law, etc.), do not seem capable of offering a comprehensive answer, capable of covering the whole rule-interaction model inserted in the SSM legal framework. This is precisely what the proposed interpretation of art. 18(1) SSM R **7.152**

---

215 Which is designed and implemented at a national level, to be applied in national administrative bodies with, more than probably, a well-developed *corpus* or *acquis* of procedural and internal rules, interpreted by national courts during decades.

216 See above in this Section.

217 This conclusion can be held only considering the *constitutionality* dimension, legal basis upon which the *mechanism* rests.

aims at fulfilling: to devise a coherent application of the SSM framework not exclusively based on the literal wording of the law but also on the objectives of the European legislator and in the legal interests protected[218] by this legal scheme.

7.153 The conclusion that follows the foregoing analysis (from a systematic, literal and finalistic perspective) favours the construction that, under art. 18(1) SSM R, the ECB would be entitled to sanction, at least, the infringements listed in art. 67(1) of CRD IV (and in art. 66(1)(b) CRD IV as well) referring to CRR, regardless of its transposition by MSs. In this case, the maximum administrative pecuniary penalty that the ECB could impose on the sanctioned entity would be the one such established provision:

> (…) *up to twice the amount of the profits gained or losses avoided because of the breach where those can be determined, or up to 10 % of the total annual turnover, as defined in relevant Union law, of a legal person in the preceding business year or such other pecuniary penalties as may be provided for in relevant Union law.*[219]

7.154 This approach must be further analysed regarding its practical approach, and in this vein, attention must be paid to the time when the infringement was committed[220] and, what is more important, to whether the provisions stated in CRD IV were transposed by the member state at stake when the infringement was committed. This analysis will be carried out right below.

(c) Practical consequences of the preferred interpretation of art. 18(1): mitigating but not avoiding regulatory arbitrage

7.155 Does the proposed interpretation above and, more broadly, the interlink between national implementation of penalties and ECB sanctioning powers under art. 18(1) SSM R affect the level playing field that the SSM legal framework tries to ensure? It seems that yes, inevitably. In this regard, two major asymmetries can be found:

---

218 As can it be inferred teleologically from art. 1 paragraph I SSM R, those interests are represented by the stability of the credit institutions, the broader interest of the sound functioning of the internal market, and so the stability of the EU Financial market (ensuring an adequate level of protection to the depositor (cf Recital 30 SSM R)).

219 See art. 18.1 *i.f.* SSM R.

220 In the present time, all member states have transposed the relevant provision to allow the ECB to exercise its sanctioning powers within the framework establish by the mentioned arts. 18(1) SSM R and 66(1) and 67(1) CRD IV. However, one must bear in mind the punitive action of the ECB, and in general, the punitive conduct of national Supervision authorities has a retrospective bias.

Due to this fact, the ECB has pursued breaches that happened at the time when the SSM became operative on 4 November 2014 or even before.

First, it can be a real asymmetry between those MSs who transposed, in due time, CRD IV sanctioning provisions and those who did not. Thus, breaches committed at the time when the relevant provisions of CRD IV (i.e., arts. 66(1) and 67(1)), which had not been transposed (or incorrectly or incompletely transposed), could not be pursued (or pursued for the whole period of infringement) and sanctioned by the ECB. This may undermine the powers of the ECB to make use of its indirect sanctioning power under art. 18(5) SSM R. Pursuant to such provision, the ECB has the exclusive competence to require the NCA at stake to open a sanctioning procedure with a view to sanction breaches of national rules transposing prudential Directives.[221] 7.156

Second, another more subtle externality can take place. CRD IV constitutes a basic pillar of the so-called Single Rulebook and, thus, constitutes a basis for the harmonisation of the internal market regarding the activity and processes of credit institutions.[222] However, the nature of this legal act (a directive) only ensures a minimum degree of harmonisation.[223] Due to this fact, we can find differences in the level and extent of the implementation of CRD IV. Whereas some member states have transposed CRD IV in a *conservative* or literal way, others have adopted a stricter approach.[224] 7.157

Focusing exclusively on sanctioning matters, some MSs could have transposed arts. 66 and 67 CRD IV in almost a literal way[225] while others have made available a wider set of penalties, ensuring that any breach of the provisions stated in CRD IV and/or in CRR are available.[226] This undermines the 7.158

221 See immediately above and in Section C. (*Allocation of sanctioning competences: a specialty over the general rule?*) in Chapter 6.

222 CRD IV itself is self-explanatory of its main aim in its Recital 13, stating its aim to harmonise the practices and standards in the internal market.

223 In fact, a further degree of harmonisation is aimed to achieve through the technical and regulatory standards that the EBA is called to develop, subject to the approval of the Commission. Several references to the role that the EBA is called to play can be found in the wording of CRD IV. Additionally, the EBA is also put in a relevant position for making use of its binding mediation powers, in order to foster harmonised supervisory practices among Supervisors (cf Recital 10 CRD IV). See also in Section B.1.(a). (*Depicting the distribution of regulatory tasks between the ECB and the EBA*) in Chapter 2.

224 Excessive reliance on Directives has been seen as a matter of concern by the ECB itself. In this vein, in its speech held in Helsinki dated on 15 September 2017, former chair of the Supervisory Board of the ECB, Danièle Nouy, said the following words: "*So, there is a clear case for further harmonising the European rulebook. To that end, we should rely less on EU directives and more on EU regulations, which are directly applicable in all Member States*". See: https://www.bankingsupervision.europa.eu/press/speeches/date/2017/html/ssm.sp170915.en.html.

225 More generally, see Allegrezza, S. (ed.). (2020).

226 See, for example, art. 92.f) of the Spanish Law 10/2014 on Solvency, Supervision and Ordination of Credit Institutions, which contemplates a general infringement consisting in the failure to comply with directly applicable EU Law. This infringement is classified as serious (if isolated); otherwise, it is deemed a very serious infringement (cf art. 93. d) of the Law 10/2014).

goal of levelling the playing field, which SSM R is supposed to ensure. Thus, despite having a common framework for the supervision of SIs conducted by one single Supervisor (and one harmonised scenario for the supervision LSIs), the punitive consequences to which those SIs would be subject would vary depending on the MSs in which they are registered.

BOX 7.5 EXAMPLE: REGULATORY ARBITRAGE AND SANCTIONING PROCEDURES UNDER THE SSM

Let's consider, *for example*, a breach consisting in a failure to report a large exposure that exceeds the limits set forth in art. 396 of CRR[227] committed by two different SIs. This infringement is not listed expressly in art. 67(1) CRD IV, and so it would depend on the national law to provide for the *punishability* of this infringement. If the legal framework of the first MS foresees the possibility of sanctioning this breach, whereas the second MS has not provided for such possibility (or has established less strict penalties), there could be an imbalance between the regulatory framework applicable to those SIs.

From an abstract perspective, the first SI would be subject, broadly speaking, to a stricter framework and higher regulatory risks in case of failure, regardless of whether the infringement is finally committed or not. Furthermore, if a penalty is finally imposed to the first SI because of this breach, and this SI has to face the cost of it, this would affect its profitability margins. Consequently, concurrence between both SIs can be affected.

7.159 This is just a mere potential example, but it shows fair enough how the sanctioning framework linked to banking supervision regulations may affect the level playing field that the SSM tries to build up.

7.160 Going further and with the aim of overcoming and limiting the effects of these externalities, several remedies could be deployed at a policy level, that is, by

---

Regardless of the alignment of the sanctioning consequences of the Spanish Law 10/2014 on Solvency, Supervision and Ordination of Credit Institutions with CRD IV, the most relevant aspect of the approach deployed by the Spanish legislator is that the Spanish framework provides for the possibility of sanctioning any infringement related to CRR, making the set of penalties, if any, established in CRD IV available to the ECB.

French legislator has also followed a very similar approach, enabling any breach of the provisions settled forth in CRR to be punished in accordance with the standards foreseen on CRD IV. In this vein, see art. L-612-40 of the *Code Monétaire e Financier* (as amended by *Ordonnance n° 2015–1024 du 20 août 2015 portant diverses dispositions d'adaptation de la législation au droit de l'Union européenne en matière financière*).

In addition, section V of the mentioned article L-612-40 provides for the possibility of imposing the fines foreseen in arts. 66(2)(a)(i) and 67(2)(a)(i) CRD IV. In the case of natural persons, section VII of the mentioned provision provides for the possibility of imposing penalties aligned with the content of CRD IV.

227 According to art. 396(1) of CRR "*If, in an exceptional case, exposures exceed the limit set out in Article 395(1), the institution shall report the value of the exposure without delay to the competent authorities* (…)".

modifying the current legal framework by establishing a more detailed set of sanctions and administrative penalties. Probably, the swiftest way to act, without altering the architecture depicted by the SSM R, would be amending CRD IV within the next revision of this directive. Directives CRD V and CRD VI, which amended CRD IV, have been lost opportunities in this regard, especially as they touched upon the sanctioning regime foreseen in arts. 66 and 67 CRD IV. Those directives (and particularly CRD VI) redrafted the mentioned provisions and detailed new infringements and associated administrative penalties, also including a specific regime for periodic penalty payments and greater clarification on the calculation of the Total Annual Net Turnover (TAT). These modifications, although laudable, may be insufficient to level the playing field.

Another possibility would be introducing in the CRR (amending it by means of a subsequent Regulation) the possibility for NCAs to sanction a wide number of breaches of the requirements established thereof and, eventually, any breach of CRR provisions. One may recall that whereas CRD IV, which contains the sanctioning regime applicable under the Single Rulebook, is grounded on art. 53(1) TFEU,[228] CRR is based on art. 114 TFEU.[229] However, art. 114 TFEU seems to provide a sufficient basis to establish a sanctioning regime. For example, the SRM Regulation, which is based also on art. 114 TFEU, contemplates a closed-ended sanctioning regime.[230] Even if the legal basis seems to be non-controversial, such modification would need to overcome the subsidiarity test (art. 5 TEU). Considering the whole background provided in this Section and, in particular, the difficulties linked to the application by the ECB of administrative penalties for breaches not expressly contemplated in CRD IV, it appears that a directly applicable regulation amending CRR is the best way to ensure that EU objectives are attained. This would require a further analysis on the opportunity, impact and proportionality of the legislative measure.[231] 7.161

2. National laws and administrative pecuniary penalties II: to which extent may national legislation limit the ECB direct sanctioning powers under art. 18(5) SSM R?

In accordance with the wording of Para. 5 of art. 18 SSM R and in the cases that fall outside the scope of the direct sanctioning powers of the ECB, the 7.162

228 Which refers to the take up and pursuit of activities as self-employed persons, and mutual recognition of professional qualifications between MSs.

229 Which refers to approximation of legislation to strength the internal market.

230 Also Regulation 1/2003, which, although based on art. 102 TFEU (former arts. 81 and 82 TEAC), rests under the same Chapter 2 of Title VII TFEU.

231 In this regard, see footnote 226. A good sample of this possibility would be the article 92.f) of the Spanish Law 10/2014, that expressly contemplates the possibility of sanctioning any breach of directly applicable Union provisions in the field of banking supervision.

ECB may request NCAs to use its own national powers, provided by Union or national law to institute proceedings against SIs, the members of the management board of those, or any other individuals who can be held responsible under national law.

7.163 It is worth mentioning that the ECB's competence is limited to sending a mere request addressed to the relevant NCA.[232] It will be the NCA itself who ultimately will assess[233] whether such proceeding can be initiated, what value is attributed to the evidence and conclusions reached in an eventual previous or simultaneous ECB sanctioning proceeding against the same SI (or natural persons related to it), and how such a proceeding is conducted and how it ends (with or without imposing a penalty[234] or any other sanctioning or administrative measure).[235]

7.164 Regarding this Para. 5, attention must be paid to the fact that its wording states that the powers of the ECB to request NCAs to open sanctioning proceedings are given when it lacks direct action under Para. 1 of the same provision. The key point is how to construe properly the statement "*In cases not covered by paragraph 1 of this article* (...)".

---

232 On the other side, see art. 9(1) SSM R. In the view of the author, one could argue that art. 9(1) III SSM R is more precise than this art. 18(5) SSM R, as the NCA is requested to exercise one specific power conferred under national law in the manner explicated by the ECB (more or less precisely, which depends entirely on ECB's will). However, as indicated above, the NCA would be constrained by national framework, including procedural and constitutional rules (and jurisprudential constructions), and hence may understand that the request submitted by the ECB cannot be carried out or can be but may not be, in the precise terms, requested by the ECB. Cf Section B.4. (*Supervisory and investigatory powers to exercise those tasks*) in Chapter 6 and in more detail Section C.2.(a). (*Legal challenges: coordination between the ECB and NCAs*) in Chapter 15.

233 But without being capable of autonomously deciding when to open such sanctioning proceedings, as the competence is attributed to the ECB.

234 The cases that may be particularly sensitive are those related to imposition of non-pecuniary penalties on SIs, which had been actually punished by the ECB pursuant to art. 18(1) SSM R (assuming that the request addressed to the NCA is issued after the ECB sanctioning procedure concludes with the issuance of a supervisory decision). There, several issues arise, in particular as regards how may the NCA treat the evidence constituted in the ECB sanctioning procedure, how it evaluates the notion of culpability and, ultimately, whether it finds that a penalty must be and can be imposed pursuant to national rules. The interplay of such elements can lead to the puzzling scenario where a SIs sanctioned by the ECB is not sanctioned by the NCA on lack of culpability or insufficient evidence grounds regarding the alleged infringement, which, in principle, the ECB would have already deemed negligent or voluntarily committed. See in more detail in Section C.2.(b). (*Safeguards: ne bis in idem and linkage with the facts established in the ECB direct sanctioning procedures*) in Chapter 15.

235 And also managing the publication of the sanctions imposed, if any. In this regard, the ECB webpage giving publicity to the sanctions imposed by NCAs, at the request of the ECB under art. 18(5) SSM R, provides links to notices on the publications hosted in the relevant NCAs webpages. As a mere sample, see the statement published by the Bank of Ireland concerning the penalty imposed on the Ulster Bank: https://www.centralbank.ie/news/article/press-release-ulster-bank-fine-05-march-2020.

According to art. 18(5) SSM R, the ECB would be always entitled to request NCAs to open sanctioning proceedings in the cases that fall within the remit of its competences under Para. 1 of the same provision. Such cases would include (a) the imposition of penalties (and, broadly, administrative measures) to natural persons relating to the SIs for breaches of directly applicable EU law; also, (b) the imposition of penalties for breaches of national rules transposing Union law and of national law which has gone beyond the minimum requirements established in CRD IV (and prudential Directives in general) but that would actually fall within the specific micro-prudential tasks allocated to the ECB;[236] and (c) the application of non-pecuniary penalties on SIs for breaches of directly applicable Union law.[237] The foregoing ensures the greater effectiveness of the SSM as a composite system[238] and results to be more harmonious with the overall supervisory powers vested on the ECB and its narrow sanctioning powers.[239] **7.165**

The powers of the ECB to request a given NCA to open a sanctioning proceeding would be, in principle, conditional upon the NCA having *administrative pecuniary penalties available* to punish the respective SI (and relating natural persons) concerned.[240] This, in turn, depends on whether the NCA's MS has transposed CRD IV and how it has transposed it, e.g., if it has gone beyond CRD IV basic requirements on punishable conducts. If a request in this sense is addressed to a NCA but national law does not provide for the possibility to sanction the breach allegedly committed, in the end, the ECB request would be unenforceable. **7.166**

To this end, it seems advisable that the ECB and NCAs engage themselves in a stocktaking exercise to map the complete set of breaches that the ECB could request NCAs to sanction (and the persons that can be held liable for such breaches). The foregoing, notwithstanding informal checks and discussions to **7.167**

236 See Section A.2. (*The (problematic) application by the ECB of national law: some considerations*) above.

237 See D'Ambrosio, R. (2013) at pp. 48–49.

238 Characterisation of the SSM as a *composite system* is beyond any doubt. Practitioners within Central Banks and scholars refer to composite proceedings within the remit of the SSM R, when the Regulations provide for the necessary interaction between the NCAs (as a kind of first contact point, closer to the credit institutions) and the ECB as the final decision maker, especially as it is entrusted to assessing whether a credit institution meets the requirements stated in the Union Law. The prior takes place in the course of authorization procedures. See D'Ambrosio, R. (2013) at pp. 59–61. See further in Chapter 11. (*Cooperation, coordination and composite procedures in the Banking Union and SSM*).

239 See footnote 219 in Chapter 6 on the impossibility for the ECB to sanction natural persons.

240 In a wider sense, those administrative pecuniary penalties would be also available to sanction the LSIs which fall within the scope of the NCA, according to the allocation of sanctioning competences structured within the SSM.

be conducted by the NCA and the ECB before making use of such possibility so as to ensure the potential enforceability of the request, in abstract at least. Further reasons of transparency and public information demand the publication of the previously referred stocktaking exercise. The foregoing, with a view to let SIs' stakeholders know and compare the degree of sanctioning scrutiny to which such institutions are subject.

8

DISTINGUISHING BETWEEN SUPERVISORY AND SANCTIONING PROCEDURES: IS IT POSSIBLE?

A. SUPERVISORY (COMMON) PROCEDURES VS. SANCTIONING PROCEDURES

When referring to supervisory proceedings, we cover two realities. One meaning may refer to the whole supervisory process, understood as a cycle where planning, risk assessment, exchanges and disclosures may interact on a continuous basis.[1] Another, more restrictive meaning only encompasses a method by means of which an administrative decision, generating obligations on the **8.001**

1 See, as matter of example, the *Bank Supervision Process Version 1.0 (June 2018)* issued by the American Office of the Comptroller of the Currency: https://www.occ.gov/publications-and-resources/publications/comptrollers-handbook/files/bank-supervision-process/pub-ch-bank-supervision-process.pdf. See, also, section 2 (*Supervisory Cycle*) of the SSM Supervisory Manual.

addressee, is validly produced. Such meaning resembles the rails upon which a train circulates and describes the necessary procedural steps to produce a valid and enforceable binding act. In this work, we will use the second meaning.

8.002 Art. 2(24) SSM Fr defines *ECB Supervisory procedure* as any ECB activity intended to conclude with an *ECB supervisory decision*.[2] Both the common procedures and the procedures developed with a view to impose administrative pecuniary penalties[3] are expressly included within such a definition.

8.003 Such supervisory procedures are subject to Part III (*General provisions applying to the operation of the SSM*) of the SSM Fr except otherwise provided in Part X, concerning administrative pecuniary penalties.

8.004 Art. 2(26) SSM Fr defines ECB supervisory decision as a

> *legal act adopted by the ECB in the exercise of the tasks and powers conferred on it by the SSM Regulation, which takes the form of an ECB decision, is addressed to one or more supervised entities or supervised groups or one or more other persons and is not a legal act of general application* (emphasis added).

8.005 Considering separately the elements that form the definition, it results that an ECB supervisory decision is an act that has the formal form of an ECB decision,[4] and hence, it is a binding act but not one of general application.[5] The fact that the ECB decisions are not legal acts of general application does not mean that they always have to indicate specific addressees. Indeed, the ECB, in the context of the SSM, has issued several ECB decisions without addressees.[6]

8.006 Below, the following will be analysed: if there is any ground, provided expressly or implicitly in the SSM R or in the SSM Fr, to establish a clear-cut distinction between sanctioning procedures and supervisory procedures (in general). In order to do so, several aspects of the definition of *supervisory decision*[7] will be analysed, such as (i) the absence of consideration of NCAs in such definition; (ii) the exclusion of supervisory activities not aiming at culminating with a supervisory decision; and (iii) the approval process of supervisory decisions.

---

2 Art. 2(26) SSM Fr.

3 See Section C. (*Allocation of sanctioning competences: a specialty over the general rule?*) in Chapter 6.

4 Cf arts. 34(1) SESCB; 132(1) and 288 TFEU; and 17a(4) ECB Rules Procedure.

5 Cf art. 288 TFEU. Cf Craig, P. & de Búrca, G. (2020).

6 For example, the Decision (EU) 2017/933 of the ECB of 16 November 2016 on a general framework for delegating decision-making powers for legal instruments related to supervisory tasks (ECB/2016/40). For an exhaustive list of these acts, see Bax, R. and Witte, A. (2019).

7 Art. 2(26) SSM R.

1. Absence of consideration of NCAs involvement in the ECB supervisory procedures

Since the wording of the mentioned definition refers only to "any ECB activity directed towards preparing the issue of an ECB supervisory decision", it seems to exclude NCAs involvement in such proceedings. **8.007**

NCA input is key not only as regards the common procedures[8] but also as regards the supervisory procedures regulated in Part VI of the SSM Fr concerning SIs.[9] **8.008**

A coherent interpretation of such a definition entails considering that: (i) reference to *any ECB activity* means that the ECB is the sole owner of the procedure. That is, that the decision is ultimately attributable and imputable to it and falls under its competences' remit. (ii) Despite the ECB being the *owner* of the procedure, one should be mindful that the NCAs may perform, in the course of such a procedure, actions in such procedures which may be of capital importance and that the ECB must necessarily consider when adopting its final decision. This interpretation is also consistent with the application of the EU administrative procedural rules in proceedings under direct administration by EU bodies.[10] **8.009**

The foregoing seems to be confirmed by the definition of "NCA supervisory procedure", which refers exclusively to procedures addressed to produce a decision by the NCA (basically, as regards LSIs and persons connected with them[11]). **8.010**

Moreover, the Court of Justice seems to share this view, for instance, in the *Berlusconi-Fininvest case*.[12] In such a case, the Court was requested to issue a preliminary ruling on the competence to review (by the Italian courts or by the Court of Justice) a national administrative decision, preparatory or non-binding, which was inserted in the SSM composite procedure. The particular case referred to the assessment of the acquisition of a qualifying holding in a credit institution, which supposedly came about as a result of a reverse **8.011**

8 Part V of the SSM Fr.

9 Which includes fit and proper assessment and the exercise of powers conferred by national law transposing prudential Directives in excess of the minimum content foreseen in such directives.

10 See Section B. (*The administrative procedural law applied by ECB*) in Chapter 7.

11 Cf Part VII (*Procedures for the supervision of less significant supervised entities*) of the SSM Fr.

12 Court of Justice judgment in case C-219/17 (*Berlusconi Fininvest*) of 19 December 2018 (ECLI:EU:C:2018:1023).

merger.[13] There, the Court clarified the exclusive competence of the ECB over the procedure and determined the exclusive jurisdiction of the CJEU to review such types of supervisory procedures.[14] Consequently, the line initiated by this case[15] depicted a unified procedure owned by the ECB in which the NCAs' input would be preparatory, in the sense that they would not have ultimate decision-making powers.

8.012 A key practical implication arising from this consideration is that the full ownership of the procedure (and the eventual liability in connection with it) remains the ECB's. The only exception relates to those cases where the procedure is terminated by the NCA directly because the applicant request does not conform with the minimum requirements established by national law.[16] In

---

13 Where the subsidiarity of Mediolanum SpA, Banca Mediolanum SpA (a credit institution), acquired it. Ibidem at Paras. 27–30. It must be noted that the facts presented in this preliminary ruling, particularly the acquisition of a qualifying holding, must be understood as corrected by the Berlusconi II appeal in which the CJEU, in the light of the very same facts, concluded that such acquisition of a qualifying holding did not occur.

14 Ibidem at Paras. 58–59. In this matter, reference must be made to the work of Brito Bastos: Brito Bastos, F. (2018). Derivative illegality in European composite administrative procedures. *Common market law review*, *55*(1), pp. 101–134; Brito Bastos, F. (2019); Brito Bastos, F. (2020). An Administrative Crack in the EU's Rule of Law: Composite Decision-making and Nonjusticiable National Law. *European Constitutional Law Review*, *16*(1), pp. 63–90; and Brito Bastos, F. (2021). Composite procedures in the SSM and SRM – an analytical overview. In *Judicial Review in the European Banking Union* (pp. 97–113). Edward Elgar Publishing.

15 The General Court in case T-913/16 (*Finanziaria d'investimento Fininvest SpA (Fininvest) and Silvio Berlusconi v ECB*) of 11 May 2022 (ECLI:EU:T:2022:279) [*Berlusconi II case*] already referred to the doctrine set up in *Berlusconi Finivest* in Paras. 242–243. The judgment of the General Court is the second step in a long saga occurring within national (Italian) and EU jurisdictions. This judgment was overturned by the CJEU in its recent judgement in joined Cases C-512/22 P and C-513/22 P (*Finanziaria d'investimento Fininvest SpA (Fininvest) and Silvio Berlusconi v ECB*) of 19 September 2024 (ECLI:EU:C:2024:774) [*Berlusconi II appeal*] on the basis of factual errors of appreciation committed by the appealed court which led to the consideration that the alteration of the structure of a qualifying holding is not to be regarded as the acquisition of a qualifying holding itself, and hence, the ECB erred in opposing such non-existing acquisition of a qualifying holding.

The factual background of this Berlusconi II saga concerned an action for annulment submitted by *Fininvest* and *Silvio Berlusconi* against the ECB decision opposing its acquisition of a (disputed) qualifying holding in *Banca Mediolanum*, which resulted from the absorption of *Mediolanum* (a mixed financial holding company) by *Banco Mediolanum* (a subsidiary of the previous entity). The applicants held a qualifying holding in *Mediolanum*, which, at the same time, was the single shareholder of *Banco Mediolanum*. As a result of the reverse merger, the applicants ended up having a direct qualifying holding in Banca Mediolanum. As clarified in the *Berlusconi II appeal* (Paras. 106–110), the alteration of the structure of a qualifying holding (i.e., whether it becomes more direct to the acquirer as a result of a reverse merger) is irrelevant to the classification of the qualifying holding as such. Accordingly, the CJEU held that the acquisition of any such qualifying holding an autonomous EU concept) did not occurr in the case at stake, and hence, the ECB issued an ill-based opposition to *Fininvest*, and Silvio Berlusconi continues holding a qualifying holding in *Banco Mediolanum* (Paras. 118–125).

16 Cf art. 75 SSM Fr as regards application for banking authorisations.

those cases, the application is not even submitted to the ECB,[17] and the NCA remains as the sole deciding authority.[18]

2. Exclusion of supervisory activities not aiming at producing legal acts of individual application

The fact that the ECB supervisory procedure is addressed to produce a legal act of individual application excludes, from the scope of the ECB supervisory procedures, any such activity destined to produce acts of general application. **8.013**

This would exclude, in particular, Regulations, guidelines, general recommendations[19] and guides (or guidance). In addition, the *non-formal* supervisory acts (i.e., supervisory acts not intended at crystallising an ECB decision) would not be captured by the definition of ECB supervisory procedure. This would be the case, for instance, of *operational acts* and informal exchanges of views between the supervised entities and the ECB (supervisory dialogue). Hence, they would not be subject to the procedural steps and principles to be applied on *standard* ECB procedural procedures. **8.014**

3. Approval via non-objection process and/or via delegation

ECB supervisory decisions regarding the exercise of the specific micro-prudential supervisory tasks allocated to the ECB under the SSM R are adopted via the non-objection procedure,[20] unless approved by means of delegation, as it will be referred below. By means of such a proceeding, the Governing Council is deemed to have approved the draft supervisory decision prepared by the Supervisory Board, unless it objects in a given time (which, in any event, must be below ten working days).[21] **8.015**

ECB supervisory decisions may be adopted also by means of delegation, pursuant to the basic delegation framework set out by the ECB Decision 2017/933 on a general framework for delegating decision-making powers for legal **8.016**

---

17 Based on art. 73 SSM Fr, as a matter of example.

18 This reasoning seems to be compliant with the *Berlusconi Fininvest case* (and the case law cited in such ruling). In this regard, Para. 45 of the *Berlusconi Fininvest case* states that: "(...) *an act of a national authority that is part of a decision-making process of the European Union does not fall within the exclusive jurisdiction of the EU Courts where it is apparent from the division of powers in the field in question between the national authorities and the EU institutions that the act adopted by the national authority is a necessary stage of a procedure for adopting an EU act in which the EU institutions have only a limited or no discretion, so that the national act is binding on the EU institution*". (Emphasis added).

19 See, on this topic, Bax, R. and Witte, A. (2019); and Section 1.3.2. (*Types of supervisory action*) of the SSM Supervisory Manual.

20 Cf art. 13g and 13i of the Rules of Procedure.

21 Cf art. 26(8) SSM R and SSM Supervisory Manual, at p. 118.

instruments related to supervisory tasks.[22] Such Decision establishes the basic framework. The different thematic areas of such Decision establish the criteria to adopt the delegated decisions.[23] Such areas cover, among others, decisions on own funds, fit and proper assessment and amendments to the significance of entities.[24] The framework is further rounded by specifically nominating the heads of certain ECB working units with the possibility to adopt such delegated decisions.

4. No particular distinction between sanctioning and supervisory procedures?

8.017 If we look at the Parts, Chapters, Sections and headings of the SSM R and the SSM Fr, it results that they do not foresee an express distinction between ECB supervisory procedures and sanctioning proceedings. In this regard, it can be noted that:

8.018 *First*, *administrative penalties* foreseen in art. 18 SSM R are included under the same Section (Section 2), which groups all ECB *Specific Supervisory Powers*. No distinction is made then between supervisory and *sanctioning* powers if one is to strictly follow the headings of the SSM R.

8.019 *Second*, one may note that the *common procedures* are contemplated under Part V SSM Fr, and other *procedures regarding the supervision of significant supervised* are regulated in Part VI SSM Fr. Part X (*Administrative Penalties*), despite regulating *sanctioning procedures*,[25] does not refer to *procedures* at such. This may be just a terminological flaw, but the truth is that a literal and systematic reading of the titles of the different Parts composing the SSM Fr does not allow distinguishing between *sanctioning* and *supervisory procedures*.

---

22 See, more extensively, Gren, J. (2018). The Eurosystem and the Single Supervisory Mechanism: institutional continuity under constitutional constraints. *ECB Legal Working Paper Series*, No. 17.

23 In principle, when such criteria are not met, the ordinary non-objection procedure foreseen in art. 13g of the Rules of Procedure must apply instead.

24 Cf respectively, (i) Decision (EU) 2018/546 of the ECB on delegation of the power to adopt its own funds decisions (ECB/2018/10), (ii) Decision 2017/935 of the ECB on delegation of the power to adopt fit and proper decisions and the assessment of fit and proper requirements (ECB/2016/42) and (iii) Decision 2017/934 of the ECB on the delegation of decisions on the significance of supervised entities (ECB/2016/41).

25 In a broad sense, as Part X encompasses the proceeding for the imposition of periodic penalty penalties, which is deemed an enforcement and not a sanctioning measure *per se*, the imposition of administrative penalties, questions relating to criminal procedures and the collaboration with NCAs with a view to request them to open sanctioning proceedings in the cases covered by art. 18(5) SSM R.

5. Conclusion: a distinction can be made between sanctioning and supervisory procedures based on art. 2(24) SSM Fr and from a material perspective

The different angles analysed in precedent Paras. (a) to (d) helped draft the contours of the definition of ECB *supervisory procedures*. However, it seems that the SSM R and SSM Fr do not expressly distinguish between *sanctioning procedures* and supervisory procedures. 8.020

On the contrary, the definition of ECB supervisory procedures contemplated in art. 2(24) SSM R encompasses both common procedures and procedures relating to the imposition of administrative pecuniary penalties.[26] It would appear hence that the term supervisory procedure encompasses both *supervisory procedures stricto sensu* (for example, common procedures) and *sanctioning procedures*. 8.021

As a matter of conclusion, leveraging on the definition foreseen in art. 2(24) SSM Fr, and in a dogmatic manner, we may distinguish those ECB administrative procedures aiming at adopting supervisory measures from those aiming at punishing and deterring entities which have been found in breach of its obligations.[27] The latest would be sanctioning proceedings.[28] 8.022

B. SANCTIONING PROCEDURES VS. PROCEDURES THAT ARE CRIMINAL "IN NATURE"

Having dealt with the elusive distinction between the supervisory procedures and measures and the sanctions provided in the SSM R, it is appropriate to analyse the differences between sanctioning administrative procedures and criminal procedures or procedures having a *coloration pénale* or being materially criminal, which will be referred to below.[29] 8.023

---

26 Which are actually a type of administrative penalties. Cf Section C. (*Allocation of sanctioning competences: a specialty over the general rule?*) in Chapter 6.

27 D'Ambrosio, focusing on the wording of arts. 66(2) and 67(2) CRD IV, also notes that the material legislation to be applied by the ECB – once transposed by MSs – does not provide for a clear distinction between supervisory and sanctioning procedures. See D'Ambrosio, R. (ed.). (2020)(i) at p. 150.

28 It is also possible distinguishing those procedures aiming at compelling entities to comply with their supervisory obligations. Those are enforcement proceedings which substantiate, basically, by imposing periodic pecuniary penalties. Cf Section 4.11 of the SSM Supervisory Manual.

29 For an in-depth analysis on the relationship between the SSM R sanctioning procedures and national criminal (and enforcement) measures regarding the banking sector, see Allegrezza, S. (ed.). (2020).

8.024 The ultimate aim of this analysis pursues a practical objective, which is to determine the specificities, potentially in the form of additional guarantees (administrative procedural principles), that the latter procedure should conform with and to verify, ultimately, whether the SSM R sanctioning procedure complies with it.

8.025 As a starting point and in accordance with the case law of the ECtHR, we must take into account the content of art. 6 of the ECHR. This provision enshrines, throughout its three Paras., the right to a fair trial. In brief, Para. 1 sets out the right of the accused in criminal proceedings (a situation that can be extended to civil proceedings affecting citizens) to be heard orally by an impartial tribunal, as determined by law.[30] Para. 2 contemplates the procedural guarantee of innocence presumption.[31] Finally, Para. 3 of this provision contains the minimum guarantees associated with these types of criminal procedures.[32]

8.026 Art. 48 of the ECHR expressly contemplates the right of the defendant to be presumed innocent (although it is doubtful whether it applies only to criminal procedures or to both administrative and criminal proceedings). The ECHR further contemplates the principle of criminal legality and the proportionality of criminal offences and penalties,[33] which have a more material dimension. Finally, the ECHR makes also reference to the principle of *ne bis in idem*, as specifically applicable to criminal proceedings.[34] These would be the basic procedural guarantees that criminal procedures should conform with.

8.027 The question arises as to when a procedure may be considered of criminal or penal nature, obliging MSs to apply the content and safeguards provided for above.[35] In other words, what is a criminal procedure? To this end, the repeated case law of the ECtHR has pointed out that the classification of a procedure as criminal has an autonomous meaning, which must therefore be dissociated from the taxonomy that the signatory states[36] may attribute to them.

---

30 Cf with art. 47 (paragraphs I and II) of the Charter.

31 Cf art. 48 of the Charter.

32 It should be noted that paragraph 3 of the article expressly refers to the "accused" (and not to the defendant) in terminology specific to criminal procedure. On the administrative procedural principles applicable by the ECB under the SSM, see Section C. (*Substantive law & sanctioning proceedings: issues and proposals to overcome them*) in Chapter 7.

33 Art. 49 of the Charter.

34 Cf art. 4 of Protocol 7 to the ECHR.

35 And basically, from a pure procedural perspective, with art. 6 ECHR.

36 See, for example, ECtHR judgment in *Mackenzie v. United Kingdom* (Application No. 22301/93): "*The Commission therefore has to ascertain whether there was a "criminal charge" against the applicant* (...).

In this regard, it should be recalled that criminal law, by virtue of the principle of minimum intervention, is the last resort when there are no other instruments or strategies that allow the dissuasive or punitive result desired by the public authorities to be achieved.[37][38] **8.028**

This is not a minor issue, since, for example, if the concept of criminal procedure were to be left to the discretion of the MSs acceding to the ECHR, a simple legislative decision would be sufficient to decriminalise a given conduct. Hence, such conduct could be placed at a lower level of punitive reproach (for example, reducing it to an administrative offence) to evade the application of the guarantees provided for in art. 6 ECHR.[39] **8.029**

In order to determine autonomously what is to be considered a criminal procedure or a criminal offence, the ECtHR has developed over time a well-formed body of case law, built on the case the *Engel and others v. the Netherlands* case of 8 June 1976 (*Engel case*).[40] **8.030**

In this case, the applicants were Dutch nationals serving in the army in 1971. Thus, all of them were imposed various penalties by their superiors for breach of military discipline. It came into question the compatibility of the procedure and sanctions provided for in the military disciplinary regulations, then in force in the Netherlands. More specifically, and for the purposes of what is relevant here, the applicants questioned whether the deprivation of liberty they suffered, in the form of a penalty of arrest, was contrary to art. 5 ECHR. They also questioned the compatibility of the procedure followed before the **8.031**

The Commission recalls that these expressions are to be interpreted as having an autonomous meaning in the context of the Convention and not on the basis of their meaning in domestic law (see Eur. Court H.R., Deweer judgment of 27 February 1980, Series A no. 35, p. 22 para. 42)".

37 The limited number of penalties imposed by the ECB pursuant to art. 18(1) SSM R and, also, the few sanctioning proceedings that the ECB has requested the NCAs to open seems to evidence that penalties are an extraordinary tool. They would be used as a sort of *last resort to be* accessed through a staged procedure, once the other instruments available to the ECB (supervisory and *enforcement* measures) have been exhausted or revealed to be insufficient. The sanctions published by the ECB can be accessed here: https://www.bankingsupervision.europa.eu/banking/sanctions/html/index.en.html.

38 This is the view of the Spanish Constitutional court. Cf Spanish Constitutional Court's ruling No. 24/2004 of 24 February (RTC 2004\24).

39 This is precisely the issue portrayed in the *Guide on Article 6* (*Right to a fair trial*) produced by the ECtHR. To this end, this guide (p. 10, Para. 5) states that: "*5. As regards the autonomous notion of 'criminal', the Convention is not opposed to the moves towards 'decriminalisation' among the Contracting States. However, offences classified as 'regulatory' following decriminalisation may come under the autonomous notion of a 'criminal' offence. Leaving States the discretion to exclude these offences might lead to results incompatible with the object and purpose of the Convention (see Öztürk v. Germany, § 49)*".

The guidance can be consulted here: https://www.echr.coe.int/documents/guide_art_6_criminal_eng.pdf.

40 Applications no. 5100/71; 5101/71; 5102/71; 5354/72; and 5370/72.

military authority with the system of guarantees provided for in art. 6 ECHR, and finally, it was alleged that the way in which the appellants were treated was discriminatory, in breach of art. 14 of the ECHR.

8.032 When determining the application of art. 6 of the ECHR, the ECtHR pointed out that the concept of "criminal matters" must be examined independently, in light of the ECHR. To that end, in order to determine whether an accusation or procedure is materially criminal in light of the Convention, the *Engel* case is based on a threefold examination, which has been carried out to date:[41]

(i) *First of all*, it must be examined whether the legal texts which set out the offence in question are part of the system of criminal law, disciplinary law[42] or both. It is therefore a question of taking into account the formal classification of the offence under domestic law. However, as the *Engel* judgment points out: "*This indication has no formal and relative value, and must be examined in the light of the common denominator of the respective laws of the various contracting Member States*". Only if national legislation classifies this offence as criminal can the domestic classification of the state in question be given a relevant and decisive effect.[43]

(ii) *Secondly*, the nature of the sanction should be examined as an element of paramount importance. The question is therefore to determine whether the subsequent sanction to be imposed has a restorative purpose (in the civil field) or a punitive one, pursuing a deterrent effect with regards to the generality or to a specific sector of individuals. In this sense, it is a question of judging the ultimate interest protected by the rule in question, determining, on a case-by-case basis, whether the protected object is specific to the criminal law, affecting the generality in an indeterminate manner.[44]

The ECtHR has specified a series of case-by-case parameters to evaluate this criterion, which includes: (i) whether the rule is addressed to a small group of individuals or to the general public, (ii) whether the procedure is initiated by a public body vested with enforcement powers, (iii) whether the rule in question has or seeks to have a punitive or dissuasive effect, (v) whether the imposition of the penalty depends on the alleged offender being found guilty and (vi) whether

41 As regards the classification of the administrative penalties contemplated in the SSM R in light of the Engel criteria, see D'Ambrosio, R. (2021); and Felisatti, V. (2018).

42 It is also understood as administrative, not exclusively in the sense of sanctioning a group of people who are particularly subject to an extraordinary service relationship with the State.

43 Ibidem footnote 39: "7. *The first criterion is of relative weight and serves only as a starting-point. If domestic law classifies an offence as criminal, then this will be decisive. Otherwise the Court will look behind the national classification and examine the substantive reality of the procedure in question*".

44 See, in this sense, *Grande Stevens et autres v. Italy of 4 March 2014* (Applications Nos 18640/10, 18647/10, 18663/10, 18668/10 and 18698/10), where, concerning the interest protected by the infringement and the recipients of a sanction imposed for practices infringing full information on the stock market, it concluded (Para. 96) that a fine aimed at mainly punishing a given infringement and/or detering the commission of a future similar infringement pursues the objectives of general criminal law. The foregoing, even if such a fine aims at ancillary remedying the damages suffered by the people affected by the infringement committed.

the classification of similar procedures established by the signatory states is similar.[45]

(iii) *Ultimately*, the degree of severity of the penalty that may be imposed should be examined. In this case, it is a question of examining the potential penalty, in the abstract, which may be imposed on the alleged offender, not so much the specific penalty imposed on him following the mandatory procedure.[46]

In this sense, attention should be paid to the degree of severity, in the abstract, that the penalty or sanction imposed on the alleged offender,[47] and the potential effects that it can have on it; for example, the ban from exercising a given profession for a certain period of time may have an effect not only on the subject's property but may also affect their reputation, thereby compromising its integrity.[48] **8.033**

The above criteria are of an alternative nature and not, in general, cumulative.[49] However, the ECtHR has stated that in cases where a separate analysis of each of the above criteria (especially the second and third ones) does not lead to a clear conclusion, a cumulative analysis of both may be used in order to determine more precisely whether or not the offence or procedure in question is criminal[50] in nature. **8.034**

It should also be noted that the ECtHR has been following this threefold analysis with hardly any significant variations.[51] **8.035**

45 See, in this respect, the *Guide on Article 6 (Right to a fair trial)* cited above. See, also, D'Ambrosio, R. (2013) at pp. 19 and ss. In addition to the case law set out in the *Guide* itself, the author adds, within the criteria set out in that case law, that the fact that the offence imposed does not give rise to a criminal record may be indicative, but not decisive, citing to that effect the case of *Ravnsborg v. Sweden* (Application No. 14220/88).

46 See, in this respect, *Ezeh and Connors v. the United Kingdom* (Applications Nos 39665/98 and 40086/98).

47 *Grande Stevens et autres v. Italy of 4 March 2014* (Applications Nos 18640/10, 18647/10, 18663/10, 18668/10 and 18698/10), at Para. 98.

48 Ibidem, at Para. 122.

49 According to the criterion established early on in the Engel case, with regard to the alternation of criteria, it seems that there would, in any case, be an exclusionary priority, at least with regard to the first criterion in relation to the following two. Thus, if national legislation classifies an infringement as criminal, the following parameters should obviously not be used.

50 See, in this sense, the case of *Jussila v. Finland* (Application No. 73053/01), in which the ECtHR pointed out in this respect that: "*This does not exclude a cumulative approach where separate analysis of each criterion does not make it possible to reach a clear conclusion as to the existence of a criminal charge (see Ezeh and Connors, cited above, § 86, citing, inter alia, Bendenoun, cited above, § 47*" (Para. 31).

51 Thus, in *Bendenoun v. France (*Application No. 12547/86), the ECtHR examined the criminal nature of penalty and tax surcharge proceedings, providing four criteria which did not strictly refer to the three-way classification contained in the *Engel case*. In this case, it could be seen that the ECtHR had deviated from its initial criterion.

8.036 The CJEU has followed the approach of the ECtHR, as it is clear from the *Bonda* case.[52] However, the CJEU seems to have been lately giving a greater weight to the second criterion (nature of the sanction) to determine when a penalty is criminal in nature, using this third criterion to confirm its conclusions.[53] Nevertheless, this preference of the CJEU does not seem to contradict the ECtHR approach and, in any event, does not prescind the analysis when appropriate of the third criterion (severity of the penalty that may be imposed). Hence, being noted that, pursuant to art. 52(3) of the Charter, in principle, the CJEU should not deviate from the interpretations provided by the ECtHR. This, insofar as the Charter contains rights provided in the ECHR, considering that the latter court provides the *authentic* interpretations of the meaning and scope of such rights (including when a penalty would be criminal in nature).[54]

8.037 All in all, the foregoing jurisprudential considerations must be applied (i) to determine the nature of the administrative penalties that the ECB may apply under the SSM R (and eventually also to the ECB supervisory procedures) and (ii) to serve as a framework for monitoring the safeguards of proceedings that are deemed to be materially criminal.

C. ARE THE SUPERVISORY AND SANCTIONING PROCEDURES FORESEEN IN THE SSM CRIMINAL "IN NATURE"?

1. SSM administrative penalties: criminal in nature

8.038 In the light of the above, it is worth considering whether the administrative penalties provided for in paragraphs (1) and (7) of art. 18 SSM R (including periodic penalty payments[55]) should be characterised as materially criminal or purely administrative.

However, in the *Jussila* case, the ECtHR made clear that those criteria did not depart from its general criterion but that it had to be assumed that they corresponded to additional elements of judgment in respect of the second and third criteria in the *Engel* case law (see *Jussila* at Para. *32).*

52 Court of Justice judgment in case C-489/10 (*Łukasz Marcin Bonda*) of 5 June 2012 (ECLI:EU:C:2012:319).

53 See D'Ambrosio, R. (ed.). (2020) at pp. 153 and ss.; and D'Ambrosio, R. (2021) at p. 321. See, also, Lamandini, M., Ramos Muñoz, D. & Solana, J. (2016) at pp. 212–213.

See Court of Justice judgments in cases C-537/16 (*Garlsson Real estate v. Commissione nazionale per le società e la borsa*), 20 March 2018 (ECLI:EU:C:2018:193) and C-524/15 (*Luca Menci*) of 20 March 2018 (ECLI:EU:C:2018:197).

54 See D'Ambrosio, R. (2013) at p. 21.

55 Cf art. 1(7) of Regulation 2532/1998 defining *sanctions* as both fines and periodic penalty payments.

To this end, (i) first, it will be analysed whether administrative penalty payments have a *coloration pénale*. Subsequently, (ii) it will be discussed whether the fines foreseen in art. 18(7) may deserve being classified as criminal in nature. Finally, (iii) the same analysis will be carried out as regards periodic penalty payments. **8.039**

(a) Administrative pecuniary penalties as criminal in nature

Thus, as regards the administrative pecuniary penalties set forth in art. 18(1) of the SSM R, it provides for the possibility of imposing on credit institutions a fine of **8.040**

> *up to twice the amount of the profits gained or losses avoided because of the breach where those can be determined, or up to 10 % of the total annual turnover, as defined in relevant Union law, of a legal person in the preceding business year or such other pecuniary penalties as may be provided for in relevant Union law.*

Accordingly, if those penalties are submitted to the analysis of the three *Engel* criteria, it turns out that, as regards their formal classification under the domestic law (which in this case would be EU law), they must be considered as *administrative sanctions*. **8.041**

However, the examination of these types of penalties in light of the second *Engel criterion* (nature or object of the penalties) leads to the conclusion that they would be materially criminal. The punitive and dissuasive effect of the imposition of these penalties,[56] together with the fact that they are linked to a positive assessment of the culpability of the entity concerned, confirms this conclusion.[57] **8.042**

Similarly, if we look at the third criterion – the severity of the potential penalty that can be imposed – it seems logical to conclude that this type of penalty is materially criminal in nature. An amount of *or up to 10% of the total annual turnover*, to be calculated at a consolidated level,[58] can mean, indeed, a significant amount both in relative and in absolute terms.[59] Consequently, the **8.043**

---

56 In this sense, vid. *Öztürk v. Germany* (Application no. 8544/79), at Para. 53.). It must be recalled that art. 18(3) SSM R states that: "*The sanctions applied must be effective, proportionate and dissuasive.* (…)". See, also, Recital 32 SSM R.

57 Vid. *Benham v. the United Kingdom* (Application no. 19380/92), at Para. 56.

58 Cf art. 18(2) SSM R and 128 SSM Fr.

59 Even for the smallest SIs, subject to ECB direct supervision due to being one of the three biggest entities located in a given MSs. Cf arts. 6(4) *i.f.* SSM R and 65 SSM Fr.

procedure for imposing such administrative pecuniary penalties must therefore be based on the guarantees of art. 6 of the ECHR.[60]

8.044 One must also recall that art. 18(1) SSM R does contemplate the possibility of using the criterion of profits gained or losses avoided to determine the amount of the penalties. Accordingly, such an article allows the ECB imposing administrative pecuniary penalties up to twice of such an amount.

8.045 The conclusion on the criminal nature of the penalties provided for in art. 18(1) SSM R must remain unchanged, despite the possibility of using the criterion of the profits gained/losses avoided as a yardstick to determine the amount of the penalties. According to the *Engel* case law, the potential amount of the penalty should be taken, which would require, in any event, using the criterion of the total annual turnover to assess the severity of the penalty at stake.

8.046 Moreover, the severity of the penalty that can be imposed on the basis of the profits gained/losses avoided were to be considered separately, it would also appear that the penalty is sufficient to be considered materially criminal.[61]

(b) Fines foreseen in art. 18(7) SSM R as criminal in nature

8.047 Art. 18(7) SESCB allows the ECB to impose economic fines on any type of supervised institutions (SIs and LSIs) due to non-compliance with regulations adopted by the ECB, which are directly applicable to them, or in respect of decisions directly imposed by the ECB on such institutions, in accordance with Regulation 2532/98.

8.048 The initial wording of Regulation 2532/98 provided that the ECB could impose fines of up to EUR 500.000.[62] Such Regulation was amended in 2015[63] in order to align it with the SSM, encompassing the possibility for the ECB to impose sanctions concerning supervisory breaches. After such amendment, art. 4a(1) foresees that, "*for infringements relating to decisions and regulations*

---

60 D'Ambrosio, R. (2013) at pp. 26 and ss.

61 In the *Steininger v. Austria* (Application No. 21539/07), the ECtHR held that a penalty surcharge on an agricultural fee, which could be as much as twice the unpaid amount, was dissuasive and punitive in nature and that the amount to which such a surcharge could be applied was not insignificant. In that regard, that line of reasoning would reinforce the fact that a penalty of up to twice the amount unduly perceived (profit gained) would be of a punitive nature.

62 Cf art. 2.1.a) of Regulation 2532/98.

63 Regulation 2015/159 amending Regulation (EC) No. 2532/98 concerning the powers of the European Central Bank to impose sanctions.

adopted by the ECB in the exercise of its supervisory tasks", it may impose fines in line with the upper limits contemplated in art. 18(1) SSM R.[64]

Before 2015, the upper limit of the fines foreseen in Regulation 2532/1998 of EUR 500.000 cast doubts as to their allegedly material criminal nature.[65] **8.049**

Considering that, currently, the amounts of the fines that can be applied by the ECB are the same that are foreseen for the commission of administrative pecuniary penalties, the same reasoning must be followed herein, and therefore, they must be considered as criminal in nature.[66] **8.050**

(c) Periodic penalty payments

For the periodic penalty payments concerning supervisory breaches,[67] the approach is different than for fines and administrative pecuniary penalties. The starting point, i.e., the first criterion of the *Engel* test, remains the same;[68] administrative pecuniary penalties are classified as *administrative* (not criminal) measures.[69] **8.051**

As regards the second criterion (the nature of the penalty), the paths may be slightly divergent. Regulation 2532/98 classifies, in a broad sense, periodic penalty payments as sanctions.[70] However, the definition of periodic penalty payments contained in that regulation attribute them a twofold nature, (i) **8.052**

---

64 "*for fines, the upper limit shall be twice the amount of the profits gained or losses avoided because of the infringement where these can be determined, or 10 % of the total annual turnover of the undertaking*". The creation of separate procedural rules for SSM supervisory sanctions implies, somehow, a division between (a) sanctions established in Regulation 2532/1998 before the modification operated by Regulation 2015/159 and (b) those established by such Regulation (mainly in arts. 4a to 4c, by derogating from arts. 2, 3 and 4).

65 In this regard, see D'Ambrosio, R. (2013).

However, in the *Steininger v. Austria* case, referred to in footnote 61, the ECtHR considered that the high surcharge actually imposed on the claimant for failure to comply with his obligations to pay an agricultural levy (60% of the amount initially due) made such a surcharge to be considered criminal in nature. In the present case, the amount at which that surcharge amounted to is just over EUR 7,000.

Following this reasoning, it must be noted that the ECB was able to impose, under Regulation 2532/1998 before 2015, a fine of up to EUR 500.000, that is, a figure more than 70 times higher than the surcharge prosecuted in *Steninger*. In this regard, one may consider that even before the amendment operated in such a Regulation in 2015, such fines were to be considered as criminal in nature, due to their potential abstract severity in light of the *Engel* jurisprudence.

66 See D'Ambrosio, R. (2021) at pp. 319–322.

67 Cf arts. 4a, 4b and 4c Regulation 2532/1998, as distinguished from periodic penalty payments regarding other fields: e.g., Infringements of the minimum reserves requirements stated in Regulation 1745/2003 of the European Central Bank of 12 September 2003 on the application of minimum reserves (ECB/2003/9), or in connection with the payment system (e.g., as regards Regulation 795/2014 of 3 July 2014 on oversight requirements for systemically important payment systems (ECB/2014/28)). See, also, footnote 64.

68 See Allegrezza, S. & Voordeckers, O. (2015) at p. 156. See, also, Felisatti, V. (2018) at pp. 388–392.

69 Cf art. 129 SSM Fr.

70 Together with fines. See footnote 55.

as a punishment measure or (ii) as an enforcement measure "*with a view to forcing the persons concerned to comply with the ECB supervisory regulations and decisions*".[71]

8.053 Periodic penalty payments are not defined in the SSM Fr nor in the SSM R. Yet, CRD VI introduced its definition in CRD IV (art. 3(1)(67)). This definition makes clear that periodic penalty payments are chiefly aimed at bringing ongoing infringements to an end and are therefore of a purely enforcement nature.

8.054 The SSM Fr seems to attribute periodic penalty payments an enforcement nature as well. The foregoing based on art. 129(1) SSM Fr, which contemplates its application "*[i]n the event of a continuing breach of a regulation or supervisory decision of the ECB*". Consequently, the SSM Fr only contemplates the use of such a supervisory tool for as long as a breach is *ongoing* to compel the supervisee to return to the complying path and not when its commission has ceased (in which case, an administrative penalty may be imposed).[72] Moreover, the SSM Supervisory Manual is consistent with such an approach,[73] crystallising the ECB's perception on this matter. Finally, and from a regulatory perspective, Recital 9 of Regulation 2015/159 attributes to these penalties a compelling character. It follows from the foregoing that they would have, as regards the SSM, an enforcement dimension.

8.055 Concerning the third and final *Engel* criterion (the severity of the measure), it seems objectively that 5% of the average daily turnover per day of infringement can be, in abstract, a substantive amount. In perspective, such an amount, imposed during the maximum envisaged time (six months), means a potential total fine of 2.5% of the annual turnover. In the view of the author, such materiality advocates in favour of considering them as criminal in nature. There would be another factor favouring such an approach: procedural guarantees consistence, in the sense of subjecting such periodic penalty payments to equivalent guarantee levels than the one foreseen for administrative penalties.[74] In

71 Art. 1(6) Regulation 2532/1998. Yet, art. 65(3) CRD IV (after the amendment performed by CRD VI) classifies periodic penalty payments as purely enforcement measures, different from (i) administrative penalties and (ii) other measures (cf arts. 66(2)(b) and 67(2)(b) CRD IV).

See, also, D'Ambrosio, R. (ed.). (2020)(i) at pp. 152 and ss. This author notes the twofold nature of periodic penalty payments (and the enforcement nature of such measures under the SSM Fr). However, based on the eventual prevalence of Regulation 2532/1998 over the SSM Fr, he seems to support a more formal approach encompassing its *sanctioning character* as defined in art. 1(7) of such Regulation.

72 Against this approach, see D'Ambrosio, R. (2021) at p. 319–320.

73 Cf footnote 28.

74 In favour of considering periodic penalty payments as criminal in nature sanctions, see Felisatti, V. (2018) at p. 390–391. Against this approach, see D'Ambrosio, R. (2021) at p. 322.

principle, pursuant to art. 129(1) SSM R, such periodic penalty payments are subject to Part III SSM Fr, which contemplates a set of procedural rights compliant with art. 6(1) ECHR, provided that they are interpreted in a manner accommodating the Charter and ultimately the ECHR.[75]

2. ECB exercise of supervisory powers: are they criminal penalties in nature?

It is also worth considering what happens to those supervisory *powers*[76] contemplated in art. 16 SSM R. These measures are formally classified as supervisory powers,[77] but consequences that their application may have for institutions could be of a materially criminal nature in light of the *Engel* case law analysed. **8.056**

Thus, this typology of measures could be grouped under the following scheme, those referring to (i) the limitation of activities and the risks inherent in the activity,[78] (ii) the removal of the members of the management body of the institution,[79] (iii) the increase on the frequency and/or level of reporting and disclosure requirements[80] and (iv) the reinforcement of governance arrangements.[81] **8.057**

Whereas for the groups (iii) and (iv) above, their classification, aim and severity points towards not being considered as penalties (nor even at having a *coloration pénale*), groups (i) and (ii) cast some doubts. **8.058**

As regards (i) the limitation of the activity or the restriction of the risks assumed by the entities concerned, it seems very difficult to make an abstract judgement on this matter, and a case-by-case analysis of the proposed measure will be necessary. In this vein, the greater the limitation or constraint imposed on the normal development of the activity by the supervised entity, the greater the severity could be attributed to the deserving supervisory measure. **8.059**

---

75 See Section D. (*Consequences of administrative penalties being qualified as criminal in "nature"*) below.

76 This is indeed the title of art. 16 SSM R. In principle, they would be a type of *powers* attributed to the ECB under the SSM. Cf Section C. (*From "tasks" to "powers"*) in Chapter 5.

77 See art. 16(2) SSM R, which mirrors art. 104 CRD IV. The supervisory powers contemplated in the second sub-paragraph of art. 16 SSM R are expected to be expressed via a relevant ECB supervisory decision, to be adopted pursuant to the ECB supervisory procedure.

78 Art. 16(2)(a), (c), (d), (e), (f), (g), (h), (i) and (k) SSM R.

79 Art. 16(2)(m) SSM R.

80 Art. 16(2)(j) and (l) SSM R.

81 Art. 16(2)(b), (c) and (g) SSM R. Indent (c) is susceptible of being classified under the first (i) and fourth (iv) groups depicted by the author herein.

8.060 With regards to (ii) the removal of the members of the entities' management body and (art. 16(2)(m) SSM R), it seems *a priori* that an analysis of the seriousness of the measure would indeed lead to considering its materially criminal nature.

8.061 However, if one considers, on the one hand, their classification as supervisory powers (hence of an *administrative* nature) and, on the other hand, that this measure would not pursue, in principle, a punitive or deterrent aim, it is not so easy classify them as penalties having a criminal nature.

8.062 In this respect, the case of *McParland v. United Kingdom*[82] must be mentioned. In this case,[83] the ECtHR held that art. 6(1) ECHR did not apply to the refusal to grant a driving licence to an applicant because he had a criminal record. This was precisely because it was understood that there could be no question of a criminal charge within an authorisation procedure, in which the criminal record was exclusively referred to the granting of that authorisation to drive a vehicle.[84]

8.063 Further, the Court of Justice considered, in the *UBS Europe* case,[85] that a measure taken by the national supervisor,[86] consisting in an order addressed to a director, in order to resign on the grounds that he would no longer meet the requirements to be considered suitable for that position, would be considered as part of the procedure for the withdrawal of the authorisation (hence not at as a *sanction*).[87]

8.064 Based on the foregoing precedents, it can be considered that, indeed, such supervisory power does not amount to be an *administrative sanction* and even less a criminal penalty in substance despite its potential severity.

---

82 Application No. 47898/99 of 30 November 1999.

83 Note the similarity, *mutatis mutandis,* with the provision set out in Section 3.2 (*Reputation*) of the ECB's *Guide to fit and proper assessments – December 2021*, which requires consideration of the criminal or disciplinary history (pending or past) of the manager undergoing the suitability *assessment.*

84 This judgment states textually that: "*The Court also dismisses the applicant's submission that the refusal of his application amounted to the imposition of a criminal sanction and he should therefore have been afforded the procedural guarantees guaranteed under Article 6 to persons facing a criminal charge. The Court observes that the impugned proceedings took the form of a licensing procedure. At no stage did they did involve the determination of a charge within the meaning of Article 6§1 of the Convention. This conclusion is not affected by the fact that the applicant's request for a Road Service Licence foundered on the basis of his previous criminal convictions*".
In a similar vein, see *BINGÖL v. Netherlands* (Application no. 18450/07), at Para. 36.

85 Court of Justice judgment in case C-358/16 (*UBS Europe*) of 13 September 2018 (ECLI:EU:C:2018:715).

86 The Luxembourgish *Commission de Surveillance du Secteur Financier* (CSSF) in this case.

87 Ibidem at Para. 46. See, also, D'Ambrosio, R. (ed.). (2020)(i) at pp. 156–157.

Distinguishing any further goes beyond this analysis, as it entails assessing the approach taken by MSs when transposing the so-defined administrative measures foreseen in arts. 66(2)(c) and 67(2)(c) of CRD IV.[88] CRD IV uses the doubtful term *administrative measures* to name such measures.[89] Ultimately, the classification of such administrative measures as supervisory powers and/or administrative penalties (in a broad sense) would depend on how the respective MSs have transposed CRD IV, not being possible to anticipate such treatment.[90] **8.065**

In light of the foregoing, the author is of the view that the supervisory powers foreseen in art. 16 SSM R, even if they entail *severe consequences* for the supervised entities, cannot be considered as administrative penalties and, even less, as penalties criminal in nature. **8.066**

In the particular case of group (i) administrative powers (limitation of the activity or the restriction of the risks assumed by the entities concerned), it does not seem possible to judge the matter in abstract terms. A case-by-case analysis needs to be carried out to ascertain whether those should be classified as administrative penalties having a *coloration pénale*. In this token, the stricter that measure would be,[91] the more similar this will be to the disqualification penalty. But even in that case, the precedents ruled by the ECtHR and the CJEU as regards cases involving the application of administrative measures[92] point towards not attributing to such measures a *penal* nature. Consequently, the courts may be tempted stick to their own precedents; hence, a prudent approach demands considering that even those will not be treated as penalties having a criminal nature, not even as administrative penalties. **8.067**

---

88 And mentioned in art. 65 CRD IV.

89 Recital 56 of the SSM R refers to *supervisory measures*, which overall seem to be used as a synonym of supervisory powers.

90 For example, Spanish Act 10/2014 on Organisation, Supervision and Solvency of Credit institutions classify such types of measures as non-pecuniary penalties or measures accessory to pecuniary penalties, hence, penalties as well. Cf arts. 97 to 102 of the mentioned law. See, also, Court of Justice judgment in case C-52/17 *(VTB Bank AG)* of 7 August 2018 (ECLI:EU:C:2018:648). There, the Court acknowledged that (i) the list of administrative measures contained in arts. 66(2) and 67(2) CRD IV is not exhaustive and (ii) a national measure providing for interest to be levied, in case the large exposure limits were overcome (even if, in abstract terms, it may be severe), does qualify as an administrative measure pursuant to art. 65 CRD IV. For a dedicated comment on this case, see Poscia, J. (2021). The VTB case: Administrative penalties and administrative measures. In *Judicial Review in the European Banking Union* (pp. 571–578). Edward Elgar Publishing.

91 I.e., entailing the total interdiction to conduct certain businesses, which may be capital for the continuity of the entity or which substantially contribute to its business model, or even more, the practical interdiction of continuing to carry out the business of credit institutions (at least until some additional safeguards or requisites are met).

92 Concerning the withdrawal of licenses or the denegation of permission to take managerial positions.

D. CONSEQUENCES OF ADMINISTRATIVE PENALTIES BEING QUALIFIED AS CRIMINAL IN "NATURE"

8.068 Penalties considered to be of a criminal nature must comply with the fundamental procedural guarantees and rights foreseen in art. 6 ECHR.[93] This set of guarantees include:

(i) *Firstly*, (a) the right to be heard in a public hearing (within a reasonable time) (b) by an independent and impartial court (Para. 1 of art. 6 ECHR). This requirement will be further analysed below.
(ii) *Secondly*, the presumption of innocence (Para. 2 of art. 6 ECHR), which would be somehow implied in art. 22(2) SSM R.
(iii) *Finally*, a set of minimum rights that guarantee that the person charged with a criminal charge can fairly understand the charges she or he is being accused of and prepare her or his legal defence with sufficient guarantees (Para. 3 of art. 6 ECHR). These minimum rights include: (i) the right to be informed promptly of the charges in an understandable language,[94] (ii) to be granted enough time to prepare the defence,[95] (iii) the right to be assisted or represented by a lawyer;[96] (iv) to examine witnesses[97] and (v) to have the assistance of an interpreter, in case the accused cannot understand the language used in court.[98]

8.069 It results from the foregoing that, in principle, the minimum procedural guarantees required in the second and third Paras. of art. 6 ECHR are actually foreseen in the SSM sanctioning procedure.

8.070 As regards the right to be heard foreseen in the first Para. of such provision (and notwithstanding the analysis contained in the next Section below), this is also contemplated in the SSM Fr. The only exception would be periodic penalties in which, in principle, because of being considered an administrative nature and subject to the procedural rules foreseen in Part III SSM Fr, the right to be heard can be supressed.[99]

---

93 These guarantees are similarly contemplated in arts. 47 to 49 of the Charter.

94 Cf arts. 22(1) SSM R; 24, 33 and 126(1)–(2) SSM Fr and 4b(3) Regulation 2532/1998.

95 Cf art. 22(2) SSM R, 31(3) and 126 SSM Fr; and 4b(3) Regulation 2532/1998.

96 Cf art. 22(2) SSM R; 27, 126(3) SSM Fr and 4b(3) Regulation 2532/1998.

97 Cf art. 22(2) SSM R and 30 SSM Fr.

98 Cf footnote 94. In principle, such right would be sufficiently guaranteed due to the flexibility of the language arrangements to be agreed by the supervised entity and the ECB. See, also, Section B.1. (*The sources of administrative procedural law for the ECB under the SSM*) in Chapter 7. As indicated there, arrangement may be *ad hoc* and as sophisticated as the supervised entity may wish.

99 Cf art. 22(1) SSM R and 31(4) SSM Fr. However, above, the author has argued that, due to the severity in abstract that these periodic penalty payments can entail, they are to be considered as sanctions materially criminal.

Such an apparent flaw regarding pecuniary penalty payments may not be a flaw if we consider that (i) the affected entity must be given the opportunity to be heard ex post, that is, after the relevant supervisory decision imposing the periodic pecuniary penalty has been taken.[100] (ii) Furthermore, such requirement can be cured if the public hearing can take place before a court that has full jurisdiction.[101] In addition, in practical terms, it is difficult to think of a case in which the necessity to impose a periodic penalty payment is so urgent in order to prevent a "significant damage to the financial system"[102] that the right to be heard cannot be granted before imposing such an adverse decision on the supervisee. Such a situation does not seem to be realistic and, therefore, the right to be heard may apply, in any event, to periodic penalty payments in the same terms than from administrative pecuniary penalties and fines. **8.071**

1. Sanctions having a criminal nature imposed by an administrative (not jurisdictional) body: right to a fair trial under the SSM R?

Art. 6(1) ECHR[103] frameworks the basic safeguards linked to the right for an effective judicial remedy. These form part of a greater right: the right to a *fair trial*.[104] This is most likely the most relevant procedural guarantee as regards criminal procedures.[105] **8.072**

The CJEU and the ECtHR have admitted that administrative bodies may impose penalties which would be materially criminal,[106] provided that the offender would have access to a court being independent and impartial and having full or unlimited jurisdiction.[107] **8.073**

100 Pursuant to art. 31(5) SSM Fr.

101 Cf D'Ambrosio, R (ed.). (2020)(i) at p. 251.

102 Cf arts. 22(2) SSM R and 31(4) SSM Fr.

103 And 47 of the Charter. It must be noted that, pursuant to art. 52(3) of the Charter, the Charter's rights corresponding to those foreseen in the ECHR shall have the same meaning and scope unless they are given a more extensive protection.

104 Which, in principle, together with the principles of culpability, *ne bis in idem*, the right to remain silent and the principle of separation between the investigative and decision-making phase would conform the minimum or core guarantees applicable to a sanction having a *coloration pénale*. Cf D'Ambrosio, R. (2013) at p. 69.

105 And would encompass the right to be publicly heard before an independent and impartial tribunal.

106 See Court of Justice judgment in case C-199/11 (*Community v. Otis*) of 6 November 2012 (*ECLI:EU:C:2012:684*).

107 This would mean that, on top of the legality review of the penalty imposed, the Court would be entitled to substitute the assessment of the fine imposed by the given EU institution or body, by the Court's own assessment. The foregoing empowers the Court to eventually increase, decrease or remove the fine imposed on the relevant claimant. See Lenaerts, K., Maselis, I. and Gutman, K. (2015) *at* p. 394.

8.074 Resource to full jurisdiction seems to be capital to ensure fair trial rights and guarantees. Further, such unlimited jurisdiction guarantees that the minimum procedural guarantees contemplated in art. 6 ECHR are respected. Those, on top of the right an effective judicial remedy, include, among others, the principle of separation between investigative and decision-making phases.

8.075 The foregoing results from the cumulative analysis of the three landmark cases: *Dubus*,[108] *Menarini*[109] and *Grande Stevens*.[110]

8.076 In *Dubus*, the ECtHR found that the French *Commission bancaire* was a tribunal for the purposes of the ECHR and that its configuration fell short to ensure that there was a separation between the instruction and the decision phase.[111] Such lack of separation was not able to be *cured* by the possibility to appeal before the *Conseil d'Etat*, as such a court would not have unlimited jurisdiction to review the penalty imposed by the Commission (only the legal grounds brought in the appeal[112]).

8.077 In *Menarini*, the ECtHR concluded that administrative authorities[113] could impose penalties that are criminal in nature, on the condition that the sanction imposed can be reviewed by a *tribunal* (within the meaning of art. 6(1) ECHR) having full jurisdiction. Such unlimited jurisdiction would imply the possibility of reviewing both the legal and factual grounds, the proportionality of the choices made by such an administrative body (and of the sanctions imposed) and even the technical assessments.[114]

8.078 Finally, in *Grande Stevens*, the ECtHR acknowledged that the Turin Court of appeal was indeed a *tribunal* within the meaning of art. 6(1) ECHR, having full jurisdiction to review administrative penalties imposed by the CONSOB[115] regarding financial markets infringements.[116] However, the Court concluded that the hearings held before the appeal court (having the unlimited jurisdiction) were not public. Hence, notwithstanding the full jurisdiction of the

108 *Dubus S.A. c. France* (application no. 5242/04) ECtHR judgment of 11 June 2009.

109 *Menarini Diagnostics s.r.l. c. Italy* (application no. 43509/08) ECtHR judgment of 27 September 2011. See, also, Bellamy, C. (2012). ECHR and competition law post Menarini: An overview of EU and national case law. *e-Competitions, N°47946*, 5 July 2012.

110 *Grande Stevens et autres c. Italy* (applications nos. 18640/10, 18647/10, 18663/10, 18668/10 and 18698/10) ECtHR judgment of 4 March 2014.

111 See *Dubus* Para. 50.

112 Ibidem at Para. 49.

113 In the case at stake a competition one, the *Autorità Garante della Concorrenza e del Mercato.*

114 See *Menarini* at Paras. 59, 62, 64 and 66.

115 *Commissione Nazionale per le Società e la Borsa*, the Italian stock market authority.

116 *Grande Stevens* at Para. 151.

appeal court, the ECtHR concluded that there was no public hearing in the sense of art. 6(1) ECHR and found the Italian Republic in breach of such a Convention. Therefore, one may read such judgment in the sense that the public hearing, as an element ensuring a fair trial, must happen in the administrative phase but in any event before the court which is granted the unlimited jurisdiction.[117]

It follows from the foregoing that compliance with the fundamental rights foreseen in the ECHR and the Charter demands that administrative penalties imposed by the ECB can be reviewed by a court having *full jurisdiction*. **8.079**

2. Has the CJEU unlimited jurisdiction to review administrative penalties imposed by the ECB?

The question above is self-explanatory, yet the answer that can be reached is, maybe, not as clear as it should be.[118] **8.080**

The starting point would be arts. 263 and 261 TFEU. According to the former, the CJEU performs a review of the *legality* of the reviewable acts provided by EU bodies and institutions. The control of legality to be performed by the CJEU may lead to any of the following three potential outcomes: the court upholds the act challenged, the given act is totally withheld or such act is withheld in part.[119] **8.081**

Art. 261 TFEU, on their side, provides for the possibility of granting the CJEU unlimited jurisdiction with regards to the penalties stated in pieces of secondary law. This possibility implies, in principle, vesting the CJEU with the additional capacity to modify the amount of the fine imposed.[120] Such **8.082**

---

117 If such public hearing takes place before an appeal or cassation court having only limited jurisdiction, this would not be compliant with art. 6(1) ECHR.

118 In general, concerning this specific matter, see: D'Ambrosio, R. (ed.) (2020)(i); D'Ambrosio, R. (2013); Lamandini, M., Ramos Muñoz, D. & Solana, J. (2015); and Lamandini, M., Ramos, D. & Solana, J. (2016).

119 See the opinion issued by AG Kokott in case C-194/17 P (*Georgios Pandalis*), delivered on 13 September 2018 (ECLI:EU:C:2018:725) at Para. 78 (reproduced below):

"*78. As I have already explained elsewhere, this reflects the cassatory nature of the action for annulment. Outside the scope of their unlimited jurisdiction (Article 261 TFEU), the European Union Courts may not amend the act concerned, but must declare it to be void if and in so far as the action for annulment is well founded (first paragraph of Article 264 TFEU). The European Union institutions, bodies, offices and agencies are then required to take the necessary measures to comply with the judgment annulling their decision (first paragraph of Article 266 TFEU)*".

120 See Schütze, R. & Tridimas, T. (Eds.). (2017) at. p. 592; and Sauter, W. (2016). *Coherence in EU competition law*. Oxford University Press. Some authors point out that the concept of full jurisdiction would imply that the CJEU would be able to review any material aspects (facts, legal grounds, proportionality and opportunity of the fines) of the case (not needing to complement such powers of review with the legality review foreseen in art. 263 TFEU). See Bellamy, C. (2012); and Lenaerts, K., Maselis, I. and Gutman,

provision entails that the provision of this unlimited jurisdiction must be expressly mentioned in the relevant secondary legislation.[121]

8.083 As one can easily spot, there is no express reference to the allocation of unlimited jurisdiction to the CJEU in art. 18 SSM R (nor in the SSM Fr).[122] This contrasts with the express reference contemplated in art. 5 of Regulation 2532/1998, which does attribute unlimited jurisdiction to the CJEU to review the "*final decisions whereby a sanction is imposed*".

8.084 Considering the different administrative penalties (and requests to impose penalties)[123] that the ECB may apply, the following considerations can be made as regards each type of administrative penalty:

8.085 *First*, regarding *sanctions* (periodic penalty payments and fines) imposed in accordance with art. 18(7) SSM R, the ECB must impose such sanctions pursuant to Regulation 2532/1998. The foregoing entails that the ECB must comply with the procedural stages foreseen in such Regulation and in the SSM Fr.[124] Also, since art. 5 of Regulation 2532/98 is not formally derogated as regards fines,[125] it can be construed that the CJEU retains unlimited jurisdiction. This interpretation seems to be aligned with the fundamental rights consecrated in the Charter and ECHR and, thus, with Recital 86 of the SSM R.

8.086 *Second*, regarding the administrative pecuniary penalties foreseen in art. 18(1) SSM R the issue is thornier. One may consider that the initial proposal of the SSM R submitted by the EC[126] somehow addressed such questions in an indirect matter. Draft art. 15(4) of the Commission proposal expressly stated that

K. (2015) at p. 394. These latter authors indicate that the review provided in the Treaties entails both the review of the facts and the law of the case. They affirm further that the review of legality provided in art. 263 TFEU supplemented by the review contemplated in art. 261 TFEU satisfies the requirements of effective judicial protection enshrined in art. 47 of the Charter. The doubt that arises there is what would happen in cases where only the review of the legality is provided for, especially when such review is exercised over *sanctions* which are deemed to be criminal in nature.

121 The classical example would be art. 31 of Regulation 1/2003 on the implementation of the rules on competition laid down in Articles 81 and 82 of the Treaty.

122 In fact, only a timid reference to the review to be performed by the CJEU as regards ECB decisions can be found in art. 24(11) SSM R. Also, reference to the role of the CJEU in reviewing ECB request to access investigated subjects is made in art. 13(2) SSM R (cf also Recital 60 SSM R).

123 See Section C. (*Allocation of sanctioning competences: a specialty over the general rule?*) In Chapter 6.

124 As the procedural rules contemplated therein must complete those of Regulation 2532/98. See, further, Section B. (*ECB direct sanctioning powers: Procedure for the imposition of administrative pecuniary penalties and fines*) in Chapter 15.

125 Unlike, for example, arts. 2(1) (cf art. 4a(1)), 3(1)–3(8) (cf art. 4b(1)) and 4 (cf art. 4) Regulation 2532/98.

126 Proposal for a Council Regulation conferring specific tasks on the European Central Bank concerning policies relating to the prudential supervision of credit institutions COM(2012) 511 final: https://www

art. 5 of Regulation 2532/1998 shall apply to the imposition of administrative pecuniary penalties for breaches of directly applicable EU rules.[127]

Para. 4 of art. 18 SSM R amended the initial wording but kept the reference to apply Regulation 2532/1998 to the procedures referred (surprisingly) in the whole art. 18 SSM R. The foregoing, only "*as appropriate*". Building upon this appropriateness, and with a view to ensure that fundamental rights are adequately protected under the SSM,[128] it can be construed that the CJEU would still retain unlimited jurisdiction as regards the administrative pecuniary penalties foreseen in art. 18(1) SSM R.[129] **8.087**

Some secondary arguments may be used to support this approach. One of them relates to the fact that the ECB did not raise any concerns towards this element when it issued its opinion regarding the draft SSM R[130] and not even when issued its Recommendation on the need to amend Regulation 2532/1998.[131] The latter could be read as if the current framework, in ECB's view, was sufficient to comply with the rights to a fair trial when imposing sanctions which would be criminal in nature. **8.088**

Until the present moment, the CJEU has not elaborated on this matter, although it has been given, at least, the opportunity. In case *VQ v. ECB*,[132] the General Court examined the imposition of an administrative pecuniary penalty on a credit institution who acted in breach of art. 77(a) CRR by repurchasing its own shares without seeking prior permission. In this case, the **8.089**

.europarl.europa.eu/registre/docs_autres_institutions/commission_europeenne/com/2012/0511/COM_COM(2012)0511_EN.pdf.

127 This draft provision reads as follows: "*The ECB shall apply this Article in accordance with Articles 3 to 5 of the Council Regulation (EC) No 2532/98*".

128 Cf Recitals 86 SSM R and 6 SSM Fr.

129 D'Ambrosio notes the interpretative complexities that entail trying to extend the full jurisdiction of the CJEU over administrative pecuniary penalties and brings up similar arguments to the ones exposed in this Section. See D'Ambrosio, R. (2021) at pp. 328–332.

130 Cf Opinion of the ECB of 27 November 2012 on a proposal for a Council regulation conferring specific tasks on the European Central Bank concerning policies relating to the prudential supervision of credit institutions and a proposal for a regulation of the European Parliament and of the Council amending Regulation (EU) No. 1093/2010 establishing a European Supervisory Authority (European Banking Authority) (CON/2012/96): https://eur-lex.europa.eu/legal-content/EN/TXT/?uri=uriserv%3AOJ.C_.2013.030.01.0006.01.ENG&toc=OJ%3AC%3A2013%3A030%3ATOC.

131 Recommendation for a Council Regulation amending Regulation (EC) No. 2532/98 concerning the powers of the European Central Bank to impose sanctions (ECB/2014/19): https://eur-lex.europa.eu/legal-content/EN/TXT/?uri=CELEX%3A52014HB0019.

132 General Court judgment in case T-203/18 (*VQ v ECB*) of 8 July 2020 (ECLI:EU:T:2020:313). For a commentary of this case, see Wissink, L. (2021). The VQ case T-203/18: Administrative penalties by the ECB under judicial scrutiny. In *Judicial Review in the European Banking Union* (pp. 542–550). Edward Elgar Publishing [Wissink (2021)(i)].

defendant contested the publication of the penalty imposed,[133] arguing that, because the Court would have unlimited jurisdiction, it could actually review the publication of the administrative pecuniary penalty imposed. Far from taking advantage of this chance to issue an interpretative judgment clarifying the *state of the art*, the General Court referred to the unlimited jurisdiction of the Court as a mere assumption, not confirming nor denying it, that is, leaving the matter as convoluted as it was.[134]

8.090 *Third*, concerning the requests addressed by the ECB to NCA in order to initiate sanctioning proceedings in the cases referred to in art. 18(5) SSM R, it has been indicated somehow above[135] that ECB powers are exhausted with the issuance of such a request. NCAs may substantiate and culminate such procedures, eventually, with the imposition (or not) of penalties pursuant to their national procedural and substantive law – including law transposing prudential Directives. It results from the foregoing that the compliance with the ECHR will depend on the national legislation and national procedures, as interpreted by the ECtHR, in particular, by the *Grande Stevens* precedent. Analysis of such compliance would require a separate study.[136]

8.091 To finalise, it seems possible indeed to conclude that the imposition of administrative penalties by the ECB ensures the most capital procedural guarantee, as is the right to a fair trial. However, such a conclusion may not come without some interpretative efforts and using a purposive reading of the relevant applicable provisions instead of following a literal and strict reading of those.

8.092 If, for the contrary, a strict or literal reading was to be followed and the conclusion would be that the CJEU does not enjoy full jurisdiction as regards administrative pecuniary penalties, that would be tantamount to acknowledging that the mechanism itself falls short of guarantees and does not comply with art. 6(1) ECHR (and 47 of the Charter).

---

133 Cf art. 132 SSM Fr. The entity at stake results to be Banco Sabadell, S. A. because, even if the judgment is anonymised, the ECB website publishing administrative penalties imposed by the ECB under the SSM published an administrative penalty imposed on this entity as regards the same grounds and for the same amount.

134 It must be noted that if the Court would have taken a position, this would be eventually as *obiter dicta* should it understand that such clarification would not be needed to adjudicate on the substance of the judgment. See D'Ambrosio, R. (2021) at pp. 328–332.

135 See Section C. (*Substantive law & sanctioning proceedings: issues and proposals to overcome them*) in Chapter 7.

136 In connection with this topic (but not strictly covering it), see Allegrezza, S. (ed.). (2020).

The immediate consequence derived from it would be the complete crumbling of the *mechanism*. This way of reasoning, even if hypothetically possible, must be disregarded for the reasons explained above, as it would be contrary, or not aligned at least, with the principle of providing an *effet utile* on EU rules. Hence, even if some interpretative effort is required, the SSM rules must be read in the most compliant way with the minimum safeguards guaranteed by EU law.[137] **8.093**

To conclude this Section, one needs also to consider that, for the moment, the ECHR does not apply to EU administrative procedures under direct administration, and the EU administrative system is not subject to the direct scrutiny of the ECtHR, as the EU has not joined the ECHR.[138] However, conversations towards the sign up of such convention by the EU have resumed recently.[139] Not being possible to advance the final agreement (and derogations from the general text and its complementary protocols), if such an agreement may arrive, one may wonder what the conclusions of the ECtHR on the specific matter addressed right above would be. **8.094**

---

137 Ibidem at pp. 116–117. The author there calls for a formal amendment of the SSM R in order to overcome expressly such deficit.

138 As it may be indirectly, when such court examines national measures transposing EU law and/or acts adopted by delegation/direct instruction received from the EU.

139 After 7–8 October 2019. The Council (in the EU Justice and Home Affairs Council (JHA) format), reaffirmed its commitment to accede the ECHR. In this regard, cf the Outcome of the JHA Council, dated on 8 October 2020 (pp. 10–11): https://www.consilium.europa.eu/media/40968/st12837-en19.pdf.

Also, for updated information as regards the *ad hoc* meetings held between the EU and the Steering Committee for Human Rights of the ECHR, see: https://www.coe.int/en/web/human-rights-intergovernmental-cooperation/accession-of-the-european-union-to-the-european-convention-on-human-rights#:~:text=The%208th%20negotiation%20meeting,for%202%2D4%20February%202021.&text=Meeting%20Report-,The%20CDDH%20ad%20hoc%20negotiation%20group%20(%E2%80%9C47%2B1%E2%80%9D,4%20February%202021%20via%20videoconference.&text=The%20next%20meeting%20is%20scheduled%20for%2023%2D25%20March%202021.

9

CONCLUSIONS OF PART II

9.001 As per the analysis carried out in Chapter 5 (*Tasks, powers and competences: building distinctions*), the following conclusions can be distilled:

9.002 *First*, the term *competence* will be utilised in a twofold way as encompassing (*a*) all the specific micro– and macro-prudential tasks conferred on the ECB as a whole. In this vein, it is possible to distinguish between micro-prudential *competences* (as regards the tasks listed in art. 4 SSM R) and macro-prudential *competences* (cf art. 5 SSM R). In addition, (*b*) *competence* will also mean the ECB overall liability for the effective and efficient functioning of the SSM.

9.003 *Second*, when referring to *tasks* in the context of the SSM R, this term will denote the functions listed in arts. 4(1) and (2) and 5(2) SSM R. These *specific* tasks can be split into micro– and macro-prudential tasks.

9.004 *Finally*, the term *powers* will comprise any of the functions granted explicitly by the SSM R itself, or by Union law, to the ECB to perform a task. Powers are an accessory to the tasks allocated to the ECB and must serve its fulfilment; hence, they are an accessory to achieve an objective and cannot constitute an end themselves.

9.005 Considering the analysis carried out in Chapter 6 (*Allocation of tasks within the SSM*), it can be concluded that:

9.006 *First,* as per the *vertical distribution of micro-prudential tasks*, in accordance with the specific procedures set out in the SSM Fr, NCAs serve the ECB to fulfil its responsibilities following a principal-agent model. In this vein, NCAs cooperate in two distinguishable manners: (i) providing personnel (and expertise) to the JSTs headed by the ECB and (ii) through the common procedures as applicable (e.g., preparing draft decisions addressed to the ECB for its adoption) and performing other assisting tasks for the ECB.

9.007 As regards the first cooperation modality (JSTs), it must be noted that the NCAs' staff serving in JSTs are still *national* staff and consequently not covered by EU privileges and immunities. This fact situates NCAs' staff in a comparably worse situation regarding its coverage by the EU legal framework.

Second, the *L-Bank Appeal* has clarified the exclusivity of the specific micro-prudential tasks allocated to the ECB under the SSM (those contemplated in art. 4(1)–(2) SSM R). By doing so, the Court has also emphasised that those tasks not comprised within the four corners of the mentioned provisions continue to be exercised by NCAs. **9.008**

As per the way those specific micro-prudential tasks must be exercised, the General Court first and the Court of Justice later have confirmed that these tasks are carried out via a *decentralised implementation* model. The paucity of the reference made by the Court does not provide enough clarity of what such decentralised implementation way of operation actually means. In the view of the author, only subsequent rulings may be able to elucidate and precise such key reference. **9.009**

Also, the author is of the view that the delegation mechanisms expressly contemplated in the TFEU do not preclude the existence of other forms of delegation. The SSM may be one of them: an abnormal mechanism of distribution of the tasks conferred on the ECB (which follow the principal-agent logic). In this case, the legislators would have conferred on the ECB the exclusive competence to carry out specific micro-prudential tasks. But instead of leaving up to it the decision of how to set up the distribution of functions pertaining to the SSM, they went a step forward and directly devised the perimeter, tools and forms of the cooperation. **9.010**

Third, the specific tasks foreseen in arts. 4(1) and 4(2) SSM R, which form the core tasks entrusted to the ECB under the SSM, do not constitute a *numerus clausus* and consequently must be read in a finalistic manner. **9.011**

That means that (i) the tasks listed in those provisions seek to exemplify, not exhaust, all possibilities. And, in accordance with art. 9(1)II SSM R, (ii) with a view to attaining the objective of ensuring financial stability, the ECB should also exercise those other tasks which are instrumental to the tasks depicted therein (even if not expressly mentioned in the abovementioned provisions). **9.012**

Fourth, the SSM formally does not alter the mission, purpose and powers attributed to the EBA. Thus, the ECB is expressly bound by the regulatory instruments promoted by the EBA and also by its guidelines and recommendations, as any other *national* competent authority. **9.013**

9.014 The role and responsibilities of the EBA and the ECB are close but, in the view of the author, do not necessarily overlap (if exercised in full compliance with the principle of conferral). Nevertheless, it is impossible not to appreciate the bizarre institutional equilibrium operating in this field. The ECB, an EU Institution, is subject to and must comply with the regulatory interpretations and rules proposed by an EU agency. The arrangement gets even more odd when one recalls that the ECB, by means of the Treaties, is granted a reinforced independent status.

9.015 *Fifth*, whereas the distribution of the specific supervisory tasks between the NCAs and the ECB follows, in general terms, a subjective approach (i.e., SIs supervision vs. LSIs supervision), this scheme does not apply as regards sanctioning competences.

9.016 ECB sanctioning competences under the SSM are allocated pursuant to three criteria: (i) a subjective criterion, depending on the nature of the allegedly infringer, (ii) an objective criterion, which depends on the nature of the legal act or regulation breached, and (iii) the type of sanction to be imposed (pecuniary or non-pecuniary sanctions). This is summarised in Figure 9.1.

9.018 The following considerations can be made in relation to Chapter 7 (*Allocation of tasks within the SSM*):

9.019 *First,* where MSs have legislatively gold-plated certain provisions to exercise themselves options and discretions that, based on CRD IV, should be exercised by the NCAs, this affects ECB discretion. Furthermore, this may affect the ECB's ability to exercise a consistent supervision over the entities with which it has been allocated direct supervisory powers.

9.020 In those cases and building upon the principle of primacy of Union law, and also considering the principle of level playing field enshrined in the SSM and the plain wording of art. 9(1) SSM R, the ECB must not be bound to apply national legislations gold-platting options of discretions allocated to NCAs.

9.021 The ECB should apply (as *competent authority* by ministry of EU law) the options granted to NCAs in prudential Directives. In doing so, the ECB acts validly, disregarding national legislation gold-plating options and discretions which were entrusted to NCAS (and designated authorities) under such Directives.

Breaches/penalties		SIs		LSIs	
		Entities	Natural persons	Entities	Natural persons
Directly applicable Union Law	Pecuniary penalties	ECB (art. 18(1) SSM Regulation)		NCAs*	
	Non-pecuniary penalties	NCAs at the request of the ECB (art. 18.5 SSM R)			
National Law implementing Union Law	Pecuniary penalties				
	Non-pecuniary penalties				
ECB Decisions and regulations	Pecuniary penalties	ECB (art. 18(7) SSM Regulation)	NCAs at the request of the ECB (art. 18.5 SSM R)	ECB (art. 18(7) SSM Regulation)	NCAs (at the request of the ECB. Art. 18(5) and (7) of the SSM R)
				NCAs (if obligation vis-à-vis the NCAs)	
	Non-pecuniary penalties	NCAs at the request of the ECB (art. 18(5) and (7) of the SSM R)		NCAs at the request of the ECB	
National Law (matters outside the scope of the SSM)	NCAs				

Note: * Except as regards the specific supervisory task contemplated in arts. 4(1)(a) and 4(1)(c) (the granting of banking licenses and assessment of qualifying holdings), concerning which the NCAs may initiate the relevant sanctioning procedure only upon request from the ECB.

Figure 9.1 Allocation of sanctioning powers within the SSM

9.022 *Second, a*scertaining when a national statute actually transposes a prudential Directive constitutes the first step for the ECB to apply a national law under arts. 4(3) and 9(1) SSM R.

9.023 Such an initial step can be sometimes challenging (at best). To undertake this task, the ECB (and legal operators) may use, interchangeably and as need be, the following techniques. *First,* verifying the title and/or the relevant preambles of national legislations to be applied. *Second,* checking the informative list of national measures transposing a given directive, displayed by EUR-lex (built upon the transposition notification submitted by MSs). *Third,* resorting to the NCAs' expertise to keep track of and help identify prudential Directives' transposition.

9.024 A second step entails determining whether the national statutes transpose the minimum requirements foreseen in the directive at stake. This assessment can be as easy as localising the relevant provisions, copy-pasting the text of the relevant prudential Directive or, on the contrary, requiring a complex case-by-case assessment.

9.025 The latter analysis would entail, at least, performing the following two operations: (a) identifying the core content of the provision of the directive to be transposed. (b) The second operation involves determining (on the basis of the previous one) if the national legislation has transposed or not a given directive (or, better said, a certain provision of a directive). The latter case would allow to finally ascertain whether the MSs are in a default position, similar to a wrongful transposition.

9.026 *Third,* concerning (a) the *lack of transposition of prudential Directives,* some remedies have been tested. Those included the potential application of the *Mangold* doctrine within the SSM and exploring the limits of the *emanation of the state* doctrine. All of those fall short of ensuring a consistent application of the regulatory framework.

9.027 Regarding (b) the *wrongful transposition of prudential Directives,* the tools to ensure compliance with Union law must be realistically curtailed. The fact that art. 4(3) SSM R binds the ECB to *apply* (i) national rules transposing Union law and (ii) the principles of primacy of EU law and conferral support this understanding.

9.028 Based on the above, the legal tool that can be tried to overcome cases of incorrect transposition of prudential Directives is the consistent interpretation or "*interprétation conforme*". Such interpretative technique has its very own limits and may not be able to deal with manifestly wrongful transpositions, where, according to (for the time being) existing precedents (*Corneli case*), the ECB would still be required to apply national legislation wrongfully or incompletely transpose a prudential directive.

Fourth, the sources of the administrative procedural rules applied by the ECB under the SSM are multiple and include the SSM R and the SSM Fr, the Treaties itself, the general principles of EU law, *ad hoc* agreements between the relevant supervisee and the ECB or even soft law rules. **9.029**

Even if the national rules that the ECB must apply seem to be those of a material nature, the ECB would be also bound to apply national administrative procedural rules relating to (i) national rules transposing EU law and (ii) national law exercising options and discretions allocated to MSs. The most relevant cases of the foregoing application relate to (a) notifications and (b) time lapses to exercise a given power or take relevant prudential decisions. **9.030**

Fifth, art. 18(1) SSM R confers on the ECB the possibility of imposing administrative pecuniary penalties for breaches of directly applicable EU acts "*in relation to which administrative pecuniary penalties shall be made available to competent authorities under the relevant Union law*". **9.031**

This wording implies a sort of acquiescence for the ECB, allowing it to act when pecuniary penalties have been made available to competent authorities under Union Law. The foregoing constitutes a novelty in the EU law realm, making ECB direct sanctioning powers eventually dependent on the availability of sanctioning tools under relevant national law. **9.032**

In this regard, the following must be noted: **9.033**

(i) Art. 18(1) SSM R can be interpreted in several manners, making the ECB's direct sanctioning powers more or less dependent on national laws defining administrative pecuniary penalties.
(ii) Art. 18(1) SSM R should be construed in the sense entitling the ECB to sanction, at least, the infringements listed in art. 67(1) of CRD IV referring to CRR (and in art. 66(1)(b) as well), regardless of its transposition by MSs.

For those infringements of CRR not listed in arts. 67(1) and 66(1)(b) CRD IV, the possibility for the ECB to apply administrative pecuniary penalties is subject to the availability of penalties under national law.

This second interpretation, in the view of the author, must be followed as it (a) makes ECB direct sanctioning powers under art. 18(1) SSM R less dependent upon national rules, rendering the exercise of the specific supervisory tasks conferred on the more autonomous, and (b) enhances the achievement of level playing field.

9.034 Finally, it results from Chapter 8 (*A Distinguishing between supervisory and sanctioning procedures. Is it possible?*) that:

9.035 *First*, it appears that the SSM R and SSM Fr do not expressly distinguishe between sanctioning procedures and supervisory procedures. On the contrary, the definition of ECB supervisory procedure contemplated in art. 2(24) SSM Fr encompasses both the so-called *common procedures* and procedures relating to the imposition of administrative pecuniary penalties (sanctioning proceedings).

9.036 As a matter of conclusion, leveraging on such definition and in a dogmatic manner, we can distinguish those ECB administrative procedures aiming at adopting supervisory measures from those aiming at punishing and deterring entities with have been found in breach of its obligations. The latest would be sanctioning proceedings *stricto sensu*.

9.037 *Second*, building upon the *Engel* test developed by the ECtHR (adopted by the CJEU and followed in several cases, including the *Bonda* case, it can be concluded that:

(i) The *administrative pecuniary penalties* contemplated in art. 18(1) SSM R and the *fines* defined in Regulation 2532/1998 and imposed in accordance with art. 18(7) SSM R are considered as criminal in nature.
(ii) As regards the *periodic penalty payments* that the ECB may impose under the SSM, even if those pursue mainly an enforcement nature, due to its potential severity a with a view to ensure procedural guarantees consistence, they can be considered as criminal in nature as well.
(iii) Concerning the *supervisory powers contemplated in art. 16(2) SSM R*, even if they entail *severe consequences* for the supervised entities, in principle, cannot be considered as administrative penalties and, even less, as penalties criminal in nature.

9.038 *Third*, the first Para. of art. 6(1) ECHR frameworks the basic safeguards linked to the right for an effective judicial remedy. These form part of a greater right: the right to a fair trial. This is the most relevant procedural guarantee as regards criminal procedures.

9.039 The CJEU and the ECtHR had admitted that administrative bodies can impose penalties which would be criminal in substance, provided that the offender would have access to a court being independent and impartial and having full or unlimited jurisdiction.

Art. 261 TFEU provides the possibility of granting full jurisdiction to the CJEU regarding penalties contemplated in pieces of secondary law. There is no express reference to the allocation of full jurisdiction to the CJEU in the SSM R (nor in the SSM Fr). **9.040**

Not without some interpretative effort, as detailed above, is it possible to maintain that the CJEU enjoys full jurisdiction as regards *fines* and the *administrative pecuniary penalties*. However, the foregoing demands some interpretative effort and using a purposive reading of the applicable provisions, in particular, as regards the administrative penalty payments. **9.041**

Fourth, penalties considered to be of a criminal nature must comply with the fundamental procedural guarantees and rights foreseen in art. 6 ECHR. It results that, in principle, the minimum procedural guarantees required in the second and third Paras. of art. 6 ECHR are actually foreseen in the SSM sanctioning procedure. **9.042**

PART III

CHALLENGES CONCERNING SUPERVISORY AND SANCTIONING PROCEDURES

INTRODUCTION

This research work heads for its conclusion and puts into practical context the constitutional and broader legal tensions that the SSM entails under the particular prism of supervisory and sanctioning procedures[1].

As anticipated at the beginning of this work, this Part aims at describing the practicalities of supervisory and sanctioning procedures and identifying the flaws derived from the novel institutional architecture and innovative law mechanisms displayed in the SSM R. Further, it is intended to present suggestions to overcome such flaws, which, if not perfect, at least should be sound (and backed by common sense).

The author notes that there are plenty of further issues, problems and interesting points to be covered, but only some of them will be covered here due to time and the scope limitations linked to this kind of work. In this sense,

1 See Chapter 8.

further separate (but interconnected) studies may be conducted with a view to provide an organised and complete compendium of all the issues pertaining to the SSM and European consolidated supervision.

The structure of this Part III unfolds as follows: *first*, in Chapter 10, the notion of composite procedures (within the notion of *administrative cooperation*) will be covered. Furthermore, it will discuss the several features that need to be appropriately balanced and assessed when establishing such kinds of procedures.

Second, Chapter 11 will analyse the features of cooperation, coordination and composition occurring within SSM composite procedures. This chapter deals with the elements that determine the classification of a procedure at such, their natural problematics and presents (and paves the way) to discuss more specifically the basic steps of supervisory and sanctioning procedures under the SSM.

Third, Chapter 12 will examine the justiciability of composite procedures from the prism of the SSM.

Fourth, Chapter 13 will look into the application of due process rights to composite procedures in general and the SSM in particular.

Finally, Chapters 14 and 15 will analyse, from a practical perspective and considering all the previous analysis carried out in this work, the potential defects affecting SSM supervisory and sanctioning proceedings, trying to offer ways to overcome them when possible.

10

COMPOSITE PROCEDURES: DESCRIPTIVE AND NORMATIVE CRITERIA

A. DESCRIPTIVE CRITERIA: COMPOSITE PROCEDURES AS A FORM OF INTER-ADMINISTRATIVE COOPERATION

10.001 This chapter aims at reflecting succinctly on the dogmatic classification of composite (or integrated) procedures under EU law. It must be anticipated that those must be regarded as an enhanced form of inter-administrative cooperation, that is, as a sub-specie of administrative cooperation between distinct levels of administrative structures.

10.002 The aim of this analysis is twofold and will be structured as follows:

10.003 First, it seems relevant to identify the basic features that define composite procedures pursuant to the academic literature and relevant case law. This would provide us with a yardstick to assess whether the procedures contemplated in the SSM R and further developed in the SSM Fr fall entirely under such a category or only part of those.

10.004 Second, it is desirable to assess the main goals to be achieved by establishing the supervisory (and sanctioning) procedures indicated above within the SSM. Those include, for instance, ensuring greater efficiency and consistency in the provision of reliable supervision across the participating MSs. Also, ensuring the legitimacy and accountability of the system (or, better said, of the ECB, as the Institution responsible for the functioning of the *mechanism*).

The foregoing would allow us to assess whether the mechanism and strategies put in place by the SSM have achieved those goals intended by the legislators. Such analysis will be carried out in Chapter 11 (*Cooperation, coordination and composite procedures in the Banking Union and SSM)* below. **10.005**

Serving the above as an introductory remark, it is worth questioning first the idea of *administrative procedure*. When thinking, from a purely conceptual perspective, on the way administrative procedures are handled, one could easily infer that the rule would be that the public authority that has been entrusted with the tasks (and the powers) also exercises them directly through its agents (i.e., civil servants and/or individuals vested with a similar status) and, eventually, as regards certain functions, through service providers.[1] **10.006**

Such a rule does not stand for the EU. In fact, the contrary approach does apply; EU law evolved from pure indirect administration[2] to a broad understanding in which co-administration or *cooperation* between the EU bodies and Institutions and MSs is the *de facto* common rule (despite such administrative model not being backed by a general and comprehensive legal administrative *corpus*[3]). **10.007**

Here, it is worth briefly recalling the historical evolution of administrative paradigms of the Union, more precisely, the model of implementation of EU rules: **10.008**

(a) From its inception until the Treaty of Lisbon, the *communities* first and then the EU were based on a model relying mainly on *indirect implementation*. Under such an approach, and oversimplifying, EU bodies and institutions executed their policies relying on national administrations.[4] However, and progressively, the system of implementation of EU policies developed intense multilevel cooperative approaches.

1 For example, as regards the function of ensuring the adequacy of vehicles to circulate, it is quite common across EU jurisdictions that certain private companies, duly authorised by the relevant administrative body or agency in charge of road safety or traffic, carry out the periodical technical inspections on vehicles and certify its ability to circulate.

2 Chiti, M. P. (2011). Towards an EU Regulation on Administrative Procedure? Study. European Parliament (Directorate General for Internal Policies. Policy Department C: citizens' rights and constitutional affairs: https://www.europarl.europa.eu/RegData/etudes/etudes/join/2010/432743/IPOL-JURI_ET(2010)432743_EN.pdf.

3 See Section B. (*The administrative procedural law applied by ECB*) in Chapter 7. See, particularly, (i) Alonso de León, S. (2017). *Composite administrative procedures in the European Union*. Iustel; and (ii) Alonso de León, S. (2016). *Composite Administrative Procedures in the European Union*. UC3M: Doctoral dissertation: https://core.ac.uk/download/pdf/44311475.pdf. At p. 188.

4 Due, in principle and among other causes, to the scarce resources that the *Communities* had at its beginning. See, more extensively, Alonso de León, S. (2016), at p. 49 and ss.

(b) The Treaty of Lisbon institutionalised the existence of a *European Administration* and consecrated the cooperation model which was already being operative years before. Such cooperative approach was enshrined at all levels of the policy cycle – from the decision-making phase to the implementation phase (being particularly intense in this latter one).

As indicated above, the Treaty of Lisbon recognised the existence of a *European administration.*[5] Furthermore, it also characterised such administration as *open* and *transparent.* The foregoing crystallised years later in the right to a Good Administration foreseen in art. 41 ECHR, enacted by the Treaty of Nice.

In addition, the Treaty of Lisbon also introduced the principle of *sincere cooperation* between the EU and MSs[6] and included a new Title into the TFEU exclusively on *administrative cooperation.*[7]

The CJEU has echoed such intense cooperative approach, in particular, in the competition field, where a mixture of direct administrative action (carried out directly by the Commission) and indirect or decentralised approaches can be easily witnessed.[8]

10.009 Such a cooperative model is deeply rooted and well-established in the EU legal framework, including as regards the financial rules which determine how the EU budget is spent. For instance, art. 62 of the Financial Regulation,[9] when defining the methods for the implementation of an EU budget, distinguishes between *direct implementation* of the budget and *shared management.*[10] Whereas the first form entails that the Commission directly spends the EU budget in accordance with the principles enshrined in such Financial Regulation in the policy areas entrusted to it, the latter form entails the MSs taking the lead. Under shared management,[11] MSs actually decide how to

---

5 "*1. In carrying out their missions, the institutions, bodies, offices and agencies of the Union shall have the support of an open, efficient and independent European administration*". This provision is currently art. 298(1) TFEU.

6 In its art. 1.5), current art. 4(3) TEU.

7 Between EU bodies and institutions and MSs. See current Title XXIV TFEU (*Administrative Cooperation*).

8 See, among others, Court of Justice judgments in cases C-428/14 (*DHL Express (Italy) Srl*) of 20 January 2016 (ECLI:EU:C:2016:27) and C-403/10 P (*Mediaset SpA v European Commission and Sky Italia, Srl*) of 28 July (2011 ECLI:EU:C:2011:533).

9 Regulation (EU, Euratom) 2024/2509 of the European Parliament and of the Council of 23 September 2024 on the financial rules applicable to the general budget of the Union (recast).

10 Art. 62(1)(c) of the Financial Regulation refers also to indirect management, which entails the implementation of the EU budget via third parties, International Financial Institutions, public and private bodies and even third countries (or the bodies designated by them).

11 Cf art. 5 of Regulation (EU) 2021/1060 of the European Parliament and of the Council of 24 June 2021 laying down common provisions on the European Regional Development Fund, the European Social Fund Plus, the Cohesion Fund, the Just Transition Fund and the European Maritime, Fisheries and Aquaculture Fund and financial rules for those and for the Asylum, Migration and Integration Fund, the Internal Security Fund and the Instrument for Financial Support for Border Management and Visa Policy (CPR).

spend the EU budget pursuant to a planification, which must meet wide EU policy objectives as approved by the Commission.[12] EU budget implemented under shared management amounts to a large portion, roughly an 80% of the total EU budget[13] and may be regarded as a metaphor of the operative of EU administration, an administrative system where cooperation between EU institutions and bodies and MSs is intensively embedded at all levels and phases of the policy cycle.

Under such an intensively cooperative approach of administrative action is where the doctrine, first, and CJEU also lately have depicted the basic features of composite procedures.[14] Such procedures are one of the several manifestations of the co-administrative (or cooperative) approaches developed in the EU. **10.010**

As an accurate approximation, composite procedures may be defined as "*administrative procedures in which both the European and the national public administrations intervene to reach a decision*".[15] Close to that approach, the ReNEUAL[16] code[17] has defined composite procedures as "(...) *an administrative procedure where EU authorities and the authorities of a Member State or of different Member* **10.011**

12 Cf arts. 8, 10–14 and 21 and ss. of the CPR. These include the preparation of Partnership Agreements comprising and liaising all the envisaged Programmes with the national cohesion strategy; and the separate preparation and approval of those Operational Programmes.

13 See, in this regard, the data provided by the Commission as regards EU budget management types: "(...) *in practice, some 80% of the budget is spent under what is known as 'shared management'* (...)": https://ec.europa.eu/info/strategy/eu-budget/how-it-works/annual-lifecycle/implementation/eu-budget-management-types_en.

14 Here, it is to be noted that Alonso de León states that, in order to define the concept of *composite procedure*, one needs to rely on the studies and analyses carried out within academia since it seems that the CJEU would have somehow avoided giving a more systematic coverture to this phenomenon. For a comprehensive and detailed analysis on the concept, complexities and remedies linked to composite procedures, these works are cornerstone: Alonso de León, S. (2016), at p. 184. See, also, Jansen, O. and Schöndorf-Haubold, B. (2011). *The European composite administration*. Intersentia; and Brito Bastos, F. (2018), pp. 101–134.

15 Ibidem. In addition, see, also, Eliantonio, M. (2015). Judicial review in an integrated administration: the case of "composite procedures". *Review of European Administrative Law*, 7(2), pp. 65–102; Della Cananea, G. (2004). I procedimenti amministrativi composti dell'Unione europea. In *Il procedimento amministrativo nel diritto europeo* (pp. 307–334). Milan, G.; Mastrodonato, G. (2008). *Procedimenti amministrativi composti nel diritto comunitario*. Bari, C.; and Hofmann, H. C. H. (2009). Composite Procedures in the EU Administrative law. In *Legal Challenges in EU Administrative Law: The Move to an Integrated Administration* (pp. 136–167). Edward Elgar, Cheltenham. It must be noted that these references are cited also in AG Campos Sánchez-Bordona's opinion issued in the *Berlusconi-Fininvest* case (see footnote 20).

16 The Research Network on EU Administrative Law (ReNUAL). This network groups some of the leading academics in the field of EU law and EU administrative law, including Jacques Ziller, Paul Craig, Herwig C. H. Hofmann, Giacinto della Cananea and Oriol Mir Puigpelat,

17 Hofmann, H., Schneider, J. P., Ziller, J., et al. (Eds.). (2015). *ReNEUAL model rules on EU administrative procedure*. ReNEUAL SC: http://www.reneual.eu/images/Home/ReNEUAL--Model-Rules-update-2015_rules-only-2017.PDF. Herein after simply referred as the *ReNEUAL code*.

States have distinct functions which are inter-dependent. A composite procedure may also mean the combination of two administrative procedures that are directly linked".

10.012 At this point in time, it does not seem possible to find a judicial definition of composite procedures. Nevertheless, this inertia may come to an end mainly thanks to the growing attention paid to this term (and their broader legal implications) undertaken by AG Campos Sánchez-Bordona in the recent years.[18] In his opinions in cases *Berlusconi-Fininvest*,[19] *Iccrea Banca*[20] and *GAEC Jeanningros*,[21] the AG seems to base the understanding of composite administrative[22] procedures on two notions: (i) interaction or involvement between EU authorities and national ones and (ii) substantive (and successive) decisions, on both sides.

B. NORMATIVE CRITERIA (I): COMPOSITE PROCEDURES, EFFICIENCY AND ACCOUNTABILITY

10.013 SSM's constitutional basis and foundational constraints have been analysed extensively in Part I.[23] Furthermore, following such analysis, coupled with a systematic and chronological assessment of the precedents of the SSM R (and the parliamentary debate), level playing fields, as adequately balanced by proportionality, have been identified to be the main principles of the SSM R.

10.014 In this Section, it is intended to introduce the topic and, from a normative perspective, analyse whether certain procedures (or, better said, the way those are organised) lead to further efficiency.

10.015 Also, it will be analysed whether (and how) a certain "formal" allocation of competences, as a necessary step to determine who is judged by their exercise, leads to a more accountable system. The angles of accountability being

18 More precisely, as from 2018.

19 AG Campos Sánchez-Bordona opinion in case C-219/17 (*Berlusconi Fininvest*), delivered on 27 June 2018 (ECLI:EU:C:2018:502).

20 AG Campos Sánchez-Bordona opinion in case C-414/18 (*Iccrea Banca*), delivered on 9 July 2018 (ECLI:EU:C:2019:574).

21 AG Campos Sánchez-Bordona opinion in case C-785/18 (*GAEC Jeanningros*), delivered on 26 September 2019 (ECLI:EU:C:2019:789).

22 AG also uses the term "*composite administrative procedures*" (interchangeably with *composite procedures*). As per the same notion, see also (i) AG Campos Sánchez-Bordona's opinion in case C-579/23 P (*Consortium des Charcutiers Corses*) delivered on 27 June 2024 (footnote 27) and (ii) the opinion of AG Căpeta in case C-551/22 P (*Commission v SRB*), paras. 110 and ss. These also refer to the term *composite procedures*.

23 See The *High Level Group on Financial Supervision in the EU chaired by Jacques de Larosière*, issued on 25 February 2009: The high level group on financial supervision in the EU. De Larosière report (europa.eu).

looked at here would be those of political accountability and administrative accountability.

1. Composite procedures and efficiency

Back in 2009, the *de Larosière* report identified some deficiencies in the exercise of prudential supervision at a national level, as carried out by NCAs.[24] Among others, such inefficiencies included divergent application of regulatory standards (and the associated risk of imbalances among entities registered in one or another MS), regulatory capture and moral hazard, and close interconnexion between credit institutions and sovereigns, leading to what appeared to be an *unbreakable vicious circle.* **10.016**

The BU, in general, and the SSM in particular, is supposed to ensure greater efficiency, and this is reflected somehow in the supervisory procedures set up to that end.[25] Recital 87 SSM R acknowledges expressly the need to put in place an effective framework for the exercise of a consolidated supervision but also an efficient one.[26] Such quest for greater efficiency shaped the manner in which horizontal and vertical tasks are allocated within the SSM R.[27] From this perspective, it must outlined that: **10.017**

First, reasons linked to *economies of scale* or *scope* with a view to attaining greater efficiency justifies that the oversight over the most relevant entities of the *system* (SIs) is actually centralised and directly exercised by the ECB.[28] In such a **10.018**

24 See Manger-Nestler, C. & Gentzsch, M. (2021). Dimensions of Independence in the Various Tasks of the ECB. In *Democratic Legitimation of Central Bank Independence in the European Union* (pp. 27–92). Springer, Cham.

25 Such efficiency-driven aim was early identified by IMF staff. See Goyal, R., Brooks, P. K., Pradhan, M., Tressel, M. T., Dell'Ariccia, M. G. & Pazarbasioglu, C. (2013). A Banking Union for the euro area. International Monetary Fund. *IMF Staff Discussion Note* (SDN/13/01). In the executive summary (at p. 4), the authors conclude that:

> "*Moving responsibility for potential financial support and bank supervision to a shared level can reduce fragmentation of financial markets, stem deposit flight, and weaken the vicious loop of rising sovereign and bank borrowing costs. In steady state, a single framework should bring a uniformly high standard of confidence and oversight, reduce national distortions, and mitigate the buildup of concentrated risk that compromises systemic stability*".

26 Recital 87 SSM R: "*Since the objectives of this Regulation, namely setting up an efficient and effective framework for the exercise of specific supervisory tasks over credit institutions by a Union institution, and ensuring the consistent application of the single rulebook to credit institutions,* (…)" (emphasis added). Unfortunately, such objective of achieving an *efficient* supervision is not expressly contemplated in art. 1 SSM R (or in any other provision).

27 See, more extensively, on the allocation of specific micro-prudential tasks, Chapter 6.

28 See, on this topic, Report from the Commission to the European Parliament and the Council on the Single Supervisory Mechanism established pursuant to Regulation (EU) No. 1024/2013 (COM/2017/0591 final).

way, further harmonisation (level playing field) can be achieved than if those tasks continue being exercised at a national level.

10.019 *Second*, the SSM intends to *benefit from the expertise accumulated by NCAs* and seizes the synergies generated. In this regard and as indicated earlier in this work,[29] when carrying out the direct supervision over SIs, the ECB acts through JSTs, composed by ECB staff and the NCAs' staff.[30]

10.020 Also, the so-called common procedures,[31] and also other forms of structured cooperation between the ECB and NCAs[32] regarding the supervision of SIs, contemplate a material and decisive NCA involvement, acknowledging that NCAs are best suited to provide advice concerning national law requirements and "*economic, organisational and cultural specificities*".[33]

10.021 In this regard, it is fair to concede that the design of the mechanism and the procedures and cooperation between the ECB and the NCAs within them achieve the desired efficiency.

10.022 *Third*, the *relationship between micro– and macro-prudential supervision*[34] is duly considered. Whereas the former constitutes the main competence allocated to the ECB under the SSM R, the latter is expected to be exercised in a more coordinated manner and in accordance with other relevant pieces of Union law.[35] Nevertheless, pursuant to art. 5(2) SSM R, the ECB may still decide to apply higher requirements for capital buffers than those contemplated in the relevant participating MS.[36]

---

29 See Section B. (*SSM basic principles: level playing field & proportionality*) in Chapter 1 and Section B.2.(a). (*Vertical distribution of micro-prudential tasks concerning SIs*) in Chapter 6.

30 Not to mention also that a big number of ECB staff allocated to the SSM area come from NCAs where they accumulated previous expertise in the field of banking supervision.

31 See again Section B.2.(a). (*Vertical distribution of micro-prudential tasks concerning SIs*) in Chapter 6.

32 Cf art. 91 SSM Fr by means of which the ECB may request the relevant NCA to prepare a complete draft decision concerning the exercise of specific micro-prudential supervisory tasks (listed in art. 4 SSM R). See further below in this Part III.

33 Cf Recital 37 SSM R.

34 On the effectiveness of the macro-prudential tasks allocated to the ECB under the SSM, see Alexander, K. (2016). The ECB and Banking Supervision: Does Single Supervisory Mechanism Provide an Effective Regulatory Framework? In *Regulating and Supervising European Financial Markets* (pp. 253–276). Springer, Cham.

35 For instance, Regulation (EU) No. 1092/2010 of the European Parliament and of the Council of 24 November 2010 on European Union macro-prudential oversight of the financial system and establishing a European Systemic Risk Board.

36 Subject, in any event, to a close cooperation between the ECB and the relevant national designated authorities pursuant to art. 5(4) SSM R.

Finally, the system is designed to extricate (or try to extricate, at least) *regulatory capture* by shifting the micro-prudential supervision to a supranational level. By distancing the decision-making centre from the relevant supervisees and ensuring the decision-making bodies[37] are not only composed by nationals from the MSs in which relevant supervisees are registered, favouring national champions is harder.[38] **10.023**

From a pure normative perspective, it seems possible to conclude that greater efficiency as regards the exercise of prudential supervision has been achieved by implementing the SSM. This is due to the special configuration of the *mechanism*, in particular, the manner that tasks are allocated between the NCAs and the ECB, the use of scale economies, the existence of synergies (coming from the mechanism benefit from the expertise accumulated by NCAs), the interaction between micro– and macro-prudential supervision and the suppression of undesired externalities (such as regulatory capture). **10.024**

Witnessing the results achieved so far, the same conclusion may be maintained. In this regard, the Commission has noted that:[39] **10.025**

> The effectiveness of supervision of euro area banks has improved already in the first years of SSM functioning. For SIs, the regulatory framework is more harmonised, and supervision is based on common methodologies applied in a consistent way. The quality of supervision is perceived as having increased in relation to several core supervisory areas, especially the SREP, internal models, fit and proper assessments and the functioning of colleges. The ECB also took important steps in harmonising supervisory practices for LSIs.[40] **10.026**

2. Composite procedures and political and administrative accountability

There is an interest in analysing whether the manner the competences are allocated in the SSM, in general, and in the different *cooperative* (including composite) procedures structured under the SSM R results in a system meeting appropriate accountability standards. In other words, holding itself, and **10.027**

37 The Supervisory Board but also the Governing Council.

38 Cf also Recital 18 SSM R, where it is expressly contemplated that: "*The exercise of the ECB's tasks should contribute in particular to ensure that credit institutions fully internalise all costs caused by their activities so as to avoid moral hazard and the excessive risk-taking arising from it*".

39 Report from the Commission to the European Parliament and the Council on the Single Supervisory Mechanism established pursuant to Regulation (EU) No. 1024/2013. Brussels, 11.10.2017. (COM(2017) 591 final).

40 Yet, some academics have criticised the fact that the ECB may lack "*sufficient regulatory powers when acting as a supervisor of the eurozone*". See, in this regard, Ferrarini, G. (2015). Single supervision and the governance of banking markets: will the SSM deliver the expected benefits? *European Business Organization Law Review*, *16*(3), pp. 513–537.

the Institution responsible for ensuring its smooth functioning (the ECB), accountable.

10.028 Such analysis would require a dedicated study which is far beyond the remits of this work. However, some incipient conclusions can be reached, backed by the text of the SSM R itself.

10.029 There would be, at least, three identifiable dimensions of accountability within the SSM R. Those are: political, administrative and judicial.[41] The latter one will be analysed briefly in the next Section below.

10.030 As regards *political accountability*, the SSM R has duly considered that shifting prudential supervision competences from MSs to the EU should be balanced by appropriate political accountability tools.[42] The foregoing, to allow examining (and questioning), by the political Institutions of the EU (the Parliament and the Council[43]), the efficient and proportionate exercise of such competence.[44]

10.031 To this end, art. 20(1) SSM R expressly acknowledges that the ECB[45] is accountable for the functioning of the *system* before the Parliament and the Council.[46] Such accountability is translated into specific obligations imposed on the ECB, with a view to keep the Parliament and the Council duly informed of the functioning of the *mechanism* and the exercise of the powers conferred on it. Those include: (i) the duty to submit an annual report on the execution

---

41 On this triple distinction, see Ter Kuile, G., Wissink, L. & Bovenschen, W. (2015). Tailor-made accountability within the Single Supervisory Mechanism. *Common Market Law Review*, 52(1), pp. 155–189.

42 See Recital D of the *Interinstitutional Agreement between the European Parliament and the European Central Bank on the practical modalities of the exercise of democratic accountability and oversight over the exercise of the tasks conferred on the ECB within the framework of the Single Supervisory Mechanism* (2013/694/EU):

"Whereas any conferral of supervisory powers to the Union level should be balanced by appropriate accountability requirements; under Article 20 of Regulation (EU) No 1024/2013 the ECB is therefore accountable for the implementation of that Regulation to Parliament and the Council as democratically legitimised institutions representing the citizens of the Union and the Member States".

43 Those backed by direct or indirect democratic legitimacy, as the representatives conforming them have been appointed (directly or indirectly) by EU citizens.

44 Cf Recital 55 SSM R.

45 As the Institution responsible for the functioning of the SSM pursuant to art. 6(1) SSM R.

46 On the political accountability of the ECB before the EP, see among many others: (i) Ter Kuile, G., Wissink, L. & Bovenschen, W. (2015); (ii) Zilioli, C. (2016); (iii) Karagianni, A. & Scholten, M. (2018); (iv) Beroš, M. B. (2019). The ECB's accountability within the SSM framework: Mind the (transparency) gap. *Maastricht Journal of European and Comparative Law*, *26*(1), pp. 122–135; (v) Amtenbrink, F. & Markakis, M. (2019). Towards a meaningful prudential supervision dialogue in the euro area? A study of the interaction between the European Parliament and the European Central Bank in the single supervisory mechanism. *ADEMU working paper series* (WP 2017/081); and (vi) Markakis, M. (2016). Political and Legal Accountability in the European Banking Union – A First Assessment. In *Hungarian Yearbook of International Law and European Law* (pp. 535–558). Eleven Publishing.

of tasks conferred upon by the SSM R;[47] (ii) the duty of the Chair of the Supervisory Board to appear before the Parliament and present the previously mentioned report;[48] (iii) the obligation to participate in hearings before the euro Group and the relevant committees of the Parliament regarding the execution of its tasks under the SSM R;[49] and (iv) the obligation to reply (orally or in writing) to the questions asked by the Eurogroup or the EP.[50]

Following art. 20(8)–(9) SSM R, the practical modalities for the implementation of the duties referred to above *vis-à-vis* the Parliament are further developed and detailed in the *Interinstitutional Agreement between the European Parliament and the European Central Bank on the practical modalities of the exercise of democratic accountability and oversight over the exercise of the tasks conferred on the ECB within the framework of the Single Supervisory Mechanism* (2013/694/EU). **10.032**

In this token, art. 21 SSM R contemplates that some of the specific obligations foreseen as regards the Parliament and the Council are also extended to the National Parliaments (of the participating MSs). **10.033**

Together with political accountability, and with the checks and balances put in place to ensure a minimum level of accountability,[51] there is also administrative accountability. Such accountability is carried out by the specialised EU body: the European Court of Auditors (ECA), which is tasked with examining the operational efficiency of the ECB.[52] To facilitate the appropriate development of the modalities of operational accountability as regards the SSM, the ECA and the ECB entered, on 9 October 2019, into a Memorandum of Understanding.[53] **10.034**

---

47 Art. 20(2) SSM R. It must be noted that the same report must be submitted to the Euro group.

48 Art. 20(3) SSM R. It must be noted that, to ensure adequate transparency and to cater for the possibility that non-euro currency participating MSs attend to the presentation before the euro Group, this Para. expressly foresees that representatives of non-euro currency MSs may also be present in this presentation.

49 Art. 20(4)–(5) SSM R. Ibidem previous footnote.

50 Art. 20(6) SSM R.

51 Which is nevertheless counterbalanced by the (a) principle of professional secrecy in carrying out the obligations allocated by the SSM R (cf art. 27 SSM R) and (b) the ECB's statutory independence, contemplated in art. 130 TFEU. See, in this vein, Zilioli, C. (2016) and Beroš, M. B. (2019).

52 Under the SSM (cf art. 21(7) SSM R) but also as regards the task entrusted by the TFEU (cf arts. 127 TFEU and 27(2) SESCB).

53 Memorandum of Understanding between the ECA and the ECB regarding audits on the ECB's supervisory tasks: https://eur-lex.europa.eu/legal-content/EN/TXT/PDF/?uri=IMMC:MOU/2019/10091&from=EN.

10.035 Concerning the perception of the ECA regarding the performance of the ECB, it must be noted that the auditor has highlighted that the ECB did not furnish it with all the relevant documentation it requested.[54] Hence, the assessment of the efficiency carried out by this EU Institution must be taken cautiously as it is based on partial documental evidence.[55] However, the ECA does not seem to question the efficiency of the political accountability arrangements put in place by the ECB and foreseen in the SSM R.[56]

10.036 From the perspective of political and administrative accountability, it seems logical to question first whether a formal allocation of tasks within the SSM may lead to further clarity as regards *who is accountable* and, in the end, to further accountability. Secondly, and linked to the previous question, one may wonder whether the SSM R sets forth such formal allocation of tasks.

10.037 As regards the first question, the answer seems affirmative. A clear allocation of tasks, in particular as regards accountability duties, leads necessarily to a more accountable system. The opposite, a system or structure where competences, interventions and responsibilities between the different intervening administrations or bodies are not clearly (formally) allocated, or where functions are blurry, creates confusion. Such confusion makes difficult to ascertain who must be held accountable for what, and so being appropriately overseen by the bodies which have democratic legitimacy (or which have been entrusted with performance assessment duties).

10.038 The answer to the second question seems to be also affirmative; the SSM has settled a more or less clear allocation of tasks[57] but, for the most, has established: (i) a system in which the ECB is responsible for the overall functioning of the *mechanism* and (ii) a distribution of the direct exercise of specific microprudential tasks between the ECB and the relevant NCAs. The foregoing sets up minimum standards regarding political and performance accountability. Yet, these minimum standards do not prevent the *mechanism*, or, better said,

---

54 See European Court of Auditors, "Special Report No 29/2016: Single Supervisory Mechanism – Good Start But Further Improvements Needed": https://www.eca.europa.eu/en/Pages/DocItem.aspx?did=39744. See, mainly, the conclusions (and recommendations) included in Paras. 184–197.

55 It remains to be seen if the signature of the Memorandum of Understanding entered into the ECA and the ECB in 2019 referred to immediately above may change this fact.

56 Ibidem footnote 55 at Paras. 189. Yet, the ECB is recommended to exhibit additional external transparency by publishing, for instance, some performance indicators and metrics.

57 See Chapter 6.

the ECB under the SSM R, from potentially incurring accountability gaps[58] or flaws and/or performance accountability deviations.[59]

C. NORMATIVE CRITERIA (II): LEGAL ACCOUNTABILITY AND JUDICIAL REVIEW AS A SUBJECT OF SPECIAL FOCUS

Finally, there is legal accountability. In the view of the author, such an accountability dimension may be split into two areas: **10.039**

First, there are "justiciability" considerations linked to the possibility of reviewing, judicially, the binding (or even, indirectly, the non-binding) legal decisions adopted within the SSM (and the BU in general). Such reviewability is closely connected to the manner the specific micro-prudential tasks are attributed within the *mechanism* and to its direct exercise by the ECB and/or the NCAs, and the overall responsibility allocated to the ECB as regards the functioning of the SSM.[60] The basic framework catering for judicial review is provided in arts. 24(11) SSM R[61] and art. 5 Regulation 2532/1998. **10.040**

Second, and inextricably linked to the "justiciability" of the decisions, are the material and procedural "safeguards" applicable to those decisions. Those procedural and material safeguards must be present in the process leading to the adoption of such decisions, and its absence or violation may result in a corrective ruling. Further, these are enunciated in art. 22 SSM R, referred to as *due process rights* or *rights of defence*.[62] **10.041**

---

58 See Karagianni, A. & Scholten, M. (2018). The authors identify that the hierarchical organisation between the ECB and NCAs requires a clarification of such a relationship from an accountability perspective. Also, they note that the ECB lacks proper coercive powers against NCAs which do not appropriately follow its instructions. This latter observation has been developed by the author in Section B.2.(b). (*Vertical distribution of micro-prudential tasks concerning LSIs*) in Chapter 6.

See, also, Beroš, M. B. (2019). The author links ECB accountability with transparency (towards its stakeholders and the general public). The author perceives that, in several areas, ECB transparency may be deficient.

59 Linked to operational aspects and to the statute of independence granted to the ECB (cf art. 130 TFEU).

60 And may lead to different judicial proceedings, depending on the relevant actor involved. For example, annulment procedures to quash ECB supervisory decisions; or actions for damages should it be perceived that there is an entitlement to compensation for the damage caused by the ECB (when performing *direct* supervisory tasks or even, potentially, in its role as the responsible body for the functioning of the SSM). We can distinguish preliminary rulings on matters relating to the interpretation of EU law brought up by national courts, which need to adjudicate on these matters, and last but not least, we may have purely national judgments as regards supervisory decisions duly adopted by NCAs as regards LSIs.

61 Cf Recitals 48 and 60 SSM R.

62 And further developed in arts. 25–35 SSM Fr. See, also, Section B.2. (*Administrative procedural rules (and principles) to be applied by the ECB: general overview and particular analysis of procedural rules contained in national law transposing prudential Directives*) in Chapter 7.

10.042 Those two dimensions constitute the core analysis developed in this work and will be extensively analysed precisely in this Part III.

10.043 As a preliminary consideration, and in the abstract, it can be concluded that the SSM R foresees a minimum set of safeguards mirroring the content of the Charter, including the right to challenge before competent courts (national, European or even supranational, in the first case) those decisions perceived as unfair and affecting (more or less directly) the interest of a supervisee or its stakeholders.

11

COOPERATION, COORDINATION AND COMPOSITE PROCEDURES IN THE BANKING UNION AND SSM

A. COOPERATION, COORDINATION AND COMPOSITION IN THE SSM

We have depicted above how (i) interaction between EU and national authorities and (ii) attribution of substantive (or material) decision powers are the key elements that determine the "composite" nature of a given procedure. **11.001**

We will look into those two elements and their applicability in classifying SSM (and generally BU) procedures using the *Berlusconi-Fininvest case*[1] as a practical benchmark to analyse how the CJEU understands, for the time being, the abovementioned concepts. **11.002**

As a matter of introduction, in such case, the Court was requested to issue a preliminary ruling on who was the competent court (CJEU or national court) **11.003**

1 Court of Justice judgment in case C-219/17 (*Berlusconi and Fininvest*) of 19 December 2018 (ECLI:EU:C:2018:1023).

to review a preparatory (non-binding) decision issued by national authorities and which was inserted in a SSM procedure.[2] Such procedure led to the adoption by the ECB of a supervisory decision by means of which it opposed the acquisition of a qualifying holding in *Banca Mediolanum* by Mr Berlusconi and its controlled company *Finanziaria d'investimento Fininvest SpA* (Fininvest). In this regard, the ECB concurred with Banca d'Italia that Mr Berlusconi (and so Fininvest) did not meet the reputational requirements to own a qualifying holding in a credit institution.

11.004 For the sake of factual completeness, reference must be made to a separate but closely connected legal saga: the Berlusconi II.[3] The object of this saga concerned an action for annulment submitted by *Fininvest* and *Silvio Berlusconi* against the ECB decision opposing its acquisition of the (disputed) qualifying holding in *Banca Mediolanum*. Whereas in first instance, the General Court dismissed the action brought up by the applicants, in the Berlusconi II appeal,[4] the CJEU overturned the previous judgement. Such decision was rooted on the factual background.

11.005 *First,* the CJEU determined that the General Court manifestly misinterpreted the factual background of the case. In the Berlusconi II case, it is indicated that, following a decision of the Supreme Court of Cassation which found Silvio Berlusconi guilty of tax fraud, Banca d'Italia considered that he no longer met the reputation condition required under art. 23(1)(a) CRD IV and, by decision of 7 October 2014, requested Fininvest to sell its shares in *Banca Mediolanum* in excess of 9.99% within 30 months.[5] In the meantime, Mr Berlusconi and Fininvest brought an action before the Council of State to suspend the effect of the referred decision of Banca d'Italia, which was duly granted. Finally, the same court annulled, on 3 March 2016, the abovementioned decision of Banca d'Italia, which compelled Fininvest to decrease its stake on *Banca Mediolanum*. In parallel, *Mediolanum* was absorbed by its subsidiary *Banca Mediolanum* on 30 December 2015, that is, without the stake of Mr Berlusconi and Fininvest being altered.[6]

2 See, in more detail, some features of the case in Section A.1. (*Absence of consideration of NCAs involvement in the ECB supervisory procedures*) in Chapter 8.

3 Composed by the Berlusconi II case and the Berlusconi II appeal.

4 Filed by Silvio Berlusconi's heirs.

5 Which would also indirectly cause Mr Berlusconi to no longer hold a qualifying holding in *Banca Mediolanum*.

6 See Berlusconi II appeal paras. 12 to 15.

As a result of this factual developments, the CJEU concluded that: "*the General Court manifestly misinterpreted the scope of the decision of the Bank of Italy of 7 October 2014 by confusing its order to the appellants to sell their shares in Mediolanum in excess of 9.99% with the sale itself of those shares, (...) while, on the date of the annulment by the Consiglio di Stato (Council of State) of that decision, that order had not had any effect*". The CJEU then concluded that the General Court distorted the relevant facts.[7] **11.006**

Second, the CJEU continued its reasoning, stating that the alteration of the legal structure of a qualifying holding, as occurred in the case at stake, should not "*be regarded as an acquisition of such a holding, even if the quantum of that holding had not been altered*". In short, the CJEU concluded that there was no new acquisition of qualifying holding for Mr Berlusconi and Fininvest as a result of the absorption of *Mediolanum* by *Banca Mediolanum*. The CJEU then concluded that the General erred in law. **11.007**

Finally, the CJEU recalled that the qualifying holding held in Banca Mediolanum by Fininvest and Berlusconi dated back from 1996. As described above, the appellants simply retained the said holding without it being modified. Hence, the ECB should not have triggered the procedure for the assessment of qualifying holdings enshrined in CRD IV, as the application of such Directive (as implemented by relevant national Italian law) cannot occur retroactively.[8] **11.008**

1. Interaction (or involvement) between EU and national authorities[9]

Concerning this first element (the involvement of several EU and national authorities), the Berlusconi judgment itself does not expressly refer to it nor devote much attention to the interlink between national bodies (mainly Banca d'Italia) and EU (ECB) steps.[10] However, such intense interaction between Banca d'Italia and the ECB is captured in the factual background provided.[11] **11.009**

---

7 Ibidem Paras. 94–102.

8 Ibidem Paras. 116–125.

9 Purposely plural, as it may be the case that a national authority cooperates (or discusses, in a broader sense) a given matter, and at certain point, European authorities may intervene in order to determine the course of action and/or settle disputes. This would be the case of the EBA as regards the procedure for the settlement of disputes between NCAs foreseen in arts. 19 and 20 of the EBA Regulation (and also in the equivalent provisions of the ESAs Regulation).

10 Accordingly, it must be noted that neither modern doctrine seems to put the accent in this feature (the involvement of EU and national authorities) but in the second one: the materiality of the decision (i.e., its ultimate attribution to national or EU authorities). See Brito Bastos, F. (2018), at p. 105, and Brito Bastos, F. (2021).

11 *Berlusconi-Fininvest* case at Paras. 27–38.

11.010 The opinion of AG Campos Sánchez-Bordona,[12] despite assuming from the beginning that SSM procedures involving the ECB and NCAs are, by definition, composite procedures,[13] puts some accent on the *interlink* between the ECB and NCAs actions adopted in the course of the relevant procedure. In this vein, the AG indicates that: *"As I have just described, the procedure for authorising acquisitions of or increases in qualifying holdings in financial institutions is a composite procedure, because it involves both the ECB, as the decision-making authority, and the NCAs, as bodies responsible for undertaking the preparatory work for the decisions"*.[14]

11.011 Also, as regards this element and in a more abstract token, it must be noted that the intervention of EU or national authorities does not need to follow always a predetermined order (i.e., national authorities initiate or launch the procedure, and EU ones continue it on the basis of the previous assessment undertaken by national authorities).

11.012 In this regard, we can find examples of *bottom-up*[15] composite administrative procedures, where national authorities receive the applications submitted by natural or legal persons, assess them and submit them to EU authorities for their final decision. This oversimplified scheme corresponds to SSM common procedures.[16]

11.013 Also, we may find examples of the contrary approach; procedures, where the lead comes from EU authorities and national authorities, intervene at a later stage (typically implementing EU decisions). We also find *circular* procedures where the interactions boundaries between national authorities and EU authorities go even beyond a classical linear scheme. This would be the case of the implementation of shared management funds under the CPR. There, national planning is further approved by the Commission,[17] implemented by Managing Authorities (broadly subject to MSs supervision) and subject to further approval and potential audits by the Commission[18] as regards the

---

12 Opinion of AG Campos Sánchez-Bordona in case C-219/17 (*Berlusconi Fininvest*) of 27 June 2018 (ECLI:EU:C:2018:502).

13 Ibidem at Para. 3.

14 Ibidem at Para. 92.

15 Cf Alonso de León, S. (2016), at p. 192.

16 See Section B. (*SSM acts resulting from composite procedures, and SSM cooperation not resulting from (or into) composite procedures*) below in this chapter. See, further, Section B.2.(a). (*Vertical distribution of micro-prudential tasks concerning SIs*) in Chapter 6.

17 See art. 23 CPR.

18 Cf arts. 51, 52, 53 and 58; and arts. 69 and ss.

eligibility of the expenditure incurred with the financial support of the shared management funds.

2. Attribution of substantive decision powers

The second element, also referred as *decisional interdependence*,[19] means that one authority (national or European) may not exercise the decision powers it has been entrusted with until the other authority has exercised its respective powers. Furthermore, such decision powers may be binding or not to the subsequent authority. This feature ultimately determines to whom the decision may be attributed[20] (national or EU authorities): classifying also the final act adopted as *national* (and thus reviewable by national courts) or European (and amenable to the review of the CJEU[21]). **11.014**

The *Berlusconi-Fininvest case* looks closely into this feature with a view to ascertain what court is competent to review the content of an administrative act, which may be solely attributed to an EU body (the ECB in this case). The foregoing, including the preparatory steps that led to such decision. **11.015**

First, the Court of Justice states that any involvement of national authorities, including drafting preparatory acts (draft decisions) which are not binding to the EU authorities, does not affect the classification of the final decisions as EU acts.[22] **11.016**

Second, the Court indicates that, in the above-mentioned case and pursuant to art. 263 TFEU, the EU body having the final decision-making powers, it is for the CJEU exclusively to review the legality of such an act.[23] And this review should be extended over any preparatory acts preceding the adoption of the decision at stake, regardless of whether such preparatory acts were adopted by national authorities (on the basis of national rules). **11.017**

Third, the Court further explains that the *rationale* for this approach is to ensure effective judicial protection, which can only be guaranteed when a single court (the CJEU) reviews the final decision adopted by the relevant EU institution. **11.018**

---

19 See Brito Bastos, F. (2018), at pp. 105–106, and Brito Bastos, F. (2021).

20 As a general rule and except for notable exceptions, composite procedures have EU "decisional dominance". See Brito Bastos, F. (2020), at p. 68.

21 See, in this regard, Court of Justice judgments (i) in joined cases 106 & 107/63 (*Alfred Toepfer and Getreide-Import Gesellschaft v Commission*); (ii) in case C-97/91 (*Oleificio Borelli SpA v EC*) of 3 December 1992 (ECLI:EU:C:1992:491) [*Borelli case*], at Paras. 10–13; and (iii) in the *Berlusconi Fininvest case* at Paras. 43–45.

22 *Berlusconi Fininvest case* at Para. 43.

23 *Berlusconi Fininvest case* at Para. 44.

Such effective legal protection would be undermined if national courts could review, separately, the preparatory acts adopted by the intervening national authorities.[24] That would entail no small risk of adopting irreconcilable judicial decisions (at national level and at EU level[25]) that would endanger the applicants' right to an effective legal remedy.

11.019 The possibility of reviewing national preparatory acts, within the action of annulment challenging an EU act, is an extremely sensitive matter. As a matter of introduction, it can be said that, at least as regards SSM matters, the Court is willing to accept the challenge and venture into uncharted waters.

11.020 Reviewability of national preparatory acts[26] entails at least three major constitutional tensions, which are depicted in detail by Brito Bastos.[27] The first one relates to the CJEU's own judicial mandate, which, by definition, does not extend to the review (or application) of national rules but of EU ones. The second and third ones concern the uniformity and autonomy of EU law.[28]

11.021 Pursuant to the principle of *autonomy* of EU law, EU rules are to be applied uniformly in all MSs from its inception. Such uniformity could be affected if the validity of EU acts or decision would be dependent on purely national requirements, which may vary from one MS to another.

11.022 Also, under the principle of autonomy of EU law, the EU legal system is deemed to be a complete system, independent from national legal systems. Such autonomy could be also compromised if national rules had to be considered in order to rule on the validity of the EU bodies' decisions.

11.023 Yet, even if those principles seem to constrain to the maximum the reviewability of national preparatory acts in composite procedures, in general, and in SSM ones, in particular, one should recall the exceptionality of the SSM, which vests the ECB with the task of applying national rules transposing prudential Directives.[29] Such exception should expand the CJEU's jurisdiction to

24 Ibidem at Paras. 48–51. See also AG Campos Sánchez-Bordona opinion in this case at Paras. 107–113.

25 The Court also states that this reasoning is grounded in the principle of sincere cooperation foreseen in art. 4(3) TEU and 6(2) SSM R. See *Berlusconi-Fininvest case* at Para. 55.

26 In principle, under national rules, as well as under EU principles and rights.

27 See Brito Bastos, F. (2018) and Brito Bastos, F. (2020).

28 See. in more detail, Brito Bastos, F. (2020), at pp. 74 and ss.

29 Cf art. 4(3) SSM R and Recital 34. See, further, Section A. (*The substantive rules applied by the ECB under the SSM*) in Chapter 7.

the revision of national rules, if needed to ensure adequate reviewability of the challenged decision and if so requested by the applicant on a concrete basis.[30]

However, valid legal concerns, linked to the strict reading of the application of national law by the ECB (only as regards national rules transposing prudential Directives) and to the subsequent *automatic* expansion of the CJEU's competence, appear.[31] If those were to apply (and eventually a sound and coherent reading of CJEU case law may so demand), we would need to accept (and so would the CJEU) that there is a gap in effective judicial protection of applicants in SSM composite administrative procedures. **11.024**

Such conclusion would entail that the system designed by the SSM, in which intense cooperation between the ECB and NCAs is at its core, falls short of safeguards and is at odds with the very rule of law. **11.025**

While acknowledging that this is a well-argued conclusion, and in order not to let crumble a system which founds its legitimacy on the will of the legislators,[32] a more purposive reading may be preferred. Such interpretation should be capable of dealing with the peculiarities of the system, which demands alternative implementing strategies.[33] **11.026**

Under this finalistic reading, it can be assumed that the CJEU should be competent to adjudicate on national law (applied by NCAs during the preparatory stages of a composite procedure) if necessary to assess the validity of an ECB decision. Also, such incidental judgment should be essentially substantiated on the national rules transposing prudential Directives and also on the linked national rules enabling the application of the former ones. The foregoing should be coupled with a specific burden to be placed on applicants; it should be for them to identify precisely and further explain the specific national preparatory acts vitiating the final act and the applicable national rules which **11.027**

30 Such argument is also sketched by AG Campos Sánchez Bordona in his opinion pertaining to the *Berlusconi-Fininvest case* (cf footnote 12): *"Moreover, this solution is also consistent with the provision in Article 4(3) of the SSM. (66) Under that provision, the ECB is entrusted with applying national law that transposes directives and, in exceptional cases, regulations that deal with the banking union, underpinning the extension of the jurisdiction of the Court of Justice to review such cases. (67)"*.

In a similar token, see General Court judgment in case T-52/16 (*Crédit Mutuel Arkéa v ECB*) of 13 December 2017 (ECLI:EU:T:2017:902) at Para. 131.

31 See Brito Bastos, F. (2020) at pp. 85–86.

32 Cf footnote 26 in Chapter I.

33 Cf Section C. (*Substantive law & sanctioning proceedings: issues and proposals to overcome them*) in Chapter 7. The challenges posed by the SSM R may require new ways of thinking and, accordingly, new approaches.

would have been infringed. Thus, the CJEU's judgment should be restricted within the four corners of the applicant's plea.[34]

11.028 Beyond the above considerations, it is not always easy to determine the materiality of the involvement of national or European authorities.

11.029 Sometimes the legislator has evidenced such substantive intervention by granting decision-making powers within the relevant stage of the procedure (e.g., allowing the relevant authority to decide on the continuation of the procedures based on the information provided by the requester[35]). This would be the case, again, of the SSM common procedures.[36]

11.030 In other occasions, the distinction is more subtle and may consist in the fact of the final decision-making authority having to respect or, at least, to take into consideration the assessment or evidence provided by the authority which intervened in a previous stage. Pursuant to Alonso de León, one example of this would be chemicals authorisations,[37] in which the results of technical analysis carried out by national authorities, even if not binding to the Commission, are *de facto* not questioned.[38]

11.031 One can conclude from the foregoing that there must be a minimum or critical decision-making power vested with the intervening authorities. Furthermore, one of the intervening authorities will be empowered to take the final decision bringing the relevant procedure to an end.[39]

---

34 However, intentionally or not, in the Berlusconi II case, the General Court missed a good chance to determine how to rule as regards national preparatory acts.

There, after the issuance of the *Berlusconi-Fininvest case* (ruling), the applicants brought an additional plea once they had already submitted their application. The applicants held that there was a close connection between their pleas and the judgment produced and, consequently, requested the Court to adjudicate on the alleged invalidity of national preparatory acts within the procedure. Building upon the defendants' arguments, the Court found that there was no clear or close connection between the cited judgment and the pleas put forward by the applicants. Also, the Court noted that the ruling had an interpretative value *ex tunc*, and hence, its conclusion should be known by the applicants and could not be brought as an element of law. Based on these two arguments, the Court declared this plea inadmissible.

35 Which may be determined by Union law or national law (or even a combination thereof).

36 E.g., granting an authorisation, measured against national law.

37 The procedure for the authorisation and registration of chemical substances under Regulation (EC) No. 1907/2006 of the European Parliament and of the Council of 18 December 2006 concerning the Registration, Evaluation, Authorisation and Restriction of Chemicals (REACH), establishing a European Chemicals Agency, amending Directive 1999/45/EC and repealing Council Regulation (EEC) No. 793/93 and Commission Regulation (EC) No. 1488/94, as well as Council Directive 76/769/EEC and Commission Directives 91/155/EEC, 93/67/EEC, 93/105/EC and 2000/21/EC.

38 See Alonso de León, S. (2016) at p. 195.

39 Ibidem at. p. 186; Mendes, J. & Eckes, C. (2011). The right to be heard in composite administrative procedures: lost in between protection? *European Law Review*, *36*(5), pp. 651–670. At p. 652; and Aperio

The foregoing also sets the upper limit, permitting to exclude other forms of administrative cooperation which do not amount to constitute composite administrative procedures.[40] One may recall here that pursuant to the principle of sincere cooperation enshrined in art. 4(3) TEU, EU bodies and Institutions and national authorities are expected to provide themselves mutual assistance. Such *assistance* cannot amount to frame each and every form of cooperation or facilitation of tasks as a composite procedure. The paradigmatic case would be the mere exchange of information or providing access to databases. The Early Detection and Exclusion System (EDEs), contemplated in art. 137(1) of the Financial Regulation,[41] constitutes a valid example. The EDEs publishes information regarding operators excluded from access to EU funding on the grounds of being in one of the exclusions listed in art. 138(1) of the Financial Regulation. National authorities and EU bodies are entitled to check this EDEs so as to prevent grant funding to unreliable operators.[42] Maintenance by the Commission of such database and, eventually, data feed by relevant national authorities to keep it updated would not constitute a composite administrative procedure but a mere form of (desirable) cooperation. **11.032**

3. Additional considerations and conclusions

The author is of the view that it is not feasible to establish a hard incontrovertible benchmark to measure the intensity of the authorities' intervention. The difference between simple cooperation and truly composite procedures may be subtle and should be assessed against the possibility for the authority taking the final decision to completely disregard the input from other authorities. **11.033**

In the specific *Berlusconi-Fininvest case*, the Court of Justice seems to stress (almost exclusively) the decisional interdependence.[43] In this vein, the Court (correctly) assumes that common procedures are composite procedures and, after identifying that the ECB holds the ultimate decision-making powers, determines that it (the Court) is exclusively competent to adjudicate as regards **11.034**

Bella, F. (2020). Composite Procedures and Procedural Guarantees: the "Borelli Doctrine" in the Light of ReNEUAL Model Rules. *ROMA TRE LAW REVIEW* (1), pp. 7–36.

40 See Eckes, C. & D'Ambrosio, R. (2020). Composite administrative procedures in the European Union. *ECB Legal Working Paper Series*, pp. 1–51. At pp. 18–19.

41 See, for more information, the Commission's dedicated EDEs webpage: https://ec.europa.eu/info/strategy/eu-budget/how-it-works/annual-lifecycle/implementation/anti-fraud-measures/edes_en.

42 Here, it must be noted that, whereas the general public may consult the *basic* EDEs database (which publishes cases relating to operators whose publication was agreed), national and EU authorities may have access to an advance version named EDES-DB which publishes information regarding operations found to be in an exclusion situation, disregarding whether the publication of such exclusion was agreed or not.

43 See above in this Section.

these types of procedures. The Court of Justice reflections have gone one step ahead by stating that it would also be for it to review the validity of the preparatory steps adopted by the relevant NCA on the basis of national law. The intention of the Court of ensuring effective judicial protection (and respecting the EU rule of law) entails tensioning the constitutional principles of autonomy and uniformity of EU law, together with the Court's own jurisdiction to the very limit. To overcome those tensions, some interpretative remedies can be sketched, considering, in particular, the singularity of the SSM and the one of art. 4(3) SSM R. Yet, it remains to be seen if those remedies are enough.

11.035 The mixed[44] nature of composite procedures may also result in discrepancies in the understanding of whether the input provided by any of the intervening authorities is substantive or not. National and EU courts may have different perceptions on this element, which may, in turn, have a significant impact on the individuals' rights to access judicial review and due process rights in general.[45] For example, if a national court considers the input of their national authority amounting to simple cooperation (and not integrated within a truly composite administrative procedure), it may review such input based on its own national law.[46] On the contrary, if the same national judicial authority understands that such contribution is material and it must be construed within a broader composite administrative procedure, it may submit a preliminary reference in case there is a question of EU law. The flip side of the coin is that, under this scenario, EU courts can also validly understand that such input is either not material or even that they are the competent ones to adjudicate on the dispute (quashing national courts' understanding and eventually endangering the continuation of the national judicial procedure).

11.036 In light of the above, the following analyses which of the administrative procedures contemplated in the SSM R fall within the definition of composite procedures and which others may amount to simple cooperation forms.

44 See Della Cananea, G. (2004). The author uses the term mixed administrative procedures to refer to composite administrative procedures. In this regard, the author seems to build upon the term used by Cassesse. See Cassese, S. (2003). Il diritto amministrativo europeo presenta caratteri originali? *Rivista trimestrale di diritto pubblico*, (1), pp. 35–52.

45 See Chapter 12 below.

46 Which may include, in principle, whether the relevant administrative decision (form of cooperation) can actually be challenged and reviewed by courts.

B. SSM ACTS RESULTING FROM COMPOSITE PROCEDURES, AND SSM COOPERATION NOT RESULTING FROM (OR INTO) COMPOSITE PROCEDURES

A quick glance at the Recitals of the SSM R reveals that the intensity of the exchanges and decision-making powers allocated and distributed between NCAs and the ECB[47] amounts to, at least as regards certain tasks, composite administrative procedures. **11.037**

One needs to take a closer look to identify the procedures that actually constitute composite administrative procedures[48] from (a) other forms of cooperation and exchange of information and (b) mixed-composed bodies playing a role in the supervisory decision-making process[49] and/or the bodies performing day-to-day supervision.[50] **11.038**

Following this scheme, in Section B.1. below, forms of cooperation not qualifying as composite procedures will be examined first; secondly, Section B.2. aims at identifying SSM supervisory composite procedures; and finally, in subsequent Section C, SSM sanctioning procedures will be examined in order to determine whether we can speak about composite procedures. **11.039**

1. Forms of cooperation which do not amount to be composite procedures within the SSM

It is worth distinguishing first which forms of cooperation happening within the SSM framework would not amount to be composite procedures. **11.040**

(a) Exchange of information and reporting

NCAs and the ECB are expected to cooperate, in a broad sense, under the SSM R.[51] More precisely, exchanges of information occurring within the SSM between NCAs and the ECB do not seem to constitute composite procedures.[52] **11.041**

47 Cf Section B. (*Allocation of micro-prudential tasks*) in Chapter 6.

48 Including composite administrative procedures relating to banking resolution in which certain decisive steps may be taken not only by the ECB (as an EU authority) but by other EU bodies (e.g., the SRB).

49 Basically, the Supervisory Board and the Governing Council.

50 Those are the JSTs composed by both NCAs staff and ECB staff. See Section B.2.(a). (*Vertical distribution of micro-prudential tasks concerning SIs*) in Chapter 6.

51 Cf art. 6(1) and (2) SSM R and art. 21 SSM Fr.

52 See, in this regard (and concerning this part), Eckes, C. & D'Ambrosio, R. (2020) at. pp. 22 and ss.

11.042 With the aim of not imposing on supervised entities the burden of reporting twice (to NCAs and to the ECB when relevant),[53] uniform reporting requirements have been established, and the NCAs formally converted in *focal* points which relevant entities may submit their due supervisory information.[54]

11.043 These exchanges cannot be considered composite procedures, since the exchange or transmission of information between the NCAs and the ECB is not intended to crystallise in a given decision (nor are the NCAs expected to produce any material judgment but merely transmit the data they have received[55]).

(b) Composition of bodies playing a role within the SSM

These interactions or acts include:

(1) In principle, the adoption by the ECB decision-making bodies[56] of decisions relating to SSM tasks would not constitute composite procedures. It does not matter, in this regard, that such bodies are composed by NCAs representatives and ECB staff.[57] One may note that the decision-making process of these collegial bodies would not allow to ascertain several intertwined steps, attributing each of them to the competence of NCAs or the ECB itself.

Furthermore, the fact that the members of the abovementioned decision-making bodies (pertaining either to the NCAs or to the ECB[58]) must act in the interest of the Union[59] implies that there would not be any national input.

(2) Also, JSTs composition[60] and functioning do not amount to composite procedure either. The adoption of internal decisions, the issuance of operational acts,[61] liaising with NCAs and preparing formal supervisory decisions to the

53 Cf Recital 47 of SSM R.

54 Cf art. 140 SSM Fr. See, also, Regulation (EU) 2015/534 of the European Central Bank of 17 March 2015 on reporting of supervisory financial information. Recital 11 of this Regulation emphasises the nature of this cooperation between NCAs and the ECB.

55 The performance of mere formal checks to ascertain that the files were readable and submitted in the format required would not imply or amount to the issuance of a decision.

56 In the context of the SSM. This approach, in principle, would exclude the General Council (cf art. 44 and ss. SESCB).

57 In particular, the Supervisory Board in which four representatives of the ECB sit (cf art. 26(5) SSM R).

58 Including, also, the persons appointed for the positions of Chair and Vice-Chair of the Supervisory Board (art. 26(3) SSM R) and of the ECB's Executive Board (arts. 283 TFEU and 11 SESCB).

59 Cf (i) Recital 68, art. 26(1) SSM R (as regards the Supervisory Board); and, in general, regarding NCAs intervention within the SSM as whole, (ii) art. 19(1) SSM R (pursuant to which NCAs and ECB shall act independently, and the members of the Supervisory Board and steering committee will act in the interest of the Union). Cf Lastra, R. M. & Louis, J. V. (2013) at pp. 72–73 and 77–78.

60 See, on the JSTs, Section B. (*SSM basic principles: level playing field & proportionality*) in Chapter 1 and Section B.2.(a). (*Vertical distribution of micro-prudential tasks concerning SIs*) in Chapter 6.

61 Cf Section A.2. (*Exclusion of supervisory activities not aiming at producing legal acts of individual application*) in Chapter 8. See, also, p. 20 of the SSM Supervisory Manual.

Supervisory Board[62] are actions (and outcomes) that are to be attributed to the relevant JST solely, with no *decisional interdependence* attributable to the NCAs.

(3) Two interactions shed, however, some doubts as regards their true nature as composite administrative procedures. The first one is the mediation procedure led by the Mediation Panel foreseen in art. 25(5) SSM R.[63] Acknowledging that the mediation proceeding may be initiated at the request of NCAs,[64] this appears to be the sole *decisive* or binding input that the NCA at stake may have.[65] Even if the mediation request submitted by the NCAs cannot be discarded and the procedure must be developed in its entirety, it is debatable whether this equates to a binding decision issued within one stage of a composite procedure. The potential assessment carried out by the requesting NCA does not condition the outcome of the procedure, and hence, this mediation procedure would not constitute a composite procedure.[66]

The second interaction[67] relates to potential discrepancies arising between the **11.044**
NCAs' appointed members (or the sub-coordinator[68]) of the JST and the coordinator of the JST (an ECB official). The matter must be resolved in this case in the light of the nature of the JSTs,[69] and hence, it can be concluded that this would not amount to a composite procedure.[70]

2. (Supervisory) SSM composite procedures

(a) Common procedures as composite procedures

The common procedures relating to (i) the authorisation (and withdrawal) **11.045**
of banking authorisations[71] and (ii) the assessment of the acquisition (and disposal) of qualifying holdings in credit institutions[72] (except in cases per-

62 See Eckes, C. & D'Ambrosio, R. (2020) At. p. 20.

63 And developed in greater detail in Regulation (EU) No. 673/2014 of the European Central Bank of 2 June 2014 concerning the establishment of a Mediation Panel and its Rules of Procedure (Regulation 673/2014).

64 Pursuant to art. 8(5) of Regulation 673/2014, in case of Eurocurrency MSs and following art. 8(6) of the mentioned Regulation, if the request comes from a non-euro currency MSs which has entered into a close-cooperation agreement.

65 As in the end, the Mediation Panel, building upon the Case Committee draft opinion (art. 9 of Regulation 673/2014) shall submit an opinion to both the Supervisory Board and the Governing Council. Nevertheless, the Governing Council has the very last word (or right to object) and the final decision is indeed attributable to it.

66 Against this approach is D'Ambrosio and Eckes. See Eckes, C. & D'Ambrosio, R. (2020).

67 Not even framed as a procedure under the SSM Fr.

68 See Art. 3(1) SSM Fr. See, also, Section 1.2.2. of the SSM Supervisory Manual.

69 Specialised bodies created with staff coming from both ECB and NCAs to conduct day-to-day supervision on SIs. Cf art. 2(6) SSM Fr.

70 In addition, it must be noted that the JST Coordinator would have the final word to settle any controversy arising within the JST (cf art. 6(1) SSM Fr).

71 Arts. 14 SSM R and 73–84 SSM Fr.

72 Arts. 15 SSM R and 85–87 SSM Fr.

taining to banking resolution[73]) are the clearest example of SSM composite procedures.[74]

11.046 As it is the general rule within the SSM, these constitute bottom-up mixed procedures where the NCAs serve as a focal point for the supervised entities.[75]

11.047 The exception to this general rule would be the rejection of authorisation applications by NCAs (solely) based exclusively on national law considerations.[76] In this case, it is not possible to speak of "composite" procedures, as the procedure would only be developed in one step and with the only intervention of one authority.[77]

(b) Other mixed approaches

11.048 Beyond common procedures, we can find some other procedures under the SSM which fit within the concept of "composite" procedures. These comprise:[78]

(a) Requests submitted by the ECB to the NCAs to prepare a draft supervisory decision concerning the tasks foreseen in art. 4(1) and (2) SSM R, pursuant to art. 91(1) SSM Fr. Also, when NCAs, on their own initiative, submit draft supervisory decisions following art. 91(2) SSM Fr addressed to the ECB; in both cases, as regards SIs.[79]
(b) Decisions to review the status of an LSI following a NCA notification under art. 43(4) SSM Fr.[80]
In the same vein, decisions relating to the reclassification as LSIs of entities classified as SIs based on the particular circumstances referred to in arts. 6(4) III and 70–72 SSM Fr constitute composite procedures. In these cases, in the understanding that cooperation from NCAs amount to more than a simple consultation, i.e., it does have a substantive impact on the ECB final decision taken.
(c) Decisions concerning "fit-and-proper" requirements of management bodies' members (as regards SIs) when adopted under the delegation framework established by Decision 2017/935.[81] Such framework foresees that NCAs prepare

73 Cf art. 4(1)(c) SSM R.
74 And apply to all supervised entities disregarding whether they are LSIs or SIs (cf art. 6(4) SSM R).
75 Meaning that request for authorisations must be addressed to the NCAs.
76 Cf arts. 14(2) SSM R and 75 SSM Fr.
77 Which, at the same time, would determine that national courts would be competent to adjudicate as regards such rejections issued by national authorities on the exclusive basis of national law (national provisions transposing CRD IV).
78 See, on this matter, Brito Bastos, F. (2021).
79 Eckes, C. & D'Ambrosio, R. (2020). Composite administrative procedures in the European Union. *ECB Legal Working Paper series* No. 20/November 2020. At pp. 20–21.
80 And eventually also as regards significant changes, such as mergers or asset transfer under art. 52 SSM Fr.
81 Decision 2017/935 of the European Central Bank of 16 November 2016 on the delegation of the power to adopt fit and proper decisions and the assessment of fit and proper requirements (Decision 2017/935).

draft decisions on the suitability of the proposed management member to be approved by ECB heads of work units.

This procedure applies in case both subjective requirements, relating to the supervised entity whose potential management member is assessed,[82] and objective requirements, relating to the complexity of the suitability assessment to be carried out,[83] are met.

(d) Similarly, the request addressed by the ECB to the NCAs to use their national powers,[84] pursuant to art. 9(1)III SSM R, triggers a composite procedure (a top-down one). In this procedure, the NCAs have the ultimate word, as they may assess how (and/or if) they can comply with the request received from the ECB.[85]

(e) The notification of draft supervisory decisions (and further issuance of ECB opinions on them), concerning material decisions or procedures as regards *High Priority* LSIs,[86] may be considered a composite procedure.[87]

(f) Finally, also, the ECB calling the direct supervision of an LSI pursuant to arts. 6(5)(b) SSM R and 67–69 SSM Fr would constitute a composite procedure. The foregoing, to the extent it triggers an exchange or consultation between the ECB and the relevant NCA at stake, could amount to a composite procedure.[88]

C. SANCTIONS UNDER THE SSM IN LIGHT OF COOPERATION, COORDINATION AND COMPOSITION

As anticipated, this part analyses whether the sanctioning procedures contemplated (or at least depicted in the SSM R[89]) can be classified as composite procedures. **11.049**

Taking a step back to the inspection stage, in principle, the ECB request of the NCAs' assistance to perform inspections to supervised entities may lead **11.050**

82 Art. 3(1) of Decision 2017/935.

83 Art. 3(1)(d) of Decision 2017/935. The adoption of the referred fit and proper decisions under the delegation framework requires that the assessment at stake to be carried out is not *complex* and not *sensitive* (cf also art. 3(2) of Decision 2017/935).

84 See Section C. (*From "tasks" to "powers"*) in Chapter 5 and Section B.4. (*Supervisory and investigatory powers to exercise those tasks*) in Chapter 6.

85 Section B.4. (*Supervisory and investigatory powers to exercise those tasks*) in Chapter 6.

86 Cf art. 98(1) SSM Fr. Following this provision, the ECB (in cooperation with NCAs) has defined *High Priority LSIs*. The criteria that trigger the classification of a given LSI as a *High Priority* LSI were only made available to the general public in 2022 in the ECB LSI Supervisory report: Supervisory approach and methodologies (europa.eu). Those criteria include (i) size (> €15 billion); (ii) importance for the economy of the relevant Participating MS; (iii) cross-border activities; and (iv) a business model (being of systemic relevance). See in Section B.2.(b). (*Vertical distribution of micro-prudential tasks concerning LSIs*) in Chapter 6.

87 See Eckes, C. & D'Ambrosio, R. (2020) at. pp. 28–29.

88 Ibidem at p. 26.

89 Cf Section A. (*Supervisory (common) procedures vs. sanctioning procedures*) in Chapter 8.

to composite procedures. Following art. 12(5) SSM R, when a person opposes an on-site inspection, the ECB may seek assistance from NCAs[90] to seize or seal files and premises of the supervised entities. This type of request resembles closely the mechanism foreseen in art. 9(1)III SSM R,[91] and hence, it may trigger a multistep composite procedure in which the ECB (by requesting the use of certain national powers available under pure national law) and NCAs (or other relevant authorities) substantively cooperate.

11.051 As discussed in Section C. (*Are the supervisory and sanctioning procedures foreseen in the SSM criminal "in nature"?*) of Chapter 8,[92] ECB sanctioning procedures would encompass the procedures for the imposition of administrative penalties[93] and ECB requests addressed to NCAs in order to open sanctioning procedures foreseen in art. 18(5) SSM R.[94] It is debatable whether procedures targeting the imposition of periodic penalty payments to compel supervised entities to return to compliance may have a sanctioning nature (and a *coloration pénale* as well). Considering their severity in abstract, and in order to ensure consistency with applicable procedural guarantees, it has been suggested to consider those penalties as criminal in nature.[95] Considering the total amount of the fines that could be imposed and also balancing consistency reasons, the author favoured considering them as criminal in nature.[96]

11.052 Whereas the direct sanctioning procedures (i.e., procedures for the imposition of administrative penalties) would not trigger, in principle, a composite procedure, the requests addressed to NCAs to open sanctioning procedures would. In this latter case (procedures triggered under art. 18(5) SSM R), we can depict them as top-down composite procedures where the final decision is taken by the NCA.[97]

90 Or other national authorities pursuant to art. 12(5) SSM R.

91 See references immediately above.

92 See, also, Section C. (*Allocation of sanctioning competences: a specialty over the general rule?*) in Chapter 6.

93 Both under Paras. 1 and 7 of art. 18 SSM R. This encompasses (i) administrative pecuniary penalties (art. 18(1) SSM R), (ii) fines and (iii) periodic penalty payments as stipulated, in both cases, in art. 2 of Regulation 2532/1998 (cf art. 120 SSM Fr).

94 Cf art. 134 SSM Fr.

95 Cf Section C.1.(c). (*Periodic penalty payments*) in Chapter 8.

96 Against this approach, see Wissink, L. (2021). *Effective Legal Protection in Banking Supervision: An Analysis of Legal Protection in Composite Administrative Procedures in the Single Supervisory Mechanism*. Europa Law Publishing [Wissink, L. (2021)(ii)]. At p. 50; and D'Ambrosio, R. (2013), at pp.19 and 27–28. The SSM Supervisory seems to embrace that view eventually, as periodic penalty payments are not contemplated under the section devoted to *sanctions*. Cf SSM Supervisory Manual at pp. 100–101.

97 As regards the leeway given to the NCAs to attend the request formulated by the ECB pursuant to art. 18(5) SSM R, see Section C.2. (*National laws and administrative pecuniary penalties II: to which extent national legislation may limit ECB direct sanctioning powers under art. 18(5) SSM R?*) in Chapter 7. See, also, D'Ambrosio, R. (2021) at p. 324.

Regarding the imposition of administrative penalties, it is possible that NCAs may participate within the relevant sanctioning procedure, providing evidence, reports or even as experts (if requested). If one considers, for example, a case involving potential fraud or misreporting by a SIs, the NCA, which acted as focal point receiving such reporting, may be asked to provide information as regards when, or by whom, such reports and/or accounts were submitted or any informal discussion that may have occurred as regards those. The participation of the NCA within such procedure would qualify them as an expert or a witness intervention (allowed under art. 30 SSM Fr). However, in those cases, it does not seem feasible to speak about composite procedures, as the NCA intervention would have been triggered by the ECB or the allegedly infringing supervisee[98] and would not have the materiality demanded by the definition of composite procedures. **11.053**

In the same vein, communication by NCAs to the ECB on potential evidence and suspicions relating to the commission of breaches, for which the ECB is exclusively competent to initiate sanctioning procedures, would not trigger any composite procedure and would constitute just another example of *sincere cooperation*. **11.054**

Also, it must be noted that measures addressed to remove obstacles pursuant to arts. 11(2) SSM R,[99] 12(5)[100] and 13 SSM R,[101] in principle, would not amount to a composite procedure but to mere assistance measures which fit under the sincere cooperation due among the ECB and NCAs (and other relevant national authorities). Exceptionally, and building on the applicable domestic legislation, such cooperation may become closer and necessary in order to apply for the relevant judicial authorisation.[102] **11.055**

98 Not then being statutorily foreseen.

99 Facilitation of ECB access to the premises of the persons referred to in such article. Cf art. 142 SSM Fr on the adoption of a decision to conduct a general investigation and its specificities (i.e., reference to the fact that any obstruction to the investigation constitutes a breach of an ECB decision leading to an infringement under art. 18(7) SSM R).

100 For example, the seizing of any business and books or records (and reports). Cf art. 143 SSM Fr. See, on this matter, Karagianni, A. M. (2022). *The Protection of Fundamental Rights in Composite Banking Supervision Procedures*. Utrecht University: Doctoral dissertation. At pp. 78 and ss.

101 In case on-site inspections or assistance under art. 12(5) SSM R require judicial authorisation.

102 Where on-site inspections require judicial authorisation, this fact should be indicated by the NCA (cf art. 145(1) SSM Fr), and it cannot be discarded that it provides further guidance to the ECB so as to how to channel such request for on-site inspections. In these cases, the contribution performed by NCAs may be material enough to trigger a composite procedure (account taken that the ECB should, in these cases, consider or follow the indication from the relevant NCA so as to apply for a judicial authorisation).

12

SSM COMPOSITE PROCEDURES AND JUSTICIABILITY

12.001 In a perfect world, the different phases of composite procedures would dovetail to create a multistep yet single procedure in which procedural rights are ensured, remedies (both administrative and judicial) are foreseen and clear lines of responsibility are defined.

The reality is far from this ideal scenario. Composite procedures, despite being early introduced in the EU legal framework,[1] have not attracted much attention from legislators and EU courts in the past decades.[2] **12.002**

Nevertheless, the intertwining between the different phases of composite procedures and its relationship with due process rights[3] create situations not always simple to file down using legal logic. **12.003**

Two types of issues may arise:[4] *justiciability* or *safeguards*. This chapter explores the former. By "justiciability", the author refers to the legal mechanism that determines whether a given decision, produced within a SSM composite procedure, may be (or may be not) tried in court; and if so, by what court (national courts or the CJEU), on what basis and who may be entitled to bring an action before the relevant court. Also, within this *justiciability* dimension, it is necessary to distinguish, at least within the EU legal framework, the type of procedures that determine the justiciability of the decision at stake. **12.004**

Joining the voices which advocate in favour of a codified and unified approach to EU composite procedures, in the following sections, some of the main tensions that such procedures generate (from the SSM perspective) will be analysed. This matter has brought increasing academic attention[5] and even dedicated monographies.[6] **12.005**

The analysis below tries to offer an overview based on recent judicial developments, which paves the way for the analysis[7] of Chapter 14 (*Supervisory procedures: common procedures*) and 15 (*Sanctioning procedures*). **12.006**

1 In principle, their origins could be traced back to the proliferation of EU agencies. See Alonso de León, S. (2016) at pp. 196 and ss.

2 Despite a rising academic interest as from, at least, the 2000s headed by professors Edoardo Chiti, Giacinto della Cananea and Alexander Türk (among others).

3 See Section B.1. (*The sources of administrative procedural law for the ECB under the SSM*) in Chapter 7.

4 Or even to the two of them eventually. One may easily acknowledge that whether a decision is justiciable is itself part of the procedural safeguards (i.e., whether the relevant decision was amenable to judicial review). From another angle, such *justiciability* character may be treated as a procedural safeguard when a court is entrusted with the task of reviewing the action of another (usually lower) court. A clear example of the foregoing happens when the ECtHR or the CJEU review the work of national courts.

5 Lamandini, M., Ramos, D. & Solana, J. (2016); Markakis, M. (2020). Composite Procedures and Judicial Review in the Single Resolution Mechanism: Iccrea Banca. *Review of European Administrative Law, 13*(4), 109–125; and Gagliardi, E. & Wissink, L. (2020) (among many others).

6 Eckes, C. & D'Ambrosio, R. (2020) at pp. 18–19; and Wissink, L. (2021)(ii).

7 Together with the historical, constitutional, operational, competences-based legal analysis of the mechanism provided in precedents Parts I and II.

12.007 Following the approach anticipated above, questions relating to the nature of *justiciability* and its connection with the principle of institutional balance and fundamental rights will be addressed in Section A. Section B will deal with the judicial review applicable specifically in composite procedures, using the *Berlusconi-Fininvest case*, once again, as a yardstick to conduct the analysis. Section C will look into the action for annulment. Finally, Sections D and E will analyse the action for damages and the preliminary reference, respectively.

A. JUSTICIABILITY: INSTITUTIONAL BALANCE (AND SEPARATION OF POWERS) AND FUNDAMENTAL RIGHTS

12.008 It is believed that the first reference to the first *institutional balance* principle may be found in the *Meroni* case. There, the Court indicated that:

> *From that provision there can be seen in the balance of powers which is characteristic of the institutional structure of the community a fundamental guarantee granted by the treaty in particular to the undertakings and associations of undertakings to which it applies.*

12.009 In the early view of the Court, such balance or division of powers within the EU acts at a double level, (i) preventing against any excess of powers granted and (ii) protecting fundamental rights of the individuals to whom the rules apply.[8] It appears that, in this early ruling, the Court incorporated Montesquieu's idea that the separation of powers should serve, indeed, to protect the rights of individuals.[9]

12.010 Such intimate connection between division of powers (or institutional balance) and fundamental rights became blurred over the years.[10] The referred institutional balance progressively acquired, then, a more autonomous reading, linked to the principle of conferral, as a principle of EU law in itself. Early in the 1990s, the Court of Justice stated that:

> *Observance of the institutional balance means that each of the institutions must exercise its powers with due regard for the powers of the other institutions. It also requires that it should be possible to penalize any breach of that rule which may occur.*[11]

8 Lamandini, M., Ramos Muñoz, D. & Solana, J. (2016).

9 Jacqué, J. P. (2004). Principle of Institutional Balance, The. *Common Market L. Rev.*, *41*, pp. 383–391.

10 Ibidem at p. 384. See, also, Lamandini, M., Ramos Muñoz, D. & Solana, J. (2016) at pp. 201–202.

11 Court of Justice judgment in case C-70/88 (*European Parliament v Council*) of 22 May 1990 (ECLI:EU:C:1990:217). At Para. 22.

In the *Vreugdenhil* case,[12] the Court openly expressed that the institutional balance contemplated in the treaties was not aimed at protecting individuals.[13] Such a line of reasoning has been kept by the CJEU in more recent rulings.[14] Hence, we need to stick, at least for the time being, to this approach when assessing fundamental rights and potential breaches of the institutional balance set up by the Treaties. **12.011**

B. JUDICIAL REVIEW IN COMPOSITE PROCEDURES: THE CJEU'S *BERLUSCONI-FININVEST* CASE LAW IN PERSPECTIVE

Whereas previously in *Section* A. (*Cooperation, coordination and composition in the SSM*) of Chapter 11, the *Berlusconi-Fininvest* case was used as a yardstick to test how the CJEU construes the basic elements defining composite procedures and the constitutional tensions linked to those procedures, we will look deeper in this Section to the distribution of judicial competences in composite procedures using, again, that ruling. **12.012**

Ensuring judicial protection in composite procedures can be, by definition, problematic.[15] The intertwined (or superimposed) interactions between national and EU authorities sometimes make it difficult to ascertain which court reviews what. The sequence of acts may lead to some national or EU acts not being capable of specific judicial reviews, impinging effective judicial protection.[16] **12.013**

With a view to offer a complete picture on the evolving CJEU's understanding regarding judicial competences to review final decisions adopted in the course of a composite procedure (or incidental, preparatory questions linked to it): *first* Section B.1. discusses the Court's initial approach in *Borelli*. Section B.2. looks at the most recent case law on the matter issued by the CJEU, not surprisingly, mainly in the light of SSM and SRM composite procedures. Section **12.014**

12 Court of Justice judgment in case C-282/90 (*Industrie- en Handelsonderneming Vreugdenhil BV v Commission*) of 13 March 1992 (ECLI:EU:C:1992:124).

13 "*In that context, it is sufficient to state that the aim of the system of the division of powers between the various Community institutions is to ensure that the balance between the institutions provided for in the Treaty is maintained, and not to protect individuals*". Ibidem at Para. 20.

14 See, among others, Court of Justice judgment in case C-221/10 P (*Artegodan GmbH v Commission*) of 19 April 2012 (ECLI:EU:C:2012:216).

15 See, among others, Alonso de León, S. (2016) at pp. 306 and ss.; Lamandini, M., Ramos, D. & Solana, J. (2016). at pp. 254; and Markakis, M. (2020).

16 See, in this regard, Brito Bastos, F. (2020) and Gagliardi, E. & Wissink, L. (2020).

B.3. will condensate the main conclusions, and finally, Section B.4. will summarise some, for the time being, unresolved issues linked to this matter.

1. CJEU initial approach: the *Borelli* case

12.015 In its landmark case *Borelli*,[17] the Court of Justice ruled that, in cases where a national act is binding on an EU decision-taking authority, the Court could not rule on the validity of that national act.[18] Consequently, any irregularity vitiating the national act cannot affect, ultimately, the validity of the decision taken by the EU body.[19] The Court of Justice also concluded in this case that:

> *it is for the national courts, where appropriate after obtaining a preliminary ruling from the Court, to rule on the lawfulness of the national measure at issue on the same terms on which they review any definitive measure adopted by the same national authority which is capable of adversely affecting third parties.*[20]

12.016 Even if the *Borelli* case remains in good law, the Court of Justice provided further guidance confirming such previous understanding. For example, in case C-269/99,[21] the Court declared that, as regards composite procedures in which the decision adopted by national authorities is quasi-biding for EU bodies and institutions, it is for the national courts to review the final decision taken (and also any preliminary steps).[22] Should national courts have, nevertheless, doubts as regards the interpretation of applicable EU law (including the interaction between national rules and EU law), they may approach the CJEU by means of a preliminary reference.[23]

---

17 Court of Justice judgment in case C-97/91 (*Oleificio Borelli SpA v EC*) of 3 December 1992 (ECLI:EU:C:1992:491).

18 Ibidem (*Borelli case*) at Para. 10. Cf also with the scheme depicted in art. III-24(4) of the ReNEUAL code.

19 Ibidem at Para. 12.

20 Ibidem at Para. 13. To close the loop and prevent potential flaws regarding effective judicial protection, the CJEU further added that, in cases where the domestic system does not provide for the admissibility of actions aiming at reviewing the validity of the national act, such actions must be deemed to be admissible.

21 Court of Justice judgment in case C-269/99 (*Carl Kühne GmbH & Co. KG and Others v Jütro Konservenfabrik GmbH & Co. KG*) of 6 December 2001 (ECLI identifier: ECLI:EU:C:2001:659).

22 Ibidem at Paras. 57–58:

"(57) *The requirement of judicial control stems from the constitutional traditions common to the Member States and is enshrined in Articles 6 and 13 of the European Convention for the Protection of Human Rights and Fundamental Freedoms. That requirement must also be complied with with* [sic] *regard to a measure, such as the application for registration at issue in the main proceedings, which constitutes a necessary step in the procedure for adoption of a Community measure, where the Community institutions have only a limited or non-existent discretion with regard to that measure.*

(58) It is, therefore, for the national courts to rule on the lawfulness of an application for registration of a designation, such as that at issue in this case, on the same terms as those by which they review any definitive measure adopted by the same national authority which is capable of adversely affecting the rights of third parties under Community law (…)".

23 See below in Section E. (*Justiciability and preliminary ruling procedure*) in this chapter.

Further, in 2007 in the *Sweden v. the EC*[24] case, the CJEU continued this line of reasoning. The case at stake related to a request to access certain documents under Regulation 1049/2001 regarding public access to Parliament, Council and Commission documents. In that case, the Court of Justice ruled that it "*is within the jurisdiction of the Community judicature to review, on application by a person to whom the institution has refused to grant access*".[25] The foregoing, regardless of which authority (the EU Institution or the national authority) made the assessment pursuant to which access to the requested documents, was denied. The Court ultimately implied that, when an EU Institution is the final decision-taking authority, it should be for the CJEU to review the final act adversely affecting the interests of the person concerned.[26] **12.017**

2. CJEU recent approaches: *Berlusconi-Fininvest, Iccrea Banca* and *GAEC Jeanningros*

The criteria to allocate judicial competence in EU composite procedures has been further enriched by the three latest cases: *Berlusconi-Fininvest*, *Iccrea Banca*[27] and *GAEC Jeanningros*.[28] **12.018**

In *Berlusconi-Fininvest*,[29] the Court of Justice stated that, when the ECB is the final decision-making body,[30] "*[a]ny involvement of the national authorities in the course of the procedure leading to the adoption of such acts cannot affect their classification as EU act*".[31] Consequently, the CJEU remains exclusively competent to review such acts pursuant to art. 263 TFEU.[32] The foregoing review should extend also to national non-binding preparatory acts, as the principle **12.019**

24 Court of Justice judgment in case C-64/05 P (*Kingdom of Sweden v. EC*) of 18 December 2007 (ECLI:EU:C:2007:802).

25 Ibidem at Para. 94.

26 More extensively and for a systematical analysis on case law concerning composite procedures and derivative illegality from preparatory measures, see Brito Bastos, F. (2018). See, also, Brito Bastos, F. (2019). Judicial review of composite administrative procedures in the Single Supervisory Mechanism: Berlusconi. *Common Market L. Rev.*, *56*, pp. 1355–1378.

27 Court of Justice judgment in case C-414/18 (*Iccrea Banca*) of 3 December 2019 (ECLI:EU:C:2019:1036).

28 Court of Justice judgment in case C-785/18 (*GAEC Jeanningros*) of 29 January 2020 (ECLI:EU:C:2020:46).

29 See previous references to this judgment made in Section A.1. (*Absence of consideration of NCAs involvement in the ECB supervisory procedures*) in Chapter 8.

30 Where national preparatory acts or decisions are not legally binding upon the ECB (unlike in the *Borelli* case). Cf *Berlusconi-Fininvest case* at Paras. 45–46.

31 *Berlusconi-Fininvest case* at Para. 43.

32 Ibidem at Para. 44.

of judicial protection demands,[33] including, in principle, the interpretation of the national law provisions applied by the ECB pursuant to art. 4(3) SSM R.[34]

12.020 The Court of Justice reiterated the same reasoning in the *Iccrea Banca* case. In this case, the Court was asked to adjudicate on a preliminary ruling brought by Iccrea Banca as regards the payment to the Italian national resolution fund of ordinary, extraordinary, additional contributions and to the SRF *ex ante* contributions.[35] Those levies were requested by the Banca d'Italia by means of several decisions and communications. In particular, and for what matters here, requests for *ex ante* contributions were backed by SRB decisions.[36] Iccrea Banca thus challenged such communications and decisions, questioning the calculation of the levies (and the return of the sums already paid) before the requesting (national) court,[37] which, ultimately, requested the preliminary ruling.

12.021 As regards *ex ante* contributions,[38] the Court, building upon *Berlusconi-Fininvest,* confirmed its previous approach and rendered itself exclusively competent to control any acts of national authorities, taking into account that the SRB was, in the case at hand, the ultimate decision-taking authority.

12.022 Finally, the *GAEC Jeanningros* case has definitely contributed to close the circle and ease the distinction (and implications) between the *Borelli* and the *Berlusconi-Fininvest/Iccrea Banca* scenarios. The topic examined by the Court concerned the challenge of a minor amendment to a product specification concerning protected designations of origin (PDO) regulated by Regulation 1151/2012.[39] In those procedures, the decision-taking power corresponds to national authorities, whereas EU institutions (the EC) are left with limited

33 Art. 47 Charter and art. 6 ECHR.

34 Nevertheless, ensuring that national law meets the requirements of predicated *effective judicial protection* seems to be a thorny matter. See, among others: Prek, M. & Lefèvre, S. (2017). The EU Courts as "national" courts: National law in the EU Judicial Process. *Common Market Law Review, 54*(2), pp. 369–402; Sarmiento, D. (2019); and Coman-Kund, F. & Amtenbrink, F. (2018).

35 Cf arts. 103 BRRD, 70 SRM and 5(1)(a) and (f) of the Commission Delegated Regulation 2015/63 supplementing Directive 2014/59/EU of the European Parliament and of the Council with regard to ex ante contributions to resolution financing arrangements and Council Implementing Regulation 2015/81 specifying uniform conditions of the application of Regulation (EU) No. 806/2014 of the European Parliament and of the Council with regard to ex ante contributions to the Single Resolution Fund.

36 See, in detail, *Iccrea Banca* case at Paras.19–22.

37 *Tribunale amministrativo regionale per il Lazio* (Regional Administrative Court for Lazio, Italy).

38 Calculated by the SRB Board and requested from Iccrea Banca by Banca d'Italia.

39 Regulation (EU) No. 1151/2012 of the European Parliament and of the Council of 21 November 2012 on quality schemes for agricultural products and foodstuffs.

discretion.[40] Consequently, the Court ruled that it is for national courts to examine any irregularity that may vitiate a national act.[41] The nexus between the *Borelli* and the *Berlusconi-Fininvest/Iccrea Banca* scenarios is perhaps better summarised in the AG Opinion:[42] "*the exercise of the final decision-making power is the crucial factor for determining whether the EU Courts or the national courts must conduct a judicial review*".[43]

3. Recapitulation and conclusions in the light of CJEU jurisprudence on distribution of judicial competence regarding EU composite procedures

Building upon the abovementioned cases, we can draw some relevant conclusions: **12.023**

First, that to determine the relevant court (CJEU or national courts) to adjudicate in composite procedures, we need to inquire which is the authority being allocated with the final decision-making power. **12.024**

Second, following the above, we can find two basic scenarios and attached consequences as per the allocation of jurisdiction: **12.025**

(i) Under a *Borelli*-like scenario, national authorities are, in terms of *attributability*, the ultimate decision takers. As such, it is for national courts to adjudicate on the final decision as regards any precedent preparatory acts.
In addition, when in doubt about the validity of the involvement of EU bodies or institutions or as regards the interpretation to be given to EU law provisions (or the interpretation of national rules in the light of EU law), those national courts *must* request a preliminary ruling from the CJEU.
(ii) In a *Berlusconi-Fininvest* scenario, where the EU body or institution is the ultimate decision maker, it is for the CJEU to adjudicate on the validity of the final decision taken and also as regards any preliminary acts adopted pursuant to national rules which may vitiate the final decision.

The application of this test in the SSM renders the CJEU solely competent to adjudicate in SSM common procedures and also in those procedures composite in nature where the ECB is the ultimate decision taker.[44] **12.026**

40 Basically limited to "*checking that the application contains the information required and does not appear to be vitiated by manifest error*". *GAEC Jeanningros* case at Paras. 25 and 36.
41 *GAEC Jeanningros* case at Paras. 26–27.
42 Cf footnote 20 in Chapter 10 above.
43 Ibidem at Para. 45.
44 Cf Section B. (*SSM acts resulting from composite procedures, and SSM cooperation not resulting from (or into) composite procedures*) in Chapter 11 above.

12.027 *Third*, the *Berlusconi Fininvest case* can no longer be considered an isolated case but authentic jurisprudence as the *ratio decidendi* is further confirmed in the *Iccrea Banca* case. It stems from the foregoing that, despite the specialties embedded in the SRM and SSM legal frameworks the same rationale could be (and should be) followed by the Court in other unrelated matters and in mixed procedures broadly.

4. Some (for the time being) unresolved issues

12.028 Beyond the conclusions indicated above, there are some valid legal concerns for which, for the time being, there may not be a satisfactory answer (nor guiding case law).

12.029 *First*, as discussed in Section A. (*Cooperation, coordination and composition in the SSM*) of Chapter 11, reviewability by the CJEU of national preparatory acts stretches the constitutional principles of uniformity and autonomy of EU law.[45] Additionally, it further enlarges, without clear treaty basis, the scope of the review of the CJEU, which should adjudicate eventually on the basis not only of EU law but also of national statutes.

12.030 *Second*, some undesired interferences and conflicts of competence between the CJEU and national courts may occur as well.

12.031 As the CJEU or national courts' jurisdiction depends on which authority (EU/national) takes the final decision, there may be some grey areas or hard cases in which the allocation of jurisdiction may not be crystal clear. Hence, conflicts of competence may arise between the CJEU and national courts.

12.032 Although it is not possible to anticipate practical examples, the primacy of EU law supports a solution that places the CJEU in a privileged position to adjudicate in those cases. Yet, this seems to require that adequate procedural safeguards are respected ensuring effective judicial protection, in particular, allowing the CJEU to review any defects vitiating preparatory or necessary acts undertaken by national authorities. This would be particularly problematic under the SSM when the decision taken by the ECB is based or rooted in national legislation transposing prudential Directives.[46]

---

45 And the very *rule of law* foreseen in arts. 2 TEU, 263 TFEU and in the preamble of the Charter.

46 See further Section C. (*Substantive law & sanctioning proceedings: issues and proposals to overcome them*) in Chapter 7.

Third and closely linked to the *first* reflection above, these judgments[47] leave unresolved two key questions: **12.033**

(a) Which irregularities may be reviewed by the CJEU when it is allocated judicial competence. Will those be only the ones attached to the preparatory acts that incardinate in the formal succession of steps in the composite procedures (i.e., only those affecting the preparatory acts referred to in the final decision (e.g., formal opinions or draft decisions))? Will those be *any* irregularities affecting the preparatory acts (i.e., defects vitiating request for information or inspections which provided the national authority with information later on used to prepare its opinion or draft decision)?
(b) Whether the CJEU will be keen to examine the conformity of the national preparatory acts against the procedural and substantive national rules remains to be seen. The uniformity and autonomy of EU law[48] may constitute an impenetrable wall which the CJEU may not be able to overcome under the current constitutional framework (at least when secondary legislation has not made possible an extension of CJEU jurisdiction).

The problematic resides in the fact that, eventually, some errors capable of vitiating the final decision may not be able to be reviewed by the CJEU or by national courts, producing and undesirable gap which severely undermines effective legal protection. The Court did not drop a hint in this regard in the *Berlusconi-Fininvest case*, so the question remains open for discussion. We will look into this immediately below. **12.034**

C. THE ANNULMENT PROCEDURE: STANDING AND REVIEWABILITY

The annulment procedure contemplated in art. 263 TFEU may be the most evident action associated to the concept of *justiciability*. It is a direct action filed by individuals concerned by a decision issued by an EU body or institution by means of which they seek its invalidation.[49] **12.035**

Within the SSM framework, this action is addressed to challenge ECB decisions[50] adopted, in principle, in a *Berlusconi-Fininvest* scenario.[51] Concerning those, there are two matters that deserve (and have attracted) some attention: **12.036**

47 The *Berlusconi-Fininvest case*, the *Iccrea Banca* case and *GAEC Jeanningros* case referred to in Section B.2. (*CJEU recent approaches: Berlusconi-Fininvest, Iccrea Banca and GAEC Jeanningros*) in this chapter.

48 Brito Bastos, F. (2020).

49 On action for annulment concept and practicalities, see, further, Lenaerts, K., Maselis, I. and Gutman, K. (2015) and Craig, P. (2018).

50 Before the General Court, in accordance with art. 256(1) TFEU.

51 In principle, addressed to identified individuals. Also, it is rather doubtful that supervisees have legal standing as regards ECB acts of general application. In this regard, see Section C.1. (*Who may challenge the*

(i) the standard of review deployed by the CJEU when reviewing ECB supervisory decisions (and actions) and (ii) the legal standing required of individuals, so their actions are deemed admissible. These will be analysed right below.

1. In search for a standard of review: challenges to effective legal protection

12.037 It goes without saying that examining the different standards of review applicable to ECB decisions would require a dedicated and thoughtful analysis.[52] This Section does not envisage to undertake such research but rather envisages (1) sketching the standard of review applied by the CJEU when reviewing ECB supervisory and sanctioning decisions under the SSM and (2) proposing some mitigants to the flaws spotted.

(a) CJEU standard of review concerning ECB supervisory tasks

12.038 In a previous work,[53] it was examined how, from a deferential or *light touch* standard of review (applicable to matters falling under ECB's monetary policy mandate), the CJEU has moved towards greater scrutiny or *hard look review* as regards Banking Union matters, but it has made such a move subtly.[54]

SSM R?) in Chapter 2. The considerations made there as regards the possibility to challenge (directly) the SSM R can be also extrapolated here.

Further, the use of the action for annulment as regards ECB instructions addressed to NCAs pursuant to arts. 9(1)III and 18(5) is not analysed here. The possibility of annulling those instructions through the annulment procedure would depend ultimately on the level of discretion granted to the requested NCA. For a useful analysis of this matter, see Hernández Saseta, C. (2021).

52 Ioannidis, M. (2021). Specifically, as regards the ECB monetary policy mandate, see: Zilioli, C. (2017); Kokkot, J. & Sobotta, C. (2017). Judicial review and institutional balance with regard to European monetary policy. In *ECB Legal Conference 2017. Shaping a new legal order for Europe: a tale of crises and opportunities* (pp. 104–112). Frankfurt am Main, ECB; Lehman, M. (2017). Varying standards of judicial scrutiny over central banks actions. In *ECB Legal Conference 2017. Shaping a new legal order for Europe: a tale of crises and opportunities* (pp. 112–133). Frankfurt am Main, ECB; Koskelo, P. (2017). Relevance of fundamental rights for central bank policy decision-making. In *ECB Legal Conference 2017. Shaping a new legal order for Europe: a tale of crises and opportunities* (pp. 133–146). Frankfurt am Main, ECB; and Ventoruzzo, M. (2017). A few notes on judicial review of central banks' activity from the perspective of corporate law. In *ECB Legal Conference 2017. Shaping a new legal order for Europe: a tale of crises and opportunities* (pp. 146–151). Frankfurt am Main, ECB.

On the supervisory SSM side, see: Triantafyllou, D. (2020). The banking union as a new field for composite administrative procedures. In *ESCB legal conference 2020* (pp. 273–278). Frankfurt am Main, ECB; and Lefterov, A. (2020). Judicial review in a multi-level administrative framework – the case of the SSM. In *ESCB legal conference 2020* (pp. 286–304). Frankfurt am Main, ECB.

53 Bosque Argachal, C. and Pizarroso Ceruti, A. (28 January 2019). Welcome to Hard Look Review, ECB. Retrieved from http://eulawanalysis.blogspot.com/2019/01/the-european-central-bank-judicial.html.

Using the same term (and citing the above work) see Ioannidis, M. (2021) at p. 138.

54 In the same vein, see Rosas, A. (2021). EMU in the Case Law of the Union Courts: A General Overview and Some Observations. *European Papers*, Vol. 6, No. 3, pp. 1397–1414. There, the author states that:

"*While these cases are not generally of constitutional significance, they demonstrate a fairly regular involvement of the General Court and/or the ECJ in the judicial control of decisions pertaining to the Banking Union and seem*

It follows naturally that greater discretion entails more scrutiny, and this has been also appreciated by the General Court when reviewing the ECB's SSM related decisions. For instance, in *La Banque Postale* case,[55] despite expressly admitting that it would not intend to substitute the BCE's appreciation, limiting itself to control whether the contested contains "*materially incorrect facts, or is vitiated by an error of law, manifest error of assessment or misuse of powers*",[56] the General; the Court applied a rather intrusive scrutiny. The intensity of the review applied therein precisely reveals the foregoing. Such line of reasoning echoed (maybe not so outspokenly) in other SSM-related judgments[57] seems to progressively move towards a *light touch* approach, at least formally, whereas in the substance we still can find examples of *hard* and *light touch* approaches. **12.039**

In the *Agricole Mutuel Alpes and others* case,[58] the General Court looked deeply into the ECB's interpretation of the concept of *effective director*[59] and the refusal of the authorisation sought by the applicants to appoint several individuals as chairmen of the board of directors of the respective entities and as "*effective directors*" simultaneously. Such refusal was based on the prohibition arising from art. 88(1)(e) of CRDV,[60] as transposed into the French framework by art. L. 511-58 of the French Monetary Code (*Code monétaire et financier*). In doing so, the Court confirmed that the ECB did not err in law by denying the request submitted by the applicants.[61] Such analysis of whether the ECB erred or not in a precise interpretation of a legal concept reveals, indeed, a great **12.040**

---

to suggest that judicial review in this area is fairly robust. This is so especially when it comes to the limits to the powers of the relevant institutions, where there is less room for administrative discretion".

55 See General Court judgment in case T-733/16 (*La Banque postale v ECB*) of 13 July 2018 (ECLI:EU:T:2018:477) *(La Banque Postale case).*

The General Court ruled five more additional judgments of (almost) identical content: (i) case T-745/16 (*BPCE v ECB*) of 13 July 2018 (ECLI:EU:T:2018:476); (ii) case T-751/16 (*Confédération nationale du Crédit mutuel v ECB*) of 13 July 2018 (ECLI:EU:T:2018:475); (iii) case T-757/16 (*Société Générale v ECB*) of 13 July 2018 (ECLI:EU:T:2018:473); (iv) case T-758/16 (*Crédit Agricole SA v ECB*) of 13 July 2018 (ECLI:EU:T:2018:472); and (v) T-768/16 (*BNP Paribas v ECB*) of 13 July 2018 (ECLI:EU:T:2018:471).

56 La *Banque Postale* case at Para. 69.

57 See Zilioli, C. and Buono, G. (2021). Chapter 2: A New Kid on the Block: The European Central Bank Before the Union Courts. In *Max Planck Institute Luxembourg for Procedural Law Research Paper Series | N° 2021 (2) Special Issue* (pp. 41–79). Luxembourg.

58 See General Court judgment in joined cases T-133 to 136/16 (*(1) Caisse régionale de crédit agricole mutuel Alpes Provence; (2) Caisse régionale de crédit agricole mutuel Nord Midi-Pyrénées, (3) Caisse régionale de crédit agricole mutuel Charente-Maritime Deux-Sèvres; and (4) Caisse régionale de crédit agricole mutuel Brie Picardie, established in Amiens v ECB*) of 18 April 2018 (ECLI:EU:T:2018:219). For a dedicated commentary on this judgment, see Gortsos, C. V. (2021).

59 See art. 13(1) CRD IV.

60 "(*e) the chairman of the management body in its supervisory function of an institution must not exercise simultaneously the functions of a chief executive officer within the same institution, unless justified by the institution and authorised by competent authorities*".

61 See the joined cases referred to in footnote 58.

scrutiny from the Court, which was not prone to accept, without too much questioning,[62] the ECB's discretionary choices.

12.041 Yet, in the recent judgment in case C-389/21 P (*Crédit Lyonnais v ECB*),[63] the CJEU showed greater deference towards ECB decisions. In this regard, and acknowledging that the ECB enjoys *broad discretion* under the SSM R, the CJEU indicated that it should not substitute its own assessment for that of the ECB. Hence, the CJEU is limited to ensure that (1) the decision is based on accurate and reliable facts, without manifest errors of assessment or misuse of powers, (2) the evidence contains all the relevant information, which must be taken into account in order to assess a complex situation, and (3) all the procedural guarantees have been duly observed, including careful and impartial examination of all relevant aspects relating to the dispute.[64] Accordingly, the CJEU quashed the judgement from the General Court under appeal, stating that: "*the General Court annulled the decision at issue in so far as it concerned Crédit lyonnais, substituting its own assessment of the risk of fire sales of assets to which Crédit lyonnais was exposed, without establishing how the ECB's assessment set out in that decision was, in that regard, vitiated by a manifest error of assessment. In so doing, it exceeded the scope of its judicial* (...)".[65] Such approach can be regarded as a shift towards a *light touch* scrutiny of deferential approach towards the ECB supervisory assessment.

12.042 After the issuance of this judgement, the General Court seems to have echoed this approach, at least formally. However, a closer look at the General Court's judgements on this matter, after the *Crédit Lyonnais v ECB*,[66] may reveal that it is still prone to exercise thorough reviews, particularly when examining the absence of manifest error of assessments. In the said cases, the General Court examined (i) exhaustively the interpretation of national requirements transposing CRD IV as regards the acquisition of qualifying holdings followed by the ECB[67] and (ii) the appropriateness of the methodologies put in place by the ECB to quantify capital risks.[68]

62 For instance, because of being manifestly disproportionate or wrongful.

63 CJEU judgment in case C-389/21 P (*Crédit Lyonnais v ECB*) of 4 May 2023 (ECLI:EU:C:2023:368).

64 Ibidem at Paras. 55–57.

65 Ibidem at Paras. 75–76.

66 General Court judgements in cases (i) T-323/22 (*Socrates Capital Ltd and others v ECB*) of 10 July 2024 (ECLI:EU:T:2024:460) at Paras. 117–118; (ii) T-186/22 (*BNP Paribas v ECB*) of 5 June 2024 (ECLI:EU:T:2024:353) at Paras. 65–66; and (iii) T-182/22 (*Deutsche Bank AG and others v ECB*) of 5 June 2022 (ECLI:EU:T:2024:352) at Paras. 59–60.

67 See case T-323/22 (*Socrates Capital Ltd and others v ECB*) cited above.

68 See cases T-186/22 (*BNP Paribas v ECB*) and T-182/22 (*Deutsche Bank AG and others v ECB*) cited above.

Conversely, in the Berlusconi II appeal, the CJEU did not refer expressly to the same *deferential* approach towards ECB assessment. There, on top assessing the facts of the dispute and finding that the General Court distorted those, the CJEU went a step beyond and analysed the notion of a qualifying holding submitted by the ECB (and used in the disputed supervisory decision). Accordingly, the CJEU concluded that "*it is not the legal structure of a holding – in particular, whether it is direct or indirect – which determines the existence of a qualifying holding, but, (...) whether that holding makes it possible to attain a particular level of control or influence over the credit institution*".[69] The foregoing situates, in the view of the author, the position of the CJEU closer to a *hard look* review rather than to a *light touch* one. **12.043**

In this regard, it can be concluded that the standard of review used by the CJEU to adjudicate on ECB supervisory decisions (outside sanctioning decisions) may be still oscillating, and only subsequent judgments, issued over time, may be able to settle this controversy. **12.044**

As regards the use of ECB sanctioning powers, the Court has been inclined to exercise an intrusive review of the ECB's interpretation and motivation. In particular, in case T-576/18 *Crédit Agricole*,[70] the Court was asked to annul an administrative pecuniary penalty imposed on the applicant by the ECB. There, the Court observed first that, considering the wide discretion that the ECB enjoyed to impose administrative pecuniary penalties[71] and the substantial amount that could be imposed, "*the obligation to state reasons for decisions imposing such a penalty is of particular importance*".[72] Further, the Court declared that stating the reasons is capital for assessing the proportionality of the penalty imposed, its compliance with EU law and the application of the mitigating and/or aggravating circumstances foreseen in art. 18(3) SSM R.[73] **12.045**

In this regard, the Court looked with much detail into the reasons stated in the sanctioning decision to determine the level of the penalty[74] and acknowledged **12.046**

---

69 See Berlusconi II appeal at Para. 108.

70 General Court judgment in case T-576/18 (*Crédit agricole SA v ECB*) of 8 July 2020 (ECLI:EU:T:2020:304). See, also, General Court judgments in cases T-577/18 (*Crédit Agricole Corporate and Investment Bank v ECB*) of 8 July 2020 (ECLI:EU:T:2020:305) and T-578/18 (*CA Consumer Finance v ECB*) of 8 July 2020 (ECLI:EU:T:2020:306).

The content of this judgment was later confirmed by the Court of Justice judgment in joined cases C-456/20 P to C-458/20 P (*(1) Crédit agricole SA; (2) Crédit agricole Corporate and Investment Bank; (3) CA Consumer Finance v ECB*) of 16 June 2021 (ECLI:EU:C:2021:502).

71 Pursuant to art. 18(1) SSM R.

72 Ibidem. Cf Para. 134 of case T-576/18 as referred to above.

73 Ibidem at Para. 134.

74 Ibidem at Paras. 142–155.

that the reasons stated therein "*neither allow the applicant to understand the methodology chosen by the ECB nor allow the Court to review the legality of the penalty imposed*".[75] Consequently, the Court annulled the sanctioning decision, but "*only to the extent that it imposes an administrative pecuniary penalty on the applicant of EUR 4,300,000*", as it considered proved that an infringement had indeed occurred.[76] Accordingly, if the CJEU was to follow a *light touch* approach to adjudicate as regards the imposition of fines and administrative pecuniary penalties by the ECB, this would equate to rendering the SSM short of the guarantees foreseen in the ECHR, as the Court would not have *full jurisdiction*.[77]

(b) On the extension of the jurisdiction of the CJEU and its limits

12.047 Further, it is worth questioning whether, by means of art. 4(3) SSM R, CJEU jurisdiction would be somehow extended to adjudicate on the use or application of national legislation transposing prudential Directives. In other words, whether the CJEU would be entitled to construe national rules as applied by the ECB when adjudicating in a concrete case.

12.048 The answer to this question is far from clear:

12.049 Above, in Section A.2. (*Attribution of substantive decision powers.*) in Chapter 11, and building upon Brito Bastos' solid analysis,[78] it has been analysed how the CJEU's own jurisdiction (circumscribed in principle to the application and interpretation of EU law) and the principles of autonomy and uniformity constitute major legal concerns.

12.050 Also, considering that art. 4(3) SSM R refers exclusively to "*national legislation transposing those Directives*", it is doubtful whether, on this basis, the CJEU could interpret any national rule relevant to adjudicate in the case as stake.

12.051 Yet, three arguments[79] may be put forward to advocate in favour of allowing the extension of the CJEU's jurisdiction as regards the interpretation and application of national law under the SSM R.

12.052 *First,* an intuitive approach would lead us to consider that if the ECB is deemed to apply national law pursuant to art. 4(3) and the CJEU is allocated

75 Ibidem at Para. 145.

76 Ibidem at Para. 157.

77 See Section D.1. (*Sanctions having a criminal nature imposed by an administrative (not jurisdictional) body: Right to a fair trial under the SSM R?*) in Chapter 8.

78 See, mainly, Brito Bastos, F. (2020).

79 Those are presented in order of strength, from weaker to stronger.

with exclusive competence to review those ECB acts,[80] it would need to review which national law was applied and how. Of course, the intensity of such a review may be debatable but would need to occur, as otherwise some national acts (and the rules constituting the basis for the ECB to adjudicate) may be left unreviewed. Although we know that the old adagio of the *completeness of the system of legal remedies* may be more a desideratum that an actual reality,[81] it is still a value that must be pursued so as to avoid gaps in the reviewability of acts, which can undermine effective legal protection and the very rule of law itself. This argument has been picked up by the General Court in case T-667/21 (*BAWAG PSK Bank v ECB*), where the Court intuitively (and without too much reasoning on the potential constrains associated to its own jurisdictional limits) assumed that it needed to review the national law applied by the ECB resulting from the transposition of CRD IV to adjudicate on the case.[82]

Second, and closely linked to the above, the right to an effective judicial remedy[83] demands that the adequacy of the final act has to be measured against the applicable law upon which the act is based. This includes scrutinising the applicable law and the preparatory acts that materially lead to that decision. The foregoing requires not only examining the law (national law in this case) but also examining the conformity of those preparatory acts against the standard of review typically applied, in the view of the author, to the ECB when carrying out supervisory tasks.[84] **12.053**

Third, authorised voices and the CJEU itself seem to have understood that an extension of the CJEU jurisdiction has operated through art. 4(3) SSM R. As indicated by AG Campos Sánchez-Bordona in hisopinion in the **12.054**

80 In a *Berlusconi-Fininvest* scenario, where the ECB is the final decision-making authority.

81 Taking into account the evolving and, sometimes, constraining standards to grant *locus standing* before the CJEU to the parties concerned but also the constitutional framework applicable to EU bodies and institutions and *related* politically bodies. The latest may be paradigmatic in the *Mallis* and the *Chrysostomides* cases, where the Court of Justice ultimate held (with the favourable opinion of AG Pitruzzela) that Eurogroup may not be subject to scrutiny under art. 263 TFEU nor trigger the liability of the EU, as it is situated outside the constitutional EU framework. Cf Court of Justice judgments in joined cases C-105/15 P to C-109/15 P (*Konstantinos Mallis and Others v European Commission and European Central Bank*) of 20 September 2016 and (ECLI:EU:C:2016:702) and joined cases C-597/18 P, C-598/18 P, C-603/18 P and C-604/18 P (*K. Chrysostomides & Co. and Others v Council*) of 16 December 2020 (ECLI:EU:C:2020:1028).

82 See General Court judgement in case T-667/21 (*BAWAG PSK Bank v ECB*) of 28 February 2024 (ECLI:EU:T:2024:131) at Para. 58.

83 Arts. 47 Charter and 6 ECHR.

84 See immediately above as regards *La Banque Postale* case. It seems reasonable and coherent subjecting preparatory acts carried out by NCAs to the same standard of review applicable to the ECB when adjudicating on the errors that may vitiate the final acts. This approach also ensures the uniformity of EU law that, as discussed below, may be hard to achieve in the context of SSM judicial procedures relating to composite procedures (or whenever national law is applied by the ECB).

Berlusconi-Fininvest case,[85] when the CJEU is attributed exclusive jurisdiction, considering the mandate contained in art. 4(3) SSM R, it should also adjudicate the lawfulness of the opinions and decisions provided by the NCAs as preparatory acts. In the AG's own words: "*Under that provision, the ECB is entrusted with applying national law that transposes directives and, in exceptional cases, regulations that deal with the banking union, underpinning the extension of the jurisdiction of the Court of Justice to review such cases*".[86]

12.055 Also, and as indicated above,[87] the Court of Justice itself seems to have embraced such approach in the *Berlusconi-Fininvest case* (although the extension or intensity of the review remains unclear).

12.056 The same reasoning can be somehow inferred from other cases. For example, in the *Credit Agricole Mutuel Alpes and others* case,[88] the Court thoughtfully examined the relevant provision of CRD IV (art. 13(1)) and art. Article L. 511-13 of the French *Code monétaire et financier*[89] (transposing the previous provision of CRD IV into the French legal system). Further, the *Credit mutuel Arkéa* cases[90] follow a similar line where the Court of Justice examined the application of the same code[91] and took into consideration the views expressed by the French *Conseil d'Etat*.

(c) On the application and interpretation of national law by the CJEU

12.057 Other problems arising out of the binomial (a) CJEU exclusive jurisdiction and (b) ECB application of national law relate to (i) which acts may be deemed to fall under the review of the Court and (ii) how to assess the conformity of national provisions serving as a base for the final decision (used by the ECB or the NCAs in the preparatory acts) in particular, in cases where there are

---

85 AG Campos Sánchez-Bordona's opinion in case C-219/17 (*Berlusconi-Fininvest*) of 27 June 2018 (ECLI:EU:C:2018:502). In the same vein, see case T-667/21 (*BAWAG PSK Bank v ECB*) at Para. 58.

86 Ibidem at AG opinion at Para. 114. This conclusion is backed (or inspired) by the elements cited in footnote 67 of this opinion: (i) the letter issued by the ECB dated on 31 March 2017: "Additional clarification regarding the ECB's competence to exercise supervisory powers granted under national law" and (ii) an article written by Smits (see Smits, R. (2017)).

87 See Section B.2. (*CJEU recent approaches: Berlusconi-Fininvest, Iccrea Banca and GAEC Jeanningros*) in this chapter above. See, also, Paras. 49–51 of the *Berlusconi-Fininvest case*.

88 General Court judgment in joined cases T-133/16 to T-136/16 (*Caisse régionale de crédit agricole mutuel Alpes Provence and Others v European Central Bank*) of 24 April 2018 (ECLI:EU:T:2018:219).

89 Ibidem at Paras. 49 and 84–103.

90 Court of Justice judgment in joined cases C-152/18 P and 153/18 P (*Crédit Mutuel Arkéa v ECB*) of 2 October 2019 (ECLI:EU:C:2019:810). Those judgments resulted from the appeal of previous cases T-712/15 (*Crédit Mutuel Arkéa v ECB*) of 13 December 2017 (ECLI:EU:T:2017:900) and T-52/16 (*Crédit Mutuel Arkéa v ECB*) of 13 December 2017 (ECLI:EU:T:2017:902).

91 Ibidem (appeal) at Paras. 151, 158–160 and 185–188.

no national jurisprudence or where there may be divergent interpretations between different legal systems prompting different legal avenues.

(i) Concerning the national preparatory *acts over which the CJEU* may need to adjudicate, it seems impossible to draw *ex ante* a clear line determining which acts would be excluded and which acts would be included.[92] As a matter of principle, these should include those materially affecting the final decision (forming a proper, identifiable step of the relevant composite procedure or not). The pleas brought by the plaintiff may identify such acts[93] (e.g., request for information, informal communications, etc.) as, otherwise, it seems difficult for the Court to further indagate those *ex officio*.

(ii) The standard of review applied to assess the conformity of the preparatory acts issued by national authority should be, in principle, the same applied by the CJEU to adjudicate on the ECB's supervisory decisions[94] (i.e., the criteria used and the intensity of the CJEU review should be the same for both cases). This is not only consistent with the ultimate purpose of the judicial procedure (assess whether the final ECB decision was vitiated by irregularities, no matter where they come from) but also permits the preservation of the uniformity of the criteria applied by the Court and, hence, the uniformity of judgment.

Whereas national laws transposing prudential Directives remain *national*,[95] the principle that Union law must be applied uniformly stills needs to be protected, to the maximum extent that the prorogation of the CJEU's mandate on SSM matters so allows. **12.058**

For instance, in the *Credit Agricole Mutuel Alpes and other* case, the Court was prompted to consider the Conseil d'Etat judgment as it reinforced its own view and the view of the AG.[96] But it is worth asking: would the CJEU have **12.059**

92 See, as regards the uncertainty of the national acts falling under the Courts review, Dermine, P. and Eliantonio, M. (2019). Case Note: CJEU (Grand Chamber), Judgment of 19 December 2018, C-219/17, Silvio Berlusconi and Finanziaria d'investimento Fininvest SpA (Fininvest) v Banca d'Italia and Istituto per la Vigilanza Sulle Assicurazioni (IVASS). *Review of European Administrative Law*, *12*(2), pp. 237–253.

93 Arts. 76(d) and 84 of the Rules of Procedure of the General Court of Justice (2018). Consolidated version available at: CURIA – Procedure – Court of Justice of the European Union (europa.eu).

94 Ibidem.

95 See also Section A.2.(c). (*When does national law transpose a Directive?*) in Chapter 7.

96 Such judgment was produced during a procedure substantiated before the General Court. The applicants disputed the validity of such national judgment as, in their view, it "*was based on a misunderstanding of their cooperative bank status*" (see *Credit Agricole Mutuel Alpes and others* case at Para. 41). The Court did not enter into greater scrutiny of the national judgment but simply considered it relevant for the purpose of interpreting the controversial provision of the French Monetary Code and, hence, noted that it should be "*taken into account*" (Ibidem at Paras. 86–87). Once the interpretation provided by that judgment was examined, the Court measured it against the wording of CRD IV, noting that the national rules and the directive were aligned (Ibidem at Paras. 91). Finally, the Court simply expressed that since the constantly referred judgment was sufficient to establish the interpretation of the national provisions applied by the ECB, the claims questioning the validity of such interpretation should be rejected at the outset (ibidem

been ready to accept such judgment in case it was in contradiction (to a certain extent) with its own reading of the national provisions? There is no answer to such a question, but for the time being, the General Court seems keen to apply a certain deferential approach to national judgments construing relevant provisions of national law applied by the ECB under art. 4(3) SSM R.

12.060 Another issue relates to what may happen if the CJEU is due to interpret a national provision for which there is no settled jurisprudence (or a precedent, at least) at national level.[97] Following the expanded mandate allocated to the CJEU, it should be ready to examine and interpret the national provisions.[98] However, it is undeniable that when construing such national law, the CJEU may lack the tools to carry out this interpretation, in particular when the interpretation concerns several interconnected provisions or demands considering further jurisprudence of basic substantive rules which demand familiarity with the national legal framework. To deal with those cases, some avenues are sketched below.

12.061 Finally, it may also happen that the CJEU, when confronted to assess the application of national legislation, may have to deal with contradictory judgments. If that contradiction arises on the basis of (substantially) different national rules, then such divergence may be acceptable.[99] However, if, based on essentially similar laws, divergent lines of jurisprudence are produced across MSs, then there may be an issue as regards how to ensure that supervisory rules are applied (and reviewed) uniformly, ensuring the desired level playing field.[100]

---

at Para. 92). The Court applied, hence, a deferential approach (and a bit of a circular logic), as it did not enter into further analysis on the interpretation of the national provision but fully relied on the national judgment.

97 Connected to this issue, another problemat arises: what would happen if the national provision applied by the ECB constitutes a wrongful transposition of a prudential Directive? As a first line of the defence, it must be noted that the ECB (working in liaison with the relevant NCA) should be prompt to apply the remedies devised in an earlier section of this work (See Section A.2.(b).(3). (*What happens when a MS has not transposed (or has deficiently transposed) a Directive. Are there any remedies?*) in Chapter 7).

On account of the foregoing, this question should be rather theoretical than real; however, flaws may happen. If such a case arises, the CJEU should be ready to expurgate the national provision from the legal framework due to its incompatibility with the EU legal framework. But then another issue arises as then the ECB may be deprived of a proper legal basis. In this latter case, the CJEU still would have resource to the usual interpretative mechanisms (see the Section cited immediately above) to try to devise a practicable solution which upholds the validity of the legal base used by the ECB. However, if there is no other possibility but to consider that indeed such national provisions constitute a wrong transposition, then the Court should annul the ECB decision because of the lack of relevant legal basis.

98 On the reasons justifying this expanded mandate, see immediately above.

99 Provided that the national law applied by the ECB has been correctly transposed by the MSs. See footnote 97.

100 See further Section B. (*SSM basic principles: level playing field & proportionality*) in previous Chapter 1.

The issue may be more apparent than real because, in the end, relying on the application of national laws determines that prudential rules may be applied differently and, so, may construed in diverse manners as well. The limit must be given by the correctness of the transposition and the conformity of the interpretation with the purpose of the prudential Directive. Provided that those two are met (and to the extent that the principle of equivalence and effectiveness is observed), it does not seem to be many grounds to push for uniformity where the EU legislators have left the MSs leeway so as to how to transpose EU rules into their internal order. **12.062**

(d) Some proposals addressed to mitigate the issues generated by the expansion of the CJEU jurisdiction over national preparatory acts

Acknowledging that the CJEU may be lacking the tools to apply relevant provisions of national law and considering that the mechanism devised in situations where the CJEU was supposed to incidentally adjudicate on national law matters[101] may fall short, some proposals can be, at least, sketched.[102] **12.063**

In the *first place*, one should trust the CJEU internal capabilities. For instance, the *référendaires* serving the institution come from all MSs. Their legal background and expertise on the different European legal traditions should provide the Court with an adequate expertise to understand the national legal considerations at stake. The foregoing could be also coupled, as the case so requires, with *ad hoc* research performed by the Research and Documentation Directorate of the CJEU.[103] **12.064**

Second, a more extensive, if also targeted, use of the *amicus curiae* mechanism could be explored. Pursuant to arts. 24(2) and 40 of the Statute of the Court of Justice,[104] MSs (together with EU bodies and Institutions) may be required to assist the Court. Such assistance is, in principle, confined to provide the form of assistance requested by the Court and is embedded in the principle of sincere cooperation.[105] Pursuant to this mechanism, the Court may request the assistance of MSs to help identify and construe the relevant provisions at stake. **12.065**

101 Constituting mainly a factual question, rather than a legal basis whose validity may be scrutinised or its meaning needs to be construed by the Court. See Gagliardi, E. & Wissink, L. (2020) and Sarmiento, D. (2019).

102 In this regard, see more extensively, Gagliardi, E. & Wissink, L. (2020).

103 Which is actually fully devoted to provide "*research notes at the request of one of the courts which the institution comprises, primarily on approaches taken in the national legal systems of the Member States to resolve a given legal issue*": https://curia.europa.eu/jcms/jcms/Jo2_11968/en/.

104 Available at: https://curia.europa.eu/jcms/upload/docs/application/pdf/2016-08/tra-doc-en-div-c-0000-2016-201606984-05_00.pdf.

105 Art. 4(3) TEU.

These requests may be addressed directly to the MSs but could precise that they should be fulfilled by requesting certain input from the judiciary (e.g., from the constitutional or highest national court) and providing the reply to the Court. In addition, they may be issued in a broad manner (i.e., addressed to the MSs and not to a given body of the judiciary), being the MSs are better-placed to decide which one of the national bodies (including national courts) is capable of fulfilling the entrusted request. As the provisions of the Statute of the Court of Justice are open as regards the content and form of assistance that may be requested, they can be bespoken to address the needs of the Court.

12.066 *Third*, some other authors[106] have also proposed introducing an *inverse* preliminary ruling which would amount to be an incidental procedure[107] facilitating the exchange between the CJEU and national courts. This mechanism has been initially devised as a tool to examine the legality of actions undertaken by national bodies under national law in composite administrative procedures.

12.067 Disregarding the considerations on the legal basis required for such mechanism (which would require a dedicated analysis), the main issue stands with the legal value that should be given to the national judgments issued under this hypothetical mechanism. It would be at odds with the exclusive jurisdiction of the CJEU in the cases at stake and with the supremacy of EU law attributing a binding character to such national interpretations. Yet, paradoxically, national law applied by the ECB under art. 4(3) SSM R remains *national*. This dichotomy, together with the fact that this remedy is, for the time being at least, an academic proposal, encourages the exploration of the possibilities offered by the two precedent proposed solutions to assist the CJEU to deal with the interpretation of the national law applied by the ECB.

2. Legal standing in actions for annulment in SSM related matters

12.068 An action for annulment to be admissible requires *locus standi*.[108] Accordingly, pursuant to art. 263(IV) TFEU, to challenge the ECB's supervisory acts, individuals must demonstrate that such act is "*of direct concern to them and does not entail implementing measures*".

---

106 See Hofmann, H. C. H. (2009) at p. 159. See, also, Alonso de León, S. (2017); Alonso de León, S. (2016); Gagliardi, E. & Wissink, L. (2020); and Lamandini, M., Ramos Muñoz, D. & Ruíz Almendral, V. (2020). The EMU and Its Multi-Level Constitutional Structure: The Need for More Imaginative "Dialogue" Among and Across EU and National Institutions. *Legal Issues of Economic Integration*, *47*(4), pp. 311–336.

107 Building upon the description of the mechanism as depicted by Alonso de León. Alonso de León, S. (2017) at p. 438.

108 Lenaerts, K., Maselis, I. and Gutman, K. (2015) at *Chapter 15. Review of legality: access.*

For the time being, the CJEU has kept a restrictive approach of what is to be considered direct concern building upon the *Plaumann* doctrine,[109] even though certain developments have shown a certain relaxation of such restrictive approach.[110] 12.069

As regards SSM (and more broadly BU) actions for annulment, the tendency of the General Court is to refuse *locus standi* to the supervised entities' shareholders to challenge supervisory (or resolution) acts addressed to the supervised entity. Initially, the General Court was favourable to grant *locus standi* to the shareholders of an entity which has been served with an ECB decision withdrawing its banking authorisation. In the *Trasta case*,[111] the General Court admitted that the shareholders were individually concerned by the withdrawal of the banking license of *Trasta Komercbanka AS*[112] and also that such withdrawal was of direct concern to them;[113] the latter, as "*it directly affects the legal position of the shareholder applicants*". There, the Court substantiated that even if the shareholders were not deprived from their status as such, the withdrawal of the banking license undermined their economic rights,[114] and their voting rights became rather formal, as the credit institution could no longer achieve its object[115] (i.e., undertaking the banking business). 12.070

However, in the *Trasta appeal case*,[116] the Court of Justice set aside the abovementioned order, rejected the admissibility of the action filed by *Trasta Komercbanka AS* against the ECB decision withdrawing its banking authorisation and referred the case back to the General Court for adjudication. 12.071

More particularly, in what matters as regards shareholders' *locus standi*, the Court does not seem to question the *individual concern* generated by the banking authorisation withdrawal, but rather the *direct concern*.[117] In this vein, the 12.072

109 On the *Plaumann* doctrine and its further development, see, for more detail, Section C.1. (*Who may challenge the SSM*) in Chapter 2. The foregoing, in particular, as regards the possibility of challenging EU acts of general application.

110 Ibidem.

111 General Court order in case T-247/16 (*Trasta Komercbanka AS and others v ECB*) of 12 September 2017 (ECLI:EU:T:2022:389) (*Trasta case*).

112 The LSI whose license was withdrew by the ECB. Cf *Trasta case* at Paras. 60–63.

113 *Trasta case* at Para. 66.

114 "*The right to receive dividends from the profits of a commercial company which is no longer authorised to carry on its business activities necessarily becomes illusory*". *Trasta case* at Para. 67.

115 Ibidem.

116 Court of Justice judgment in joined cases C-663/17 P, C-665/17 P and C-669/17 P (*ECB and Others v Trasta Komercbanka and Others*) of 5 November 2019 (ECLI:EU:C:2019:923) (*Trasta appeal case*).

117 See, for an updated analysis on SSM developments of shareholders' *locus standi*, Arnal, J., Russo, C. & Thomadakis, A. (2024). The Judicial Scrutiny of the SSM and the SRB A Missed Chance or a Success Story? *Economic Governance Support Unit (EGOV).*

Court determined that: "*the right of shareholders to receive dividends and to participate in the management of Trasta Komercbanka, as a company constituted under Latvian law, has not been affected by the decision at issue*".[118] Having said that, the Court further notes that the withdrawal of the baking licenses may generate negative effects for the shareholders, but those are of economic nature and do not affect the legal situation of the shareholders.[119] Hence, they should not be taken into consideration, as the General Court (allegedly) did wrongly.

12.073 The General Court has stuck to the *Trasta appeal case* and has systemically denied *locus standi* to shareholders filing actions for annulment against the ECB decision withdrawing the banking licenses of the entity in which they have a stake. This is the case, for instance, of cases T-27/19,[120] T-351/18 and T-584/18,[121] and T-797/19[122]. Yet, there seems to be a recent yet inexplicable exception: the *Anglo Austrian AAB AG* saga.[123] There, the General Court first and the CJEU later admitted, without questioning (and without further explanations being provided), that the main (and practically sole) shareholder of the credit institution concerned by the withdrawal of its banking license was able to challenge that measure and appeal against the ruling in first instance later. The reason for this exception may be found in the fact that the said shareholder was a holding company owing 99.99% of the share of the concerned credit institution, which eventually could have afforded the necessary direct and individual concern.

12.074 Another relevant line of judicial doctrine relates to the SRB. In the *Iccrea* case,[124] the Court of Justice was asked to adjudicate in a preliminary ruling as regards the contributions to be levied to a national resolution fund. As a starting point, it must be recalled that, according to art. 5(1) of Council Implementing Regulation 2015/81,[125] requests to levy those contributions are

118 *Trasta appeal case* at Para. 110.

119 *Trasta appeal case* at Paras. 111–112.

120 General Court judgment in case T-27/19 (*Pilatus Bank plc and Pilatus Holding ltd. v European Central Bank*) of 2 February 2022 (ECLI:EU:T:2022:46). Cf at Para. 33.

121 General Court judgment in cases T-351/18 and T-584/18 (*Ukrselhosprom PCF LLC and Versobank AS v European Central Bank*) of 6 October 2021 (ECLI:EU:T:2021:669). Cf at Para. 100.

122 General Court judgment in case T-797/19 (*Anglo Austrian AAB AG and Belegging-Maatschappij "Far-East" BV v European Central Bank)* of 22 June 2022 (ECLI:EU:T:2022:389). Cf at Para. 16.

123 Composed by the CJEU judgement in case C-579/22 P (*Anglo Austrian AAB AG and others v ECB*) of 12 September 2024 (ECLI:EU:C:2024:731); and General Court judgement in case T-797/19 (*Anglo Austrian AAB and Belegging-Maatschappij "Far-East" v ECB*) of 22 June 2022 (EU:T:2022:389).

124 Court of Justice judgment in case C-414/18 (*Iccrea Banca*) of 3 December 2019 (ECLI:EU:C:2019:1036).

125 Council Implementing Regulation 2015/81 specifying uniform conditions of application of Regulation (EU) No. 806/2014 of the European Parliament and of the Council with regard to *ex ante* contributions to the Single Resolution Fund.

addressed to national resolution authorities (and not to the concerned credit institutions[126]).

There, the Court acknowledged that these acts are of direct concern to credit institutions and do not entail implementing measures. Consequently, such acts would be open to be challenged by the concerned credit institutions pursuant to art. 263(4) TFEU.[127] In those circumstances, the Court indicated that Iccrea Banca could only have claim before a national court, that the decisions of the SRB on the calculation of the *ex ante* contributions to the SRF for the year 2016 were illegal, only if it had also brought an action for annulment of the SRB's decision.[128] That, in fact, did not happen, as Iccrea Banca did not bring any action against the second SRB decision and brought an action that resulted time-barred as regards the first one.[129] In that respect, the Court of Justice stuck to the well-settled *TWD* jurisprudence[130] and declared inadmissible the referral insofar as it related to the calculation of the *ex ante* contributions. Questions relating to the levies due to the Italian resolution authority were admitted and ruled against the Iccrea Banca. **12.075**

From all of the above and following CJEU's case law, it can be concluded that, in a scenario where an entity having its banking license withdrawn is capable of challenging the relevant ECB decision and so protecting its legitimate interests, shareholders are not granted *locus standi* to challenge such supervisory decision.[131] **12.076**

Also, as regards the decisions on the *ex ante* calculations of the contributions to the SRF addressed to national authorities, those would be, in principle, open to the direct challenge of the concerned entities. The foregoing, building upon the *Iccrea Banca* case.[132] **12.077**

---

126 *Iccrea Banca* case at Para. 65.

127 Ibidem at Paras. 63 and 70.

128 Ibidem at Para. 70. Actually there were two SRB decisions on the calculation of *ex ante* contributions: one on 15 April 2016 and another one (correcting the previous one) on 20 May 2016.

129 Due to the lapse of the two-month period foreseen in the sixth Para. of art. 263.

130 Court of Justice judgment in case C-188/92 (*TWD Textilwerke Deggendorf GmbH v Bundesrepublik Deutschland*) of 9 March 1994 (ECLI:EU:C:1994:90).

131 Being the *Anglo Austrian AAB AG* saga, in principle, the sole exception to this line of reasoning, for the time being.

132 Court of Justice judgment in case C-414/18 (*Iccrea Banca*) of 3 December 2019 (ECLI:EU:C:2019:1036). Cf Paras. 66–67 and 69–70.

D. JUSTICIABILITY AND DAMAGES ACTION: THE CONFERRAL OF "RIGHTS" ON INDIVIDUALS

12.078 The ECB is made accountable for the functioning of the entire *mechanism*.[133] However, such clear statement made under the SSM R does not clarify two key aspects: (i) which is the administrative authority to which the final supervisory or sanctioning decision is attributable and, in this regard, (ii) who is liable in the case of failures happening.[134]

12.079 Starting from the second question, since the SSM has no legal personality, it cannot be attributed direct liability pursuant to art. 340 TFEU.[135] Consequently, liability resulting from acts (and omissions[136]) under the SSM triggering liability need to be ascribed to the NCAs and/or the ECB.[137] As a starting point, Recital 61 SSM R proclaims the liability ECB as regards the tasks performed under the SSM pursuant to art. 340 TFEU.[138] The last sentence of this recital further concretes that such liability "*should be without prejudice to the liability of national competent authorities to make good any damage caused by them or by their servants in the performance of their duties in accordance with national legislation*".

---

133 See art. 6(1) SSM R. Cf also Recital 55 SSM R.

134 See, for an exhaustive analysis of financial supervisors' liability, Busch, D., Gortsos, C. V. and Mcmeel, G. (2022). *Liability of Financial Supervisors and Resolution Authorities*. Oxford: OUP.

135 For a comprehensive study on the liability regime of the ECB under the SSM, its compliance with the Basel Principles and the applicable standard of review, see, further, D'Ambrosio, R. (2015) and Türk, A. (2017). Liability and accountability for policies announced to the public and for press releases. In *ECB Legal Conference 2017. Shaping a new legal order for Europe: a tale of crises and opportunities* (pp. 43–59). Frankfurt am Main, ECB.

136 The CJEU has admitted that omissions may trigger EU bodies and Institution liability but "*only where the institutions have infringed a legal obligation to act under a provision of Community law*". See General Court judgment in case T-279/03 (*Galileo International and others v. EC*) of 10 May 2006 (ECLI:EU:T:2006:121) at Para. 137 (among many others).

137 Reference is made as encompassing potential *joint* liability. Such cases cannot be determined in advance because the casuistry can be rich. As a mere sample, this can arise when the ECB issues a delayed request to the relevant NCA to make use of its supervisory powers (pursuant to art. 9(1)III SSM R) and the NCA fails to act when it could do it. The foregoing, presuming that such acts caused quantifiable damages to a given claimant.

138 Such liability is triggered provided that the following three elements are determined: (i) infringement of an EU law rule intended to confer rights on individuals, (ii) being sufficiently serious and (iii) the existing causal link between that infringement and the damage suffered by those individuals. See Court of Justice judgments in cases C-501/18 (*BT v. Balgarska Narodna Banka*) of 25 March 2021 (ECLI:EU:C:2021:249) (Para. 113); C-571/16 (*Nikolay Kantarev v Balgarska Narodna Banka*) of 4 October 2018 (ECLI:EU:C:2018:807) – Para. 92 and 94; and C-350/16 P (*Salvatore Aniello Pappalardo and Others v European Commission*) of 13 September 2017 (ECLI:EU:C:2017:672) at Para. 48.

Following such statement[139] logic dictates that the SSM R implies a differentiated liability regime: one as regards the ECB (subject to EU law) and the other as regards NCAs (subject to national law[140]). **12.080**

In absolute terms, such liability regime entails an asymmetrical distribution of the share of responsibility, where the ECB, in principle, holds a greater share of the overall Eurozone (and beyond) micro– (and macro–) prudential tasks. This is based on (i) the purpose of the mechanism, which attributes to the ECB the exclusive competence as regards the tasks listed in arts. 4(1), 4(2) and 5 of the SSM R. Also, (ii) considering the direct and indirect supervisory tasks the ECB is allocated with.[141] Finally, (iii) regarding the volume of assets which actually are directly supervised by the ECB, which amount to almost 82% of the banking sector of participating MSs.[142] **12.081**

As regards the first question introduced above (i.e., which is the administrative authority to which the final supervisory or sanctioning decision is attributable), it appears that the assessment and further adjudication on liability will mostly depend on the attribution (*accountability*) of the given act or omission to the ECB and/or to the NCA. The attribution of acts (and omissions) between the ECB and the NCAs may be sketched as follows.[143] **12.082**

1. The ECB will remain accountable (and hence liable) as regards any acts or omissions relating to SIs to whom it has been allocated direct supervisory (and sanctioning[144]) powers. The same would stands as regards granting banking authorisations and assessing the acquisition of qualifying holdings regarding LSIs.

   Such a statement may be tempered as regards the use of instructions addressed to NCAs pursuant to art. 9(1)III and 18(5) SSM R.[145] As indicated earlier in this work, in such cases, the power of the ECB amounts to simply *request* NCAs to act. Ultimately, it will be for the respective NCAs to assess if and how such

139 To be noted that Recital 61 SSM R: *on the one hand*, as regards the ECB, refers to art. 340 TFEU and the general principles of common to MSs legal traditions; and *on the other hand*, also refers to the liability principles embedded under MSs domestic legislation. This implies that a differentiated standard of liability will rule on the ECB and NCAs' liability.

140 Which could be less restrictive (imposing less strict conditions) but could not add additional conditions, making it harder for the individuals to access compensation in case of MS/NCAs liability (cf cases *Kantarev* at Para. 121 and *BT v. Barlagska Narodna Banka* at Para. 114).

141 Where, on top of the overall responsibility over the *mechanism*, the ECB is entirely competent to grant (and withdraw) banking licenses and assess the acquisition of qualifying holdings in credit institutions regarding each and every credit institution of a participating MS.

142 Cf the briefing made available by the ECB on its banking supervision webpage: https://www.bankingsupervision.europa.eu/about/thessm/html/index.en.html.

143 See, further, in Chapter 7.

144 See Section C. (*Allocation of sanctioning competences: a specialty over the general rule?*) in Chapter 6.

145 See, further, footnote 232 and Section C. (*Substantive law & sanctioning proceedings: issues and proposals to overcome them*) in Chapter 7.

a request can be fulfilled carefully considering national legislation as a whole to this end.[146]

From a more abstract perspective, the ECB retains also overall oversight over the SSM,[147] and in this sense, it should bear the liability arising out of its incorrect functioning or the paralysation or collapse[148] of the mechanism, rendering it incapable of attaining its goals and fulfilling its financial stability objectives.

2. As regards LSIs, in principle, NCAs will bear the liability for any acts or omission relating to the direct supervision of LSIs.

   It must be noted that, as regards the NCAs' direct supervision over LSIs, the ECB must be properly and periodically informed.[149] Also, as regards material supervisory procedures or decision, NCAs must inform the ECB, and on the basis of the information provided, it may request further aspects to be analysed and/or may express its views.[150] Nevertheless, as indicated above,[151] such (potentially) material input provided by the ECB does not turn it into the final decision maker; the NCA issuing such supervisory decisions as regards LSIs will then remain accountable.

12.083 Following the abovementioned scheme, some of the main issues pertaining to liability allocation within the SSM will be presented in the subsequent two Sections.

1. The conferral of rights as a requisite needed to trigger ECB liability pursuant to art. 340 TFEU

12.084 In practical terms, individuals seeking compensation due to ECB acts and because of its broader oversight over the system would need to prove three elements. These elements triggering EU bodies or institution liability have been elaborated by the CJEU on the basis of art. 340 TFEU. Those are: (i) the infringement of an EU law rule intended to confer rights on individuals, (ii) being sufficiently serious and (iii) existing causal link between that infringement and the damage suffered by those individuals.[152]

12.085 In particular, the first element deserves some additional analysis, as it is not self-evident that the SSM R actually *confers* rights on individuals.[153]

146 Encompassing not only substantive rules but also procedural rules and national case law construing such rules.

147 Cf art. 6(5)(c) SSM R.

148 It is to be noted that these situations may look quite remote but are not absolutely impossible, especially if the relationship between NCAs (or some of them) would antagonise as a result of the ECB not keeping a collegial and cooperative approach.

149 Arts. 6(5)(a) SSM R and 99–100 SSM Fr.

150 Arts. 6(5)(c) SSM R and 97–98 SSM Fr.

151 See Section B.2.(a). (*Common procedures as composite procedures*) in Chapter 11 above.

152 Cf footnote 138.

153 Cf *Kantarev* at Paras. 113 and 115.

Despite its apparent rigidity, the landmark case *Francovich*[154] implied that the content of the rights (not the rights conferred on individuals itself) should be identifiable on the basis of the EU law.[155] This is not at odds with the fact that a piece of EU law may protect different legal interests.[156] **12.086**

The SSM R protects, indeed, a plurality of interests. Following Recital 30 SSM R, such interests comprise the integrity of the internal market, the individual soundness of credit institutions, the financial stability of the Union and (particularly relevant for this analysis) the protection of investors.[157] **12.087**

In this sense, one can easily detect some provisions enshrined in the SSM R aiming at conferring rights on the entities (and individuals) subject to ECB supervision.[158] Whereas the conferral of rights on entities (and individuals) falling under the scope of the supervision carried out by the ECB[159] seems to be unproblematic, the matter gets thornier as regards other individuals, mainly depositors potentially affected by a deficient ECB supervision. **12.088**

In the *Peter Paul* case,[160] the Court of Justice held that the banking directive under scrutiny[161] was not aimed at conferring direct rights on depositors in the case deposits became unavailable as a result of defective supervision by the competent authority.[162] The foregoing even if such directive actually (i) regulated depositors' protection and (ii) made further reference to the interests of **12.089**

154 Court of Justice judgment in joined cases C-6/90 and C-9/90 (*Francovich v Italy*) of 19 November 2011 (ECLI:EU:C:1991:428).

155 In this regard, see SSM, its compliance with the Basel Principles and the applicable standard of review; see, further, D'Ambrosio, R. (2015) at p. 53.

156 Ibidem. D'Ambrosio further notes that the existence of a plurality of interest protected by the EU law allegedly infringed may have an impact on "the assessment of the seriousness of the breach" (but not in the recognition of the rules conferred).

157 It is to be noted also that the CJEU has declared that, when assessing the interests protected by a given piece of EU law, one needs to take into account the content of Recitals. See the reasoning used in Court of Justice judgment in case C-222/02 (*Peter Paul*) of 12 October 2004 (ECLI:EU:C:2004:606) at Paras. 31, 36–38. In this judgment, the Court builds a significant part of its argumentation by making reference to several Recitals of EU Directives.

158 Among others, the due process rights enshrined in art. 23 SSM R and arts 24 and 30–35 SSM Fr. But more broadly, any other substantive rule enshrined in the single Rulebook to which the ECB is required to apply on the basis of the SSM R.

159 Directly, as regards SIs but also as regards those tasks for which the ECB is made the direct supervisor of LSIs (banking licensing and assessment of qualifying holdings).

160 See footnote 157.

161 Directive 94/19/EC of the European Parliament and of the Council of 30 May 1994 on deposit-guarantee schemes.

162 Directive 2009/14/EC of the European Parliament and of the Council of 11 March 2009 amending Directive 94/19/EC on deposit-guarantee schemes as regards the coverage level and the payout delay.

depositors in its recitals, as depositors are, in principle, ensured compensation in case of unavailability of their deposits.[163]

12.090 Nevertheless, more recently, the Court ruled in the *Kantarev* case that the Directive 2009/14 "*constitutes a rule of law intended to confer rights on individuals allowing depositors to bring an action for damages for the harm sustained by late repayment of deposits*".[164] Yet, the Court observed that, following the *Peter Paul* precedent, EU law does not preclude national law limiting depositors' right to seek liability for damages caused due to defective supervision by national supervisors. In *BT v. Balgarska Narodna Banka*, the Court reiterated the *Peter Paul* case's findings.[165]

12.091 Against this background, it seems that depositors may be unable to seek liability from the ECB in case of defective supervision.[166] Yet, one may note that the relevant case law in this field is intended to provide guidance on national courts and relates to depositors whose deposits have become unavailable. The author can only wonder whether the CJEU[167] will take a different approach not only as regards depositors but also as regards other individuals affected by a potential ECB-defective supervision (e.g., investors). The author is of the view that an extremely restrictive approach, as regards whether EU law in general and the SSM R in particular confer rights on the formers, may hamper the *complete system of legal remedies*.[168]

2. Issues concerning NCAs' acts (and omissions)

12.092 The general attribution of accountability (and liability) to NCAs, pursuant to the general description performed above, admits at least two exceptions.

12.093 The *first one* relates to the common procedures[169] as regards which the ECB is vested with the exclusive competence to decide on them.[170]

---

163 *Peter Paul* at Para. 50. See, also, *BT v. Balgarska Narodna Banka* at Para. 57.

164 *Kantarev* at Para. 148.

165 *BT v. Balgarska Narodna Banka* at Paras. 57 and 60.

166 Including (a) specific wrongful decisions (contrary to EU law and principles) and (b) deficient oversight of the mechanism, materialising in actual damages for individuals.

167 The General Court in the first instance.

168 See, among many others, Court of Justice judgment in case C-50/00 P (*Unión de Pequeños Agricultores)* of 25 July 2002 (ECLI:EU:C:2002:462) at Para. 40.

169 Cf arts. 4(1)(a) and (c), 14 and 15 SSM R.

170 As further elaborated in the *Berlusconi-Fininvest case*. See, further, in Section B. (*Judicial review in composite procedures: the CJEU's Berlusconi-Fininvest case law in perspective*) in this chapter above.

Although the case principally discusses the competence of EU courts to review composite procedures in their entirety (including the steps pursued by national bodies under national law), where the EU body

The *second one* relates to the requests to act in a certain manner issued by the ECB. We may distinguish between two types of requests. On the one hand, those not leaving any margin of discretion to the NCA.[171] In those cases, the NCA acts as a mere link with the supervisee in the supervisory chain. On the other hand, those others which leave some leeway or margin of discretion to the NCA to decide how to implement such request.[172] **12.094**

Whereas in the latter cases it is clear that the NCA may be accountable and consequently liable for such decisions,[173] the latter type of request follows a divergent approach. Pursuant to settled case law,[174] where an EU Institution issues compulsory instructions to national authorities, leaving no margin of discretion to them, the EU Institution may be held liable for the damages caused by relating to such instruction. Consequently, the ECB may be accountable and held liable for narrow instructions addressed to NCAs in case they cause damages (pursuant to art. 340 TFEU). **12.095**

E. JUSTICIABILITY AND PRELIMINARY RULING PROCEDURE

Having recourse to the preliminary ruling procedure foreseen in art. 267 TFEU closes the circle of judicial protection concerning supervised entities. **12.096**

By means of this procedure, national courts may request the CJEU[175] to issue an opinion on the interpretation of EU law[176] and the validity of the acts performed by EU bodies and institutions.[177] **12.097**

is the final decision maker, the assessment actually entails that the supervisory decision is solely attributable to the ECB.

171 For instance, instruction given under art. 6(3) SSM R.

172 Which may happen when NCAs issue decisions (or decide to open supervisory proceedings) following ECB guidelines or general instructions (cf art. 6(5)(a) SSM R and 22 SSM Fr). See, also, Lamandini, M., Ramos, D. & Solana, J. (2016) at pp. 251–252; and, on this topic, see Hernández Saseta, C. (2021) at pp. 308–315.

173 And potentially also the ECB. This would need to be assessed on a case-by-case basis, but joint liability may not appear unrealistic or unthinkable.

174 See Court of Justice judgments in cases C-175/84 (*Krohn & Co. v EC)* of 15 January 1987 (ECLI:EU:C:1987:8) at Paras. 23–24 and T-680/13 (*Dr. K. Chrysostomides & Co. LLC v Council of European Union et al.*) of 13 July 2018 (ECLI:EU:T:2018:486) at Para. 84.

175 Cf art. 93 and ss. Rules of procedure/statute of the Court of Justice. Consolidated version available at: https://curia.europa.eu/jcms/upload/docs/application/pdf/2012-10/rp_en.pdf.

176 The majority of cases linked to the compatibility of a certain national provision with EU law.

177 For a more detailed explanation, see Lenaerts, K., Maselis, I. and Gutman, K. (2015). See, also, Craig, P. & de Búrca, G. (2020) at *Chapter 14: Preliminary rulings*.

12.098 By providing to national courts guidance on the *authentic* interpretation of EU law, the preliminary ruling becomes a strategic tool which contributes in maintaining the uniformity and protects the autonomy of EU law.[178]

12.099 This general statement is particularly true as regards the interpretation of the SSM and BU-related rules and, in general, of the single rulebook. For example, some of the SSM landmark cases have been, indeed, the result of a preliminary ruling. That is the case of the *Berlusconi-Fininvest case*[179] and the *Iccrea banca*[180] case, which contributed to define the contours of composite procedures and the allocation of judicial competences between national and EU courts as regards them.

12.100 From a rather practical perspective, the preliminary ruling procedure may be particularly useful to close potential justiciability gaps as regards three particular scenarios:

12.101 The *first one* relates to *Borelli*-based scenarios, in which the NCAs act on request of the ECB but retain the ultimate capacity to decide how to implement such request.[181] Assuming that national courts would be competent to control the acts adopted by the NCAs, in case incidental questions arise on the interpretation on EU law in the course of a judicial action challenging those decisions, the CJEU may be requested to issue a preliminary ruling.[182]

12.102 The *second one* refers to cases in which NCAs issue supervisory decisions concerning LSIs which are subject to its direct supervision.

---

178 Particularly, in a system which is embedded, as regards at least preliminary references, on a diffuse constitutional control. See Covelo de Abreu, J. (2017). An approach to today's EU constitutionality control – understanding this EU inter-jurisdictional phenomenon in light of effective judicial protection. *UNIO–EU Law Journal*, *3*(2), pp. 104–124. At p. 108.

179 On the relevance and implications of this judgment, see Section A. (*Cooperation, coordination and composition in the SSM*) in Chapter 11 and Section B.2. (*CJEU recent approaches: Berlusconi-Fininvest, Iccrea Banca and GAEC Jeanningros*) in this chapter above.

180 See the references made to this relevant judgment in B.2. (*CJEU recent approaches: Berlusconi-Fininvest, Iccrea Banca and GAEC Jeanningros*) and Section C.2. (*Legal standing in actions for annulment in SSM related matters*) above in this chapter.

181 For an analysis of these types of supervisory requests, based mainly on art. 9(1)III SSM R, see Section B.4. (*Supervisory and investigatory powers to exercise those tasks*) in Chapter 6.

Also, as regards the ECB's requests addressed to NCAs to initiate sanctioning procedures under art. 18(5) SSM R, see Section C. (*Allocation of sanctioning competences: a specialty over the general rule?*) in Chapter 6 and Section C.2.(a). (*Legal challenges: coordination between the ECB and NCAs*) in Chapter 15.

182 This was actually, *mutatis mutandis*, what occurred in the *Berlusconi-Fininvest case*.

The *third one* refers to cases in which NCAs act purely relying on national legislation or exercise competences excluded from the scope of the SSM and/or relating to compensation for damages claims exercised as regards those acts.[183] 12.103

183 And eventually also as regards the exercise of direct supervision concerning LSIs.

13

PROCEDURAL AND SUBSTANTIVE SAFEGUARDS IN COMPOSITE PROCEDURES

13.001 This chapter looks into the sensitive issue relating to the need of safeguarding due process and procedural rights.[1]

13.002 In the broader context of SSM composite procedures, the following questions appear naturally linked to the rule of law: (i) what rights and procedural guarantees must be safeguarded (as a minimum) within the composite procedure; (ii) at what level (at the level of the authority initiating the procedure? at the level of the authority issuing the final decision? at both levels?); and (iii) can any flaws as regards procedural guarantees be *cured* by having recourse to a fair judicial trial.

13.003 Right below, Section A will offer an overview on the procedural rights depicted in the Charter and at what level those must be guaranteed. Subsequently, Section B will analyse whether flaws in procedural rights and safeguards can be cured or rectified during the judicial stage, if any.

1 Which may be considered as *fundamental* under the Charter in some cases (e.g., *ne bis idem in idem*, the privilege against self-incrimination, etc.).

A. PROCEDURAL SAFEGUARDS: WHAT RIGHTS AND SAFEGUARDS, AND AT WHAT LEVEL?

1. What rights and procedural guarantees (due process rights)?

The SSM R frames the basic content of due process rights applicable to the mechanism in art. 22. The provision refers expressly to the right to be heard, applicable to both sanctioning and supervisory proceedings,[2] the right to access to the file[3] and the right to obtain a motivated decision.[4] Further broad reference is made in this provision to the rights of defence of the persons concerned (which, as a matter of fact, must be respected). **13.004**

The SSM Fr further develops some of the due process rights applicable to SSM supervisory and sanctioning proceedings. In particular, art. 31 SSM Fr refers to the right to be heard, art. 32 SSM Fr focuses on the right to access to files and art. 29(2) SSM Fr implicitly refers to the privilege against self-incrimination. As regards sanctioning procedures, art. 126 SSM Fr encompasses the right to legal assistance. **13.005**

From the perspective of the Charter, we can identify the basic rights that compose the defence right. The foregoing include: (i) the right to equality before the law (art. 20 Charter), (ii) the right to be treated equally (and the prohibition of discrimination) (art. 21 Charter), (iii) the right to good administration[5] (art. 41 Charter) and (iv) the right of access to documents (art. 42 Charter).[6] Further and at judicial or at quasi-judicial level, art. 47 Charter contemplates the right to an effective remedy and a fair trial,[7] art. 48 Charter foresees the presumption of innocence (as regards criminal charges) and the right of defence and, finally, art. 50 contemplates the *ne bis in idem* principle. **13.006**

The due process rights are also present in the ECHR. There, art. 6 seems to encapsulate the majority of the rights of defence. Firstly, it recognises the right **13.007**

---

2 With the specialty that, as regards supervisory procedures, this procedural guarantee may be restrained, where the right to be heard may be granted only *ex post* the adoption of the relevant supervisory decision in urgent cases.

3 Art. 22(2) SSM R.

4 Which would be integrated within the right to a good administration enshrined in art. 41 ECHR.

5 Which expressly includes the right to be heard, the right to access the file, the right to obtain a motivated decision, the right to use official languages when communicating with EU bodies and institutions and the right to make good of the damaged caused by the relevant authority.

6 Which must be differentiated from the right to access to the file relating to the person concerned handled by EU bodies and institutions or MSs' authorities.

7 Which includes the right to a public hearing, the right to an impartial tribunal pre-established by the law and the right to receive legal assistance and advice (including access to free assistance in certain cases).

to a fair trial (as regards civil and criminal procedures). As regards criminal procedures,[8] the ECHR further elaborates on the defence rights applicable to such procedures, which include the right to be presumed innocent and a set of minimum guarantees which include: (i) the right to be informed promptly of the charges in an understandable language, (ii) the right to be granted enough time to prepare the defence, (iii) the right to be assisted or represented by a lawyer, (iv) the right to examine witnesses and (v) the right to have the assistance of an interpreter, in case the accused cannot understand the language used in court.[9] Finally, Protocol 7 to the ECHR, in art. 4, further contemplates the *ne bis in idem* principle.

13.008 Table 13.1 offers an overview of the different procedural rights contemplated in the Charter, the ECHR and the SSM R/SSM Fr and the correspondence among them.

13.009 In the academic literature, there is relative consensus on the procedural guarantees embedded in the rights of defence and due process[10] to be applied in the procedures handled (even indirectly) by EU bodies and institutions (including judicial procedures[11]). Those, among others, would include the right to be heard (which would be the keystone of due process rights[12]), the right to access the file and the duty to state reasons. The foregoing, together with the access to trial and fair trial rights, form the hard core of safeguards;[13] these must be provided and guaranteed to the person facing a procedure (of whatever nature) that may have a negative impact on their interests.[14]

---

8 Those considered *criminal in nature* or having a *coloration pénale* (cf Section B. (*Sanctioning procedures vs. procedures that are criminal "in nature"*) in Chapter 8). It results that sanctioning proceedings need to observe stricter (or additional) due process rights. Such rights should extend also to the investigatory phase of a sanctioning proceeding (that phase aimed at building evidence capable of defeating the presumption of innocence (cf arts. 10–13 SSMR)). See Wissink, L. (2021)(ii) at p. 55.

9 The content of this article (together with the *ne bis in idem* principle contemplated in Protocol 7 to the ECHR) mirrors arts. 47, 48 and 50 Charter. Cf Section D. (*Consequences of administrative penalties being qualified as criminal in "nature"*) in Chapter 8.

10 See among others the qualified view of Lenaerts, K. (2013). Due process in competition cases. *Neue Zeitschrift für Kartellrecht-NZKart, 1*, 5, pp. 175–182.

11 Including both civil and criminal procedures (which would include such administrative procedures having a *coloration pénale*).

12 Craig, P. (2018). Particularly Chapters 11 (*Access*) and 12 (*Process*). See, also, Craig, P. & de Búrca, G. (2020). at pp. 578 and ss. In the context of administrative procedures (with a view to later on challenge them), see the detailed analysis included in Lenaerts, K., Maselis, I., and Gutman, K. (2015) at pp. 169–170.

13 For a comparison with the American standard, see Shipley, D. E. (2008). Due process rights before EU agencies: the rights of defense. *Ga. J. Int'l & Comp. L., 37*, 1, pp. 1–53.

14 Craig, P. & de Búrca, G. (2020) at p. 577.

Table 13.1 Procedural rights

No.	Due Process Rights	Charter	ECHR	SSM R	SSM Fr
1	Equality before the law	Art. 20	Art. 14	Art. 1(1) and Recital 30	-
2	Prohibition of discrimination	Art. 21	Art. 14	Art. 1(1) and Recital 30	-
3	Right to good administration/due process rights	Art. 41	Art. 6	Art. 22 and Recitals 54 and 58	-
	(i) Right to be heard	*Art. 41(2)(a)*	*Art. 6(1)*	*Art. 22(1)*	*Art. 31*
	(ii) Access to the file	*Art. 41(2)(b)*	*Art. 6(3)(b)*	*Art. 22(2)*	*Art. 32*
	(iii) Motivation	*Art. 41(2)(c)*	-	*Art. 22(2)*	*Art. 33*
	(iv) Legal assistance	*Art. 47(III)*	*Art. 6(3)(c)*	-	*Art. 126(3)**
4	Right to access to documents	Art. 42	-	-	-
5	Right to a fair trial	Art. 47	Art. 6	Recital 63 and 86	-
	(i) Be informed of the nature of accusation	*Art. 48(2)* (implicitly)	*Art. 6(3)(a)*	-	*Arts. 35 and art. 126(1) and (2)*
	(ii) Examination of witnesses	*Art. 48(2)* (implicitly)	*Art. 6(3)(d)*	-	*Art. 30*
	(iii) Assistance of an interpreter	*Art. 48(2)* (implicitly)	*Art. 6(3)(e)*	-	-
6	Presumption of innocence	Art. 48(1)	Art. 6(2)	-	-
7	Privilege against self-incrimination	Art. 48(2) (implicitly)	Art. 6(2) (implicitly)	-	Art. 29(2) (implicitly)
8	Ne bis in idem	Art. 50	Protocol 7, Art. 4	-	-

Note: * Regarding sanctioning proceedings but, implicitly, also applicable to supervisory procedures.

Such basic rights are composed by several sub-rights, which constitute a more defined expression of those defence rights. For example, the right to be heard is further composed by the right to be informed about the nature and basic features of the procedure beforehand, the right to incriminate oneself and the **13.010** right to professional privilege with a designated lawyer.[15] The list would be too long to be covered by this analysis and deserves a separate work.

13.011 Within the SSM, the rights and procedural guarantees to be observed in supervisory proceedings (composite or not) and sanctioning ones (principally relating to ECB direct sanctioning powers) comprise at least the right to be heard, the duty to state reasons (right to motivation) and the right to have the procedure handled impartially.[16]

13.012 One last reflection must be done as regards the applicability of the Charter to the NCAs when conducting micro-prudential tasks under the SSM scheme.[17] As indicated in this work, the SSM is a multifaceted supranational *mechanism* allowing the exercise of micro– and macro-prudential tasks. Decision and acts may be taken by both the ECB and NCA by means of composite procedures, by direct administration (solely by the ECB) or solely by the NCAs (as regards LSIs[18]). In any case, it seems that whatever decision or act[19] is taken *under* the umbrella of the SSM would need to abide to the fundamental rights established in the Charter (including, evidently, due process rights). The foregoing is rather obvious in the case of the ECB and is based on arts. 51(1) and 52(5) Charter, and the same basis would apply as regards NCAs. There, cited, art. 51(1) indicates that the Charter would apply to MSs "*when they are implementing Union law, in the exercise of their respective powers*". Exercising the tasks contemplated in the SSM, in the form and with the intensity described therein would amount, in the view of the author, to *implement* EU law. Also, more clearly, the Charter would apply when NCAs base their supervisory action on EU prudential regulations (basically CRD IV and CRR).[20]

2. At what level must due process be respected?

13.013 The ReNEUAL code[21] provides an authorised guidance on the level at which due process rights must be ensured in composite procedures. Art. III-24

---

15 See Bernatt, M. & Svetlicinii, A. (2018). The Right of Defence in the Decentralized System of EU Competition Law Enforcement: A Call for Harmonization from Central and Eastern Europe. *World Competition*, *41*(3), pp. 309–315.

16 See Wissink, L. (2021)(ii) at pp. 75 and 274; and D'Ambrosio, R. (2013). Outside the SSM, see, also, Alonso de León, S. (2016) at p. 155.

17 These exclude those tasks which fall outside the SSM Framework; see Section B.1. (*Tasks included vs. tasks excluded*) in Chapter 6.

18 Subject to the general overview of the ECB over the whole *mechanism*. Cf art. 6(1) SSM R.

19 Including operational acts; see Section A.2. (*Exclusion of supervisory activities not aiming at producing legal acts of individual application*) in Chapter 8.

20 See, in this regard, Lamandini, M., Ramos, D. & Solana, J. (2016) at pp. 205–209.

21 Book-III at para. 35. See previous footnote 17 in Chapter 10 above.

(*Right to be heard in composite procedures*) foresees that the right to be heard must be respected "*at all stages of a composite procedure between the EU and the Member States*". In this sense, the explanatory introduction to Book III of the ReNEUAL code further outlines that "*general rights of the parties that shall be respected in all stages of the procedure*".[22]

Nevertheless, and on the account taken of the variety of composite procedures,[23] the ReNEUAL code further fine-tunes the applicability of such "*at all stages*" requirement. The foregoing will depend on the allocation of responsibilities between intervening EU and MSs authorities. **13.014**

For instance, when the EU body is the final decision-making body, but is bound by the MSs' recommendation, the right to be heard must be protected before the MSs' authority (and vice versa in the case is the MSs' authority making the final decision but bound by a previous EU body recommendation[24]). **13.015**

In cases where the recommendation made by the EU or national authorities is not legally binding to the final decision-making body ("*and where there was no opportunity for a hearing before such a public authority*"), such final decision-making authority must ensure that the person concerned can have access to and allege on the recommendation.[25] **13.016**

The above specifications do not alter the conclusion that the right to be heard must be respected at all stages of the procedure. In the particular case of the SSM, the academic literature backs the previous approach.[26] **13.017**

Yet, flaws in due process right occur (more often that one would expect or desire). In those cases, it is worth wondering whether resources to a fair trial, where, by definition, parties are granted with a broad right to be heard and further procedural guarantees, can cure those flaws. **13.018**

---

22 Those general rights of the parties can be found in art. 8-III and match, very closely, the rights composing the *due process*.

23 See Section A. (*Descriptive criteria: composite procedures as a form of inter-administrative cooperation*) in Chapter 10 above.

24 Art. III-24(4) ReNEUAL code.

25 Art. III-24(5) ReNEUAL code.

26 See Eckes, C. & D'Ambrosio, R. (2020) at p. 38.

B. ARE FAIR TRIAL RIGHTS A CURE?

13.019 In Part II,[27] it was analysed how a resource to a judicial process, meeting the procedural guarantees foreseen in the Charter,[28] was able to cure the fact that an administrative body could (and effectively) impose criminal in nature sanctions. The foregoing analysis looked, in particular, at the *Menarini*[29] and *Grande Stevens*[30] landmark cases.

13.020 The main issue arising here as regards the SSM relates to the fact that sanctions of a criminal nature demand full jurisdiction to meet the procedural safeguards enshrined in art. 47 of the Charter[31] (and indirectly in art. 6 ECHR[32]). Whether the CJEU enjoys full jurisdiction to review ECB administrative penalties is not entirely clear, as it was reasoned in Part II.[33] Nevertheless, for the time being and as long the EU does not ratify the ECHR,[34] the issue seems to be of a theoretical nature, as one can reasonably expect that the CJEU does not declare its own judicial system to be in breach of procedural guarantees.[35]

13.021 Notwithstanding the foregoing, the General Court in case T-576/18 *Crédit Agricole*[36] has recently reminded that, following unchanged CJEU case law, certain substantive requirements concerning the adoption of administrative measures cannot be cured in the judicial phase.[37] That is the case, for instance,

27 See Section D.1. (*Sanctions having a criminal nature imposed by an administrative (not jurisdictional) body: Right to a fair trial under the SSM R?*) in Chapter 8.

28 And in particular, those foreseen in arts. 47 to 50 of the Charter.

29 *Menarini Diagnostics s.r.l. c. Italy* (application no. 43509/08) ECtHR judgment of 27 September 2011. See, also, Bellamy, C. (2012). ECHR and competition law post Menarini: An overview of EU and national case law. *e-Competitions, N°47946*, 5 July 2012.

30 *Grande Stevens et autres c. Italy* (applications nos 18640/10, 18647/10, 18663/10, 18668/10 and 18698/10) ECtHR judgment of 4 March 2014.

31 See Lamandini, M., Ramos, D. & Solana, J. (2016) at pp. 251–252.

32 Noting that art. 52(3) Charter demands that the rights foreseen therein are construed in accordance with the ECHR, which indeed has demanded full jurisdiction as regards sanctions having a criminal nature.

33 See Section D. (*Consequences of administrative penalties being qualified as criminal in "nature"*) in Chapter 8. See, also, D'Ambrosio, R. (2021).

34 As regards the status of the EU Accession to the ECHR, see further Section D.2. (*Has the CJEU unlimited jurisdiction to review administrative penalties imposed by the ECB*) in Chapter 8.

35 See Lamandini, M., Ramos, D. & Solana, J. (2016) at p. 254.

36 General Court judgment in case T-576/18 (*Crédit agricole SA v ECB*) of 8 July 2020 (ECLI:EU:T:2020:304). This ruling has been confirmed by Court of Justice judgment in joined cases C-456/20 P to C-458/20 P ((*1) Crédit agricole SA; (2) Crédit agricole Corporate and Investment Bank; (3) CA Consumer Finance v ECB*) of 16 June 2021 (ECLI:EU:C:2021:502).

37 Should the relevant decision be challenged before EU courts. Cf, also, Court of Justice judgment in joined cases C-456/20 P to C-458/20 P ((*1) Crédit agricole SA; (2) Crédit agricole Corporate and Investment Bank; (3) CA Consumer Finance v ECB*) of 16 June 2021 (ECLI:EU:C:2021:502), at Para. 76.

of the motivation requirement.[38] In this regard, the General Court indicated that:

> (...) *is also clear from the case-law that the statement of reasons must, in principle, be notified to the person concerned at the same time as the decision adversely affecting him or her. A failure to state the reasons cannot be remedied by the fact that the person concerned learns the reasons for the decision during the proceedings before the EU Courts (judgments of 29 September 2011, Elf Aquitaine v Commission, C-521/09 P, EU:C:2011:620, paragraph 149; of 19 July 2012, Alliance One International and Standard Commercial Tobacco v Commission, C-628/10 P and C-14/11 P, EU:C:2012:479, paragraph 74; and of 13 December 2016, Printeos and Others v Commission, T-95/15, EU:T:2016:722, paragraph 46).*

It would follow from the CJEU's consistent case law that, indeed, resource to an impartial tribunal, i.e., the review of the legality itself of a given decision by a court, may not be able to remedy severe or material flaws of due process rights occurring in the administrative phase. **13.022**

Yet, the abovementioned example did not relate to a composite procedure itself but rather a direct sanctioning procedure[39] instituted by the ECB. It is worth discussing whether a flaw occurring in a composite procedure (for instance, at the national stage) may be cured (i) at the EU level stage or (ii) at the judicial stage, if any. **13.023**

The conclusion to the above question seems to be negatively based on the reasons that will be detailed below. **13.024**

As pointed out by Brito Bastos,[40] when the final decision is attributable to an EU body or institution, having the ultimate capacity to determine its outcome,[41] it is for them to correct any flaw of material procedural safeguards occurring in the national phase. The absence of this correction may lead the court to annul the final decision. For instance, if the competent national authority granted no hearing to the concerned individual, the EU authority may correct such a procedural flaw granting a proper hearing phase. Lack of doing so may vitiate radically the final decision adopted by such EU authority.[42] **13.025**

38 The very state of the reasons that led to the adoption of a given decision (or a substantive part of it).

39 Instituted on the basis of art. 18(1) SSM R and hence pertaining to the ECB's direct sanctioning remit.

40 See Brito Bastos, F. (2018) at p. 126; and Brito Bastos, F. (2020) at pp. 85–86.

41 For instance, when the EU body or institution can actually vary the material content of the draft decision submitted by the national authorities. The foregoing would be the case of the so-called *common procedures* foreseen in the SSM R.

42 Ibidem footnote 40.

13.026 It stems from the foregoing that, in a *Berlusconi-Fininvest scenario*, (i) the occurrence of a material procedural defect at the national administrative stage can be, in principle, cured at the EU stage. However, (ii) if such a defect is not cured at the EU stage, that may determine the annulment of the relevant decision.

13.027 Furthermore, (iii) in the previous case and building upon the case law consistently maintained by the CJEU, resource to court proceedings may not be able to correct such material procedural flaws, leading to the annulment of the relevant decision challenged.

13.028 This conclusion seems to stand in SSM composite procedures; material procedural flaws occurring at the NCA stage, if not duly corrected by the ECB, determine the annulment of the relevant ECB decision.

14

SUPERVISORY PROCEDURES: COMMON PROCEDURES

A. INTRODUCTION

ECB supervisory procedures contain clear examples of the constitutional, procedural and consistency challenges analysed in Parts I and II of this work. **14.001**

As regards these, probably the so-called common procedures[1] offer greater opportunities to see the *mechanism* in *motion*. They provide the possibility of analysing the application of national law by the ECB, the intertwined relationship between NCAs and ECB in composite procedures, the procedural guarantees to be respected and the procedural and material inconsistencies eventually resulting from the application of the SSM R and the SSM Fr. With **14.002**

1 See Section B.2.(a). (*Common procedures as composite procedures*) in Chapter 11 above.

the purpose of evidencing the wide variety of types of supervisory procedures carried out by the ECB, the following non-exhaustive list is provided:

1. Common procedures dealing with (i) authorisation and withdrawals of authorisations (in a broad sense[2]) and (ii) the acquisition (and disposal) of qualifying holdings.
2. Sanctioning procedures.[3]
3. Fit and proper assessments of the people appointed to the management bodies of SIs.[4]
4. Requests addressed to NCAs to prepare draft decisions on matters falling under ECB competences (to be later on adopted by it).[5]
5. Adoption of administrative measures following the SREP procedure.[6]
6. Early intervention measures, following a SREP or information gathered through (i) the use of investigatory powers,[7] (ii) ordinary reporting and (eventually) compulsory public disclosure and (iii) potentially also the breach reporting mechanism.[8]
7. Preparation of resolution and recovery plans (as regards SIs) and resolution assessments as regards falling or likely-to-fall entities.[9]

14.003 From these procedures, in this chapter, it will be described, in practical terms, how the common procedures are developed.

14.004 These supervisory procedures are selected because they are particularly useful to illustrate, in a practical context, the previous friction points and challenges identified in the precedent Part II[10] and in this Part III and the mechanisms to overcome them.

---

2 Cf Section B.2. (*Vertical allocation? Examining the decentralise mode of implementing the specific supervisory tasks*) in Chapter 6.

3 Which, for the purpose of this work, have been distinguished from supervisory procedures. See Section A. (*Supervisory (common) procedures vs. sanctioning procedures*) in Chapter 8.

4 "*both in their management function (executive directors) and supervisory function (non-executive directors) of all institutions under the direct supervision of the ECB (significant institutions), whether credit institutions or (mixed) financial holding companies and in the case of licensing or qualifying holdings*". Cf ECB Guide to Fit and Proper assessments. December 2021: Guide to fit and proper assessments (europa.eu).

5 See Section B.2.(b). (*Other mixed approaches*) in Chapter 11 above. On this topic, see Hernández Saseta, C. (2021).

6 For a detailed analysis of the SREP and, equally relevant, the supervisory measures that its outcome may trigger, see Lamandini, M., Ramos Muñoz, D. and D'Ambrosio, R. (2022).

7 Cf arts. 10–13 SSM R. Those include requests of information, general investigations and on-site inspections.

8 Arts. 23 SSM R and 36–38 SSM Fr.

9 Arts. 4(1)(i) SSM R and 18(1) SRM R.

10 More precisely, in Chapter 6 and in Chapter 7 of this work.

B. AUTHORISATION AND WITHDRAWAL OF BANKING LICENSES

The legal framework governing the acquisition and withdrawal of banking licenses is regulated in (i) art. 14 SSM R,[11] (ii) arts. 73–78 and 88 SSM Fr and (iii) the ECB Guide to assessments of licence applications.[12] **14.005**

1. Authorisation/licensing of credit institutions

Any undertaking wishing to (i) take deposits or other repayable funds from the public and (cumulatively) (ii) grant credit for its own account[13] must apply for a banking license.[14] A wide variety of credit and financial activities can be performed under the umbrella of a banking license. In this sense, the license granted can be rather *universal*,[15] or specific (or modular). In the latter sense, some MSs have opted, pursuant to their national rules, to follow a modular approach, specifically authorising applicants to perform those credit activities for which they applied for, as foreseen in Annex I of CRD IV. In this case, if the applicant decides to expand the scope of its activities, pursue new ones or stop providing any of the activities for which it was already authorised, a new license (or an updated one) may be needed. **14.006**

Additionally, other corporate and structural changes may also trigger the need to apply for a banking license. For instance, for the change of the legal form of a credit institution when pursuant to its applicable national law, a license decision is required; also, mergers of credit institutions when the entity taking up the business of credit institution was not authorised to carry out the same activities authorised to the merged entities. Even the approval of modifications **14.007**

---

11 Cf art. 4(1)(a) SSM R. See, also, arts. 8 and 10–15, 18 and 20 CRD IV.

12 ECB Guide to assessments of licence applications. Licence applications in general. Second revised edition (January 2019) (ECB Guide on License Applications): https://www.bankingsupervision.europa.eu/ecb/pub/pdf/ssm.201901_guide_assessment_credit_inst_licensing_appl.en.pdf. See, also, EBA: *Final report on draft Regulatory Technical Standards under Article 8(2) of Directive 2013/36/EU and draft Implementing Technical Standards under Article 8(3) of Directive 2013/36/EU (EBA/RTS/2017/08 and EBA/ITS/2017/05).* The ECB Guide mentioned above refers that the "ECB, together with the NCAs, has developed policies regarding authorisation applications and supervisory practices and processes". Those, for the time being, do not seem to have been disclosed.

For a dedicated commentary on this topic article by article, see Binder, J., Gortsos, C. V., Lackhoff, K. & Ohler, C. (Ed.). (2022) at pp. 189–215.

13 Art. 4(1)(1) CRR. On the different elements which integrate the definition of credit institution (e.g., repayable funds, public, "on its own account"), see Section D.1 of the ECB Guide on License Applications.

14 Both activities need to be carried out, although not necessarily from the very beginning (cf Section D.1 of the ECB Guide on License Applications).

For a targeted overview of the basic requisites in the context of the SSM, see Laguna de Paz, J. C. (2014). El mecanismo europeo de supervisión bancaria. *Revista de administración pública*, (194), pp. 49–77.

15 Covering any type of financial activities that a credit institution can carry out (and falling under the scope of the notion of *credit institution* (see above)).

of credit institutions' statutes, when so foreseen under national law, constitutes an authorisation which the ECB is competent to grant (or deny).[16]

14.008 The foregoing is rooted in art. 9(1)II SSM R, pursuant to which the ECB has been vested with the national powers allocated to NCAs when those powers underpin a supervisory function which fall under the specific micro-prudential tasks allocated on the ECB under the SSM R.[17]

14.009 Based on the referred art. 9(1)II SSM R, the ECB has expanded its authorising functions outside the strict reading of art. 4(1)(a) SSM R and also beyond the list of specific micro-prudential tasks contemplated in art. 4(1) and 4(2) SSM R.[18] As indicated above in this work,[19] such, sometimes necessary, expansion of *implied* tasks needs to strike a fair balance with the competences that remain outside the scope of the SSM R and which continue to be exercised by NCAs. Otherwise, there can be a breach of the principle of proportionality,[20] as the ECB action would exceed what is necessary to attain the goal of ensuring the stability of the financial system.[21]

14.010 Due to the wide variety of matters which are subject to the authorisation process, and also considering their relevance, this process is erected as the basic or standard procedure, and the rest of procedures developed under the umbrella of the SSM R mirror it or, at least, are somehow based on it. There is then a clear interest in analysing this procedure in detail.

14.011 In the following Sections, we outline the basic steps of the authorisation process (2.1.1), highlight its key aspects (2.1.2) and then, on that basis, analyse the legal challenges and safeguards (2.1.3).

---

16 See Hernández Saseta, C. (2021) at pp. 306–307.

17 This topic has been addressed in Section B.2.(d). (*On the scope of the micro-prudential supervisory task contemplated in arts. 4(1) and 4(2) SSM R: Teleological interpretation*) in Chapter 6 and extensively in Section A.2.(b).(2). (*What happens when the national statute allocates powers in excess to the ones foreseen in a prudential Directive?*) in Chapter 7.

18 Ibidem. Cf, also, art. 78(5) SSM Fr, which, when referring to the decision granting an authorisation to take up the business of credit institutions, also mentions the "*additional requirements for authorisation under the relevant national law for activities other than the business of taking deposits or other repayable funds from the public and granting credits for its own account*".

19 See Section B.2.(d). (*On the scope of the micro-prudential supervisory task contemplated in arts. 4(1) and 4(2) SSM R: Teleological interpretation*) in Chapter 6.

20 Art. 5(4) TEU. Understood in that provision as the adequacy between the EU action at stake and the ultimate goal pursued with that action.

For a multifaceted analysis of the principle of proportionality, including the correlation between the administrative powers with the purposes for which those powers were entrusted to public authorities, see Sarmiento Ramírez-Escudero, D. (2007). *El principio de proporcionalidad en el Derecho administrativo. Un análisis jurídico desde el Derecho español*. Bogotá: Universidad Externado.

21 Art. 1(I) SSM R.

(a) Basic steps of the authorisation process

Pursuant to the SSM *decentralised* scheme of distribution of specific micro-prudential tasks, the ECB is exclusively competent to grant (and withdraw) banking licenses[22] as regards both LSIs and SIs.[23] Consequently, all credit institutions captured in the scope of the SSM undergo the very same process for obtaining and/or modifying its banking authorisation (including when they enlarge their functions to take up activities exclusively foreseen under national law, which underpin a supervisory function under EU law[24]). **14.012**

Before applying for a banking license, usually, the promoter or promoters[25] establish a supervisory dialogue *vis-à-vis* the NCA (and/or the ECB) with a view to obtaining further guidance as to how to formally submit the application and to clarify the indicative information they need to submit.[26] Such an informal phase would not be subject to any formal procedures, yet some guarantees, relating to the right to a good administration, transparency rights and the right to access information, apply, if any.[27] **14.013**

The basic steps of the authorisations can be summarised as follows: **14.014**

(i) [Stage 1] **Submission of the application**: Banking authorisation applications are submitted to the NCA of the MS where the institution is to be established (or is established), in accordance with the requirements foreseen in national law.[28]

Once the application is received, the NCA shall inform the ECB of such an application within fifteen working days and also will indicate the time limit to take a decision on the application pursuant to national law.[29] In principle, pursuant to art. 15 CRD IV, the maximum time limit to take a decision is 12 months.[30]

---

22 See in more detail in Section B.2. (*Vertical allocation? Examining the decentralised mode of implementing the specific supervisory tasks*) in Chapter 6.

23 See García Alcorta, J. (2013). Observaciones en torno al mecanismo único de supervisión bancaria en la Unión Europea. *Actualidad jurídica Uría Menéndez* no. 34-2013, pp. 51–70. At p. 64.

24 See ECB letter to banks "Additional clarification regarding the ECB's competence to exercise supervisory powers granted under national law": https://www.bankingsupervision.europa.eu/press/letterstobanks/shared/pdf/2017/Letter_to_SI_Entry_point_information_letter.en.pdf?d01637f249f9109f54a70a6803078b66. At p. 2.

25 The promoter of the application can be the entity itself (that will become a credit institution if so authorised), a parent undertaking of the shareholder or even a shareholder of a newly or to-be-created entity once the authorisation is granted.

26 See Section 6.1 of the ECB Guide on License Applications.

27 See, extensively, Section A.1. (*What rights and procedural guarantees (due process rights)?*) in the precedent Chapter 13.

28 Art. 14(1) SSM R.

29 Art. 73(1)–(2) SSM Fr.

30 It is implied in art. 73(3) SSM Fr that the NCA must also provide the ECB with the application (documents) submitted by the application. Although it is not clear when the ECB must be furnished with that

(ii) [Stage 2] **NCA examination and preparation of a draft authorisation decision**: If the application is complete, the NCA will assess it. If it complies with all the relevant requirements established under national law, the NCA will prepare a draft authorisation decision and will submit it to the ECB for its final approval.

(iii) [Stage 3] **ECB examination of the draft authorisation decision and adoption of a decision on the authorisation requested**: Following the examination of the draft decision prepared by the NCA, if the ECB considers that the application meets all the relevant requirements foreseen under EU law, it will grant the relevant authorisation and will arrange the relevant notification. Otherwise, it will reject the application submitted.

14.015 The sequence of the authorisation process is summarised in Figures 14.1 and 14.2.

14.016 Beyond describing the basic steps in which the authorisation process can be divided, it must be noted that subjecting all credit institutions falling under the remit of the SSM to the authorisation of the ECB (as referred to at the beginning of this Section) serves, at least, two purposes:

14.017 *First, effectiveness*; by positioning the ECB as the *gatekeeper* of the system, being the ultimate body to grant banking licenses streamlines the authorising tasks.[31]

14.018 *Second, harmonisation* between the different participating MSs (and their national practices), ensuring that all entities are treated equally and scrutinised under the same lens (and by the same decision-making bodies).

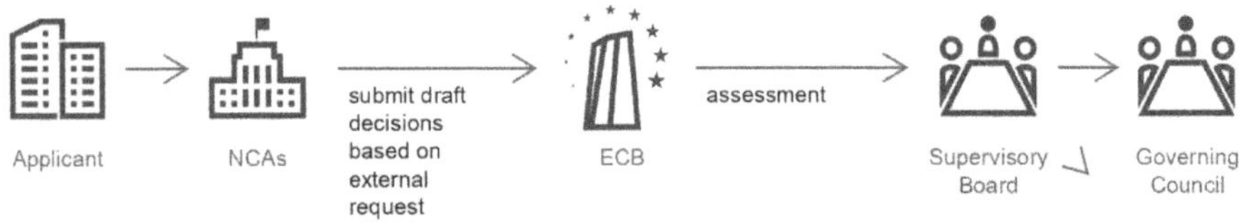

Figure 14.1 The authorisation process

documentation, a sound approach would require sharing such information with the ECB from the very beginning, so that it can potentially request additional information at an early stage and not later on, when it receives, eventually, the draft assessment prepared by the relevant NCA.

31 On the overall efficiency of the SSM, see the reflections made in Section B.1. (*Composite procedures and efficiency*) in Chapter 10.

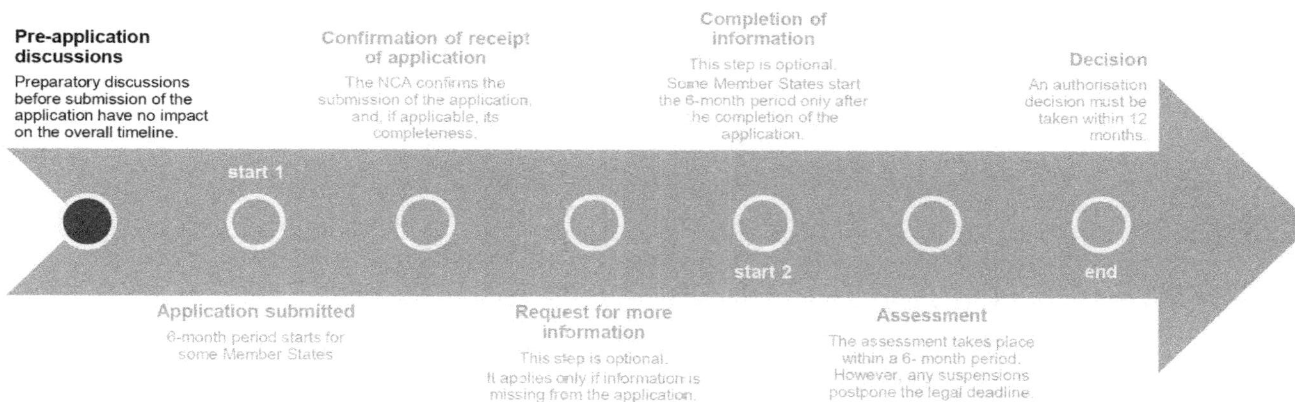

Source: ECB Guide on License Applications, figures 4 and 6 (pp. 27 and 28, respectively).

Figure 14.2 Timeline application phase

14.019 As a result, the level playing field, which has been identified in this work as one of the basic values enshrined in the SSM R[32] that the *mechanism* aims at ensuring, is reinforced and protected.[33]

(b) Key aspects of the process (stage by stage)

14.020 In Stage 1 [*Submission of the application*], the NCA is expected to ensure that the information contained is complete prior to performing any analysis on the content of the application and its conformity with national law.

14.021 In this sense, and pursuant to art. 73(3) SSM Fr, the NCA, at its own initiative or at the request of the ECB, may request the applicant to provide additional required information, should any of them consider that the application is not complete.

14.022 It must be noted here that, following the vertical allocation of tasks under the SSM R,[34] NCAs act as the entry point[35] for the authorisation requests. Further and following the *principal-agent* model upon which common procedures are built,[36] NCAs must assist the ECB (and execute its instructions) ensuring the completeness of the file to perform, later on, a duly funded assessment on that basis.

---

32 The analysis that has led to that conclusion can be found in Section B. (*SSM basic principles: level playing field & proportionality*) in Chapter 1.

33 Without neglecting the other *basic* principle: *proportionality* (cf art. 1.III SSM R). Such a principle being understood as the need to take into due account the size and nature of the business of all the entities subject to the SSM when carrying out the supervisory tasks foreseen in the SSM R.

Yet, academia (and the industry itself) have pointed out that the referred proportionality principle would demand lowering the complexity of the substantive supervisory rules to be applied on small and less complex credit institutions. In this regard, see (i) Joosen, B., Lamandini, M., Lehmann, M., Lieverse, K. & Tirado, I. (2018); (ii) Joosen, B. & Lehmann, M. (2019). Proportionality in the single rule book. In *The Palgrave Handbook of European Banking Union Law* (pp. 65–90). Palgrave Macmillan; and (iii) Lehmann, M. (2017). Single Supervisory Mechanism Without Regulatory Harmonisation? Introducing a European Banking Act and a "CRR Light" for Smaller Institutions. *EBI Working Paper Series. no. 3.*

In the latter work, the author even postulates to create a sort of European Banking Act for, at least, the Eurozone MSs. Within that proposed Act and in order to comply with the demands of the principle of proportionality, the author proposes creating a *light* regime for non-significant credit institutions.

34 See Section B.2. (*Vertical allocation? Examining the decentralised mode of implementing the specific supervisory tasks*) in Chapter 6.

35 Cf Section 6 of the ECB Guide on License Applications.

Conversely, SIs (directly supervised by the ECB), pursuant to art. 95(1) SSM Fr, must address their notifications and applications directly to the ECB (except those relating to common procedures, fit and proper assessments (art. 93 SSM Fr) and passporting (art. 11 SSM Fr)). Cf ECB letter to banks "Additional clarification regarding the ECB's competence to exercise supervisory powers granted under national law": https://www.bankingsupervision.europa.eu/press/letterstobanks/shared/pdf/2017/Letter_to_SI_Entry_point_information_letter.en.pdf?d01637f249f9109f54a70a6803078b66. At p. 3.

36 See Section B.2.(c). (*Rationale of the system*) in Chapter 6.

As per Stage 2 [*NCA examination and preparation of a draft authorisation decision*], once the complete application has been received,[37] the relevant NCA shall assess it on its merits under the prism of relevant national law, and two outcomes are possible: **14.023**

(i) The NCA may directly reject the application if it judges that it does not comply with applicable national rules.[38] The NCA then shall notify such decision to the applicant(s)[39] (and will send a copy of such decision to the ECB[40]).
Such rejection must be exclusively based on requisites pertaining to national law transposing the relevant EU law.[41]

(ii) Should the NCA understand that the application meets all the relevant requirements foreseen under national law,[42] it will prepare a draft authorisation decision proposing the ECB to grant such authorisation.
Whereas the rejection referred to in (i) above does not seem to trigger an actual "composite" procedure (and thus the NCA remains fully accountable for such decision[43]), a draft authorisation requires a subsequent act by the ECB and, thus, entails a composite procedure. In such case, it seems that the draft authorisation decision must not only assess the national law requirements but also, in general, the EU law requirements. The foregoing is implied in art 76(3) SSM Fr but also follows from the rationale of the authorisation procedure, where the NCA is expected to prepare a full draft authorisation decision to be assessed by the ECB.[44]

Such a draft decision must be notified to the ECB and to the applicant at least twenty working days before the time limit to resolve on the application expires.[45] In accordance with the right to be heard,[46] the applicant can express their opinion and put forward further arguments as regards the draft authori sation decision. These additional considerations should be further considered **14.024**

---

37 Pursuant to art. 73(3) SSM Fr, it cannot be discarded that, at any point before the final decision on the authorisation is taken, additional information may be required.

38 Art. 14(2) SSM R and art. 75 SSM Fr.

39 Art. 88(3)(b) SSM Fr.

40 Art. 75 SSM Fr.

41 CRD IV, basically. Or, on top of those requisites stemming from harmonised EU law, national requirements added to it and underpinning a supervisory function under EU law. See immediately above on the reflection made to art. 9(1)II SSM R.

42 For an overview on the material requisites that the application and the applicant must meet, and which are foreseen in arts. 8 and ss., see Section 5 of ECB Guide on License Application.
In particular, for a comprehensive analysis on the definition and composition of the capital requirements for applying to credit institutions (and hence as a requisite for obtaining a banking license), see Lamandini, M. & Ramos Muñoz, D. (2022). 2. The Definition of Common Equity Tier 1 Capital and of Contingent Capital. In *Capital and Liquidity Requirements for European Banks* (pp. 44–75). Oxford University Press.

43 See Section B.2.(a).(*Common procedures as composite procedures*) in Chapter 11 above.

44 Possibility also generally foreseen (outside the framework of licensing processes) in art. 91 SSM Fr. See Section B.2.(b). (*Other mixed approaches*) in Chapter 11 above.

45 As determined under national law. Cf arts. 14(2) SSM R and 76(2) and 88(3)(a) SSM Fr.

46 See, extensively, Section A.1. (*What rights and procedural guarantees (due process rights)?*) in Chapter 13 above.

by the ECB when issuing the decision granting the authorisation or objecting to it.[47]

14.025 As discussed in Part II of this work, national rules regulating the maximum deadline to decide on the approval or denegation of the request, and even national rules determining whether the potential request for additional information suspends the procedure, have a substantive nature and should be treated accordingly as material rules to be applied and observed by the ECB when dealing with the procedure.[48]

14.026 Finally, in stage 3 [*ECB examination of the draft authorisation decision and adoption of a decision on the authorisation requested*], the ECB assesses whether the application meets the conditions established under EU law.[49]

14.027 If the ECB has doubts regarding whether the application meets the conditions established by EU law, it must give the applicant an opportunity to submit their observations in writing (and may arrange a meeting to discuss those).[50]

14.028 The ECB must decide, within ten working days, whether it agrees or objects to a draft authorisation decision submitted by a NCA.[51] The ECB must base its decision on[52] (i) its own assessment of the application, (ii) the draft authorisation decision prepared by the NCA and (iii) the comments provided by the applicant,[53] if any.[54]

14.029 The ECB must adopt its decision granting the banking license, provided that the applicant (or the entity on behalf of which the application is submitted)

47 It must be noted that the NCA may also assess them and present its considerations to the ECB.

48 See Section B.2. (*Administrative procedural rules (and principles) to be applied by the ECB: general overview and particular analysis of procedural rules contained in national law transposing prudential Directives*) in Chapter 7.

49 Cf art 77(1) SSM Fr.

50 Cf art. 77(2) SSM Fr. Accordingly, the ECB may extend the maximum period for deciding on the application.

51 Arts. 14(3) SSM R and 78(1) SSM Fr. Unless such period for deciding is extended pursuant to art. 77(2) SSM Fr.

52 Art. 78(2) SSM Fr.

53 Where art. 78(2) SSM Fr refers only to those comments provided by the applicant pursuant to art. 77 SSM Fr, it seems that the ECB must consider any comment provided by the applicant within the authorisation period addressed to it.

54 In this regard, pursuant to reiterated CJEU jurisprudence on SSM matters, the ECB must "*take into consideration, carefully and impartially, all elements of fact and of law that relevant to the case*". See L-Bank case at Para. 147; General Court judgment in case T-768/16 (*BNP Paribas v ECB*) of 13 July 2018 (ECLI:EU:T:2018:471) at para. 84; General Court judgment in case T-758/16 (Crédit Agricole SA v ECB) of 13 July 2018 (ECLI:EU:T:2018:472) at para. 84; and recent General Court judgment in case T-504/19 (*Crédit lyonnais v ECB*) of 14 April 2021 (ECLI:EU:T:2921:185) at Paras. 99 and 106. See, in this regard, Bosque Argachal, C. & Pizarroso Ceruti, A. (2019).

met all the relevant requirements applicable under national and EU law.[55] The referenced decision may also cover additional requirements established under national law to take up other activities than taking repayable deposits from the public and granting loans on one's own account.[56]

Also, if the ECB does not take a decision within ten working days from the reception of the NCA's draft authorisation, the authorisation is deemed adopted.[57] **14.030**

Although not explicitly foreseen in the SSM R nor in the SSM Fr,[58] the ECB may include, in the authorisation conditions, obligations or even recommendations. The formers refer to provisions suspending the effectiveness of the ECB supervisory decision[59] until its fulfilment by the applicant. The obligations do not affect the effectiveness of the given decision but require the applicant to comply with certain requirements on a continuous basis. Finally, recommendations do not have a binding character but express the supervisor expectations and suggestions as regards the operation of the intended banking business.[60] **14.031**

In the case that the ECB decides to object to the granting of an authorisation, it is not clear how such an objection may materialise and what the procedural avenues being triggered in this case are.[61] Both the SSM R and the SSM Fr do not provide much guidance in that respect. **14.032**

---

55 Art. 78(4) SSM Fr.

56 Art. 78(5) SSM Fr.

57 Nevertheless, should this occur, it would not impede the ECB to eventually trigger the procedure for lapsing or withdrawing the banking license. See Section B.2. (*Withdrawal (and lapsing) of banking*) authorisation below in this chapter.

58 Lo Schiavo, G. (2017). Conditions and Obligations in ECB Supervisory Decisions as Ancillary Provisions under SSM Law. *European Company and Financial Law Review*, *14*(1), pp. 94–120. At p. 111. See, also, Section 6.2 of the ECB guide on License application at p. 31–32.

59 Art. 2(26) SSM Fr. See further Section A. (*Supervisory (common) procedures vs. sanctioning procedures*) in Chapter 8.

60 Lo Schiavo, G. (2017) at pp. 97–98.

The author also notes the careful approach that the ECB must take as regards the *right to be heard*, at least when conditions and obligations are included in a given banking license. The author indicates that, pursuant to well established case law, only obligations and conditions generating adverse effects on the applicant, and for which the supervisor enjoys certain discretions, should trigger the right to be heard of the concerned applicant. Accordingly, it should be given the chance to opine on those obligations and conditions before the adoption of the final supervisory decision (ibidem at pp. 118–119).

61 For example, whether a new draft authorisation decision is to be prepared by the NCA, informal exchanges are to be held between the ECB and the NCA in order to reach a compromise, the procedure is terminated (and, eventually, a new application could be submitted again by the applicant), etc.

14.033 Finally, and as per the notification of the final outcome of the procedure, the possibilities are as follows:[62]

(a) The ECB must notify the relevant NCA its decision (positive or negative) on the application for a credit institution authorisation.
(b) The relevant NCA, in turn, must notify the applicant of (i) the ECB decision objecting to the authorisation requested or (ii) the ECB decision granting the requested authorisation, as the case may be.

(c) Legal challenges and safeguards

(i) Some reflections on the safeguards applicable in the authorisation procedure

14.034 The legal safeguards embedded in the SSM apply with particular intensity in this type of authorisation procedure. They apply even in the preliminary informal phase preceding the formal application, which consists of a supervisory dialogue between the applicant and the relevant NCA and the ECB. Such an informal phase is not part of the procedure, yet the applicant is covered by the right to a good administration, transparency rights and the right to access to information.

14.035 More particularly, in Stage 2 [*NCA examination and preparation of a draft authorisation decision*], it must be noted that the right to be heard, envisaged in art. 31 SSM Fr, must be observed, and so the applicant must be given the opportunity to (a) contest the denegation of the application purely based on national law requirements, (b) formulate observations on the additional information that NCAs/ECB may require at this stage and (c) formulate observations on the draft authorisation decision prepared by the relevant NCA and that must be timely notified to it.[63]

14.036 The previous Chapter 11 (*Cooperation, coordination and composite procedures in the Banking Union and SSM*) explained why the authorisation process contemplated in the SSM R and the SSM Fr fully falls within the category of *composite procedures*. Accordingly, and as developed further in Chapter 13 (*Procedural and substantive safeguards in composite procedures*), due process rights, including particularly the right to be heard, must be carefully respected at all stages of the procedure, including when relevant, before the NCAs.[64]

---

62 Arts. 14(4) SSM R and 88(2) and (3) SSM Fr.

63 Including the content of obligations and/or conditions, if adversely affecting the applicant and if its exercise entails discretion from the ECB. See footnote 45.

64 I.e., when the NCA considers that the applications are incomplete and requests additional information or the clarification of details included in the application.

On the reviewability by the CJEU of any flaws happening in the preparatory (national) phase of a SSM composite procedure (including as regards the right to be heard), see Brescia Morra, C. (2018).

Ultimately, closing the circle, in case the applicant is denied the authorisation it requested for, it is entitled to challenge such a decision before the CJEU.[65] In such action, it may bring any alleged violations of safeguards occurring in the course of the procedure.[66] **14.037**

(ii) Legal challenges (and potential remedies)

Each of the three stages into which the process for obtaining a banking license has been divided raises some specific legal challenges.[67] These are explored immediately below. **14.038**

Concerning stage 1 [*Submission of the application*], the legal texts raise some questions. In particular: **14.039**

(i) Concerning art. 73(3) SSM Fr, it is not entirely clear what type of information the NCA[68] may request from the applicant, should it find that some information is not complete.

It must be noted here that the provision only refers to "*required additional information*". This could be read as preventing the NCA from requesting any information that strictly is not required but that can be useful to be analysed.[69]

However, considering the wide range of information that can be necessary to perform a compressive assessment on the application and following a rather logical interpretation, *required* information may be read in a broad sense, encompassing any information relating to the capital, programme of operations, and fit and proper assessment of the proposed management body and of the envisaged shareholders.[70]

The Interplay between the ECB and NCAs in the "common procedures" under the SSM Regulation: are there gaps in legal protection? In *Judicial review in the Banking Union and in the EU financial architecture, Conference jointly organized by Banca d'Italia and the European Banking Institute* (pp. 79–94). Quaderni di Ricerca giuridica della Banca d'Italia, n. 84.

For a classical overview on the characterisation of composite procedures and the interaction between the national and EU phases in those, see Chiti, E. (2004). Administrative proceedings involving European agencies. *Law and Contemporary Problems*, *68*(1), pp. 219–236.

65 See above and in Section A. (*Procedural safeguards: what rights and safeguards, and at what level?*) in Chapter 13 above.

66 See, on this very matter, the detailed analysis carried out by Brito Bastos when commenting on the landmark *Berlusconi Fininvest case*: Brito Bastos, F. (2019).

67 On top of the rather general questions concerning the application of national law by the ECB, the allocation of final decision-making powers and the justiciability of those decision which have been explored in Chapter 11. (*Cooperation, coordination and composite procedures in the Banking Union and SSM*) and in the precedent Part II more deeply.

68 Acting on its own initiative or even at the ECB's request. It must be noted also that the ECB can also request such information directly, particularly when assessing the draft authorisation decision. See Section 6.1 of the ECB Guide on License Application (p. 29). See also Gurlit, E. (2022)(i).

69 It must be noted also that eventually the ECB could also request additional information.

70 See Section 5 of ECB Guide on License Applications.

(ii) The moment an application is considered *complete* has an impact on time limits applicable to approve or deny it. As analysed before,[71] procedural national rules determining the relevant deadlines must be regarded as "substantive" national rules, which must be considered and applied by the ECB.[72]

It is worth mentioning that MSs (and so NCAs) have several approaches as to whether the request for additional information should interrupt (or not) the time limit to decide on the application. This has a substantial impact on the procedure, as it affects ultimately the regulatory deadline to complete the procedure under relevant national law. Due to this fact, this very feature and the linked national law intricacies should be communicated by the NCA to the ECB, potentially, when informing it about the application received.

14.040 Similarly to stage 1, stage 2 [*NCA examination and preparation of a draft authorisation decision*] presents some interpretative legal challenges, specifically:

(i) First, it is not clear what happens if the NCA finds that the application may not comply with requisites arising from EU law. The relevant SSM R and SSM Fr provisions seem to imply (a) that the NCA *must* prepare a draft decision proposing invariably to the ECB to grant an authorisation and (b) that the NCA power to reject the application must be exclusively based on relevant national law requirements.

Yet, the relevant NCA should include any non-compliance with EU law requirements in the draft authorisation decision so that the ECB can make its own assessment, and the applicant can make additional considerations, as applicable. This understanding seems to be compliant with art. 77 SSM Fr, which attributes to the ECB the ultimate decision as regards evaluating compliance with EU law requirements.

This reasoning is not only compatible with the SSM Fr but also makes sense from the perspective of how the *mechanism* itself was set up to benefit from the accumulated expertise of NCAs.[73] In this vein, it must be recalled that NCAs not only have the expertise pertaining to their national law, but also, since prudential supervision has been exercised at a national level until the advent of the SSM,[74] they have accumulated vast knowledge in directly applicable EU law instruments (e.g., CRR) and prudential Directives (e.g., CRD IV, as transposed by national statutes).[75]

Additionally, as the ECB assessment may run in parallel to the NCA's, the ECB may question whether application complies with relevant EU law requirements even *before* the NCA prepares a draft authorisation decision, inviting,

71 See Chapter 7.

72 Of the same view, Lackhoff, K. (2017)(i) at pp. 107–109.

73 See Section B.1. (*Composite procedures and efficiency*) in Chapter 10 and further cross-references made to parts of this work therein.

74 For participating MSs (art. 2(1) SSM R). Cf also Recital 5 SSM R.

75 Cf Ferrarini, G. (2015). Similarly, see Wymeersch, E. (2014) at pp. 32 and 39.

then, the applicant to submit their comments.[76] This latter approach would be also desirable for effectiveness reasons.

(ii) Second, art. 76(3) SSM Fr states that the NCA may attach recommendations, conditions and restrictions to the draft authorisation. Those can be based both in national and EU law. The provision further states that *"the NCA shall be responsible for assessing compliance with the conditions and/or restrictions"*.[77]

Considering that the final decision is taken by the ECB and, consequently, the ECB remains accountable for that decision,[78] the meaning of the statement seems ambiguous, when not superfluous.

A way to reconcile the language of the provision with its spirit is to interpret it as meaning that the NCA that included such conditions and restrictions must check whether those conditions are fulfilled. This rationale of this interpretation works well as regards LSIs, where the NCAs are, in principle, competent to conduct ongoing supervision. On the contrary, for SIs, which are directly supervised by the ECB, it is difficult to determine how art. 76(3) SSM Fr may work in practical terms. The fact that NCAs do not directly supervise SIs renders difficult for them to assess the compliance with such recommendations, restrictions or conditions.

Finally, stage 3 [*ECB examination of the draft authorisation decision and adoption of a decision on the authorisation requested*] presents the following legal challenge: 14.041

(i) As the ultimate decision maker, the ECB remains fully accountable for the authorising decision taken, and the CJEU is the only competent court to review such a decision.[79]

Although the ECB has the last word as regards the decision granting the authorisation, it is only given (in principle) ten working days to assess the draft authorisation decision submitted by the relevant NCA. In this sense, and without prejudice of the parallel or simultaneous assessment that the ECB may carry

---

76 And eventually summoning it to a meeting and extending the maximum period for deciding on the draft authorisation decision submitted by the NCA (cf art. 14(3) SSM R).

Art. 77(2) SSM Fr refers to extending the maximum period *"for deciding on an application in accordance with art. 14(3) of the SSM R"*. Actually, art. 14(3) SSM R, rather, refers to the period given to the ECB to decide on the draft authorisation decision submitted by the NCA (although it may ultimately entail extending the period for deciding on the application).

77 It must be also noted that the provision does not demand NCAs to check *compliance* with the recommendations included by them, as they are not binding.

78 On the general accountability of the ECB for the functioning of the mechanism, see Section B.2. (*Composite procedures and political and administrative accountability*) in Chapter 10 above.

More precisely, on the fact that the ECB is ultimately responsible for the decisions relating to common procedures, see Section B. (*Judicial review in composite procedures: the CJEU's Berlusconi-Fininvest case law in perspective*) in Chapter 12 above. Specifically, and for a targeted analysis not only of the interplay between NCAs and the ECB within authorisation procedures but also from the perspective of the judicial accountability of the ECB, see Brito Bastos, F. (2021).

79 See extensively in Section B. (*Judicial review in composite procedures: the CJEU's Berlusconi-Fininvest case law in perspective*) in Chapter 12 above. On the application of national law by the ECB, see, further, Chapter 7.

out (on the compliance of the requisites stemming from EU law), it heavily relies on the assessment performed by NCAs.

Such reliance is at its greatest when it comes to the assessment of the requisites foreseen under relevant national law to take up the business of credit institutions and other activities falling outside the strict scope of the banking business (for which the applicant may also apply simultaneously for authorisation). On those matters, the ECB assumes the NCA assessment and the conditions and restrictions it may impose in this regard.

From a pure proportionality perspective,[80] one must acknowledge that the ECB is made accountable for such a significant decision for which it is actually given so little time to perform a thoughtful analysis.

2. Withdrawal (and lapsing) of banking authorisations

14.042 If the previous Section analyses the procedure for granting a bank license, the flip side of the coin is the withdrawal of such license, which renders the entity unable to continue business as a credit institution. The process to formally withdraw a banking authorisation (or to lapse it) will be referred immediately below.

(a) Key aspects of the lapsing of authorisation process

14.043 Lapsing an already granted authorisation implies that a given authorisation ceases to exist.[81] Relevant national rules may clarify or define temporary or quantitative thresholds that may automatically trigger the lapse of an already granted authorisation.[82]

14.044 The lapse of the authorisation occurs when:[83] (i) the applicant (or the entity allocated with the relevant authorisation) renounces the license; (ii) the credit institution does not make use of the authorisation within twelve months; and (iii) the institution ceases to engage in business for more than six months.

14.045 It must be noted that the possibility of lapsing banking authorisation is fully governed by national law, on which the ECB must rely pursuant to art. 4(3) SSM R.[84] In this token, art. 18(a) CRD IV (and the entire art. 18 itself) is configured, granting broad leeway to MSs. The introductory sentence of this

---

80 And acknowledging the efficiency and accountability rationale that demands that one single authority (the ECB) remains accountable and that the review of its decisions is carried by one single judicial authority (see previous Section B.1. (*Composite procedures and efficiency*) in Chapter 10 above).

81 Section 7 of ECB Guide on License Application.

82 The author notes the absence of dedicated academic studies to the lapsing of authorisation (in a SSM context but also outside it). However, some considerations can be found in Gurlit, E. (2022)(i).

83 Art. 18(a) CRD IV.

84 See in more in detail in Section A.2. (*The (problematic) application by the ECB of national law: some considerations*) in Chapter 7. Particularly, see also there how divergent transposition of CRD IV rules, eventually

art. 18 indicates that *"competent authorities may"* withdraw or lapse banking licenses only in the situations referred thereto. The foregoing paves the way for national legislators to transpose such provision in different ways, limiting eventually the discretion of competent authorities.[85]

The procedure for the lapsing credit institution authorisations is described in art. 79 SSM Fr. In this vein, NCAs must inform the ECB about individual lapsing cases. Subsequently, the ECB shall make such information available to the public after updating the relevant NCA and the concerned entity. **14.046**

(b) Basic steps of the withdrawal of authorisation process

The process to withdraw a banking license resembles the procedure to grant banking authorisations, but it has its own particularities.[86] The relevant legal framework applicable to this procedure is constituted by (i) paras. 5 and 6 of art. 14 SSM R and (ii) arts. 80–84 SSM Fr. Its three basic steps can be summarised as follows:[87] **14.047**

(i) [Stage 1] Initiation of the withdrawal procedure: The relevant NCA or the ECB may consider, based on national or EU law, as applicable, that the authorisation of a credit institution needs to be wholly or partially withdrawn.

(ii) [Stage 2] Assessment of the withdrawal of the banking authorisation: There are two avenues depending on which authority (NCA or ECB) has taken the lead in the withdrawal process:
  a. In case the initiative comes from the NCA, after liaising with the NRA, it shall prepare a draft withdrawal decision that will be submitted to the ECB for its final decision.
  b. In case the initiative comes from the ECB, it shall inform the relevant NCA and coordinate with the NRA.

(iii) [Stage 3] ECB decision on the withdrawal of a banking authorisation: Where the ECB considers that it is justified to withdraw a banking authorisation, if the NRA does not object to the withdrawal of the authorisation, or the ECB judges that the NRA and/or NCA have not taken action to maintain the financial stability, it will take a decision withdrawing (totally or partially) the relevant authorisation.

---

subjecting the ECB to divergent national regulations, would jeopardise equal treatment of credit institution, producing regulatory arbitrage.

85 See, in this regard, Section A.2.(a). (*Gold-plating national options and discretions*) in Chapter 7.

86 Cf Section 7 of ECB Guide on License Applications: "*The applicable process for the withdrawal of the licences is defined in national law, while cooperation between the NCA and the ECB is largely the same as that for granting authorisations*".

87 See, on this matter, Gurlit, E. (2022)(i).

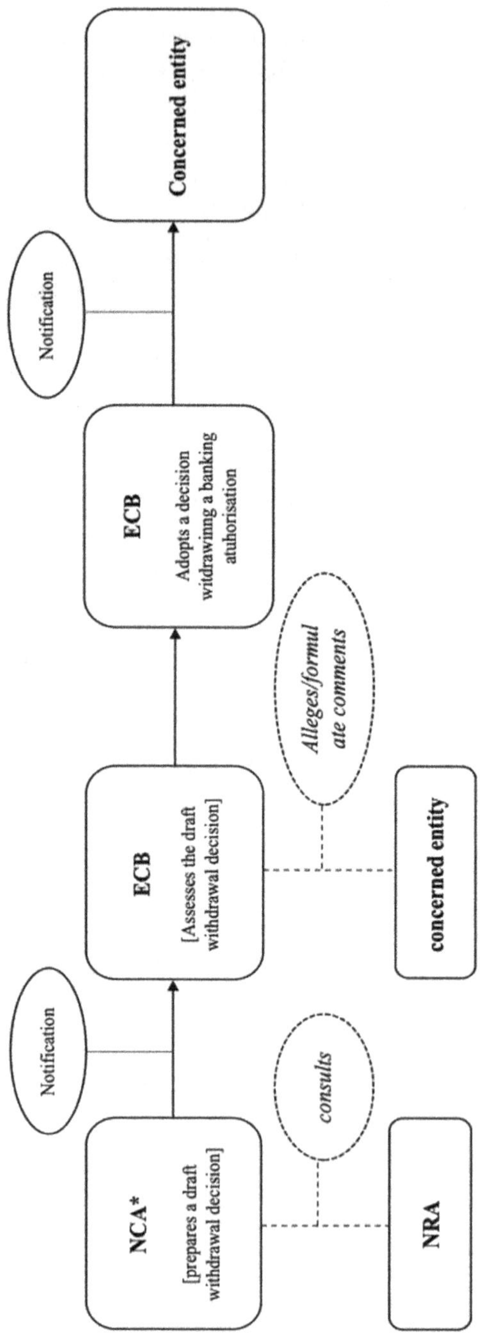

Note: * Acting also at the request of a credit institution.

Figure 14.3 Procedure initiated by the NCA

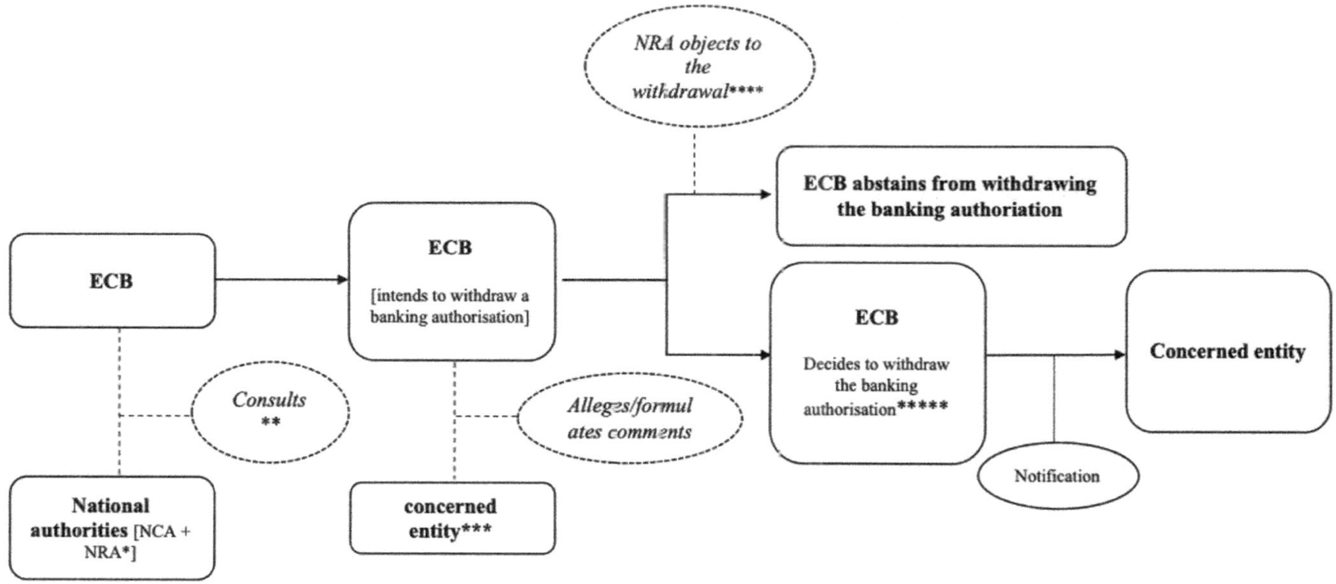

Notes: * Where the NCA is not the NRA.
** The NCA may be consulted at any time (art. 82(2) SSM Fr). Finally, where the NCA is not the NRA, it must be informed by the ECB immediately after it starts contact with the relevant NRA (art. 82(4) SSM Fr).
*** The NCA will be informed of any comments produced by the concerned credit institution (art. 82(3) SSM Fr).
**** The NRA may object to the ECB decision. In that case, the ECB and the NRA may agree that, for a period of time, the ECB will refrain from withdrawing the authorisation (art. 84(1)–(2) SSM Fr).
***** If the NRA does not object to the withdrawal, or even if it objects, the ECB may withdraw the banking authorisation where it "*determines that proper actions necessary to maintain financial stability have not been implemented by national authorities*" (arts. 83(3) and 84(4) SSM Fr).

Figure 14.4 Procedure initiated by the ECB

14.048 Figures 14.3 and 14.4 offer a simplified picture of the procedure, depending on which authority (NCA or ECB) initiates the procedure.

(c) Key aspects of the process

14.049 The procedure for the withdrawal of a banking authorisation varies depending on which authority initiates the procedure (the ECB or the NCA). With the purpose of offering a clearer picture, the key legal aspects pertaining to the two potential avenues are presented below.

14.050 Yet, and as an introduction, it must be noted that, as it happened with the authorisation of the process, the ECB is placed as the *gatekeeper* to control the exit of entities from continuing carrying out the business of credit institutions.[88] Following this logic, any withdrawal of a banking license (as regards both LSIs and SIs) must be ultimately decided by the ECB. This includes, in the author's view, when such a withdrawal is imposed as a sanction after the instruction of the relevant sanctioning proceeding by a given NCA.[89]

(i) Withdrawal procedure initiated by a NCA

14.051 The relevant NCA[90] may consider that a banking authorisation should be withdrawn[91] and initiate the corresponding procedure. The NCA may come to such conviction on the basis either of EU law or national law requirements.[92]

88 See in more detail in previous Section B.2. (*Vertical allocation? Examining the decentralised mode of implementing the specific supervisory tasks*) in Chapter 6. See, also, Recital 21 SSM R.

The L-Bank case even made succinct reference to the fact the ECB, on top of being exclusively competent to carry out the specific micro-prudential supervisory foreseen in art. 41(1) (and in art. 4(2) SSM R), is also competent to directly authorise and withdraw banking licenses as regards *all* credit institutions subject to the scope of the SSM R (Paras. 59–60 of the *L-Bank appeal*).

Noting the paucity of the concise reference contained in the L-Bank case to the division of competences in the SSM, its logic and the nature of the relationship between the ECB and the NCAs (not corrected in the *L-Bank appeal*), see Annunziata, F. (2020).

89 Art. 64(1) CRD IV foresees, in fact, that competent authorities must be vested with the supervisory power of withdrawing banking licenses (in accordance with art. 18 CRD IV). In this vein, some MSs have incorporated the withdrawal or revocation of banking licenses as a (strong) form of punishment in case (serious) breaches are committed). This is, for example, the case of Spain, whose art. 97(1) of Law 10/2014 on Solvency, Supervision and Ordination of Credit Institutions (*Ley 10/2014, de 26 de junio, de ordenación, supervisión y solvencia de entidades de crédito*) contemplates the withdrawal of banking licenses as a serious sanction to be imposed on entities.

For a compared analysis on the transposition of CRD IV sanctioning provisions and its interplay with the sanctioning powers allocated on the ECB (and broadly on the SSM), including on the nature of licenses withdrawal, see Allegrezza, S. (ed.). (2020). In particular, as regards the Spanish case and the imposition of the withdrawal of license as a sanction, see pp. 401 and ss. and 495–496.

90 Acting on its own initiative or at the initiative of the concerned credit institution (cf art. 80(1) SSM Fr).

91 Arts. 14(5) SSM R and 80(1) SSM Fr.

92 Cf arts. 18 and 67(1) CRD IV.

In addition, where the NRA is competent for the resolution of the concerned entity,[93] the relevant NCA will further coordinate with it[94] as regards any impediments under the resolution framework.[95] **14.052**

Considering the *modular* approach to banking licenses contemplated in some MSs,[96] the relevant NCA may only consider withdrawing partially a given banking authorisation. **14.053**

As the case may be, the NCA will prepare a draft withdrawal decision and address it to the ECB for its assessment. The ECB must assess such a draft decision without undue delay, in particular when particular urgency reasons are put forward by the NCA.[97] **14.054**

(ii) ECB initiative to withdraw a credit institution authorisation

Pursuant to art. 82(1) SSM Fr, the ECB may, on its own initiative, assess whether a banking authorisation must be withdrawn. ECB assessment must be based on circumstances it became aware of, in accordance solely to applicable EU law.[98] **14.055**

The ECB may consult with the NCA of the MS where the concerned entity is established. However, such consultation becomes compulsory if the ECB indeed foresees withdrawing a given banking authorisation.[99] Under this consultative procedure, the ECB must inform the NCA of the comments provided by the credit institution concerned[100] and any further liaising with the relevant NRA.[101] **14.056**

In this specific step, things seem to occur in the opposite manner they usually happen in a common procedure: It is not the NCA that presents a draft proposal to the ECB but the ECB that presents a draft proposal to the NRA (if **14.057**

93 Mainly, as regards LSIs pursuant to the distribution of competences operated by the SRM R (art. 7(2)(a)). See, on this matter, Capolino, O. (2019). The Single Resolution Mechanism: Authorities and Proceedings. In *The Palgrave Handbook of European Banking Union Law* (pp. 247–270). Palgrave Macmillan.
See also, for a comprehensive and complete analysis of the SRM, Gortsos, C. V. (2019).

94 Art. 80(2) SSM Fr.

95 For instance, risks regarding the disruption of operations and deposit blocking, protection of depositaries (e.g., setting up deadlines to retrieve deposits), reconciliation of ongoing operations, transfer of banking business to other entities, etc.

96 See immediately above in Section B.1. (*Authorisation/licensing of credit institutions*) of this chapter.

97 On the ECB assessment, see further below.

98 Arts. 14(5) SSM R and 82(1) SSM Fr.

99 Art. 82(2) SSM Fr. In principle, such consultation is due, at least, 25 working days before the date it plans to make its decision.

100 Arts. 14(5) SSM R and 82(3) SSM Fr.

101 And informing the NCA immediately after initiating such contact, pursuant to art. 82(4) SSM Fr.

any), on which such NRA may opine and propose postponing the withdrawal of the license due to reasons related to the entity's resolution.

14.058 Such an intense exchange with the relevant NRAs is rooted in the constitutional basis upon which the SSM is created (and which should not be trespassed in any event).[102] Pursuant to art. 127(6) TFEU, only *prudential supervisory* tasks could be allocated to the ECB, which excluded the assumption of resolution tasks.[103] Yet, some competences attributed to the ECB, in particular those relating to early intervention and the yearly approval of recovery plans,[104] blur the distinction between supervision and resolution, stretching the SSM constitutional basis.

(iii) ECB assessment and decision on the withdrawal of the banking license

14.059 Regardless of the entity taking the initiative (NCA or ECB), the ECB is bound to take a decision on the withdrawal without undue delay.[105]

14.060 To do so, the ECB has to consider the following elements: (a) its own assessment of the circumstances motivating the withdrawal; (b) the NCA's withdrawal decision, if any:[106] (c) the outcome of the consultations with the NCA and the NRA; and (d) the comments provided by the concerned entity.[107]

14.061 The withdrawal of a bank's license may take place in the broader context of bank crisis management. Thus, it is important to consider the interplay with the resolution framework. In this scenario, the resolution authorities need to take into account a plurality of evolving factors when deciding on a resolution strategy.[108] In cases where a partial transfer strategy has been decided (or simply occurred), the banking authorisation may be partially maintained to ease the operation of the credit institution placed under liquidation.[109] The

102 On the assessment of the robustness of the SSM constitutional basis (i.e., art. 127(6) TFEU) to set up the mechanism as it was and its potential flaws, see Chapter 2.

103 Ibidem. See, on this specific matter, Teixeira, P. G. (2017). The author states in this work that: "*This implied that the ECB could only perform banking supervision tasks within its central banking jurisdiction. (...). This defined the jurisdiction of the Banking Union, particularly since the jurisdiction of the Single Resolution Mechanism followed that of the SSM*" (p. 548).

104 Art. 4(1)(i) SSM R.

105 Cf Arts. 81(1) and 83(1) SSM Fr, which seem to be somehow redundant.

106 In principle, in those cases where the NCA proposed, to the ECB, withdrawing the authorisation.

107 For the sake of consistency with art. 31 SSM Fr (right to be heard).

108 Which should be "*to ensure the continuity of essential financial services, to maintain the stability of the financial system, to reduce moral hazard by minimising reliance on public financial support to failing entities, and to protect depositors*". (cf Recital 58 SRM regulation).

109 This entity, presumably, would have retained the distressed or impaired assets of the original entity, being the performing or profitable assets partially transferred (as a block) to another entity. On this matter and on the notion of keeping a partial authorisation to facilitate the transfer of business or assets, see Ramos

foregoing amounts, *sensu contrario*, to admitting that partial withdrawal of a banking license may happen within the resolution process.

Beyond the case described above, where potential resolution measures are taken by the NRA,[110] the ECB may take the decision directly provided that (i) the NRA does not object to the withdrawal of the banking license or (ii) the ECB judges that the relevant NRA did not implement proper actions to maintain financial stability. **14.062**

(iv) Interaction with resolution authorities

Art. 84 SSM Fr contemplates the interplay and further involvement of NRA in the withdrawal process. Here, it must be noted that the SSM Fr does only make reference to NRAs and not to the SRM. The reason behind this seems to be that, at that time, the SRM was not in place at the time the SSM Fr was adopted.[111] **14.063**

As per the involvement of the resolution authorities: **14.064**

(i) Regarding NRA, art. 84(1) SSM Fr foresees that, if the relevant NRA objects to ECB intention to withdraw the authorisation, they must agree on a period during which the ECB shall abstain from withdrawing the banking license.[112]
After such a period lapses, the ECB will assess whether it withdraws the authorisation or extends the deadline[113] (following a consultation with the NCA and/or NRA).
(ii) When the entity concerned falls under the remit of the SRB,[114] a similar consultation mechanism is in place. The master lines of such a process are contemplated in the Memorandum of Understanding between the Single Resolution Board and the European Central Bank in respect of cooperation and information exchange.[115]

Muñoz, D. & Lamandini, M. (2022). Evolving key risks in the banking sector and related priorities for the SRB: the lack of an effective transfer-based bank crisis framework. *Economic Governance Support Unit (EGOV)*.

Additionally, as regards the transfer of the banking business as a resolution tool, see Gortsos, C. V. (2019) at pp. 194–195. See, also, Gortsos, C. V. (2021). Impediments to resolvability – what is the status quo. *Economic Governance Support Unit (EGOV)*. At pp. 29 and ss.

110 Those cases are referred to in art. 84 SSM Fr (cf art. 83(3) SSM Fr).

111 The SRM Regulation was adopted on 15 July 2014 (OJ L 225/1 of 30 July 2014), whereas the SSM Fr was adopted on 16 April 2014 (OJ L 141/1 14 May 2014).

112 It must be noted that the SSM Fr does not contemplate any maximum (or minimum) deadline. Hence, the ECB and NRA are granted broad leeway to come to terms.

113 Pursuant to art. 14(6) SSM R (cf art. 84(2) SSM Fr).

114 For instance, when the entity is classified as a SI pursuant to the SSM R (and other cross-border groups) in accordance with art. 7(2) SRM Regulation.

115 It can be accessed here: https://www.srb.europa.eu/system/files/media/document/mou_with_the_single_resolution_board_on_cooperation_and_information_exchange_2018_.pdf.

The MoU stipulates that the ECB and the SRB will exchange information before the ECB decides to withdraw a banking license.[116]

Some recent resolution experiences[117] evidence that intense exchanges and continuous information flows take place between the ECB and the SRB.[118] For example, (i) the relevant SRB decision concerning the resolution of *Sberbank Europe AG* highlights that, as from the start of the deterioration of *Sberbank Europe AG* position, "*The information exchange between the SRB, the ECB and the relevant NRAs has been continuous since then*".[119] Additionally, (ii) in the resolution of Banco Popular, the ECB and the SRB kept regular exchanges, and when the situation became critical, and the sale of Banco Popular was about to take place,[120] the ECB exchanged on a continuous daily basis to oversight the transfer of the distressed credit institution.[121]

By the same token, as indicated in the MoU, the SRB will be consulted if the ECB intends to withdraw a banking license.

(v) Notification and publication

14.065 Following art. 88(1)(a) SSM Fr, the ECB will notify the concerned entity and the NCA of the withdrawal of the banking license. The former will also update its registry of credit institutions accordingly.[122]

---

116 See Paragraph 9.5.1. and 9.5.3. of this MoU (cf also Recital 4).

117 See for instance: (i) SRB decision SRB/EES/2022/19 of 1 March 2022 on the Assessment of the conditions for resolution in respect of Sberbank Europe AG (https://www.srb.europa.eu/system/files/media/document/2022-06-10_SRB-Non-confidential-version-of-the-decision-in-respect-of-Sberbank-Europe-AG.pdf); (ii) SRB decision SRB/EES/2018/09 of 23 February 2018 concerning the assessment of the conditions for resolution in respect of ABLV Bank, AS (https://www.srb.europa.eu/system/files/media/document/decision_srb-ees-2018-09_ablv_lv_non_confidential_version_final_0.pdf); and (iii) SRB decision SRB/EES/2017/08 of 7 June 2017 concerning the adoption of a resolution scheme in respect of Banco Popular Español, S. A. (https://www.srb.europa.eu/system/files/media/document/resolution_decision_updated_on_30_10_2018.pdf).

118 See, for instance, Paras. 27–40 of the SRB decision SRB/EES/2022/19 of 1 March 2022 on the Assessment of the conditions for resolution in respect of Sberbank Europe AG (https://www.srb.europa.eu/system/files/media/document/2022-06-10_SRB-Non-confidential-version-of-the-decision-in-respect-of-Sberbank-Europe-AG.pdf).

119 See SRB decision SRB/EES/2022/19 of 1 March 2022 on the Assessment of the conditions for resolution in respect of Sberbank Europe AG (https://www.srb.europa.eu/system/files/media/document/2022-06-10_SRB-Non-confidential-version-of-the-decision-in-respect-of-Sberbank-Europe-AG.pdf), at Para. 27. The decision does not provide much detail on the exact content and details pertaining to these exchanges, as some parts of it have been censored to protect business and banking secrecy.

120 See Ramos Muñoz, D. & Lamandini, M. (2022) at p. 8. See also, on this matter, Binder, J. H. (2017). Wunderkind is Walking? The Resolution of Banco Popular as a First Test for the Single Resolution Mechanism. Oxford Business Law Blog: Wunderkind is Walking? The Resolution of Banco Popular as a First Test for the Single Resolution Mechanism | Oxford Law Blogs.

121 See SRB decision SRB/EES/2017/08 of 7 June 2017 concerning the adoption of a resolution scheme in respect of Banco Popular Español, S. A. (https://www.srb.europa.eu/system/files/media/document/resolution_decision_updated_on_30_10_2018.pdf). At Paras. 36–37.

122 And will communicate this fact to the EBA (art. 88(5) SSM Fr) so that it can update the *EBA Credit Institution Register*. Such register can be accessed here: https://euclid.eba.europa.eu/register/cir/search.

Also, pursuant to art. 88(4) SSM Fr, the relevant NCA will inform the respective NRA on the withdrawal. Taking into account the implementation of the SRM and the set-up of the SRB, the ECB will inform the SRB of the effective withdrawal of the relevant banking authorisation. **14.066**

(d) Legal challenges and safeguards

(i) Some reflections on the safeguards applicable in the procedure for lapsing and withdrawing banking licenses

When dealing with the lapsing and withdrawal of banking licenses, a number of safeguards come into play. These safeguards, closely linked to fundamental rights (or an expression of them), are particularly relevant as a counterbalance or *limit* to the broad discretionary powers enjoyed by the ECB as supranational supervisor under the SSM.[123] Thus, these safeguards rather act as a source of legitimacy for the ECB, considering its independent role as prudential supervisor.[124] In addition, and closely linked to the precedent considerations, procedural and substantive safeguards play a capital role in the judicial review of ECB acts, as the CJEU is to scrutinise the ECB actions using those safeguards and rights as a yardstick.[125] **14.067**

The referred safeguards relate, mainly, to the right to be heard, the right to a good administration and the equal treatment of the concerned entity. For the sake of precision, it will be analysed below, first, the interplay of due process rights concerning lapsing of banking licenses and, after, the safeguards which raise the most concern during the process of withdrawing banking authorisations **14.068**

Regarding the *lapsing of banking authorisation*, a thorny matter is how the procedure can ensure that the right to be heard is respected. As a matter of principle, it must be recalled that the right to be heard must be granted as regards any decision (ECB supervisory decision, in this case) adversely affecting the supervisee.[126] The lapsing of a banking authorisation intrinsically constitutes **14.069**

---

123 See Lamandini, M., Ramos Muñoz, D. & Solana, J. (2015) at pp. 7–8; and Lamandini, M., Ramos Muñoz, D. & Solana, J. (2016) at pp. 201–203

124 See Moloney, N. (2021). Banking Union and the Charter of Fundamental Rights. In *Judicial Review in the European Banking Union* (pp. 209–220). Edward Elgar Publishing.

See, also, Section A. (*Justiciability: institutional balance (and separation of powers) and fundamental rights*) in Chapter 12 above.

125 See Moloney, N. (2021) at pp. 214 and ss. See, also, Papathanassiou, C. (2022). Fundamental rights and banking supervision. *Journal of Banking Regulation*, pp. 1–12 [Papathanassiou, C. (2022)(i)].

126 See Papathanassiou, C. (2022)(i) at pp. 4–5. See, also, Lo Schiavo, G. (2017) at pp. 117–119. Finally, as per relevant case law, see (i) General Court judgement in cases: (i) T-323/22 (*Socrates Capital Ltd and others v ECB*) of 10 July 2024 (ECLI:EU:T:2024:460) at Paras. 421 and ss.; and Court of Justice judgment in case

an act that adversely affects the interest of the supervisee,[127] and consequently, the right to be heard should be protected.

14.070 Art. 79 SSM Fr does not expressly foresee that this safeguard applies to the lapsing of banking licenses. Yet, the application of the right to be heard is not expressly ruled out either.[128] As stated above, considering that this basic safeguard must be applied in any procedure that may produce unfavourable effects for the concerned supervisee, it must be applied herein.

14.071 In addition, in case of disagreement with the decision lapsing the authorisation, the concerned entity should be able also to challenge it.[129]

14.072 The matter gets thornier here since (a) it is not foreseen that a *lapsing* decision may be issued by the ECB and (b) the ECB lapsing action is fully based on the relevant verification of the circumstances giving rise to the lapsing of the credit institution authorisation.

14.073 Against this background, it seems desirable that the ECB formally issues a decision agreeing on publishing the lapse of the authorisation and succinctly motivating it in light of the previous assessment carried out by the NCA. This would facilitate filing a claim before the relevant court and would satisfy the requisite of motivating a decision adversely affecting the rights of individuals.

14.074 Pursuant to recent case law,[130] it would appear that such a decision would be amenable to the judicial review of the CJEU. If a formal decision is not issued by the ECB, the concerned credit institution could still try to challenge the notification furnished by the ECB so as to ensure that the action could be amenable to judicial review.

14.075 When it comes to the safeguards to be observed during the withdrawal of a banking license, those relating to the right to be heard, the need to motivate

---

C-650/19 P (*Vialto Consulting Kft. V EC*) of 28 October 2021 (ECLI:EU:C:2021:879). At Para. 120 (and cited case law therein).

127 However, in some cases, the supervisee itself may seek such lapsing. For instance, a credit institution to which a banking license has been awarded may decide not to start exercising the banking activity if the provisions upon which it made its business plan dramatically worsen. Also, disputes between promoters or main shareholders of a newly created credit institution may end up in the cancellation of the project and the credit institution, refraining from pursuing any activity. The scenarios and casuistics are wide.

128 Cf art. 31(1) SSM Fr. For instance, this provision sets forth that the right to be heard does not apply to Section 1, Chapter III SSM R (*Investigatory powers*).

129 See Section B. (*Judicial review in composite procedures: the CJEU's Berlusconi-Fininvest case law in perspective*) in Chapter 12.

130 Ibidem.

the decisions, the equal treatment of the concerned entity and the right to a good administration raise the acutest concerns:[131]

(i) The *right to be heard*, contemplated in art. 31 SSM Fr and 41(2)(a) Charter, is paramount in a procedure of this kind and so has deserved attention in recent case law.

Granting sufficient time to provide comments to the draft withdrawal decision served by the ECB is capital to enable the exercise of this procedural guarantee. In this vein, the minimum time to be allowed the concerned entity to provide comments must be of, at least, three working days pursuant to art. 31(3) SSM Fr. Even if that period of time does not look quite substantial, the General Court has confirmed the validity of such deadline, judging that the *legislators* established it after accurately weighting two "*opposing interests: on the one hand, the private interests of the credit institutions in having as much time as possible to make their observations and, on the other, the public interest in having legality restored as quickly as possible*".[132]

Even if the right to be heard must be respected, Paras. 4 and 5 of art. 31 SSM Fr provide that such a right may be granted to the concerned entity *ex post,* that is, after adopting the relevant withdrawal decision.

This way forward is only possible in urgent cases and subject to the need to avoid "*a significant damage to the financial system*". Such urgent need to prevent damages to the financial system may be appreciated as regards SIs, especially those of a systemic nature (*Global systemically important institutions*). However, it may be more difficult (although not unthinkable) to assess the existence of the need to prevent damages to the financial system when the entity involved is an LSI.

(ii) The ECB (and, indirectly, NCAs) must ensure that entities facing this type of procedures are *treated equally*. The right to be treated equally before the supervisory action of the ECB and not to be discriminated is enunciated in art. 1(1) SSM R[133] and fully provided in arts. 20–21 Charter.

Pursuant to this principle, "*comparable situations must not be treated differently*" and "*different situations must not be treated in the same way unless such treatment is objectively justified*".[134]

Yet, considering the wide variety of facts coming into play in these kinds of withdrawal procedures,[135] it seems very difficult to conceive two situations identical or even substantially similar. Consequently, the entities concerned by

131 See for an overview of the safeguards presented right below Papathanassiou, C. (2022)(i).

132 See General Court judgment in cases T-351/18 and T-584/18 (*Ukrselhosprom PCF LLC and Versobank AS v European Central Bank*) of 6 October 2021 (ECLI:EU:T:2021:669). Cf at Para. 374.

133 Cf also Recital 30 SSM R.

134 Court of Justice judgment in case C-406/15 (*Petya Milkova v Izpalnitelen direktor na Agentsiata za privatizatsia i sledprivatizatsionen control*) of 9 March 2017 (ECLI:EU:C:2017:198) at Para. 55.

See, also, General Court judgment in cases T-351/18 and T-584/18 (*Ukrselhosprom PCF LLC and Versobank AS v European Central Bank*) of 6 October 2021 (ECLI:EU:T:2021:669) at Paras. 349–350.

135 See footnote 117. Pursuant to the overview of cases offered therein, there is a wide variety of resolution cases to which the withdrawal of banking licenses appears closely linked.

a withdrawal procedure should manage their expectations when it comes to the protection granted by the equal treatment principle. It seems more promising in theory than effective in practice. Considering that withdrawal procedures are by definition confidential,[136] and that only if scrutinised before the CJEU entities (and public in general) can have limited access to the substantive and factual background surrounding the case,[137] the possibilities to establish comparison look rather limited.

The flip side of the coin is that the ECB, when deciding on the withdrawal of the banking license, would not be bound by precedents.[138] Nevertheless, it needs to be considered that there will always be uncertainty on which cases may be tried in court. This uncertainty can constitute a strong interest for the ECB to assess all cases *equally*, so that when the CJEU[139] scrutinises its actions, it can demonstrate that it has treated all entities equally. Otherwise, it may incur in a violation severe enough to lead to the annulment of the concerned withdrawal decision.

Furthermore, it must be noted that an absence of precedent does not entail in itself the breach of the principle of equal treatment as indicated by the General Court.[140] That being said, the CJEU seems to maintain a rather casuistic approach when assessing whether the principle of equal treatment has been violated. As a starting point, the Court outlines the need to treat similarly what is similar (unless there is an objective justification to carry out a differentiated approach).[141] Using such broad principles as a compass, the CJEU further analyses (with more or less detail) the factual and legal situation of the case and

---

Also, we can think also of cases in which the relevant entity wants to give up its banking license and may request the relevant NCA or the ECB to commence the relevant procedure (or even in the course of a group restructuring, as it was the case of Piraeus Bank, S. A. and Alpha Bank AE).

In this Regard, the ECB Annual Report on supervisory activities 2021 (ECB Annual Report on supervisory activities 2021 (europa.eu)) indicates that:

"*Withdrawal procedures arose mainly from voluntarily terminations of business activity and mergers or other types of restructuring*". At p. 57.

136 And request for access to the file filed by not directly concerned entities will be rejected on the grounds of art. 32 SSM Fr and 4(1)(a) of Decision of the European Central Bank of 4 March 2004 on public access to European Central Bank documents (ECB/2004/3).

137 On top of the regulatory updates/press releases that the ECB may decide to issue and, of course, the information appearing in the press.

138 See General Court judgment in cases T-351/18 and T-584/18 (*Ukrselhosprom PCF LLC and Versobank AS v European Central Bank*) of 6 October 2021 (ECLI:EU:T:2021:669) at Para. 353:

"(...) *The gravity of conduct does not need to be assessed in relation to the gravity of the conduct of other persons, but only in relation to the legal standards required by the applicable legal provisions, with that gravity being relevant only for determining the appropriate sanction. Furthermore, it is apparent from the case-law referred to in paragraph 351 above that, even if there had been other decisions concerning the withdrawal of authorisation of other credit institutions for infringements of AML/CFT regulatory requirements, the ECB would not be bound by such decisions*".

139 The General Court in first instance. See Lehmann, M. (2021).

140 See General Court judgment in cases T-351/18 and T-584/18 (*Ukrselhosprom PCF LLC and Versobank AS v European Central Bank*) of 6 October 2021 (ECLI:EU:T:2021:669) at Para. 352.

141 See Court of Justice judgment in case C-823/18 P (*GEA Group AG v EC*) of 25 November 2020 (ECLI:EU:C:2020:955). At Para. 58.

compares it to precedent (or coetaneous) situations decided by the EU administration.[142] As a result, it can be said that the review carried out by the CJEU is rather *light*, providing EU bodies and Institutions with a broad margin of discretion when deciding on cases that look similar (and provided that their decisions are sufficiently motivated).

(iii) The *justification* or statement of reasons of the decision (i.e., the *motivation*) is a core safeguard. This procedural safeguard entails that the decision-making administration must state the reasons on which its decision is based.[143][144]

In the process to withdraw a banking authorisation, the motivation of a final decision is anticipated, to a great extent, in the draft decision submitted to the concerned entity for comments before the final decision is adopted by the ECB.

The statement of reasons of a decision regarding the withdrawal of a banking license fulfils a double safeguarding objective. On the one hand, from a purely procedural view, it enables the concerned entity to know the reasons leading to the adoption of the relevant withdrawing decision. On the other hand, it has also a judicial reviewability dimension, allowing the competent court (the General Court, in first instance) to analyse whether it was vitiated or not.[145]

The minimum requirements of motivation can be satisfied by the ECB with a succinct motivation, comprehensive enough to allow the concerned entity to understand why the supervisor acted in such manner.

In addition, it must be highlighted that the appropriate formal or informal supervisory dialogue preceding the adoption of a withdrawal decision, occurring between the relevant NCA (as regards LSIs) or the ECB (as regards SIs), can actually complement the motivation of such decision.[146] Such exchanges, properly documented or evidenced, can actually show that the concerned entity was aware of the situation and of the supervisory expectations communicated by the ECB, and its intended course of action, should the situation leading to the withdrawal of the authorisation persist. This results in the process following a rather "relational" supervisory approach,[147] even if the legal text distils a quantitative and strictly structured methodology.

142 See General Court judgment in case T-466/17 (*Printeos, SA et al. v EC*) of 24 September 2019 (ECLI:EU:T:2019:671). At Paras. 100 and ss.

143 See Section A.1. (What rights and procedural guarantees (due process rights)? and Section B. (*Are fair trial rights a cure?*) in Chapter 13.

Additionally, see Section C.1.(a). (*CJEU standard of review concerning ECB supervisory tasks*) in Chapter 12.

144 Ibidem.

145 See *L-Bank case* at Para. 123 and General Court judgment in cases T-351/18 and T-584/18 (*Ukrselhosprom PCF LLC and Versobank AS v European Central Bank*) of 6 October 2021 (ECLI:EU:T:2021:669) at Para. 386.

See, also, Section C.1.(a). (*CJEU standard of review concerning ECB supervisory tasks*) in Chapter 12 for a dedicated examination of the relevant General Court judgment in case T-576/18 (*Crédit agricole SA v ECB*) of 8 July 2020 (ECLI:EU:T:2020:304).

146 General Court judgment in cases T-351/18 and T-584/18 (*Ukrselhosprom PCF LLC and Versobank AS v European Central Bank*) of 6 October 2021 (ECLI:EU:T:2021:669) at Para. 388.

147 Using the same term used by Lamandini, D'Ambrosio and Ramos Muñoz in Lamandini, M., D'Ambrosio, R. & Ramos Muñoz, D. (2022). 2. 18 Supervisory Review and Evaluation Process (SREP) in the Context

Such a "relational" method is desirable, considering the delicate weighting of interests[148] and, especially, the qualitative factors[149] to be taken into account when withdrawing a banking license. The need to intensify the supervisory dialogue peaks when it comes to withdrawing (partially or totally) banking licenses as a result of a resolution process, where, on top of the interests of the entity and its depositors, resolution (and supervisory) authorities need to also balance the interests of shareholders, bondholders, taxpayers and the financial stability of the EU as a whole.

(iv) *Right to a good administration*

It follows from constant case law that the right to a good administration imposes on EU authorities the duty to "*examine carefully and impartially all the relevant aspects of the individual case*"[150] before adopting a given decision.

The General Court has started to delimit the contours of this safeguard lately. It has indicated that the right to a good administration does not impose on the ECB the obligation to share with the concerned entity the draft decision prepared by the relevant NCA proposing the withdrawal of its banking licenses, nor even informing it about such draft decision.[151]

Additionally, the right to a good administration also entails the concerned person's right to access the administrative file he or she is affected by.[152] In the particular context of the procedure for withdrawing banking licenses, it must be highlighted that the right of access to the file, in principle, does not extend to the ECB and/or NCA internal documents, which are considered confidential. Those comprise, for example, internal drafts and preliminary analysis, draft versions of the relevant final decision and internal requests submitted to services and departments different from the one dealing with the withdrawal process.[153]

In principle, the same logic applies as regards communications and exchanges held between the ECB and the relevant NCA. However, if proving a given violation of safeguards requires to accede such exchanges and/or communications, the court should weight the interest at stake and may grant the applicant access to the relevant communications.[154]

---

of the Exercise of Supervisory Powers and Extraordinary Measures. In *Capital and Liquidity Requirements for European Banks* (pp. 526–547). Oxford University Press [Lamandini, M., Ramos Muñoz, D. and D'Ambrosio, R. (2022)(ii)].

148 See above. These include the entity interests, those of their depositors and those of the general public.

149 Including, for example, having in place robust governance arrangements, where it is likely that the entity will not be able to meet the obligations towards its creditors, the capital situation of the entity is *expected* to deteriorate leading to minimum thresholds not being met, etc.

150 CJEU judgment in case C-389/21 P (*Crédit Lyonnais v ECB*) of 4 May 2023 (ECLI:EU:C:2023:368) at Paras. 57 and 74.

151 See General Court judgment in case T-797/19 (*Anglo Austrian AAB AG and Belegging-Maatschappij "Far-East" BV v European Central Bank)* of 22 June 2022 (ECLI:EU:T:2022:389) at Paras. 233–236.

152 Art. 41(2)(b) Charter. See, also, art. 32 SSM Fr.

153 See Papathanassiou, C. (2022)(i) at p. 6. See, also, Wissink, L. (2021)(ii) at p. 57.

154 Ibidem. Or, at least, to part of them. A redacted version of the relevant exchanges between the NCA and the ECB, containing only the information which may be relevant to establish a certain irregularity, can be considered sufficient from the perspective of the right to access to the file.

See also, on the topic of access to the file and its practicalities, Lackhoff, K. (2017)(i) at pp. 116–119.

Finally, one final reflection can be made as regards the judicial reviewability of the decision adopting the withdrawal of a banking license. It must be noted that no proved violation of the abovementioned (and eventually others) safeguards will lead to the annulment of the relevant supervisory decision. **14.076**

The General Court has constantly noted that, only if it is established by the applicant that the "*outcome of the procedure might have been different without the alleged irregularity*",[155] it may annul the challenged decision. Consequently, non-substantial violations of safeguards, or even material ones not affecting the final outcome of the procedure, would not lead to its annulment. **14.077**

(e) Legal challenges (and potential remedies)

The procedures for lapsing and withdrawing banking authorisations present some legal challenges concerning coordination among intervening authorities. For instance: **14.078**

Concerning *lapsing of banking authorisations*, it is worth noting that art. 79 SSM Fr foresees that NCAs must inform the ECB on the occurrence of a lapsing event, as foreseen under national law. It is difficult to think how the procedure operates in practice as regards SIs, which are not directly supervised by NCAs.[156] **14.079**

As an alternative venue, staff from the NCA performing their duties in the relevant JST could gather such information, acting in a coordinated manner or under the direction of the JST supervisor.[157] **14.080**

As regards the *withdrawal of banking authorisations*, there are two issues that deserve separate attention: **14.081**

(i) Concerning procedures that begin at the NCAs' initiative, the *legislators* seem to have conceived such initiative only as regards LSIs, which fall under their direct supervision. In this sense, NCAs could have all the relevant elements to

155 See General Court judgment in case T-728/17 (*Marinvest and Porting v Commission*) of 14 May 2019 (ECLI:EU:T:2019:325) at Para. 57 and cited case law therein.

156 The concern can be particularly acute when the national law transposing CRD IV has included additional lapsing requirements to those foreseen in art. 18(a) CRD IV. Such causes for lapsing, based exclusively on national law, are particularly difficult for the ECB, as there may not be a clear connection with the CRD IV text.
On this matter, see Gurlit, E. (2022)(i) at Paras. 56–58.

157 In a similar token, see Section B.1.(c). (*Legal challenges and safeguards*) in this chapter. A similar issue occurred when the relevant NCA proposed the insertion of recommendations, conditions and restrictions to the relevant authorisation granted to a SI. As regards conditions and obligations, see also Section B.1.(b). (*Key aspects of the process (stage by stage)*) in this chapter.

assess whether the requisites stemming from both EU or national law leading to the withdrawal are met. However, it cannot be ruled out that the same initiative may be used as regards SIs, where the relevant NCA has available information allowing it to verify that EU or national law requisites regarding the withdrawal of the banking license are met. This can happen, for example, when the national staff of a JST can have access to certain information or where periodic reporting obligations or statistics obligations are channelled through the NCA where the institution is registered.

(ii) It results from arts. 14(6) SSM R and 83(3) and 84(3) SSM Fr that the ECB may decide to withdraw a banking authorisation even with the opposition of the relevant NRA (or the SRB) if it is convinced that such action is needed in order to maintain financial stability.[158]

14.082 For the time being, the ECB has not made use of this possibility in any case that the author is aware of.[159] In any event, such prerogative raises relevant questions from the perspective of the checks and balances of the *mechanism*:

14.083 *First*, it entails that that the ECB is granted certain assessment powers as regards the adequacy of resolution measures implemented by national authorities to ensure financial stability.

14.084 *Second*, it can be inferred that resolution objectives, when assessed at a national level, may be secondary to the overall stability of the systema as whole (on a case-by-case basis and upon a duly weighted assessment).

14.085 In practical terms, controversies may arise *vis-à-vis* the concerned entities should this option materialise. Under this prism, the entities concerned may also challenge the ECB decision withdrawing the authorisation on grounds of an inappropriate assessment of the adequacy of the national resolution measures implemented.

14.086 It is difficult to anticipate the outcome of such type of judicial claim. From the perspective of the ECB (and national authorities as well), it seems to be preferrable to not make use of such a drastic measure and reachi a common understanding.

---

158 Actually, those provisions only refer expressly to the lack of implementation of proper actions addressed to maintain financial stability by national authorities (NCAs and NRAs). The implementation of the SRM and the appearance of the SRB need to be encompassed accordingly, and thus, the ECB must be given the opportunity to withdraw a relevant SI's banking license even with the opposition of the SRB if it judges that this is appropriate from a financial stability perspective.

159 Pursuant to the information made available to the general public.

C. ASSESSMENT OF THE ACQUISITION OF QUALIFYING HOLDINGS

The ECB has to approve the acquisition of qualifying holdings[160] or the increase of qualifying holdings in a credit institution when the resulting holdings exceed the regulatory thresholds.[161] **14.087**

The process regarding the assessment of the acquisitions (and disposals) of qualifying holdings[162] is quite similar to the process for granting banking authorisations discussed in Section B.1. (*Authorisation/licensing of credit institutions*) of this chapter. Furthermore, and procedurally speaking, the same procedural issues can be extrapolated to this process, *mutatis mutandis*. **14.088**

As in the authorisation procedure, the ECB acts a *gatekeeper*, being entrusted with the task of directly controlling that shareholders holding a significant share in credit institutions or who are capable of decisively influencing such entities meet some minimum standards.[163] With a view to ensure consistency and level playing field in the participating MSs, this crucial task is vested to the ECB as regards all credit institutions, disregarding whether they are LSIs or SIs.[164] **14.089**

In the following paragraphs, we (1) describe the basic steps of the process for the acquisition of qualifying holdings, (2) outline its key aspects and then (3) analyse the legal challenges and safeguards. **14.090**

1. Basic steps of the procedure for acquiring a qualifying holding in a credit institution

The basic steps of the procedure for acquiring a qualifying holding in a credit institution can be summarised as follows: **14.091**

---

160 Cf arts. 3(33) and 4(1)(36) CRR. Pursuant to these provisions, qualifying holding "*means a direct or indirect holding in an undertaking which represents 10 % or more of the capital or of the voting rights or which makes it possible to exercise a significant influence over the management of that undertaking*".

For an analysis of the substantive requirements linked to the procedure of acquisition of qualifying holding, see Gurlit, E. (2022). Art. 15 Assessment of acquisitions of qualifying holdings. In *European banking union: Brussels commentary* (pp. 215–235). Baden-Baden: Nomos [Gurlit, E. (2022)(ii)].

Generally, on the procedure for the acquisition of qualifying holdings regulated in the SSM R, see (i) Buono, G. (2021); and (ii) Lackhoff, K. (2017)(i) at pp. 171–176.

161 Cf previous footnote: the increase in the qualifying holding exceeds 20%, 30% or 50% [of capital and/or voting rights] "*or so that the credit institution would become its subsidiary*" (cf art. 22(1) CRD IV).

162 Cf arts. 4(1)(c), 6(4) and 15 SSM R.

163 Cf Recital 22 SSM R.

164 The same considerations were made as regards the authorisation process, see Section B.1.(a). (*Basic steps of the authorisation process*) of this Chapter 14.

On the vertical distribution of tasks within the SSM, see Section B.2. (*Vertical allocation? Examining the decentralised mode of implementing the specific supervisory tasks*) in Chapter 6.

(i) [Stage 1] **Notification of the intention to acquire a qualifying holding:** Intended acquirers must submit to the NCA in which the relevant credit institution is established a notification to acquire a qualifying holding.[165]

Subsequently, a relevant NCA will notify the ECB of the notification received, indicating "*the date by which the decision to oppose or not to oppose the acquisition of a qualifying holding has to be notified to the applicant pursuant to the relevant national law*".[166]

(ii) [Stage 2] **NCA assessment of the intended acquisition of a qualifying holding:** The competent NCA will assess whether the intended acquisition complies with both national and EU law conditions. Following such analysis, it will submit to the ECB a draft decision suggesting whether to oppose or not the intended acquisition before the period for completing the assessment, as established under EU rules, comes to an end.[167]

(iii) [Stage 3] **ECB decision of the proposed acquisition of a qualifying holding:** On the basis of the draft decision prepared by the NCA, the ECB will decide to oppose or not the proposed acquisition.[168]

(iv) [Stage 4] **Notification of the decision on the intended acquisition:** The ECB will notify the concerned acquirer[169] and the relevant NCA as well.[170]

14.092 Figures 14.5 and 14.6 sketch the procedure.

14.093 To closure this Section, it is maybe important to emphasise the quantitative relevance that the qualifying holding procedures have within the SSM; the number of these procedures is only second to that of passporting procedures.[171]

2. Key aspects of the process (step by step)

14.094 In Stage 1 [*Notification of the intention to acquire a qualifying holding*], the intended acquirer must submit to the NCA the MS in which the relevant entity is established a notification to acquire a qualifying holding.[172] NCAs act as the entry point for the communication of intended acquisitions. This apparently simple act is particularly relevant as it determines the applicable rule

165 Cf arts. 15(1) SSM R and 85 SSM Fr. This step resembles the initial stage of the process for obtaining a banking authorisation.

166 Cf art. 85(1) and (3) SSM Fr.

167 Arts. 15(2) SSM R and 86 SSM Fr.

168 Arts. 15(3) SSM R and 87 SSM Fr.

169 Cf art. 88(1)(b) SSM Fr. The provision refers to the need to notify the "*parties*", which would encompass the need to notify not only the concerned acquirer but the relevant credit institution as well.

170 Art. 88(2)(c) SSM Fr.

171 The number of notifications concerning qualifying holdings by the ECB amounted to 111 in 2021, against 404 notifications concerning passporting. See the ECB Annual Report on supervisory activities 2021 (ECB Annual Report on supervisory activities 2021 (europa.eu).

See, also, Gurlit, E. (2022)(ii) at Para. 7.

172 And/or any other information related to the assessment process (art. 15(1) SSM R).

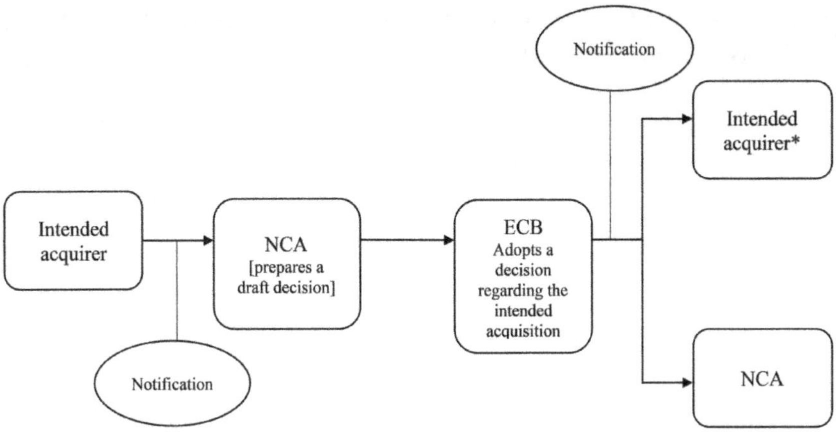

Note: *And eventually the relevant credit institution (see above).
Source: SSM Supervisory Manual, Figure 10 (p. 49).

Figure 14.5 Acquisition of a qualifying holding: SSM workflow

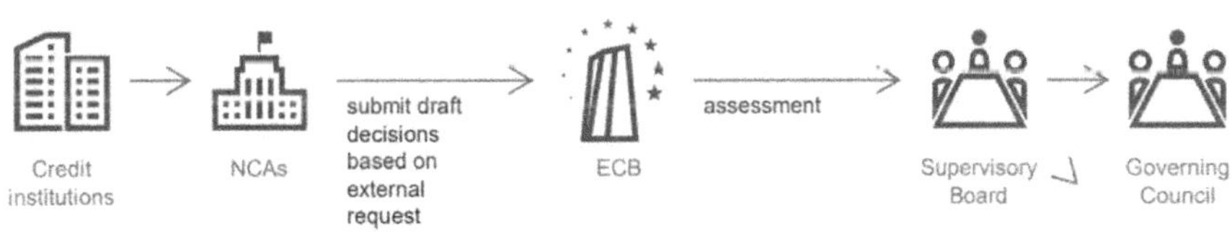

Figure 14.6 Authorisation and acquisitions of qualifying holdings

to which the relevant acquisition will be subject.[173] Consequently, qualifying holdings notifications must be carried out in accordance with such national law requirements.[174] On top of that, after the implementation of the IMAS

173 That is, the national law transposing the relevant requirements foreseen in CRD IV. As CRD IV establishes maximum harmonisation requirements concerning the assessment of qualifying holdings, MS could not impose additional requirements based solely on national law and/or add any conditions that interfere with those.

Yet, CRD IV transposition affects the procedural aspects of the procedures, in particular, the deadlines to be applied in the national stage of this composite procedure (cf art. 23(3)–(4) CRD IV). See, in this regard, the ECB Guide on qualifying holding procedures. September 2022: Guide on qualifying holding procedures (europa.eu).

On the rules to be applied by the ECB in composite procedures, see Chapter 7.

174 Ibidem.

portal,[175] these notifications are expected to be channelled via this digital platform (provided that national law so foresees[176]).

14.095 Additionally, it must be also emphasised that, pursuant to art. 4(1)(c) SSM R, this procedure is not applicable to cases pertaining to bank resolution. In those cases, NCAs will take over the tasks of conducting the assessment of the acquisition of the qualifying holding, with a view to ease the resolution of the concerned entity.[177]

14.096 Even if not specifically foreseen in the said art. 4(1)(c), national-based procedures regulating the authorisation to acquire a qualifying holding in non-credit institutions or a qualifying holding in credit institutions established in third countries are not subject to this common procedure. Those will be dealt by the ECB, when they concern SIs which fall under their direct supervision (and not as regards LSIs).[178][179]

14.097 Process-wise, after assessing the completeness of the file submitted, or simultaneously to this assessment,[180] the NCA must notify to the ECB the request received within five working days of the acknowledgement of the submission sent by the intended acquirer.[181]

---

175 The IMAS portal went live on 27 January 2021, and functionalities have been added subsequently. Nowadays, it covers all of the *common* procedures (as regards both LSIs and SIs) and some additional procedures concerning SIs (e.g., evaluation of fit and proper assessments and internal models).

176 A complete list of the MSs in which using the IMAS portal is compulsory (depending on the relevant procedure) can be consulted here: https://www.bankingsupervision.europa.eu/banking/portal/imas/shared/pdf/Regime_of_use.pdf.

177 For instance, as regards the sale of business tools, see art. 38(8) BRRD. In addition, regarding the bail-in tool, see art. 47(4) BRRD.
On this aspect, see Gurlit, E. (2022)(i) at Para. 15.

178 In principle, and following art. 9(1)II SSM R, the ECB is competent to apply those authorising powers as (i) they fall under the scope of the specific micro-prudential tasks allocated to it under the SSM R (cf art. 4(1)(a)) and (ii) underpin a supervisory function foreseen under EU law (i.e., ex ante authorisation). Gurlit, E. (2022)(i) at Para. 11–12.
See, further, Section B.4. (*Supervisory and investigatory powers to exercise those tasks*) in Chapter 6 and Section A.2.(b).(2). (*What happens when the national statute allocates powers in excess to the ones foreseen* a *prudential Directive?*) in Chapter 7. A similar reflection has been made above as regards certain national-law-based powers concerning authorisations; see Section B.1. (*Authorisation/licensing of credit institutions*) in this chapter.

179 Additionally, the approval procedure of financial holding companies and mixed financial holding companies foreseen in art. 21a CRD IV (as introduced by CRD V) would not fall under this qualifying holding procedure. Nevertheless, the ECB should be competent to grant or deny such approval pursuant to art. 4(1)(g) SSM R (if the entities qualify as SIs). See, on this topic, Gortsos, C. V. (2021). The New EU Regulatory Framework Governing the Approval and Consolidated Supervision of Financial Holding Companies and Mixed Financial Holding Companies. *Available at SSRN 3834246*. At pp. 18–19.

180 Art. 85(2) SSM Fr.

181 Art. 85(2) SSM Fr.

Finally, the NCA must also inform the ECB the date by which the decision on the qualifying holding must be notified to the intended acquirer.[182] That date will be determined by national provisions transposing CRD IV. Such procedural provisions materially affect the procedure, establishing a maximum deadline for its completion. In this regard, as argued above in this work, even these formally constitute procedural national provisions (and, in principle, the ECB should not abide to them), they have a substantive nature, and hence, the ECB must observe those.[183] **14.098**

This initial stage shares a good number of elements with the initial stage of the process for granting a banking license: the fact that NCAs act as entry point for the requests,[184] the fact that deadlines (and suspension periods) are subject to national rules transposing CRD IV and the fact that the examination of the completeness of the application is to be carried out by NCAs at the outset. **14.099**

Further, in Stage 2 [*NCA assessment of the intended acquisition of a qualifying holding*], the relevant NCA must submit to the ECB, some working days before the end of the period foreseen in national law to decide to oppose or not the proposed acquisition, a draft decision containing its assessment of the matter.[185] It is in this stage where the *composite* nature of the procedure starts to unfold,[186] as the relevant NCA needs to prepare first the foregoing assessment (on the basis on national law transposing CRD IV), which will trigger the subsequent assessment and final decision of the ECB.[187] **14.100**

From a substantive perspective, the process' main goal is to ensure that the proposed acquirer (and the acquisition itself) would not produce a negative impact in the target entity, jeopardising its prudential safety, financial soundness and **14.101**

182 Art. 85(3) SSM Fr.

183 See Section B.2. (*Administrative procedural rules (and principles) to be applied by the ECB: general overview and particular analysis of procedural rules contained in national law transposing prudential Directives*) in Chapter 7.

184 See above in Section B.1.(b). (*Key aspects of the process (stage by stage)*) in this chapter. Particularly, see also footnote 35.

185 Art. 22(2)II CRD IV foresees a maximum period of 60 working days to carry out the relevant assessment. National law may shorten such a period.

186 See, for an analytic overview on SSM (and SRM) composite procedures, Brito Bastos, F. (2021). See also, on the same topic, but rather focusing on the judicial review of these procedures, Buono, G. (2021). See further in Chapter 10 above.

187 See Chapter 11.

good repute.[188] For the assessment of the proposed acquisition, the following elements must be taken into account:[189]

(i) The reputation of the proposed acquirer.
(ii) The suitability of any member of the management body to be appointed to the target entity as a result of the acquisition.[190]
(iii) The financial soundness of the proposed acquirer.
(iv) The feasibility that the target entity continues to comply with its prudential requirements, basically under CRD IV and CRR.
(v) The existence, if any, of reasonable grounds to suspect that money laundering or terrorist financing is occurring or likely to happen (or even the risks of those may increase) in connection with the proposed acquisition.[191]

14.102 The abovementioned elements are the only ones that must be taken into consideration when performing the assessment of the proposed acquisition.[192] NCAs (and so the ECB) must refrain from examining (or even opposing) the proposed acquisition on different grounds and should not require any information which is not "*relevant for the prudential assessment*".[193]

14.103 It is worth also mentioning that, if the intended acquirer intends to appoint members to the management body of the target, exceptionally, the ECB will carry out also the fit and proper assessment concerning the relevant LSI.

188 Art. 23(1) CRD IV, Section 5.2.1. (*Reputation of the proposed Acquirer (criterion A)*) of the ECB Guide on qualifying holding procedures and Section 3.1.2 of the SSM Supervisory Manual. For a detailed analysis of the reputation requirement, see General Court judgement in case T-323/22 (*Socrates Capital Ltd and others v ECB*) of 10 July 2024 (ECLI:EU:T:2024:460) at Paras. 360–366.

189 Ibidem. See further ESAS Joint guidelines on the prudential assessment of acquisitions and increases of qualifying holdings in the financial sector (JC/GL/2016/01) of 20 December 2016: JC GL 2016 01 Joint Guidelines on prudential assessment of acquisition and increases of qualifying holdings – Final (europa.eu).

It must be noted that, pursuant to art. 22(9) CRD IV, the EBA was tasked with the preparation of ITS "*establish common procedures, forms and templates for the consultation process between the relevant competent authorities as referred to in Article 24*". These ITS were approved by the Commission Implementing Regulation (EU) 2017/461 of 16 March 2017, laying down implementing technical standards with regards to common procedures, forms and templates for the consultation process between the relevant competent authorities for proposed acquisitions of qualifying holdings in credit institutions as referred to in Article 24 of Directive 2013/36/EU of the European Parliament and of the Council.

190 See footnote 4 as regards the reference to fit and proper assessments.

191 Noting that the ECB has not been entrusted with an anti-money laundering task under the SSM R, this assessment is carried out on the basis of the information provided by the NCA. At the same time, when the NCA is not the competent authority for carrying out anti-money laundering monitoring tasks, it should liaise with the relevant authority. See Section 5.2.5.1 (*Scope of the assessment of criterion E*) of the ECB Guide on qualifying holding procedures. See, further, Section B.1. (*Tasks included vs. tasks excluded*) in Chapter 7.

192 Art. 23(2) CRD IV.

193 Art. 23(4) CRD IV.

Following the allocation of vertical tasks within the SSM,[194] the ECB carries out the fit and proper assessment as regards SIs,[195] whereas those assessments are carried out by NCAs when it comes to LSIs. This approach is not followed in qualifying (and authorisation) procedures. With a view to ensure broad consistency and level playing field, the ECB carries out, within the same qualifying procedure, the fit and proper assessment of the members of the management body to be appointed by the potential acquirer.[196]

In addition, in Stage 3 [*ECB decision of the proposed acquisition of a qualifying holding*], the ECB may decide to oppose or not the proposed acquisition on the basis of the draft decision submitted by the relevant NCA and its own assessment.[197] The ECB may simply not oppose the acquisition or impose conditions to authorise the acquisition of the proposed stake. Those conditions must relate, in any event, to the five elements of the assessment referred to above. **14.104**

It must be noted that, if the ECB does not expressly oppose before the deadline for the assessment contemplated under the applicable national law, the proposed acquisition will be deemed to have been approved.[198] Additionally, to prevent any supervisory preference towards one or another proposed acquirer, the ECB (and the NCA, accordingly) is expected to treat them in a non-discriminatory manner,[199] which eventually means that the ECB should act in a *first come, first served* manner. **14.105**

The right to be heard of the potential acquirer must be respected,[200] which means that if the ECB intends to oppose the acquisition of the qualifying holding, it must be given the opportunity to opine on such an adversely affecting decision. **14.106**

Furthermore, and similarly to banking license decisions, the ECB may attach conditions and obligations to its decision not to oppose the acquisition of the **14.107**

194 See Section B.2. (*Vertical allocation? Examining the decentralised mode of implementing the specific supervisory tasks*) in Chapter 6.

195 Cf arts. 93–94 SSM Fr.

196 Noting that not in all cases is it intended (or possible) to appoint a member of the management board following the acquisition of a qualifying holding in a credit institution. If this is not envisaged, then there is no need to carry out such fit and proper assessment. Cf Section 5.2.3.1. (*Assessment of financial soundness*) of the ECB Guide on qualifying holding procedures.

197 Art. 86 SSM Fr.

198 Art. 21(6) CRD IV.

199 Art. 23(5) CRD IV.

200 Cf arts. 22 SSM R, 87 and 31 SSM Fr. See, also, Section A. (*Procedural safeguards: what rights and safeguards, and at what level?*) in Chapter 13.

qualifying holding.[201] The imposition of those conditions should trigger the right to be heard for the intended acquirer when they entail the application of a certain discretion by the ECB.[202]

14.108 Finally, in Stage 4 [*Notification of the decision on the intended acquisition*], pursuant to art. 88(1)(b) SSM Fr, the ECB is expected to notify to the concerned parties[203] its decision to oppose or not the proposed stake acquisition.

14.109 Furthermore, in accordance with indent (c) of paragraph 3 of the same provision, the ECB is also required to notify to the relevant NCA its decision on this matter. In both cases, such notifications are expected to be produced "*without undue delay*".[204]

3. Legal challenges and safeguards

(a) Some reflections on the safeguards applicable in the procedure for acquiring a qualifying holding in a credit institution

14.110 Although the purpose of this Section is to analyse the legal challenges and safeguards present in the procedure for the acquisition of qualifying holdings regardless of the circumstances, the framing of these have been shaped in recent times by the *Berlusconi case*. The factual grounds, legal considerations and issues (mainly concerned to judicial review) have been analysed above in this Part III, and reference is made to them.[205] The *Berlusconi case* has shown that the composite nature of qualifying holding procedures work in practice raises some practical legal question on the scope, nature and intensity of the review to be carried out by the ECB. But also, these procedures can (and actually raise) some other questions linked to the respect of due process rights. The procedural concerns include, among others, the need to motivate unfavourable decisions, the right to access to the relevant file and the right to be heard.

---

201 See Lo Schiavo, G. (2017).

202 See footnote 60.

203 See footnote 169.

204 An ECB decision deciding to oppose a potential acquisition may be challenged before the General Court under the annulment procedure. On reviewability of common procedures decision, see more extensively Section 2. (*Judicial review in composite procedures: the CJEU's Berlusconi-Fininvest case law in perspective*) and Section C. (*The annulment procedure: standing and reviewability*) in Chapter 12.
See also, on this topic, Buono, G. (2021).

205 See Section B. (*Judicial review in composite procedures: the CJEU's Berlusconi-Fininvest case law in perspective*) in Chapter 12.
On this topic, see also the following academic works: (i) Brito Bastos, F. (2021); (ii) Brito Bastos, F. (2019); (iii) Buono, G. (2021); and (iv) Dermine, P. and Eliantonio, M. (2019).

(i) As indicated previously, the *motivation* of a potentially unfavourable decision must be sufficient to understand the reasons backing such a decision.[206] However, it can be rather succinct.

In particular, the General Court held in *Berlusconi II* that the NCAs/ECB assessment of the proposed acquisition must be confined to the five requisites foreseen in art. 23(1)(a)–(e).[207] In that particular case, the applicants argued that the ECB did not assess the "*likely influence of the proposed acquirer on that credit institution*",[208] which they believed was an element to be included within the motivation of the ECB decision opposing the acquisition of the given qualifying holding. Against this argument, the General Court argued that the final ECB decision was not required to contain any motivation on the "*likely influence of the proposed acquirer on that credit institution*", as this was not a specific point of assessment foreseen in art. 23 CRD IV.[209]

In practical terms and within the realm of the ECB, the foregoing means that the motivation duty imposed on the ECB extends only to the specific points of assessment defined by CRD IV as applicable.[210] And this stands in good law, even if the concerned entity or person brings additional considerations, provided that those are outside the scope of the assessment elements.

(ii) The General Court also held in *Berlusconi II* that the *right to access to the relevant file*,[211] in principle, does not extend to the ECB and/or NCA internal documents nor the exchanges held between them.[212] This means that applicants will be systematically denied access to any draft decision preceding the final one or the one to which they are given access and provided time to provide comments[213] and which could be interesting for them to have if they want to challenge the final decision adopted.[214]

(iii) Concerning the *right to be heard*,[215] the General Court confirmed that the restricted deadline of three working days to formulate comments on the draft decision[216] may comply with the minimum standards of the right to be heard.

---

206 See previously in Section B.1.(c).(2). (*Legal challenges (and potential remedies)*) in this chapter.

207 See Section C.2. (*Key aspects of the process (step by step)*) above in this chapter.

208 Art. 23(1) CRD IV.

209 See *Berlusconi II* at Paras. 166–168. Despite being such reference contained in art. 23(1) CRD IV.

210 Which must be recalled is a maximum harmonisation rule in the particular case of qualifying holdings' assessments. See Bassani, G. (2019).

211 Art. 32 SSM Fr.

212 See *Berlusconi II* at Paras. 194.

213 Which would be the case when the ECB intends to adopt a decision opposing the acquisition of a qualifying holding. In those cases, the concerned applicant should have access to the draft decision containing the negative assessment and give the occasion to provide comments on that. The ECB should then take those comments into consideration when adopting the final decision on the qualifying holding.

214 Particularly when the different draft versions show diverging considerations or assessments. But even if they are not, they are valuable pieces of evidence capable of showing the confirmation of the progressive conformation of the ECB's will and, eventually, the comments and opinions of the relevant services involved in their elaboration, which may not be always in agreement.

215 Cf arts. 22(1) SSM R and 31 SSM Fr.

216 Art. 31(3)I SSM R sets forth that this deadline is, as a general rule, two weeks. However, for common procedures, such a deadline is shortened to three working days pursuant to art. 31(3)III SSM Fr.

Developing the arguments already put forward in *Ukrselhosprom*,[217] the General Court understood that the right of the intended acquirers to be heard can be adequately protected.[218] The court reached that conclusion on the basis of the three following arguments: *first*, it noted that intended acquirers can expose their favourable arguments as early as in the application that starts the procedure. *Second*, it noted that the intended acquirer must be given the opportunity to contest any objections put forward by the ECB before the adoption of the final decision. And *third*, the Court also outlined that in the event that the ECB intends to base its decision on factual and legal considerations on which the intended acquirer has not been given the opportunity to be heard, it can (or rather must) convey a meeting to provide the concerned party with an appropriate opportunity to be heard.

(b) Legal challenges (and potential remedies)

14.111 The procedure for assessing the acquisition of qualifying holdings in credit institutions presents some challenges of legal interpretation. For instance:

14.112 In Stage 1 [*Notification of the intention to acquire a qualifying holding*], process-wise and pursuant to art. 85(1) SSM Fr, the relevant NCA must notify to the ECB any request received within five working days of the acknowledgement of its receipt.

14.113 The referred provision does not indicate expressly whether the notification that the NCA must send to the ECB needs to include also the relevant documentation submitted by the requester.

14.114 Yet, later on, art. 85(2) SSM Fr indicates that:

> *2. The NCA shall notify the ECB if it has to suspend the assessment period due to a request for additional information. The NCA shall send any such additional information to the ECB within 5 working days following receipt thereof by the NCA.*

14.115 From the abovementioned provision, it can be inferred that the notification referred to in art. 85(1) SSM Fr must be accompanied by the relevant documentation submitted by the requester. This is due to the fact that mentioned art. 85(2) SSM Fr expressly foresees that the *additional information* must be sent to the ECB. Following the same reasoning, the initial *information* received with the application should be shared with the ECB as well.

217 General Court judgment in cases T-351/18 and T-584/18 (*Ukrselhosprom PCF LLC and Versobank AS v European Central Bank*) of 6 October 2021 (ECLI:EU:T:2021:669). Cf at Paras. 374. See, also, Section B.1.(c).(2). (*Legal challenges (and potential remedies)*) in this chapter above.

218 See Berlusconi II at Paras. 225–228.

Concerning Stage 2 [*NCA assessment of the intended acquisition of a qualifying holding*], another potential mismatch arises between the deadlines envisaged in art. 15(2) SSM R and art. 86(2) SSM Fr. Whereas art. 15(2) SSM R states that the ECB must be notified at least ten working days before the expiry of the relevant assessment period, art. 86(2) SSM Fr contemplates that such a period must be of fifteen working days. The mismatch is evident, and the SSM Supervisory Manual remains silent on this matter.[219] **14.116**

It must be recalled that the SSM Fr is a regulatory text that is supposed to develop the SSM R, i.e., it is based on art. 6(7) SSM R.[220] Thus, a development rule cannot contradict (at any point) the law on which it is based. It follows from this that the compulsory minimum deadline for the submission to the ECB of the relevant assessment is ten working days (before the expiry of the relevant assessment period). **14.117**

However, before concluding that the deadline in the SSM simply "trumps" that of the SSM Fr, as a hierarchically superior provision, we must assess whether such a contradiction exists and whether this may result in a detriment to any of the parties concerned. The deadline of fifteen days contemplated in the SSM Fr does not jeopardise any procedural rights of the concerned parties nor puts them in a worse situation than foreseen in the SSM R. On the contrary, it allows the ECB to have more time to examine the assessment submitted by the relevant NCA. **14.118**

Consequently, the deadline of fifteen days foreseen in art. 86(2) SSM Fr must be actually applied. The abovementioned contradiction is, hence, surmountable. **14.119**

Finally, another interpretative challenge can be found in Stage 3 [*ECB decision of the proposed acquisition of a qualifying holding*]. **14.120**

When looking at the assessment mechanism, like in the process for granting a banking license, the ECB is heavily reliant on the NCAs. NCAs are expected to provide a draft decision (to oppose or not the acquisition) and specialised guidance on the deadline to complete the procedure. **14.121**

219 See Section C.1.(b). of the Supervisory Manual.
220 Cf Recital 7 SSM Fr.

14.122 Yet, even if the ECB is expected to perform its own assessment, and the SSM Fr explicitly refers so, it may *only* be granted fifteen working days to do so (whereas the relevant NCA is granted way more time). In these circumstances and despite the ECB being the ultimate decision maker, the same concerns and issues that were expressed as regards the authorisation process can be brought here.[221]

221 See Section B.1.(c).(2). (*Legal challenges and safeguards*) in this chapter above.

15

SANCTIONING PROCEDURES

A. INTRODUCTION

This final chapter, which deals with sanctioning procedures, enjoys particular importance. Although all the procedures entail their own challenges and complexities, sanctioning proceedings tend to "raise the stakes" both doctrinally and practically. The success or failure of these will likely be used as a proxy for the success or failure of composite supervisory procedures in the Banking Union. The sanctioning procedures addressed here are both (i) sanctioning 15.001

procedures directly managed by the ECB in accordance with art. 18(1) and (7) SSM R and (ii) requests issued by the ECB to NCAs to open sanctioning procedures pursuant to art. 18(5) SSM R (and their interactions thereof).

15.002 The procedures regarding the imposition of periodic penalty payments, contemplated in Regulation 2532/1998 and further referred to in arts. 120(b) and 129 SSM Fr are not analysed herein.[1] This is because: (1) *first*, periodic penalty payments do not pursue a *punitive* aim but rather an *enforcement* one. Hence, they are treated differently from the rest of the administrative penalties;[2] and (2) *second*, the procedural regime to be followed with a view to impose periodic penalty payments is different from the one sketched for the rest of the administrative penalties.[3]

15.003 SSM sanctioning proceedings raise particularly serious legal issues. Those issues are linked to the legal interpretation of the relevant provisions but are also closely linked to the procedural safeguards enshrined in the SSM legal framework and in the Charter.

15.004 The procedural issues linked to legal safeguards are particularly serious, as a breach of the key due process rights may result in the annulment of a given

---

1 Even if the author is of the view that, due to its severity, these periodic penalty payments can be classified as criminal in nature sanctions. Cf Section C.1.(c). (*Periodic penalty payments*) in Chapter 8.

2 Against this approach, see D'Ambrosio, R. (2021) at pp. 320–321.

The author understands that periodic penalty payments have a dual nature, as enforcement measures (measures) or as sanctions, depending on the main aim they pursue (compelling or punitive). The author reaches that conclusion noting that art. 1(6) of Regulation 2532/1998 defines periodic penalty payments as enforcement measures or as sanctions. Subsequently, it notes that Regulation 2532/1998 prevails over the SSM R in the case of conflict.

Yet, it can be argued against this reasoning that: (i) Recital 9 of Regulation 2015/159 amending Regulation 2532/1998 seems to contemplate periodic penalty payments as a compelling mechanism to oblige entities to comply with ECB decisions or Regulations or to end ongoing infringements. Additionally, (ii) the SSM Fr contemplates periodic penalty payments as an enforcement instrument (cf art. 129 SSM Fr), and consequently, the procedure for imposing those is different to the one applicable to administrative pecuniary penalties and fines. The foregoing is not at odds with Regulation 2532/1998, which attributes periodic penalty payments a twofold nature (as fines and as enforcement measures). It is just that the SSM Fr has decided that these periodic penalty payments will be used as enforcement measures in the context of the SSM. Yet, the author has argued in this work that, due to its potential severity, periodic penalty payments should be classified as penalties being materially criminal (see Section C.1.(c). (*Periodic penalty payments*) in Chapter 8).

3 In this regard, art. 129 SSM Fr contemplates specific procedural rules applicable to periodic penalty payments. Additionally, Title 2 of Part X (*Administrative Penalties*) of the SSM Fr is titled as follows: "*Procedural rules for the imposition of* administrative penalties, other than periodic penalty payments, *on supervised entities in euro area member states*" (emphasis added). In the light of the foregoing, periodic penalty payments would be excluded from the general procedural rules depicted in the SSM Fr for administrative penalties. See, on this matter, Papathanassiou, C. (2022). Art. 18 Administrative penalties. In *European banking union: Brussels commentary* (pp. 264–277). Baden-Baden: Nomos [Papathanassiou, C. (2022)(ii)].

procedure and of the administrative penalties imposed. Furthermore, these types of issues, if not properly addressed, can put the entire model under pressure, in case it is concluded that it falls short of minimum safeguards at any point.[4]

This Section analyses the legal challenges arising from the sanctioning procedures indicated above, following that same order, i.e., (1) Section B focuses on ECB direct sanctioning procedures and (2) Section C deals with ECB requests addressed to NCAs to open sanctioning procedures. **15.005**

Both Sections follow the same sequence; *first,* each sanctioning procedure is broken down into several phases or stages, and each stage is analysed separately to favour a more granular analysis. Such an analysis comprises *first*, a targeted overview, *second*, the main legal challenges on interpretation and (due process) safeguards and, *third*, some conclusions to overcome those legal challenges. **15.006**

B. ECB DIRECT SANCTIONING POWERS: PROCEDURE FOR THE IMPOSITION OF ADMINISTRATIVE PECUNIARY PENALTIES AND FINES

Arts. 123 to 128 SSM Fr regulate the procedural rules applicable to administrative pecuniary penalties (art. 18(1) SSM R) and fines regarding breaches of ECB regulations or decisions (art. 18(7) SSM R). **15.007**

As regards the above-mentioned fines (art. 18(7) SSM R), it must be noted that arts. 4a to 4c were included in Regulation 2532/1998 by means of Council Regulation (EU) 2015/159 of 27 January 2015 to adapt the regime of ECB sanctions to the realities of the SSM R. In essence, arts. 4a–4c provide exceptions to the general regime on sanctions that the ECB may apply, mainly relating to minimum reserves and monetary obligations. They mirror (in a more succinct way) the basic stages and procedural guarantees contemplated under the SSM Fr.[5] **15.008**

---

4 On the acute safeguards issues that administrative penalties can raise in the context of the SSM (and particularly from the perspective of effective judicial protection), see, among others, D'Ambrosio, R. (2021); D'Ambrosio, R. (2013); Allegrezza, S. & Voordeckers, O. (2015); Wissink, L. (2021)(ii); Karagianni, A. M. (2022); van Bockel, B. (2017). The Single Supervisory Mechanism Regulation: Questions of *ne bis in idem* and implications for the further integration of the system of fundamental rights protection in the EU. *Maastricht Journal of European and Comparative Law*, *24*(2), pp. 194–216; Lasagni, G. (2019). *Banking Supervision and Criminal Investigation. Comparing the EU and the US experience.* Springer; and Felisatti, V. (2018).

5 On the interactions between Regulation 2532/1998 and the SSM Fr, see Allegrezza, S. & Voordeckers, O. (2015).

15.009 In addition, art. 121(2) SSM Fr states that the provisions established therein complement those foreseen in Regulation 2532/1998. This means that the procedural rules established in the SSM Fr (by definition, more detailed than the ones established in Regulation 2532/1998) should be applied unless they conflict with those established in the Regulation 2532/1998.[6] The basic procedural steps concerning administrative pecuniary penalties and fines are compared in Table 15.1.[7]

15.010 The procedure set forth in both SSM Fr and Regulation 2532/1998 provisions presents a series of interpretative challenges, which may also raise issues concerning procedural safeguards. From a systematic perspective, the overall procedure can be split into five stages:

i. An initial phase, which comprises the decision to initiate a sanctioning procedure against a supervised entity.
ii. A subsequent sanctioning investigatory phase.
iii. A third phase, which comprises the formulation of a *statement of objections* (SO) and the issuance of a first round of comments by the concerned entity.
iv. A fourth phase would entail the circulation of a draft sanctioning to the concerned entity and a new round of comments from its side.
v. Finally, the procedure itself terminates with the issuance of the final decision by the ECB and its notification.

6 Furthermore, art. 6(1) Regulation 2532/1998 (not modified by Regulation 2015/159) ultimately foresees that, in the case of conflict between the Regulation 2532/1998 and other Council Regulations attributing to the ECB the power to impose sanctions, the latter shall prevail.

So far, no conflicts between the procedural rules foreseen in arts. 4a to 4c of Regulation 2532/1998 and the SSM are spotted. However, in case the SSM Fr would be amended, leading to an evident conflict, the referred closure provision (art. 6(1) of Regulation 2532/1998) could not be used to settle the controversy, as the SSM Fr is but an ECB Regulation and not a Council Regulation. The conflict should be then resolved by applying primarily the rules contemplated in the Regulation 2532/1998 complemented with the SSM Fr provisions.

7 Parts highlighted in grey correspond to elements on which the SSM Fr would complement the procedural rules foreseen in Regulation 2532/1998.

Table 15.1 Comparison of basic procedural steps concerning administrative pecuniary penalties and fines

–	Administrative pernalties (SSM Fr)	Fines (Regulation 2532/1998)
Investigation of suspected breaches	Art. 125: *1. For the purpose of investigating alleged breaches as referred to in Article 124, the investigating unit may exercise the powers granted to the ECB under the SSM Regulation.*	Art. 4b(2): *Where the ECB, in carrying out its tasks under Regulation (EU) No 1024/2013, considers that there is reason to suspect that one or more breaches of an ECB regulation or decision as referred to in Article 18(7) of Regulation (EU) No 1024/2013 are being or have been committed (...) the ECB shall exercise the relevant investigations in accordance with the following provision.*
–	*2. Where a request is made to the supervised entity concerned under the powers granted to the ECB pursuant to the SSM Regulation in the context of an investigation, the investigating unit shall specify the subject matter and the purpose of the investigation.*	–
	3. When carrying out its tasks, the investigating unit shall have access to all documents and information gathered by the ECB and, where appropriate, by the relevant NCAs in the course of their supervisory activities.	–
Notification of the Statement of Objections	Art. 126(1): *On completion of an investigation and before a proposal for a complete draft decision is prepared and submitted to the Supervisory Board, the investigating unit shall notify the supervised entity concerned in writing of the findings under the investigation carried out and of any objections raised thereto.*	Art. 4b(3)I: *On completion of an investigation and before a proposal for a complete draft decision is prepared and submitted to the Supervisory Board, the ECB, in its capacity to investigate breaches in the field of supervision, shall notify the undertaking concerned in writing of the findings under the investigation carried out and of any objections raised thereto.*

–	Administrative pernalties (SSM Fr)	Fines (Regulation 2532/1998)
Submission of observations by the concerned entity	Art. 126(2): *2. In the notification referred to in paragraph 1, the investigating unit shall inform the supervised entity concerned of its right to make submissions in writing to the investigating unit on the factual results and the objections raised against the entity as set out therein, including the individual provisions which have been allegedly infringed, and it shall set a reasonable time limit for receipt of such submissions. The ECB shall not be obliged to take into account written submissions received after the time limit set by the investigating unit has expired.*	Art. 4b(3)II: *In the notification referred to in the first subparagraph, the ECB, in its capacity to investigate breaches in the field of supervision, shall inform the undertaking concerned of its right to make submissions in writing to the ECB on the factual results and the objections raised against the entity as set out therein, including the individual provisions which have been allegedly infringed, and it shall set a reasonable time limit for making such submissions. The ECB shall not be obliged to take into account written submissions made after the time limit set by the ECB in its capacity to investigate breaches in the field of supervision has expired.*
(potential) Oral hearing	Art. 126(3): *3. The investigating unit may also, following notification in accordance with paragraph 1, invite the supervised entity concerned to attend an oral hearing. The parties subject to investigation may be represented and/or assisted by lawyers or other qualified persons at the hearing. Oral hearings shall not be held in public.*	Art. 4b(3)III: *The ECB, in its capacity to investigate breaches in the field of supervision may also, following notification in accordance with the first subparagraph, invite the undertaking concerned to attend an oral hearing. The parties subject to investigation may be represented and/or assisted by lawyers or other qualified persons at the hearing. Oral hearings shall not be held in public.*
Access to information	Art. 126(4): *The right of access to the file of the investigating unit by the supervised entity under investigation shall be determined in accordance with Article 32.**	Art. 4b(3)IV: *The right of access to the file by the undertaking concerned under investigation shall be guaranteed. It shall not extend to confidential information.*

–	Administrative pernalties (SSM Fr)	Fines (Regulation 2532/1998)
(Potential) Review by the ABoR	[Regulated extensively in (i) art. 24(5)-11 SSM R and (ii) in the Decision of the European Central Bank of 14 April 2014 concerning the establishment of an Administrative Board of Review and its Operating Rules (ECB/2014/16)].	Art. 4b(5): *5. The undertaking concerned shall have the right to request a review by the Administrative Board of Review of the decision taken by the Governing Council pursuant to paragraph 4, in accordance with the procedure laid down in Article 24 of Regulation (EU) No 1024/2013.*
Limitation periods	Art. 130(1)–(3): *1. The ECB's power to impose administrative penalties on supervised entities shall be subject to a limitation period of five years, which shall begin to run on the day on which the breach is committed. In the case of on-going or repeated breaches, the limitation period shall begin to run on the day on which the breach ceases.*	Art. 4(c)(2): *1. By way of derogation from Article 4, the right to take a decision to impose a sanction in case of a breach of an ECB decision or regulation relating to its supervisory tasks, shall expire five years after the infringement occurred or, in the case of a continued infringement, five years after the infringement ceased.*
–	*2. Any action taken by the ECB for the purposes of the investigation or proceedings in respect of a breach under Article 124 shall cause the limitation period for imposing administrative pecuniary penalties to be interrupted. The limitation period shall be interrupted with effect from the date on which the action is notified to the supervised entity concerned.*	*2. Any action taken by the ECB for the purposes of the investigation or proceedings with respect to an infringement shall cause the time limit laid down in paragraph 1 to be interrupted. The limitation period shall be interrupted with effect from the date on which the action is notified to the supervised entity concerned. Each interruption shall cause the time limit to recommence. However, the time limit shall not exceed a period of 10 years after the infringement occurred or, in the case of a continued infringement, 10 years after the infringement ceased.*

–	Administrative pernalties (SSM Fr)	Fines (Regulation 2532/1998)
–	*3. Each interruption shall cause the limitation period to begin to run afresh. However, the limitation period shall expire at the latest on the day on which a period equal to twice the duration of the limitation period has elapsed without the ECB having imposed an administrative penalty. That period shall be extended by any period of time for which the limitation period is suspended pursuant to paragraph 5.*	–
Suspension/extension of the limitation period	Art. 130(4)–(5): *4. The limitation period for imposing administrative penalties shall be suspended for any period during which the decision of the ECB's Governing Council is subject to review proceedings before the Administrative Board of Review or appeal proceedings before the Court of Justice.*	Art. 4(c): *3. The time limits described in the preceding paragraphs can be extended if:*
–	*5. The limitation period shall also be suspended for such period as criminal proceedings are pending against the supervised entity in connection with the same facts.*	*(a) a decision of the Governing Council is subject to review before the Administrative Board of Review or appeal proceedings before the Court of Justice of the European Union; or*
–	–	*(b) criminal proceedings are pending against the concerned undertaking in connection with the same facts. In such a case, the time limits described in the previous paragraphs shall be extended for the period of time it takes for the Administrative Board of Review or the Court of Justice to review the decision or until conclusion of the criminal proceedings against the concerned undertaking.*

Note: * Noting that art. 32 SSM Fr is way more detailed than the wording included in art. 4b(3)IV of Regulation 2532/1998.

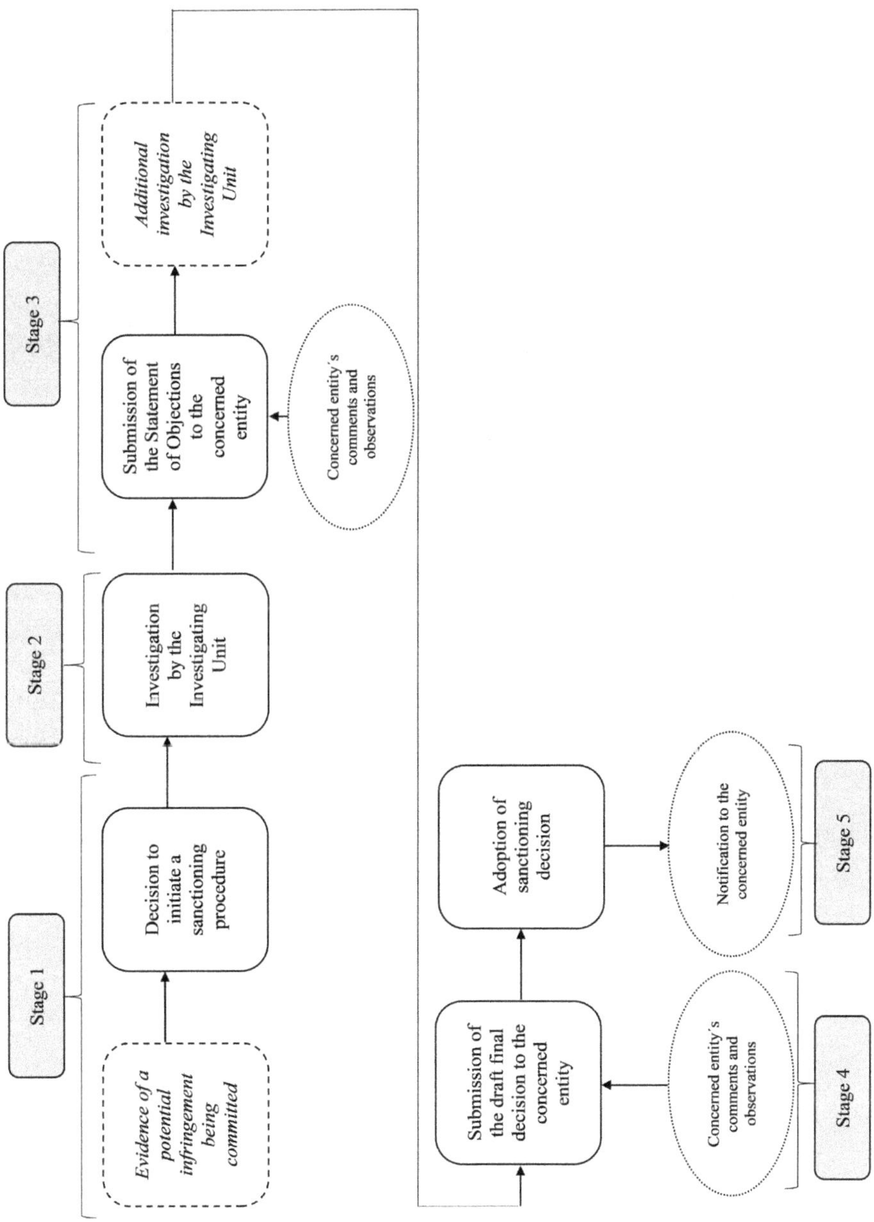

Figure 15.1 Sanctioning procedure

15.011 The whole sanctioning procedure is presented in an oversimplified diagram Figure 15.1.

15.012 Also, with a view to offer a systematic approach, the following Sections: *first*, describe how the process is meant to work, in accordance with the provision enshrined in the SSM Fr[8] (and the SSM R); *second*, analyse the tensions and challenges relating to such stages of the process, trying to find ways to overcome them whenever possible.[9]

1. Stage 1: reporting of potential breaches and the decision to initiate a sanctioning procedure

(a) Key aspects of stage 1

15.013 The ECB can become aware of potential breaches through different channels.[10] For example:

(i) When carrying out the micro-prudential tasks it has been allocated under the SSM R.[11] The foregoing applies to a wide variety of situations; for instance, the ECB may become aware of those potential breaches not only when conducting on-site inspections (general or thematic ones) but also when engaging with the relevant entities in informal supervisory dialogues, or even when examining the consistency of the periodical reporting those entities are obliged to provide.
(ii) Through the breach reporting mechanism.[12]
(iii) Through reporting by NCAs, i.e., bank supervisors or even other national authorities, e.g., securities markets authorities, which may spot potential irregularities when carrying out supervisory tasks outside the SSM remit and/or while acting as a primary point of contact.

15.014 Those potential breaches must be referred to the independent Investigating Unit,[13] which, based on a preliminary internal assessment, may decide to start a sanctioning proceeding.

---

8 And in Regulation 2532/1998, in parallel.

9 For an overview on the procedure, see Papathanassiou, C. (2022)(ii). See also, for an analytical overview on this matter, Gortsos, C. V. (2015)(ii).

10 See, for a more detailed overview on the ways the ECB may become aware of potential breaches, Karagianni, A. M. (2022) at pp. 71–89.

11 As it can be inferred from art. 124 SSM Fr.

12 Foreseen in arts. 23 SSM R and 36–38 SSM Fr. Breaches may be reported anonymously through the following platform settled by the ECB: https://whistleblowing.bankingsupervision.europa.eu/.

13 As a safeguard for the supervised entities, those officers cannot be directly or indirectly involved in the supervision of the entities they may investigate; neither have been directly or indirectly involved in their supervision for the two years immediately before taking up such a position (art. 123(2) SSM Fr).

(b) Legal challenges and safeguards

(i) Some reflections on the relevant safeguards: independence of the Investigating Unit (and investigating officers) in a hierarchical organisation

One of the most relevant aspects (if not the most) coming into play at this stage relates to the independence[14] of the body in charge of investigating the alleged infringement and proposing its sanction: the Investigating Unit.[15] **15.015**

Pursuant to art. 123 SSM Fr, the Investigating Unit is an "*internal independent*" body composed of investigating officers. In order to implement a practical separation between the supervisory overview and the investigatory/sanctioning powers allocated to the ECB, art. 123 SSM Fr builds upon the idea of attributing investigatory powers to an independent Investigating Unit.[16] **15.016**

To avoid any bias and to ensure operational separation of supervisory and sanctioning tasks, those officers are not involved in the execution of the specific micro-prudential supervisory tasks vested on the ECB.[17] Additionally, they cannot be involved in any investigating file relating to entities which they have supervised, directly or indirectly, in the two years preceding their appointment as investigating officers. **15.017**

Furthermore, the whole sanctioning procedure contemplates the separation of the investigatory phase *per se* (conducted by the Investigating Unit) from the decision-making phase, which is entrusted to the Governing Council (upon proposal made by the Supervisory Board).[18] **15.018**

Art. 123(3) SSM Fr stipulates that the investigating officers "*shall perform their investigative functions independently of the Supervisory Board and Governing Council and shall not take part in the deliberations of the Supervisory Board and* **15.019**

---

14 To ensure adequate separation between the investigation and decision-making phases of materially criminal sanctioning procedures. See, in this regard, *Dubus S.A. c. France* (Application no. 5242/04) ECtHR judgment of 11 June 2009.

See further, in Section D.1. (*Sanctions having a criminal nature imposed by an administrative (not jurisdictional) body: right to a fair trial under the SSM R?*) in Chapter 8, the analysis of the practical outcome arising from this landmark case: lack of separation between instruction and the decision phases was not able to be cured by having the possibility of getting such a sanctioning decision reviewed by an appeal court. Additionally, see Allegrezza, S. & Voordeckers, O. (2015) at p. 157.

15 Cf art. 123(3) SSM Fr. See also Karagianni, A. M. (2022) at pp. 83–84 and 182–183.

16 Cf art. 123(3) SSM Fr. See further immediately below. See, also, Lackhoff, K. (2017)(i) at pp. 215–217.

17 See in more detail in Section B.2. (*Vertical allocation? Examining the decentralised mode of implementing the specific supervisory tasks*) in Chapter 6.

18 On the topic of the separation between the investigatory phase from the decision-making phase from the angle of the ECHR, see Bindi, E. & Pisaneschi, A. (2019). The Fair Trial as a Guarantee of the Administrative Procedure. In *Judicial Power in a Globalized World: Liber Amicorum Vincent De Gaetano* (pp. 47–62). Springer, Cham.

Governing Council". What, in conceptual terms, is easy to understand, in practical terms, may not be so easy to achieve, especially in a big hierarchical organisation.

15.020 As a starting point, the Investigating Unit would be located within the Enforcement & Sanction Division of the ECB. Thus, it would be incardinated within the corporate structure of the ECB (within the Directorate General SSM Governance & Operations). This entails its placement within a highly structured and hierarchical organisation.

15.021 In principle, the fact that the Investigating Unit is placed under a given Directorate General and a Division would not go against art. 123(1) SSM Fr, *provided* that it is granted independence to self-organise (to a certain extent) its tasks and duties.

15.022 The sense of *independence* would be met, in the view of the author, by the fact that the unit is differentiated from other units and performs specialised tasks relating to the investigation of potential breaches.[19]

15.023 The independence of investigating officers is more problematic, though. In principle, those officers, when carrying out their investigatory activities on a given file, should act independently and should not follow any instructions from the Supervisory Board and/or the Governing council.[20] Furthermore, they should not participate in the deliberations of those bodies.[21]

15.024 From this standpoint, the ECB needs to apply self-restraint to guarantee the necessary independence of the Investigating Unit. Investigating officers should not be contacted (nor pressured) by the Supervisory Board or the Governing Council to present (or not to present) a draft sanctioning a decision in a particular sense or to conduct the investigation in a particular way. Furthermore, the officers who participated in the investigation should not participate in the

19 Even if not performing, solely, those tasks but additional ones, for instance, providing specialised advice as regards bills submitted for the ECB assessment, carrying out internal and external formative activities and serving as a contact point for the referral of potential breaches (and to perform a preliminary assessment on the referrals received).

20 This does not prevent that investigating officers may be obliged to follow the instructions of their immediate hierarchy (e.g., head of unit or division). The foregoing may be even desirable (provided that the judgment of the officer is not completely erased by the one of its managers) with a view to ensure transparency and equal treatment among investigated subjects. In this regard, there would be a common point (a manager) at the top of the pyramid, capable of overseeing the whole investigatory and sanctioning action undertken by the investigating unit and, hence, ensuring that similar cases are treated similarly.

21 See Riso, A. L. (2014).

relevant deliberations concerning the approval or rejection of the sanctioning decision that they may present to the ECB governing bodies.

The requirement that the relevant investigating officers should not interact with the ECB governing bodies applies only with regards to the ongoing investigations in which they may be involved. This would not prevent the investigating officers from providing guidance and advice to those bodies as regards other matters that are not the sanctioning procedure they may be handling. **15.025**

Following a similar logic, these safeguards should not prevent the Supervisory Board from issuing guidance as regards the tasks entrusted to the Investigating Unit either[22] or asking the Investigating Unit to focus their activities as regards a specific type of breaches, in accordance with the ECB supervisory priorities. **15.026**

(ii) Legal challenges (and potential remedies)

This stage of the sanctioning procedure raises some specific legal challenges. These are explored immediately below. **15.027**

The first question that arises is *what breaches is the ECB obliged to pursue*: all of them (at least all that may detected or may be brought to its attention)? Does the ECB have discretion to decide which breaches should be pursued? **15.028**

It is unclear whether, following the SSM R and the SSM Fr, the ECB would be obliged to investigate and sanction each and every infringement of which it may become aware.[23] **15.029**

As a starting point, it must be noted that Paras. 1 and 7 of art. 18 SSM R indicate that the ECB "*may impose administrative pecuniary penalties* [or *sanctions*]". Thus, it follows that the ECB is entitled to impose those administrative penalties (but is not obliged to do so). Recital 36 of the SSM R further reinforces such a conclusion by stating that: **15.030**

> (…) *the ECB is entitled to impose fines or periodic penalty payments on undertakings for failure to comply with obligations under its regulations and decisions. Moreover,* (…), *the ECB should be empowered to impose pecuniary penalties on credit institutions, financial holding companies and mixed financial holding companies for breaches of such rules.* (Emphasis added).[24]

---

22 For example, a guidance note on the criteria to be considered to pursue an investigation with a view to impose administrative pecuniary penalties or fines. See below in this Section.

23 Noting that some national systems foresee that public authorities must prosecute all materially criminal administrative breaches they become aware of. See D'Ambrosio, R. (2021) at p. 318.

24 To be noted, also, that art. 19(1) SESCB uses a similar language and so makes available to the ECB the possibility to impose sanctions for breaches of the minimum reserves that credit institutions must retain (but does not constrain the ECB to impose a sanction anytime it detects an infringement).

15.031 The provisions of Regulation 2532/1998 are less explicit as regards the margin of discretion allocated to the ECB to impose the fines and periodic penalty payments for infringements pertaining to art. 18(7) SSM R. However, Recital 5 expressly refers that the mentioned Regulation must grant the ECB "*certain discretion, both in relation to the relevant procedures and to their implementation within the limits and conditions laid down in this Regulation*"[25] (emphasis added).

15.032 Nevertheless, art. 122 SSM Fr indicates that the ECB "*shall impose administrative penalties, as defined in Article 120(b), if there is a failure to comply with obligations under ECB regulations or decisions*". The foregoing may have two readings: (i) following a strict plain reading, each and every time there is a failure to comply with regulations, an administrative penalty should be imposed to the concerned entity. This interpretation is opposed to the strict reading of art. 18(1) SSM R, which allowed (but not obliged) the ECB to impose sanctions as regards detected breaches.

15.033 (ii) Instead, a finalistic interpretation would imply that the ECB *could* impose an administrative fine *provided that* a breach has happened (as regards those potential breaches that it discretionarily considered appropriate to pursue). In this regard, the ECB would enjoy discretion as regards what alleged infringements it decides to investigate and prosecute. Additionally, if the ECB came to the conviction that a breach has been committed (after the instruction of the relevant sanctioning procedure), it would still enjoy broad supervisory discretion to decide whether to sanction such infringement or not.

15.034 This second interpretation, which does not require the ECB to sanction each infringement it may detect or became aware of, seems to be more compatible with the SSM R, Regulation 2532/1998 and art. 132(3) TFEU[26] and should be therefore preferred. Three arguments can be provided to justify this conclusion:

15.035 *First*, as argued above, the SSM R (and the rest of the pieces of legislation referred to immediately above) support granting the ECB discretion so as to decide when to pursue potential infringements. They do not see to oblige the consolidated supervisor to punish any potential breach.

15.036 This approach is consistent with the case law of the CJEU as regards the ESAs' powers to investigate breaches of the Single Rulebook committed by NCAs. In

25 Cf art. 132(3) TFEU.

26 See immediately above.

the *SV Capital OÜ* saga,[27] the Court of Justice was asked to examine whether, pursuant to art. 17 of the EBA Regulation,[28] the EBA was obliged to initiate an investigation upon request from an individual (or from the privileged bodies referred to in art. 17(2) of the EBA Regulation). Even if the Court dismissed the appeal filed, finding it inadmissible, it nevertheless indicated that: "*It follows from that provision that the EBA has a discretion as regards the initiation of investigations, both when it receives a request from one of the entities expressly mentioned in Article 17(2) of Regulation No 1093/2010 and when it acts on its own initiative*".[29] Consequently, the Court of Justice was convinced that the EBA (and the ESAs in general) should enjoy broad discretion as regards what breaches it may investigate, even in cases when it received specific request to investigate a particular case.[30] The same understanding can be extrapolated to the ECB, noting also that the verb "may" is used both in art. 17 of the EBA Regulation and in Paras. 1 and 7 of art. 18 SSM R to indicate such discretion.[31]

Second, the ECB (as any other prudential supervisor) must be granted latitude for deciding *which supervisory tool* to apply. In some cases, it may decide to resort to its supervisory powers, issuing a supervisory decision, or impose a periodic penalty payment with a view to compel the infringing entity to return **15.037**

---

27 See Court of Justice judgment in case C-577/15 P (*SV Capital OÜ v EBA*) of 14 December 2016 (ECLI:EU:C:2016:947) and General Court judgment in case T-660/14 (*SV Capital OÜ v EBA*) of 9 September 2015 (ECLI:EU:T:2015:608).

28 Which, at the time the action was filled, read as follows:

"*2. Upon a request from one or more competent authorities, the European Parliament, the Council, the Commission or the Securities and Markets Stakeholder Group, or on its own initiative, and after having informed the competent authority concerned, the Authority* may investigate *the alleged breach or non-application of Union law*".

It must be outlined that the wording of this provision looks quite similar to the one foreseen in Paras. 1 and 7 of art. 18 SSM R.

Art 17(2) of the EBA Regulation was nevertheless modified by Regulation (EU) 2019/2175 of the European Parliament and of the Council of 18 December 2019 (…). The foregoing regulation supressed the reference made to "*may investigate*" and added that the EBA "*shall outline how it intends to proceed with the case and, where appropriate, investigate the alleged breach or non-application of Union law*".

29 Court of Justice judgment in case C-577/15 P (*SV Capital OÜ v EBA*) of 14 December 2016 (ECLI:EU:C:2016:947). At Para. 47.

30 The Board of Appeal of the ESAS maintains the same approach, building upon the mentioned *SV Capital OÜ* saga. See Board of Appeal decisions (i) BoA-D-2022-01 of 21 July 2022 (BoA-D-2022-01 (Decision – Appeal C against EBA)_FINAL.pdf (europa.eu)); (ii) D 2021 02 of 12 March 2021 (boa_d_2021_02 _decision_on_a_v_esma.pdf (europa.eu)); and (iii) BoA D 2018 02 of 10 September 2018 (Appeal by SV Capital OÜ against European Banking Authority decision (europa.eu)).

31 Ibidem footnote 27. Noting that the content of art. 17 of the EBA Regulation is identical to art. 17 of Regulation 1095/2010 (ESMA regulation), for a dedicated analysis of these provisions, see Gortsos, C. V. (2016). The Powers of the ESMA in Case of Breach of European Union Law: The Particular Case of Breaching the "Non Bis in Idem" Principle. Forthcoming, Journal of Financial Law (2017), Nomiki Bibliothiki, Athens. Available at SSRN: https://ssrn.com/abstract=2890444.

to the path of compliance, or also maybe decide to initiate a sanctioning proceeding (or a combination of the three thereof). In other cases, and if the ECB judges it appropriate, it may simply refrain from acting (at least immediately), exchanging with the concerned entity on this topic, giving it additional time to return to the path of compliance.[32] In this vein, the ECB supervisory discretion would be curtailed if the ECB had to necessarily sanction any breach falling under its remit.

15.038 *Finally*, it must be noted that, in practice, it would be impossible for the ECB to sanction each and every potential infringement of which it may become aware (at least with the human resources allocated to the ECB for the time being). As a logical conclusion and in order not to render an allocated supervisory competence impossible to perform, it can be concluded that the ECB must enjoy sufficient supervisory discretion when deciding which potential breaches to sanction.[33]

15.039 Another thorny matter is the *lack of available criteria determining thresholds for the initiation of sanctioning procedures.*

15.040 The SSM R and the SSM Fr remain silent as per the criteria that may result in the beginning of a sanctioning procedure. However, when assessing the need or opportunity to start a sanctioning procedure, as regards any referral received, the Investigation Unit may consider (i) the potential gravity of the alleged breach,[34] (ii) the risks such a breach may entail to the stability of the financial market as a whole, (iii) the reputational risk it may imply for the SSM, (iv) the supervisory priorities settled by the ECB for the year at stake and (iv) overall, the aggravating/mitigating circumstances foreseen in art. 70 of CRD IV.

---

32 This may happen when the ECB carries out the SREP. In this process, the ECB is well-placed to judge whether some breaches have potentially occurred (or continue occurring), which of those infringements are relevant and whether these breaches can be cured by alerting the concerned entity of the detected deviations and giving it some time to comply with the applicable rules (or even when the imposition of sanctions could be counterproductive). As the SREP follows a rather "relational" approach, these types of issues and exchanges between the supervised entity and the ECB may occur. On the SREP process and its relational dimension, see Lamandini, M., D'Ambrosio, R. & Ramos Muñoz, D. (2022). See also above in Section B.2.(d).(1). (*Some reflections on the safeguards applicable in the procedure for lapsing and withdrawing banking licenses*) in Chapter 14.

33 A different angle, related to this matter, would refer to which potential breaches must be referred to the Investigating Unit. In principle, JSTs, ECB business units or even NCAs would need to refer any potential breach of which they became aware to the Investigating Unit. It will be, then, for the investigating unit to determine which of those potential breaches must be pursued.

34 Cf art. 70(a) CRD IV.

So far, the ECB has not made available any public guidance on the elements and circumstances that may be taken into account as regards the initiation of a sanctioning procedure, including potential thresholds that may trigger the sanctioning action as regard breaches that do not entail the assessing subjective circumstances.[35] **15.041**

Purely internal criteria may have been set up. In fact, such a step would be even advisable to provide guidance to the officers serving at the Investigating Unit, in order to facilitate their tasks, and to provide for further alignment and equal treatment among the supervised entities. However, making such criteria public could have negative consequences; i.e., it could provide entities with a "roadmap for unlawfulness", as they could decide to breach prudential rules, but only up to the limits that would eventually trigger the ECB sanctioning action. In addition, should that be the case, entities sanctioned as regards breaches not reaching the threshold foreseen in that theoretical guidance could feel tempted to allege that they are being mistreated in comparison to other entities,[36] and an additional motivational effort would need to be deployed by the ECB, justifying the need to initiate such sanctioning proceedings (and the ultimate imposition of administrative penalties). **15.042**

2. Stage 2: investigatory phase: research conducted by the Investigating Unit

(a) Key aspects of stage 2

To investigate the alleged breaches, the Investigating Unit (i.e., the investigating officers) is vested with the investigatory powers contemplated in the SSM R.[37] Those include, among others:[38] **15.043**

35 For example, overcoming the thresholds established for large exposures (art. 395 CRR), the purchase of one's own shares (or similar CET 1 instruments) without requesting prior authorisation when applicable, etc.

36 Noting that the CJEU seems to display a loose standard of review as regards potential violations of the principle of equal treatment. See Section B.2.(d).(1). (*Some reflections on the safeguards applicable in the procedure for lapsing and withdrawing banking licenses*) in Chapter 14.

37 Art. 125(1) SSM Fr. Those investigatory powers are regulated specifically in arts. 10–13 SSM R.
In addition, it must be noted that whenever the Investigating Unit makes use of the investigatory powers, in the course of any investigation, it must indicate the subject matter and the purpose of the investigation to the addressee of the request (art. 125(2) SSM Fr). See, in this regard, Papathanassiou, C. (2022)(ii).

38 See more generally in Section B.4. (*Supervisory and investigatory powers to exercise those tasks*) in Chapter 6. On this topic, see also Wissink, L. (2021)(ii) at pp. 198–204.

(i) The power to request to the relevant supervisory entity[39] to provide relevant information (and not only certain documents).[40]
(ii) Examine the books and records of the concerned entity and conduct interviews.[41]
(iii) Perform on-site inspections.[42]

15.044 As a necessary complement to the foregoing investigatory powers, the investigating officers may have access to any information and document available to the ECB and the relevant NCAs.[43]

15.045 On the basis of the investigation conducted (or at any stage after a referral to investigate a potential breach takes place), the investigating officers in charge of the investigation may decide to:

(a) continue the sanctioning procedure;[44]
(b) further investigate (or repurpose the scope of the investigation);
(c) initiate an enforcement procedure with a view to compel the investigated entity to comply with regulatory requirements;[45] or
(d) closure the sanctioning proceeding.[46]

15.046 The basic decision scheme is presented in Figure 15.2.

39 And/or to the persons referred to in art. 10(1) SSM R.

40 Art. 10 SSM R.

41 Art. 11(1) SSM R.

42 Art. 12 SSM R.

43 Art. 125(3) SSM Fr.

44 The continuation on the sanctioning procedure should not preclude that it could be closed if, at any time during the subsequent phases (e.g., hearing phase), there is enough evidence showing that the alleged breaches were not committed (or that the potential breach, as such, can no longer be punished (e.g., due to its prescription)).

45 In the case of ongoing breaches (to the extent that ongoing infringements are detected and proved). In principle, enforcement procedures (aiming at imposing a pecuniary penalty payment) would be compatible with the imposition of administrative pecuniary penalties and fines (and even with pure supervisory measures) due to the different aim pursued by those proceedings (enforcement vs. punitive purpose). Another question is whether strategically, it is preferred to compel the infringing institution to comply with a prudential requirement through a periodic penalty payment and, in case it does not comply within the maximum given deadline (6 months), to initiate a sanctioning procedure, in parallel (or not) with a procedure to impose additional supervisory measures. See Court of Justice judgment in joined cases C-217/15 and C-350/15 (*Orsi Baldetti*) of 5 April 2017 (ECLI:EU:C:2017:264), at Paras. 22–23. See also Felisatti, V. (2018) at pp. 400 and 402.

46 In those cases, the Investigating Unit should further justify, in an internal note, its decision with a view to (a) be able to produce evidence of its decision (and of the grounds motivating it) and (b) keep the Supervisory Board informed (and also to eventually share or distribute those data among the relevant services of the NCAs).

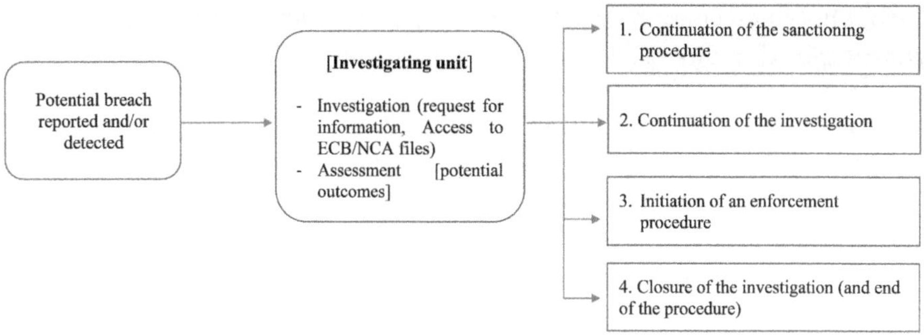

Figure 15.2 *Investigating unit workflow and outcomes following a potential breach*

(b) Legal challenges and safeguards: conflicts between requests for information and fundamental rights and other safeguards

This stage of the sanctioning procedure raises a number of due process concerns caused by the existing tensions between the investigations carried out by the investigating officers, and the procedural rights enjoyed by the concerned entities and their staff and representatives. **15.047**

As it will be analysed below, such tensions relate mainly to the privilege against self-incrimination, the right to remain silent, professional secrecy and the attorney-client privilege.[47] **15.048**

(i) The privilege against self-incrimination in sanctioning procedures handled directly by the ECB

This topic has deserved quite some academic attention[48] and will continue to receive more as SSM case law continues to be developed by the CJEU. **15.049**

As a matter of introduction, it must be recalled that within arts. 47 and 48, which regulate the right to a fair trial and the presumption of innocence,[49] also lays the right to remain silent or not to incriminate oneself. Such a right, **15.050**

47 On this topic, from a SSM perspective, see Allegrezza, S. & Voordeckers, O. (2015) at p. 154. See, also, Segoin, D. (2021). Chapter 17. The investigatory powers, including on-site inspections, of the ECB, and their judicial control. In *Judicial Review in the European Banking Union* (pp. 285–303). Edward Elgar Publishing.

48 See among many others: Eckes, C. & D'Ambrosio, R. (2020) at pp. 8–10. Lamandini, M., Ramos, D. & Solana, J. (2016); Lasagni, G. (2019); Lasagni, G. (2020). Investigatory, supervisory and sanctioning powers within the SSM. In *The enforcement dimension of the single supervisory mechanism* (pp. 49–91). CEDAM. At. pp. 87 and ss; Lamandini, M., Ramos Muñoz, D. & Solana, J. (2016) at pp. 242–246.

49 See Section A.1. (*What rights and procedural guarantees (due process rights)?*) in Chapter 13 above. See, also, the foregoing Section for an analysis on the applicability of the rights consecrated in the Charter to SSM procedures (including sanctioning procedures).

even if not foreseen expressly in the Charter, is a common standard across EU constitutional traditions.[50]

15.051 As a starting point, reference must be made to the case law preceding the recent landmark case *DB v. Consob*.[51] Until the issuance of the *DB v Consob* ruling, the Court of Justice had systematically maintained (particularly in competition cases) that a given investigated undertaking could not be forced to provide answers "*which might involve an admission on its part of the existence of an infringement which it is incumbent upon the Commission to prove*".[52] In the *DB v Consob* ruling, the CJEU[53] stated at least three key elements to understand the right not to incriminate oneself[54] or the right to remain silent.

15.052 *First*, the Court of Justice expressly admitted that arts. 47 and 48 of the Charter do enshrine the right of natural persons to remain silent within proceedings that are criminal in nature.[55] To reach that conclusion, the Court emphasised that the rights foreseen in the Charter must be consistently interpreted with the rights contemplated in the ECHR,[56] in particular with art. 6 therein, as interpreted by the ECtHR.[57] Building upon such ECtHR case law,[58] the Court of Justice concluded that the right to remain silent (and not to produce or deliver incriminatory evidence) in proceedings having a *coloration pénale* is a necessary guarantee enshrined in the right to a fair trial that must be respected.[59]

---

50 See della Cananea, G. (2022). Common Constitutional Traditions Taken Seriously: The Right to Remain Silent in Administrative Procedures. *Italian J. Pub. L.*, *14*, pp. 275–288.

51 Court of Justice judgment in case C-481/19 (*DB v Consob*) of 2 February 2021 (ECLI:EU:C:2021:84) (*DB v Consob*).

52 Court of Justice judgment in case 374/87 (*Orkem v Commission*) of 18 October 1989 (ECLI:EU:C:1989:387). At Paras. 35. See also Court of Justice judgment in case C-301/04 P (*Commission v SGL Carbon et al.*) of 29 June 2006 (ECLI:EU:C:2006:432). At para. 402.

It must be noted that relevant CJEU case law relating to the right to remain silent has been issued before the adoption of the Charter (by means of the Treaty of Lisbon).

53 Acting in Grand Chamber formation.

54 On the material scope of the right to remain silent within ECB sanctioning procedures, see Karagianni, A. M. at p. 205 and ss.

55 *DB v Consob* at Para. 45.

56 See Veenbrink, M. (2021). The Freedom from Self-Incrimination – A Strasbourg-Proof Approach? Cases C-466/19 P Qualcomm and C-481/19 P DB v Consob. *Journal of European Competition Law & Practice*, *12*(10), pp. 750–752. At p. 751.

57 *Ibidem* at Paras. 37–43.

58 For instance, ECtHR judgments, *John Murray v. the United Kingdom* (Application no. 18731/91) and *Saunders v. the United Kingdom* (Application no. 19187/91), and further case law cited in Paras. 39–43 therein.

59 It is to be noted that the Court of Justice seems to depart from its initial reasoning settled in its judgment in case 374/87 (*Orkem v Commission*) of 18 October 1989 (ECLI:EU:C:1989:387). Here, the Court of Justice indicated that art. 6 ECHR did not contemplate the right not to give evidence against oneself. Cf *Orkem v Commission* at Paras. 27–31.

Second, the Court of Justice concluded that national and EU authorities must respect the right to remain silent not only *within* administrative (sanctioning) proceedings which are criminal in nature but also in administrative (supervisory) proceedings, if the evidence or information gathered in such proceedings may be used subsequently (or parallelly) to determine the criminal liability of that person.[60] To that end, the Court of Justice indicated that: "*[T]he right to silence cannot reasonably be confined to statements of admission of wrongdoing or to remarks which directly incriminate the person questioned, but rather also covers information on questions of fact which may subsequently be used in support of the prosecution and may thus have a bearing on the conviction or the penalty imposed on that person*".[61] In the light of the foregoing, the relevant authority cannot impose any sanction on the investigated subject due to its failure to provide evidence and information or produce oral statements that may incriminate itself.[62] **15.053**

The Court recalls, nevertheless, that the right to remain silent "*cannot justify every failure to cooperate with the competent authorities, such as a refusal to appear at a hearing planned by those authorities or delaying tactics designed to postpone it*".[63] **15.054**

Third, the Court made a clear distinction as regards legal persons; the doctrine devised above would not be applicable to them.[64] Such distinction can be traced back to *Orkem v Commission*.[65] Actually, the majority of legal traditions and jurisdiction do not confer to legal persons the right to silence, as it would be considered a *personal* right.[66] **15.055**

The Court then concluded that its doctrine, settled as regards competition cases, involving solely legal person, stands in good law.[67] Thus, it recalled that *undertakings* may be compelled "*to provide all necessary information concerning such facts as may be known to it and to disclose, if necessary, such documents relating thereto as are in its possession, even if the latter may be used to establish, inter* **15.056**

60 Understood as liability within an administrative proceeding, which is criminal in nature.

61 *DB v Consob* at Para. 40.

62 AG Pikamäe's opinion, delivered on 27 October 2020 (ECLI:EU:C:2020:861), seems to have been followed by the Court. For an interesting analysis of this opinion, see Sakellaraki, A. (2021). Halcyon Days for the Right to Silence: AG Pikamäe's Opinion in Case DB v. Consob. *European Papers – A Journal on Law and Integration, 2020*(3), pp. 1543–1554.

63 *Ibidem* at Para. 41.

64 *DB v Consob* at Paras. 46–48.

65 See footnote 59 (at Para. 29).

66 This would be the case in, among other countries, the US and the UK. See Lamandini, M., Ramos, D. & Solana, J. (2016) at pp. 242–243.

67 *DB v Consob* at Para. 46.

alia in its regard, the existence of anti-competitive conduct [or infringements in general]".[68] The limit to this (and, in general, the *core* of the right to silence applicable to legal persons) is circumscribed to the fact that "*undertaking cannot be compelled to provide answers which might involve an admission on its part of the existence of such an infringement*".[69]

15.057 The application of the CJEU case law to the ECB direct sanctioning proceedings implies that, in principle, investigated entities should provide the Investigating Unit with any information, document or clarification they may request. The only limit to the foregoing being that they could not be compelled to acknowledge (even indirectly) the commission of the wrongdoing they are being investigated for. The same limit would apply to supervisory proceedings where the entity is requested to hand in certain information or documentation.

15.058 Two further questions arise in connection with the above: (i) what would happen if the investigated entity refused to provide the information or documents requested,[70] and (ii) to what extent would the investigated entity have a duty to produce new documents or pieces of evidence upon request from the investigating officers?

15.059 As per the first question, one potential outcome can be foreseen.[71] Within the sanctioning proceedings instructed by the ECB, such lack of cooperation may be considered as an element that may aggravate or mitigate the amount of the administrative pecuniary penalty or fines to be finally imposed on the investigated entity. Such an avenue is expressly contemplated in art. 69(f) CRD

---

68 *Ibidem.*

69 *Ibidem* at Para. 47.

70 On the understanding that they have such documents or pieces of evidence.

71 If such lack of cooperation happens in the course of a supervisory proceeding, the possibilities are more diverse. *First,* if it is a procedure initiated by the relevant entity (and in their interest), for example, a request for certain authorisation in the meaning of art. 4(1)(a) SSM R, failing to submit the requested document may entail the termination of the procedure or the denegation of the authorisation so requested (if the information requested by the ECB is material for making up its final decision).

Second, lack of providing certain information or documentation (e.g., periodical reporting on large exposures) may entail the commission of a breach due to a failure to comply with a regulatory duty. Hence, the possibilities are fourfold: address such failure by resorting to supervisory powers, initiating an enforcement procedure with a view to impose a pecuniary penalty payment, initiating a sanctioning procedure or any combination thereof. Failure to provide information requested by means of an ECB supervisory decision may trigger the same consequences.

However, such consequences would not be triggered when the request is made through an operational act issued by the JSTs (or any of its members), or even informal request for info requested by ECB/NCA staff. In those cases, such potential lack of cooperation may be considered for the purpose of assessing the supervisory compliance of the relevant entity or its overall cooperation with the ECB in the course of an enforcement or sanctioning proceeding.

IV, and it is also referred to in the Guide for the calculation of administrative pecuniary penalties.[72]

As regards the second question, in *DB v Consob*, the Court of Justice held that the obligation to provide documents relates to documents which are in the *possession* of the investigated undertaking.[73] **15.060**

In this regard, as a general consideration in any matter affecting procedural fair trial rights, any limitation of such rights must be applied restrictively.[74] Thus, it seems fair to conclude that the right to silence should also cover the right not to produce new documents or re-engineer them, so as to comply with a request from the investigating officer. The foregoing on the understanding that the production of such evidence would contribute to incriminate the investigated entity. **15.061**

For the time being, the Court of Justice seems to have come to terms and aligned with the ECtHR doctrine. In this vein, the Court's restrictive doctrine settled in *Orkem* would only apply to legal entities, whereas a broader, more protective approach is taken as regards the right to remain silent concerning natural persons. Such alignment may not hold if the ECtHR expands its doctrine to legal entities. **15.062**

The foregoing may not be unthinkable, considering that the privilege against self-incrimination is understood as a procedural safeguard enshrined in the notion of fair trial and, as such, independent from the subjective nature of the investigated party (natural or legal persons). **15.063**

(ii) Limits to the information requested by the Investigating Unit II: reliance on national systems and fundamental rights' conflicts

Pursuant to art. 10(1)(e) SSM R, the ECB may request information (or interrogate) natural persons belonging to the investigated entity.[75] The SSM R **15.064**

---

72 See further below in Section B.4.(b).(1). (*Determination of the fines: Basis for the calculation of administrative pecuniary penalties*) in this chapter. See, also, on the topic of the Guide for the calculation of administrative pecuniary penalties, Fromage, D. (2021). The ECB's guide on pecuniary penalties in banking supervision: Increased transparency on its (still) limited powers. *EU Law Live, 2021, Weekend Edition no. 60.* Hal-03696931.

73 *DB v Consob* at Para. 46. In the same vein, see *Orkem* at Para. 34.

74 See on this topic, more broadly connected to criminal matters, Bonelli, M., Eliantonio, M. & Gentile, G. (Eds.). (2022). *Article 47 of the EU Charter and Effective Judicial Protection, Volume 1: The Court of Justice's Perspective.* Bloomsbury Publishing; and Pagliacci, A. (2020). *Efficacia delle sanzioni nel settore bancario: criticità e spunti comparatistici.* LUISS: Doctoral dissertation.

75 It is to be noted that the SSM R use the term *belonging to* rather than *employed by*. The use of this term would imply that the ECB would be entitled to request information from staff employed by the investigated

and the SSM Fr do not contemplate, at least expressly, the consequences of the refusal to provide evidence by those persons, and this raises due process concerns.[76]

15.065 Due to the division of sanctioning competences[77] between NCAs and the ECB, the latter cannot directly punish in any way such natural persons for not complying with their requests for information. For purposes of compelling those persons to produce evidence, the ECB may rely on the relevant NCAs, which may act in accordance with their national law,[78] compelling the person requested to provide the evidence demanded.

15.066 The majority of jurisdictions contemplate penalties in the case of obstruction or lack of cooperation during criminal or sanctioning procedures.[79] However, it is not entirely clear whether such penalties or enforcement measures may be available in the case of lack of cooperation under a procedure that falls outside the national remit. A case-by-case analysis of the applicable legislation would need to be carried out to ascertain whether such compulsory measures would be available to the NCA to use at the request of the ECB.

15.067 Another angle to be carefully considered is the following: even if the ECB cannot itself sanction directly natural persons,[80] it can nevertheless instruct NCAs to open sanctioning procedures against natural belonging to a supervised entity regarding breaches of supervisory rules.[81]

15.068 As the declarations or information submitted by the requested natural persons (or lack of reply thereof) in the course of ECB investigations and/or direct sanctioning procedures may be used later on to establish their liability under a national procedure initiated by the NCA at the request of the ECB, the

---

entity but also from the senior managerial team (members of the board), theoretically including independent board members.

76 See, on this topic, Karagianni, A. M. (2022) at pp. 83–87 and 105–106.

77 See Section C. (*Allocation of sanctioning competences: a specialty over the general rule?*) in Chapter 6.

78 Cf arts. 10(2), 11(2) and 9(1)III SSM R. See also Karagianni, A. M. (2022) at pp. 87–88.

79 Lasagni, G. (2020) at p. 88.

80 See Section C. (*Allocation of sanctioning competences: a specialty over the general rule?*) in Chapter 6.

81 And this may happen, in principle, even if the ECB decides not to act against the relevant entity to which those natural persons (key function holders) belong to. This is due to the fact that the liability of the natural persons object of the request submitted by the ECB to the NCAs under art. 18(5) SSM R would be independent from the liability allocated to the supervisory entity itself. In this regard, it must be noted that art. 18(5) SSM R does not make possible to request NCAs to open a sanctioning procedure against natural persons dependent on the imposition of an administrative pecuniary penalty or fine upon such entity (and hence, upon its liability for the breach at stake being declared). See, further, in Section C. (*ECB requests addressed to NCAs to open sanctioning procedures under art. 18(5) SSM R*) of this chapter.

treatment of such requests to provide information (and the potential information gathered in this sense) proves to be problematic.

One thing to consider is that the sequence of steps to activate the request to initiate a sanctioning proceeding against natural persons under art. 18(5) SSM R is not entirely clear, and several options are possible.[82] These interactions deserve a separate discussion, which will be undertaken in Section C. (*ECB requests addressed to NCAs to open sanctioning procedures under art. 18(5) SSM R*) below in this chapter. **15.069**

However, building on relevant case law by the Court of Justice (*DB v Consob*) and the ECtHR,[83] any evidence obtained by means of a request of information under art. 10(1) SSM R in a sanctioning proceeding, in which it was not the investigated subject, should not be later on used to determine its liability. **15.070**

Additionally, it is to be considered whether the requested natural person may be entitled to remain silent or can be compelled by the relevant NCA to produce the evidence requested by the ECB. The foregoing requires *interpretation*, particularly in cases where the requested people are not formally investigated subjects, but they may have reasonable concerns that they will end up being investigated (and eventually sanctioned) by the NCA.[84] It seems to be more of a matter of national law (calibrated by the NCA concerned)[85] to distinguish **15.071**

82 Also, the latitude of leeway seems to be far from clear. See, in this regard, D'Ambrosio, R. (2021) at pp. 323–325.

In Section C.2. (*National laws and administrative pecuniary penalties II: to which extent national legislation may limit ECB direct sanctioning powers under art. 18(5) SSM R?*) in Chapter 7, the author has argued that the ECB competence is limited to requesting the relevant NCA to open a sanctioning procedure with a view to punish a given (potential) breach. The NCA hence would not be bound by such a request and would need to assess whether it is actually possible, pursuant to its domestic framework, to pursue and sanction such infringement. See in more detail in Section C.2.(a). (*Legal challenges: coordination between the ECB and NCAs*) below in this chapter.

83 In particular, its latest developments represented by the ECtHR judgment of 5 April 2012 (*Chambaz c. Suisse*), application 11663/04.

84 See Karagianni, A. M. (2022) at pp. 105 and ss. The foregoing author does not explore the same scenario portrayed herein but, rather, scenarios where the evidence gathered by the ECB in the course of investigatory or sanctioning procedures is later used by NCAs. These scenarios raise some concerns from the perspective of the validity of such information and its use in the domestic framework and also as regards the safeguards surrounding the obtention of such evidence. In particular, the author examines potential violations of the *ne bis in idem* principle, concluding that such procedural safeguards would not be at risk, taking into account the allocation of sanctioning tasks between the ECB and the NCAs under the SSM.

85 Ibidem at p. 105. As regards unlawfully obtained evidence, the cited author understands that the matter needs to be assessed through the lens of the domestic framework.

Additionally, the author brings up the case law produced in the *Prokuratuur* case (Court of Justice judgment in case C-746/18 (*Prokuratuur*) of 2 March 2021 (ECLI:EU:C:2021:152)), pursuant to which national courts enjoy discretion when deciding how (if) to treat unlawful evidence.

whether in such situations a restrictive approach must be taken, granting to such a person the benefit of the right to silence.

15.072 Finally, and to conclude, this reliance on national legal systems can generate diverging approaches, inconsistencies and gaps in the fair trial rights of the natural persons who are the addressees of an information request coming from the ECB (and which may be eventually subject to a sanctioning procedure handled by the relevant NCA on the grounds of the same or related facts to those investigated by the ECB). As the system is, in this specific aspect, reliant on domestic legal frameworks, such divergence cannot be avoided. At best, NCAs should be aware of such problems and, when the conflict arises, try to apply its domestic framework in the manner which ensures the greater playing field[86] across the SSM. In that regard, further guidance could be issued by the ECB[87] after discussion with the relevant NCAs.

(iii) Lawyers' advice and legal professional privilege

15.073 Another angle susceptible of presenting procedural frictions relates to the limits of the provision of information and the legal professional privilege.[88]

15.074 The SSM R provides that the request of information by the ECB from the persons (natural or legal) referred to in art. 10(1) SSM R: (i) would not be covered by the professional secrecy provisions and (ii) would not entail a breach of the professional secrecy obligations.[89]

15.075 The strict reading of that provision would entail the total abolition of any professional privilege. The matter is controversial, since professional secrecy duties are often regulated in national statutory law, for which MSs retain (at least) shared competences, and normally has strong constitutional implication. The matter itself would deserve a separate study.[90]

15.076 In this work and as regards this matter, only the legal professional privilege linked to it will be examined, in the context of investigations carried out by the Investigating Unit.

86 Which has been identified in Part I as one of the top principles guiding the application of the SSM R.

87 On the basis of art. 4(3) and Paras. 1 and 5(c) of art. 6 SSM R.

88 See, on this matter, Allegrezza, S. & Voordeckers, O. (2015) at p. 154. Additionally, see also De Bellis, M. (2021). Multi-level administration, inspections and fundamental rights: Is judicial protection full and effective? *German law journal*, *22*(3), pp. 416–440. At pp. 434–435.

89 Art. 10(2) SSM R.

90 See, for instance, the following work, which covers a wide variety of EU jurisdictions: The Bar of Brussels & Barreau de Bruxelles (Eds.). (2013). *Professional secrecy of lawyers in Europe*. Cambridge University Press.

Independent lawyers, registered and admitted to the practice to the national bar, enjoy a professional secrecy with a view to ensure that communications and information received and provided to their clients remains confidential. This constitutes one of the basic pillars of the legal profession, and it is widely protected (and disciplined) in all EU legal systems and beyond.[91] **15.077**

The Court of Justice and the General Court have confirmed the scope of the legal professional privilege in connection with (i) written communication with their clients;[92] (ii) internal memos produced by companies referring to external legal advice;[93] and (iii) documents furnished and/or created exclusively to allow external counsel to produce legal advice.[94] **15.078**

As regards in-house lawyers, in its heavily criticised judgment[95] *Akzo Nobel*,[96] the Court of Justice held that legal professional privilege would only apply to external legal counsels and not to internal (in-house) lawyers.[97] These would not enjoy the necessary independence that external lawyers have, and in the Court's view, they would not enjoy the legal professional secrecy (at least, as within concurrent investigations led by the Commission). **15.079**

Based on this, in-house legal advice pertaining to any of the entities referred to in art. 10(1)(a) to (d) SSM R would not be covered by the legal professional privilege. This would be compatible with the wording of art. 10(2) SSM R. However, the application of such provisions regarding external counsel proves to be problematic. A consistent interpretation with the CJEU case law demands **15.080**

---

91 *Ibidem.* Within the EU legal order, the professional privilege enjoyed by lawyers would be even supported by arts. 47–48 of the Charter.

92 Court of Justice judgment in case 155/79 (*AM&S v Commission) of 18 May 1982 (*ECLI:EU:C:1982:157*), Paras. 21–26.*

93 General Court judgment in case T-30/89 (*Hilti AG v Commission) of 12 December 1991 (ECLI:EU:T:1991:70), Paras. 78–131.*

94 Court of First Instance judgment in Joined Cases T-125/03 and T-253/03 (*Akzo Nobel Chemicals Ltd & Akcros Chemicals Ltd v Commission*) of 17 September 2007 (ECLI:EU:T:2007:287), paras. 123–134. To be noted that this judgment was appealed before the Court of Justice and confirmed in *Akzo Nobel.*

95 See, among others, Stefanelli, J. N. (2013). Expanding Akzo Nobel: in-house counsel, government lawyers, and independence. *International & Comparative Law Quarterly*, *62*(2), pp. 485–492. Also, to be noted, the sceptical position held by the *Conseil des barreaux européens* (CCBE). See CCBE (2005). The history of the CCBE. CCBE: Brussels.

96 Court of Justice judgment in case C-550/07 P (*Akzo Nobel Chemicals Ltd and Akcros Chemicals Ltd v European Commission*) of 14 September 2010 (ECLI:EU:C:2010:512) – *Akzo Nobel.* The doctrine settled therein has been further confirmed by the Court of Justice judgment in joined cases C422/11 P and C-423/11 P (*Prezes Urzędu Komunikacji Elektronicznej and Republic of Poland v Commission*) of 6 September 2012 (ECLI:EU:C:2012:553). The Court of Justice went even beyond than in Akzo Nobel, acknowledging that in-house lawyers were not entitled to represent the company they belong to before the Court, as they would lack the relevant independence.

97 *Ibidem* at Paras. 46–50.

construing art. 10(2) SSM R as referring exclusively to in-house lawyers. Thus, external lawyers assisting supervised entities (including as regards sanctioning proceedings) would be covered by the legal professional privilege, including as regards the communications addressed to (and from) their clients.[98] Any other interpretation risks colliding with the Court's doctrine, as it stands today.

15.081 Additionally, and following the same logic,[99] independent advisers or members of the board, being registered lawyers and not linked with the relevant entity by means of a labour contract, would remain outside the scope of art. 10(2) SSM R, and consequently, the legal advice provided by them would be covered by the legal professional privilege.

15.082 Finally, it must be emphasised that the doctrine settled by the Court of Justice in *Akzo* may suffer further adaptations or be complemented within the SSM R remit and even outside. In this regard, in the recent *Orde van Vlaamse Balies* case,[100] the CJEU confirmed the legal professional privilege as regards a Directive (*DAC 6*[101]), which required lawyers acting as intermediaries to notify any other intermediary (who is not her own client) of such intermediary's reporting obligations as regards potentially aggressive tax arrangements.[102] There, the Court rendered the relevant provision of DAC 6 conflicting with such privilege invalid.

3. Stage 3: issuance of the Statement of Objections and the first round of comments by the concerned entity

(a) Key aspects of stage 3

15.083 Art. 126 SSM Fr[103] regulates the (first) hearing in direct sanctioning procedures. Pursuant to the first paragraph of that provision before a complete draft sanctioning decision is dispatched to the Supervisory Board, the Investigating Unit must notify the entity under investigation of (i) the findings of the investigations carried out and (ii) the objections raised in connection with those findings. Such notification is meant to be done through a SO.

---

98 Which, in principle, would include written communications, upon-request memos or legal opinions and internal memos drafted by the supervised entity addressed exclusively to the external counsel.

99 In the absence of any specific ruling addressing the issue depicted in the previous Para., this argument is made building upon the case law cited in footnote 96.

100 Judgement of the Court of Justice in case C-694/20 (*Orde van Vlaamse Balies, IG, Belgian Association of Tax Lawyers*) of 8 December 2022 (ECLI:EU:C:2022:963).

101 Council Directive (EU) 2018/822 of 25 May 2018 amending Directive 2011/16/EU as regards mandatory automatic exchange of information in the field of taxation in relation to reportable cross-border arrangements.

102 Ibidem footnote 100 at Para. 66.

103 And art. 4b(3) of Regulation 2532/1998 as regards fines.

Art. 126(2) SSM Fr provides some hints about the minimum content of the SO. Based on this provision, as complemented by the procedural safeguards foreseen in Title 2 of the same Regulation, the SO should contain: 15.084

(i) The factual grounds upon which the observations addressed to the investigated entity are based and the evidence sustaining them.
(ii) The objections raised and the directly applicable provisions or the ECB decisions or regulations allegedly infringed.
(iii) The deadline provided for the submission of written submissions.[104]
(iv) The means by which the investigated entity may submit its written submission. Those would include, at least, the means referred to in art. 35(1) SSM Fr[105] and could be extended to the IMAS portal, if further functionalities are added.
(v) The possibility of accessing the file,[106] i.e., the documents incorporated to the file, with the exception of those (or those parts of the documents listed in the file) considered confidential.
(vi) Information on the limitation period and interruption of such limitation period.[107]
(vii) The regime on the publication as per art. 132 SSM Fr.[108]

Finally, following art. 126(3) SSM Fr, the Investigating Unit may invite the investigated entity to attend an oral hearing. Also, if the SO does not contain such invitation,[109] the investigated entity may request such an oral hearing to be held. 15.085

At the end of this stage, there are several potential outcomes; the investigating officers in charge of the investigation may decide to (a) continue the sanctioning procedure, (b) repurpose the scope of the investigation, then submitt a new SO or a complement to the previous one in case they understand that the facts investigated correspond to other (including additional) breaches, (c) request the relevant NCA to open a sanctioning proceeding in the light of the facts 15.086

104 See above, usually no less than two weeks following art. 31(3) SSM Fr. Such info may be presented also in a cover letter to the SO.

105 That is: "(…), *(b) by serving or delivering by hand a copy of the supervisory decision, (c) by registered mail with a form for acknowledgment, (d) by express courier service, (e) by telefax, or (f) electronically,* (…)". The oral notification foreseen in letter (a) of this provision is not practicable, for obvious reasons, as regards the SO.

106 Art. 126(4) SSM Fr.

107 Art. 132(2)–(5) SSM Fr.

108 This provision mirrors art. 68 CRD IV.

109 Or the ECB cover letter attaching such SOs and/or any other communication following the notification of the SO.

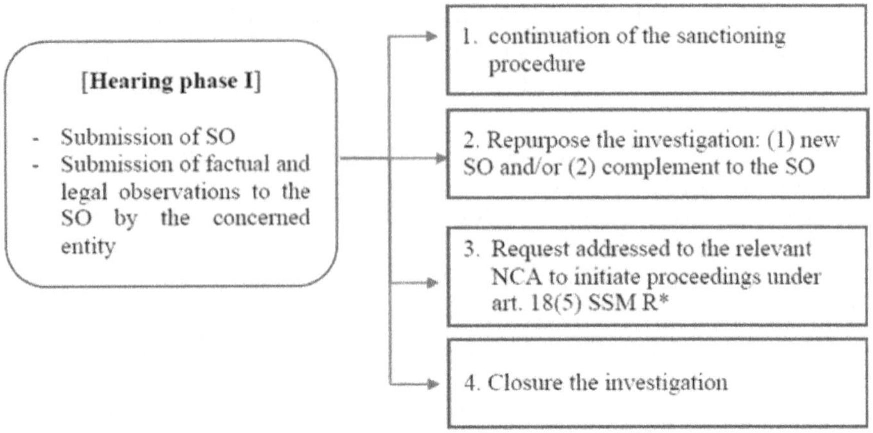

Note: * In parallel to the sanctioning proceeding handled by the ECB or repurposing the nature of the sanctioning proceeding (in the understanding that the ECB would not be competent under Paras. 1 and 7 of art. 18 SSM R to sanction the breach committed by the relevant entity

Figure 15.3 Hearing phase I: post-SO decision paths

investigated[110] or (d) decide to closure such a proceeding.[111] The basic scheme is presented in Figure 15.3.

(b) Legal challenges and safeguards

(i) Procedural safeguards: the subjective element of the infringement (intention and negligence)

15.088 Art. 18(1) SSM R requires that, in order to impose a fine, a given entity must have acted *intentionally or negligently*. Such a subjective element must be proved by the Investigating Unit. The legal interpretation that can be given to this subjective element, together with the need to prove its existence, can raise important legal issues,[112] which are analysed below:

---

110 In parallel to the sanctioning proceeding handled by the ECB or repurposing the nature of the sanctioning proceeding (in the understanding that the ECB would not be competent under Paras. 1 and 7 of art. 18 SSM R to sanction the breach committed by the relevant entity). See Section C. (*ECB requests addressed to NCAs to open sanctioning procedures under art. 18(5) SSM* R) in this chapter below.

111 In those cases, the Investigating Unit should further justify, in an internal note, its decision with a view to (a) be able to produce evidence of its decision (and of the grounds motivating it) and (b) keep the Supervisory Board informed (and also to eventually share or distribute those data among the relevant services of the NCAs).

112 Closely linked to this topic, there is another one connected: the assessment of the potential concurrence of offences.

When assessing the breaches presumably committed by the relevant entity, the investigating officer may realise that one specific conduct may lead, eventually, to more than one breach, that several sanctioning provisions seem to be applicable to the same breach, that the duration of the breach may be extended

First, it must be noted that the requirement of the *subjective* element is only expressly contemplated in the SSM R and not in the SSM Fr.[113] This requirement is also contemplated in the Guide for the calculation of administrative pecuniary penalties.[114] The referred Guide indicates to that end that either intention or negligence must be present in the action of the concerned entity so that it can be punished for any fault.[115] **15.089**

In this regard, it must be noted that art. 18(7) SSM R *and* Regulation 2532/1998, regulating the infringement of ECB decisions or regulations, do not contemplate that the entity that commits an infringement must act negligently or wilfully.[116] This creates an undesired mismatch; whereas for the infringements regulated in art. 18(1) SSM R a certain subjective element is needed, art. 18(7) SSM R does not expressly require such a subjective element to sanction breaches of ECB decisions or regulations. **15.090**

However, even if not expressly contemplated in art. 18(7) SSM R, such subjective requirement must apply to avoid an unjustifiably divergent treatment in the imposition of fines and administrative pecuniary penalties.[117] **15.091**

Additionally, requiring the ECB to prove the existence of a subjective element in the commission of a given infringement reinforces the procedural safeguards of the entities concerned, and thus, such an approach should be kept[118] also for the infringements set forth under art. 18(7) SSM R. **15.092**

---

over time or that successive breaches were committed but eventually should be treated as a single continuous infringement. Those situations are broadly referred to as a concurrence of offences or concurrence of breaches by doctrine and case law (See ECtHR judgments in *Chowdury and others v. Greece* (Application no. 21884/15) and *M. Özel and others v. Turkey* (Applications nos. 14350/05, 15245/05 and 16051/05). This topic would require a dedicated analysis that seems to exceed the limits of this Section and the objective, also. of this work.

113 Not even expressly in Regulation 2532/1998.

114 At Paras. 4 and 14.

115 Para. 14. On the subjective element required (intent or negligence), see Papathanassiou, C. (2022)(ii) at Para. 18.

The Court of Justice has also highlighted that the concept of negligence "(...) *entails an act or omission by which the party responsible breaches the duty of care which it should have discharged, and could have discharged, in view of its attributes, knowledge and abilities*" (see Court of Justice judgment in case C-47/07 P (*Masdar (UK) Ltd v Commission*) of 16 December 2008 (ECLI:EU:C:2008:726). At Para. 90 (and case law cited therein)).

Similarly and specifically as regards the SSM, the General Court built upon the same definition of negligence that has been indicated in the previous Para., see General Court judgment T-576/18 (*Crédit agricole SA v ECB*) of 8 July 2020 (ECLI:EU:T:2020:304). At Para. 80.

116 And hence any breach, disregarding the cause, may lead to the imposition of a fine.

117 Whose procedural rules applied practically equally. Cf art. 121(2) SSM Fr.

118 It is to be noted that this approach seems to have been chosen also by the ECB as in the Guide for the calculation of administrative pecuniary penalties; requiring the allegedly infringing entity to act negligently

15.093 *Second*, the standard to be applied by the ECB[119] to determine when an infringement has been committed negligently is not clear. Considering the complex regulatory environment in which credit institutions and the rest of the entities subject to the oversight of the ECB operate, the need for appropriate corporate structures to carry out their activities and their access to (presumed) first class legal advice, such standard of diligence must be extraordinarily high, equivalent to *exact diligence*.

15.094 This view is also supported by the General Court, which has insisted on the fact that credit institutions must apply an extraordinary degree of care when interpreting and applying regulatory provisions, not to incur in an infringement.[120] In a similar way, the Board of Appeal of the ESAs has concluded that, indeed, credit institutions are subject to a high standard care when carrying out its specialised and regulated business.[121] Yet, the Board of Appeal also hinted that when a regulatory provision presents "*interpretative difficult[ies]*",[122] an interpretation of such provision made logically and in good faith (even if favourable to the allegedly infringing entity), considering the particular circumstances, could not trigger the liability of the investigated entity (on the basis of negligence).[123]

(ii) Legal challenges (and potential remedies): some concerns on the (first) hearing

15.095 Reference will be made immediately below to some questions regarding the hearing phase contemplated in art. 126 SSM Fr. Those relate to: (i) the need to grant one or two hearing phases within the sanctioning proceeding; additionally, (ii) the language in which the hearing phase may be substantiated, in particular, regarding the submission of written statements and the conduct of the oral hearing:

---

or intentionally is equated for both fines and administrative pecuniary penalties (cf Para. 4 of the Guide for the calculation of administrative pecuniary penalties).

119 And ultimately by the CJEU itself.

120 See General Court judgment in case T-576/18 (*Crédit agricole v ECB*) of 8 July 2020, at Paras. 79–84.

121 See Board of Appeal decisions D 2019 01, D 2019 02, D 2019 03 and D 2019 04 of 27 February 2019 at Paras. 193, 281 and 322 (Appeal by SV Capital OÜ against European Banking Authority decision (europa .eu)).

122 Ibidem, at Para. 2.

123 Ibidem, at Paras. 2–5.

How many hearing phases need to be granted: one or two?

The SSM Fr expressly contemplates granting only one hearing phase[124] to the entity concerned. However, the case law available up to date[125] reveals that the ECB would be granting two hearings:[126] (i) one as regards the SO and (ii) another one on the draft sanctioning decision to be submitted to the Supervisory Board. **15.096**

In principle, it would appear that only the draft sanctioning decision (not the SO) would include a reference to the amount imposed as a fine or administrative pecuniary penalty. Yet, the Guide for the calculation of administrative pecuniary penalties does not give further indications as to whether such dual hearing is linked to the need to give the investigated entity an opportunity to provide submissions on the calculation of the penalties proposed. **15.097**

Leaving aside the ECB's practice (i.e., granting two hearings), the question is whether there are legal arguments to suggest whether the preferred number of hearings should be one or two. **15.098**

Option 1: Pursuant to this approach, the Investigating Unit would grant one single hearing, allowing the entity to submit its written observations on the SO. This approach would follow the strict wording of the SSM Fr. **15.099**

To carry out the analysis of this approach, one should be mindful that it is not clear whether the SO must include a determination of the amount of the penalty proposed. Art. 126 SSM Fr, as anticipated, does not state so. Furthermore, it seems difficult to conceive the determination of the amount of the penalty in the SO without the concerned entity being given the opportunity to comment on the facts and objections raised. Also, it must be noted that this approach would resemble the procedure followed by the Commission as regards competition cases, where the investigated entities are granted a single hearing on the SO, and such SO does not include a specific determination of the amount of the fine.[127] **15.100**

---

124 As per art. 126 SSM Fr.

125 See (i) General Court judgment in case T-203/18 (*VQ v ECB*) of 8 July 2020 (ECLI:EU:T:2020:313), at Paras. 3 and 5, and (ii) General Court judgments in cases T-576/18 (*Crédit agricole v ECB*), T-577/18 (*Crédit agricole Corporate and Investment Bank v ECB*) and T-578/18 (*CA Consumer Finance v ECB*) of 8 July 2020 (ECLI:EU:T:2020:304, ECLI:EU:T:2020:305, and ECLI:EU:T:2020:306, respectively), at Paras. 3–4.

126 Understood as the opportunity to submit comments and observations.

127 See Forrester, I. S. (2009). Due process in EC competition cases: a distinguished institution with flawed procedures. *European Law Review*, *34*(6), pp. 817–843. At pp. 833–834.

See, also. (i) de La Serre, É. B. & Lagathu, E. (2021). The Law on Fines Imposed in EU Competition Proceedings: A Judicial Paradox. *Journal of European Competition Law & Practice*, pp. 710–717 and (ii)

15.101 The approach of not including the amount of the fine in the SO received the blessing of the Court of First Instance (currently the General Court) regarding competition cases.[128] Justifying the previous practice, the Court indicated that, if the amount of the fine was to be included in the SO, it would inappropriately anticipate the level of the fines to be imposed.[129] In other words, the Commission may only indicate the level of fines in cases where the concerned entity has been given the opportunity to be heard (and not before). Such an approach seems to factor in the fact that (i) the Commission has issued detailed guidelines for the calculation of fines[130] and (ii) the unlimited jurisdiction enjoyed by the CJEU as regards the imposition of fines in competition cases.[131]

15.102 Following the previous reasoning, it appears that, in principle, provided that the SO does not precisely indicate the amount of the penalties imposed, one hearing would suffice. Nevertheless, nothing would preclude granting a second hearing on the complete draft sanctioning decision, including the amount of the penalties.[132]

15.103 *Option 2*: Under this approach, the investigated entity would be granted two hearings: one on the SO and a second one on the draft complete sanctioning decision.[133] This latter approach seems to be the one followed by the ECB, building on the *obiter dictum* of recent judgments.[134] In the *VQ v ECB* and

---

Barbier de La Serre, É. & Lagathu, E. (2022). The Law on Fines Imposed in EU Competition Proceedings: A Post-Pandemic Boost of Case Law. *Journal of European Competition Law & Practice*, *13*(6), pp. 448–458.

128 Handled under Regulation No 17: First Regulation implementing Articles 85 and 86 of the Treaty (and currently Council Regulation (EC) No. 1/2003 of 16 December 2002 on the implementation of the rules on competition laid down in Articles 81 and 82 of the Treaty).

129 See Court of First Instance judgment in Joined cases T-109/02, T-118/02, T-122/02, T-125/02, T-126/02, T-128/02, T-129/02, T-132/02 and T-136/02 (*Bolloré SA et altera v. Commission*) 26 April 2007 (ECLI:EU:T:2007:115), Paras. 402–403. See, also, Court of Justice judgment in joined cases 100/80 to 103/80 (*Musique diffusion française et al. v. Commission*) of 7 June 1983 (ECLI:EU:C:1983:158), at Para. 21, and Court of First Instance judgment in case T-203/01 (*Michelin v Commission*) of 30 September 2003, at Para. 19.

130 Cf Guidelines on the method of setting fines imposed pursuant to Article 15(2) of Regulation No. 17 and Article 65 (5) of the ECSC Treaty and more recent Guidelines on the method of setting fines imposed pursuant to Article 23(2)(a) of Regulation No. 1/2003.

131 See further, Section D.2. (*Has the CJEU unlimited jurisdiction to review administrative penalties imposed by the ECB?*) in Chapter 8. Not without some interpretative efforts, the author submitted that the CJEU should also enjoy unlimited jurisdiction regarding the administrative penalty payments imposed by the ECB.

132 This hearing being granted before the Investigating Unit.

133 Ibidem.

134 See previous footnote 125.

Crédit agricole cases,[135] the judgment details how, after submitting comments to the SO, the concerned entities also submitted comments to the *draft decision*.[136] In the *VQ v ECB* case, the General Court even indicated that the purpose of the ECB sharing that draft decision was to allow the concerned entity "(...) *to submit its written observations on the amount of the proposed administrative pecuniary penalty* (...)".[137]

As indicated above, granting a second hearing on the draft complete sanctioning decision complies with the doctrine settled by the CJEU, which requires that the person affected by a decision adversely affecting it must be heard before such a decision is taken.[138] The foregoing includes the amount of the fine, on which the concerned entity was not given the opportunity to opine.[139] Also, such approach adds an extra layer of protection by reinforcing the right of the concerning entity to be heard. **15.104**

All in all, even if not expressly provided in the SSM Fr, it appears that granting two hearings would be more protective of the right to be heard[140] of the investigated subjects while, at the same time, compliant with a settled case law. Furthermore, at the price of some added administrative cost, the supervisor would be on the safe side. In this regard, it seems advisable following this approach. **15.105**

---

135 Ibidem. For a dedicated commentary on the VQ v ECB case and, particularly, on the issue of the publication of the penalties imposed by the ECB, see Wissink, L. (2021)(i).

136 See (i) General Court judgment in case T-203/18 (*VQ v ECB*) of 8 July 2020 (ECLI:EU:T:2020:313), Paras. 3 and 5, and (ii) General Court judgments in cases T-576/18 (*Crédit agricole v ECB*), T-577/18 (*Crédit agricole Corporate and Investment Bank v ECB*) and T-578/18 (*CA Consumer Finance v ECB*) of 8 July 2020 (ECLI:EU:T:2020:304, ECLI:EU:T:2020:305 and ECLI:EU:T:2020:306, respectively), at Paras. 3–4.

137 General Court judgment in case T-203/18 (*VQ v ECB*) of 8 July 2020 (ECLI:EU:T:2020:313), at Para. 4.

138 See Section B.2.(d).(1). (*Some reflections on the safeguards applicable in the procedure for lapsing and withdrawing banking licenses*) in Chapter 14 and the case law cited therein.

139 And, *a fortiori*, taking into account that, pursuant to art. 22(1) SSM R, "*The ECB shall base its decisions only on objections on which the parties concerned have been able to comment*". Similarly, see also arts. 33(3) and 127(2) and (9) SSM Fr.

140 In particular, if it is to be considered that the CJEU would not enjoy unlimited jurisdiction (opposite approach to the one submitted by the author in Section D.2. (*Has the CJEU unlimited jurisdiction to review administrative penalties imposed by the ECB?*) in Chapter 8).

The language of the hearing phase

15.106 As a starting point, it must be recalled that multilingualism is embedded in the EU.[141] The operational dimension of this multilingualism, i.e., the official languages in which the EU legal texts will be published,[142] and EU institutions will exchange with individuals, MSs and internally is framed in Regulation 1/58.[143]

15.107 The abovementioned regulation foresees in its art. 2 that documents drafted by individuals and sent to EU Institutions may be drafted in one the EU official languages selected by that sender. The Institution must reply, accordingly, in the same language selected by the sender.

15.108 This art. 2 sets up the basis for the language regime to be used in communications between EU Institutions and senders; in principle, and unless an exception applies,[144] individuals can choose any of the official languages of the EU and can expect that a given Institution replies in the same language.

15.109 This approach is captured (and detailed) in art. 24 SSM Fr. Pursuant to this provision, supervisees (and individuals in general) may send their communication in any of the EU official languages. Additionally, supervisees may agree with the ECB in using a given official language for all their communication.[145] Such agreement may be revoked at any time.[146]

15.110 As per the language in which the SO and further communication may be held with the investigated entity, it must be noted that the relevant entity may have made its choice before the procedure was substantiated.[147] The question may

---

141 See Athanassiou, P. (2006). The application of multilingualism in the European Union context. *ECB legal working paper series no. 2.* At p. 5.

142 And would enjoy legal authenticity. Ibidem at p. 9.

143 The constitutional basis of that Regulation can be found in art. 342 TFEU. This Regulation, subsequently amended as needed by the EU accession process, is actually the first Regulation adopted by the Council of the European Economic Community. See Athanassiou, P. (2006) at p. 5

144 Cf art. 6 of the Regulation 1/58. Pursuant to that provision, the rules of procedures of the Institutions may stipulate in their rules of procedures the language(s) that must be used in certain cases.

Athanassiou further analyses the reasons that may justify the adoption of a restrictive language regime by an EU institution (e.g., practical and efficiency restrictions). See Athanassiou, P. (2006) at pp. 12–16.

145 Art. 24(2) SSM Fr. See, on this topic, Lackhoff, K. (2017)(i) at pp. 110–112.

146 Yet, pursuant to art. 24(2)II SSM Fr, the procedures ongoing before such a revocation takes place will continue to be handled in accordance with the language regime agreed previously between the ECB and the relevant person.

147 Cf art. 24 SSM Fr. See, in this vein, Section B.1. (*The sources of administrative procedural law for the ECB under the SSM*) in Chapter 7. As indicated therein, language arrangements between the ECB and supervised entity constitute a source of procedural law for the ECB, and beyond that, they may be as sophisticated or simple as the relevant entity may want to (i.e., agreeing to conduct daily supervision in English but reserving another EU official language to carry out sanctioning or enforcement procedures).

have more relevance for both the investigated entity and the ECB that it may appear at a first look.

As per the concerned entity, choosing a given language would mean that it would need to translate[148] all the evidence provided with its reply to the SO, as the case may be.[149] The absence of a translation of that evidence (or, at least, its key parts), would impede the ECB to consider it. Accordingly, in these circumstances, it is hard to find a flaw on the right to be heard, as the burden of translating the evidence lies within the concerned entity. **15.111**

The same approach can be anticipated for the ECB; it should also translate the relevant documents composing the file (or its key parts, at least) to the language agreed with the supervisee (or chosen by it). This creates an additional complexity layer, as the Investigating Unit may be obliged to prepare further translations of the key documents of the file so that it can submit a *complete draft decision* to the Supervisory Board.[150] **15.112**

Specifically regarding the oral hearing, art. 24(2)III SSM Fr contemplates that it may be held in an official language different from the one of the sanctioning procedure. The foregoing must be notified sufficiently in advance[151] so that the ECB may arrange the required simultaneous translation and other logistics aspects. **15.113**

4. Stage 4: second hearing and preparation of a draft final decision

(a) Key aspects of stage 4

Pursuant to art. 127(1) SSM Fr, upon reception of the observations submitted by the investigated entity, the investigating officer in charge prepares a preliminary *complete draft decision*. Such draft contains a complete decision, including (a) a determination of the penalties to be imposed and (b), eventually, a reply to the factual and legal arguments brought by the relevant entity. **15.114**

The entity is provided, then, with a new hearing to submit its comments as regards this complete draft sanctioning. Pursuant to art. 31(3) SSM Fr, the deadline to submit observations to this draft should be no less than two **15.115**

---

148 Unless in English or otherwise agreed with the Investigating Unit (i.e., because it is maybe the native language of the investigating officer in charge, or she may be proficient in that language).

149 As per the documents that may be attached, see immediately above in this Section.

150 Cf art. 127(1) SSM Fr.

151 The term is rather ambiguous and does not contemplate a minimum deadline.

weeks.[152] Observations submitted by the concerned entity, particularly those relating to the calculation of the administrative pecuniary penalties or fines imposed, must be carefully considered by the investigating officer handling the case.

15.116 On the basis of the foregoing, and following the regular course of the events, the Investigating Unit prepares a complete draft decision, together with a complete file, to be submitted to the Supervisory Board (and later on the Governing Council, if any) for their approval.[153]

15.117 Notwithstanding the above, there are other potential outcomes; the investigating officers may decide to (a) repurpose the scope of the investigation and then submit a new SO or a complement to the previous one in case it may be understood that the facts investigated correspond to other (including additional) breaches,[154] (b) request the relevant NCA to open a sanctioning proceeding in the light of the facts investigated[155] or (c) decide to closure such a proceeding.[156]

15.118 The basic structure and options are presented in Figure 15.4.

(b) Legal challenges

(i) Determination of the fines: basis for the calculation of administrative pecuniary penalties

15.120 As discussed immediately above, the ECB seems to grant a second hearing in the course of the sanctioning procedures falling under its direct remit.

15.121 One of the key elements of the draft complete sanctioning decisions is the determination of the penalties to be imposed on the concerned entities.

---

152 This seems, indeed, to be ECB practice, building upon the factual background presented by the General Court in its judgment in case T-203/18 (*VQ v ECB*) of 8 July 2020 (ECLI:EU:T:2020:313), at Paras. 4–5.

153 See art. 127(1)–(2) SSM Fr. Lackhoff, K. (2017)(i) at pp. 215–216.

154 In this regard, the author is of the view that if the investigation mutates to address additional and/or other different breaches, in connection with the same or other (new) facts, the first hearing phase should be redone in its entirety with a view to ensure the highest level of protection for the investigated entity.

155 In parallel to the sanctioning proceeding handled by the ECB or repurposing the nature of the sanctioning proceeding (in the understanding that the ECB would not be competent under Paras. 1 and 7 of art. 18 SSM R to sanction the breach committed by the relevant entity). See further, Section C. (*ECB requests addressed to NCAs to open sanctioning procedures under art. 18(5) SSM R*) in this chapter below.

156 In those cases, the Investigating Unit should justify, in an internal note, its decision with a view to (a) be able to produce evidence of its decision (and of the grounds motivating it) and (b) keep the Supervisory Board informed (and also to eventually share or distribute those data among the relevant services of the NCAs).

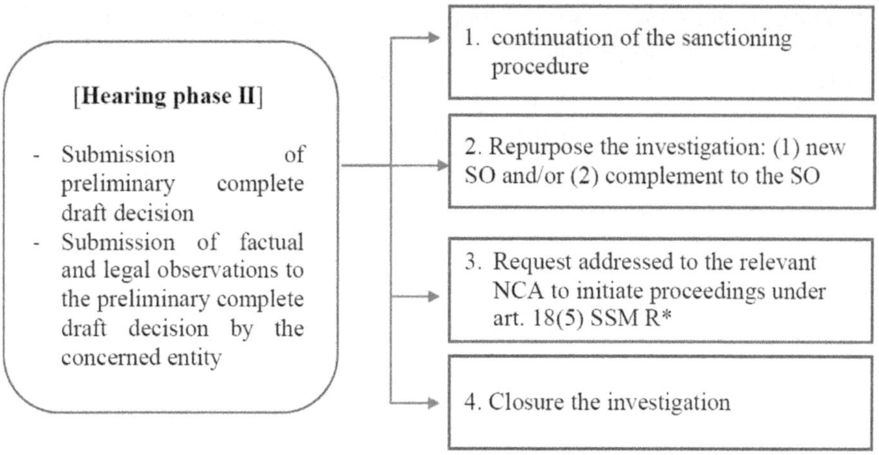

Figure 15.4 Hearing phase II: preliminary draft decision and outcome routes

Under art. 18(1) SSM R, the ECB enjoys a wide margin of appreciation regarding the fines that it can impose.[157] Such fines range from "(…) (i) *up to twice the amount of the profits gained or losses avoided because of the breach where those can be determined, or* (iii) *up to 10 % of the total annual turnover, as defined in relevant Union law, of a legal person in the preceding business year or* (iii) *such other pecuniary penalties*". (Roman numbers added).[158] **15.122**

Pursuant to art. 18(3) SSM R, penalties imposed by the ECB must be "*effective, proportionate and dissuasive*". In the light of those principles, the penalty imposed must be *proportionate* to the nature of the breach committed by the sanctioned entity. Also, the penalty must be *dissuasive* and thus generate the appropriate deterrent effect. In this vein, the penalty imposed should prevent any entity (general deterrent effect) and, in particular, the sanctioned entity (specific deterrent effect) from incurring any breach in the future. The appropriate achievement of these two principles would determine that the penalty is indeed *effective*, i.e., appropriate to meet the required punitive and deterrent objectives. **15.123**

Rules regarding such calculation have been made publicly available in the Guide for the calculation of administrative pecuniary penalties.[159] This delicate point deserves, at least, a succinct separated analysis. **15.124**

157 Cf Para. 5 of the Guide for the calculation of administrative penalty payments. See further, General Court judgment in case T-576/18 (*Crédit agricole v ECB*) of 8 July 2020 (ECLI:EU:T:2020:304), at Para. 133.

158 See also Section C.1.(b). (*Exploring the limits of article 18(1) SSM R: is there any interpretation that can ensure a minimum level playing field? Possible interpretations of article 18(1) SSM R*) in Chapter 7.

159 See Fromage, D. (2021).

Relevant elements leading to the adoption of the Guide for the calculation of administrative pecuniary penalties

15.125 The ECB enjoys supervisory discretion when determining the amount of the penalty to be imposed in a sanctioning entity.[160] The determination of the penalty impinges on some fundamental principles, as one can attest from the General Court recent case law. In case T-576/18 (*Crédit agricole v ECB*) of 8 July 2020,[161] the Court annulled the administrative pecuniary penalty imposed to Crédit Agricole.[162] In that judgment, the Court pointed out that the sanctioning decision did not allow the applicant to know the method for the calculation of the administrative pecuniary penalty.[163] The foregoing, on the understanding that the sanctioned entity should not be obliged to litigate to know the methodology leading to the calculation of the penalty imposed.[164]

15.126 The General Court indicated that, considering that the sanctioning decision was not based on the conclusions issued by the ABoR[165] nor in a previous precedent[166] nor in a published methodology, the sufficiency of the motivation of the penalty imposed should be assessed against the content of the sanctioning decision itself. Consequently, the General Court ruled that the motivation established therein was insufficient to let the applicant know how the amount

160 Papathanassiou, C. (2022)(ii) at para. 19.

161 See footnote 120.

162 The same outcome occurred as regards *Crédit agricole Corporate and Investment Bank* and *CA Consumer Finance* as per cases T-577/18 (*Crédit agricole Corporate and Investment Bank v ECB*) and T-578/18 (*CA Consumer Finance v ECB*) of 8 July 2020 (ECLI:EU:T:2020:305 and ECLI:EU:T:2020:306, respectively).

Those judgments (including the judgment pertaining to case T-576/18) have been confirmed by the Court of Justice order in joined cases C-456/20 P to C-458/20 P (*Crédit agricole SA et al. v ECB*) 16 June 2021 (ECLI:EU:C:2021:502).

163 Case T-576/18 at Paras. 146–147.

164 Ibidem at Para. 146.

165 As it was the case in the *L-Bank Appeal* (at Para. 92). Ibidem at Para. 138. See, in more detail, the topic of the integration of the ABoR opinion within the final ECB (sanctioning) supervisory decision in Section B.5.(b).(2).(ii). (*Integration of the ABoR opinions in the final ECB supervisory (sanctioning) decision review*) below in this chapter.

166 As this is deemed to be the first case to be heard by the General Court on the application of administrative pecuniary penalties by the ECB under the SSM. However, and surprisingly, in its judgment in case T-203/18 (*VQ v ECB*), issued the same day, the General Court did not annul the ECB sanctioning decision. In both cases, the applicants alleged breach of the principle of proportionality concerning the imposition of the penalties. However, in the *Crédit agricole v ECB* case, the applicant specifically alleged that it was impossible to know how the ECB calculated the penalty to be imposed. In *VQ v ECB*, the applicant made a general reference to the principle of proportionality, in the light of which and considering that, in its view, it could not be considered that a breach has been committed; the ECB violated the principle of proportionality in abstract.

Notwithstanding the foregoing, it would have been more appropriate (and coherent) if the General Court itself would have put forward the same argumentation it used in *Crédit agricole v ECB* in *VQ v ECB*. In the end, both sanctioning decisions would present the exact same defect concerning the methodology applied for the calculation of the penalties.

of the penalty imposed was calculated and for the Court to exercise its legality control.[167]

In order to prevent future similar court rulings, on March 2021, the ECB published the Guide for the calculation of administrative pecuniary penalties. Such a Guide seems to be inspired by the Commission's *Guidelines on the method of setting fines imposed pursuant to Article 23(2)(a) of Regulation No 1/2003.*[168] The Guide for the calculation of administrative pecuniary penalties reproduces the same steps contemplated in the Commissions Guidelines to determine the final amount of the penalty to be imposed. In this way, the ECB can rely on an approach that is familiar to the CJEU. **15.127**

Rationale of the Guide for the calculation of administrative pecuniary penalties

The Guide for the calculation of administrative pecuniary penalties contemplates two steps for the imposition of penalties:[169] (i) the determination of the base amount of the breach and, subsequently, (ii) the adjustment of the base amount in the light of the aggravating and mitigating circumstances concurring. **15.128**

Step one: determination of the base amount

The base amount takes into account the severity of the breach, which helps to classify fines that are classified as (1) minor, (2) moderately severe, (3) severe, (4) very severe and (5) extremely severe.[170] Determining the base amount (which will be adjusted in the second step to the specific concurring circumstances) is key in ensuring that the penalty complies with its main purpose: ensuring deterrence.[171] This base amount should provide a base that, even if tempered, ensures that the penalty finally imposed is dissuasive to the concerned entity (and to other potential infringing entities). **15.129**

---

167 Cf General Court judgment in case T-576/18 (*Crédit agricole v ECB*) of 8 July 2020 (ECLI:EU:T:2020:304), at Paras. 145 and 156.

168 https://eur-lex.europa.eu/legal-content/EN/ALL/?uri=CELEX%3A52006XC0901%2801%29. For a comparison between the SSM enforcement model and the one followed in competition (under regulation 1/2003), see Annunziata, F. and Maggiolino, M. (2021). The single supervisory mechanism and the European framework for the enforcement of competition law: a comparison between two models for economic governance in the EU. *Bocconi Legal Studies Research Paper Series,* March 2021.

169 As per footnote two of the Guide for the calculation of administrative pecuniary penalties, the Guide is used for the calculation of both fines and administrative pecuniary penalties (which are equated for this purpose).

170 See Para. 11 of the Guide for the calculation of administrative pecuniary penalties.

171 Following arts. 18(3) and 129(2) SSM Fr. On the desired deterrent effect, see Felisatti, V. (2018) at pp. 390–391; and Allegrezza, S. and Radopolos, I. (2017). Enforcing prudential banking regulations in the Eurozone: A reading from the viewpoint of criminal law. In *Challenges in the field of economic and financial crime in Europe and the US* (pp. 233–264). London, Hart Publishing. At p. 240.

15.130 Such severity is determined by looking at two different elements: (i) the impact of the breach and (ii) the degree of misconduct incurred.

15.131 As per the *impact of the breach*,[172] breaches may be classified as low medium or high. Such classification depends on a number of factors, including the impact of the breach on the entity's prudential situation and supervision, the duration of the breach, the damage caused by the breach and "*the actual and potential consequences of the breach on the reputation of and confidence in the banking sector*".[173]

15.132 The impact of the breach on the infringing entity's prudential situation and supervision will be, in particular, assessed against the deviation from legal requirements. In this regard, the ECB clarifies that: "*The more important a legal requirement is for the safety and soundness of a supervised entity, the smaller the degree of deviation will need to be in order to classify the impact of the breach as 'high'*".[174]

15.133 However, there is no further explanation of what is meant by the entity's "prudential situation" and "supervision", e.g., whether these only refer to their own funds and capital requirements or something else. Nor is it clear whether the *assessment* itself may change, even under the same situation, depending on the cycle or on the prudential priorities undertaken that year, e.g., if the ECB decides to adopt a stricter approach towards certain breaches. Thus, it may be advisable for the ECB to update, clarify and refine the Guide for the calculation of administrative pecuniary penalties as regards those points (among potentially others).

15.134 For determining the *degree of misconduct*,[175] the ECB will look at the subjective element of the breach in order to ascertain whether the breach was committed intentionally or negligently. It has been analysed above[176] how the SSM R requires that breaches are committed "*intentionally or negligently*". Concerning *negligence*, the General Court (and also the Board of Appeal of the ESAs)[177] has insisted on the fact that credit institutions must display a high standard of care when interpreting and applying prudential provisions. If that extraordinary

---

172 Ibidem at Paras. 12–13.

173 Ibidem at Para. 12.

174 Ibidem at Para. 13.

175 Ibidem at Paras. 14–17.

176 See Section B.3.(b).(1). (*Procedural safeguards: the subjective element of the infringement (intention and negligence)*) in this chapter.

177 Ibidem.

standard of care is evidenced, the concerned cannot be sanctioned, as the subjective element would be lacking.[178] And this, even if the interpretation or practice followed by the entity results, in the view of the ECB, in a breach. For example, that would be the case when a substantive provision is not clear (leaving room for interpretation) and the entity, after having considered the background of that provision and its intention, decides to follow a logical (yet favourable to its interests) interpretation of the given provision.[179]

In accordance with the *degree of misconduct*, breaches may be classified as low, medium or high. In principle, the higher the intentional (or negligent) element is, the more severe this element will be considered.[180] **15.135**

The interactions between the two elements described above will determine the classification of the breach,[181] e.g., when the degree of misconduct of the breach at stake and its impact are low, such breach may be classified as *minor*. There is a direct correlation; the more severe the impact and/or the degree of the misconduct is, the more severe will be the classification of the relevant penalty. **15.136**

Once the severity of the breach is defined, the Guide sets up the base amount.[182] To do so, the Guide contemplates five groups of entities, determined pursuant to their total assets: from above EUR 500 billion (group 1), to equal or less than EUR 3 billion (group 5). **15.137**

The amount of the penalties considered *minor* to *very severe*[183] is determined in accordance with a modelled penalty grid,[184] which takes into account, as referred to above, (a) the severity of the breach and (b) the size of the entity at stake. The base amount is further adjusted proportionally taking into account the size of the average entity of the given group and the average entity of the group above or below, depending on whether the entity is bigger or smaller (respectively) than the average entity of its own group.[185] **15.138**

---

178 And assuming that the potential infringement has not been committed intentionally either.

179 See Board of Appeal decisions D 2019 01, D 2019 02, D 2019 03 and D 2019 04 of 27 February 2019 at Para. 2 (Appeal by SV Capital OÜ against European Banking Authority decision (europa.eu)).

180 Ibidem at 17.

181 Ibidem at Para. 18.

182 Except for those cases where the penalty is calculated as a multiple of the profits obtained or losses avoided by the relevant entity. Ibidem at Paras. 19 and 27.

183 For extremely severe breaches, the penalty is defined as the percentage of the total annual turnover. Ibidem at Paras. 20 and 26. See, on this matter, Fromage, D. (2021) at pp. 4–5. Additionally, see also Papathanassiou, C. (2022)(ii) at Para. 19.

184 Ibidem at Para. 20 and Table 2.

185 Ibidem at Paras. 24–25.

15.139 As a concluding remark to this point, it must be noted that the classification system is not categorial or automatic, and the ECB may depart from the examples given therein, provided that this is adequately justified. As noted above in this Section, the ECB would enjoy broad discretion when deciding the amount of the pecuniary penalty to be imposed. Further, it must be recalled that the application of the *equal treatment* principle allows the ECB to diverge from precedent, provided that such divergence is sufficiently motivated and rooted in objective factors.[186]

Step two: adjustment of the penalty

15.140 Once the base amount is settled, the ECB will adjust it by considering *all* the relevant mitigating and aggravating circumstances.

15.141 The Guide does not include an exhaustive list of aggravating and mitigating circumstances.[187] It must be noted that, as the level of negligence or intention was taken into account to determine the base amount, it should not be taken into account as mitigating or aggravating circumstance. Otherwise, the same subjective element would be considered twice.

15.142 In addition, in the case of *concours idéal*, that is, where the same set of facts committed by the relevant entity constitutes two or more breaches, the ECB may adjust the amount of the penalty, if it is considered that imposing the sum of the penalties corresponding to each and every breach committed may be disproportionate.[188]

15.143 Overall, it must be recalled that the maximum penalty that the ECB can impose may not be higher that (i) "10 % of the total annual turnover" or (ii) "twice the amount of the profits gained or losses avoided because of the breach where those can be determined", as per art. 18(1) SSM R.[189]

15.144 Finally, the Guide also indicates the ECB should carry out an overall proportionality assessment of the penalty finally imposed. This is to ensure that such penalty does not cause the entity becoming insolvent or aggravates its liquidity and/or capital situation (if already weak).[190] Linked to the above, in certain

186 See Section B.2.(d).(1). (*Some reflections on the safeguards applicable in the procedure for lapsing and withdrawing banking licenses*) in Chapter 14 above. It must be also noted that the CJEU seems to apply a *light* review of the application of this principle, which contributes (and reinforces) the margin of discretion enjoyed by the ECB.

187 Which, in principle, would include at least those foreseen in art. 70 CRD IV.

188 See footnote 112. Ibidem at Para. 31.

189 Ibidem at Para. 32.

190 Ibidem at Para. 33.

cases, the ECB may decide to depart from the Guide and impose a symbolic penalty.[191]

Final considerations on the Guide for the calculation of administrative pecuniary penalties

Looking at the relevant judicial precedents,[192] it can be concluded that the referred Guide (a) enhanced ECB transparency regarding the imposition of penalties and (b) seems to comply with the request for further transparency embedded in the General Court judgment in case T-576/18 (*Crédit agricole v ECB*) of 8 July 2020.[193] The foregoing entails that further claims based on lack of motivation of the penalties imposed would be more difficult for success. **15.145**

Recalling the fact that the ECB enjoys supervisory discretion when carrying out the specific micro-prudential tasks allocated to it under the SSM R[194] and how to punish infringements,[195] it must be outlined that there are three elements of the Guide analysed in this Section that are susceptible to improvement: **15.146**

(1) As indicated above, further clarification on what the threats to "prudential situation" and "supervision" on which the ECB is allowing less divergence from legal requirements (and which would justify the *impact of the breach* being considered higher) are.
(2) Even if the ECB enjoys wide discretion in deciding how to calculate the penalties to be imposed,[196] it is not clear when it may opt to calculate those on the basis of the profits gained or the losses avoided.
    Would this be the preferred option? Would the general criteria foreseen in the Guide apply as a fallback option, then? Such clarification would be welcomed for the sake of transparency. Additionally, including this clarification within the Guide would also help to reduce legal uncertainty, as entities would

191 Which has not occurred for the time being. See the list of supervisory sanctions imposed by the ECB: Supervisory sanctions (europa.eu).

192 See the indent devoted to the *Rationale of the Guide for the calculation of administrative pecuniary penalties* in this Section and footnote 162.

193 See previous footnote 120.

194 See Section B. (*Allocation of micro-prudential tasks*) in Chapter 6.

195 See above in this Section and also in Sections C.1.(a). (*CJEU standard of review concerning ECB supervisory tasks*) in Chapter 12 and B.2.(d).(1). (*Some reflections on the safeguards applicable in the procedure for lapsing and withdrawing banking licenses*) in Chapter 14 (as regards the discretion enjoyed by the ECB when conducting common procedures).

On the academic side, particularly looking at the discretion enjoyed by the ECB to impose sanctions (and the amount of those), see Ioannidis, M. (2021) and Bosque Argachal, C. & Pizarroso Ceruti, A (2019). For a detailed analysis on the interplay between the discretion enjoyed by the ECB and the NCAs under the SSM, see also Wissink, L. (2021)(ii).

196 See Section B.4.(b).(1).(i). (*Relevant elements leading to the adoption of the Guide for the calculation of administrative pecuniary penalties*) in this Chapter 15 above.

know in advance when they can expect the ECB to apply to this approach. Finally, clarifying in which cases pecuniary penalties could be imposed, on this basis of profits obtained or losses avoided because of the infringement, could shield ECB sanctioning decisions from claims relating to the violation of the principle of equal treatment.[197]

(3) Finally, circumstances leading to the imposition of a symbolic penalty should be also sketched beforehand. The reasons are equivalent to the ones indicated in the preceding paragraph.

Such circumstances may include, among others, cases in which the relevant entity has been nationalised, and hence allowing the national and EU backstops, as applicable, and national taxpayers not to bear an additional burden.[198]

(ii) Determination of the Total Annual Turnover (TAT)

15.147 The determination of the TAT is of capital importance. *First*, because it acts as the upper limit for the administrative pecuniary penalties and fines to be imposed by the ECB. *Second*, because it also acts as the yardstick to determine the amount of those penalties when breaches are considered *extremely severe*.[199]

15.148 The determination of the TAT (or the precise way to calculate it) is also relevant from the perspective of ensuring legal certainty and to broadly respect the principle of legality and foreseeability of the consequences of the infringement. Entities subject to a sanctioning proceeding[200] should know beforehand the maximum penalty to which they may be subject and know that the definition of the TAT must be clear and ascertainable (and also the method to calculate it).

15.149 The CJEU has well established that "*The principle of legal certainty requires, on the one hand, that the rules of law be clear and precise and, on the other, that their application be foreseeable for those subject to the law, in particular, where they may have adverse consequences*".[201] Pursuant to CJEU's case law, the application of

197 From entities which requested (but were not granted) to be imposed just a symbolic pecuniary penalty. It must be nevertheless recalled that the CJEU seems to apply a loose review of EU bodies' decisions from the perspective of the equal treatment principle. See Section B.2.(d).(1). (*Some reflections on the safeguards applicable in the procedure for lapsing and withdrawing banking licenses*) in Chapter 14 above.

198 The foregoing, without prejudice of the ECB requesting to the relevant NCA to open a sanctioning procedure against the members of the board or other relevant natural persons that may be deemed responsible for the breach (pursuant to art. 18(5) SSM R).

199 Pursuant to the Guide for the calculation of administrative pecuniary penalties (see immediately above), except in those cases where the penalty is determined in accordance with the profits gained or losses avoided.

200 And broadly, all entities supervised under the SSM.

201 Court of Justice judgment in case C-156/21 (*Hungary v European Parliament and Council*) of 16 February 2022 (ECLI:EU:C:2022:97), at Para. 223. In the same vein, see also the Court of Justice judgment

rules must be foreseeable, which includes, for the concerned individuals, the possibility of knowing beforehand the consequences that infringements of those rules may potentially entail in terms of punishment.[202]

Similarly, and on the basis of art. 7(1) ECHR, the ECtHR has also systematically indicated that in cases where (criminal) penalties are imposed: "(...) *relevant penalties must be clearly defined by law. This requirement is satisfied where the individual can know from the wording of the relevant provision, if need be with the assistance of the courts' interpretation of it and after taking appropriate legal advice, what acts and omissions will make him criminally liable and what penalty he faces on that account*".[203] **15.150**

Yet, it is also admissible that the sanctioning provision presents some "abstract legal notion[s]" to allow capturing a variety of cases that cannot be determined beforehand.[204] Additionally, the Court of Justice has also outlined that: "(...) *the fact that a law confers a discretion on the authorities responsible for implementing it is not in itself inconsistent with the requirement of foreseeability, provided that the scope of the discretion and the manner of its exercise are indicated with sufficient clarity, having regard to the legitimate aim in question, to give adequate protection against arbitrary interference*".[205] In the light of the forgoing, it is not contrary to the principle of legal certainty, applied within sanctioning procedures, that a given provision grants some leeway for interpretation, provided that its **15.151**

---

in case C-158/06 (*Stichting ROM-projecten v Staatssecretaris van Economische Zaken*) of 21 June 2007 (ECLI:EU:C:2007:370), at Para. 25: "*The principle of legal certainty requires, on the one hand, that the rules of law be clear and precise and, on the other, that their application be foreseeable for those subject to the law, in particular, where they may have adverse consequences*".

Similarly, see also Board of Appeal decisions D 2019 01, D 2019 02, D 2019 03 and D 2019 04 of 27 February 2019 at Paras. 217–218 (*obiter dicta*) and 306 (Appeal by SV Capital OÜ against European Banking Authority decision (europa.eu)).

202 For a general study on the principle of legal certainty, see Raitio, J. (2003). *The principle of legal certainty in EC law*. Kluwer Academic Publishers. See, also, Whelan, P. (2012).

Specifically on the relevance of the principle of certainty within the SSM, see (i) Allegrezza, S. & Voordeckers, O. (2015) at p. 157; (ii) Lamandini, M., Ramos Muñoz, D. & Solana, J. (2016). at pp. 241–242; (iii) Lamandini, M., Ramos Muñoz, D. & Solana, J. (2015) at pp. 99–103; and (iv) Karagianni, A. M. (2022) at pp. 201–218.

203 ECtHR judgment in *Del Río Prada v. Spain* of 21 October 2013 (Application no. 42750/09), at Para. 79. See, in the same vein, the ECtHR judgment in *Cantoni v. France* of 11 November 1996 (Application no. 17862/91), at Para. 29.

For a complete analysis of the CJEU and ECtHR case law concerning the principle of certainty, see Timmerman, M. (2018). *Legality in Europe: on the principle'nullum crimen, nulla poena sine lege'in EU law and under the ECHR*. European University Institute: Doctoral dissertation: Timmerman_2018_LAW .pdf (eui.eu) At. pp. 84–87.

204 Court of Justice judgment in case C-156/21 (*Hungary v European Parliament and Council*) of 16 February 2022 (ECLI:EU:C:2022:97), at Para. 224.

205 Ibidem at Para. 225.

consequences are foreseeable. Additionally, attributing discretion to relevant authorities to apply such a (sanctioning) provision would not contravene the referred principle either.

15.152 It follows from the foregoing that the principle legal certainty principle demands that the TAT definition and its calculation, in the context of ECB sanctioning procedures, are clear, which, as we will see below, raises some interpretative and due process concerns.

15.153 Coming back to the definition of TAT, it is referred to in art. 18(1) SSM R.[206] Such provision states that the TAT will be "*as defined in relevant Union law*". Such (vague) reference is further clarified in art. 128 SSM Fr, which reads as follows:

> *The total annual turnover as referred to in Article 18(1) of the SSM Regulation shall mean the annual turnover, as defined in Article 67 of Directive 2013/36/EU, of a supervised entity according to the most recent available annual financial accounts of such supervised entity. Where the supervised entity that has committed the breach belongs to a supervised group, the relevant total annual turnover shall be the total annual turnover resulting from the most recent available consolidated annual financial accounts of the supervised group.*

15.154 Again, such provision contains a cross-reference, this time made to art. 67 CRD IV. In particular, indent (e) of Para. 2 of the same provision seems to provide the keys to appropriately determine the TAT. Indent (e) reads as follows:

> *(e) in the case of a legal person, administrative pecuniary penalties of up to 10 % of the total annual net turnover including the gross income consisting of interest receivable and similar income, income from shares and other variable or fixed-yield securities, and commissions or fees receivable in accordance with Article 316 of Regulation (EU) No 575/2013 of the undertaking in the preceding business year.*[207]

15.155 The definition of TAT generates some uncertainties (and consequent legal challenges) as regards (i) the business year to be considered for the purposes of calculating the relevant TAT and (ii) the elements that must be considered when calculating the TAT.

(i) As per the *relevant year that must be taken into account when calculating TAT*, art. 128 SSM Fr specifies that such TAT must calculated "*according to the most recent available annual financial accounts*".Such specific reference seems to constitute

206 But also in art. 18(3) SSM R.

207 It is to be noted that the final sentence of art. 67(2) CRD IV constitutes the source of inspiration of art. 18(3) SSM R (which basically reproduces this art. 67(2) CRD IV).

an addition, not contemplated under art. 67(2)(e) CRD IV. What the provision does not specify is the point in time to be taken to determine the most recent annual financial statement to be considered to calculate the TAT; are those the ones available at the moment of notifying the final decision to the relevant entity? Are those available when the complete draft decision is submitted to the Supervisory Board for approval? The answer is uncertain and the principle of legal certainty looks compromised.

The strict wording of the provision suggests that the TAT may be that of the most recent financial statement produced at the moment the ECB decision is adopted (and notified to the relevant entity). Nevertheless, this may imply certain recalculations if, during the instruction of the sanctioning proceeding, more recent annual financial statements become available. 15.156

A more practical, and potentially more balanced, approach would be considering, for the calculation of the TAT, the annual financial statement of the year in which the infringement was committed or the average of the relevant years in the case of ongoing breaches. This approach brings further *foreseeability* as per the level of punishment to which the relevant entity may be subject (i.e., based on the TAT of the year in which the infringement was committed). 15.157

Adopting such an approach would require a modification of art. 128 SSM Fr. As it is an ECB Regulation, the revision of such a provision would be swifter than, for example, amending the SSM R. Another avenue would be for the ECB to clarify this matter (and also the point indicated below) in the Guide to the method of setting administrative pecuniary penalties.[208] 15.158

(ii) Another angle to be look at is ***the elements that integrate the TAT***. On this, there may be two potential and reasonable interpretations.

Following art. 67(2)(e) CRD IV (the *positive approach*), the TAT would include three items:[209] (i) *interest receivable and similar income*,[210] (ii) *income from shares and other variable or fixed-yield securities*[211] and (iii) *commissions or fees receivable*.[212] [213]

The foregoing would constitute the *gross income* and would imply that, by definition, it can only be positive. Such approach to the TAT is well-known

208 Noting that the Guide only laconically indicates that the TAT would be calculated in accordance with art. 128 SSM Fr. See Guide to the method of setting administrative pecuniary penalties at Paras. 20 and 32.
209 Constituting the *gross income*, by definition, an always positive item.
210 Cf art. 316(1) CRR, first item of Table 1.
211 Cf art. 316(1) CRR, third item of Table 1.
212 Cf art. 316(1) CRR, fifth item of Table 1.
213 All these three items, in accordance with art. 316 CRR. See previous footnotes.

in the competition field.[214] For instance, art. 5(1) of the Council Regulation No. 139/2004 of 20 January 2004 on the control of concentrations between undertakings (the Merger Regulation) does contemplate an *aggregate* turnover encompassing a *positive* definition. A similar example can be extracted from art. 2(5) of Directive 2013/34/EU of the European Parliament and of the Council of 26 June 2013 on the annual financial statements, consolidated financial statements and related reports of certain types of undertakings, amending Directive 2006/43/EC of the European Parliament and of the Council and repealing Council Directives 78/660/EEC and 83/349/EEC.

Nevertheless, another approach, the *negative approach*, is also possible. The reference contained in art. 67(2)(e) CRD IV[215] to art. 316 CRR invites to consider also the elements foreseen in Para. 1 of such provision that may have a negative impact on the TAT, even leading to a negative figure. It must be highlighted that, following CRR III, art. 316 CRR has been modified and no longer refers to the TAT calculation.[216] This constitutes a insurmountable mismatch that requires a legislative correction. For the purpose of this analysis, as it may be relevant, references made to art. 316 herein are made to the wording of art. 316 CRR before it was modified by CRR III.[217]

Furthermore, if such interpretation is to be followed, one needs to consider that, for entities applying the standards foreseen in the Council Directive 86/635/EEC of 8 December 1986 on the annual accounts and consolidated accounts of banks and other financial institutions, the elements foreseen in the first Para. of art. 316 CRR may apply. For the contrary, for entities applying different accounting standards from those foreseen in the mentioned Directive, they should calculate the TAT "*on the basis of data that best reflect the definition set out in this Article*".

This *negative approach* seems to be more tailored to cope with the banking industry. In this vein, it must be noted that Basel Framework (Basel III standards) would actually support such notion.[218] One also may argue that, by making specific reference to art. 316 CRR, the legislator preferred using a concept

---

214 See Commission Staff Working Paper. Impact Assessment Accompanying the document Proposal for a Directive of the European Parliament and the Council on the access to the activity of credit institutions and the prudential supervision of credit institutions and investment firms and amending Directive 2002/87/EC of the European Parliament and of the Council on the supplementary supervision of credit institutions, insurance undertakings and investment firms in a financial conglomerate (COM(2011) 453 final), at p. 32: https://eur-lex.europa.eu/legal-content/EN/TXT/PDF/?uri=CELEX:52011SC0952&from=ES.

215 After due consideration to the reference made to "relevant Union law" in art. 18(1) SSM R.

216 But to the so-called *relevant indicator.*

217 Such change entered into force on 1 January 2025.

218 Cf Basel Framework. OPE 20. Basic indicator approach. 20.3: "*Gross income is defined as net interest income plus net non-interest income. It is intended that this measure should:*

(1) be gross of any provisions (e.g., for unpaid interest);

(2) be gross of operating expenses, including fees paid to outsourcing service providers;

(3) exclude realised profits / losses from the sale of securities in the banking book; and

(4) exclude extraordinary or irregular items as well as income derived from insurance".

falling under the *banking* remit, discarding the use of concepts linked to general business or pertaining to the field of competition.

The use of the positive or negative approach must be carefully weighed in light of the overall legal framework used by the ECB, the deterrent effect that penalties must have,[219] the principle of legal certainty and the *pro reo* interpretation of sanctioning (criminal in nature) provisions.[220] **15.159**

As per the first element, it seems rather obvious that the ECB should apply a homogenous definition of the TAT so as to use the same approach regarding not only its purely supervisory activities but also the specific sanctioning ones. In this regard, the point would be to use the same approach (*positive* or *negative*) consistently concerning any task allocated to the ECB under the SSM and potentially beyond. **15.160**

Considering that the ultimate purpose of the penalty is to have a deterrent effect, applying the *positive approach* would entail that, indeed, higher limits (and eventually penalties) may be applied. Consequently, such approach may enhance higher compliance with the objectives and principles enshrined in art. 18(3) SSM R. **15.161**

Conversely, the principle of *favor rei* must also be considered. In this regard, the use of the *negative approach* may be more favourable, generally speaking, for the sanctioned entities, as lower upper limits would be settled.[221] Also, for extremely severe breaches, such an approach may actually have a higher impact, as those are expected to be imposed as a percentage of the TAT. **15.162**

Recent case law[222] does not shed any light on this point, and the literature does not seem to have addressed this matter in detail either, at least not yet. Also, **15.163**

219 Cf art. 18(3) SSM R.

220 Also known as the *rule of lenity*. See Ornowska, A. (2010). Introducing Hermeneutic Methods in Criminal Law Interpretation in Europe. *Interpretation of Law in the Global World: From Particularism to a Universal Approach* (pp. 251–275). Springer. At pp. 254–255.

221 Actually, as the main elements constituting an entity operating income are excluded from the elements listed in Table 1 of art. 316(1) (e.g., fixed costs such as staff salaries, provisions, etc.), it would appear that negative figures would be difficult to obtain. Verification of this hypothesis would need a global exercise, calculating the TAT under the positive approach and under the negative approach of a representative number of entities directly supervised by the ECB.

222 See immediately above in this Section. Particularly, see (i) General Court judgment in case T-203/18 (*VQ v ECB*) of 8 July 2020 (ECLI:EU:T:2020:313); and (ii) General Court judgments in cases T-576/18 (*Crédit agricole v ECB*), T-577/18 (*Crédit agricole Corporate and Investment Bank v ECB*) and T-578/18 (*CA Consumer Finance v ECB*) of 8 July 2020 (ECLI:EU:T:2020:304, ECLI:EU:T:2020:305 and ECLI:EU:T:2020:306, respectively). For a dedicated commentary on the *VQ v ECB* case and, particularly, on the issue of the publication of the penalties imposed by the ECB, see Wissink, L. (2021)(i).

further empirical evidence would need to be gathered on the actual divergence of these two approaches.[223] Acknowledging that a prudent and restrictive approach is more compliant with the principles that guide sanctioning proceedings, the negative approach may be less controversial and, at the same time, protective of the interests of the infringing entities.[224] Consequently, such *negative* approach to the concept of TAT, based on art. 316 CRR, should be preferred.

5. Stage 5 (Decision phase): submission to the Supervisory Board (and Governing Council approval)

(a) Key aspects of stage 5

15.164 The decision phase would strictly comprise the adoption of the relevant ECB supervisory decision. This phase, however, may be less linear than ideally presented and will be enlarged to describe also (potential) interactions with the ABoR and the submission of a claim before the CJEU.

15.165 Pursuant to art. 127(1) SSM Fr, upon conclusion of the sanctioning proceeding by the investigating officer, if it is demonstrated that a given entity has committed a breach capable of being directly pursued by the ECB, a complete draft ECB decision proposing the imposition of penalties will be submitted to the Supervisory Board. Additionally, the file relating to this sanctioning proceeding will also be made available to the Supervisory Board.[225]

15.166 At the Supervisory Board, several outcomes are possible:

(i) If the Supervisory Board considers that the file is incomplete, it may return it to the Investigating Unit and submit a reasoned request for resubmission or inclusion of additional information.[226]

---

223 Cf footnote 221.

224 And, as indicated immediately above, more suitable for the banking sector.

225 Pursuant to art. 127(2) SSM Fr, it must be recalled that such a complete draft decision must be based only on facts and legal objections on which the concerned entity was given the opportunity to submit observations. If material facts and objections resulting in negative consequences for the concerned entity (e.g., appreciation of aggravating circumstances) are not disclosed before the final ECB supervisory decision is issued, it may vitiate (totally or partially, depending on the type of flaw) such a decision – making it amenable for annulation. See, also, the end of Section B.2.(d).(1). (*Some reflections on the safeguards applicable in the procedure for lapsing and withdrawing banking licenses*) in Chapter 14.

See also, on the need to provide the concerned entity with the possibility to submit comments as regards the amount of the sanction proposed, Section B.3.(b).(2).(i). (*How many hearing phases need to be granted; one or two?*) in this chapter.

226 Cf art. 127(3) SSM Fr.

(ii) If the Supervisory Board agrees with the complete draft decision it shall adopt such draft decision.[227]
(iii) If the Supervisory Board does not agree with the complete draft decision, considering that the facts described therein do not reveal the commission of one or more breaches, it may decide to close the case.[228]
(iv) If the Supervisory Board does agree with the proposal contemplated in the complete draft decision but disagrees with the amount of the proposed penalties, it will adopt the decision specifying the amount of the penalties it deems more appropriate.[229]
(v) If the Supervisory Board does not agree with the proposal submitted but understands that (a) a different breach has been committed or (b) there are different factual bases, it shall inform the supervised entity concerned. In this case, it will invite the concerned entity to submit its observations, and in general, the previous hearing phase will be redone.[230]

After the adoption of the complete draft decision by the Supervisory Board,[231] if any, it will submit this draft decision to the Governing Council for its adoption, pursuant to the non-objection procedure.[232] **15.167**

Following such approval, the concerned entity will be notified of the relevant sanctioning decision (an ECB supervisory decision).[233] The sanctioning decision will become executive then, and the potential submission of a request for review before the ABoR will not suspend its application.[234] **15.168**

After the notification of the sanctioning decision takes place, there are three potential avenues: **15.169**

(i) The relevant entity may decide to abide to the sanctioning decision and not to pursue any further steps.[235]
(ii) The entity at stake may decide to request the review of the sanctioning decision by the ABoR.[236] If the ABoR considers the request admissible, it will issue a non-binding opinion addressed to the Supervisory Board.

227 As regards the breaches it considered to be committed (art. 127(4) SSM Fr).
228 Cf art. 127(5) SSM Fr.
229 Cf art. 127(6) SSM Fr.
230 Cf art. 127(7) SSM Fr. See, also, art. 126(2)-4 SSM Fr and Sections B.3. (*Stage 3: Issuance of the Statement of Objections and the first round of comments by the concerned entity*) and B.4. (*Stage 4: Second hearing and preparation of a draft final decision*) immediately above in this chapter.
231 Namely, as per cases described in romans (ii) and (iv) above. Cf art. 127(8)–(9) SSM Fr.
232 See, on this matter, Section B.3. (*Approval via non-objection process and/or via delegation*) in Chapter 8.
233 Cf art. 35 SSM Fr.
234 Cf art. 34 SSM Fr. The foregoing, unless the Governing Council decides to suspend the application of the sanctioning decision *motu proprio*.
235 It may also decide to pay the penalty imposed right away or wait for the ECB enforcement, if any.
236 See Paras. 1 and 5 of art. 24 SSM R.

On the basis of that opinion,[237] the Supervisory Board will issue a new complete draft decision addressed to the Governing Council which "*shall abrogate the initial decision, replace it with a decision of identical content, or replace it with an amended decision*".[238] Such new decision will be adopted by the Governing Council, if any, under the non-objection procedure and the concerned entity will be notified.

(iii) After requesting the review of the ABoR or even directly (without undergoing the ABoR review),[239] the entity may decide to submit a claim before the General Court[240] within two months[241] after the notification of the relevant decision.[242]

15.170 Finally, and pursuant to art. 132 SSM Fr, it must be outlined that upon notification to the concerned entity, the ECB must publish such a decision, including information on (i) the type and nature of the breach and (ii) the identity of the concerned entity.[243] Should such a decision be challenged before the CJEU, the ECB will publish in its website such a fact and any change on statutes regarding such judicial proceeding.[244] This information will be kept published by the ECB for at least five years.[245]

(b) Legal challenges and safeguards

(i) Safeguards: jurisdiction enjoyed by the CJEU to review ECB sanctioning decisions

15.171 The CJEU and the ECtHR admitted that administrative bodies may impose penalties that are criminal in nature, provided that the wrongdoer has access to a court that is independent and impartial and has full or unlimited jurisdiction. The lack of such unlimited jurisdiction can render the sanctioning regime incompatible with fundamental rights.

---

237 Contrary to what one might think due to the ABoR's independence and high standards, the ECB does not always follow its opinions (due to the non-binding nature of its opinions). In this respect, in the General Court judgement in joined Cases T-647/21 and T-99/22 (*Sber Vermögensverwaltungs AG v ECB*) of 28 February 2024 (ECLI:EU:T:2024:127) at Para. 15, it seems clear that the ECB expressly departed from the ABoR's approach.

238 Cf Art. 24(7) SSM R.

239 It must be noted that filing for the review of the ABoR is optional and does not constitute a precondition to file a claim before the CJEU (as it is the case, for instance, for the ESAs when the concerned individual is able to file for the review of the Board of Appeal). See Brescia Morra, C., Smits, R. & Magliari, A. (2017) at pp. 572–573. See also Koupepidou, E. (2021). Administrative pre-litigation review mechanism in the SSM: the Administrative Board of Review. In *Judicial Review in the European Banking Union* (pp. 28–43). Edward Elgar Publishing.

240 Actually before the General Court. Cf art. 24(11) SSM R. See further in Lenaerts, K., Maselis, I. and Gutman, K. (2015).

241 Art. 263.VI TFEU.

242 Including the *revised* decision, if, prior to submitting a claim before the CJEU, the relevant entity submitted a request for review addressed to the ABoR.

243 Art. 132(1) SSM Fr. Cf art. 68(1)–(2) CRD IV.

244 Art. 132(2) SSM Fr.

245 Art. 132(3) SSM Fr. Cf art. 68(3) CRD IV.

Whether the CJEU enjoys full jurisdiction to review ECB sanctioning decisions is debatable. Such a topic has been extensively discussed in Section D.2. (*Has the CJEU unlimited jurisdiction to review administrative penalties imposed by the ECB*) in Chapter 8.[246] **15.172**

Pursuant to that analysis, it is concluded here that the CJEU enjoys full jurisdiction as regards *fines* and the *administrative pecuniary penalties*. Yet, such an approach requires some interpretative efforts to render the system fully compliant with the minimum safeguards required in the Charter and in the ECHR. **15.173**

(ii) Legal challenges

This Stage 5 of the sanctioning procedure raises a number of interpretative legal issues. Those relate to: (i) the content of the file that must be submitted to the Supervisory Board for the approval of a draft sanctioning decision, (ii) the role played by the ABoR decisions, and the integration of its reasoning in the final sanctioning decision, (iii) the limits that bar the imposition of administrative penalties and (iv) the interactions between ECB sanctioning proceedings and criminal offences. **15.174**

Content of the file to be submitted to the Supervisory Board

The content of the sanctioning file is actually quite relevant. Art. 127 SSM Fr requires that the Supervisory Board is provided with *a complete file*. However, it is not clear from the SSM Fr what is meant by a complete file or what documents, at least, should be provided to the Supervisory Board so that the file can be considered complete. **15.175**

Pursuant to art. 32 SSM Fr,[247] the file is composed by "*all documents obtained, produced or assembled by the ECB during the ECB supervisory procedure, irrespective of the storage medium*". **15.176**

The issue may arise when the file contains relevant documents, which are written in a different language of the working language used by the ECB, that is English.[248] It could happen that the Supervisory Board could be served a file that is materially complete[249] but which, nevertheless, it cannot fully understand as (some) documents would not be translated into English. It could **15.177**

246 Of the same opinion is D'Ambrosio. See D'Ambrosio, R. (2021) at pp. 328–332.

247 Applicable to ECB sanctioning proceedings in accordance with art. 25(1) SSM Fr.

248 In this regard, it must be recalled that different language arrangements may be set up *vis-à-vis* the different supervised entities. See further in Section B.1. (*The sources of administrative procedural law for the ECB under the SSM*) in Chapter 7.

249 In the sense that it contains all the relevant documents produced or incorporated during the procedure.

hence happen that, if those documents are not duly translated, the Supervisory Board ends up taking a decision on the basis of evidence that it is not able to duly examine and understand. The issue can become sharp when the draft sanctioning decision is based on a particular set of documents (or a document) which is used to destroy the concerned entity's presumption of innocence[250] and that has not been translated into English.

15.178 In these cases, the principle of impartiality and the necessary separation between the investigation and decision-making phase, required for sanctioning (materially criminal) procedures,[251] would be impinged, as the decision-making body would not be provided with all the elements of judgement necessary to make a fair decision.[252]

15.179 Ideally, in order to decide, the Supervisory Board should have all the documents composing the file translated into English. However, the same result can be materially achieved if the Supervisory Board has made available English versions of the SO, the complete draft supervisory decision, the observations submitted by the investigated entity and any other document included in the file that may have a material relevance for the determination of the breach and which is used[253] to determine and prove the existence of breaches.

15.180 It is the determination of those last documents which may cause problems. As such, practice shows that *limit cases* exist, and disagreement may arise between the Supervisory Board and the Investigating Unit[254] as regards the need to translate a given document. For example, when preparing the file, the Investigating Unit considered unnecessary to translate a given document that

---

250 See Karagianni, A. M. (2022) at pp. 206 and ss. On the topic of the *presumption of innocence*, see Villamarín López, M. L. (2017). The presumption of innocence in Directive 2016/343/EU of 9 March 2016. In *ERA Forum* Vol. 18, No. 3 (pp. 335–353). Berlin/Heidelberg: Springer.

251 See Section D.1. (*Sanctions having a criminal nature imposed by an administrative (not jurisdictional) body: right to a fair trial under the SSM R?*) in Chapter 8.

252 Which ultimately affects the independence of the decision-making body (the Supervisory Board) to comply with the task it has been entrusted, as it would be relying on the draft sanctioning decision provided by the Investigating Unit without having the chance to verify the details and conclusions reached on the basis of those untranslated documents. See, on the necessary impartiality of the decision-making body, the ECtHR landmark cases *Dubus*, at Para. 54 (and case law cited therein), and *DB v Consob*, at paras. 135–136 (and cited case law therein). See, on this topic, Lasagni, G. (2019) at pp. 202 and ss.

Outside the remit of the ECHR, on the EU side, only two AG opinions (not a single judgment) have linked the considerations made in *Dubus* as regards the need to separate the investigation from the decision-making phase to comply with the principle of impartiality. See (i) Opinion of AG Kokott in case C-358/16 (*UBS (Luxembourg) SA and Others*), delivered on 26 July 2017 (ECLI:EU:C:2017:606), at Para. 88; and (ii) Opinion of AG Campos Sánchez-Bordona in case C-524/15 (*Luca Menci*), delivered on 12 September 2017 (ECLI:EU:C:2017:667), at Para. 125.

253 And indicated in the draft supervisory decision.

254 And within the Supervisory Board itself.

one member of the Supervisory Board judged particularly relevant to determine the commission of a breach or its severity or even the mitigants concurring in the case at stake.

There is no general formula that can be sketched to determine which those documents are, and to tackle this issue, a case-by-case analysis must be carried out by the investigating officer and further assessed by the Supervisory Board itself.[255] **15.181**

Integration of the ABoR opinions in the final ECB supervisory (sanctioning) decision review

For the purposes of determining whether a given ECB supervisory decision complies with the requirement of providing sufficient motivation,[256] the CJEU has reiterated that one needs to look not only to the text of the resolution at stake but also at its *context* and the legal framework governing it.[257] **15.182**

As a starting point, it must recalled that it is not compulsory for the concerned entity to request the review of the ECB sanctioning decisions before the ABoR to be able to challenge them later before the General Court.[258] It must be also outlined that ABoR results are not binding for the ECB,[259] since art. 24(7) indicates that the ABoR should issue only *opinions*.[260] **15.183**

Against this background, it is worth considering whether ABoR decisions, aimed at re-examining the case at stake, are integrated in the final decision adopted by the Governing Council. **15.184**

Concerning that notion of *context* in which ECB supervisory decisions are issued, the CJEU[261] indicated early that ABoR's opinions integrate that context and form part of the final supervisory decision taken by the ECB[262] (after considering such ABoR's opinions). Such doctrine seems to be settled as the **15.185**

255 Who, in any event, could request the completion of the file (including the translation of relevant documents, as appropriate) pursuant to art. 127(3) SSM Fr.

256 As broadly foreseen in art. 296 TFEU, and more specifically within the SSM in arts. 22(2) SSM R and 33 SSM Fr. On the need to motivate EU administrative decision, see Section B.2.(d).(1). (*Some reflections on the safeguards applicable in the procedure for lapsing and withdrawing banking licenses*) in Chapter 14.
See, also, Lasagni, G. (2019) at pp. 194–195.

257 Cf Court of Justice judgment in case C-439/11 P (*Ziegler* v *Commission)* of 1 July 2013 (EU:C:2013:513), at Para. 116.

258 Cf art. 24(11) SSM R. See immediately above in this Section and in Brescia Morra, C., Smits, R. & Magliari, A. (2017) at pp. 572–573.

259 As EU Institutions are subject to Treaty limitations, which do not allow establishing binding review mechanisms. See, on this topic, Koupepidou, E. (2021).

260 Which the Supervisory Board must take into account, but which do not bind it. Ibidem.

261 The General Court confirmed first, and the Court of Justice confirmed later.

262 See *L-Bank case* at Paras. 124–127. See, also, L-Bank Appeal at Paras. 95–96.

General Court is prone to consider ABoR's opinions part of the contested supervisory decision *per relationem*.[263]

15.186 ABoR's opinions are not made public,[264] which means that a negative decision does not put an added pressure on the ECB based on its reputational effects. Furthermore, and as indicated right above, any justification that the ABoR may provide for the ECB's act is assimilated by the Court into the statement of reasons of the ECB itself. Thus, the way it has been shaped, one could say, rather than a mechanism of review, is purposed as a second chance for the ECB. Since filing a request for review is not mandatory, a legitimate question arises: is it worth submitting such a request for review?

15.187 The answer to this question depends on the concrete situation and on the factual and legal objections to be raised. Strategically wise, the concerned entity may understand that the reasons stated in the relevant ECB supervisory decision fall short of justifying the sanctioning decision finally taken. In that scenario, there is a solid argument not to request the review of the ABoR and directly filing a claim before the General Court.

15.188 The foregoing would prevent the integration of the opinion of the ABoR within the contested decision, thus barring any possibility that a sanctioning decision be appropriately complemented and potential motivational flaws cured. Reaction to such a strategical consideration would require the ECB to eventually increase attention as regards motivation.[265]

---

263 General Court judgment in cases T-351/18 and T-584/18 (*Ukrselhosprom PCF LLC v ECB* and *Versobank AS v ECB*, respectively) of 6 October 2021 (ECLI:EU:T:2021:669), at Paras. 387–388.

264 Brescia Morra, C., Smits, R. & Magliari, A. (2017) at pp. 573: "*The proceedings of the ABoR are confidential and its opinions are not published, unless the Governing Council authorises the President to make the outcome of such proceedings public*".

In the same vein, see Arrigoni, M. (2020). The Administrative Board of Review of the European Central Bank. A critical analysis. *Rivista Orizzonti Del Diritto Commerciale, 2*, pp. 519–538. At pp. 536–537. The author proposes that the Governing Council should make the ABoR decision public (as a general rule) to improve the transparency of the ECB and help to overcome its accountability deficit (as pointed out by the ECA (see, on the ECA observations, Section B.2. (*Composite procedures and political and administrative accountability*) in Chapter 10).

265 General Court judgment in cases T-576/18 (*Crédit agricole v ECB*) of 8 July 2020 (ECLI:EU:T:2020:304), T-577/18 (*Crédit agricole Corporate and Investment Bank v ECB*) of 8 July 2020 (ECLI:EU:T:2020:305) and T-578/18 (*CA Consumer Finance v ECB*) of 8 July 2020 (ECLI:EU:T:2020:306 constitutes a valid precedent in this regard, as those lead to the partial annulation of an ECB sanctioning decision due to lack of motivation on the methodology used to calculate the amount of the penalties imposed). See previous Section B.4.(b).(1). (*Determination of the fines: Basis for the calculation of administrative pecuniary penalties*) above in this chapter.

Time limits for the imposition and enforcement of penalties by the ECB[266]

Art. 130 SSM Fr establishes the time limits for the imposition of penalties. In general, breaches capable of being sanctioned directly by the ECB are subject to a lapsing period of five years.[267] Such a lapsing period will start (i) the day the breach is committed and (ii), in the case of ongoing breaches, the day such infringement ceased. **15.189**

This period will be interrupted in the case the ECB takes any investigatory action as regards such breach.[268] These interruptions restart the countdown of the lapsing period. Nevertheless "*the limitation period shall expire at the latest on the day on which a period equal to twice the duration of the limitation period has elapsed without the ECB having imposed an administrative penalty*".[269] **15.190**

The limitation period will be suspended in the case (i) a request for review is submitted to the ABoR, (ii) an action is filed to the CJEU[270] and (iii) criminal proceedings are brought against the relevant entity as regards the same facts for the period such proceedings are ongoing.[271] **15.191**

Art. 131 SSM Fr, on its side, regulates the limitation periods for the enforcement of penalties imposed by the ECB. As a general rule, the ECB enjoys a limitation period of five years to enforce any penalty it imposed.[272] Any action taken by the ECB with a view to enforce the payment of the relevant fines[273] interrupts such a limitation period[274] and restarts it.[275] As an exception, this lapsing period will be interrupted (i) for so long as a grace period for the payment is granted and (ii) if the enforcement of the relevant payment is suspended by decision of the Governing Council[276] or of the CJEU. **15.192**

---

266 This topic has not attracted much academic attention. However, reference can be made to the following works: (i) Papathanassiou, C. (2022)(ii) at Para. 23; (ii) Hayden, H. (2021). Enforcement of Fines and Other Pecuniary Obligations Imposed by the ECB (Part I): European Level. *European Company and Financial Law Review*, *18*(6), pp. 1011–1050, at p. 1040; and (iii) Allegrezza, S. (ed.). (2020) at pp. 69 and 90.

267 Art. 130(1) SSM Fr.

268 Art. 130(2) SSM Fr. Hence, it must be noted that only ECB actions addressed to clarify or investigate the potential breach may interrupt the lapsing period (and not other related or linked acts).

269 Art. 130(3) SSM Fr. Yet, "*that period shall be extended by any period of time for which the limitation period is suspended pursuant to paragraph 5*".

270 Art. 130(4) SSM Fr.

271 Art. 130(5) SSM Fr.

272 Art. 131(1) SSM Fr.

273 Which would include any formal or informal intimation for payment, as well as the fulfilment of any milestone scheduled in a payment calendar agreed with the relevant entity.

274 Art. 131(2) SSM Fr.

275 Art. 131(3) SSM Fr.

276 Which, in principle, should be duly notified to the concerned entity.

Commission of potential criminal offences

15.193 If at any point in time when carrying out its prudential supervisory tasks[277] the ECB suspects that criminal offences have been committed by supervised entities or natural persons linked to them, it may request NCAs to send the matter to national competent criminal authorities.[278]

15.194 On this, the *cooperative* nature of the SSM comes into play;[279] the ECB must refer the matter to the relevant NCA and relies on it to reach out the national prosecutor. It must be noted here that the ECB lacks the possibility of deferring the matter directly to national prosecuting authorities.[280] Additionally, two observations can be made as regards (i) the nature of the potential criminal offences to be communicated to the NCAs and (ii) the value attributed to the ECB request addressed to the NCA.

15.195 As per the *first* consideration, it must be noted that the type of offences of which the ECB may become aware can be very wide, including: money laundering and terrorism financing offences, crimes related to political corruption, tax offences, white collar crimes, etc. Due to its specific mandates, the ECB and the NCAs may only have the expertise to recognise a fraction of those potential offences, and hence, signs of the commission of potential offences may be unnoticed. This issue seems structurally difficult to overcome as both NCAs and the ECB lack relevant expertise. One potential avenue to mitigate, to the extent possible, this undesired flaw would entail some training to ECB staff (i.e., JST coordinators)[281] to raise awareness and facilitate the detection of evidence that could reveal the commission of offences pursuant to national rules.

15.196 The *second* consideration is linked to the nature of the request submitted by the ECB to the NCAs to report the potential commission of criminal offences to the national prosecuting activities. The situation here resembles the one occurring when the ECB sends a request addressed to NCAs to open sanctioning procedures under national law pursuant to art. 18(5) SSM R.[282]

---

277 Within or outside a sanctioning proceeding, as the provision simply refers to the tasks allocated to the ECB under the SSM. See Allegrezza, S. (ed.). (2020) at pp. 36–37.

278 Art. 136 SSM Fr. Similarly, see also art. 3(10) Regulation 2532/1998.

279 See Section B.2.(a). (*Vertical distribution of micro-prudential tasks concerning SIs*) in Chapter 6.

280 See Lasagni, G. (2019) at p. 138.

281 Cf art. 6 SSM Fr.

282 See Section C.2. (*National laws and administrative pecuniary penalties II: to which extent national legislation may limit ECB direct sanctioning powers under art. 18(5) SSM R?*) in Chapter 7 and D'Ambrosio, R. (2021).

Like in art. 18(5) SSM R, art. 136 SSM Fr consists of a *request*, which the relevant NCA (may) undertake in accordance with *national law*. Similarly, it appears that the ECB action is limited to send such a request, but the NCA would not be bound by it. On the contrary, it should assess such a request against the applicable domestic framework.[283] The margin of latitude granted to the NCA under the domestic framework is what ultimately will determine its involvement to the request received from the ECB. For example, if pursuant to the national rules, the NCA is obliged to report to the national prosecuting authorities any evidence of which it becomes aware; it will need to necessarily attend the request received. If, on the contrary, the national framework attributes to the NCA some degree of discretion to assess when the criminal evidence is relevant enough to be transferred to the prosecuting authorities, it may or may not refer the matter to the national prosecutor, depending ultimately on its own assessment.[284] **15.197**

Further issues arise here as regards potential frictions with the *ne bis in idem* principle and the prosecution of offences by national authorities. Those will be examined later on in Section C.2.(b). (*Safeguards: ne bis in idem and linkage with the facts established in the ECB direct sanctioning procedure*) of this chapter. **15.198**

C. ECB REQUESTS ADDRESSED TO NCAS TO OPEN SANCTIONING PROCEDURES UNDER ART. 18(5) SSM R

Following the distribution of sanctioning tasks operated by the SSM R,[285] the ECB may request the NCAs to open sanctioning proceedings, under relevant national law, with a view to sanction natural persons and entities. It must be recalled that pursuant to the referred allocation of tasks, the NCAs may only initiate such sanctioning proceedings upon ECB request[286] and, hence, never on its own initiative.[287] **15.199**

283 Ibidem.

284 See, in more detail, Allegrezza, S. (2020). Information Exchange Between Administrative and Criminal Enforcement: The Case of the ECB and National Investigative Agencies. *Eucrim: the European Criminal Law Associations' fŏrum*, (4), pp. 302–309.

285 See Section C. (*Allocation of sanctioning competences: a specialty over the general rule?*) in Chapter 6.
See, on this topic, Gortsos, C. V. (2015)(ii); Papathanassiou, C. (2022)(ii); Lamandini, M., Ramos Muñoz, D. & Solana, J. (2015); Lamandini, M., Ramos Muñoz, D. & Solana, J. (2016); Lasagni, G. (2019); and D'Ambrosio, R. (2021).

286 See art. 134(1) SSM Fr. See, also, Recital 36 SSM R.

287 However, they may request that the ECB makes use of such possibility. See art. 134(2) SSM Fr.

15.200 This Section will describe, *first*, the key aspects of those requests issued by the ECB and the potential outcome they may trigger. *Second*, the legal and safeguard-related issues that these requests may trigger will be analysed. Those issues concern, particularly, the coordination between the national sanctioning procedures with ECB direct sanctioning procedures.

1. Key aspects and basic steps of the requests addressed by the ECB to initiate sanctioning proceedings

15.201 The procedure for NCAs to open a sanctioning procedure under art. 18(5) SSM R follows almost the same procedural route and legal principles observed when the ECB makes use of its direct sanctioning powers under arts. 18(1) and 18(7) SSM R. This procedure is sketched in Figure 15.5

15.202 In this regard and *as a starting point*, the ECB may be reported potential breaches and/or become aware of them through the use of its investigatory powers.[288]

15.203 *Secondly*, and in light of the information gathered at a given point in time, the Investigating Unit may decide (i) to initiate the steps to submit a request addressed to the relevant NCA to initiate a sanctioning proceeding or (ii) not to further pursue such an avenue and to close the case. The Investigating Unit may resolve to close the case should it consider that there is no evidence that a breach falling under the scope of tasks allocated to the ECB under the SSM has been committed, or when, even if it considers that a potential breach has been committed, it has elapsed.[289]

15.204 The assessment described above may take place at any of the following moments:[290]

(i) While conducting the relevant investigation prior to adopting a decision to initiate a direct sanctioning proceeding.
(ii) Upon the formal initiation of a sanctioning proceeding, simultaneously to the submission of the SO to the investigated entity or, subsequently, within that

288 See the analysis and description provided in Sections B.1. (*Stage 1: Reporting of potential breaches and decision to initiate sanctioning procedure*) and B.2. (*Stage 2: Investigatory phase: research conducted by the Investigating Unit*) in this chapter above.

289 When the lapsing period of five years foreseen in art. 130(1) SSM Fr has passed without interruption. See further, Section B.5.(b). (*Legal challenges and safeguards*) in this chapter above. See, also, Papathanassiou, C. (2022)(ii) at Para. 23.

290 Those have been already identified in the different stages composing the direct sanctioning proceeding. See previous Section B. (*ECB direct sanctioning powers: Procedure for the imposition of administrative pecuniary penalties and fines*) in this chapter.

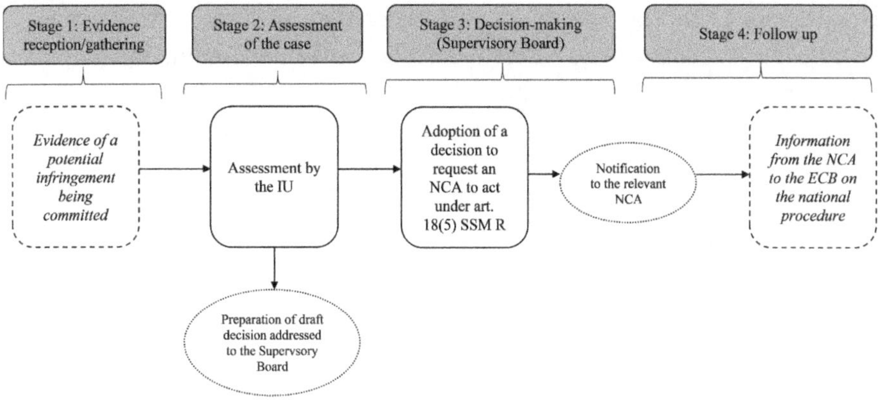

Figure 15.5 *SSM art. 18(5): Referral workflow*

first hearing phase (i.e., after the reception of the observations submitted by the entity).

(iii) During the *second hearing phase*, i.e., simultaneously to the preparation of the draft complete decision shared with the concerned entity or upon the reception of the written observations submitted by it.

(iv) During the *decision-making phase*, should the Supervisory Board not agree with the complete draft proposal of the supervisory (sanctioning) decision submitted by the Investigating Unit but understand that a different breach has been committed,[291] for whose sanction needs to address a request to the relevant NCA.

Thirdly, if the Investigating Unit considers that the ECB should act and hence request the relevant NCA to initiate a sanctioning procedure under art. 18(5) SSM R, it will prepare a complete draft decision detailing the terms and scope of the request to act. **15.205**

Such a request will be submitted to the Supervisory Board for its approval. The outcome from the Supervisory Board can be the same as the one foreseen for direct sanctioning proceedings in the *decision-making phase*.[292] Basically, the Supervisory Board may decide to: (i) approve the complete draft decision, (ii) reject it (ending the proceeding) or (iii) amend the complete draft decision.[293] **15.206**

291 Cf art. 127(7) SSM Fr.

292 See Section B.5. (*Stage 5 (Decision phase): Submission to the Supervisory Board (and Governing Council approval)*) above in this chapter.

293 That would be the case if it understands that other different (or additional) breaches may have been committed by the relevant persons identified in such a draft proposal.

15.207 Upon approval by the Supervisory Board of the complete draft decision, if any, such a proposal will be submitted to the Governing Council for approval under the non-objection procedure.

15.208 *Finally*, the relevant decision is formally notified to the concerned NCA.[294] This is not formally foreseen in Title 6 of the SSM Fr,[295] however, legal certainty and alignment with the mechanism settled in art. 88(2) SSM Fr so demands.

15.209 Pursuant to the principle of sincere cooperation,[296] the ECB may request the relevant NCA to periodically inform it on the status of the procedure. Additionally, art. 134(3) SSM Fr expressly contemplates that the relevant NCA must inform the ECB "*of the penalties* [finally] *imposed, if any*". Based on the same cooperative principle, art. 135 SSM Fr establishes that the NCAs must inform, periodically, the ECB on penalties they may impose on LSIs as regards the supervisory tasks falling under the SSM R.[297]

2. Legal challenges and procedural safeguards

(a) Legal challenges: coordination between the ECB and NCAs

15.210 Before assessing the coordination challenges arising from art. 18(5) SSM R, it is helpful to recall the literal wording of this provision:

> *5. In the cases not covered by paragraph 1 of this Article, where necessary for the purpose of carrying out the tasks conferred on it by this Regulation, the ECB may require national competent authorities to open proceedings with a view to taking action in order to ensure that appropriate penalties are imposed in accordance with the acts referred to in the first subparagraph of Article 4(3) and any relevant national legislation which confers specific powers which are currently not required by Union law. The penalties applied by national competent authorities shall be effective, proportionate and dissuasive.*
>
> *The first subparagraph of this paragraph shall be applicable in particular to pecuniary penalties to be imposed on credit institutions, financial holding companies or mixed financial holding companies for breaches of national law transposing relevant Directives, and to any administrative*

294 Even if, evidently, the NCA participates in the Supervisory Board and in the Governing Council. The foregoing, except in the case of non-euro currency participating MSs, which do not have a seat in the Governing Council (and hence may not be immediately aware of the approval of the relevant decision to request the NCA at stake to open a sanctioning procedure under art. 18(5) SSM R).

295 Titled "*COOPERATION BETWEEN THE ECB AND NCAs IN EURO AREA MEMBER STATES UNDER ARTICLE 18(5) OF THE SSM REGULATION*" and comprising arts. 134 and 135 SSM Fr.

296 On the principle of sincere cooperation within the SSM, see Weismann, P. (2017). The European Central Bank (ECB) Under the Single Supervisory Mechanism (SSM): Its Functioning and Its Limits. *TARN Working paper 1/2017.* At pp. 4–8.

297 Such continuous reporting obligation seems to be aligned (and would even be redundant) with the general obligation imposed on the NCAs to continuously inform on supervisory measures adopted *vis-à-vis* LSIs (art. 99(1) SSM Fr) and, in particular, those which have a material impact on LSIs (art. 98 SSM Fr).

penalties or measures to be imposed on members of the management board of a credit institution, financial holding company or mixed financial holding company or any other individuals who under national law are responsible for a breach by a credit institution, financial holding company or mixed financial holding company.

Pursuant to its statutory foundation, the ECB is unable to sanction natural persons and to impose other penalties than pecuniary ones.[298] In this vein, the abovementioned provision allows to circumvent such limitation and ensures that, indirectly, the ECB is somehow vested with a complete panoply of sanctioning powers. **15.211**

The cases in which the ECB may require a given NCA to open a sanctioning procedure, under national law, include the following ones:[299] **15.212**

(i) Imposition of pecuniary and non-pecuniary penalties on natural persons belonging to SIs (e.g., managers or members of the board of a credit institution[300]) for breaches of directly applicable Union rules.
(ii) Imposition of pecuniary and non-pecuniary penalties on natural persons belonging to SIs for breaches of national laws transposing prudential Directives or of national rules that attribute to the relevant NCA specific powers not required by EU law but closely connected with prudential rules .[301]
(iii) Imposition of non-pecuniary penalties to SIs for breaches of directly applicable EU law.
(iv) Imposition of pecuniary and non-pecuniary penalties to SIs as regards breaches of national law transposing EU law[302] or of national rules that attribute to the relevant NCA specific powers not required by EU law but closely connected with prudential rules.[303]
(v) Concerning LSIs, imposition of penalties concerning "breaches of 'common procedures'", for which the ECB remains exclusive competence.[304]

---

298 See in more detail in Section C. (*Allocation of sanctioning competences: a specialty over the general rule?*) in Chapter 6.

299 Cf art. 134 SSM Fr. See Lackhoff, K. (2017)(i) at pp. 217–219; Gortsos, C. V. (2015)(ii) at p. 27; and Allegrezza, S. & Voordeckers, O. (2015) at pp. 157–158.

300 In general, the individuals "*who under national law are responsible for a breach by a credit institution, financial holding company or mixed financial holding company*" (art. 18(5)II SSM R). See above as regards the statutory limitation discussed (art. 34(3) SESCB).

301 I.e., (i) they fall under the scope of the specific micro-prudential tasks allocated to the ECB under the SSM R and (ii) underpin a supervisory function foreseen under EU law. See Section A.2.(b).(2). (*What happens when the national statute allocates powers in excess to the ones foreseen in a prudential Directive?*) in Chapter 7.

302 As regards the three cases indicated above, see in more detail in Section C. (*Allocation of sanctioning competences: a specialty over the general rule?*) in Chapter 6.

303 Ibidem footnote 300.

304 See ECB Annual Report on Sanctioning Activities in the SSM in 2021: Annual Report on Sanctioning Activities in the SSM in 2021 (europa.eu). At footnote 2. See also Fernandez-Bollo, E. & Teixeira, P. G. (2021). Fostering a compliance culture in the European banking system. ECB. The supervision blog: Fostering a compliance culture in the European banking system (europa.eu).

15.213 ECB requests to NCAs to open sanctioning procedures require an intense cooperation and coordination between the two of them, capable of constituting top-down composite procedures where the NCA has the final word.[305] Anticipating that mismatches and flaws concerning such coordination may happen, it is worth wondering (i) what kind of control the ECB can exercise over NCAs; additionally, (ii) whether the ECB would be vested with any prerogatives and powers to correct any flaws concerning such coordination or even the NCAs' inactivity.

15.214 Concerning the first question, it must be noted that, beyond formulating its request, the ECB has very little control over the sanctioning procedure to be undertaken, eventually, by the concerned NCA.

15.215 This is supported by the fact that, unlike art. 9(1)III[306] SSM R, art 18(5) SSM R does not qualify the request of the ECB as an *instruction*. The plain wording of art. 18(5) simply indicates that the ECB can *require* NCAs to initiate sanctioning procedures. Consequently, art. 18(5) SSM R limits the coordinating power of the ECB to the mere issuance of such request.[307]

15.216 It could not be otherwise, as the sanctions to be imposed by the relevant NCA either (i) relate to subjects over which the ECB has no capacity to sanction (natural persons), (ii) concern infringements of national rules transposing prudential rules or (iii) are not pecuniary, and hence, they fall outside the statutory powers vested on the ECB.[308]

15.217 Another factor limiting ECB oversight over the procedures started by the NCA (or its lack of initiation) is that those are sustained exclusively on national rules and fall under the exclusive jurisdiction of national courts.[309]

15.218 The foregoing allows to anticipate the reply to the second question formulated above; in principle, the ECB would not be vested with any coordinating power to oversee how (and if) the relevant NCA has attended their request to initiate a sanctioning proceeding under art. 18(5) SSM R.

---

305 See further in Section C. (*Sanctions under the SSM in light of cooperation, coordination and composition*) in Chapter 11.

306 As noted by Lasagni. See Lasagni, G. (2019) at pp. 128–129.

307 In favour of this approach, see (i) D'Ambrosio, R. (2021) at pp. 324–325; (ii) Wissink, L. (2021)(ii) at pp. 260 and ss.; Felisatti, V. (2018) at pp. 387–388; and Lehmann, M. (2021) at p. 84.

308 See in more detail in Section C. (*Allocation of sanctioning competences: a specialty over the general rule?*) in Chapter 6.

309 See Lehmann, M. (2021) at p. 84.; and Wissink, L. (2021)(ii) at pp. 263–264.

Despite the ECB not being allocated with powers to oversee how the NCAs fulfil the request under art. 18(5) SSM R, one can expect that NCAs feel constrained to attend those requests and to, at least, initiate the requested sanctioning procedures. This approach is natural considering the subordinated role attributed to the NCAs in the SSM. **15.219**

In addition, even if it is not possible not to refer to *coordination*, building upon the principle of sincere cooperation enshrined in the SSM R and on the general periodical information duties of the NCAs towards the ECB,[310] the ECB must be informed of any development regarding sanctioning procedures triggered by the NCAs as regards LSIs, SIs and/or their staff.[311] **15.220**

Does this mean that there is no coordination between the ECB and NCAs regarding the request foreseen in art. 18(5) SSM R? Absolutely not. The ECB and the NCAs intensively cooperate and exchange in formal[312] and informal manners before launching any such request. The foregoing ensures a minimum degree of coordination in which both the ECB and NCAs exchange on equal footing. **15.221**

(b) Safeguards: *ne bis in idem* and linkage with the facts established in the ECB direct sanctioning procedure

This Section examines whether, within the sanctioning interactions displayed by the SSM *ad intra* (between the ECB and NCAs) and *beyond* (between the ECB/NCAs and national prosecuting or national administrative authorities), there can be frictions which jeopardise the principle of *ne bis in idem*. On the basis of the previous analysis, it is aimed at concluding whether such *frictions* are structural or, rather, isolated events capable of, eventually, being prevented. **15.222**

To do so, in the following lines: (i) *first*, the definition of the principle of *ne bis in idem* will be examined (in the light of the CJEU and ECtHR case law). (ii) Further, the two elements composing the principle of *ne bis in idem* (the *bis* and the *idem* elements) will be assessed to circumscribe its scope and practical application. (iii) Building upon the vertical allocation of sanctioning competences depicted by the SSM R, some particular cases that raise concern on their compliance with the *ne bis in idem* principle will be presented and **15.223**

310 Cf art. 92 SSM Fr (regarding SIs) and art. 99 SSM Fr (as regards LSIs).

311 See arts. 134 (SIs) and 135 (LSIs) SSM Fr.

312 Account taken that ECB requests issued under art. 18(5) SSM R will adopt the form of an ECB supervisory decision, and so the concerned NCA will participate in the decision-making procedure (at least within the Supervisory Board).

separately analysed. (iv) Finally, on the basis of the precedent analysis, some conclusions will be drawn.

15.224 For what matters for the EU legal framework, the *ne bis in idem* principle is enunciated in art. 50 ECHR.[313] Additionally, and as the rights contemplated in the Charter need to be construed in compliance with the ECHR,[314] reference must be made to art. 4(1) and to Protocol 7 ECHR.[315]

15.225 Following the abovementioned provisions, the principle of *ne bis in idem* precludes that an individual is prosecuted (and punished) twice for the same facts or offence.[316] Within the remit of the Charter, this principle has a *transnational* dimension,[317] applying across EU jurisdiction and to the procedures carried out by EU bodies and institution itself.[318]

15.226 The principle of *ne bis in idem* applies to *criminal* procedures, which entails that, in principle,[319] administrative sanctions which are criminal in nature cannot be cumulated with criminal sanctions *stricto sensu* (or with other penalties having a *coloration pénale*).[320]

---

313 Reading as follows: "*No one shall be liable to be tried or punished again in criminal proceedings for an offence for which he or she has already been finally acquitted or convicted within the Union in accordance with the law*".

Cf also arts. 54–58 of the Convention, implementing the Schengen Agreement of 14 June 1985 between the Governments of the States of the Benelux Economic Union, the Federal Republic of Germany and the French Republic on the gradual abolition of checks at their common borders. On the interplay of this piece of EU secondary legislation with the Charter and with the *ne bis in idem* principle, see Felisatti, V. (2018) at p. 393.

314 Art. 52(3) Charter. See Court of Justice judgment in case C-279/09 (*DEB Deutsche Energiehandels- und Beratungsgesellschaft mbH v Bundesrepublik Deutschland*) of 22 December 2010 (ECLI:EU:C:2010:811). At Paras. 35. See, also, van Bockel, B. (2017) at p. 205.

315 Reading as follows: "*1. No one shall be liable to be tried or punished again in criminal proceedings under the jurisdiction of the same State for an offence for which he has already been finally acquitted or convicted in accordance with the law and penal procedure of that State*".

316 van Bockel, B. (2017); van Bockel, W. B. (2015). *Fundamental rights aspects of the SSM: Differentiated standards of protection under the Charter of Fundamental Rights of the EU.* Retrieved from: (PDF) Fundamental rights aspects of the Single Supervisory Mechanism: differentiated standards of protection under the Charter of Fundamental Rights of the EU | Willem Bastiaan van Bockel – Academia.edu.

317 See the Explanations Relating to the Charter of Fundamental Rights ((2007/C 303/02)). See, also, Felisatti, V. (2018) at p. 392–393.

318 When the matter falls under the scope of application foreseen in art. 51 Charter, see, in this regard, Section A.1. (*What rights and procedural guarantees (due process rights)?*) in Chapter 13. See also Lamandini, M., Ramos Muñoz, D. & Solana, J. (2016) at pp. 204–206.

319 See immediately below; exceptionally, when those sanctioning procedures can be regarded as constituting a *consistent whole*, both the CJEU and the ECtHR have accepted that there would be no violation of the *ne bis in idem* principle.

320 See, also, Lamandini, M., Ramos Muñoz, D. & Solana, J. (2016) at p. 240. See also Case C-489/10 (*Łukasz Marcin Bonda*) of 5 June 2012 (ECLI:EU:C:2012:319), at Paras. 44–46.

As per the constitutive elements of the principle, the *bis* and in the *idem* elements, the following reflections can be made. 15.227

As regards the *bis* element, it protects the individual from new criminal proceedings being initiated or continued once one of the simultaneously ongoing proceedings becomes final.[321] The concept of a procedure being final entails that no further legal remedies are available to the defendant.[322] However, and tempering the foregoing, the ECtHR has indicated that, where the procedures are both *sufficiently connected* as regards substance and time, the safeguard provided by the *ne bis in idem* principle does not apply.[323] That is, where the procedures can be regarded as forming a *coherent whole* in reaction to the same facts, the principle is rendered inapplicable.[324] This approach has been also embraced by the Court of Justice in landmark cases *Menci*,[325] *Garlsson*[326] and *Enzo di Puma*.[327] 15.228

Concerning the *idem* element, in synthesis, refers to the fact that both concurring proceedings should be rooted in the *same facts*. This approach is followed by both the CJEU[328] and the ECtHR.[329] However, in competition cases, the CJEU has developed a (criticised)[330] doctrine, requiring, on top of the *same facts* criterion, that the legal interest protected also coincides.[331] The application of this latter approach has not been tested (yet) within the SSM.[332] However, considering the notable resemblances existing between the EU 15.229

321 Resulting in a ruling adjudicating on the substance of the matter. In this regard, the General Court has exhibited a lenient approach when the first procedure, regarding the same fact, has been annulled due to procedural reasons. See Lamandini, M., Ramos Muñoz, D. & Solana, J. (2016) at p. 239 (footnote 257).

322 See Court of Justice judgment in joined cases C-187/01 and C-385/01 (*Hüseyin Gözütok and Klaus Brügge*) of 11 February 2003 (ECLI:EU:C:2003:87), at Para. 33.

323 *A and B v Norway* of 15 November 2016 (Applications nos. 24130/11 and 29758/11). At Paras. 120–133.

324 And subject to certain additional guarantees aiming at ensuring that the punishment is proportionate and not excessive. Ibidem at Para.132. See, on this matter, Karagianni, A. M. (2022) at p. 109.

325 Court of Justice judgment in case C-524/15 (*Luca Menci v Procura della Repubblica*) of 20 March 2018 (ECLI:EU:C:2018:197). At Para. 44. See, also, Karagianni, A. M. (2022) at p. 109.

326 Court of Justice judgment in case C-537/16 (*Garlsson Real estate v. Commissione nazionale per le società e la borsa*) 20 March 2018 (ECLI:EU:C:2018:193). At Paras. 60–62.

327 Court of Justice judgment in joined cases C-596/16 and C-597/16 9 (*Enzo di Puma and Antonio Zecca*) of 20 March 2018 (ECLI:EU:C:2018:192). At Para. 43.

328 See Court of Justice judgments in joined cases C-187/01 and C-385/01 (*Hüseyin Gözütok and Klaus Brügge*) of 11 February 2003 (ECLI:EU:C:2003:87); and in case C-150/05 (*Jean Leon Van Straaten*) of 28 September 2006 (ECLI:EU:C:2006:614).

329 *Sergey Zolotukhin v. Russia* of 10 February 2009 (Application no. 14939/03).

330 See Karagianni, A. M. (2022) at pp. 109–110.

331 See Felisatti, V. (2018) at pp. 395–396; and Lamandini, M., Ramos Muñoz, D. & Solana, J. (2016) at p. 240.

332 See Karagianni, A. M. (2022) at p. 244.

competition enforcement framework and the SSM,[333] the application of this latter jurisprudence to the SSM looks quite probable.

15.230 Having exposed the basic features of the *ne bis in idem* principle, considering the vertical distribution of tasks operated by the SSM R, there are at least three types of situations that can eventually create frictions with this safeguard. Those are:

(i) Situations in which, on top of the imposition of an administrative pecuniary penalty or a fine on an entity (a SI), the ECB requests to the relevant NCA, pursuant to art. 18(5) SSM R, the opening of a sanctioning procedure with a view to impose a non-pecuniary penalty.
(ii) Situations in which a SI is punished and, simultaneously or subsequently, the ECB issues a request addressed to the relevant NCA to initiate sanctioning proceedings against a natural person belonging to that entity for the same facts and potentially for the same infringement.
(iii) Situations in which an infringement falling under the specific tasks allocated within the SSM is committed by an entity (LSI or SI) and the relevant sanctioning procedure is carried out by the ECB or by the relevant NCA; and a criminal (or criminal in nature) procedure is followed at national level.

15.231 Concerning the *first* case, there is broad academic consensus on the idea that the allocation of sanctioning tasks within the SSM and the coordination existing between the ECB and NCAs prevent the duplication of criminal in nature proceedings.[334] The author agrees with this approach as well, although it is worth digging into the practical scenarios and the potential issues that may raise.

15.232 National legal systems, on top of pecuniary penalties and following the path indicated in CRD IV,[335] have foreseen that non-pecuniary penalties[336] can be applied to breaches of prudential rules. These include cease and desist orders, publications of the penalty in the official journal, and, for what matters here, the revocation of the banking license.

333 See, for a notable analysis of this matter, Annunziata, F. and Maggiolino, M. (2021). See also the considerations made in van Bockel, B. (2017).

334 See Lamandini, M., Ramos Muñoz, D. & Solana, J. (2016) at p. 240; Felisatti, V. (2018) at p. 399; van Bockel, B. (2017) at pp. 212–213; and Karagianni, A. M. (2022) at pp. 106–107.

335 CF art. 64(1), 66(2) and 67(2) CRD IV.

336 See, for example, arts. 97(1)(b), 97(2) and 98(2) of Spanish Law 10/2014 on Solvency, Supervision and Ordination of Credit Institutions (*Ley 10/2014, de 26 de junio, de ordenación, supervisión y solvencia de entidades de crédito*).

It must be recalled here that the withdrawal of banking authorisations is a competence exercised exclusively by the ECB as regards both LSIs and SIs.[337] Consequently, it is for the ECB alone to deal with such punitive revocation. Furthermore, in the case a NCA envisaged withdrawing the banking license of an LSI (as a result of the commission of infringement falling under its remit), the NCA should request this to the ECB, following the relevant common procedure.[338] From this perspective, it is possible to conclude that when the revocation of a banking authorisation takes place as a consequence of the commission of an infringement,[339] it would constitute a *coherent whole* and would not contravene the *ne bis in idem* principle, as per the recent case law of both the ECtHR and the CJEU.[340] **15.233**

Additionally, it has been argued that the revocation of a banking license *per se* would not necessarily constitute a criminal in nature penalty, following the *Engel/Bonda* test.[341] Consequently, if this measure (the withdrawal of a banking license) was to be applied, it would not jeopardise the *ne bis in idem* principle as, in this scenario, there would be no double *criminal* punishment. **15.234**

Concerning the *second* situation indicated above,[342] as a matter of introduction, it must be emphasised that the ECB cannot sanction natural persons[343] (members of the board or key holder functions in supervised entities) nor other entities other than credit institutions, financial holding companies or mixed financial holding companies;[344] nor can it impose non-pecuniary sanctions on supervised entities. **15.235**

The issue arises when the ECB requests the NCAs, under art. 18(5) SSM R, to initiate a sanctioning proceeding against natural persons[345] on the basis of facts and legal observations already put forward in the ECB direct sanctioning **15.236**

---

337 See Section B. (*Allocation of micro-prudential tasks*) in Chapter 6.

338 See Section B.2. (*Withdrawal (and lapsing) of banking authorisations*) in Chapter 14.

339 On top of the imposition of a pecuniary penalty by the ECB or by the NCA, as the case may be.

340 See immediately above the references made to *A and B v Norway* (ECtHR) and *Menci*, *Garlsson* and *Enzo di Puma* (CJEU).

341 Of the same opinion, van Bockel, B. (2017) at pp. 210 and 212; and Felisatti, V. (2018) at p. 391.
Similarly, it has been argued before in this work that the removal of the member of the management board of an entity would constitute neither a criminal-in-nature sanction nor an administrative penalty. See Section C.2. (*ECB exercise of supervisory powers: are they criminal penalties in nature?*) in Chapter 8.

342 Situations in which a SI is punished and, simultaneously or subsequently, the ECB issues a request addressed to the relevant NCA to initiate sanctioning proceedings against a natural person belonging to that entity for the same facts and potentially for the same infringement.

343 Art. 34(3) SESCB and Recital 53 SSM R.

344 Cf arts. 18(1) and 18(5)II SSM R.

345 Or other entities for which the ECN is not competent to impose administrative penalties.

proceeding and for which those natural persons were not provided the opportunity to be heard and/or influence the ECB decision during the procedure.

15.237 In those circumstances, (i) one may wonder whether there is any breach of the *ne bis in idem* principle. (ii) Additionally, it is worth questioning what would be the value of the facts (and legal considerations) established in the ECB direct sanctioning procedure.

15.238 To answer the abovementioned first question, we need to look carefully at the requisites that trigger the application of the *ne bis in idem* which have been indicated immediately above.[346]

15.239 The fact that the direct sanctioning procedure handled by the ECB refers to different (legal) persons prevents that the *ne bis in idem* principle can be actioned in the request to open sanctioning procedures issued by the ECB under art. 18(5) SSM R.[347]

15.240 Eventually, other requisites can be also not met, contributing to reinforcing the idea that the *ne bis in idem* principle cannot apply in the case at stake. For instance, it may happen that, although connected to the facts directly sanctioned by the ECB, the facts upon which the ECB may request the relevant NCA to open a sanctioning proceeding differ. In those circumstances, the facts could not be exactly the same, as they would be referring to actions (or omissions) carried out by natural persons or other persons different from the supervised entities.

15.241 In addition, it can also occur that, by the time the ECB requests the relevant NCA to open a sanctioning proceeding against a given individual, its sanctioning decision is not final and can still be challenged before the CJEU.[348] This determines that the requisite of the first decision being final is not met.

---

346 On the CJEU jurisprudence on the application of the *ne bis in idem* principle, see, among others, Court of Justice judgments in cases (i) C-617/10 (*Åklagaren v Hans Åkerberg Fransson*) of 26 September 2013 (ECLI:EU:C:2013:105), (ii) C-524/15 (*Luca Menci*) of 20 March 2018 (ECLI:EU:C:2018:197), (iii) joined cases C-217/15 and C-350/15 (*Orsi Baldetti*) of 5 April 2017 (ECLI:EU:C:2017:264), (iv) C-436/04 (*Van Esbroeck*) of 9 March 2006 (ECLI:EU:C:2006:165) and (v) C-505/19 (*Bundesrepublik Deutschland*) of 12 May 2021 (ECLI:EU:C:2021:376).

347 In this vein, see Court of Justice judgment in joined cases C-217/15 and C-350/15 (*Orsi Baldetti*) of 5 April 2017 (ECLI:EU:C:2017:264), at Paras. 22–23. See, also, Felisatti, V. (2018) at p. 400 and 402.

348 Or the ECB sanctioning procedure may be even running in parallel. Another potential scenario entails that the sanctioning decision issued by the ECB is being challenged before the General Court (or appealed before the CJEU).

Consequently, the *ne bis in idem* principle does not prevent the issuance of ECB requests under art. 18(5) SSM R nor protects the concerned individual from the scrutiny, under the relevant sanctioning procedure, initiated by NCAs.[349] 15.242

From another angle, (ii) it is worth analysing the legal value that, eventually, NCAs must give to the facts proved and legal considerations determined in the ECB direct sanctioning proceeding. In other words: should NCAs consider proved the facts so declared in the relevant ECB direct sanctioning procedure, which led to the issuance of their request to act under art. 18(5) SSM R?[350] In the affirmative, would the NCAs be bound as well by the legal considerations stated in those procedures? 15.243

The case law of the CJEU has already dealt with similar cases from where we can draw some conclusions. For example, in recent case C-546/18 (*Adler Real Estate AG*),[351] the Court of Justice was requested to adjudicate on the value of facts and conclusions declared in a final administrative decision in a subsequent sanctioning decision of a criminal nature. 15.244

There, the applicant (*Adler Real Estate AG*), acting in coordination with other four persons, acquired stocks of an Austrian listed company above the threshold of 30% without notifying this fact to the financial market supervisor. This conduct was against the Austrian laws transposing relevant EU Directives. On 22 November 2016, the Takeover Commission (as the competent national authority) issued an administrative decision stating that the applicant and the rest of the acquirers failed to submit a bid as "*legal entities acting in concert*". Such decision was challenged before the Supreme Court. However, the high court confirmed the previous administrative decision and it became final. 15.245

On 29 June 2018, the Takeover Commission imposed administrative pecuniary sanctions to three natural persons. Two of them were members of the management of the acquiring entities and were not part of the previous procedure substantiated before the Takeover Commission. 15.246

The Takeover Commission argued that the sanctioning persons failed to comply with the requisite of notification or to ensure that the acquirers complied with it. Further, the Takeover Commission indicated that, pursuant to relevant 15.247

349 In case they consider it appropriate, or feasible, at its own discretion, considering the substantive and procedural rules applicable under the domestic legal framework.

350 See, more extensively on this matter and also incorporating a perspective from the Dutch and Greek jurisdictions, Karagianni, A. M. (2022) at pp. 102–111, 138 and 171.

351 Court of Justice judgment in case C-546/18 (*Adler Real Estate AG*), delivered on 9 September 2021 (ECLI:EU:C:2021:711).

national rules, in issuing its sanctioning decision, it was bound by the administrative decision previously issued on 22 November 2016, which became final.

15.248 The sanctioning decision was challenged before national courts and, during the procedure, requested a preliminary ruling from the CJEU was requested. The referring court wondered whether, when examining the sanctioning decision of 29 June 2018, it should be bound by the facts declared in the resolution issued on 22 November 2016 by the Takeover Commission, which had become final, even as regards the sanctioned persons which were not part in the procedure leading to this latter decision.

15.249 Building upon AG opinion,[352] the Court of Justice highlights that the rights of the defence enshrined in art. 47 of the Charter are subjective.[353] The concerned person must genuinely exercise them, and consequently, they cannot be exercised by the company or entity in which anyone is a manager or member of the board.[354]

15.250 Further, the Court of Justice states that:

> (…) *in proceedings for the imposition of an administrative penal sanction on a natural person, the administrative authority must disregard the binding effect attaching to assessments made in a decision which has found the alleged infringement to have been committed, and which has become final, without that person having had the opportunity to challenge those assessments in his or her personal capacity.*[355]

15.251 Extrapolating the abovementioned judgment to the SSM environment would imply that the NCAs, when dealing with national sanctioning procedures initiated at the request of the ECB,[356] should be completely free to determine the facts considered proved.[357] Further, they should not be bound also by any previous legal considerations reached by the ECB in its direct sanctioning procedure.

15.252 This conclusion is not easily palatable. There are several valid reputational considerations. These concern as to whether NCAs would *dare* to go as far as

352 Opinion of AG Bobek in case C-546/18 (*Adler Real Estate AG*), delivered on 18 March 2021 (ECLI:EU:C:2021:219).

353 Court of Justice judgment in case C-546/18 (*Adler Real Estate AG*) of 9 September 2021 (ECLI:EU:C:2021:711) at Para. 59.

354 Similarly, see also Court of Justice judgment in case C-687/13 (*Fliesen-Zentrum Deutschland*) of 10 September 2015 (EU:C:2015:573) at Para. 73. See also, General Court judgment in case T-228/17 (*Zhejiang Jndia Pipeline Industry v Commission*) of 19 September 2019 (EU:T:2019:619) at Para. 36.

355 Ibidem at Para. 60.

356 Also, when considering whether to initiate or not the requested sanctioning procedure.

357 On the academic writing supporting this view, see footnote 306.

denying facts and considerations reached by the ECB (and which, ultimately, they supported within the decision-making process). Additionally, if the foregoing scenario would happen, the intended *unity* of the SSM would be put under pressure, debilitating its institutional image.

Furthermore, this approach can lead also to the potential situation where some facts that are considered proven by the ECB may not be for the relevant NCA. This scenario can turn even more bizarre if the CJEU confirms a given ECB sanctioning decision and, by extension, the facts indicated therein, but those facts are not considered proven within a domestic legal order. **15.253**

Taking into account the constrained set up of the SSM, which is built within the limits provided by the enabling clause,[358] and the ECB statutory limitations regarding the possibility of sanctioning natural persons,[359] the possibilities of remedying this mismatch without proposing a SESCB modification are very limited. **15.254**

One potential avenue to limit flaws, to the extent possible, entails increasing ECB cooperation within the NCAs sanctioning procedure, with a view to harmonising the conclusions and facts reached in the ECB sanctioning procedure with those resulting from those led by NCAs. In this vein, NCAs can request the ECB to furnish them with the documentation and reports they used to determine the facts that lead to the sanction of a given conduct. Further, investigating officers may be called to ratify particular facts or to issue targeted reports, which could be incorporated to the national file to align the conclusions reached in both proceedings. **15.255**

Finally, as regards the *third* situation indicated above,[360] before initiating this analysis, it is worth specifying the concrete cases that can potentially arise. To do so, we will look at the concrete body (NCA or ECB) giving rise to the *ne bis in idem* concern within the SSM framework. **15.256**

(a) On the NCA side: a NCA may initiate a sanctioning procedure, which could be characterised as criminal in nature depending on the type of sanctions to be imposed (i) on its own account as regards LSIs and natural persons belonging to

358 Art. 127(6) TFEU. See more extensively on the limitations of the SSM constitutional basis in Chapter 2.
359 See immediately above in this Section.
360 Situations in which an infringement falling under the specific tasks allocated within the SSM is committed by an entity (LSI or SI), and the relevant sanctioning procedure is carried out by the ECB or by the relevant NCA; and a criminal (or criminal in nature) procedure is followed at national level.

them or (ii) at the request of the ECB, for example, to punish members of the board of a SI.[361]

In those cases, it could occur that a judicial criminal authority prosecutes the same subjects (LSIs or natural persons) as regards the same facts. That would be the case, for example, of criminal offences relating to tax fraud, money laundering, documentary fraud, etc. Additionally, it can even happen that national administrative authorities also initiate sanctioning procedures, which could lead to the imposition of materially criminal sanctions as regards the same facts.

(b) On the ECB side: the ECB may initiate a sanctioning procedure under art. 18(1) or 18(7) SSM R when it becomes aware that criminal procedure is being followed under the relevant national court aiming at punishing the same SI (or LSI, as regards art. 18(7) SSMR) for the same facts. Also, it may also occur that a national administrative authority follows a sanctioning procedure against the same entity for the same (or strictly connected) facts, which leads to the imposition of a criminal in nature sanction.

15.257 Against this background and in what concerns the entities (legal persons), it must be noted as regards criminal procedures (strictly speaking) that national legislation does not always contemplate that legal persons can be found criminally liable.[362] This fact should preclude the violation of the principle of *ne bis in idem* from occurring in a number of cases (and subject to a casuistic analysis).

15.258 Moreover, and as regards ECB direct sanctioning procedures and instructions issued under art. 18(5) SSM R, one may recall that pursuant to art. 136 SSM Fr,[363] the ECB may request the relevant NCA to communicate the facts having potential criminal relevance to the national prosecuting authorities.[364] This provision falls short of ensuring appropriate coordination and the avoidance of duplicated criminal procedures as, ultimately, the ECB itself does not have direct resource to the national prosecutors, and the referral remains at the relevant NCA discretion.[365] Additionally, this guarantee only works in one direction (from the ECB to national prosecuting authorities) but not the other way around. Consequently, the issue of coordination is only partially avoided, unless national rules cater for a similar reverse referral *vis-à-vis* the ECB.

361 This scenario is framed by Felisatti. See Felisatti, V. (2018) at p. 399–401.

362 Ibidem at p. 403. On the interplay between criminal systems and the SSM, see, in more detail, Allegrezza, S. (ed.). (2020).

363 Cf art. 3(10) of Regulation 2532/1998.

364 As noted in the precedent Section B.5.(b).(2).(iv). (*Commission of potential criminal offences*) of this chapter, the ECB must request the NCA to refer the facts to the prosecuting authorities, not having itself direct recourse to the national prosecutors. See Lasagni, G. (2019) at p. 267.

365 Ibidem. And subject to the applicable national rules, which may require the relevant NCA to assess the matter by itself or report the matter only when it judges that the facts allow to the determine the commission of a given offence in a clear manner.

In both cases (a) and (b) indicated above, it seems difficult, somehow, to sustain that the national criminal procedures and the ECB sanctioning ones form a *coherent whole* giving the lack of coordination between the concerned bodies. Further, it remains to be seen whether the total of the penalties finally imposed (or that can be imposed) can be regarded as proportionate. Drawing this ultimate conclusion would require a casuistic analysis of all national criminal orders that is well beyond this work. Accordingly, the more lenient jurisprudence followed by the ECtHR (*A and B v Norway*) and the CJEU (*Menci*, *Garlsson* and *Enzo di Puma*) may not be applied in these cases, resulting in a potential violation of the *ne bis in idem* principle protected under the Charter.[366] **15.259**

Finally, it cannot be taken for granted that the CJEU, if confronted with these cases, would apply the approach followed in competition cases.[367] As indicated immediately above, in competition cases, the CJEU, as regards the *idem* requirement, has required the identity of facts and of *legal interests protected* to apply the protection dispensed by the *ne bis in idem* principle. If the CJEU followed this approach, the risk of infringing the *ne bis in idem* principle would decrease. This should be subject, again, to a case-by-case analysis to determine whether the *legal interest* identity between the national criminal procedure and the ECB (or NCA) one concurs. **15.260**

In light of the analysis carried out in this Section, it can be noted that, indeed, the allocation of sanctioning tasks within the SSM prevents the violation of the *ne bis in idem* occurring at the level of the ECB/NCAs. However, the conclusion is different in situations which involve the prosecution of entities (and legal persons belonging to them) by national prosecutors pursuant to national criminal law or by national authorities (distinct from NCAs) capable of imposing criminal in nature sanctions.[368] **15.261**

366 Assuming also that the criminal proceeding tried by the national prosecutor falls under the remit of the Charter because it has a minimum EU legal order connection (art. 51(1)). Otherwise, the situation becomes even trickier, as the *ne bis in idem* may be subject to different standards: national and based on EU law. See, in this regard, van Bockel, B. (2017) at pp. 26–207.

367 See Karagianni, A. M. (2022) at p. 244.

368 In the same vein, as regards national prosecuting authorities and criminal offences, see van Bockel, B. (2017); and Felisatti, V. (2018).

15.262 There seems to be no quick or easy fix for this issue for which, for the time being, there is no CJEU guidance either. As for many other matters analysed in the course of this work, this topic and maybe the SSM itself are subject to interpretation that requires and will continue requiring an exercise of legal creation, which will make EU law change and evolve.

16

CONCLUSIONS OF PART III

As per the analysis carried out in Chapter 10 (*Composite procedures: descriptive and normative criteria*), the following conclusions can be drawn: **16.001**

First, from a pure normative perspective, it seems possible to conclude that greater efficiency as regards the exercise of prudential supervision has been achieved by implementing the SSM. This is due to the special configuration of the *mechanism*, in particular, the manner tasks that are allocated between the NCAs and the ECB, the use of scale economies, the existence of synergies (coming from the mechanism benefit from the expertise accumulated by NCAs), the interaction between micro– and macro-prudential supervision and the suppression of undesirable externalities (such as regulatory capture). **16.002**

Second, the foregoing sets up minimum standards regarding political and performance accountability. Yet, the existence of minimum standards does not prevent the *mechanism*, or better said, the ECB under the SSM R, from potentially incurring in accountability gaps or flaws and/or performance account ability deviations. **16.003**

Chapter 11 (*Cooperation, coordination and composite procedures in the Banking Union and SSM*) looks into the features of cooperation, coordination and composition occurring within SSM composite procedures. This Chapter deals also with the elements that determine the classification of a composite procedure as such. Following this dedicated analysis, several conclusions were reached: **16.004**

First, the two elements that determine that a procedure may be classified as a *composite procedure* are: (i) interaction (or involvement) between EU and national authorities and (ii) (successive) attribution of material decision powers among the involved authorities, also referred to as *decisional interdependence*. The latter element seems to be the most relevant element to determine the nature of a procedure as composite, as recent CJEU case law shows (i.e., the *Berlusconi-Fininvest case*). **16.005**

16.006 *Second*, in the *Berlusconi-Fininvest case*, the Court indicated that, the ECB having the final decision-making powers, it is for the CJEU exclusively, pursuant to art. 263 TFEU, to review the legality of ECB supervisory decisions adopted under the SSM R. And this review should be extended over any preparatory acts preceding the adoption of the decision at stake, regardless of whether such preparatory acts were adopted by national authorities (on the basis of national rules).

16.007 As indicated by the CJEU, such *rationale* obeys the need to ensure effective judicial protection, which can only be guaranteed when a single court (the CJEU) reviews the final decision adopted by the relevant EU institution.

16.008 *Third*, the possibility of reviewing national preparatory acts, within the action of annulment challenging an EU act, is an extremely sensitive matter that entails at least three major constitutional tensions. The first one relates to the CJEU's own judicial mandate, which, by definition, does not extend to the review (or application) of national rules but EU ones. The second and third ones concern the principles of uniformity and autonomy of EU law, which may be hampered.

16.009 *Fourth*, the following exchanges developed within the SSM do not constitute composite procedures: (i) information exchanges and periodical reporting between the ECB and NCAs, (ii) the procedure for adopting decisions by ECB/SSM decision-making bodies, (iii) the mediation process led by the Mediation Panel foreseen in art. 22(5) SSM R and (iv) further cooperation occurring under the JSTs.

16.010 On the contrary, (i) SSM common procedures and (ii) other mixed approaches – including (a) requests submitted by the ECB to the NCAs to prepare a draft supervisory decision pursuant to art. 91(1) SSM Fr, (b) decisions to review the status of an LSI following a NCA notification under art. 43(4) SSM Fr, (c) decisions concerning fit and proper requirements of management bodies' members (as regards SIs), (d) requests addressed by the ECB to NCAs to use their national powers pursuant to art. 9(1)III SSM R, (e) the notification of draft supervisory decisions (and further issuance of ECB opinions on them) concerning material decisions or procedures as regards high priority LSIs and (f) the ECB calling the supervision of an LSI pursuant to arts. 6(5)(b) SSM R and 67–69 SSM Fr – fall under the concept of composite procedures (or trigger those).

As regards purely SSM sanctioning proceedings, it appears that the procedures for the imposition of administrative penalties would not be composite procedures whereas ECB requests addressed to NCAs in order to open sanctioning procedures as foreseen in art. 18(5) SSM R would constitute composite procedures. **16.011**

Chapter 12 (*SSM composite procedures and justiciability*) analyses the justiciability perspective of SSM procedures. Following this dedicated analysis, it can be concluded that: **16.012**

First, until 2023, the CJEU (and particularly the General Court) moved from a deferential or *light touch* standard of review (applicable to matters falling under the ECB's monetary policy mandate) to a more intense scrutiny or *hard look review* as regards SSM matters. **16.013**

However, in case C-389/21 P (*Crédit Lyonnais v ECB*), the CJEU showed greater deference towards ECB decisions. In this regard, and acknowledging that the ECB enjoys *broad discretion* under the SSM R, the CJEU indicated that it should not substitute its own assessment for that of the ECB. There, the CJEU expressed that its control would be limited to ensure that (1) the ECB decision is based on accurate and reliable facts, without manifest errors of assessment or misuse of powers, (2) the evidence contains all the relevant information, which must be taken into account in order to assess a complex situation, and (3) all the procedural guarantees have been duly observed (including careful and impartial examination of all relevant aspects relating to the dispute). Conversely, in the Berlusconi II appeal, the CJEU did not refer expressly to the same *deferential* approach towards ECB assessment. **16.014**

In this regard, it can be concluded that the standard of review used by the CJEU to adjudicate on ECB supervisory decisions (outside sanctioning decisions) may be still oscillating, and only subsequent judgments, issued over time, may be able to settle this controversy. **16.015**

Second, if the CJEU was to follow a *light touch* approach to adjudicate as regards the imposition of fines and administrative pecuniary penalties by the ECB, this would equate to rendering the SSM short of the guarantees foreseen in the ECHR, as the Court would not have *full jurisdiction*. This would lead to a bizarre situation in which the EU legal framework is at odds with the ECHR (to which the Charter is pegged pursuant to art. 53 Charter, even if the EU has not ratified the ECHR yet). **16.016**

16.017 Chapter 13 (*Procedural and substantive safeguards in composite procedures*) explores the procedural safeguards to be applied in composite procedures and the legal challenges that it implies. It follows from the analysis carried out in this chapter that:

16.018 *First*, whatever decision or act is taken under the umbrella of the SSM R would need to abide by the fundamental rights established in the Charter (which include due process rights). The foregoing is rather obvious in the case of ECB decision and is based on arts. 51(1) and 52(5) Charter, and the same basis would apply as regards NCAs. The cited art. 51(1) indicates that the Charter would apply to MSs "*when they are implementing Union law, in the exercise of their respective powers*". Exercising the tasks contemplated in the SSM, in the form and with the intensity described therein would amount to implementing EU law. Also, more clearly, the Charter would apply when NCAs base their supervisory action on EU prudential regulations (basically CRD IV and CRR).

16.019 *Second*, it must be outlined that due process rights should be respected at all stages of the relevant procedure. However, a material violation of those due process rights may occur only if those procedural guarantees are not respected before the final decision-taking authority (national or European).

16.020 In a *Berlusconi-Fininvest scenario* (e.g., as regards common procedures), (i) the occurrence of a material procedural defect at the national administrative stage can be, in principle, cured at the EU stage. However, (ii) if such defect is not cured at the EU stage, that may determine the annulment of the relevant decision.

16.021 Furthermore, (iii) building upon the case law consistently maintained by the CJEU, resource to court proceedings may not be able to correct such material procedural flaws, leading to the annulment of the relevant decision challenged. This conclusion stands for SSM composite procedures; material procedural flaws occurring at the NCA stage, if not duly corrected by the ECB, may determine the annulment of the relevant ECB decision.

16.022 Chapter 14 (*Supervisory procedures: common procedures*) looks, in a detailed manner, into the practicalities and challenges raised by the so-called common procedures, and Chapter 15 (*Sanctioning procedures*) focuses specifically on sanctioning procedures. The analysis carried out in these Chapters builds on and cross-references the material analysis carried out in precedent Parts of this work while, at the same time, concentrates their assessments in the practical challenges that arise when conducting common procedures and sanctioning procedures and sketches creative and implementable solutions to overcome those. As regards those Chapters, the following can be concluded:

As regards the supervisory (common) procedures analysed therein: **16.023**

First, it results that the majority of the interpretative issues or legislative ambiguities, related to the coordination between the ECB and the NCAs, occurred in the course of the relevant procedure or in the application of national rules by NCAs in the context of these composite procedures (e.g., when the file may be considered completed and, hence, when the deadline to authorise or reject the request for authorisation starts counting). **16.024**

Second, by definition, those interpretative or legislative ambiguities and/or mismatches are possible to be overcome by applying some legal interpretation and/or pursuing a consistent principle-driven application of the mentioned rules. **16.025**

Concerning sanctioning procedures (including the request addressed to NCAs to open sanctioning procedures pursuant to art. 18(5) SSM R), it is concluded that: **16.026**

First, concerning ECB *direct* sanctioning procedures (i.e., those relating to the administrative penalties contemplated in art. 18(1) & (7) SSM R), unlike in the common procedures, the fact that the ECB carries out this procedure on its own account has eliminated the majority of the coordination-related flaws, as the intensity of the exchanges with NCAs is very limited. **16.027**

However, some interpretative legal issues are spotted. Those relate to wording mismatches between the SSM R and its legal development, the SSM Fr. These types of issues can be corrected or minimised by resorting to traditional interpretation techniques (e.g., literal reading or avoidance of absurd interpretation) or to a finalistic (yet plausible) reading of the legal text, in conjunction with its main objectives and the need to ensure level playing field and proportionality. **16.028**

Second, as regards ECB requests to NCAs to open sanctioning procedures pursuant to art. 18(5) SSM R, it must be outlined that beyond formulating its request, the ECB has very little control over the sanctioning procedure to be sustained, eventually, by the concerned NCA pursuant to its national rules. In this vein, it has been argued that the request issued by the ECB under the referred provision would not be binding to the NCAs, and these retain the ultimate decision-making power. **16.029**

16.030 Accordingly, the ECB would not be vested with any coordinating power to oversee how (and whether) the relevant NCA has fulfilled their request to initiate a sanctioning proceeding under art. 18(5) SSM R.

16.031 Further and in respect of the capital *ne bis in idem principle*, I concluded that the allocation of sanctioning tasks within the SSM prevents *breaches from occurring* at the level of the ECB/NCAs. However, the conclusion is different in situations that involve the prosecution of entities (and legal persons belonging to them) by national prosecutors pursuant to national criminal law or by national authorities (distinct from NCAs) capable of imposing criminal in nature sanctions.

BIBLIOGRAPHY

Alexander, K. (2018). The European Central Bank's supervisory powers: the need for enhanced macro-prudential supervision. In *ECB Legal Conference 2017, Shaping a new legal order for Europe: a tale of crises and opportunities* (pp. 349–369). Frankfurt am Main, ECB.

Alexander, K. (2016). The ECB and Banking Supervision: Does Single Supervisory Mechanism Provide an Effective Regulatory Framework? In *Regulating and Supervising European Financial Markets* (pp. 253–276). Springer, Cham.

Allegrezza, S. (ed.). (2020). *The enforcement dimension of the single supervisory mechanism*. Wolters Kluwer.

Allegrezza, S. (2020). Information Exchange Between Administrative and Criminal Enforcement: The Case of the ECB and National Investigative Agencies. *Eucrim: the European Criminal Law Associations' forum*, (4), pp. 302–309.

Allegrezza, S. and Radopolos, I. (2017). Enforcing prudential banking regulations in the Eurozone: A reading from the viewpoint of criminal law. In *Challenges in the field of economic and financial crime in Europe and the US* (pp. 233–264). London, Hart Publishing.

Allegrezza, S. & Voordeckers, O. (2015). Investigative and sanctioning powers of the ECB in the framework of the Single Supervisory Mechanism: mapping the complexity of a new enforcement model. *EUCRIM*, *4*, pp. 151–160.

Alonso de León, S. (2016). *Composite Administrative Procedures in the European Union*. UC3M: Doctoral dissertation: https://core.ac.uk/download/pdf/44311475.pdf.

Alonso de León, S. (2017). *Composite administrative procedures in the European Union*. Iustel.

Altunbas, Y., Gambacorta, L. & Marques-Ibanez, D. (2010). Does monetary policy affect banks' risk-taking. *BIS working paper* 298.

Amtenbrink, F. (2019). The application of national law by the European Central Bank: challenging European legal doctrine? In *Building bridges:*

central banking law in an interconnected world. ECB Legal Conference 2019 (pp. 136–151). Frankfurt am Main, ECB.

Amtenbrink, F. & Markakis, M. (2019). Towards a meaningful prudential supervision dialogue in the euro area? A study of the interaction between the European Parliament and the European Central Bank in the single supervisory mechanism. *ADEMU working paper series* (WP 2017/081).

Annunziata, F. and D'Ambrosio, R (2019). L'applicazione del diritto degli Stati membri da parte della Banca Centrale Europea. *Giur. Comm.*, Vol. 46. Fas. 4.

Annunziata, F. (2020). European Banking Supervision in the Age of the ECB: Landeskreditbank Baden-Württemberg – Förderbank v. ECB. *Bocconi Legal Studies Research Paper No. 0*, pp. 1–39.

Annunziata, F. and Maggiolino, M. (2021). The single supervisory mechanism and the European framework for the enforcement of competition law: a comparison between two models for economic governance in the EU. *Bocconi Legal Studies Research Paper Series, March* 2021.

Annunziata, F. & Braga de Arruda, T. (2023). The Corneli Case and the Application of National Law by the European Central Bank. *Bocconi Legal Studies Research Paper*, (4477503).

Annunziata, F., Lamandini, M. & Ramos Muñoz, D. (2020). Weiss and EU Union Banking Law. A Test for the Fundamental Principles of the Treaty. *EBI Working Paper Series* 2020 – no. 67.

Aperio Bella, F. (2020). Composite Procedures and Procedural Guarantees: the "Borelli Doctrine" in the Light of ReNEUAL Model Rules. *ROMA TRE LAW REVIEW*(1), pp. 7–36.

Arnal, J., Russo, C. & Thomadakis, A. (2024). The Judicial Scrutiny of the SSM and the SRB A Missed Chance or a Success Story? *Economic Governance Support Unit (EGOV).*

Arranz Alonso, L. (2017). Level playing field: towards a more uniform application of banking legislation. In *ESCB Legal Conference 2016* (pp. 260–270). Frankfurt am Main, ECB.

Arrigoni, M. (2020). The Administrative Board of Review of the European Central Bank. A critical analysis. *Rivista Orizzonti Del Diritto Commerciale, 2*, pp. 519–538.

Athanassiou, P. (2006). The application of multilingualism in the European Union context. *ECB legal working paper series no. 2.*

Bagehot, W. (1873). Lombard Street: a Description of the Money Market. *Henry S. King & Co.*, London.

Banks, K. (2019). Incorrect implementation of EU directives: what effects for the ECB and the CJEU, and what mechanisms for rectification? In

ECB Legal Conference 2019. Building bridges: central banking law in an interconnected world (pp. 121–129). Frankfurt am Main, ECB.

Barbier de La Serre, É. & Lagathu, E. (2022). The Law on Fines Imposed in EU Competition Proceedings: A Post-Pandemic Boost of Case Law. *Journal of European Competition Law & Practice, 13*(6), pp. 448–458.

Bassani, G. (2019). *The Legal Framework Applicable to the Single Supervisory Mechanism: Tapestry Or Patchwork?* Kluwer Law International BV.

Bax, R. and Witte, A. (2019). The taxonomy of ECB instruments available for banking supervision. *Economic Bulletin Articles, 6.*

Bellamy, C. (2012). ECHR and competition law post Menarini: An overview of EU and national case law. *e-Competitions, N°47946*, 5 July 2012.

Beroš, M. B. (2019). The ECB's accountability within the SSM framework: Mind the (transparency) gap. *Maastricht Journal of European and Comparative Law, 26*(1), pp. 122–135.

Binder, J. H. (2017). Wunderkind is Walking? The Resolution of Banco Popular as a First Test for the Single Resolution Mechanism. Oxford Business Law Blog: Wunderkind is Walking? The Resolution of Banco Popular as a First Test for the Single Resolution Mechanism | Oxford Law Blogs.

Binder, J., Gortsos, C. V., Lackhoff, K. & Ohler, C (Ed.). (2022). *European banking union: Brussels commentary.* Baden-Baden: Nomos.

Bindi, E. & Pisaneschi, A. (2019). The Fair Trial as a Guarantee of the Administrative Procedure. In *Judicial Power in a Globalized World: Liber Amicorum Vincent De Gaetano* (pp. 47–62). Springer, Cham.

Blanke, H. J. & Mangiameli, S. (Eds.). (2020). *Treaty on the Functioning of the European Union: A Commentary.* Springer.

Blanke, H. J., Villalón, P. C., Klein, T. & Ziller, J. (2015). *Common European Legal Thinking.* Springer.

Bonelli, M., Eliantonio, M. & Gentile, G. (Eds.). (2022). *Article 47 of the EU Charter and Effective Judicial Protection, Volume 1: The Court of Justice's Perspective.* Bloomsbury Publishing; and Pagliacci, A. (2020). *Efficacia delle sanzioni nel settore bancario: criticità e spunti comparatistici.* LUISS: Doctoral dissertation.

Bosque Argachal, C. (2019). Sanctioning powers of the Banco de España within the SSM. General overview and challenges faced. In *Aspecte cheie in activitatea financiar-bancara. Conferinta internationala* (pp. 26–40). C. H. Beck.

Bosque Argachal, C. and Pizarroso Ceruti, A. (2019). Welcome to Hard Look Review, ECB. Retrieved from http://eulawanalysis.blogspot.com/2019/01/the-european-central-bank-judicial.html.

Boucon, L. & Jaros, D. (2017). The Application of National Law by the European Central Bank within the EU Banking Union's Single Supervisory Mechanism: A New Mode of European Integration. *Eur. J. Legal Stud.*, *10*, pp. 155–187.

Brescia Morra, C. (2014). From the Single Supervisory Mechanism to the Banking Union: The Role of the ECB and the EBA. *Luiss Guido Carli Working Paper 2/2014*.

Brescia Morra, C. (2018). The Interplay between the ECB and NCAs in the "common procedures" under the SSM Regulation: are there gaps in legal protection? In *Judicial review in the Banking Union and in the EU financial architecture, Conference jointly organized by Banca d'Italia and the European Banking Institute* (pp. 79–94). Quaderni di Ricerca giuridica della Banca d'Italia, n. 84.

Brito Bastos, F. (2018). Derivative illegality in European composite administrative procedures. *Common market law review*, *55*(1), pp. 101–134.

Brito Bastos, F. (2019). Judicial review of composite administrative procedures in the Single Supervisory Mechanism: Berlusconi. *Common Market L. Rev.*, *56*, pp. 1355–1378.

Brito Bastos, F. (2020). An Administrative Crack in the EU's Rule of Law: Composite Decision-making and Nonjusticiable National Law. *European Constitutional Law Review*, *16*(1), pp. 63–90.

Brito Bastos, F. (2021). Composite procedures in the SSM and SRM – an analytical overview. In *Judicial Review in the European Banking Union* (pp. 97–113). Edward Elgar Publishing.

Busch, D. and van Rijn, M. (2018). Regulating systemic risk: A cross sectoral approach. In *European Financial Regulation: Levelling the Cross-Sectoral Playing Field. A Research Agenda* (pp. 107–129). Oxford: Hart Publishing.

Busch, D., Gortsos, C. V. and Mcmeel, G. (2022). *Liability of Financial Supervisors and Resolution Authorities*. Oxford: OUP.

Capolino, O. (2013). Il Testo unico bancario e il diritto dell'Unione Europea. In *Dal Testo unico bancario all'Unione bancaria: tecniche normative e allocazione di poteri* (Pp. 51–73). Quaderni di Ricerca Giuridica della Consulenza Legale (Banca D'italia), n.75.

Capolino, O. (2019). The Single Resolution Mechanism: Authorities and Proceedings. In *The Palgrave Handbook of European Banking Union Law* (pp. 247–270). Palgrave Macmillan.

Cassese, S. (2003). Il diritto amministrativo europeo presenta caratteri originali? *Rivista trimestrale di diritto pubblico*, (1), pp. 35–52.

Chiti, E. (2004). Administrative proceedings involving European agencies. *Law and Contemporary Problems*, *68*(1), pp. 219–236.

Chiti, M. P. (2011). Towards an EU Regulation on Administrative Procedure? Study. European Parliament (Directorate General for Internal Policies. Policy Department C: citizens' rights and constitutional affairs: https://www.europarl.europa.eu/RegData/etudes/etudes/join/2010/432743/IPOL-JURI_ET(2010)432743_EN.pdf.

Coman-Kund, F. & Amtenbrink. F. (2018). On the Scope and Limits of the Application of National Law by the European Central Bank within the Single Supervisory Mechanism. *Banking & Finance Law Review*, Vol. 33, Iss. 2, pp. 133–172.

Covelo de Abreu, J. (2017). An approach to today's EU constitutionality control–understanding this EU inter-jurisdictional phenomenon in light of effective judicial protection. *UNIO–EU Law Journal*, *3*(2), pp. 104–124.

Craig, P. (2018). *EU administrative law*. Oxford. University Press.

Craig, P. & de Búrca, G. (2020). *EU Law-Text, Cases, and Material*. Oxford: Oxford University Press.

D'Ambrosio, R. (ed.). (2020). Law and Practice of the Banking Union and of its governing Institutions (Cases and Materials). *Quaderni di Ricerca Giuridica*, (88). [D'Ambrosio, R. (2020)(i)].

D'Ambrosio, R. (2013). Due process and safeguards of the persons subject to SSM supervisory and sanctioning proceedings. *Quaderni di Ricerca giuridica della Consulenza Legale* (Banca d'Italia), n° 74.

D'Ambrosio, R. (2015). The ECB and NCA liability within the single supervisory mechanism. *Quaderni di Ricerca giuridica della Consulenza Legale* (Banca d'Italia), n° 78.

D'Ambrosio, R. (2019). Single Supervisory Mechanism: Organ and Procedures. In *The Palgrave Handbook of European Banking Union Law* (pp. 157–183). Palgrave Macmillan.

D'Ambrosio, R. (2020). The application of national law by the ECB. In *Law and Practice of the Banking Union and of its governing Institutions (Cases and Materials)* (pp. 129–147). *Quaderni di Ricerca Giuridica*, (88) [D'Ambrosio, R. (2020)(iii)].

D'Ambrosio, R. (2020). The involvement of the NCAs in the ECB's supervisory proceedings. In *Law and Practice of the Banking Union and of its governing Institutions (Cases and Materials)* (pp. 163–181). Quaderni di Ricerca Giuridica, (88) [D'Ambrosio, R. (2020)(ii)].

D'Ambrosio, R. (2021). The legal review of SSM administrative sanctions. In *Judicial Review in the European Banking Union* (pp. 316–332). Edward Elgar Publishing.

De Bellis, M. (2021). Multi-level administration, inspections and fundamental rights: Is judicial protection full and effective? *German law journal*, *22*(3), pp. 416–440.

de La Serre, É. B. & Lagathu, E. (2021). The Law on Fines Imposed in EU Competition Proceedings: A Judicial Paradox. *Journal of European Competition Law & Practice*, pp. 710–717.

della Cananea, G. (2004). I procedimenti amministrativi composti dell'Unione europea. In *Il procedimento amministrativo nel diritto europeo* (pp. 307–334). Milan, Giuffrè.

della Cananea, G. (2022). Common Constitutional Traditions Taken Seriously: The Right to Remain Silent in Administrative Procedures. *Italian J. Pub. L.*, *14*, pp. 275–288.

Dermine, P. and Eliantonio, M. (2019). Case Note: CJEU (Grand Chamber), Judgment of 19 December 2018, C-219/17, Silvio Berlusconi and Finanziaria d'investimento Fininvest SpA (Fininvest) v Banca d'Italia and Istituto per la Vigilanza Sulle Assicurazioni (IVASS). *Review of European Administrative Law*, *12*(2), pp. 237–253.

Di Bucci, V. (2018). Quelques questions concernant le contrôle jurisdictionnel sur le mécanisme de surveillance unique. In *Liber Amicorum Antonio Tizzano. De la Cour CECA à la Cour de l'Union: le long parcours de la justice européenne* (pp. 317–331). Torino.

Dworkin, R. (2013). *Taking rights seriously*. Bloomsbury.

Eckes, C. & D'Ambrosio, R. (2020). Composite administrative procedures in the European Union. *ECB Legal Working Paper Series*, pp. 1–51.

Eijffinger, S. & Nijskens, R. (2012). Monetary policy and banking supervision. *VoxEU*, 19 December: https://voxeu.org/article/monetary-policy-and-banking-supervision.

Eliantonio, M. (2015). Judicial review in an integrated administration: the case of "composite procedures". *Review of European Administrative Law*, *7*(2), pp. 65–102.

Felisatti, V. (2018). Sanctioning Powers of the European Central Bank and the Ne Bis In Idem Principle within the Single Supervisory Mechanism. *EuCLR European Criminal Law Review*, *8*(3), pp. 378–403.

Fernandez-Bollo, E. & Teixeira, P. G. (2021). Fostering a compliance culture in the European banking system. ECB. The supervision blog: Fostering a compliance culture in the European banking system (europa.eu).

Ferrarini, G. (2015). Single supervision and the governance of banking markets: will the SSM deliver the expected benefits? *European Business Organization Law Review*, *16*(3).

Finke, D. & Dannwolf, T. (2015). Who let the dogs out? The effect of parliamentary scrutiny on compliance with EU law, *Journal of European Public Policy*, 22:8, pp. 1127–1147.

Forrester, I. S. (2009). Due process in EC competition cases: a distinguished institution with flawed procedures. *European Law Review, 34*(6), pp. 817–843.

Fromage, D. (2021). The ECB's guide on pecuniary penalties in banking supervision: Increased transparency on its (still) limited powers. *EU Law Live, 2021, Weekend Edition no. 60.* Hal-03696931.

Gagliardi, E. & Wissink, L. (2020). Ensuring effective judicial protection in case of ECB decisions based on national law. *Review of European Administrative Law, 13*(1), pp. 41–71.

Galetta, D.-U., Hofmann, H. C., Mir Puigpelat, O. & Ziller, J. (2015). The General Principles of EU Administrative Procedural Law In-depth Analysis. European Parliament, Brussels.

García Alcorta, J. (2013). Observaciones en torno al mecanismo único de supervisión bancaria en la Unión Europea. *Actualidad jurídica Uría Menéndez* no. 34-2013, pp. 51–70.

Goodhart, C. A. E. (2010). The changing role of central banks. *BIS Working Papers* No. 326.

Goodhart, C. & Schoenmaker, D. (1995). Should the functions of monetary policy and banking supervision be separated? *Oxford Economic Papers.*

Gortsos, C. (2022). Evolving key risks in the banking sector, and related priorities for the SRB: the impact of the current "inflation crisis". *Economic Governance Support Unit (EGOV).*

Gortsos, C. V. (2015). Competence sharing between the ECB and the national competent supervisory authorities within the Single Supervisory Mechanism (SSM). *European Business Organization Law Review, 16*, pp. 401–420 [Gortsos, C. V. (2015)(i)].

Gortsos, C. V. (2015). The Power of the ECB to Impose Administrative Penalties as a Supervisory Authority: An Analysis of Article 18 of the SSM Regulation. *ECEFIL Working Paper Series No 2015/11* [Gortsos, C. V. (2015)(ii)].

Gortsos, C. V. (2016). The Powers of the ESMA in Case of Breach of European Union Law: The Particular Case of Breaching the "Non Bis in Idem" Principle. Forthcoming, Journal of Financial Law (2017), Nomiki Bibliothiki, Athens.

Gortsos, C. V. (2016). The role of the European Banking Authority (EBA) after the establishment of the Single Supervisory Mechanism (SSM). In

Regulating and Supervising European Financial Markets (pp. 277–297). Springer, Cham.

Gortsos, C. V. (2018). Legal Aspects of the European Central Bank (ECB) – The ECB within the European System of Central Banks (ESCB) and the European System of Financial Supervision (ESFS) – Second (Extended and Updated) Edition. *SSRN 3162024*.

Gortsos, C. V. (2019). European Banking Union Within the System of European Banking and Monetary Law. In *The Palgrave Handbook of European Banking Union Law* (pp. 19–40). Palgrave Macmillan, Cham.

Gortsos, C. V. (2020) European Central Banking Law: The Role of the European Central Bank and National Central Banks under European Law. Cham: Palgrave Macmillan.

Gortsos, C. V. (2021). Impediments to resolvability – what is the status quo. Economic. *Economic Governance Support Unit (EGOV).*

Gortsos, C. V. (2021). The Crédit Agricole cases: banking corporate governance and application of national law by the ECB. In *Judicial Review in the European Banking Union* (pp. 510–520). Edward Elgar Publishing.

Gortsos, C. V. (2021). The New EU Regulatory Framework Governing the Approval and Consolidated Supervision of Financial Holding Companies and Mixed Financial Holding Companies. *Available at SSRN 3834246*.

Gortsos, C. V. & Lagaria, K. (2020). The European Supervisory Authorities (ESAs) As “”Direct” Supervisors in the EU Financial System. *European Banking Institute Working Paper Series* No. 57.

Gortsos, C. V. (2023). Options and Discretions under the Capital Requirements Directive IV. *EBI working* no. 155.

Gortsos, C. V. (2024). 10 years of Banking Union case-law: How did CJEU judgments shape supervision and resolution practice in the Banking Union? Economic Governance Support Unit (EGOV).

Goyal, R., Brooks, P. K., Pradhan, M., Tressel, M. T., Dell’Ariccia, M. G. & Pazarbasioglu, C. (2013). A Banking Union for the euro area. International Monetary Fund. *IMF Staff Discussion Note* (SDN/13/01).

Gren, J. (2018). The Eurosystem and the Single Supervisory Mechanism: institutional continuity under constitutional constraints. *ECB Legal Working Paper Series*, No. 17.

Gruber, G. (2022). Art. 9 SSMR Supervisory and investigatory powers. In *European banking union: Brussels commentary* (pp. 146–158). Baden-Baden: Nomos.

Grundmann, S. (2019). European Banking Union and Integration. In *European Banking Union and Constitution* (pp. 85–120). Oxford: Bloomsbury Publishing.

Gurlit, E. (2022). Art. 14 Authorisation. In *European banking union: Brussels commentary* (pp. 189–215). Baden-Baden: Nomos [Gurlit, E. (2022)(i)].

Gurlit, E. (2022). Art. 15 Assessment of acquisitions of qualifying holdings. In *European banking union: Brussels commentary* (pp. 215–235). Baden-Baden: Nomos [Gurlit, E. (2022)(ii)].

Hayden, H. (2021). Enforcement of Fines and Other Pecuniary Obligations Imposed by the ECB (Part I): European Level. *European Company and Financial Law Review, 18*(6), pp. 1011–1050.

Heller, H. R. (1991). 5 Prudential Supervision and Monetary Policy. In *The Evolving Role of Central Banks.* International Monetary Fund.

Hernández Saseta, C. (2021). The legal review of ECB instructions under article 9 SSM regulation. In *Judicial Review in the European Banking Union* (pp. 304–315). Edward Elgar Publishing.

Hofmann, H. C. H. (2009). Composite Procedures in the EU Administrative law. In *Legal Challenges in EU Administrative Law: The Move to an Integrated Administration* (pp. 136–167). Edward Elgar, Cheltenham.

Hofmann, H. C. & Mihaescu, C. (2013). The relation between the charter's fundamental rights and the unwritten general principles of EU law: good administration as the test case. *European Constitutional Law Review, 9*(1), pp. 73–101, and Hofmann, H. C. (2014). General Principles of EU law and EU administrative law. *European Union Law*, pp. 196–225.

Hofmann, H., Schneider, J. P., Ziller, J., et al. (Eds.). (2015). *ReNEUAL model rules on EU administrative procedure.* ReNEUAL SC: http://www.reneual.eu/images/Home/ReNEUAL--Model-Rules-update-2015_rules-only-2017.PDF.

Hohfeld, W. N. (1917). Fundamental legal conceptions as applied in judicial reasoning. *The Yale Law Journal, 13*(1).

Horspool, M. & Humphreys, M. (2012). *European Union Law.* Oxford University Press.

Ioannidis, M. (2021). Chapter 9: the judicial review of discretion in the banking union: from ""soft" to "hard(er)" look? In *Judicial Review in the European Banking Union* (pp. 130–145). Elgar Financial Law and Practice Series.

Ioannidis, M., Murphy, S. J. H. & Zilioli, C. (2021). The mandate of the ECB: Legal considerations in the ECB's monetary policy strategy review. *ECB Occasional papers* No. 276. European Central Bank.

Jacqué, J. P. (2004). Principle of Institutional Balance, The. *Common Market L. Rev., 41*, pp. 383–391.

Jansen, O. and Schöndorf-Haubold, B. (2011). *The European composite administration.* Intersentia.

Joosen, B. & Lehmann, M. (2019). Proportionality in the single rule book. In *The Palgrave Handbook of European Banking Union Law* (pp. 65–90). Palgrave Macmillan.

Joosen, B., Lamandini, M., Lehmann, M., Lieverse, K. & Tirado, I. (2018). Stability, Flexibility and Proportionality: Towards a Two-Tiered European Banking Law? *European Banking Institute Working Paper Series* 2018 no. 29.

Joosen, B., Pulgar Ezquerra, J. & Tröger, T. (2024). 10 years of Banking Union case law How did CJEU – judgments shape supervision and resolution practice in the Banking Union? Economic Governance Support Unit (EGOV).

Karagianni, A. M. (2022). *The Protection of Fundamental Rights in Composite Banking Supervision Procedures.* Utrecht University: Doctoral dissertation.

Karagianni, A. & Scholten, M. (2018). Accountability Gaps in the Single Supervisory Mechanism SSM Framework. *Utrecht J. Int'l & Eur. L., 34*, pp. 185–194.

Kaufhold, A.-K. (2022). Art. 22 SSMR Due process for adopting supervisory decisions. In *European banking union: Brussels commentary* (pp. 307–318). Baden-Baden: Nomos.

Kaufhold, A.-K. (2022). Art. 3 SSM R Cooperation. In *European banking union: Brussels commentary* (pp. 23–37). Baden-Baden: Nomos.

Klamert, M. (2014). *The principle of loyalty in EU law.* OUP Oxford.

Kokkot, J. & Sobotta, C. (2017). Judicial review and institutional balance with regard to European monetary policy. In *ECB Legal Conference 2017. Shaping a new legal order for Europe: a tale of crises and opportunities* (pp. 104–112). Frankfurt am Main, ECB.

Kokott, J. & Sobotta, C. (2012). The Kadi case–constitutional core values and international law–finding the balance? *European Journal of International Law, 23(4)*, pp. 1015–1024.

Konstadinides, T. (2009). *Division of powers in European Union law: the delimitation of internal competence between the EU and the member states.* Kluwer Law International BV.

Kornezov, A. (2017). The application of national law by the ECB – a maze of (un) answered questions. In *ESCB Legal Conference 2016* (pp. 260–270). Frankfurt am Main, ECB.

Koskelo, P. (2017). Relevance of fundamental rights for central bank policy decision-making. In *ECB Legal Conference 2017. Shaping a new legal order for Europe: a tale of crises and opportunities* (pp. 133–146). Frankfurt am Main, ECB.

Koupepidou, E. (2021). Administrative pre-litigation review mechanism in the SSM: the Administrative Board of Review. In *Judicial Review in the European Banking Union* (pp. 28–43). Edward Elgar Publishing.

Kucko, M. (2017). The Status of Natural or Legal Persons According to the Annulment Procedure Post-Lisbon. *LSE Law Review*, *2*, pp. 101–119.

Lackhoff, K. (2017). The SSM Framework regulation as a source of ECB administrative procedural Law. In *ESCB Legal Conference 2016* (pp. 202–211). Frankfurt am Main, ECB [Lackhoff, K. (2017)(ii)].

Lackhoff, K. (2017). *Single supervisory mechanism: European banking supervision by the SSM: a practitioner's guide*. C. H. Beck [Lackhoff, K. (2017)(i)]

Laguna de Paz, J. C. (2014). El mecanismo europeo de supervisión bancaria. *Revista de administración pública*, (194), pp. 49–77.

Lamandini, M. & Ramos Muñoz, D. (2019). Appeal bodies of EU financial regulatory agencies: are we where we should be? In *ECB Legal Conference 2019. Building bridges: central banking law in an interconnected world* (pp. 384–399). Frankfurt am Main, ECB.

Lamandini, M. & Ramos Muñoz, D. (2022). 2. The Definition of Common Equity Tier 1 Capital and of Contingent Capital. In *Capital and Liquidity Requirements for European Banks* (pp. 44–75). Oxford University Press.

Lamandini, M. & Ramos Muñoz, D. (2024) 10 years of Banking Union's case-law: How did European courts shape supervision and resolution practice in the Banking Union? Economic Governance Support Unit (EGOV).

Lamandini, M. Ramos Muñoz, D. and D'Ambrosio, R. (2022). 18 Supervisory Review and Evaluation Process (SREP) in the Context of the Exercise of Supervisory Powers and Extraordinary Measures. In *Capital and Liquidity Requirements for European Banks* (pp. 526–547). Oxford University Press.

Lamandini, M. & Muñoz, D. R. (2024). *Finance, Law, and the Courts*. Oxford University Press.

Lamandini, M., Ramos Muñoz, D. & Ruíz Almendral, V. (2020). The EMU and Its Multi-Level Constitutional Structure: The Need for More Imaginative "Dialogue" Among and Across EU and National Institutions. *Legal Issues of Economic Integration*, *47*(4), pp. 311–336.

Lamandini, M., Ramos Muñoz, D. & Solana, J. (2015). Depicting the Limits to the SSM's Supervisory Powers: The Role of Constitutional Mandates and of Fundamental Rights' Protection. *Quaderni di Ricerca Giuridica*, (79).

Lamandini, M., Ramos, D. & Solana, J. (2016). The European Central Bank (ECB) as a Catalyst for Change in EU Law, Part 1: The ECB's Mandates. *Colum. J. Eur. L.*, *23*, 1.

Lasagni, G. (2019). *Banking Supervision and Criminal Investigation. Comparing the EU and the US experience.* Springer.

Lasagni, G. (2020). Investigatory, supervisory and sanctioning powers within the SSM. In *The enforcement dimension of the single supervisory mechanism* (pp. 49–91). CEDAM.

Lastra, R. M. (2011). The Evolution of the European Central Bank. *Queen Mary University of London, School of Law Legal Studies Research* Paper No. 99/2012.

Lastra, R. M. & Louis, J. V. (2013). European Economic and Monetary Union: history, trends, and prospects. *Queen Mary University of London, School of Law. Legal Studies Research Paper* No. 136/2013.

Lastra, R. M. & Psaroudakis, G. (2020). Prudential supervisory tasks (Article 127 (6) TFEU, monetary policy vs prudential supervision): "Kissing awake the Sleeping Beauty provision". In *The EU Law of Economic and Monetary Union* (pp. 751–787). OUP.

Lefterov, A. (2020). Judicial review in a multi-level administrative framework – the case of the SSM. In *ESCB legal conference 2020* (pp. 286–304). Frankfurt am Main, ECB.

Lehman, M. (2017). Varying standards of judicial scrutiny over central banks actions. In *ECB Legal Conference 2017. Shaping a new legal order for Europe: a tale of crises and opportunities* (pp. 112–133). Frankfurt am Main, ECB.

Lehmann, M. (2017). Single Supervisory Mechanism Without Regulatory Harmonisation? Introducing a European Banking Act and a "CRR Light" for Smaller Institutions. *EBI Working Paper Series. no. 3.*

Lehmann, M. (2021). Jurisdiction, *locus standi* and the circulation of judgments in the Banking Union. In *Judicial Review in the European Banking Union* (pp. 77–96). Edward Elgar Publishing.

Lenaerts, K. (2011). National remedies for private parties in the light of the EU law principles of equivalence and effectiveness. *Irish Jurist (1966–)*, Vol. 46, pp 13–37.

Lenaerts, K. (2013). Due process in competition cases. *Neue Zeitschrift für Kartellrecht-NZKart*, *1*, 5, pp. 175–182.

Lenaerts, K. (2022). Proportionality as a matrix principle promoting the effectiveness of EU law and the legitimacy of EU action – Keynote speech. In *ECB Legal Conference 2021. Continuity and change – how the challenges of today prepare the ground for tomorrow* (pp. 27–45). Frankfurt am Main, ECB.

Lenaerts, K. & Gutiérrez-Fons, J. A. (2010). The constitutional allocation of powers and general principles of EU law. *Common Market Law Review*, *47*(6), pp. 1629–1669.

Lenaerts, K., Maselis, I. and Gutman, K. (2015). *EU procedural law.* OUP Oxford.

Lo Schiavo, G. (2017). Conditions and Obligations in ECB Supervisory Decisions as Ancillary Provisions under SSM Law. *European Company and Financial Law Review, 14*(1), pp. 94–120.

Lo Schiavo, G. (2019). The ECB and its application of national law in the SSM. In *The European Banking Union and the Role of Law* (pp. 177–196). Edward Elgar Publishing.

Loosveld, S. (2013). The ECB's investigatory and sanctioning powers under the future single supervisory mechanism. *Journal of International Banking Law and Regulation, 28*(10), pp. 422–425.

Mancini, M. (2013). Dalla vigilanza nazionale armonizzata alla Banking Union. *Quaderni di Ricerca Giuridica della Consulenza Legale Banca d'Italia, No 73.*

Manger-Nestler, C. & Gentzsch, M. (2021). Dimensions of Independence in the Various Tasks of the ECB. In *Democratic Legitimation of Central Bank Independence in the European Union* (pp. 27–92). Springer, Cham.

Markakis, M. (2016). Political and Legal Accountability in the European Banking Union – A First Assessment. In *Hungarian Yearbook of International Law and European Law* (pp. 535–558). Eleven Publishing.

Markakis, M. (2020). Composite Procedures and Judicial Review in the Single Resolution Mechanism: Iccrea Banca. *Review of European Administrative Law, 13*(4), 109–125.

Mastrodonato, G. (2008). *Procedimenti amministrativi composti nel diritto comunitario.* Bari, Cacucci.

Mayer, F. C. (2003). The debate on European powers and competencies. Seeing the trees but not the forest. *Walter Hallstein Institut: Working Paper* 18/03.

Mendes, J. & Eckes, C. (2011). The right to be heard in composite administrative procedures: lost in between protection? *European Law Review, 36*(5), pp. 651–670.

Moloney, N. (2021). Banking Union and the Charter of Fundamental Rights. In *Judicial Review in the European Banking Union* (pp. 209–220). Edward Elgar Publishing.

Montemaggi, S. Case-study: Judgments of the General Court and of the ECJ on the Landeskreditbank (General Court, T-122/15 and ECJ, C-450/17 P). In D'Ambrosio, R. (ed.). (2020). In *Law and Practice of the Banking Union and of its governing Institutions (Cases and Materials)* (pp. 217–231). Quaderni di Ricerca Giuridica, (88).

Montesquieu (de Secondat, C.-L.). (2012). *De l'esprit de lois.* Norph Nop.

Morra, C. B., Smits, R. & Magliari, A. (2017). The administrative board of review of the European Central Bank: experience after 2 years. *European Business Organization Law Review, 18*(3), pp. 567–589.

Ornowska, A. (2010). Introducing Hermeneutic Methods in Criminal Law Interpretation in Europe. *Interpretation of Law in the Global World: From Particularism to a Universal Approach* (pp. 251–275). Springer.

Papathanasiou, C. (2022). Art. 18 Administrative penalties. In *European banking union: Brussels commentary* (pp. 264–277). Baden-Baden: Nomos [Papathanassiou, C. (2022)(i)].

Papathanassiou, C. (2022). Fundamental rights and banking supervision. *Journal of Banking Regulation*, pp. 1–12 [Papathanassiou, C. (2022)(i)].

Parchimowicz, K. M. (2019). Missed targets and misplaced incentives? The case of parent undertaking requirement in the USA and in the EU. *Journal of Banking Regulation*, pp. 1–12.

Petit, C. A. and Beck, T. (2024). 10 years of Banking Union case law – how did CJEU judgments shape supervision and resolution practice in the Banking Union? Economic Governance Support Unit (EGOV).

Porzio, M. (2010). *Testo unico bancario: commentario.* Giuffrè Editor and Banca D'Italia, R. (2012). Legislazione bancaria, finanziaria e assicurativa: la storia, il presente, il futuro. *Quaderni di Ricerca Giuridica* della *Consulenza Legale Banca d'Italia No 72.*

Poscia, J. (2021). The VTB case: Administrative penalties and administrative measures. In *Judicial Review in the European Banking Union* (pp. 571–578). Edward Elgar Publishing.

Prek, M. & Lefèvre, S. (2017). The EU Courts as "national" courts: National law in the EU Judicial Process. *Common Market Law Review, 54*(2), pp. 369–402.

Raitio, J. (2003). *The principle of legal certainty in EC law.* Kluwer Academic Publishers.

Ramos Muñoz, D. & Lamandini, M. (2022). Evolving key risks in the banking sector and related priorities for the SRB: the lack of an effective transfer-based bank crisis framework. *Economic Governance Support Unit (EGOV).*

Riso, A. L. (2014). The power of the ECB to impose sanctions in the context of the SSM. *Bančni vestnik, Letnik, 63*, pp. 32–35.

Rosales, L. (2005). *Antología poética.* Rialp, Madrid.

Rosas, A. (2021). EMU in the Case Law of the Union Courts: A General Overview and Some Observations. *European Papers*, Vol. 6, No. 3, pp. 1397–1414.

Sakellaraki, A. (2021). Halcyon Days for the Right to Silence: AG Pikamäe's Opinion in Case DB v. Consob. *European Papers – A Journal on Law and Integration*, *2020*(3), pp. 1543–1554.

Sarmiento Ramírez-Escudero, D. (2007). *El principio de proporcionalidad en el Derecho administrativo. Un análisis jurídico desde el Derecho español.* Bogotá: Universidad Externado.

Sarmiento, D. (2008). *El "soft law" administrativo: un estudio de los efectos jurídicos de las normas no vinculantes de la Administración.* Thomson Civitas.

Sarmiento, D. (2019). National Law as a Point of Law in Appeals at the Court of Justice. The case of Crédit Mutuel Arkéa/ECB. *EU law live.*

Sauter, W. (2016). *Coherence in EU competition law.* Oxford University Press.

Schneider, Sven H. (2014). Sanctioning by the ECB and National Authorities Within the Single Supervisory Mechanism. *European Journal of Business Law.* EuZW-Beilage 18.

Scholten, M. (2017). Mind the trend! Enforcement of EU law has been moving to """Brussels". *Journal of European Public Policy*, *24*(9), pp. 1.348–1.366.

Schütze, R. (2015). Union Competences. In *An Introduction to European Law* (pp. 65–89). Cambridge: Cambridge University Press.

Schütze, R. & Tridimas, T. (Eds.). (2017). *Oxford principles of European Union law* (Vol. 1). Oxford: Oxford University Press.

Segoin, D. (2021). Chapter 17. The investigatory powers, including on-site inspections, of the ECB, and their judicial control. In *Judicial Review in the European Banking Union* (pp. 285–303). Edward Elgar Publishing.

Shipley, D. E. (2008). Due process rights before EU agencies: the rights of defense. *Ga. J. Int'l & Comp. L.*, *37*, 1, pp. 1–53.

Shuman, S. I. (1955). Jurisprudence and the analysis of fundamental legal terms. *Journal of Legal Education, 8(4)*, pp. 437–468.

Smith, M. (2018). Challenges in the implementation of EU Law at national level. *European Parliament Briefing.*

Smits, R. (1997). *The European Central Bank: Institutional Aspects.* The Hague: Kluwer Law International.

Smits, R. (2005). The role of the ESCB. In *Banking supervision. Legal Aspects of the European System of Central Banks.* In *Liber amicorum Paolo Zamboni Garavelli* (pp. 199–212).

Smits, R. (2017). Competences and alignment in an emerging future after L-Bank: how the Eurosystem and the Single Supervisory Mechanism may develop. *Ademu Working Paper Series,* WP 2017/077.

Smits, R. (2018). Interplay of administrative review and judicial protection in European prudential supervision. Some issues and concerns. In *Judicial review in the Banking Union and in the EU financial architecture*. Quaderni di Ricerca Giuridica della Consulenza Legale, Banca d'Italia.

Steiner, J., Woods, L. & Watson, P. (2012). *Steiner & Woods EU Law*. Oxford University Press.

Teixeira, P. G. (2017). The legal history of the Banking Union. *European Business Organization Law Review, 18,* pp. 535–565.

Ter Kuile, G., Wissink, L. & Bovenschen, W. (2015). Tailor-made accountability within the Single Supervisory Mechanism. *Common Market Law Review*, 52(1).

The Bar of Brussels & Barreau de Bruxelles (Eds.). (2013). *Professional secrecy of lawyers in Europe*. Cambridge University Press.

Timmerman, M. (2018). *Legality in Europe: on the principle'nullum crimen, nulla poena sine lege' in EU law and under the ECHR*. European University Institute: Doctoral dissertation: Timmerman_2018_LAW.pdf (eui.eu).

Triantafyllou, D. (2020). The banking union as a new field for composite administrative procedures. In *ESCB legal conference 2020* (pp. 273–278). Frankfurt am Main, ECB.

Tröger, T. (2017). How not to do banking law in the 21st century. *SAFE Policy Letter*, no. 56.

Türk, A. (2017). Liability and accountability for policies announced to the public and for press releases. In *ECB Legal Conference 2017. Shaping a new legal order for Europe: a tale of crises and opportunities* (pp. 43–59). Frankfurt am Main, ECB.

Ugena Torrejón, R. (2014). El Mecanismo Único de Supervisión Europeo. *Actualidad Jurídica Uría Menéndez*, no. 36-2014, pp. 7–18.

van Bockel, B. (2017). The Single Supervisory Mechanism Regulation: Questions of ne bis in idem and implications for the further integration of the system of fundamental rights protection in the EU. *Maastricht Journal of European and Comparative Law, 24*(2), pp. 194–216.

van Bockel, W. B. (2015). *Fundamental rights aspects of the SSM: Differentiated standards of protection under the Charter of Fundamental Rights of the EU.* Retrieved from: (PDF) Fundamental rights aspects of the Single Supervisory Mechanism: differentiated standards of protection under the Charter of Fundamental Rights of the EU | Willem Bastiaan van Bockel – Academia.edu.

Veenbrink, M. (2021). The Freedom from Self-Incrimination – A Strasbourg-Proof Approach? Cases C-466/19 P Qualcomm and C-481/19 P DB v Consob. *Journal of European Competition Law & Practice, 12*(10), pp. 750–752.

Ventoruzzo, M. (2017). A few notes on judicial review of central banks' activity from the perspective of corporate law. In *ECB Legal Conference 2017. Shaping a new legal order for Europe: a tale of crises and opportunities* (pp. 146–151). Frankfurt am Main, ECB.

Véron, N. (2017). *The governance and ownership of significant euro-area banks* (No. 2017/15). Bruegel Policy Contribution, Issue no. 14, May 2017.

Villamarín López, M. L. (2017). The presumption of innocence in Directive 2016/343/EU of 9 March 2016. In *ERA Forum* Vol. 18, No. 3 (pp. 335–353). Berlin/Heidelberg: Springer.

Weismann, P. (2017). The European Central Bank (ECB) Under the Single Supervisory Mechanism (SSM): Its Functioning and Its Limits. *TARN Working paper 1/2017.*

Weismann, P. (2018). The European Central Bank under the Single Supervisory Mechanism. Cooperation, Delegation, and Reverse Majority Voting. *European Journal of Current Legal Issues, 24*(1).

Whelan, P. (2012). Legal certainty and cartel criminalisation within the EU member states. *The Cambridge Law Journal, 71*(3), pp. 677–702.

Wissink, L. (2017). Challenges to an Efficient European Centralised Banking Supervision (SSM): Single Rulebook, Joint Supervisory Teams and Split Supervisory Tasks. *European Business Organization Law Review, 18*(3).

Wissink, L. (2021). The VQ case T-203/18: Administrative penalties by the ECB under judicial scrutiny. In *Judicial Review in the European Banking Union* (pp. 542–550). Edward Elgar Publishing [Wissink, L. (2021)(i)].

Wissink, L. (2021). *Effective Legal Protection in Banking Supervision: An Analysis of Legal Protection in Composite Administrative Procedures in the Single Supervisory Mechanism.* Europa Law Publishing [Wissink, L. (2021)(i)].

Witte, A. (2014). The Application of National Banking Supervision Law by the ECB: three Parallel modes of executing EU law? *Maastricht journal of European and comparative law, 21*(1), pp. 89–109.

Witte, A. (2017). When does a national law transpose a directive? In *ESCB Legal Conference 2016* (pp. 247–260). Frankfurt am Main, ECB.

Witte, A. (2021). The application of national law by the ECB, including options and discretions, and its impact on the judicial review. In *Judicial Review in the European Banking Union* (pp. 236–250). Edward Elgar Publishing.

Wojcik, K.-P. (2017). Primary law requirements for administrative procedures in the case-law of the court of justice. *In ESCB Legal Conference 2016* (pp. 211–220). Frankfurt am Main, ECB.

Wymeersch, E. (2014). The Single Supervisory Mechanism or "SSM", Part One of the Banking Union. *National Bank of Belgium Working Paper,* (255).

Zilioli, C. (2016). The independence of the European Central Bank and its new banking supervisory competences. In *Independence and Legitimacy in the Institutional System of the European Union* (pp. 125–179). Oxford University Press.

Zilioli, C. (2017). Justiciability of central banks' decisions and the imperative to respect fundamental rights. In *ECB Legal Conference 2017. Shaping a new legal order for Europe: a tale of crises and opportunities* (pp. 91–104). Frankfurt am Main, ECB.

Zilioli, C. and Buono, G. (2021). Chapter 2: A New Kid on the Block: The European Central Bank Before the Union Courts. In *Max Planck Institute Luxembourg for Procedural Law Research Paper Series | N° 2021 (2) Special Issue* (pp. 41–79). Luxembourg.

INDEX